THE FORGOTTEN JEWS

of

AVOYELLES PARISH, LOUISIANA

CAROL MILLS-NICHOL

2012
JANAWAY PUBLISHING
Santa Maria, California

Copyright © 2012, Carol Mills-Nichol

ALL RIGHTS RESERVED.
No part of this publication may be reproduced, stored in a retrieval system, or transmitted in any form or by any means whatsoever, whether electronic, mechanical, magnetic recording, or photocopying, without the prior written approval of the Copyright holder or Publisher, excepting brief quotations for inclusion in book reviews.

Published by:

Janaway Publishing, Inc.
732 Kelsey Ct.
Santa Maria, California 93454
(805) 925-1038
www.janawaygenealogy.com

2012

Library of Congress Control Number: 2012945057

ISBN: 978-1-59641-282-8

Cover design by Janaway Publishing, Inc.

Made in the United States of America

For my husband, Jack, who spent more time than he would have liked in cemeteries and courthouses supporting my project. And to the Cavaliers who waited patiently under the desk for my attention.

Finally, to the no-longer forgotten Jews of Avoyelles Parish who live on in their descendants.

CONTENTS

Introduction vii

Acknowledgments xiii

List of Illustrations xvii

1. First Arrivals at Hydropolis 1

2. Abe Felsenthal – A Pointe Maigre Merchant 39

3. Sam & Alex Haas – Louisiana Moguls .... .65

4. Mansura Bound 143

5. Family Feuds 183

6. Simon Siess - World Traveler 217

7. Saw Mills, Gushers and Broken Bones 239

8. Words and Music – The Descendants of David Siess 291

9. The Goudchaux Network 327

10. The Curious Case of Moses Wolf 367

11. Moise Levy – Evergreen Merchant 379

12. Simon Karpe – A Refugee in Louisiana 407

13. The Rich Family – Bunkie Pioneers 423

14. The Avoyelles Outrage 469

15. The Last Wave of Jewish Immigrants 491

Bibliography 539

Index 549

Map of Avoyelles Parish, Louisiana in 1895

INTRODUCTION

The Jewish men and women who came to Louisiana before the Civil War left Alsace and Bavaria for many reasons. In France the Declaration of Rights of Man which granted equality to all citizens had not changed the lives of the French Jew very much at all. The majority of them still lived in small towns in Alsace or Lorraine. They continued working as merchants or cattle dealers, as most other professions were still closed to them. Because they were not Christians, they were still regarded with some suspicion by other townsfolk. Most young men were educated in small Hebrew-run establishments where the basics of French and other disciplines along with the tenets of their religion were taught. Poor Jews were blamed for being shiftless. Prosperous ones were accused of making their fortunes on the backs of Christians. Men, reaching the age of conscription, often found it unthinkable to fight for a country where they were second class citizens. A Christian, with money, could pay a substitute to do his military service. Most poor Jews could not. In order to curb the non-Christian population, some towns even had marriage restrictions for Jews, allowing only the eldest son to take a wife. The younger boys had to wait until an elderly male member of their community died, or had to move on to another village that would be willing to accept them. Across the border in the Rheinland-Pfalz (Bavaria) such discriminatory laws were the same or worse. So the freedom that America offered these immigrants was enough for them to overcome the fear of an arduous and lengthy sea voyage.

For French and German Jews, antebellum Louisiana was an attractive destination. First, it was cheaper by one third to take a ship to New Orleans although the voyage was one third longer than to alternative northern ports. Second, French, and to a lesser degree German, was widely spoken. In his book, *The Business of Jews in Louisiana 1840-1875,* Elliot Ashkenazi studied both urban and country storekeepers, exposing the reasons why a large numbers of Alsatian and

German Jews were drawn to a sparsely settled state such as Louisiana. While it goes without saying that the attraction of the French and German languages that coexisted beside English in this state had a lot to do with facilitating the newcomers' business interests, it may be equally important that one half of all the Jews who lived in France in the early nineteenth century had lived in rural Alsace as opposed to cities such as Paris, Bordeaux or Metz, and consequently were more comfortable in the "country" setting. It is not surprising that thousands were willing to travel half way across the world to settle in towns and villages that closely resembled their previous homes. Mr. Ashkenazi sums up the situation of the rural Jewish merchant in this way:

> *The Jewish residents of rural Louisiana were, if anything, even more mobile than their counterparts in New Orleans. They generally began as peddlers, an occupation that made them itinerant by necessity. Even when Jews managed to open stores, they did so with little or no capital investment and hence with little or no risk. The overwhelming majority of Jewish storekeepers in rural Louisiana owned dry goods or general stores. Their customers included slaves, large and small landowners, and other village residents. They bought their inventory from larger stores in Shreveport, Baton Rouge or Donaldsonville, but most often in New Orleans. Some went directly to the Northeast or Europe for merchandise They depended for their sales and terms of payments, from their customers and to their suppliers, on the prevailing agricultural economy based on the growth and marketing of cotton and sugar. Many of the rural store keepers also became active traders in these staples. Records can be found of Jewish businesses in at least thirty-one of the forty-seven parishes that existed in 1860.*(Elliot Ashkenazi, *The Business of Jews in Louisiana, 1840-1875,* [Tuscaloosa: The University of Alabama Press, 1988], 14, 15)

It is also important to realize that almost every immigrant who came knew someone else who had left before him and had prospered in America. Often, earlier Jewish arrivals kept in touch with the "old country" encouraging others to follow, often paying passage for relatives to join them. Some men of means eventually sent for family or friends, welcoming cousins, nieces and nephews, or elderly parents. Others brought over brides for themselves or for other single Louisiana Jews of their acquaintance.

Often starting out their American experience in New Orleans, a bustling metropolitan port city even then, these small town immigrants were like fish out of water. Some stayed and adapted to city life but many more fanned out in the countryside as peddlers in order to make enough money to open up a store, picking a small town in a rural setting to settle and start a family. In Avoyelles Parish, the object of this study, more often than not, this meant marrying outside of one's faith.

After the Civil War, the Jewish experience in Avoyelles Parish changed. In 1872 Alsatians had just lost their French citizenship to their country's defeat in the Franco-Prussian War. Told to accept German nationality or leave, thousands did just that, fleeing their comfort zone in the countryside to inhabit the larger cities of France, especially Paris. But if they no longer had a home in Alsace, why not go to America? So they came by the thousands, many following a long-established immigration chain to the Gulf South. These displaced French citizens were followed by the Austro-Hungarian and Russian Jews, who, because of persecution and the continued unrest in Europe, sought refuge in a new land. In New Orleans, these new arrivals were, at first, looked down on, and even discriminated against, by the old, established French and German speaking Jewish Louisiana families. But they were Jews, after all, and eventually became prospective partners for the old guard's unmarried sons and daughters. Following in the footsteps of their Alsatian brethren, many Eastern European Jews traveled the countryside, and settled in the parishes. But unlike earlier arrivals, these men often emigrated from their homelands with spouses, or had, perhaps, spent several years in a northern city where they had gotten married. As a consequence they began to establish a Jewish presence in the small towns they inhabited, something that earlier Jews who had settled there were never able to do.

Throughout the nineteenth century, Avoyelles Parish had never had a synagogue, or a Jewish burying ground, as had St. Landry or Rapides Parishes. Yet, at the dawn of the twentieth century, thanks to this new wave of Jewish immigrants, it was on the very cusp of developing a social support network for its Hebrews, when a cataclysmic event occurred. Cotton crops were decimated by the boll weevil. Businesses failed. Jewish merchants went into bankruptcy. Some fled north while others relocated in New Orleans. If the older generation could still eke out a living in small town Louisiana, their children, many of whom were given the opportunity to pursue careers in medicine, dentistry, pharmacy, and teaching, could not.

In Avoyelles Parish today, there is but one person who practices the Jewish faith. There are, however, many residents in whom the Jewish blood of long-forgotten relatives courses through their veins. It is a parish where, it has long been said, that if you are descended from the twelve or so original Pointe Coupée and Avoyelles families, you are related to at least one third of the people currently living in Louisiana. Avoyelles is also a parish where you can not only be yourself but also your own cousin. However, if you are descended from one of those original French families who married one of the early Jewish immigrants to the parish, then you are doubly blessed with Jewish cousins from all over the Gulf South, as both Catholics and Jews in the nineteenth century tended to marry within the same family groups. It is only by studying these relationships does one come to understand how the Jewish migration into Central Louisiana developed over the course of the last two centuries.

This book, which had started out as a quest to uncover the story of the Siess family of Lembach, grew into the history of all of the many Jews who lived and worked in Avoyelles Parish. As relationships were explored it became clear that only two of the later arriving families, the Schreibers and the Schlessingers, had escaped being woven into the larger Judeo-Christian network of Avoyelles Parish cousins. These are the stories of people who were never famous or extraordinary. They were merchants and farmers, owners of public gins and saw mills, slave masters and Confederate patriots, jayhawkers and prisoners of war. They were members of the Police Jury, mayors, constables, and postmasters. They founded towns and promoted railroads. They grew cotton and cane, raised cattle, and struck oil. As merchants, they were relied upon by farmers to furnish the necessities on credit to produce next year's harvest. Yet these same merchants were also reviled when forced to foreclose on their debtors due to crop failure. Unfortunately, their positions of importance in the small towns of the parish did not always insulate them from the wave of anti-Semitism which swept through Louisiana during the difficult period of Reconstruction. Whether they stayed for ten years or a lifetime these Jewish immigrants left a mark on the parish, helping it to grow and develop its resources.

copyright MemorialLibrary.com

Map of Grant Parish, Louisiana in 1895

Photo courtesy of Steven Marcotte Family

Albert Frank – ca. 1900

Only surviving child of Charles Frank and Pauline Bordelon

ACKNOWLEDGEMENTS

During my first a trip to Avoyelles Parish in 1999 to search for my maternal ancestors, the editor of the *Marksville Weekly News*, Randy DeCuir, asked a question which was pivotal for me: "You do know you are Jewish, don't you," he inquired? As the only child of an only child, who was told she had no relatives, I thought I had no one who could tell me what I needed to know. I started a quest to find out the truth and now have a family tree groaning with the weight of thirty-three thousand people. In Avoyelles Parish, I was introduced to many cousins. Barbara Escudé Lemoine was the first. She led me to the Seiss family members who remained in the area: Marjorie Ann Seiss, her daughters, Felicia and Lorraine Seiss, and sons, Irby and Michael, as well as many of Marjorie's siblings including Juanita Seiss Barbin and Yolanda Seiss Barbin and their children.

My research also took me to Temple Gemiluth Chassodim in Alexandria, where I met Rabbi Arnold Task, who was immediately helpful. He showed me a book, which his predecessor, Dr. Martin Hinchin, had published in 1984: *Fourscore and Eleven, A History of the Jews of Rapides Parish 1828-1919*. There I found bits and pieces of the lives of my forgotten Jewish ancestors. I was hooked. Rabbi Task also directed me to Jim Levy, retired owner of the *Bunkie Record*. Jim was kind enough to submit to several interviews, where he shared his memories about living in a small southern town. Through the internet I reconnected with various heretofore unknown family members: Judy Siess, Mary Nell Davenport, Joe & Bill Friend, Bettye Jo Bango Maki, Murrell Smith Siess, Lenox Leopold Siess, Jr., and Donald Clement. I started a family tree, discovering that I had family connections to both the numerous southern Jewish families, as well as the many Catholic families from Avoyelles Parish and the surrounding areas.

An answer to a question I sent out on a Jewish mailing list, searching for the town of origin of the Jewish Siess family, brought a reply from Roseanne Leeson, who told me that the Siess brothers had appeared in a French publication of an 1851 Jewish Census for Alsace in the town of Lembach. I was unable to go back any further.

In 2005, my cousin, Judy Siess, travelled to France and went to Lembach. She met Daniel Lubrez, a librarian at a near-by Lycée, in the local bakery. Able to speak English, he took her to his home, which was very near the Town Hall and promised to try to find some records of the family for her. Upon return Judy gave me his email address, and we began to correspond. Very soon Daniel found the pivotal document for me, the marriage of Mindele Loeb (aka Amalie Dalsheimer or Minette Thalsheimer) and her second husband, Salomon Lehmann. That document contained Mindele's birth place, the name of her first husband, Michael Süss, his place of birth and date of death, all important clues. A year later Daniel, his wife, Denise, and two children, Bettina and Jonathan, hosted us at their home in Lembach. Before our arrival, Daniel contacted Wolfgang Heiss in Obrigheim to arrange for a record search there, which turned up the birth records for the Siess children. While, we were unable to find Mindele and Salomon's graves in the Jewish Cemetery at Wissembourg, which was overgrown with weeds, Daniel spearheaded an effort, along with the local Jewish community, which convinced the town to undertake its upkeep. Unfortunately their place of interment remained a mystery for several years after that.

I am indebted to the Clement family, Donald, his wife Patsy, their children Elaine, Donald, Jr. and Merrie, for their support, their sharing of family photos and information on the Emmanuel Siess branch of the family. Judge Jerry Winsberg and his brother David offered up photos and information on the Isidore Rich family. Rose Rubel Rich provided information on the Leon Rich descendants. Bettye Jo Bango Maki provided photos, insight and connections to members of the Isaac Edouard Siess family, as did her cousin James Bango. Judy and her late father, Chester Paul Siess, gave me family photos and shared stories of the Auger Siess family. Marney Siess Kepner and her brother, Charles Preston Siess, Jr., shared their knowledge of the Louis Preston Siess family. Jay Lehman provided guidance concerning the descendants of Paul Marius Lehman.

Three fellow family researchers, Teri Downs Tillman of Mississippi, Dr. Leonard Robbins of Texas and Ann Williams of North Carolina have been email correspondents for many years and we have shared and built our family trees, which has resulted in our discovery that we are all related. Teri has been largely responsible for the incredible research done on the Goudchaux family. Karen Brown, a Rosenbaum family researcher from California, was primary in my understanding of the Karpe and Carb families. She spent hours gathering Karpe records from the Family History Library, which I, in turn, translated and we jointly reconstituted this family one member at a time. Brad Fanta and Alice Holland contributed important memorabilia, photos, and information on the Samuel and Alexander Haas family. Dr. David B. Davis, II shared his insights on Haas family protégé, Dr. David Davis, Sam Haas' clerk at the Bayou Chicot store. Steven Mayeux, author of *Earthen Walls, Iron Men – Fort DeRussy, Louisiana, and the Defense of Red River*, provided me with records from the French and American Claims Commission, as well as newspaper accounts of Siess involvement in one of the most barbarous acts of the Civil War. In December 2010, I contacted Micheline Gutmann, one of the major contributors to *Genami.org* who was able to shed light on the fate of Minette Thalsheimer Lehmann and her second husband, Salomon Lehmann, the news of which sent me reeling for weeks.

This book would have never been possible in a pre-internet world. Armed with very little personal information about these Avoyelles Parish Jews, I was able through *Ancestry.com*, *LAgenweb.net, Familysearch.org, and Rootsweb.com* to discover censuses, draft cards, birth and death records, all manner of information and connections to long-lost relatives. *Fold3.com* (formerly *Footnote.com*), with its valuable city directories and civil war records, as well as *Genealogybank.com* and *Chroniclingamerica.loc.gov* with their local and national newspaper availability made it possible to be able to further reconstruct these forgotten lives. I consulted *Jewishgen.org* to use their online world-wide burial registry which is a valuable tool as well. The map resources at USGenNet.org, of which two, Avoyelles and Grant Parish, have been reproduced in this book, have been used to locate places which no longer exist, or whose names have been changed. Finally, my gratitude to Jim Skidmore, editor and publisher of Janaway Publications, for his faith in this project, and his encouragement and expertise in guiding me through the editorial process. For a complete genealogical picture of how all these French Catholic and Jewish families are intertwined, please visit the free website:

http://worldconnect.rootsweb.ancestry.com/cgi-bin/igm.cgi?db=siessfamily

ABBREVIATIONS USED IN FOOTNOTES

Louisiana State University Libraries On-Line Catalog – Special Collections – Louisiana and Lower Mississippi Valley................ LLMV

The (New Orleans, LA) *Times Picayune* .... *TP*

The (New Orleans, LA) *Daily Picayune* .... *DP*

The (Alexandria) *Louisiana Democrat* .... *LD*

Ancestry.com (http://www.ancestry.com) .... A

Chroniclingamerica.loc.gov (http:// chroniclingamerica.loc.gov/ ...... CA

Familysearch.org (http://www.familysearch.org) .... F

Fold3.com (http://www.fold3.com) F3

Genealogybank.com (http://www.genealogybank.com) .... GB

LIST OF ILLUSTRATIONS

Unless noted otherwise, all images are from the author's collection

Map of Avoyelles Parish, Louisiana in 1895 vi

Map of Grant Parish, Louisiana in 1895 xi

Albert Frank, ca. 1900 xii

Mae Rose Clement and sons, Donald (left) and Clay, Jr., ca. 1935.... xx

Dr Harry Siess, Sr., ca. 1920.. xx

Adolph Frank, undated 37

Signature page – Marriage of Maurice Fortlouis and Aurore Porché.. 38

Alexander M. Haas - General Store Letterhead.................................. 138

Alexander M. Haas, ca. 1861 – Confederate Soldier......................... 138

Grey Gables, Haasville, LA – Home of Alexander M. Haas............. 139

Mary Maccie "Bunkie" Haas, ca. 1888 140

Alexander M. Haas, ca. 1905.. 141

Alice Haas, ca. 1885 141

Meyer Weis, bill for shipped cotton from A.M. Haas 1882 142

Leopold Siess, ca. 1884 181

Simon Siess, undated photo 182

David Siess at Mansura, LA Post Office/Store, ca. 1922 182

Louis P. Siess, Dr. Isaac Siess, Philippe Escudé, Auger Siess 214

Alice Siess marker – Jewish Cemetery, Pineville, LA 214

Emmanuel and Auger Siess, Alexandria, ca. 1900 215

Leopold Siess marker, Jewish Cemetery, Pineville, LA 216

Florestine Siess Escudé at her home in Mansura, ca. 1930 216

Wedding Photos of Ernest M. Weil and Mathilde Siess, ca. October 1888 238

Josette Chatelain Siess, ca. 1886 287

Isaac Edouard Siess, Country Doctor, ca. 1902 288

Winnfield, LA, ca. 1903 (Left to right) Clotile Siess, Dr. I.E. Siess, Guy Siess, Helena Berger Siess holding Estelle Siess, unidentified African-American Girl 288

Interior of City Drug Co., Winnfield, LA. Owned by Dr. I.E. Siess (second from right), ca. 1912 289

Winnfield Oil Co., Well #1, ca. 1908 290

David Siess Store and Post Office, ca. 1910. David Siess underneath sign, Dr. Harry James Siess, Sr. to the right 324

Dr. Harry James Siess, Jr., ca. 1946 325

Louis André Seiss (half-brother of Dr. Harry Siess, Sr.) and wife Helen Prévot 325

Eugenie Siess in costume, ca. 1899 326

Esther (Estelle) Goudchaux Kahn, mother of Max, Henry and Aaron Kahn and Helvena Kahn Hiller, ca. 1865 366

Moses Wolf marker, Amite City Cemetery, Amite, LA 378

Moses Levy marker, Jewish Cemetery, Pineville, LA 406

Aaron Charles Karpe marker, Jewish Cemetery, Pineville, LA 422

Abe Rich, ca. 1890 466

Aaron Gross and Sadye Rae Goldstein, Louisiana, ca, 1939 466

Aaron Gross and Sadye Rae Goldstein, ca. 1928 in Guatemala 467

Sarah Coberly, her grandmother, Hermina Siess Rich (in Cajun bonnet), and mother, Raye Rich Coberly, ca. 1926 in Bunkie, LA ... 468

David and Minette Rich Goldstein, ca. 1926, en route to Central America 468

Aaron Kahn, ca. 1885 489

Elster's Sale – Main Street Marksville, ca. 1925 536

Schreiber & Sons – Main Street Marksville, ca. 1930 537

Schreiber's Policy of Cash Transactions – *Marksville Weekly News* – February 1, 1926 537

Saint Louis, Avoyelles & Southwestern RR Co. Stock Certificate ... 538

Mae Rose Siess Clement and her sons, Donald (left) and Clay, Jr., ca. 1935 (*Courtesy of Donald Clement family*)

Dr. Harry James Siess, Sr., ca. 1920

(*Courtesy of the late Murrell Smith Siess*)

CHAPTER 1

FIRST ARRIVALS AT HYDROPOLIS

Until 1803, when the United States purchased the Louisiana Territory from France, Jews were prevented from settling permanently in the area by the *Code Noir* promulgated by King Louis XIV in 1685. Although its aim was to regulate slavery in the French colonies, it had also forbidden Jews to settle in any of France's overseas possessions. In 1819 Moritz J. Fortlouis left Karlsruhe, Kingdom of Baden-Württemberg, aboard the ship *Louisa* out of Le Havre to settle in Louisiana.[1] Not so incidentally, Germany had seen the beginning of the so-called Hep-Hep riots which started in Würzburg that same year. Crowds, whose battle cry was "Hep Hep," attacked and killed Jews, ransacking their homes and stores. This hysteria spread through Bavaria, parts of the Duchy of Baden, eventually all the way to Denmark. The pogrom in Karlsrhue, Moritz Fortlouis' home town, lasted three days, finally being put down by the infantry with their canons and the personal intervention of the Duke of Baden, himself.[2] This violence, a general unrest in Europe at the close of the Napoleonic wars, as well as the failure of the Jews to secure their civil rights, promised, but not effectively granted in the Duchy of Baden's constitution of May 14, 1807, propelled Fortlouis to abandon Karlsruhe. His arrival in the former French Colony made him, at that time, one of a handful of Hebrew residents in the entire state.

The surname "Fortlouis" does not automatically denote Jewish ethnicity. It is a surname taken by only one known Hebrew family who settled in the small village of Fort-Louis in Eastern Alsace, during the reign of the French King, Louis XIV. The town, formerly a sleepy hamlet, became an army depot in 1686, chosen for its strategic location on the Rhine River which separated the little town from the Duchy of Baden, eventually becoming home to almost four thousand military personnel. Many Jewish merchants settled there to become purveyors of foodstuffs and dry goods to the burgeoning population, amongst them, the family of Aron Lazarus. However, by 1740, he and his family had moved permanently to Karlshrue, in the kingdom of Baden-Württemburg.[3]

A January 13, 1809 addendum to the Duchy of Baden's constitution, first published in 1807, called the *"judenedikt"* required that the head of each Jewish household report to the Town Hall in order to declare the members of his family, listing their former names and the surname by which they would be known henceforth.[4] The immigrant family from Fort-Louis, Alsace, now three generations strong and numbering twenty people, officially adopted the name "Fortlouis." This document had an entry for Moritz J. Fortlouis, born on May 28, 1793.[5] His birth date falls within the age range given in an 1820 census taken in East Baton Rouge Parish, Louisiana, for Maurice Fortlouis who was enumerated as a single free white male foreigner between sixteen and twenty-six years of age.[6]

Since Maurice, as he was called in French Louisiana, had just arrived one year previous to the census, he was probably still peddling on foot or on horseback from town to town. Ten years later he surfaced in Pointe Coupée, a neighboring parish, where he fathered a child with a local woman of color. His namesake, Maurice Fortlouis, a black male born in 1830, was enumerated in the 1880 Federal Census, along with his wife, Helen Porché, and their four children.[7] Pointe Coupée historian, Brian J. Costello has written that by the middle of the nineteenth century "the civil and religious records of Pointe Coupée indicated colored Creoles bearing nearly every surname held by the white Creole community."[8] This was true for most of antebellum Central Louisiana. French planters routinely had relationships with free women of color or their own slaves. Even though such unions could not be legalized because of the laws against miscegenation, a few of them, nevertheless, became lifelong commitments. More often than not, due to societal pressure, some men abandoned their partners and children in order to contract legitimate marriages. This way of life was not confined to the rich plantation owner. French, German, and Jewish merchants of the nineteenth and early twentieth centuries are known to have engaged in such relationships as well.[9]

On December 17, 1834, four years after the birth of his illegitimate son, Maurice wed Marie Aurore Porché. The marriage was recorded in the church records of St. François de Pointe Coupée. The groom's name was given as Jean Fortlouis Maurice, a native of Carlesruhe in the Duchy of Baden, the legitimate son of Jean Fortlouis Maurice and his wife Minette Auerbach.[10] The bride's parents, Michel Porché and Rosalie Langlois, were descended from two Pointe Coupée families long established in the community.[11] At the ceremony itself, the couple was given the nuptial blessing by Fr. Jean Émile Martin. Church law dictates that, in the case of mixed marriages, despite any dispensation, neither a nuptial Mass may be held nor a blessing of the spouses or the ring be given.[12] While the document itself mentions some sort of dispensation, it does not appear to be for a difference of religion. Father Martin may have been unaware that Maurice was a Jew, or may not have received a response from his Bishop in New Orleans before he performed the ceremony. During the first half of the nineteenth century priests in the outlying parishes often had to wait weeks to receive a marriage dispensation for a parishioner. A problem from the beginning, this situation finally came to a head when Father Ennemond Dupuy of Iberville Parish wrote to Bishop Anthony Blanc in 1838, asking for blanket permission to perform marriages in the third degree of consanguinity, as well as those with an impediment for a disparity of religion. Fr. Dupuy wrote that since the Creole families were nearly all related to one another, there was rarely a marriage without some degree of impediment. He added that his parishioners made elaborate preparations before notifying him. Consequently he often did not have enough time to write to New Orleans, so the couple would simply marry before a Judge.[13] It is not known what Bishop Blanc replied, but it may be assumed that eventually he had to make some adjustments in order to accommodate his priests living in remote areas.

After several years in Pointe Coupée, Maurice Fortlouis moved his wife across the Atchafalaya River to Hydropolis in Avoyelles Parish, where he became its first permanent Jewish resident. Hydropolis, near present day Cocoville, was founded in 1797 in conjunction with the establishment of the first Catholic Church in the area, Nuestra Senora del Carmen, Our Lady of Mt. Carmel, when Louisiana was under Spanish rule. In the waning years of the 1830s Maurice purchased three and a half arpents[14] of land where he farmed, keeping cattle and a few horses. He also constructed a store. His first son, Michel, was born there on July 20, 1837, and his first daughter, Mathilde, the next year on December 13, 1838.[15]

Six months later, on July 6, 1839, according to naturalization forms filed in the Avoyelles Parish courthouse, two brothers, Charles and Adolph Frank, arrived in New Orleans, from Germany, to join Maurice Fortlouis and his family at Hydropolis. Civil records from the town of Nordstetten, less than seventy-five miles from Karlsruhe, indicate that Charles and Adolph's father, Abraham Frank, was a master butcher. His second marriage to seventeen year old Madele Fortlouis, born in 1787 in Karlsruhe to Isaak Fortlouis and his wife Mamel, produced twelve children. Abe and Madele's third child, Aron was born on October 30, 1809, and their fourth, Juda, on June 4, 1811.[16] These birth dates coincide with those given by Adolph, who abandoned his former name, Aron, upon coming to America, and Juda, who did likewise, when he adopted the name Charles.[17]

It is unquestionable that Madele Fortlouis Frank, born in 1787 in Karlesruhe and Maurice Fortlouis born in 1793 in the same town are part of the same family with the same unique name. Unfortunately, there is not enough information available to determine whether they were siblings, cousins or otherwise related. Madele's son, Charles Frank, joined Maurice Fortlouis, becoming a partner in the store at Hydropolis, while Adolph set up shop nearby, plying his father's trade as a butcher.

***

On February 16, 1841, Maurice and Aurore's daughter, Rosalie, was born. Father Nicolas Français, the latest in a long line of embattled pastors at Nuestra Senora del Carmen, also commonly known as the "Avoyelles Church" finally baptized her almost a year later on February 12, 1842.[18]

The ease with which these Jewish immigrants were accepted into the Central Louisiana agrarian society may be, at least, partially explained by the state of organized religion in the small community. Avoyelles residents, most of whom were French immigrants were neither observant nor obedient to Church law. They had been deeply influenced by the anti-clericalism of the French Revolution which had led to the expulsion, even murder, of hundreds of Roman Catholic priests who refused to sign the "Civil Constitution of the Clergy," passed in 1790 which subordinated the Catholic Church in France to the French government.[19] As a consequence the Avoyelles Parish citizenry was in almost constant conflict with ecclesiastical authority. Since its founding in the previous century, the little church had suffered from a lack of a permanent pastor. Even those who were assigned to Nuestra Senora del Carmen were, more often than not, on the road, travelling to various remote locations of the parish to see members of their flock. So sacraments were often delayed, often for months at a time. Eleven clerics had preceded Father Français who had baptized Rosalie Fortlouis. They had not only been mistreated by the harsh environment, but had to contend with a generally apathetic French immigrant population. In 1831 the citizens of Avoyelles Parish elected two wardens, called *marguilliers*, to oversee its church and run it as a business. A clash of wills erupted between these wardens, who seemed indifferent to the deplorable condition of the church, and the existing pastor, Jean Émile Martin. The wardens refused to provide Fr. Martin with a decent place to live. After more than a year of strife, they dismissed him and put a lock on the church door. Fr. Leon deNeckere, Bishop of New Orleans, put the church under interdiction, thereby denying the sacraments to its parishioners. Reopened in 1834 after two years, the installation of a permanent pastor did not happen for another eight. Fathers D'Hauwe, Alaux, Français and Cheutier came and went, but the struggle between the laity and its priests continued, making their tenures brief and fraught with unpleasant discord.[20]

Complaints about the parishioners' lack of religious conviction lasted well into the 1860s. In November 1855, a group of French Missionary teachers, members of the Congregation of Daughters of the Cross, led by Mother Marie Hyacinthe le Conniat, arrived in Avoyelles Parish to open a school. The Reverend Mother wrote to her brother in 1856, "Here in a population of 10,000 Catholics, 200 or 300 only fulfill their Easter duties. Our little chapel is frequented more than is the Church. I saw only one man go to confession; yet there are no idolaters or heretics. They are simply indifferent." [21] And to her parents she explained, "They listen to the word of God and they do not practice it [...] I do not know if they believe in Hell. One thing is sure. They fear sickness and death. These are the only evils for them..."[22] It is little wonder that marital unions between Catholics and people of other faiths seemed to cause little, if any, consternation in the community.

On March 29, 1842, Adolph Frank, the town's German Jewish butcher, wed seventeen year old Caroline Gaspard, the Catholic daughter of Jean Baptiste Gaspard and his wife Marianne Garcellier. Adolph and Caroline were united in a Roman Catholic service performed by Father Nicolas Français. The original record does not indicate that Adolph was a Jew, nor does it indicate any conversion, or dispensation other than for a second publication of banns. In contravention of ecclesiastical rules, Father Français gave the couple the nuptial blessing, as had Father Martin in the case of the Fortlouis-Porché marriage.[23] Adolph and Caroline's first child, Mathilde, was born nine months later, on January 2, 1843. She was baptized by Father Français on April 17th of the same year with her Jewish paternal uncle, Charles Frank, standing as her godfather, and her mother's sister, Leonore Gaspard, as her godmother.[24] Since Church law dictates that godparents be baptized and confirmed in the Catholic faith, Charles Frank's participation in this sacrament was highly irregular as well.

In the summer of 1843 the little enterprise belonging to Charles Frank and Maurice Fortlouis, crushed by an overwhelming debt, fell into bankruptcy. Charles was able to hold onto some of his assets which had been managed separately, but Maurice and his family were completely ruined. On Monday, November 27, 1843, a U.S. Marshal's sale was held at Maurice Fortlouis' residence at Hydropolis to dispose of his property. The sum total of his assets included: three or so arpents of land in town, a black women named Fanny, age twenty-six, and her son William, age two, fifteen head of "gentle" cattle, three horses, one gig and harness, one calèche[25], one wagon and harness, one cart and harness, one-half of the buildings and improvements held in partnership between himself and Charles Frank, one clock, some household furniture and several uncollected notes and accounts in favor of the bankrupt.[26]

Maurice and his family left Avoyelles Parish soon after. Their fourth child, Leopold, was born during all their financial troubles in 1843, but there is no record of his baptism. By the time of the birth of their fifth child, Geneviève Stephanie Fortlouis on August 18, 1845, the family had returned to Pointe Coupée Parish. Their last child, a son, Théophile, was born there one year later.[27]

***

Adolph Frank's family continued to grow as he enjoyed success as a Marksville butcher. His second child, Aurore, was born on November 11, 1844, and baptized on September 29, 1845, by the newly appointed pastor of Avoyelles, Father Charles Dalloz.[28] Included in the baptismal record of the child was the notation that Adolph was a Jew. Fr. Dalloz made the same entry for their third child, Émile's record, born in 1846, but not on Emelie's, born in 1848.[29]

After his business with Maurice Fortlouis failed, Charles Frank started over, investing in a tannery with Fabius Ricord, a longtime parish resident and church warden originally from France. Frank and Ricord cured animal hides and made harnesses, saddles, and other small leather goods, selling for cash or in exchange for skins.[30] His enterprise finally off the ground, Charles married in a civil ceremony on April 2, 1845. He took a young Catholic bride, Pauline Bordelon, descended on her father's side from one of the original Pointe Coupée families. Parish Judge, Gervais Baillio, united the couple in matrimony.[31]

Charles and Pauline's first two children, Louis, born March 14, 1846, and baptized May 3, 1846, by Father Dalloz,[32] who recorded that the father was Jewish, and Ovilia, born in 1848, but not baptized until 1850, died one day apart in August 1852. Whatever epidemic carried them away is not known, but that summer there were sixteen children buried in St. Paul's Cemetery.[33] Their last child, Albert, was born on August 22, 1849, just days before Charles, himself, succumbed to cholera in September of the same year.[34] This disease was rampant in and around Hydropolis starting in January of 1849. Charles' burial location is unknown. Since the Jewish cemetery in Pineville was not founded until three years later, and given the state of the epidemic, he may have simply been interred in a far corner of the local Catholic Cemetery.

On November 26, 1849, a family meeting was held at the home of Victor Prostdame in Mansura by Edouard DeGenérès, a notary public, where financial arrangements were made on behalf of Charles' surviving spouse and children. It was decided by Pauline's relatives and Adolph Frank, the decedent's brother, that the community property should immediately be given over to the widow, with the exception of that which was held in partnership between Charles Frank and Fabius Ricord. Those assets, including the slave and the leather and tan yard were to be sold as soon as practicable.[35]

Pauline Bordelon Frank remarried on March 19, 1853.[36] Her son, Albert Frank, was raised by his step father, Valery Guillot, on the family farm with his six half-siblings born to the couple. It is not surprising that descendants of Albert Frank, who never knew his Jewish father, were completely unaware of their Hebrew roots. Maurice Fortlouis' children suffered the same fate, when their father died in Pointe Coupée Parish before the 1850 Federal census, after which, his widow and children went to live nearby on her elderly mother's plantation.[37] On August 15, 1852, Aurore Fortlouis married Paul Aguillard, a carpenter, fifteen years her senior.[38] They had three children, Adele, Lucien and Charles. In 1860 this blended family appeared in the Pointe Coupée census, living next door to Aurore's eighty-three year old mother, Rosalie Porché.[39]

***

Adolph Frank's fifth child, Alicia, was born on December 13, 1849. He was now in competition with Gremillion Bros. for the butcher business in Marksville. Advertising in the weekly newspaper, *The Villager*, Adolph proclaimed "Fat Beef!!! Adolph Frank begs to inform his numerous customers that he will go his round and sell at his stall on every Monday, Tuesday, Wednesday, Thursday and Saturday. […] He is happy to proclaim his determination for the future to sell his Fat Beef, etc., at five cents per pound !!!!" Gremillion Bros. advertised both beef and pork at the same price. It is significant that, as a Jew, Frank was not observing the Hebrew Sabbath, instead remaining closed on Sundays, yet, he did not sell pork which he left to his competition.[40]

Four more children were born to Adolph and Caroline during the 1850s: Cleophine (b.1851), Louis (b. 1853), Rebecca (b. 1856), and Clara (b. 1858). They were all baptized at St. Paul the Apostle Catholic Church.[41] With nine children now in the household, Adolph needed to expand his business interests. On April 24, 1858, he and Caroline opened the "Frank Hotel." Not the first in town, it had been preceded by the Bell Tavern (which closed during the Civil War), the Hotel des Planteurs, attended by French immigrant Dominique Ingouf, and the Avoyelles House, run by an American, John McDonnell. It did, however, outlast all of its competition, being in almost continuous operation for sixty-four years.[42] Announcements of the venture were published in *The Villager* in 1858. The original one dated April 24th read: "Frank's Hotel, Marksville, LA. The undersigned, having opened a house of entertainment in the town of Marksville respectfully solicits a share of public patronage. Particular attention will be given to the internal and external wants of both man and beast. The stables are large and the greatest attention paid to the cleanliness and good feeding of horses. Buggies are placed in safe places and well sheltered." [43] The hotel, described as a "wide frame building with a front porch clear across, affording much rocking chair space in summer," was located on Washington Street, north of the courthouse. [44] Publicity was hard to come by in those days. As luck would have it, however, J.W. Dorr was touring Louisiana for his newspaper, *The New Orleans Crescent*. On

May 22, 1860, he sent a dispatch back to his publication. In speaking of Marksville, he wrote, among other things, "There are three hotels, and of one of them, 'Frank's House,' I can speak knowingly as being an admirable institution. The landlord combines the functions of butcher with those of Boniface, and, of course, his table gets the finest joints and the nicest steaks."[45]

About the time the first shots were fired at Fort Sumter in April 1861, fifty-two year old Adolph Frank undertook the renovation of his hotel. Taking out a small advertisement in *The Avoyelles Pelican*, the bilingual newspaper published in Marksville, he reported that he had just renovated and refurnished all his rooms, that his restaurant was abundantly supplied, and he had a large stable and pasture for horses, as well as horses and carriages for rent, all at very moderate prices.[46] In the early years of the war, the recruitment of able bodied male citizens for the Confederate army and the formation of local militias were in high gear. Starting in the summer of 1862, lists of those drafted into the army appeared monthly in the *Pelican*. There was an exemption for age, which was modified periodically until finally only those under seventeen and over fifty were protected. As situations became more desperate for the Confederacy, a government physician was employed to assess the prospective conscripts' health. Adolph Frank's hotel was chosen as the location for these physical examinations, which began on January 26 and 27, 1863, and were held every successive Monday and Tuesday until everyone had been seen.[47]

Living conditions in 1863 had become more difficult in Central Louisiana, and certainly no time to run a hotel. Essential supplies had been cut off from the interior parishes since the fall of New Orleans in April 1862. The *Avoyelles Pelican* was forced to publish, when it could, on the back of wallpaper. On one of these sheets, on June 29, 1863, Adolph Frank announced the closing of his hotel saying, "The undersigned, thankful for the patronage hitherto extended to him as Hotel Keeper in Marksville La, takes this mode of announcing to his friends and the travelling community in general, that he has ceased keeping hotel since he found it almost impossible to furnish himself with the necessary articles needed for that line of business. He, therefore, cannot any longer receive travellers [sic] and entertain them." [48] The hotel remained shuttered until the end of the war. Frank took this opportunity to sell off some of his possessions. On June 30, 1863 he furnished one ambulance and two tan mules to pull it, for which he was paid $750 by Major T.P. Heard, Quartermaster CSA at Alexandria.[49] On the same day he sold one army wagon to the Chief Engineer, Edward Gottheil of the Engineer's Corps, Western District of Louisiana for $450.[50]

***

Preparations were also being made for an imminent invasion of the Avoyelles area by the Federals in their attempt to cut off the Confederacy's new international trading routes through Texas and Mexican ports. Louisianans had been subsisting on what they could smuggle to and from Mexico, including their cotton, which now made its way to Europe via Matamoros and Veracruz. In order to stop the Federal advance down the Red River, Avoyelles Parish slaves had been "rented" temporarily from their owners to build up the fortifications at Fort DeRussy, north of Marksville, in hopes of stopping the advancing Union army. Adolph and Caroline's eldest son, Émile, was seventeen in November 1863. He enrolled as a private in an unattached Confederate Cavalry, known as Dubecq's Company, commanded by Second Sr. Lieut. H. Ducôté. As far as is known, these men never saw any action, but became headquarters' guards for the Western District of Louisiana.[51] During Emile's service to the Confederacy, two more children were born to his parents, Bertha, in 1863, and Emma in 1865.[52] There were now eleven children, nine daughters and two sons, all baptized as Catholics who all married members of their same faith. The fact that their father had been a Jew was just a forgotten footnote to their stories.

***

In Pointe Coupée Parish the six children born to the late Maurice Fortlouis and his wife Aurore Porché were raised by her second husband, Paul Aguillard. The three boys, all older than their Frank cousins, volunteered for service with the Confederate army. The two eldest sons, Michel and Leopold, enlisted as privates in Captain R.A. Stewart's Pointe Coupée Artillery on June 29, 1861, at New Orleans.[53] Mustered into Confederate service in August 1861, the contingent became part of Captain Alcide Bouanchaud's Company A, Light Artillery of Pointe Coupée Louisiana Volunteers. On August 7, 1861, Michel Fortlouis was elected Corporal.[54] That same month Company A was ordered to Columbus, Kentucky and fought in November at the Battle of Belmont. They were also amongst those who defended Fort Pillow, Tennessee, near Island #10 in June 1862. After other Confederate troops lost the battle of Corinth, Fort Pillow was left surrounded on all sides by advancing federal troops. On June 5, 1862, the rebel garrison including Captain Bouanchaud's Company A slipped away from the fort and marched back into Mississippi to join Companies B, from Livingston Parish, and Company C from Pointe Coupée under Alexander Chust.[55] The Confederate garrison was ordered back to Port Hudson, Louisiana, where seventeen year old Théophile Fortlouis joined his two older brothers, enlisting as a private in Company C on March 10, 1863.[56] By the middle of April all three companies were in or near Jackson, Mississippi, but attached to different brigades under Major General William W. Loring. Parts of these three companies joined the garrison at Vicksburg during the siege which lasted from May 19 to July 4, 1863.[57] Leopold and Théophile were captured by the victorious Union Army. As was customary, both were paroled on the spot.[58] After Vicksburg, Companies B and C were disbanded. Théophile and Leopold returned to Louisiana where they joined the Trans-Mississippi Department of the CSA under Lieutenant-General Kirby Smith for the duration of the war.[59]

Since Corporal Michel Fortlouis was not amongst those paroled at Vicksburg, he may have been serving elsewhere in Mississippi with the other half of Major General Loring's division which did not take part in the siege. At this point his military activity is unclear due to poor record keeping by the rebel forces. Michel was first reported AWOL between April and August of 1864 in West

Feliciana Parish. Two differing documents show him being captured by union forces at either Clinton, north of Baton Rouge in East Feliciana Parish, or Morganza in Pointe Coupée Parish, on the same date, June 18, 1864.[60] Loyal confederates from Avoyelles Parish and those returning from combat in Mississippi had tried in four successive skirmishes beginning on May 24 and ending on June 4, to dislodge General Nathaniel Banks' federal encampment, which, after the disastrous Red River campaign, had fled across the Atchafalaya River, in order to head back to New Orleans. It was probably subsequent to this last skirmish in June 1864, that Michel was captured by Union General M.K. Lawler's forces who had been sent out to put an end to the Confederate harassment in the parish.[61] What is not in dispute is that Michel Fortlouis was amongst rebel prisoners taken to Ship Island, Mississippi on October 7, 1864, and sent to New York, arriving there November 5, 1864, under Captain M.A. Marston, U.S. Army. Michel was transported to the infamous Elmira Prison camp where he arrived on November 19, 1864, in the dead of an upstate New York winter.[62]

The camp at Elmira, on the Chemung River, had originally been a training ground for Union recruits, but in July 1864 it was transformed into housing for thousands of Confederate prisoners. There was barracks space enough for five thousand, but a year later, before it was closed in July 1865, over twelve thousand prisoners had been assigned there. Many were housed in tents, five to a shelter some facing the frigid waters of the Chemung. They got a single stick of wood per day in order to keep from freezing, and only a minimal amount of food. A tower was built by two enterprising brothers from the town, and chairs and binoculars were supplied to curious sightseers for a ten cent fee. Vendors provided refreshments for the spectators. Several photographic postcard versions of the camp were sold as well. In all, almost three thousand Confederate soldiers who died there are buried at Woodlawn National Cemetery on Elmira's north side, including Michel Fortlouis who lived only ten days after his arrival at the camp. He succumbed to pneumonia on November 29, 1864, at the age of twenty-seven. His grave marker, #995, reads "L. Forthewis, Co. A. Pointe Coupée Artillery, LA." [63] Elmira resident, Diane Janowski, discovered the identity of "L. Forthewis" with the help of Brian Costello, a local Pointe Coupée historian, whom she visited in 2006. In her book, *In Their Honor: Soldiers of the Confederacy, The Elmira Prison Camp*, she detailed her quest to find out the stories of some of the dead buried there. She "adopted" Michel Fortlouis, whose grave she visits annually on Memorial Day. In honor of those buried so far from home, she brought back a container of Pointe Coupée dirt to spread on Michel's grave, and affixed his correct information to his marker.[64]

Théophile Fortlouis was paroled at Natchitoches, La on June 6, 1865,[65] and returned to Pointe Coupée Parish at the end of the war.[66] Théophile never married. He tended his mother's place as long as she lived, then moved in with his half-sister, Adele Aguillard Carmouche, and her husband, Numa, who owned a rice farm which supported them all, including Adele's seven children, as well as her bachelor brother, Charles Aguillard.[67] Théophile died on October 27, 1917, at the age of seventy-two.[68]

Leopold Fortlouis married Philomène Victoria Major. They had two children, Philomène (b. 1878) and Maurice, born on January 15, 1880.[69] There is no record of either Leopold or Philomène's death, but by 1900, their children were living with their Uncle Théophile and grandmother, Aurore Fortlouis Aguillard, on their farm.[70] Leopold's son, Maurice, was married briefly to a twenty-eight year old widow, which produced no children. After his wife's death, he went to work on his cousin, Leo David's farm. Maurice died at the age of sixty-nine at Jarreau in Pointe Coupée Parish.[71] Philomène, Leopold's daughter, married Alexandre Isaac, a veteran of the Civil War, who had fought with her uncles. They lived on a farm in Ventress in Pointe Coupée and had three children, Alexandre (b. 1905), Leopold (b.1907), and Jacob (b. 1911). Philomène died at the age of forty on July 30, 1918, at Ventress, and her husband succumbed on January 4, 1924, leaving the children to room with other relatives and work on local farms[72].

Two of Maurice Fortlouis' three daughters married local men from Pointe Coupée. Rosalie wed one of her brothers' Civil War comrades-in-arms, Charles W, Villère (also spelled Villeret), a second

Lieutenant in the first Louisiana Cavalry, also known as the "Morgan Rangers." The couple had eleven children before Charles died of the "fever" on September 12, 1884. Rosalie Fortlouis passed away on October 4, 1928. Although born into a Catholic family, she and several of her children were buried in the Grace Episcopal churchyard.[73] It is not likely that Rosalie's Jewish roots were even known to her descendants as her Jewish father had been dead for over half a century.

Forty-five year old Stephanie Fortlouis married fifty year old Louis Carmouche, also a Confederate veteran from her brothers' own regiment, Bouanchaud's Pointe Coupée Artillery, in 1910. The couple, childless, tended a farm in Pointe Coupée parish until their deaths in the late 1920s.[74] Stephanie's sister, Mathilde, never married and last appears in the 1880 census with her widowed mother, sister Stephanie, and half-brother, Charles Aguillard.[75]

***

Karlsruhe native Maurice Fortlouis' illegitimate son, Maurice, married Helen Porché, a descendant of that racially mixed line. Young Maurice and Helen had two sons and two daughters, François (b.1870), Ellen (b 1872), Augustine (b. 1873), and Moïse (b. 1875). At some time before the 1880 census, Helen Porché Fortlouis died, leaving her husband to raise the children on the family farm near the town of Wickliffe, between False River Lake and the Mississippi River.[76] Three of their offspring left their trace in the parish.

François married around 1890 and fathered five sons: Henry (b. 1892), Ernest (b. 1894), Albert (b. 1896), Mac Bennett (b 1898) and Lionel (b.1900). The François Fortlouis family lived not far from Wickliffe, making their home in Ventress near the False River. Augustine Fortlouis married another Pointe Coupée farmer, Paul Martin, in 1893. They were the parents of six children, two sons, William and Philibert, and four daughters, Elizabeth, Georgina, Mary and Augustine. Moïse Fortlouis and his wife Rose were the parents of two daughters, Georgiana and Estella. They farmed in the little hamlet of Happy Jack.[77] These racially mixed descendants of Maurice

Fortlouis were all raised in the Christian faith, and likely unaware of their German Jewish roots. Some of the descendants eventually dropped "Fort" and simplified their names to "Lewis."

***

Adolph Frank's eldest child, Mathilde, was the first to marry. She wed John Schwartzenburg, a Rapides Parish butcher, on November 17, 1864, at St. Paul the Apostle Catholic Church in Mansura.[78] The groom was one of the ten children of John and Margaretha Schneider Schwartzenburg who had immigrated to Rapides Parish, Louisiana in the late 1830s from Switzerland. The elder Schwartzenburg owned the Rapides Hotel in Pineville, Louisiana. The couple made their home in Pineville where their children were born: Caroline in 1866, Edward in 1868 and Charles in 1874, before John's death at age thirty-eight in 1876. Their last child, Mary (Mollie), born December 27, 1876, never knew her father.[79] Mathilde eventually remarried. Her husband, Leon Molenor, a farmer, became the Marksville town photographer. They had two daughters, Alice and Beulah. Matilda lived to be ninety-seven years old, dying in Marksville on February 1, 1940.[80] She was buried in St. Joseph's Catholic Cemetery in town.

Aurore Frank married a French widower and father of three, Jean-Baptiste Claverie, on November 7, 1865, in a Catholic service. They went on to have three sons and five daughters of their own, before he died in 1878. Claverie was a butcher in Marksville. Aurore died on November 22, 1921, at the home of her eldest living son, Jean Marie Claverie, in Evergreen, Avoyelles Parish.[81]

On May 31, 1869, Adolph Frank sold the contents of his hotel to his son, Emile. This transaction included five beds, three round tables, three commercial tables, three armoires, fourteen country chairs, five lavatories with pitchers, bowls and trestles, all the crockery, glassware, knives and forks and spoons, two looking glasses, one toilette and side board, two safes, axes and shovels and one piano. On the same day Emile Frank bought five horses, mules, and a hack from his brother-in-law, John Schwartzenburg. Emile may have purchased at least a half ownership in the hotel business from his father, with the latter keeping the building and the land.[82] He also took over his father's butcher shop. On September 2, 1869, Emile married Ludoviska Saucier in a Catholic ceremony conducted by Father Jules Janeau. His sister, Emelie, followed him to the altar seven months later when she married Charles Frederick Huesman, a German immigrant from Hanover, on April 21, 1870.[83] Emile and Ludoviska had three children, Eustis Louis (b. 1871), Robert (b. 1872) and Fremont Filbert (b. 1874). Emelie and Charles Huesman also had three children, Harriet (b.1872), Herman (b. 1873) and Bertha (b. 1876).

Emile's brother-in-law, Charles Huesman, opened "Huesman's emporium" in Marksville in 1876. It was in direct competition with another family owned enterprise run by George L. Mayer, who had married Cleophine, Adolph Frank's daughter, on April 18, 1871.[84] Competing advertisements for both the Huesman and Mayer stores often ran side by side in the *Marksville Bulletin*, with Mayer hawking his fancy and staple dry goods, clothing, shoes, hats, boots, and groceries, including wine and liquors, and Huesman decrying all the corpses littering Main Street in Marksville because they had "died from exhaustion, trying to look at all the pretty things just brought up from New Orleans." [85] This business rivalry between two brothers-in-law was finally put to rest in the early 1880s. Charles Huesman became the postmaster at Marksville in 1881, and in 1882 was hired as the druggist in George Mayer's store. The editor of the *Marksville Bulletin* opined "Marksville at last has a first class drug store. (…) Mr. G. L. Mayer has attached an apothecary department to his well assorted store, and that accomplished gentleman and druggist, Mr. Chas. F. Huesman performs the functions of the knight of the mortar and pestle. Mr. H.is a graduate in pharmacy and has had besides an extended experience in that line." [86]

Alicia Frank, Adolph's fifth child, had a brief marriage to Jean Marie Couget, a French national, in 1868.[87] The couple had no children, and, by June 1880, Alicia, now divorced, was back living with her parents and unmarried sisters, Rebecca and Bertha, in Marksville.[88]

Louis Frank, Adolph's other son, married Mary Virginia Delhoste on November 3, 1874, in Acme, Concordia Parish.[89] Louis Frank, a barber, was enumerated living outside of Marksville in 1880 in Ward One with his wife and daughters, Rebecca (b. 1877), Matilda (b. 1878), and Emma (b. January 1880). Next door, his sister, Matilda, kept house with her second husband, Leon Molenor, and their children. Louis' sister, Aurore, the widow of Jean Baptiste Claverie also lived close by.[90]

Adolph's daughter, Clara Frank, was married to Jules Émile Didier on November 19, 1879.[91] The groom was the son of Avoyelles Parish native, Caroline Brouillette, and her husband, Jean Pierre Didier, a native of Lunéville, France. Clara and Jules made their home in Marksville where they became the parents of six children.[92]

Adolph's late brother Charles Frank's son, Albert, married Felonise Roy, daughter of Jean-Baptiste Roy and his wife Marie Guillot on January 4, 1876, in a ceremony conducted by Father J.E. Chauvin.[93] He and Felonise had five daughters: Marie Siphaée, Emma, Bertha, Inez and Alicia. The family lived and worked their Avoyelles farm, and after Felonise died on March 26, 1898, Albert wed nineteen year old Josephine Marcotte, with whom he had four boys and three girls. All of Albert Frank's children chose Catholic partners from the Avoyelles area.

On May 4, 1880, Adolph Frank, now seventy-one, sold the hotel and the sixty-five acres it sat on to his daughter, Matilda Frank Molenor. Adolph kept two arpents of land adjacent to the hotel for himself, his wife, and unmarried daughters. Shortly thereafter, on February 9, 1881, Rebecca Frank married her sister, Mathilde Frank's late husband's youngest brother, George Washington Xavier Schwartzenburg, in a Catholic ceremony. Witnessing the union was her father, Adolph Frank, and brother-in-law, George Mayer.[94]

On June 18, 1881, Adolph Frank's wife, Caroline Gaspard, died at her home in Marksville at the age of fifty-five years, nine months and eighteen days. An obituary appeared in the June 25, 1881 edition of the *Marksville Bulletin,* which praised her as a kind, hospitable, Christian woman, a model wife and affectionate mother. [95]

In February 1882, Louis Frank moved his family into Marksville, occupying the house formerly owned by his sister, Clara Frank Didier, and her husband. A rumor appeared in the *Marksville Weekly News* that he had returned to open up a hotel and restaurant, having already secured the services of a first class cook for his enterprise. Nothing further, however, was heard about this, as it would have put him in direct competition with other family members.[96] Louis and his wife, Virginia's, four youngest children: Pearl, Edward Joseph, Anaïs Albertine, and Webster Francis (Webbie) were born in town.

***

The French and American Claims Commission occupied rooms in the Frank Hotel in early 1882 to hear the cases that French nationals living in Avoyelles Parish had brought against the United States government for damage to or confiscation of goods or property during the Civil War. The principal players, the Honorable George Williamson, Government Counsel, and Judge John Laresche, Special Commissioner, arrived on January 16th to take down the testimony.[97] The editor of the *Bulletin* joked in an item supposedly submitted by Adolph Frank in the same edition, writing "Sacre Voinché! He is the cause of my hotel being made a Court House with French claims strewn all about it." [98] The hearings, however, were delayed until the middle of April 1862 due to spring flooding in Avoyelles Parish. High water was causing an influx of wild creatures into the town and a disruption in the delivery of the weekly paper.[99] Twenty-three cases were finally heard at the Frank Hotel on behalf of its foreign citizens, beginning on April 17th. These claims amounted to around six hundred thousand dollars not including interest at 6% per year. Only three, however, were paid by the commission, the smallest being $49.79 to Jean-Baptiste Pierrot for cows taken by General Banks. Father Jean Chauvin received $298.75 for horses stolen from the Mansura Church by Union soldiers. The largest payment went to Angelique Brochard for cotton, corn and cattle seized by Admiral Porter in the amount of $3,506.01. All the others were dismissed or disallowed.[100]

The Special Commissioner in charge of these hearings, John Baptist Félix Léonce Laresche, was born in New Orleans on January 13, 1840. He was a veteran of the Civil War, and lately, a Judge with the Justice of the Peace Courts, Third Division, in New Orleans. Official records indicate that he stayed in Marksville from April 17, 1882, until May 10th of the same year hearing the cases, for which he was paid $42.87 for travel expenses and incidentals while in town. The Frank Hotel received a total of $10.00 for use of the room where testimony was taken during that same time at fifty cents per day.[101]

Judge Laresche, however, did not leave Avoyelles Parish with just souvenirs from the Frank Hotel. On Thursday, May 4, 1882, he wed Bertha Frank, Adolph's nineteen year old daughter, and took her back to New Orleans.[102] Their only child, John Léonce Guilbert Laresche, was born there on June 27, 1886.[103] Bertha was widowed nine months later when her husband, age forty-seven, breathed his last.[104] Bertha Frank Laresche, was listed in the 1891 *Soards New Orleans Directory* as a dressmaker, living at 200 Dumaine Street.[105]

After the French and American Claims Commission left town, Adolph Frank closed his hotel for a brief period only to reopen two years later. *La Revue de Marksville* reported in 1884 that "Mr. Frank, now seventy-five years old, whose hotel was known so favorably in the Parish for twenty-five years, had just reopened it."[106] Louis Frank, on the other hand, had been hired by his brother-in-law, George L. Mayer, to superintend a new feed and livery stable that the former had opened, at the place originally occupied by George H. Stevens who had moved his business to Bunkie.[107] Another brother-in-law, Jules Didier, Clara Frank's husband, had become the "mixologist" in George Mayer's saloon.[108]

Adolph's last single daughter, Emma Frank, married Charles Maximilien Weisenberg, a native of Sarreguemines, France on May 23, 1891, in a Catholic ceremony conducted by Rev. A. Chorin.[109] Charles and Emma left the parish, making their home in Chicago, Illinois where he was a customs' house broker. The couple was childless, and after ten years of marriage, Charles died on March 26, 1901, just shy of his forty-third year.[110] Emma remained in Chicago for almost a decade before moving back to Avoyelles Parish where she married widower Ernest Moncla, the father of eight children, and a local farmer. Ernest died on March 25, 1926, at the age of sixty-nine.[111] Emma outlived him by another twenty-six years, expiring on June 10, 1952, in Orange, Texas where she had been staying with relatives. She and Ernest are buried in St. Joseph's Catholic Cemetery in Marksville.[112]

As he grew into old age, Adolph Frank found himself no longer to be able to see to his own business interests. In September 1892, his property was put up at a Sheriff's sale for not having paid the taxes in the amount of $7.50.[113] The situation was rectified, but the die was cast. His children applied for a judicial interdiction to disqualify him from managing his affairs. On May 8, 1894, an interdict inventory was taken of the community property he held with his deceased wife, Caroline Gaspard. It included two town lots (including the Washington St. property with the hotel, valued at $1100), four bedsteads and bedding ($60.00), one armoire ($4.00), one bureau ($4.00), two parlor tables ($3.50.), two dining tables ($3.50), one side board ($5.00). two wash stands ($1.00), nine old chairs and two old rockers ($2.25), two flower stands ($2.00), five pictures ($2.50), one old cooking stove (50 cents), two spittoons (50 cents), on pair dog iron (andirons for fireplace - $1.00), and one looking glass ($2.00).[114] After Adolph's death in late 1899, another inventory was taken of his holdings, identical to the previous one, with only the addition of a "bell" worth five dollars. The value of the estate had appreciated from the 1894 figure of $1194.75 to $1267.[115] Adolph, who seems never to have had any desire to associate himself with any Jewish organizations, or the thriving synagogue in Alexandria, was not interred in any of the Hebrew cemeteries in the area. The location of his place of rest remains unknown.

At the time of the elder Frank's death, nine of the couple's eleven children, along with the late Charles Frank's only surviving child, Albert Frank, were still living in Avoyelles Parish. Most were Catholic. Mathilde Frank Schwartzenburg's children and grandchildren, had stayed, in and around Marksville, marrying into the Gremillion, Garrot, Neck, Dupuy and Edwards families. Mathilde's great-granddaughter, Elaine married Edwin Washington Edwards, who went on to become the Governor of Louisiana.

Aurore Frank Claverie's children remained in Louisiana, some settling in New Orleans. Her son, Jean Marie, also married into the Edwards family, taking Camille Henriette Edwards, daughter of Henry Clay Edwards and his wife Clara LaFargue as his bride in 1890.[116] All the children and grandchildren were practicing Catholics.

Emile Frank and his family were lifelong residents of Marksville. Emile ran the Frank Hotel until his death on July 30, 1913. His wife, Ludoviska Saucier, kept it open an additional seven years until her death on September 29, 1921. Their son, Eustis Louis Frank, married Marie Irene Gremillion. By 1920 their twenty-five year plus marriage, which had produced five children, Charles Wyman, Kirtly Mark, Karl Francis, Lolie Lee, and Katheryne, had ended in separation or divorce, and Eustis was living with his widowed mother at the hotel/boarding house on Washington Street.[117] Eustis owned a butcher shop in Marksville until his death in 1933. Emile's son, Robert Frank, was a grocer in Marksville, whose shop at the turn of the twentieth century was on Main Street adjoining the Post Office. Robert married Merle Smith, whose mother kept a boarding house in Shreveport. Robert ran a pool room in Marksville for a time where their three children, Roberta, Robert, Jr., and Shirley were born.[118] The family finally relocated to New Orleans, where, Robert, Sr. retired and Merle ran a boarding house on Magazine Street.[119] Emile's youngest son, Fremont, who married Henriette Ducôté in 1894, was employed as a carpenter, building and repairing houses in Marksville. He died at the age of thirty-eight on July 28, 1912, just a year before his father, leaving his wife and four children, Adolph, Eugenie, Floyd and Allen. His widow moved to Bunkie with her family, where her son, Adolph, became a salesman is a local store, and Allen worked at a furniture company.

The children of Emelie Frank Huesman present an interesting picture of religious diversity. Harriet C. Huesman, Emelie Frank's oldest daughter married Henry Aaron on October 19, 1896, at St. Joseph's Catholic Church in Marksville.[120] The groom's parents and grandparents were Jewish, but after Henry's mother died, his father, Robert Aaron, wed Hannah Olevia Walkling Fitzum, a non-Jewish widow. Upon Robert's death in 1907, Hannah raised her step-children as Christians. In 1922 she and her step-children petitioned the Thirteenth Judicial District Court in Rapides Parish to have their surname changed from "Aaron" to "Adrion." The petitioners stated that they all had been baptized in and practiced Christianity. The Mike and Mary Foisy Aaron and Henry and Harriet Huesman Aaron families were Catholic, while Edwin and Adele Richards Aaron and their children were Episcopalians. They alleged that they had suffered unnecessary confusion of religious identity by reason of their surname, and wished to remain Christian and be recognized as such. The petition to change their last name permanently to "Adrion" was granted on June 30, 1922.[121]

In *Jewish Life in Small-Town America*, Lee Shai Weissbach writes, "The first Jews who planted themselves in towns that would one day host small Jewish communities found themselves initially isolated from Jewish contacts, and many divorced themselves from Jewish life as a result. If they had arrived as bachelors, they often married non-Jewish women and saw their children raised as Christians."[122] True to this paradigm, Maurice Fortlouis, and Charles and Adolph Frank, had all emigrated as bachelors. They married women from families who had lived in Louisiana for many generations, and, although Jews, these immigrants were accepted into the community as equals. Their children were raised as Catholics. As a result of their choices, they led a life of alienation from the faith of their ancestors never constructing a place of worship or consecrating a Jewish burial ground in Avoyelles Parish. Despite these hardships, many more Jewish immigrants would come to Central Louisiana to make their homes and raise their children. Shunning the larger cities, they sought to replicate the lives they had left behind in the small towns of Alsace and Bavaria.

[1] Jeraldine Dufour LaCour, *Avoyelleans of Yesteryear* (Bunkie: Jeraldine Dufour LaCour [P.O. Box 5022, Alexandria, LA], 1983), 123 (File #28) Petition for naturalization filed at Marksville, March 27, 1841.

[2] Amos Elon, The Pity of it All: A History of the Jews in Germany, 1743-1933 (New York: Metropolitan Books, 2002), 103. Note: The cry "Hep Hep" may have been an acronym for the rallying cry of the Crusaders who shouted "Jerusalem is lost" (Hierosolyma est perdita), or simply the traditional herding cry of German shepherds. Its actual meaning remains unknown.

[3] Karl Gustave Fecht, geschichte der Haupt – und Residenzstadt Karlsruhe, (Karlsruhe: Macklot'sche Druckerei 1887), 238. (E-book at http://books.google.com). Note: Line 11 includes this listing for one of the heads of household residing in Karlsruhe in 1740. "Aron Lazarus Fortlouis aus Gernsbach von Fort Louis hierer gezogen." [Aron Lazarus Fortlouis from Gernsbach who moved here from Fort Louis.] Translation courtesy of Teri Downs Tillman.

[4] Baden Jewish Virtual Library, (http://www.jewishvirtuallibrary.org/jsource/judaica/ejud_0002_0003_0_01848.html : accessed 3/2012).

[5] "Karlsruhe Baden-Württemberg, Germany, Juden in Karlsruhe, 1809 (The Jewish Community in Karlsruhe, 1809)," Generallandesarchiv, Karlsruhe, Baden-Württemberg, Germany; FHL microfilm 1,180,442, Item 1.

[6] 1820 U.S. Census, East Baton Rouge Parish, Louisiana, pop. sch., p. 14 (penned), line 5, Maurice Fortlouis. digital image, *Ancestry.com* (http://www.ancestry.com [hereinafter cited as "A"]: accessed 12/ 2011), citing NARA microfilm publication M33, roll 32. Date of Enumeration: None.

[7] 1880 U.S. Census, Pointe Coupée Parish, Louisiana, pop. sch. 7th ward, ED 55, p. 406D (penned), Dwelling #124, Family #124, Maurice Fortlouis household, digital image, (A: accessed 2011), citing NARA microfilm publication T9, roll 465. Date of enumeration: 4 June 1880.

[8] Brian J. Costello, *A History of Pointe Coupée Parish, Louisiana* (Donaldsonville, LA: Margaret Media, Inc. 2010), 105.

[9] Berthold Lehmann of Pond, Mississippi had four children with Emmaline Montgomery. Morris Weinberg of Rapides Parish fathered eight children with Martha Sullivan. Simon Gumbel of Pointe Coupée Parish had a son with an unknown woman of color. In Avoyelles Parish, Isaac Lehmann had a child with Marie Charlot, and Isaac's half-nephew, Dr. Harry Siess, Sr. had a son with Josephine Olivier, Marie Charlot's daughter by her legitimate husband, Louis Olivier.

[10] "Karlsruhe Baden-Württemberg, Germany, Juden in Karlsruhe, 1809 (The Jewish Community in Karlsruhe, 1809)," Generallandesarchiv, Karlsruhe, Baden-Württemberg, Germany; FHL microfilm 1,180,442, Item 1. Note: There were two Auerbach families in the list of Jews accepted as residents of Karlesruhe in 1809: Meier Auerbacher and his wife Fanni Levi and Wolf Auerbach and his wife Mamel.

[11] Two brothers, Pierre and Vincent Le Porché, emigrated from Pluneret, a town on the Breton coast of France. They were prominent planters and slave owners in Pointe Coupée, as well as the progenitors of a number of persons of color who carried the same family surname. The Langlois family emigrated from France to New Orleans at the beginning of the eighteenth century, moving first to the Opelousas Post then to Pointe Coupée Parish.

[12] Saint François of Pointe Coupée Catholic Church Marriage Records, New Roads, LA. Marriage of Jean Fortlouis Maurice and Aurore Porché, 17 December 1834, p. 234, Item #9, Entry #4, currently held at the Diocese of Baton Rouge, Department of the Archives, Baton Rouge, LA 70821.

[13] Joe Wiegman, compiler, "Marriage Dispensations for the Catholic Diocese of New Orleans, Louisiana, 1786-1865," (Page 2 1800-1865),*Usgwachives.net* (http://files.usgwarchives.net: accessed 5/ 2011). Letter dated 1 Sep 1838, Dupuy, Father Ennemond, Iberville, LA to Bishop Anth. Blanc, New Orleans, LA.

[14] An "arpent" is a measurement used in French Louisiana and several other Gulf states, the equivalent of approximately .85 acres.

[15] "Family Search International Genealogical Index v5. Family Group record for Maurice Fortlouis and Aurore Porche," database, *Familysearch.org* (http://www.familysearch.org [hereinafter cited as F]: accessed 1/ 2011), Entries for Michel and Mathilde Fortlouis.

[16] Family registers RSA 2329, 2330; Marriage Register RSA 2324, p. 9/19 # 17 from Horb-Nordstetten (Württemberg, Germany), researched on 7/17/2010 by R. Vitt concerning an inquiry from Manuela Wettstein dated July 5, 2010.

[17] Patrick Marcotte's father, a descendant of Charles Frank's only surviving son, Albert, went to Germany with his wife in the 1980s to do genealogical research. The couple searched Catholic and Protestant records in Nordstetten, Germany to no avail. Fortunately a translator helping them suggested that they check the Jewish archives. Because the brothers had given their accurate birth dates on their naturalization records, it became an easy task to match Juda and Aron Frank from Nordstetten with Charles and Adolph Frank from Avoyelles Parish.

[18] Alberta Rouseau Ducôté, compiler and translator, *Early Baptism Records of St. Paul the Apostle Catholic Church, 1824-1844 – Avoyelles Parish* (Mansura, LA: St. Paul the Apostle Church [P.O. Box 130. Mansura, LA 71350], 1982), Part II, 63.

[19] William Lemuel Greene, *Antoine Blanc 1792-1860* (Baton Rouge, LA: Claitor's Publishing Division, 2008), 1.

[20] For a complete discussion of the Avoyelles Church's interdiction see: Dr. George C. Poret, *St. Paul the Apostle Church* (New York: Carlton Press, Inc., 1979), 54-64.

[21] Sister Dorothea Olga McCants, DC, compiler and translator, *They Came to Louisiana: Letters of a Catholic Mission 1854-1882* (Baton Rouge, Louisiana: Louisiana State University Press, 1970), 39.

[22] McCants, 57.

[23] St. Paul the Apostle Catholic Church, *Wedding register #2*, p. 92, Marriage of Adolph Frank and Caroline Gaspard. Thanks to Fr. Chad Partain for locating the original record at the Catholic diocese office at Alexandria, Rapides Parish, LA which has never been published in its entirety.

[24] Alberta Rouseau Ducôté, compiler and translator, *Early Baptism Records of St. Paul the Apostle Catholic Church, 1824-1844 – Avoyelles Parish*, Part II, p. 64.

[25] A "calèche" is a two wheeled horse drawn vehicle.

[26] "Marshal's Sales – District Court of the United States, Western District of Louisiana. Maurice Fortlouis in Bankruptcy vs. his creditors," Louisiana State University Libraries On Line Catalog – Special Collections – Louisiana and Lower Mississippi Valley (hereinafter cited as "LLMV"), Microfilm # 5964, *The Villager,* Vol. 11, no. 8, 11 November 1843, p. 1, col. 2.

[27] "Family Group Record for Maurice Fortlouis," database, (F : accessed 1/2011), record submitted after 1991 by unknown LDS Church member.

[28] Under Father Dalloz, the Avoyelles Church, Nuestra Senora del Carmen, was rebuilt and in 1846 Antoine Blanc, Bishop of New Orleans, arrived in the parish to dedicate it. It was placed under the protection of and renamed for St. Paul the Apostle, a name which has carried over into the twenty-first century.

[29] Alberta Rouseau Ducôté, compiler and translator, *St. Paul the Apostle Church, Mansura, Louisiana – Baptism Book #5, 1845-1850* (Marksville, Louisiana: Avoyelles Publishing Company, 1994), 34.

[30] [Title illegible – Text in French], LLMV, Microfilm # 5964, *Le Villageois (The Villager)*, 9 November 1844, p. 2, col. 2.

[31] Avoyelles Parish Courthouse Records (Marksville, Avoyelles Parish, LA), *Marriages,* Book B-2 : 64, Charles Frank to Pauline Bordelon (Recorded in French).

[32] Alberta Rouseau Ducôté, compiler and translator, *St. Paul the Apostle Church, Mansura, Louisiana – Baptism Book #5*, p. 34.

[33] Willie J. Ducôté, compiler and translator, *Burial register of St. Paul's Church Mansura, Louisiana, Parish of Avoyelles, Book II – Entries recorded April 1850-December 1859* (Baton Rouge, Louisiana: No publisher, 1997), 9.

[34] "U.S. Federal Census Mortality Schedule 3 - Persons who died during the year ending June 1850 in the Parish of Avoyelles," database, (A.: accessed 1/ 2011), citing NARA microfilm publication T655, roll 21. Entry for Charles Frank, p. 3, no. 5.

[35] Avoyelles Parish Courthouse records (Marksville, Avoyelles Parish, LA), *Family Meetings,* Book A, pp. 65-69, Proceedings of Family Meeting held 26 November, 1849.

[36] Jeraldine DuFour LaCour, *Brides Book of Avoyelles Parish, Louisiana Volume I, 1808-1855* (Bunkie: Jeraldine Dufour LaCour [203 South Gayle Blvd., Bunkie, LA], 1979), 10.

[37] 1850 U. S. Census, Pointe Coupée Parish, Louisiana, pop. sch. p. 7A (stamped), Dwelling #106, Family #106, (Widow) Mitchell (sic) Porché household, digital image, (A: accessed 12/ 2010), citing NARA microfilm publication M432, roll 239. Date of enumeration: August 9, 1850. Note: The Fortlouis children were enumerated in error using the last name Porché.

[38] "Louisiana Marriages – 1718-1925," database, (A: accessed 12/ 2010), citing a variety of sources including individual marriage records located in Family History Library microfilm, microfiche, or books. Original marriage records are available from the Clerk of Court, Orleans Parish, Marriage of Paul Aguillard and Julie Aurore Porché, Pointe Coupée Parish.

[39] 1860 U.S. Census, Pointe Coupée Parish, Louisiana, pop. sch. pp. 749, 750 (penned), Dwelling #52, Families #59 & #60, Paul Aguillard & Michel Fortlouis households, digital images, (A: accessed 12/ 2010), citing NARA microfilm publication M653, roll 414. Date of enumeration: 16 June 1860.

[40] "Fat Beef," LLMV, Microfilm # 5964, *Le Villageois (The Villager)*, 27 June 1857, Vol. XIII, no. 25, p. 1, cols. 1, 2, 5.

[41] Alberta Rouseau Ducôté, compiler and translator, *St. Paul the Apostle Church, Mansura, Louisiana – Baptism Books #6 & #7, 1850-1872* (Marksville, LA; The Avoyelles Publishing Co.,1994), F-59.

[42] Corinne L. Saucier, *History of Avoyelles Parish* (Gretna, Louisiana: Pelican Publishing Co., 1998), 298.

[43] "Frank's Hotel," LLMV, Microfilm # 5964, *Le Villageois* (*The Villager*) 26 June 1858, Vol. XIV, no. 27, p. 1, col. 2.

[44] Saucier, 298.

[45] Walter Prichard, ed. "A Tourists Description of Louisiana in 1860," by J.W. Dorr, *Louisiana Historical Quarterly* Vol. 21 (Oct. 1938):1110-1214, specifically 1149.

[46] "Hotel de A. Frank – Rue Washington," LLMV, Microfilm # 5763, *The Avoyelles Pelican*, 9 November 1861, Vol. 18, no. 28, p. 2, col. 3. (Advertisement in French translated by the author).

[47] "Notice," LLMV, Microfilm # 5763, *The Avoyelles Pelican*, 24 January 1863, Vol. 23, no. 37, p. 2, col. 6.

[48] "Frank's Hotel," LLMV, Microfilm # 5763, *The Avoyelles Pelican*, 4 July 1863, p. 2, col. 6.

[49] "Confederate Papers relating to Citizens or Business Firms, 1861-1865," digital image, *Fold3.com* (http://www.fold3.com [hereinafter cited as "F3"]: accessed 1/ 2011), citing NARA publication M346, record group 109. File for Adolph Frank (Document # 5 of 5).

[50] "Confederate Papers relating to Citizens or Business Firms, 1861-1865," (F3: accessed 1/2011). File for Adolph Frank (Document # 3 of 5).

[51] Arthur W. Bergeron, Jr., *Guide to Louisiana Confederate Militaery Units 1861-1865* (Baton Rouge, LA: Louisiana State University Press, 1989), Appendix 1, p. 176.

[52] Alberta Rouseau Ducôté, compiler and translator, *St. Paul the Apostle Church, Mansura, Louisiana – Baptism Books #6 & #7, 1850-1872*, F-59.

[53] "Compiled Service Records of Confederate Soldiers who served in organizations for the State of Louisiana," digital image, (F3: accessed 1/2011), citing NARA publication M320, record group 109. File # 215 - Leopold Fortlouis, p. 2 and File #219 - Michel Fortlouis, p. 3.

[54] "Compiled Service Records of Confederate Soldiers who served in organizations for the State of Louisiana," (F3: accessed 1/2011), Michel Fortlouis File #219, p. 3.

[55] Bergeron, 13.

[56] "Compiled Service Records of Confederate Soldiers who served in organizations for the State of Louisiana," (F3: accessed 1/2011), Theophile Fortlouis File #220, p. 2.

[57] Bergeron, 13.

[58] "Compiled Service Records of Confederate Soldiers who served in organizations for the State of Louisiana," (F3: accessed 1/2011), Theophile Fortlouis File #220 p. 10; Leopold Fortlouis, File #215, p. 1.

[59] *Ibid.*, Theophile Fortlouis, File #220, p. 2; Leopold Fortlouis, File #215, p. 5.

[60] *Ibid.*, Michel Fortlouis, File #219, p. 6.

[61] Costello, 20, 212.

[62] "Compiled Service Records of Confederate Soldiers who served in organizations for the State of Louisiana," (F3: accessed 1/2011), Michel Fortlouis, File #219, pp. 7, 9, 11-14.

[63] Diane Janowski, *In their Honor: Soldiers of the Confederacy. The Elmira Prison Camp* (Elmira, New York: New York History Review Press, 2009), 8, 9, 12, 13, 96, 97.

[64] Janowski, 96.

[65] "Confederate Pension Application for Théophile Fortlouis, Pointe Coupée Parish, LA, File 11428," Louisiana State Archives, Reel CP1.50, Microdex 3, Sequence 20, Baton Rouge, Louisiana – 6 pages. Théophile Fortlouis' application for pension dated 13 March 1912.

[66] "Compiled Service Records of Confederate Soldiers who served in organizations for the State of Louisiana," (F3: accessed 1/2011), Theophile Fortlouis, File # 220, p. 5.

[67] 1910 U.S. Census, Pointe Coupée Parish, Louisiana, pop. sch, Ward 5, ED 79, p 2A (penned), Dwelling #16, Family #16, Numa P. Carmouche household, digital image, (A: accessed 1/ 2011), citing NARA microfilm publication T624, roll 526. Date of enumeration: 16 April 1910.

[68] "Louisiana Deaths 1850-1875; 1894-1954," database, (F: accessed 1/ 2011). Death of Theofile Fortlouis - Film number: 2364416, Certificate Number: 11039, Digital Folder Number: 4218215.

[69] "World War I Draft Registration Cards, 1917-1918," digital image, (A: accessed 1/ 2011), Morris Fortlouis, Serial No. 1426, Order No., 1614 Draft Board "0", Pointe Coupée Parish, citing NARA microfilm publication M 1509, no roll given. Imaged from FHL microfilm roll 1684929. Note: Maurice was described in 1918 as being, short, stout and having red hair and blue eyes.

[70] 1900 U.S. Census, Pointe Coupée Parish, Louisiana, pop. sch, Ward 9, ED 72, p 10A (penned), Dwelling #188, Family #188, Theofile (sic) Fortlouis household, digital image, (A: accessed 1/ 2011), citing NARA microfilm publication T623, roll 577. Date of enumeration: 12 June 1900.

[71] "Louisiana Deaths 1850-1875; 1894-1954," database, (F: accessed 1/2011). Death of Maurice Fortlouis - Film number: 1418363, Certificate Number: 6154, Digital Folder Number: 4215552.

[72] "Louisiana Deaths 1850-1875; 1894-1954," (F, accessed 1/2011), death of (Mrs.) Alex Isaac - Film number: 2364703, Certificate Number: 10747, Digital Folder Number: 4218221; and death of Alexandre Isaac, Film number: 2367540, Certificate Number: 731, Digital Folder Number: 4219346.

[73] "Louisiana Genealogy Links," database, *Angelfire.com* (http://www.angelfire.com/la/Rougon: accessed 26 January 2011), "Boots" Villere's Family Links.

[74] Stephanie died on May 25, 1929 at age 84. She was predeceased by her husband, whose date of death cannot been located.

[75] 1880 U.S. Census, Pointe Coupée Parish, Louisiana, pop. sch, Ward 7, ED 55, p 410D (penned), Dwelling #217, Family #217, (Mrs.) Paul Aguillard household, digital image, (A: accessed 1/ 2011), citing NARA microfilm publication T9, roll 465. Date of enumeration: 11 June 1880.

[76] 1880 U.S. Census, Pointe Coupée Parish, Louisiana, pop. sch, Ward 7, ED 55, p 406D (penned), Dwelling #124, Family #124, Maurice Fortlouis household, digital image, (A: accessed 1/ 2011), citing NARA microfilm publication T9, roll 465. Date of enumeration: 11 June 1880.

[77] 1910 U.S. Census, Pointe Coupée Parish, Louisiana, pop. sch, Happy Jack, ED 84, p 32B (penned), Family #547, Moise Fortlouis household, digital image, (A: accessed 1/ 2011), citing NARA microfilm publication T624, roll 526. Date of enumeration: 12 May 1910.

[78] Jeraldine DuFour LaCour, *Brides Book of Avoyelles Parish, Louisiana Volume 2, 1856-1880* (Bunkie: Jeraldine Dufour LaCour [203 South Gayle Blvd., Bunkie, LA], 1979), Wedding of Matilda Frank and John Schwartzenburg, p. 58.

[79] Jane McManus, submitter, "Index To Some Probate Dockets: Rapides, LA", database, *Usgwarchives.net* (http://files.usgwarchives.net: accessed 1/2011), File 271 - John Schwartzenburg, Jr. – Succession. 1876.

[80] "Louisiana Deaths 1850-1875; 1894-1954," database, (F: accessed 1/2011). Death of Mathilda Molener - Film number: 2358539, Certificate Number: 1873, Digital Folder Number: 4216109.

[81] "Louisiana Deaths 1850-1875; 1894-1954," database, (F: accessed 1/2011). Death of Aurore Claverie - Film number: 2366284, Certificate Number: 12137, Digital Folder Number: 4219129.

[82] This family information was researched by Patrick Marcotte, descendant of Albert Frank and sent to the author on December 20, 2003.

[83] LaCour, *Brides Book of Avoyelles Parish, Louisiana Volume 2, 1856-1880*, Wedding of Emile Frank and Lodoviska Saucier, p. 139, Wedding of Emelie Frank and Charles F. Huesman, p. 58.

[84] LaCour, *Brides Book of Avoyelles Parish, Louisiana Volume 2, 1856-1880*, Wedding of Cléophine Frank and George L. Mayer, 57.

[85] "Advertisements," LLMV, Microfilm # 5730, *The Marksville Bulletin*, 28 October 1876 p. 2, col. 1.

[86] "Parochial Items," LLMV, Microfilm # 5730, *The Marksville Bulletin*, 25 March 1882, p. 3, col. 1.

[87] LaCour, *Brides Book of Avoyelles Parish, Louisiana Volume 2, 1856-1880*, Wedding of Alicia Frank and Jean Marie Couget, p. 57.

[88] 1880 U.S. Census, Avoyelles Parish, Louisiana, pop. sch, Marksville, ED 1, p 4D (penned), Dwelling #32, Family #34, A. Frank household, digital image, (A: accessed 1/2011), citing NARA microfilm publication T9, roll 448. Date of enumeration: 14 June 1880.

[89] Virginia's parents Joseph François Charles Delhoste and Josephe Elizabeth Magdeleine Barate were natives of Perpignan, France, who immigrated to

Louisiana in 1834. Joseph Delhoste, a merchant, settled on the west bank of the Mississippi River in Jefferson Parish, where his nine children were born before the family moved to Concordia Parish.

[90] 1880 U.S. Census, Avoyelles Parish, Louisiana, pop. sch, Marksville, ED 1, p 14B (penned), Dwelling #141, Family #143, Louis Frank household; Dwelling #142, Family #144 Leon Molenor household; Dwelling #143, Family #145, Aurora Claverie household, digital image, (A: accessed 1/ 2011), citing NARA microfilm publication T9, roll 448. Date of enumeration: 17 June 1880.

[91] LaCour, *Brides Book of Avoyelles Parish, Louisiana Volume 2, 1856-1880*, Wedding of Clara Frank and Jules Émile Didier, p. 57.

[92] 1880 U.S. Census, Avoyelles Parish, Louisiana, pop. sch, Marksville, ED 1, p 2B (penned), Dwelling #15, Family #17, Jules Didier household, digital image, (A: accessed 1/ 2011), citing NARA microfilm publication T9, roll 448. Date of enumeration: 14 June 1880.

[93] LaCour, *Brides Book of Avoyelles Parish, Louisiana Volume 2, 1856-1880*, Marriage of Albert Frank and Felonise Roy, p. 136.

[94] Jeraldine DuFour LaCour, *Brides Book of Avoyelles Parish, Louisiana Volume 3, 1881-1899* (Alexandria: Jeraldine Dufour LaCour [P.O. Box 5022, Alexandria, LA], 1986), 56.

[95] "Died," LLMV, Microfilm # 5730, *The Marksville Bulletin,* 25 June 1881, p. 2, col. 2.

[96] "Parochial Items," LLMV, Microfilm # 5730, *The Marksville Bulletin,* 11 February 1882, p. 3, col. 1.

[97] "Parochial Items," LLMV, Microfilm # 5730, *The Marksville Bulletin,* 21 January 1882, p. 3, col. 3.

[98] "Christmas Stockings," LLMV, Microfilm # 5730, *The Marksville Bulletin,* 21 January 1882, p. 3, col. 2. Note: Auguste Voinché, a French

citizen, and a Marksville merchant, was nearly ruined in the Civil War after Union forces confiscated his cotton.

[99] "Wolves," LLMV, Microfilm # 5730, *The Marksville Bulletin,* 1 April 1882, p. 3, col. 2.

[100] *Executive Documents of the House of Representatives for the Second Session of the Forty-eighth Congress 1884-1885* (Washington DC : Government Printing Office, 1885), Exhibit B – Claims pp. 152-194.

[101] "French and American Claims Commission. Message from the President of the United States, transmitting a communication from the Secretary of State in relation to the French and American Claims Commission. February 9, 1885. – referred to the Committee on appropriations and ordered to be printed," *Genealogybank.com* (http://www.genealogybank.com [hereinafter cited as " GB"] : accessed 1/ 2011), Serial set Vol. No. 2306, Session Vol. #31; report H. exec. Doc. 248, dated 2/19/1885, p. 630, vouchers 37, 38, 39.

[102] LaCour, *Brides Book of Avoyelles Parish, Louisiana Volume 3, 1881-1899,* 56.

[103] Merle Farrington et. al., submitters, "1886 Orleans Parish Birth Index H through L", database, *Usgwarchives.net* (http://files.usgwarchives.net: accessed 1/ 2011), Birth of John Léonce Guilbert Laresche, Vol. 85 p. 295

[104] Erin Dazzo, Charlie and Loretta Picou, submitters, "1887 Orleans Parish death Index H through L," database, *Usgwarchives.net* (http://files.usgwarchives.net: accessed 1/ 2011). Death of John L. Laresche – 47 years.

[105] "Soard's New Orleans City Directory 1891," digital image, (F3: accessed 1/ 2011), 519. Listing for "Laresche, Bertha, wid. John, r. 200 Dumaine."

[106] " Untitled," LLMV, Microfilm # 1032, *La Revue de Marksville*, Vol. V, no. 26, 18 Oct 1884, p.1, col. 1. Note: In 1885, a small article appeared indicating that the running of the hotel had been taken over by George Stevens, former publisher of the *Villager* newspaper.

[107] "Parochial items," LLMV, Microfilm # 5730, *The Marksville Bulletin,* 28 March 1885, p. 3, col. 1.

[108] "Parochial items," LLMV, Microfilm # 5730, *The Marksville Bulletin,* 25 April 1885, p. 3, col. 1.

[109] LaCour, *Brides Book of Avoyelles Parish, Louisiana Volume 3, 1881-1899,* 56.

[110] "Illinois Cook County Deaths 1878-1922," digital image, (F: accessed 1/ 2011). Death certificate for Max Charles Weizenberg (Film # 1239665, Digital folder # 4004383).

[111] "Louisiana Deaths, 1850-1875; 1894-1954," database, (F: accessed 1/ 2011). Death of Ernest Moncla (Film #2381318, Digital folder # 4219313).

[112] "Texas Deaths," digital image, (F: accessed 1/ 2011). Death certificate for Emma W. Moncla (Film # 2075087, Digital folder # 4162790).

[113] "State and Parish Tax Sales of Immovable Property," LLMV, Microfilm # 1032, *The Marksville Review,* 17 September 1892, p. 2, col. 4.

[114] Avoyelles Parish Courthouse Records (Marksville, Avoyelles Parish, LA), *Inventories,* Book K, p. 36-38, "Estate of Adolph Frank, Interdict Inventory," filed 8 May 1894.

[115] Avoyelles Parish Courthouse Records (Marksville, Avoyelles Parish, LA), *Inventories,* Book K, p. 272-274, "Succession of Adolph Frank & Caroline Gaspard, both. Dec'd - Inventory," filed 28 November 1899.

[116] Camille Henriette Edwards was former Governor of Louisiana, Edwin W. Edwards', 1st, 2nd, 3rd and 4th cousin!

[117] 1920 U.S. Census, Avoyelles Parish, Louisiana, pop. sch, Marksville, Ward 2, ED 2 , p 9A (penned), Dwelling #180, Family #203, Lodoiska Frank household, digital image, (A: accessed 1/ 2011), citing NARA microfilm publication T625, roll 605. Date of enumeration: 9 January 1920.

[118] 1920 U.S. Census, Avoyelles Parish, Louisiana, pop. sch, Marksville, Ward 2, ED 2 , p 3B (penned), Dwelling #57, Family #64, Robert E. Frank household, digital image, (A: accessed 1/2011), citing NARA microfilm publication T625, roll 605. Date of enumeration: 3 January 1920.

[119] 1930 U.S. Census, Orleans Parish, Louisiana, pop. sch, New Orleans, Ward 2, ED 18 , p 10A (penned), Dwelling #87, Family #109, Robert E. Frank household, digital image, (A: accessed 1/ 2011), citing NARA microfilm publication T626, roll 801. Date of enumeration: 11 April 1930.

[120] LaCour, *Brides Book of Avoyelles Parish, Louisiana Volume 3, 1881-1899,* 77.

[121] Transcript in possession of Charles Bressler Jackson great-grandson of Mires and Caroline Aaron Rosenthal, furnished to the author in 2004.

[122] Lee Shai Weissbach, *Jewish Life in Small-Town America* (New Haven, CT: Yale University Press, 2005), 39.

Adolph Frank, undated. (*Courtesy of Randy Decuir, from a tintype in possession of Adolph's great-granddaughter, Faye Didier Devereaux*)

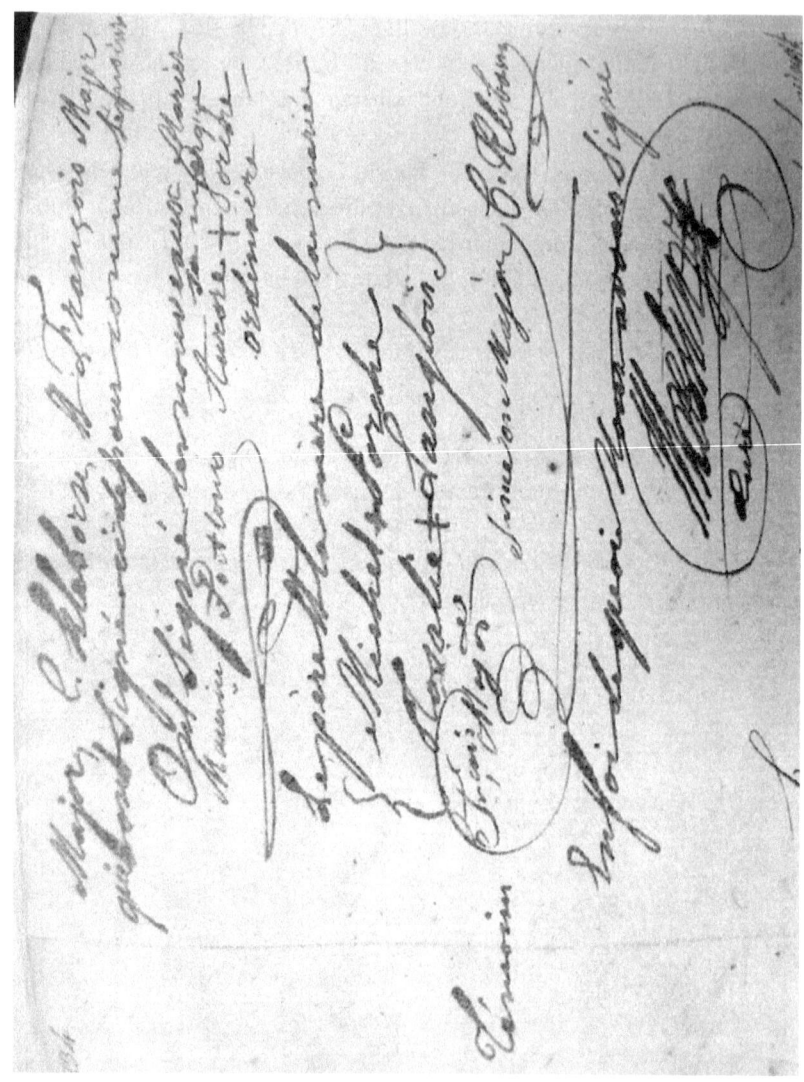

Signature page from the December 17, 1834 marriage of Maurice Fortlouis, who signed for himself (fourth line from top). His bride and the bride's parents signed with an "x." The witnesses, François Major and Simeon Major, as well as C. Kléborn (Claiborne), and the priest, Fr, Martin signed for themselves.
(*Diocese of Baton Rouge, Department of the Archives*)

CHAPTER 2

ABE FELSENTHAL – A POINTE MAIGRE PIONEER

Abe Felsenthal's life in Avoyelles Parish closely mirrored that of his co-religionists in Hydropolis and Marksville. According to his application for American citizenship, filed on March 24, 1850, he landed in New Orleans on February 11, 1841. Born on April 28, 1815, in Odenbach, Rheinland-Pfalz, Germany, Abe was the first of many Felsenthal family members to immigrate to the United States but the only one to settle in Louisiana.[1]

His father, David Felsenthal, born in 1776, married Johanetta Gruenebaum, and settled in Odenbach, where their first child, Jacob, was born on October 16, 1809. Their third, Abraham, who would eventually come to Louisiana, preceded his elder brother, Jacob, to America by twenty-three years and his niece, Jacob's daughter, Hannah, by fifteen. In 1856, Hannah Felsenthal joined the Jacob Gruenebaum family, cousins of her paternal grandmother who lived in Chicago.[2] Hannah's father, Jacob, followed with his second wife, Gertrude Herz, and their nine children, arriving in America on August 5, 1864, on the Ship "Elena"[3] By that time, Abe Felsenthal had been in Avoyelles Parish for twenty-three years. The most well-known Felsenthal to come to America was Rabbi Bernhard Felsenthal who emigrated from Münchweiler, Germany to Chicago, Illinois in 1854. A noted Zionist and leader in the Reform movement of Judaism, Rabbi Felsenthal was Abe Felsenthal's half first cousin once removed.[4] The year before the Rabbi came to America, his youngest brother, David, had arrived in Arkansas to start a dynasty whose descendants made their homes in Camden, El Dorado and Felsenthal, the Arkansas town named for the family.[5] Another brother, Marcus, arriving in 1853, chose Louisville, Kentucky and his descendants travelled as far as Memphis, Tennessee to settle down. It is through Rabbi Bernhard Felsenthal's reminiscences written in 1891, and his daughter Emma's book which followed in 1924, that the early history of the family is available.[6]

It is not known why Abe Felsenthal chose Central Louisiana as his home, or why other relatives decided to move elsewhere. After arriving in New Orleans, Abe, like Maurice Fortlouis before him, spent some time as a peddler, roaming the countryside until he found a place to his liking. He opened his store in an area of Avoyelles Parish called Pointe Maigre, also known as Ward 1, whose towns include Cassandria, Effie and Center Point.[7] Separated from the rest of the parish by the meandering Red River, Pointe Maigre was accessible from the village of Moncla via a ferry to the other side. Sparsely inhabited, only eighteen or so families were farming in the area by 1848.[8] There being no other merchants in the community, Abe took up residence, marrying, his first wife, Selena Aymond.

Selena was the eighth of nine children of Jean-Baptiste Aymond II, born at Bayou Boeuf to his first wife, Roseline Dauzat. Jean II's father, Jean-Baptiste Pierre Aymond I, was one of the many Frenchmen who had emigrated from France to settle in Avoyelles Parish. He arrived several years before the fall of the Bastille looking to escape a despotic government and a shaky economy. He and his wife, Marianne Joffrion, came to Pointe Maigre where their sons, Pierre, Jean II, Michel and Étienne all remained to farm and raise cattle. Although a Catholic, Jean I and his family were steeped in the anti-clerical culture of the French Revolutionary period, which was brought to Louisiana by the many French immigrants in the area. So it is not surprising to find that the father of the bride was not opposed to his daughter marrying a Jew. The civil union of twenty-eight year old Abe Felsenthal and fifteen year old Selena Aymond took place on April 20, 1843.[9]

Abe's new father-in-law, Jean-Baptiste Aymond II, was not only a second generation land owner at Pointe Maigre, but also a political force in the area. A minority player, being of French extraction, in a locale where mostly Anglos had settled, he had, nevertheless, been elected to the Police Jury in the 1830s.[10] He and his brother-in-law, John Reed, his oldest sister, Mary Catherine's husband, had farmed land in the area since 1800, each obtaining formal title to 640 acres in 1816.[11]

Abe and Selena's first child, Herman, was born around 1848. Unlike some Catholic women in mixed marriages, who had their children baptized, there are no records of the Felsenthal children born in the first marriage ever having had the benefit of this sacrament. Two years later, in July 1850, Selena gave birth to twins. According to the 1850 census they were named "Belvensein" and "Rothsein." Nothing is known of the latter but since he does not appear in the 1860 census, he must have died as a child. Belvensein, however does appear in the 1860 census as a female child with the same peculiar name, as well as in a succession document written in 1863 after Selena Felsenthal's death. This name, in subsequent years, was Americanized to "Barbara."[12] Three more children, Martha born in 1853, Hannah Louisiana in 1855 and Jacobias in 1856, joined the Felsenthal family and are enumerated in the 1860 census.[13]

As his family grew, and his finances permitted, Abe Felsenthal began to buy land in Pointe Maigre. On August 9, 1851, he purchased seventy acres, south of Cassandria on Bayou Wiggins, from William Hays for $120.[14] In late 1854, he acquired an additional thirty-nine acres from the estate of Joseph Marschal, mortgaged, with the entire sum of one hundred dollars payable in full on September 11, 1855.[15] On February 14, 1857, Abe Felsenthal made his first purchase of a slave from the estate of Mary LaCroix, widow of Samuel Glass, one of the largest landowners in Pointe Maigre. Bill, a thirty year old "mulatto" who was a "slave for life," was mortgaged for $1250. At the time of the sale, Abe paid one third of the price in cash. The other two-thirds were due in equal instalments in 1858 and 1859.[16] In the 1860 Federal Slave Schedule for Avoyelles Parish, Abe was listed as the owner of three slaves, a thirty-two year old black female, a fifteen year old black female and a three year old black male. During the same period of time, his wife's Aymond family members, all farmers, were owners of at least two dozen slaves themselves.[17]

By 1857, Abe's acquisition of land had grown exponentially. He mortgaged one thousand acres of farmland in and around Cassandria adjacent to the Experiment Sugar Plantation, bought from his neighbors William and Elizabeth Alexandre for $1125.[18] Judging from Abe's investments before the Civil War, he was doing very well, being the only general merchant of note north of the Red River in Avoyelles Parish. No acquisition, however, was too small. Later on in 1857, Abe bought James A. Hopson's share in his father, Littleton Hopson's estate, for $140.[19] In the 1860 census, Abe estimated his net worth at four thousand dollars invested in real estate with an accumulation of two thousand dollars in personal property, a considerable sum for the time. That same year, Abe who, had been corresponding with his Felsenthal and Gruenebaum relatives in Chicago, bought property in Illinois. Perhaps, on the eve of the War Between the States, he was thinking of heading to Chicago to be with other family members. He paid eight hundred dollars for ten acres in Cook County, Illinois.[20] The fact that so many of his transactions were made "cash in hand" was a testimony to his wealth.

Being the leading retail merchant, as well as one of the largest land owners in Pointe Maigre, his home and store became the political gathering place for Ward One. On February 28, 1858, *The Villager* announced the upcoming election for the Judge of the Thirteenth Judicial District, to be held on March 8, 1858. The polling place for Ward One was Abe Felsenthal's house.[21] In 1861, Sheriff P. P. Normand advertised that business licenses would be sold, and parish taxes collected for Pointe Maigre on April 15th and 17th at "Abe Felsendall's store." Included in the notice was the information that the parish tax would be levied at the rate of 100% on the State tax, a question that had probably been on everyone's mind since Louisiana had just seceded from the Union two months earlier. This same issue of the newspaper announced the adoption of the Confederate flag as well as the training of one of the first divisions from the Parish to make itself ready for combat, the Avoyelles Riflemen.[22] Felsenthal's home and store continued to be a polling place and a satellite parish office for the residents who lived north of the Red River until his death. The

War, however, and subsequent period of reconstruction took a great toll on everyone including Abe, whose last child with Selena, David Franklin Felsenthal, was born on February 26, 1861.

Abe was safe from conscription being forty-six at the outset of the Civil War. The Confederate States of America had enacted the first ever "draft" in April 1862 requiring all able-bodied men between the ages of eighteen and thirty-five years to spend three years in the armed forces. Exempted were railroad and marine workers, civil servants, teachers, telegraphers, druggists, and non-citizens.[23] A September amendment, the same year, raised the age limit to forty-five. A month later, land owners with more than twenty slaves to oversee, were relieved from service. Anyone with the means could hire a substitute to do his fighting for him. These latter two provisions caused much unrest and dissention amongst the local residents. The poor farmer, with little or no material stake in the War, felt that he was being used as cannon fodder to defend the way of life of the large plantation owner who sat at home watching his slaves do the work. A conscript's wife and children were left mostly to their own devices, with no other help but themselves, to eke out a living on a plot of ground which, in good times, could barely keep them in food. For those reasons the desertion rate amongst the soldiers was high.

Many prominent Anglos in Pointe Maigre, including the Sayes, Masters and Edwards families, turned to the Union cause.[24] It is not known with certainty whether Abe Felsenthal and his family were Unionists or Rebel sympathizers. Pointe Maigre was, however, the center of much political intrigue and guerrilla warfare between the two rival factions. It is known that Abe contributed to the rebel cause because he appears as "A. Felsenthal of the town of Cassandria" in the "Rebel Citizens File," a list of private individuals or business firms who provided goods and services to the Confederacy.[25]

Such were the turbulent times, which drained the South of its young men as well as its financial stability. Abe Felsenthal, like many of his neighbors, would never again be able to afford to invest money in land, and the acres that he did own, were, by the time of his death, practically worthless in the postwar economy. His first wife, Selena Aymond, died in the fall of 1862. Although there is no record of her passing, or any indication of where she was buried, her succession papers were filed on November 21, 1862, and an inventory of her estate was taken several weeks later. Her holdings, consisting of community property held jointly with her husband, Abe, and property inherited from her deceased parents, was exceptionally large, estimated to be worth $6,122.60. Included in this total were approximately 1100 acres of land north of the Red River valued at eleven hundred dollars, an additional one hundred twenty acres at Pointe Maigre valued at $756.25, and thirty-nine acres at Bayou Choctaw valued at $479. Her slave holdings included Hannah, an African American, age thirty-eight and her child, Mary, age six, valued at thirteen hundred dollars, and a griffe [26] girl, Emeline, age sixteen valued at twelve hundred dollars. In addition, there were seventy head of horned cattle worth seven hundred dollars, one yoke of oxen ($70), five horses ($300), one wagon ($100), one buggy ($75), eighty hogs ($480), four sets of bedding ($150), one armoire, two bureaus, twelve chairs and other miscellaneous furniture ($72).[27]

Left with five young children, Abe took a second wife on June 29, 1864, in a ceremony conducted by Jean Pierre Aymond, Justice of the Peace, his late wife's first cousin. The bride was Mary Ann Eleanor Blunt, twenty-five years his junior.[28] Mary Ann was the third child of Alexander Blunt and his wife Mary Simmons. Originally from Mississippi, Blunt had moved to Rapides Parish in the late 1830s where he married and fathered his six children. Twenty years later the family moved to Pointe Maigre where they tended a farm, owning nine slaves to help them work it.[29] Abe's marriage to Mary Ann was a brief one. In November 1865, they became the parents of one son, Lawrence A. Felsenthal. They divorced less than three years later.

Abe married for a third time at the age of fifty-three on February 10, 1868. The bride was Elodie Guillot, the twenty-seven year old widow of Philogène Mayeux. The civil union was conducted by François Barbin de Bellevue, J. P.[30] Elodie, born on June 12, 1841, was the daughter of parish residents, Zénon Guillot and his wife,

Edvige Dupuy.[31] Elodie moved in with Abe, his children, Jacobias, Hannah, Herman and David, bringing her daughter, Marie Elizordie Mayeux, from her first marriage. Abe and Elodie's first child, Benjamin C. Felsenthal, was born on January 12, 1869.[32]

The 1870 census enumerated Abe as a farmer with two thousand dollars invested in real estate and five hundred dollars in personal property, a far cry from his pre-war worth. He and his wife, Elodie, their one year old son, Benjamin, Elodie's four year old daughter, Marie Elizordie, as well as his sons Herman, Jacobias, David Franklin, and daughter Hannah from his first marriage were all living in his Pointe Maigre home. "Belvensein/ Barbara" Felsenthal, Abe's daughter with Selena Aymond, was no longer living with the family.[33] She was the first of Abe's children to leave for Chicago. According to the 1880 federal census, Barbara lived with her Uncle Jacob's daughter, Marianna Felsenthal, and her husband, Sigmund Birkenstein. She was employed as their servant, a custom not unusual in European Jewish households, where affluent family members often used poor relations as domestic help.[34] Although Abe never seemed to forge a bond with his co-religionists in Avoyelles Parish, few as they might have been, or in Rapides Parish where they were more numerous, he apparently did make an effort to see that some of his children were introduced into the Hebrew faith through his connection to the Chicago branch of the family.

Herman Felsenthal, Abe's eldest son, just starting out his life in post-war Reconstruction Louisiana, worked first on his father's farm, and, upon attaining his majority, inherited enough money from his late mother's estate to purchase four town lots in Cassandria on June 8, 1869, from Sydalise Hayes for fifty dollars.[35] After his enumeration in his father's household in 1870 he disappears from all written records and is presumed to have predeceased his father before 1877.

Abe and Elodie's last child, Esther Felsenthal, was born in March 1874. She barely knew her father who was fifty-nine at the time of her birth. His older children from his first marriage were now in their late twenties. Jacobias and David were still trying to eke out an existence on the family farm in post-war Louisiana. On July 22, 1875, Abe Felsenthal turned over one hundred twenty acres in Pointe Maigre to his son, Jacobias, the latter's entire share of his late mother, Selena Aymond's estate. On that same day Jacobias sold the acreage to his neighbor, twenty-one year old Alcée Laborde, for $100 cash.[36]

Mary Ann Eleanor Blunt was enumerated in 1870 living next door to her ex-husband, Abe Felsenthal, with her father, Alex Blunt, her youngest sister, Laura, and her son, Lawrence Felsenthal, named on the document in error as Lawrence Blunt. On March 4, 1875, Mary Ann remarried. The groom was thirty-nine year old widower Andrew Richey, who had grown up next door to Abe Felsenthal, his first wife, Selena, and their young children.[37] Moreover, Andrew's first wife, the late Rosaline Sayes, was Abe Felsenthal's deceased wife's niece. Andrew Richey had been a teamster during the Civil War in Company "G," the First Louisiana Cavalry until he deserted in October of 1863.[38] As the tide turned against the Confederacy he threw his lot in with his Unionist father-in-law, Martin Sayes. Andrew and Mary Ann Blunt Richey were married for thirty five years and had three children of their own. Richey's step-son, Lawrence Felsenthal, grew up in a Christian household, never having any Jewish roots to put down.

Abe Felsenthal died on February 11, 1877, just several months short of his sixty-second birthday. According to a brief newspaper account, the long-time resident of Pointe Maigre was buried the next day in Alexandria.[39] There is, however, no record of his interment at the Jewish Cemetery in Pineville. There are, however, a few family members buried in the Old Rapides Cemetery. Abe's son, Benjamin, the latter's wife, Sarah, and two of their children, Tency and Dennis, are interred there. There is another grave marked A.E. Felsenthal, whose stone is so eroded that it cannot be deciphered. It is, however, in the shape of a cross, so it is doubtful that it could be his resting place.

Abe's succession papers were filed at Marksville, on March 20, 1877, subsequent to the taking of an inventory. The entire estate was valued at $734.25, with the lion's share being the 1011 acres purchased from William Alexandre in 1857. It is clear from this document that

Abe was no longer a merchant, as the rest of the inventory consisted of personal household goods and farm implements worth less than $100. There were a few promissory notes, probably carry-overs from his days as a store owner, worth fifteen dollars more or less.[40] On April 25th, the administrator of Abe's estate, Montillion I. Ryland, petitioned the court to allow that the land and personal effects of the deceased be advertised and sold to satisfy certain debts. At the same time, he requested that Elodie Guillot, Abe's widow, be appointed tutor to her son and daughter, Benjamin and Esther Felsenthal, then eight and three years old, and to act on their behalf.[41] At the family meeting, held on July 3, 1877, for the benefit of the children, it was deemed advisable to allow Abe's widow, Elodie, to purchase land at Abe's succession sale in the amount coming to the minor children under their said right of homestead.[42] The succession dragged on for more than four years, with another inventory, being made in March 1878, where the worth of the estate, including the 1011 acres in Pointe Maigre were assessed at a mere one-tenth of what it was said to have be worth a year before.[43] A newspaper announcement in December 1881 indicated that the estate had finally been settled.[44]

Abe's living children from his three marriages profited little from his death. Jake stayed on through 1880, trying his luck as a farmer. A year later, however, he decided to give it all up and followed his sister, Barbara, to Chicago. He became a peddler, and on October 6, 1886, he was married to eighteen year old Margaret Conlan at St. Malachy's Church by Father Michael Mackin.[45] Jake died, however, less than five years later, of meningitis. Despite his Catholic marriage, he was buried at the Free Sons of Israel (Waldheim) Cemetery in Forest Park, Illinois.[46] Although in moving to Chicago he could have become integrated into the Jewish community, his past seems to have better suited him for something else. He certainly did not hesitate to imitate his father by marrying outside of the Jewish faith.

Barbara, on the other hand, after three years in her cousin, Marianna Birkenstein's household, in Chicago, married Bernard Friedman on April 30, 1882. Her late father's half first cousin once-removed, the renowned Rabbi Bernhard Felsenthal performed the ceremony.⁴⁷ Five children were born to the couple. Helena (b. 1883), Abraham (b. 1885), and Herman (b. 1886) died as children. Lena (b. 1887) married Donald McIntosh and died at age forty-six in Chicago on December 20, 1934.⁴⁸ Barbara's last child, Jacob (b. 1891), wed Theora Timmons. In 1920, Jacob, a locomotive engineer for the Chicago, Milwaukee and St. Paul Railway, his wife, Theora, and his four month old daughter, Jessie Bernette, born on August 19, 1919,⁴⁹ appeared together for the first and only time in a Federal Census. ⁵⁰ Jacob died on February 1, 1926, at the age of thirty-five. He was buried in the Acacia Park Masonic Cemetery in Chicago. ⁵¹ Despite her Jewish marriage, Barbara's surviving children did not carry their faith into the next generation.

Following Barbara and Jake to Chicago sometime after the death of his father, David Franklin Felsenthal boarded with his Uncle Jacob Felsenthal and was taken into the family business. The elder Jacob had already retired, but his son, Samuel, his son-in-law, Sigmund Birkenstein, and David worked together as dealers in paper.⁵² On December 24, 1882, at the age of twenty-one, David married nineteen year old Wilhelmine Knoll in a ceremony conducted by Rabbi Bernhard Felsenthal of the Zion Congregation of Chicago.⁵³ David and Minnie had three children, Dora, who died at less than two months old in 1884, Flora born in 1886, and Lucille born on March 14, 1893.⁵⁴ David left the family business some time before the turn of the twentieth century, and set himself up as a dealer in tailor clippings. His daughter Flora's husband, Max Albert Seeger, a Jewish immigrant from Berlin, Germany joined his father-in-law in the business after his marriage to her on June 21, 1905.⁵⁵ Their only surviving child, Lillian, disappears from all records after 1930. David and Minnie's daughter, Lucille, wed David L. Armitage on December 31, 1918, in a Jewish ceremony conducted by Rabbi Samuel Cohen of the Zion Congregation of Chicago. Armitage was a second generation quarry worker, employed as a teamster. Despite the Jewish nuptials, it is not known if he was a member of that faith. The couple lived with their in-laws until David Felsenthal's death on November 27, 1921.⁵⁶ Thereafter, his widow, Minnie Knoll Felsenthal, lived with David Armitage, his wife

Lucille, and their daughter, Audrey, born in 1925. Minnie Felsenthal passed away on August 15, 1930. David and Minnie Felsenthal were both interred at the Free Sons of Israel Cemetery. Lifelong residents of Chicago, David Armitage went on to become a machinist in a rail shop, and Lucile was a beautician.[57]

Although Abe's oldest children who had left Louisiana as young adults had had the opportunity to return to their father's faith, their attachment was not as strong as if they had been raised in a solidly Jewish household. One can only speculate how easily these Louisiana country cousins had really adapted to their new environment, and exactly how their more sophisticated relatives in Chicago viewed them. With one foot planted solidly in the Christian South and the other seeking a strong toehold in this northern industrial city, it is no wonder that their adherence to the Jewish way of life never really took hold. The number of mixed marriages within this group bears testament to their religious ambivalence.

In Avoyelles Parish, however, there would be no question about the fate of Abe's other children. Having lost their father's influence at a young age, his sons became farmers in the tradition of their Aymond, Guillot and Blunt relatives. The daughters married into Christian families, and their Jewish identity was completely submerged into the prevailing culture of the area. Mary Blunt Felsenthal Richey's son, Lawrence, was a prime example of this type of assimilation. Lawrence was a lifelong resident of Pointe Maigre, who worked as a farmer. He married Julia Clarice Robertson on June 9, 1890, in a civil ceremony.[58] Julia, the only child of a brief union between Charles Robertson and his wife Julie Azéma Luneau, was raised by her grandparents, Jean Baptiste Luneau, a Pointe Maigre farmer, and his wife, Azéma Legros.[59] Several years after their marriage, Julia Felsenthal purchased eighty acres in Pointe Maigre, from her grandfather's estate, for $200. It was this property, bought in 1893, that the Lawrence Felsenthal family farmed through the end of World War I.[60] Three children were born to them: Estelle (b. 1891), Eva, (b. 1894) and Hobson (b. 1899).[61] Estelle died as a child, but Eva lived to marry another local resident, William Scroggs. By 1915 the

Scroggs family had moved to nearby Oakdale, Allen Parish, where their first child, William, died as an infant in 1915. Their daughter, Wilfred, was born in Oakdale in 1918, but by 1920, Eva was a widow (or perhaps divorced, as people were rarely forthcoming about that in the early twentieth century), living with her daughter.[62] Eva's brother, Hobson, also living in Oakdale, was a self-employed tailor. Hobson may also have died young as he disappears from records after 1918.[63] Eva remarried in 1921. The groom was one of her Allen Parish neighbors, George L. Dixon, a salesman of petroleum products. Their child, George, Jr., was born in 1925. Eva supplemented her husband's income by working as a milliner.[64] Eva and her son, George Dixon Jr., lived out their lives in Oakdale, the former dying there in 1983, the latter in 2010.

Abe Felsenthal's widow, Elodie Guillot, never remarried. In 1880 she could be found living alone, with her two children by Abe Felsenthal, Benjamin, now eleven, and Hester (Esther), now eight, in Pointe Maigre. At the age of twenty-three, on January 28, 1892, her son, Benjamin, married Sarah Kelone, the daughter of another farming family in the area. Sarah's grandfather, Patrick Kelone, born in 1824, immigrated to Avoyelles Parish from County Roscommon in Ireland in the 1840s.[65] Patrick, a pioneer farmer at Egg Bend (Fifth Ward, north and west of Marksville), married into the Juneau family, and sired six sons. His first born, Thomas, and the latter's wife, Elizabeth Guillory, were Sarah's parents. Ben and Sarah Kelone Felsenthal had six children. Their first daughter, Eva, born in 1892, married Camille A. Bordelon at the age of twenty.[66] They moved to Alexandria, where Camille worked most of his life for various businesses run by the Jewish Rosenthal Brothers, first as a clerk in their bar room, then as a clerk in the Rosenthal grocery, and finally as a salesman in their hardware store. The Bordelon children, Ruth and Hubert, were raised as Christians.

Toby, Ben and Sarah's second child, born in 1894 at Egg Bend also moved to nearby Rapides Parish. He learned telegraphy and was employed by Western Union.[67] Toby and his wife, Alice, had one child, Eugene Lynn Felsenthal, born on February 17, 1924, at Alexandria.[68] Toby died suddenly at age 36 on December 3, 1930.[69]

Ben and Sarah's third and fourth children, Christopher Columbus Felsenthal (b. 1897) and Tency Deigo Felsenthal (b.1899) were born when the family was still farming their land in Avoyelles Parish.[70] Their next, a daughter, Flora, was born in the parish on November 22, 1902, on the eve of the worst scourge to visit the area since the Civil War and Reconstruction.[71] For the next fifteen years the boll weevil would wreak havoc on southern cotton crops, forcing farmers off their lands and destroying the businesses supported by these agricultural endeavors. Ben and his family were amongst the many who would abandon their farms and head for the nearest city to pick up the pieces of their lives. Sarah and Ben's last child, Dennis, was born in 1908 just before they moved to nearby Alexandria in Rapides Parish.[72] From then on, Ben supported his wife and children as a carpenter, living in town with many other families who had also lost their livelihoods during the crisis.[73]

Sarah Kelone Felsenthal died in Alexandria on September 26, 1916,[74] and soon after, Ben married Anna Florence Couvillion, who had been previously married to Thomas Willie Guillot, another Pointe Maigre farmer, with whom she had had seven children. The 1920 census shows the blended family, Ben, Anna, and three of Anna's children, Levi, age twenty-six, Pauline, age twelve and Drucy (Elmira) Guillot, age nine, and Ben's son, Dennis, age twelve. Ben and his stepson, Levi, were employed as carpenters, building homes in the Alexandria area.[75]

Ben's son, Tency, also living in Alexandria, became an electrician.[76] He died prematurely on February 26, 1939 at Columbia, in Caldwell parish.[77] Tency's brother, Columbus, wed Odette Delaune, a native of St. Martinville, LA. He made a living by clerking for a local railroad. The couple were the parents of twins, Wallace Russell and Wallice Sarah Felsenthal, and a son, Gerard Keith Felsenthal. Columbus, Odette and Gerard were lifelong residents of Alexandria.[78] The Felsenthal children were raised as Roman Catholics, their mother's religion. Ben's youngest daughter, Flora, married John McDonald, a Scotsman, who immigrated to the United States in 1907. They had one son, Lawrence, born in 1923 and lived in Galveston, Texas, where John worked in a brokerage office.[79]

Benjamin Felsenthal died on January 5, 1926, at Alexandria, and was buried in the Old Rapides Cemetery in Pineville.[80] Soon after he died, his youngest son, Dennis, who was mentally challenged, became an inmate at the State Colony and Training School, located on the grounds of Camp Beauregard outside of Pineville, Louisiana. He died on March 27, 1967, and was buried next to his father and mother at the Old Rapides Cemetery.[81]

Abe Felsenthal's youngest child, Esther Felsenthal, had a brief marriage to George Townsend. She and their daughter, Mary Townsend, born in July of 1897 in Avoyelles Parish, were living with her mother, Elodie Felsenthal, on a farm in Avoyelles in 1900. The census taker made a notation in 1900 that Esther was separated from her husband.[82]

The Jewish influence in the lives of the Felsenthal children had died with Abe in 1877, and with the exception of the three, from his first marriage, who left to live in Chicago with other Felsenthal relatives, the rest enjoyed lives of complete assimilation into the Christian agrarian community of Avoyelles Parish. The men farmed, until that was no longer tenable, then sought employment in nearby larger cities. The women married into long established Avoyelles and Rapides Parish families. As it was in the Frank and Fortlouis families, their Jewish ancestor was all but forgotten. Had Abe Felsenthal lived longer, had he prospered more, had he been able to set his children up into their own businesses in the area, his children's lives might have been very different. His own attachment to the Jewish faith, however, seemed to be non-existent. He was never an active member of the Congregation Gemiluth Chassodim in Alexandria, was not buried in the Jewish Cemetery in Pineville, did not give his children a Jewish education, or, in some cases, any education at all. He never sought out a Jewish bride in New Orleans as some of his co-religionists had done, instead marrying three Christian women. Although he made it possible for three of his oldest children, Barbara, Jacob and David, to leave the area to join Jewish relatives in Illinois, their tenuous connection to Judaism made it difficult and indeed impossible for them to sustain their father's faith over the course of subsequent generations.

---

[1] Jeraldine Dufour LaCour, *Avoyelleans of Yesteryear* (Bunkie: Jeraldine Dufour LaCour [P.O. Box 5022, Alexandria, LA], 1983), 122 (File #84). Note: The entry indicated he was from the Department "Counsel" actually "Kusel," Kingdom of "Byon," a misspelling of the German "Bayern," or as we know it " Bavaria."

[2] 1860 U. S. Census, Cook County, Illinois, pop. sch., Chicago, Ward 6, p. 70 (penned), Dwelling #623, Family #633, Jacob Greenbaum household, digital image, *Ancestry.com* (http://www.ancestry.com [hereinafter cited as "A"]: accessed 8/ 2010), citing NARA microfilm publication M653, roll 1163. Date of enumeration: 12 July, 1860.

[3] "New York Passenger Lists, 1820-1957," digital images, (A: accessed 8/2010). Arrival of SS *Elena* 5 August 1864 at New York from Havre, citing *Passenger Lists of Vessels Arriving at New York, New York, 1820-1897* NARA Microfilm Serial: M237, roll 243, lines 21-24 and 47-53; List number 778. Arrival of Jacob, Gertrude, Benjamin, Sarah, Samuel, Salomon, David, Isaac, Marianna, Judith and Charlotte Felsenthal.

[4] Abe's grandfather, Jacob Felsenthal, married twice. Abe's father, David, was a child of Jacob's second wife, Leah Wolf, while Rabbi Bernhard was a great-grandchild descended from Jacob's, first wife, Johanna Bayer Herz. This made Abe and Jacob only half first cousins. The two were "once removed" because Jacob Felsenthal was Abe's grandfather, but Bernhard's great-grandfather.

[5] Felsenthal, Arkansas was founded in 1900 by David's sons, Adolph, Isaac, Sidney and Lee, as a sawmill town, but never developed due to severe repeated flooding during the early part of the 20th century. In 1978 it was reincorporated as a result of the development of a sixty-five thousand acre Felsenthal Wildlife Refuge donated by the Felsenthal Family Estate, and made possible by a lock and dam system to control the flooding of the Ouachita River. See: Carolyn Gray LeMaster, *A Corner of the Tapestry – A History of*

the Jewish Experience in Arkansas, 1820s-1990s (Fayetteville: University of Arkansas Press, 1994), 199-200, 445-446.

[6] "Reminiscences of Rabbi Bernhard Felsenthal," Chicago, 1891. Manuscript in possession of Rabbi David Shapiro, Jerusalem, Israel, parts of which were emailed to the author on 11 July 2006. See also, Emma Felsenthal, *Bernhard Felsenthal – Teacher in Israel* (New York: Oxford University Press, 1924), 3-19.

[7] In 1830 Avoyelles Parish was divided into 5 election districts: Pointe Maigre, Avoyelles Prairie, Bayou Rouge, the prairie of Bayou Rouge, and Bayou Boeuf.

[8] Corinne L. Saucier, *History of Avoyelles Parish* (Gretna, Louisiana: Pelican Publishing Co., 1998), 70.

[9] Jeraldine DuFour LaCour, *Brides Book of Avoyelles Parish, Louisiana Volume I, 1808-1855* (Bunkie: Jeraldine Dufour LaCour [203 South Gayle Blvd., Bunkie, LA], 1979), 3. Note: Fourteen months later, Jean Aymond II's sister Hélène Aymond Fouquier's granddaughter, Justine Dupuis, became the bride of another German Jewish immigrant, Michael Aaron in Pineville, Rapides Parish, LA.

[10] A police jury is the governing body of a parish, much like the councils found in many northern U.S. counties.

[11] "American State Papers, Volume 3 – Public Lands," database, *Genealogybank.com* (www.genealogybank.com [hereinafter cited as "GB"]: accessed 8/ 2010), 214, # 493-1117 (Claim of John Amon) and # 494-1118 (Claim of John Reed).

[12] 1850 U. S. Census, Avoyelles Parish, Louisiana, pop. sch. Town not stated, Page not legible, Dwelling #641, Family #641, A. Felsendall (sic) household, digital image, (A: accessed 8/2010), citing NARA microfilm publication M 432, roll 229. Date of enumeration: 12 October 1850.

[13] 1860 U. S. Census, Avoyelles Parish, Louisiana, pop. sch., Marksville, p. 111 (penned), Dwelling #760, Family #760, Abram Felsenthall (sic)

household, digital image, (A: accessed 9/ 2010), citing NARA microfilm publication M653, no roll given. Date of enumeration: 26 October 1860.

[14] Avoyelles Parish Courthouse Records (Marksville, Avoyelles Parish, LA), *Conveyances,* Book W, p. 301, no. 7744, "William Hays to Abraham Felsenthal, Sale of Land," filed August 9, 1851.

[15] Avoyelles Parish Courthouse Records (Marksville, Avoyelles Parish, LA), *Conveyances,* Book Z, p. 280, no. 8648, "Jean Bte. David, Adm., Sale of land with mortgage to Abraham Felsenthall," filed November 18, 1854.

[16] Avoyelles Parish Courthouse Records (Marksville, Avoyelles Parish, LA), *Conveyances,* Book BB, pp. 61, 62, no. 9583, "Peter Lacroix, administrator, Sale of slave with mortgage to Abraham Felsenthal," filed February 14, 1857.

[17] 1860 U. S. Census, Avoyelles Parish, Louisiana, slave schedule, p. 74 (penned), Abram Felunthall, (sic), owner, digital image, (A: accessed 8/ 2010), citing NARA microfilm publication M653, no roll given. Date of enumeration: 11 October 1860.

[18] Avoyelles Parish Courthouse Records (Marksville, Avoyelles Parish, LA), *Conveyances,* Book BB, p. 158, no. 9658, " William Alexandre and wife – Sale of land with mortgage – to Abraham Felsenthal," filed April 9, 1857.

[19] Avoyelles Parish Courthouse Records (Marksville, Avoyelles Parish, LA), *Conveyances,* Book BB, pp. 360,361, no. 9797, " James A. Hopson, Sale of Rights to Abraham Felsenthal," filed September 11, 1857.

[20] Avoyelles Parish Courthouse Records (Marksville, Avoyelles Parish, LA), *Conveyances,* Book EE, p. 429, no. 10973, "Charles Banks, Sale of Land to Abraham Felsenthal," filed April 9, 1860.

[21] Louisiana State University Libraries On Line Catalog – Special Collections – Louisiana and Lower Mississippi Valley (hereinafter cited as "LLMV"), Microfilm #5964, *The Villager (Le Villageois),* Marksville, Avoyelles Parish, LA, 27 February 1858 - Volume 14, no. 9, p. 4, col. 4.

[22] LLMV, Microfilm #5753, *The Pelican –Official Journal*, Marksville, Avoyelles Parish, LA, 6 March 1861, p. 2.

[23] The exemption for non-citizens was short-lived. By December 1862, the Confederacy, which was outnumbered by more than two to one on the battlefield started drafting non-citizens who owned land or businesses, because they had a material stake in the outcome of the war. The December 20, 1862 issue of *The Pelican,* Vol 22, no.32, page 2 col. 3, listed amongst the latest conscripts the following foreign nationals: John Weil, Jules Descant, E. Bringol, David Siess, Simon Siess, Victor Garnier, Alphonse Monin. Louis Cayer, Jean Gajean, and Marcellin Gajean, all French citizens with the exception of John Weil, who was born in Ingenheim, Bavaria.

[24] "Letter from an Exiled Unionist – A Painful Story, Addressed to the Editor of the Delta from T.J. Edwards," *The (New Orleans, LA) Daily Delta,* 15 July 1862, p. 2, col. 2, digital image, (GB: accessed 9/ 2010).

[25] "Confederate Papers relating to Citizens or Business Firms, 1861-65," database, Washington D.C.: NARA M346, ID # 2133274, Record Group: 109, Documents # 321, 322, *Fold3.com* (www.fold3.com: accessed on 9/2010).

[26] A "griffe" was a term used to describe a person of mixed African-American and Native American heritage.

[27] Avoyelles Parish Courthouse Records (Marksville, Avoyelles Parish, LA), *Inventories,* Book E, pp. 91-94, " Inventory of the estate of Celina Aymond," filed 7 December 1862.

[28] Avoyelles Parish Courthouse Records (Marksville, Avoyelles Parish, LA), *Marriage Book B-3,* p. 210, "Abraham Felsenthall (sic) to Mary Ann E. Blunt," filed July 5, 1864. Note: The family name is alternately spelled "Blunt" or "Blount".

[29] 1860 U. S. Census, Avoyelles Parish, Louisiana, pop. sch. Marksville P.O., p. 15 (penned), Dwelling #98, Family #98, Mrs. Mary C. Blount household, digital image, (A: accessed 9/ 2010) , citing NARA microfilm publication M 653, roll 407. See also: 1860 U.S. Census, slave schedule, p. 6 (penned), lines 29-37, Mrs. Mary C. Blount, owner, digital image, (A: accessed 9/ 2010), citing NARA microfilm publication M 653, no roll given. Date of enumeration: 21 June 1860.

[30] Jeraldine DuFour Lacour, *Brides Book of Avoyelles Parish, Vol 2, 1856-1880* (Bunkie:Jeraldine Dufour LaCour [203 South Gayle Boulevard, Bunkie, LA], 1979),73. Entry for Elodie Guillot.

[31] Alberta Rousseau Ducôté, compiler, *Early Baptism Records: St. Paul the Apostle Catholic Church, 1824-1844, Avoyelles Parish*, Part II (Mansura,LA: St. Paul the Apostle Catholic Church, [P.O. Box 130. Mansura, LA 71350], 1982), #85. Baptism of Elodie Guillot on August 26, 1841. Note: This Guillot family (also spelled Guilleau) can be traced back to Pierre Guillot, dit Dufresne, who came from Lyon, France and settled in Pointe Coupée Parish, Louisiana around 1750, where he married Marguerite Richard. Pierre's son, Joseph Guillot, and his wife, Marie Françoise Dardenne, moved to Avoyelles Parish in 1780. Zénon Guillot, Elodie's father, was this last couple's grandson.

[32] Gilbert and Jane McManus, compilers, "Rapides (old) cemetery, Rapides Parish, Louisiana," database, *Usgwarchives.org* (http://files.usgwarchives.org: accessed 9/2010). Entry for B.C. Felsenthal (12 Jan 1869/5 Jan 1926, Woodmen of the World [sunken slab]).

[33] 1870 U.S. Census, Avoyelles Parish, Louisiana, pop. sch., Subdivision 6, p. 38 (penned), Dwelling #299, Family #335, A. Felsenthall (sic) household, Dwelling #300, Family #336, Alex Blunt household, digital image, (A: accessed 9/2010), citing NARA microfilm publication M593, roll 506. Date of enumeration: 24 June 1870.

[34] 1880 U.S. Census, Cook County, Illinois, pop. sch., Chicago, ED 97, p. 27 (penned), Dwelling #186, Family #283, J. Birkenstein household, digital image, (A: accessed 9/ 2010), citing NARA microfilm publication T9, Family History Film: 1254192. Date of enumeration: 7 June 1880. Note: See Line 9 – Barbara Felsenthal, Age 30 - Domestic Servant– Born in Louisiana, Father born in Bavaria, Mother born in Louisiana.

[35] Avoyelles Parish Courthouse Records (Marksville, Avoyelles Parish, LA), *Conveyances*, Book JJ, pp. 432,433, no.1388, "Sydalise Hayes, widow of R. Ferguson to Herman Felsenthal, Sale of Town lots in Cassandria. Cash," filed June 8, 1869.

[36] Avoyelles Parish Courthouse Records (Marksville, Avoyelles Parish, LA), *Conveyances,* Book OO, pp. 398-400, no. 3638, "A Felsenthal to Jacobias

Felsenthal – Sale of Land," filed July 22, 1875, and no. 3639 "Jacobias Felsenthal to Alcée Laborde – Sale of Land." filed July 22, 1875.

[37] 1850 U S. Census, Avoyelles Parish, Louisiana, pop. sch., Town not stated, p. 145B, Dwelling #462, Family #642, Daniel K. Ritchie household, digital image, (A: accessed 9/ 2010), citing NARA microfilm publication M 432, roll 229. Date of enumeration: 12 October, 1850.

[38] Nelson Gremillion, *Company G – 1st Regiment Louisiana Cavalry CSA – A Narrative* (Lafayette: Center for Louisiana Studies, The University of Southwestern Louisiana, 1986), 64.

[39] LLMV, Microfilm #5730, *The Marksville Bulletin,* Marksville, Avoyelles Parish, LA, 17 February 1877 - Vol. 1, no. 11, p. 3, col. 2.

[40] Avoyelles Parish Courthouse Records (Marksville, Avoyelles Parish, LA), *Inventories,* Book G, p. 725-728, "Succession of Abraham Felsenthal – Inventory," filed March 20, 1877.

[41] Avoyelles Parish Courthouse Records (Marksville, Avoyelles Parish, LA), *Probates, Petitions and Wills,* Book G, pp. 138-140, " Succession of Abraham Felsenthal – Petition for Sale, also, Petition for Tutorship," filed April 25, 1877.

[42] Avoyelles Parish Courthouse Records (Marksville, Avoyelles Parish, LA), *Family Meetings,* Book C, pp. 687-689, "Succession of Abraham Felsenthal deceased- Family Meeting," filed July 3, 1877. Note: The right of homestead for widow and minor children in necessitous circumstances is found in the Civil Code of Louisiana. It applies to widows and minor children who do not possess, in their own right, property to the amount of $1000 and allows them to demand and receive from the succession of the deceased, a sum, which added to the amount of property owned by them already, does not exceed $1000. This amount must be paid to them in preference to all other debts incurred by the estate, except for the vendor's privilege and expenses incurred in selling the property.

[43] Avoyelles Parish Courthouse Records (Marksville, Avoyelles Parish, LA), *Inventories,* Book I, pp. 61-63, " Succession of Abraham Felsenthal, deceased – Inventory," filed March 18, 1878.

[44] LLMV, Microfilm #5730, *The Marksville Bulletin,* 31 December 1881, p. 2, col. 6 .

[45] "Illinois, Cook County Marriages, 1871-1920," License #107009 (1886) digital image, *Familysearch.org* (https://www.familysearch.org [hereinafter cited as "F"]: accessed 9/2010), Film # 4271128. Marriage of Jacob Felsenthal to Margaret Conlan.

[46] "Illinois, Cook County Deaths, 1878-1922," (1891) digital image, (F: accessed 9/ 2010). Note: A call to the Free Sons cemetery administrator has failed to uncover any record of his burial there, although it was clearly noted on the Death Certificate # 4602. The grave may be unmarked.

[47] "Illinois, Cook County Marriages, 1871-1920," License #61397 (1882), digital image, (F: accessed 9/ 2010). Marriage of Bernard Friedman to Barbara Felsenthal.

[48] "Illinois, Deaths and Stillbirths, 1916-1947," (1934), digital image, (F: accessed 9/2010). Certificate of Death: #m34754 for Lena McIntosh.

[49] "Illinois, Cook County Birth Certificates, 1878-1922," (1919) digital image, (F: accessed 9/ 2010). Certificate of Birth # 28361 for Jessie Bernette Friedman. Note: Jessie Friedman is listed in the Social Security Death Index as "Jessie Vernette Friedman", born August 19, 1919, died 13 June 2003.

[50] 1920 U. S Census, Cook County, Illinois, pop. sch., Chicago, Ward 14, ED 813, p. 10A (penned), Dwelling #112, Family #230, Jacob Friedman household, digital image, (A: accessed 9/ 2010), citing NARA Microfilm T625, roll 323. Date of enumeration: 12 January 1920.

[51] "Illinois, Deaths and Stillbirths, 1916-1947," (1926), digital image, (F: accessed 9/2010). Certificate of Death, M3108, for Jacob Friedman. Note: David and Lucille Felsenthal Armitage are also buried in the Acacia Park Masonic Cemetery.

[52] 1880 U.S. Census, Cook County, Illinois, pop. sch., Chicago, E.D. 92, p. 14B (penned), Dwelling #82, Family #133, Jacob Felsenthal household,

digital image, (A: accessed 9/ 2010), citing NARA microfilm publication T9, roll 192. Date of enumeration: 4 June 1880.

[53] "Illinois, Cook County Marriages, 1871-1920," License #68108 (1882), digital image, (F: accessed 9/2010). Marriage of David F. Felsenthal to Minnie A. Knoll.

[54] "Illinois, Cook County Birth Certificates, 1878-1922," (1893) digital image, (F: accessed 9/2010). Birth certificate # 4584 for Lucile Felsenthal.

[55] "Illinois, Cook County Marriages, 1871-1920," (1905), digital image, (F: accessed 9/2010). Marriage License #411762 for Flora Felsenthal and Max A. Seeger.

[56] "Illinois, Cook County Deaths, 1872-1922," (1921), digital image, (F: accessed 9/2010). Certificate of Death #27752 for David Felsenthal.

[57] 1930 U. S. Census, Cook Co., Illinois, pop. sch. Chicago, Ward 98, Block 273, ED 1068, page 15B (penned), Dwelling #169, #Family 293, David L. Armitage household, digital image, (A: accessed 9/2010), citing NARA Microfilm publication T626, roll 458. Date of enumeration: 9 April 1930.

[58] Jeraldine Dufour LaCour, *Brides Book of Avoyelles Parish, 1881-1899*, Volume 3 (Alexandria: Jeraldine Dufour LaCour [P.O. Box 5022, Alexandria, LA], 1986), 130. Entry for Julia Clarice Robinson, bride of Laurence A. Felsenthal.

[59] 1880 U. S. Census, Avoyelles Parish, Louisiana, pop. sch. Ward 2, ED 2, page 6B (penned), Dwelling #62, Family #64, Jean Luneau household, digital image, (A: accessed 9/2010), citing NARA Microfilm publication T9, roll 448. Date of enumeration: 16 June 1880.

[60] Avoyelles Parish Courthouse Records (Marksville, Avoyelles Parish, LA), *Conveyances,* Book HHH, pp. 672-674, "Emile Luneau, et.als. to Mrs. Lawrence A. Felsenthal – Sale of Land," filed 17 November 1893.

[61] 1900 U. S Census, Avoyelles Parish, Louisiana, pop. sch., Police Jury Ward 1, ED 12, page 11A (penned), Dwelling #134, Family #134, Lawrence A. (no

last name given) household, digital image, (A: accessed 9/2010), citing NARA microfilm publication T623, roll 558. Date of enumeration: 12 June 1900.

⁶² 1920 U. S. Census, Allen Parish, Louisiana, pop. sch., Oakdale, Police Jury Ward 5, ED 22, page 22B (penned), Dwelling #534, Family #561, Andy Bryant household, (Eva Scroggs listed as second head of household), digital image, (A: accessed 9/2010), citing NARA microfilm publication T625, roll 603. Date of enumeration: 13 January 1920.

⁶³ "World War I Draft Registration Cards, 1917-1918," Avoyelles Parish, LA, Draft Board "O," Serial No. 3123, Order No. 2609, digital image, (A: accessed 9/ 2010), citing NARA microfilm M 1509, FHL roll 1653580. Entry for Hobson Felsenthal.

⁶⁴ 1930 U. S. Census, Allen Parish, Louisiana, pop. sch.,Oakdale, Police Jury Ward 5, ED 9, page 5A (penned), Dwelling #103, Family #104, George L. Dixon household, digital image, (A: accessed 9/2010), citing NARA microfilm publication T626, roll 782. Date of enumeration: 5 April 1930.

⁶⁵ LaCour, *Avoyelleans of Yesteryear,* 127, Entry for Patrick Kalone (sic), Files #89, & #5235.

⁶⁶ Social Security Administration, "U.S. Social Security Death Index," database, (A: accessed 9/ 2010). Entry for Eva Bordelon, 1980.

⁶⁷ "World War I Draft Registration Cards, 1917-1918," digital image, (A: accessed 9/2010) No. 78, Draft Board 1, Alexandria, Rapides Parish, citing *World War I Selective Service System Draft Registration Cards, 1917-1918,* NARA microfilm publication M 1509, roll 1684930. Entry for Toby Felsenthal.

⁶⁸ Social Security Administration, "U.S. Social Security Death Index," database, (A: accessed 9/ 2010). Entry for Eugene L. Felsenthal (1988).

⁶⁹ "Louisiana Deaths, 1850-1875; 1894-1954," database, (F: accessed 9/2010). Entry for Tobby (sic) Felsenthal, certificate # 16195.

⁷⁰ "World War I Draft Registration Cards 1917-1918," digital images, (A: accessed10/ 2010), Columbus Felsenthal, Registration No. 190 and Tency

Deigo Felsenthal, serial No. 2875, order No. 2960, Draft Board 1, Alexandria, Rapides Parish, LA, citing *World War I Selective Service Draft Registration Cards, 1917-1918,* NARA microfilm publication M1509, roll 1684937.

[71] Social Security Administration, "U.S. Social Security Death Index," (1977) database, (A: accessed 9/ 2010). Entry for Flora McDonald, Houston, Harris Co., TX (1977).

[72] McManus, compilers, "Rapides (Old) cemetery, Rapides Parish, Louisiana," database, Entry for Dennis Felsenthal (31 Dec. 1908 - 27 Mar 1967).

[73] 1910 U.S. Census, Rapides Parish, Louisiana, pop. sch., Alexandria, Ward 1, ED 78, p. 14A (penned), Dwelling #312, Family #313, Ben Felsenthal household, digital image, (A: accessed 10 / 2010), citing NARA microfilm publication T 624, roll 527. Date of enumeration: 22 April 1910.

[74] McManus, compilers, "Rapides (Old) cemetery, Rapides Parish, Louisiana," database, Entry for Sarah Kelone Felsenthal, wife of B.C. Felsenthal (21 May 1874-26 September 1916).

[75] 1920 U.S. Census, Rapides Parish, Louisiana, pop. sch., Alexandria, Ward 1, ED 56, p. 25A (penned), Dwelling #463, Family #605, Ben Felsenthal household, digital image, (A: accessed 10/ 2010), citing NARA microfilm publication T 625, roll 626. Dates of enumeration: 9 & 10 February 1920.

[76] 1920 U.S. Census, Rapides Parish, Louisiana, pop. sch., Alexandria, Ward 1, ED 56, p. 19B (penned), Dwelling #368, Family #446, William Nash household, digital image, (A: accessed 10/ 2010), citing NARA microfilm publication T 625, roll 626. Date of enumeration: 4 February 1920.

[77] "Louisiana Deaths, 1850-1875, 1894-1954," database, (F: accessed 9/ 2010). Entry for T. D. Felsenthal, (Certificate # 1863).

[78]Anita Jean Hudspeth, compiler, *My Genealogy Homepage,* Genealogy.com (http://familytreemaker.genealogy.com/users/h/u/d/Anita-J-Hudspeth/WEBSITE-0001/UHP-0797.html: accessed 10/2010). Entries for Columbus Felsenthal, Wallace Russell, Wallice Sarah Felsenthal, and Odette Delaune.

[79] 1930 U.S. Census, Galveston County, Texas, pop. sch., Galveston, District 21, ED 21, p. 2B (penned), Dwelling #416, Family #424, John A. McDonald household, digital image, (A: accessed 10/ 2010), citing NARA microfilm publication T 626, roll 2335. Date of enumeration: 15 April 1930.

[80] McManus, compilers, "Rapides (Old) cemetery, Rapides Parish, Louisiana," database, entry for B.C. Felsenthal (12 Jan 1869- 5 Jan 1926).

[81] *Ibid.*, entry for Dennis. Felsenthal (31 Dec 1908- 27 Mar 1967).

[82] 1900 U.S. Census, Avoyelles Parish, Louisiana, pop. sch. Ward 5, ED 16, p. 3A (penned), Dwelling #41, Family #41, Virginia Filsental (sic) household, digital image, (A: accessed 10/2010), citing NARA microfilm publication T623, roll 558. Date of enumeration: 1 June 1900. Note: Esther was also known as "Hester", and married as "Estelle Volcy" Felsenthal. See: LaCour, *Brides Book of Avoyelles Parish 1881-1899*, Volume 3, p. 53, entry for Estelle Volcy Felsenthal.

CHAPTER 3

SAM AND ALEX HAAS – LOUISIANA MOGULS

Alexander and Samuel Cerf Haas were unquestionably the most prosperous and successful Jewish immigrants to make their fortune in Central Louisiana. Originally from Rothbach in France they were the first Alsatians to make Avoyelles Parish their home. Other Jewish men from that region would follow, who, from neighboring villages in northeast France, would become neighbors, as well as relations by marriage, in rural Louisiana.

There had been Jews in Rothbach since, at least, 1742. Not always prosperous, this small village had only eleven Jewish families in 1784. Samuel Haas, Sr., the Louisiana immigrants' father, was born on October 8, 1798, in Rothbach to Aron Sender and Ziphele Lazarus. "Sender" was a civil recorder's clumsy phonetic spelling of Samuel's father's name, "Alexander."[1] A check of the 1808 Census of Jews in Rothbach, which gave the pre-1808 names used by the Jewish families, as well as their 1808 name adoptions, showed that previously Aron Haas had been known as Aron Alexander (Aron, son of Alexander). His wife, Sara Haas, was formerly known as Zefele Lazarus, and his son, Samuel Haas, Sr., had originally been known as Samuel Aron.[2] An extract of the marriage contract made between Aron, son of Alexander, and Zivia, daughter of Eliezer (Lazé = Lazarus), which was made on November 27, 1789, in Rothbach confirmed Samuel, Sr.'s parent's names.[3]

Samuel Haas, Sr. married Henriette Uhry at Rothbach on September 3, 1829.[4] The couple's first child, Aron, lived less than a year. Their second son, Samuel Cerf, was born on June 29, 1836 at Rothbach,[5] and their last, Alexander, came into the world on August 18, 1838.[6] Shortly afterwards, Samuel and his family moved to Ingwiller, his wife's home town, only three and a half miles away. He became a successful cattle dealer which finally lifted the family out of its humble beginnings in Rothbach. Happiness, however, did not follow prosperity. His wife, Henriette, died in the town of her birth on July 29, 1841,[7] leaving Samuel and Alexander Haas, her two young sons, still toddlers, without a mother. She was barely forty-one years old.

Samuel Haas, Sr., did not remain a widower for very long, marrying Zerlina (Caroline) Wolff on December 18, 1843, in Weinbourg, Alsace. The groom was forty-five years old. His bride was thirty-four.[8] Together they had four children all born in Ingwiller: Sophie born December 15 1844 (deceased at the age of seven on July 9, 1852), Salomon, born September 25, 1846, Fanny, born July 28, 1848, and Sara, born October 12, 1849 (deceased at the age of fifteen on March 29, 1865). [9]

In the early 1850s, nearing the age of conscription, Samuel Haas made preparations, like many other young Jewish men, to immigrate to the United States. That he left sooner rather than later may also have been the result of the family's financial condition, or even a strained relationship with his step-mother. When Samuel, applied for naturalization on the eve of the Civil War in 1860, he stated that he had been in the USA for seven years, arriving before his eighteenth birthday, thereby entitling him to immediate citizenship.[10] Two witnesses on his behalf indicated that they had known him to be in America since 1853.

Sam Haas settled in the northwest corner of St. Landry Parish at Bayou Chicot,[11] where he began his merchandising career. He had started out as a peddler first on foot, and then after he made enough to purchase a mount, he travelled the back roads of Central Louisiana on horseback for several years until he had earned the means to set himself up in a store. His younger brother, Alex, set sail as soon as Sam had gotten together enough money together for his passage. The arrival in New Orleans of Alexandre Haas on June 26, 1855, on the Ship *Baden* from Le Havre, is probably the record of Sam's younger brother, who had been sent to join him in Louisiana, just two months shy of his seventeenth birthday.[12] An examination of the 1856 Census from

Ingwiller shows that both Sam and Alex had departed, leaving Samuel Haas, Sr., his wife Zerlina Wolff, and their three children, Salomon, Fanny, and Sara in the family home in Ingwiller.[13]

By 1860, Sam, only twenty-two, had acquired seventy-five dollars in real estate and six thousand five hundred dollars in personal property.[14] The 1860 Slave Schedule for St. Landry Parish records that he was the owner of two slaves: one forty year old black female, and one nine year old black male, thus accounting for some of the net worth in personal property reported by the 1860 census taker.[15]

On the eve of the Civil War the two brothers had made enormous financial strides, having been in America less than a decade. Sam's store records indicate that he sold virtually everything, from needles and pins, to clothing, shoes, pots, ploughs, saddles, ammunition, buggies, patent medicines, and lumber. Soon the brothers were not only store owners, but, as a result of their credit dealings with the local population, were traders in cotton, horses, cattle and mules. And when crops failed, and farmers could not pay their debts, they became land owners.

When the war broke out, Sam enlisted in the Prairie Rangers from St. Landry Parish as a First Lieutenant. In the fall of 1863, the Rangers became Company K of the third regiment of the Louisiana Cavalry, known as Harrison's Regiment commanded by Colonel Isaac F. Harrison.[16] First Lieutenant Sam Haas was present on the first muster roll, dated August 20-Dec 3, 1862. The Company was then known as Capt. Todd's Independent Company Cavalry. Two surviving pay vouchers indicate that Sam was paid for the month of December 1862 in the amount of $100 with an additional $14.40 for forage for two horses. He was subsequently paid $200 for his service during the months of January and February 1863.[17] Sam's experiences in France as the son of a cattle and horse dealer in Ingwiller, as well as his years on foot and on horseback selling his wares in the small communities in Central Louisiana, made him a natural for the Cavalry, and particularly valuable to the Confederacy as a scout and guide.

A *Confederate Military History*, published in 1899, is probably the most accurate assessment of what is known about Samuel Haas' service:

> He [Haas] entered the Confederate service in 1861 as a sergeant in Company K, Third Louisiana Cavalry, Col. Isaac F. Harrison, which at a l ater date was a part of General Liddell's brigade. At the first reorganization he was elected first lieutenant of his company, and after having command of it for eighteen months in that rank, he was promoted to captain. He took part in a great many skirmishes in western Louisiana, on the Mississippi from Natchez to Vicksburg, and along the Red river, and performed outpost duty and dangerous and important scouting, much of the time under the direct orders of General Taylor. He was once wounded in Rapides parish, but escaped capture by taking refuge in the swamps. Captain Haas was particularly distinguished by his energetic and effective work in suppressing the bands of deserters and jayhawkers who had become very a ctive between Alexandria and Fort DeRussy, capturing Confederate officers and men who happened to cross the region they infested. Taking twenty men Captain Haas made a campaign against these outlaws, and after an arduous hunt through the swamps and keen manhunting, succeeded in bringing in twenty of them, besides those killed in attempting to escape. [..] Throughout he was faithfully supported by First Lieut. Eli Clark, Lieuts. Jacques Levy and A ustin Allen, Orderly Sergeant William Thomas, Sergts. Ethall Allen and Jonas Rosenthal, and Corporals James G. West, Landry Baillon and Patrick Danahy. [18]

Arthur W. Bergeron, who wrote extensively on the Civil War in Louisiana, reported that "between February and May 1863, Lieutenant Samuel Haas and at least a portion of the Prairie Rangers Company were operating as couriers in north Louisiana. They appear to have done this between Harrisonburg and Alexandria and later between

Harrisonburg and Natchitoches." Moreover, just before the cessation of hostilities between the North and South, Capt. Haas and his men, in the spring of 1865, had been stationed near Catahoula Lake, performing picket duty. Their mission had been to prevent Jayhawkers and others from transporting cotton from Louisiana into the Union lines at Natchez. [19] An article published in 1902 in *The* (Alexandria, LA) *Town Talk* profiled Sergeant Jonas Rosenthal, from Oberlauterbach, Alsace, a fellow Jew, who served under Capt. Sam Haas:

> [...] in April, 1862 he [Sgt. Rosenthal] joined the Confederate Army, enlisting as a member of Company K, Third Louisiana Cavalry, of which Capt. Sam Haas of Bayou Chicot, St. Landry Parish, was captain. [...] When the army of the Federals, under General Banks, retreated the second time from Alexandria, Mr. Rosenthal was the first Confederate soldier to arrive in Alexandria, after their evacuation, and he was so close to the retreating army that when he came in the corporation limits on one side of the town the retreating Federals had not all got out of the town. Mr. Rosenthal at the time was acting as guide for the advance guard of Colonel Gilling's Texas regiment.[20]

***

A record housed in the National Archives indicates that Sam's brother, Alex M. Haas, first joined Company E of the 10th Louisiana Infantry (Louisiana Swamp Rifles) on July 22, 1861. He was reported present in July, August, September and October of 1861 but he deserted on November 3, 1861.[21] Another record exists for Alexander Hays (sic), who enlisted on November 18, 1861 at Baton Rouge as a Private in the Creole Chargers (Company G), 1st Louisiana Cavalry and fought with them until their surrender in 1865. A list of Company G's members appeared in Howell Carter's, *A Cavalryman's Reminiscences of the Civil War*, originally published in 1900. Carter offered up the muster rolls for all of the companies of the First Louisiana Cavalry at the end of his book identifying at least 60 of the 103 members of the Creole Chargers for whom entries appeared in Andrew B. Booth's book, *Records of Louisiana Soldiers and Confederate Commands*, including Alex Haas. He wrote:

> *Alex. M. Haas is still living and prospering. Most of his time is spent in New Orleans, but he has interests in and around Haasville and Bunkie, where he and his brother have been successful in business. The latter town was named for his daughter. During the war Haas left the 1st Louisiana by promotion to a Lieutenancy in another regiment and served in the Trans-Mississippi Department.*[22]

The movements of the Creole Chargers may be traced by articles which Captain Fénélon Cannon, their leader, sent back to the local Avoyelles Parish newspaper *Le Pélican*.[23] Cannon and his men left Avoyelles Parish via the Red River on the *General Hodges* in early October 1861,[24] arriving several days later with 66 men and horses to become part of Colonel Scott's battalion.[25] A letter from Captain Cannon, appeared in the *Pelican* on October 26th confirming their presence at Baton Rouge.[26] Cannon's regiment did not depart Baton Rouge until November 29, 1861 on the Steamer *Magnolia*. Thus, while Cannon's men waited at Baton Rouge in the fall of 1861 to depart for the front, it is likely that Alex Haas, bivouacked with his infantry division some 70 miles away at Camp Moore, left to join the First Louisiana Cavalry. Since only soldiers who could provide their own horse were eligible for cavalry service, he must have been able to secure a mount somewhere in the area to insure his acceptance. Unfortunately his previous superior officer carried him erroneously as being AWOL.

Col. Alex Haas' service was also described in a biography of his son, Dr. W.D. Haas, as having been with the First Louisiana Cavalry, Company G, taking part in battles from Bowling Green, through Tennessee, Alabama and Mississippi as a scout or in the advance party. He saw the fall of Nashville to the Union army, set fire to the bridge across the Duckhill River at Columbia, TN to stop Buell's army from crossing, thereby allowing his regiment to escape unscathed and finally returned home very ill. While in St Landry Parish he recovered sufficiently to volunteer his services to Colonel Bagbie at the first battle near Opelousas. He was later transferred to the staff of Texas hero, General Tom Green, fighting in the battles of Mansfield and Pleasant Hill, then General Wharton's staff to fight at Mansura, Yellow Bayou and Simmesport.[27] It is clear that after his return from Tennessee to Central Louisiana he was attached to the Trans-Mississippi department as this is verified in Howell Carter's book. Although there are no official War Department records to support many of the details of his service, Alex Haas was always referred to after the close of the Civil War, as Colonel Haas. Moreover there is one picture of him dressed as a Confederate Lieutenant Colonel still in the possession of Haas descendants. While Captain Sam's "parole papers" signed and dated by him on June 11, 1865 at Alexandria, Louisiana are on file at the National Archives,[28] there is, unfortunately, nothing of the sort for his brother, Lieutenant Colonel Alex M. Haas.

Alex and his brother, Sam Haas, were both active after the War with the United Confederate Veterans, Alex belonging to the R.L. Gibson Camp # 33, and Sam to R.E. Lee Camp # 13.[29] In addition, Col. Alex Haas was a member of the Veteran Confederate States Cavalry Association, Camp # 9 of the U.C.V. and served on several committees, along with the aforementioned Howell Carter, to organize events amongst the many camps in the southern states.[30] He was also part of the New Orleans contingent that escorted the body of Jefferson Davis from the Crescent City to Richmond, Virginia on a special train which traversed the southern United States in May 1893. Three years later, in July 1896, Colonel Haas travelled to Richmond as part of the Louisiana delegation to attend the laying of a cornerstone for the Jefferson Davis monument.[31]

Captain Sam Haas married Martha Ann Cole, during his military service, on March 27, 1862, in St. Landry Parish.[32] She was born on March 15, 1845, to John Cole, a native North Carolinian and his wife, Lavinia Hudson, a native Louisianan. Lavinia died in 1859 at Bayou Rouge, Avoyelles Parish, leaving her estate to her husband and three children, Martha Ann, Charles Carroll and Millard Ludger Cole.[33] John Cole passed on less than two years later in October 1861, at which time there was an inventory of the estate which was valued at $27,505.70, including eighteen slaves. [34] Seventeen year old Martha Cole, heiress to one-third of a rather large plantation, was, indeed, a "good catch" for the 25 year old Jewish immigrant, who was, by then, a Confederate patriot. The Haas-Cole marriage, one of the many mixed unions between Jewish men and Christian women in mid-nineteenth century central Louisiana, started what an Alex Haas descendant, Brad Fanta, characterized as a rather complicated relationship with Judaism even after they had left the faith.

Sam and Martha's first child, John, was born on January 2, 1863.[35] There second, a girl, Hattie, was not born until October 30, 1868, long after the conflict was over.[36] Capt. Haas and his family always remained in or near Bayou Chicot, but he often did business with his brother, Alex, who, upon returning from the front, married Mary Maccie Marshall on July 12, 1866. Mary Marshall was a native of Avoyelles Parish, whose parents were influential merchants and plantation owners in the Evergreen area. Family stories brought down through Haas family descendants indicate that the Louisiana Marshalls were distant cousins of Chief Justice John Marshall.[37] They were amongst the largest slave owners in the area, claiming, at one time, more than one hundred souls. Because of Evergreen's location on Bayou Rouge, the Marshall family had become, before the advent of the railroad, local shipping magnates constructing large warehouses and landings where, for a fee, they would store or transport their own and other farmers' and merchants' goods to the New Orleans markets. This business was immensely lucrative because the waterways were the best, and, at times, the only way to ship goods into or out of the parish. There is no doubt that the Haas-Marshall marriage was a very advantageous one for Alex Haas, who, himself, was an up-and-coming merchant-farmer. Their first child, William David, (named after two of Mary Marshall's brothers), was born on May 9, 1867.[38] After living a short while in Cheneyville in Rapides Parish where William, or W.D. as he was later called, and their second child, a daughter, Nanie, was born on March 5, 1869,[39] the couple settled near Mary's family in Evergreen in an area called Tiger Bend, which became the town of

Haasville in 1888. Another daughter, Mary Maccie Haas, and a son, Alexander Marshall Haas, were born at Tiger Bend on August 28, 1871, and December 20, 1873, respectively.[40]

***

In 1872 Capt. Sam Haas brought his twenty-five year old half-brother, Solomon, to America to set him up in business. The previous year, France had been embroiled in the Franco-Prussian War, and after a ten month conflict went down to defeat. Alsace and parts of Lorraine/Moselle were ceded to the Germans. Residents of the region were given the choice to become German citizens or to leave the area. Solomon chose to come to Louisiana, accompanied by his mother, Zerlina Wolff Haas' nephew, Leon Wolff, the latter of whom became a leading merchant in nearby Washington, LA.[41] The two immigrants are remembered in stories told to Mabel Alice Thompson which were recorded in *Looking Back – A Narrative History of Bayou Chicot.* Ms. Thompson's grandfather, Thomas Thompson, the local schoolmaster, had taught the two young immigrants from Alsace English and arithmetic, after school, while sitting on the steps of the local Baptist Church.[42]

After an apprenticeship with Sam, Solomon moved to New Orleans where he opened up a livery stable in partnership with Frederick Kuhne at 92-94 Conti Street.[43] He later went on his own to 424-428 Bourbon Street where his establishment was a two story brick building with a slate roof. He stabled and sold horses and mules.[44] One particular troublesome horse was left with him on October 17, 1898 and apparently abandoned. This resulted in a judicial notice from the Second City Court of New Orleans # 32,116 entitled "Solomon Haas vs. A Brown Horse belonging to some Unknown Person" asking any person with knowledge of the affair to appear within fifteen days.[45] The horse was finally auctioned off on March 11, 1899, to Solomon's benefit. At any given time, all three Haas brothers dealt in livestock. Capt. Sam, according to Mabel Thompson, got his mules in Missouri and sold them in the fall of the year. He kept them in a pasture near the store, and never missed a chance to continue this trade, which was a family tradition that stretched back to Alsace. It is said that he preferred horse-trading over all other business. Ms. Thompson offered that if he heard of a runaway horse, he would rush right over to try and purchase it, preferring the fiery ones.[46]

***

Sam and Martha Haas had three more children in Bayou Chicot, Charles (b. September 1873), Alexander Murdock (b August 1876), and Leon Samuel (b. May 1878). Alex and Mary Marshall Haas, had one more child at Evergreen on September 19, 1876, whom they named Samuel. Mary succumbed to the rigors of childbirth the same day and the baby lived less than a month. An inventory of her estate revealed that Mary owned property in the amount of 350 acres on Bayou Rouge valued at $3850, as well as $23,200 in cash and property held jointly with her husband.[47]

With four children under ten years of age, it is not surprising that Alex sought to remarry as soon as possible. Like many wealthy planters, he had, early on, become active in New Orleans, travelling there frequently. He invested in the Lexington Stables at 146 Baronne Street, and started a commodities brokerage business. As early as 1875 a personal item appeared in the *New Orleans Times* which read: "Mr. A. M. Haas, the well-known St. Charles Street broker, left last evening via the Jackson route for St. Louis, where he intends to sojourn a few weeks, after which he will look after the interests of his plantation in Avoyelles Parish."[48] After his wife's death, however, he spent even more time in the Crescent City in the hope of finding a mother for his children, leaving his late wife Mary's brother, Roger Banks Marshall, with power of attorney to look after his affairs in Avoyelles Parish.[49]

While residing in New Orleans in August 1877, Alex Haas put his Lexington Stables up for sale, offering great bargains on buggies, spring wagons, and a choice lot of Texas horses.[50] In September of the same year, he was involved in a dispute with Gustave Moses, of the B. and G. Moses Gallery, the famous New Orleans photographer, whose brother, Bernard, was a noted artist. Bernard

Moses had accepted a commission from Alex to paint two family portraits, for which he had charged $200. Haas gave him a horse in partial payment which he said he would keep at his Lexington stables at $25.00 per month until the paintings were paid in full. Subsequently, the two men had a disagreement about the frames, for which Gustave Moses wanted an extra fifty dollars. As the dispute escalated, Moses accused Alex of entering his property during the daytime to steal back the horse. He complained to the authorities and Alex was arrested and placed under a $500 bond.[51] A week later, Gustave took an advertisement in the *Daily Picayune*, exonerating Haas from any criminal intent, and apologizing for any injury caused to him, saying that the original accusation was made in a fit of pique.[52] It can be well imagined that, upon reflection, publicly humiliating a successful member of the Jewish community over fifty dollars would not have been in the Moses Brothers' best interest. Many prominent Hebrew citizens of New Orleans had been their clients, the most well-known being Fire Captain Samuel Levy, whom Bernard had painted in his ceremonial uniform.[53]

During his time in the Crescent City Alex Haas continued to ship goods via the New Orleans and Mobile Railroad under the name of Alex Haas and Bro. back to Central Louisiana for his and his brother, Sam's, general stores. For example, on March 26 and 27, 1878 he sent seventeen sacks of coffee and fifty-three sacks of peas back to Central Louisiana and shipped two bales of cotton from Washington, LA on the steamer *Fanchon* back to the city to be sold.[54] Dealings such as these were done on a weekly basis, year after year, not only by the Haas Brothers, but by practically every small town Louisiana merchant.

While still in the city, Alex met his second wife, Hannah Pokorny, who was well-known in social circles and famous for her beautiful soprano voice. Articles often appeared in the local newspapers chronicling her solos at social and religious occasions. She was young, beautiful, and Jewish. Her father, Michael Pokorny, born in Puklice, in the Austro-Hungarian Empire, now a town in the Czech Republic, had immigrated to England with his wife, Fannie Singer, and his first child, John. After a short stay in London, where he celebrated the birth of a second child, Bertha, the family spent several years in New York City where his daughter, Hannah, was born on April 6, 1858.[55] Moving to New Orleans in late 1860, he worked as a shoe and boot maker, turning his small business into an empire, with two large stores, one at 124 St. Charles Avenue, the other at 105 Royal Street, with many employees. Eventually his two sons, John (b. 1853) and David (b. 1861), joined the business.[56] Michael Pokorny was also a trustee of the American Mutual Insurance Association of New Orleans, and his social connections were legion.[57]

Alex and Hannah were married in New Orleans on August 10, 1879. The couple soon left the city behind to return to Oak Hall, the family plantation, which spanned parts of three parishes: from Avoyelles into St. Landry, and later when it was founded in 1911, into Evangeline.[58] Oak Hall had been in Alex's late wife, Mary Maccie Marshall's family for almost half a century, since Roger Banks Marshall, her grandfather, had obtained the land grant patent from President Andrew Jackson in November 1835.[59] In addition to the Haas store where, according to his letterhead, Alex sold dry goods, groceries, hats, caps and plantation supplies, and the home itself, the acreage was planted with sugar cane and cotton. The little settlement, originally called Tiger Bend, was situated between the future towns of Bunkie and Eola. In December 1879, Alex Haas became Tiger Bend's first postmaster.[60] The post office, just like his brother Sam's at Bayou Chicot, was kept at the store itself, which was the social center of the community. Col. Haas' new wife, Hannah, never liked living in the town of Tiger Bend, nor in the fine manor house called Grey Gables near the Haas store where social contacts were few and violence was rife. On Christmas Eve 1880 at around eight or nine o'clock, a shooting occurred at the Alex Haas store, which was eventually deemed an accident. The clerk, John Maloney, had gone into an adjacent room leaving two young boys alone in the store, Johnny Thomas and Aaron Franklin, one white, the other African-American. Minutes later a shot rang out, and upon returning young Thomas had killed Aaron Franklin. Col. Haas was called and took charge of the boy, holding him until the coroner could arrive the next day, at which time there was an inquest and the boy was acquitted.[61]

Eventually Col. Alex Haas spent less and less time in Tiger Bend, directing his financial interests from afar, in order to try to satisfy his wife's preference for city life. On the other hand, Capt. Sam, his wife, Martha, and children, lived quietly in Bayou Chicot, where the head of the household made his fortune as a merchant and as a horse trader. His place was not merely a general merchandise establishment. There was also a saloon, where whiskey was sold by the glass or bottle. Sam's wife, Martha Ann Cole, tended to the Post Office located there until 1907, when she was succeeded by their "adopted" son, Henry Erlich, who held that post until 1920. According to Mabel Alice Thompson's history of Bayou Chicot: "Buggies and wagons would be tied along the fence on either side of the road for a quarter of a mile when people came to get their mail and supplies." [62]

***

Although Sam and Alex Haas lived in an area where there was little or no Jewish social or spiritual network, they both still had somewhat tenuous ties to their religion and to the "folks back home" in Alsace. Sam had welcomed his half-brother, Solomon Haas, and his step-mother's nephew, Leon Wolff, to St. Landry Parish at the conclusion of the Franco-Prussian War. In April 1874, Sam Haas filed a document in the St. Landry Parish Courthouse in Opelousas, in order to donate a plot of land together with all the buildings and improvements in Ingwiller, Alsace, to his father, Samuel Haas, Sr. In it, he stipulated that, upon his father's demise, his half-sister, Fanny Haas, would inherit the said land and buildings. This property had been a part of his inheritance from his late mother, Henriette Uhry.[63] Later on, he encouraged and sponsored Fanny, her husband, Elias Moch, and their two children in their efforts to come to the United States.

Perhaps no story better illustrates that the Haas brothers' still had a connection to their Jewish roots, than their adoption of the four

Erlich brothers, Samuel, Philip, Henry and Nathan, orphaned in 1865. Marks Erlich had immigrated to Mississippi from Prussia and married Rosalie Franklin in Yazoo County on December 30, 1853.[64] Rosalie, also from Prussia, had come to America with her two brothers who soon set themselves up as successful Mississippi merchants. In 1860 the Erlich and Franklin families were all living in Yazoo City and Marks and Rosalie were the parents of four sons.[65] During the course of the Civil War the family left Mississippi for New Orleans where Marks died on July 7, 1865.[66] Rosalie may have predeceased her husband because three of the couple's four sons were ultimately sent to the Jewish Widows and Orphans home at the corner of Jackson and Chippewa Streets, where they were enumerated as "inmates" in 1870.

The members of the Hebrew Benevolent Association of New Orleans had, at the conclusion of one of the city's worst yellow fever epidemics in the summer and fall of 1853, determined to build a facility for widows and homeless children. The cornerstone was finally laid on August 7, 1856, and the building was opened on February 1, 1857. There were approximately one hundred residents there in July 1870, when Henry Erlich, age twelve, Nathan Erlich, age nine, and Philip Erlich, age ten, became inmates.[67] Their older brother, Samuel, age fourteen, had been released to a young cotton and general commission merchant in the city, Benjamin Newgass, and his wife Sarah.[68]

Whether it was through Alex Haas' connections as a "prominent St. Charles Avenue broker," or simply the fortuitous visit to the orphanage by Sam Haas is not now known, but all four brothers were taken back to Central Louisiana in the mid-1870s to work for various members of the Haas family. By 1880 Philip had gone to Washington, LA to become the clerk of the Haas brothers' step-mother's nephew, Leon Wolff.[69]

After Benjamin Newgass and his wife left Louisiana to make their home in England, Samuel Erlich went to work as a clerk for Sam Haas' occasional business partner, Leopold Goudchaux. He lived next door to the Goudchaux household along with three other employees including Jake Kahn (b. 1866), and Abraham Kahn (b. 1836), both first cousins of Henry and Aaron Kahn of Evergreen, all children of Leopold Goudchaux's many sisters.[70] Sam Erlich later returned to New Orleans and was the first of the four brothers to pass on. He died there at age 32, on August 12, 1888, and is buried in the Dispersed of Judah Cemetery. He is most likely the Sam Ehrlich, aka "Jew Sam," who was memorialized in the *Daily Picayune* of July 11, 1886 which described a broken man, a drunkard and a gambler who could not hold a job. Given fifty cents to run an errand, he instead bought a keno card and lost it all. Fearing arrest, he walked down to French Market and out onto the ferry wharf at St. Ann Street. There he hurled himself into the Mississippi but was rescued and restored to health in Ward 18 of Charity Hospital. A little more than two years later he was gone for good.[71]

Henry and Nathan Erlich stayed in St. Landry Parish, in the village of Chicot, working for Sam Haas. In the 1880 census twenty-two year old Henry was enumerated as a clerk in the store, and Nathan, now 19 year old, was the mail carrier.[72] Henry later married Sallie Anselm, started a family, working for Sam Haas all his life. He became manager of the store, succeeded Martha Haas as the Postmaster and was, later on, a member of the Evangeline Parish School Board. He died at Bayou Chicot on July 9, 1920, [73] where his descendants, all Christians, continued to live.

Nathan, worked first for Sam, then moved to Bunkie, living in 1910 adjacent to both Alex Haas' son, W. D., and his family, and Sam's son, Charles Haas, and his wife, Maccie Rhodes. He was a salesman in the local hardware store.[74] When the W.D. Haas family moved to Alexandria shortly before 1920, Nathan moved with them, and was listed as a servant in their household.[75] Nathan died on September 8, 1924 and was buried near Alex Haas and his first wife, Mary Marshall, in the Thomas Douglas Marshall Cemetery in Evergreen.[76] On his tombstone is written "A Faithful Friend." Nathan never married.

***

On February 17, 1882 Alex and Hannah's only child, Alice Rosalind Haas, was born at Haasville. At the time of her birth, his older children, William David, Nanie, Mary Maccie and Alexander Marshall were fifteen, thirteen, eleven and nine respectively. His brother Sam's children were a bit older. John was nineteen and Hattie fifteen years of age. Charles was nine, Alex Murdock, Jr., six, and Leon Samuel, four. Alice was the only one of the brothers' ten children who was raised in Judaism. With a few exceptions, Protestantism, especially Methodism and Presbyterianism appear to have been the preponderant influences in the lives of the Haas sons and daughters. Mary Maccie Marshall and Martha Cole were both Protestants. All the Haas boys were sent away to secondary schools and colleges some of which had religious ties. Alex and Mary's son, William David, went to local schools in Louisiana, then to the Mississippi Military Institute in Pass Christian for two years, before going to Tulane University for his undergraduate degree in 1883 and the Jefferson Medical College in Philadelphia, from which he graduated in 1887.[77] Founded in 1824 by a group of Scottish Presbyterian physicians the school, whose student body was mostly Christian, had some fifty years later only loose connections to its religious beginnings. William David Haas' youngest brother, Alexander Marshall Haas, was also a physician, but attended the non-sectarian, Tulane Medical School, from where he graduated in 1895.

Sam and Martha Haas' first son, John, was also a graduate of the Jefferson Medical College, attending from 1880-1882. Their second son, Charlie Haas, was sent away to school, first to Port Gibson College which was under the control of the Presbytery of Mississippi, and then at about age thirteen, to Hiwassee College in Madisonville, Tennessee, which educated boys from grammar school through the baccalaureat. While this institution was originally founded in 1826 as an academy run by Methodist settlers, it had become a full-fledged "college" in 1849. Its first president was a Presbyterian scholar, and the college was advertised simply as offering a Christian education.[78] Nothing is currently known of their third son, Alex Murdock Haas' education. Their youngest son, Leon Samuel Haas, was schooled at the Chamberlain-Hunt Academy, a Christian military academy, founded in

1879 by the Presbyterian Church, and he later studied law at the University of Virginia Law School.

After Alex Haas' first wife, Mary Marshall, died, the boys had been sent away to their various educational institutions, but his daughters, Nanie and Mary Maccie, had lived with their Protestant grandmother, Mrs. Thomas Douglas Marshall (née Joyce Sophie Hoggatt), for several years until their father's remarriage. When they were of age, his girls, as well as Sam Haas' daughter, Hattie, attended the prestigious Franklin Female College at Holly Springs, Mississippi. The college was founded in 1849 by the Reverend Stephen G. Starks, a Methodist Minister. An 1884 advertisement in the *Daily Picayune*, seeking students for the 36th annual session at $300 per year for room and board, ended by saying "Refer to A.M. Haas, Haasville, LA."[79] There was, at least on the part of William David Haas, a sentimental attachment to Holly Springs. In a letter dated June 18, 1885, he wrote to Miss Lizzie Clark of that town how much she meant to him. From the content it was also clear that she was a school friend, of both his sister, Nanie, and his first cousin, Hattie. It is obvious that W.D., who signed his letter, "Your fond and loving Dave", and who promised to go to the city to have a photo of himself taken so that Lizzie would not forget him, was hopelessly smitten.[80]

***

Alex Haas' plantation holdings eventually grew to over 4,000 acres. In the early 1880s he decided to expand the little settlement of Tiger Bend. In an article dated June 18, 1881, which appeared in the afternoon edition of the *Daily Picayune,* it was reported that Capt. Alex Haas, who had seven hundred acres of corn and cotton under cultivation that year, had just donated fifteen acres on the west side of Bayou Boeuf to the Morgan Railroad for a depot and rail yard which would be finished by August. Plots of ground were also being surveyed which were to be offered to anyone who would like to settle in the area and farm. Larger lots were set aside for anyone who would build sawmills and factories to make use of the timber in the area to turn it into wagons, barrel staves, spokes, etc. There was also a move afoot to start the cultivation of tobacco, which according to the reporter could be grown better and more cheaply in Louisiana than elsewhere. It ended by saying that anyone who might be interested should contact Capt. Haas at Tiger Bend, "a place [which] has for its motto, prosperity."[81]

Several months later, on October 8, 1881, Haas was the first to ship out his cotton on the Morgan Road, whose depot still had not been completed. One hundred twenty-four bales were loaded and sent to New Orleans, " good for the first day's work," opined the *Marksville Bulletin*, who extolled Haas as "a live an energetic planter and merchant and one of the best business men in the State."[82] Haas was associated with many of the larger cotton factors in New Orleans. A sales slip (See page 142) from Meyer, Weis and Co., dated January 28, 1882, shows the sale of one bale of cotton on behalf of A.M. Haas, which had been shipped via the Morgan railroad from Tiger Bend. The bale was valued at $44.92, and after freight ($2.25), fire insurance ($0.17), drayage, storage and labor ($0.75) and a commission of 2 ½% ($1.12) the net proceeds were $40.63. The Meyer, Weis Company was owned by a distant relative by marriage of the Haas Brothers, Julius Weis, who was also related to the Siess brothers of Marksville and Mansura.

By the 1880s the Haas brothers were two of the richest merchant planters in Central Louisiana. Alex and Sam Haas inherited land through their wives, invested in more land, came into possession of even more when their debtors defaulted, all of which gave the brothers thousands of acres in Avoyelles and St. Landry parishes. As the brothers grew more prosperous and no longer lived one step ahead of their New Orleans creditors, they could afford to be generous to their community. In 1882 Sam and Alex gave land that they owned north of Eola to the Texas and Pacific Railway for a depot, and in doing so founded the town of Bunkie. Originally the place was called "Irion" after one of its early settlers, but it was renamed after Col. Haas' daughter, Mary Maccie Haas, whose nickname was "Bunkie." As the story goes, she had been given a toy monkey by her father, but was unable to pronounce the word, calling her new little friend, "Bunkie."

As the land had been given upon condition that Col. Haas could name the station, he did so, in honor of his daughter. Sam gave his brother a limited power of attorney "to sell off lots in an around Bunkie Station." In addition, on October 5, 1886, he ratified and confirmed "any sale or sales of lots he [Alex Haas] has already made in which we are jointly interested in and around said Bunkie Station."[83]

On March 16, 1888, Sam and Alex Haas sold a parcel of land in Bunkie for the sum of fifty dollars to the Methodist Episcopal Church, which was organized on April 1 of that same year.[84] The Haas name would henceforth be associated with Methodism, to such a degree that many of their descendants were shocked to discover that their immigrant ancestors had actually been Alsatian Jews. Col. Haas was equally generous to all faiths, later donating land on which the Bunkie Catholic Church would be built. Although his eldest son, W. D., was clearly smitten with Lizzie Clark, on July 10, 1889 he married his first cousin, Hattie, Sam Haas' daughter, in a Jewish ceremony conducted by Rabbi Isaac Leucht at Touro Synagogue in New Orleans. The reception for 500 people was hosted the following day at "Martha Manor"[85] in Bayou Chicot by the bride's parents, Sam and Martha Cole Haas.[86] Thus, the two brothers would follow a very old Jewish tradition by marrying together their separate family fortunes, which were now considerable.

Although married to a Christian, and buried beside her in the non-denominational, Vandenburg Cemetery in Bayou Chicot, Sam Haas was, throughout the years more known for his loyalty to his fellow Jews and their causes than his brother. He had often donated to the Jewish Widows and Orphans Home in New Orleans, and adopted the Erlich children. He had even sent money for the renovation of the Synagogue in Ingwiller, and supported and encouraged the immigration to America of his extended Jewish family.[87] On April 17, 1886, in a letter to Leon Wolff, Sam Haas, upon learning of the death of Caroline Preus Plonsky, Leon's first wife's aunt, expressed these sentiments which illustrate the depth of his Jewish belief: "Truly a Mother in David has passed to a better world and is at rest with Rebecca and the many other noble women of our Faith surrounding the throne of Him who giveth and taketh away."[88] Although, perhaps apocryphal, a story that has survived many years of telling, appeared in Mabel Thompson's history of Bayou Chicot. She quoted Sam's grandson, Johnny Haas, who told the following story: Capt. Haas had lent a certain gentleman five thousand dollars, and sometime later, that man's son appeared in the store in Bayou Chicot, to ask for a smaller loan of $500 for himself. Smelling alcohol on the young man's breath, the Captain refused. When the young man asked why, Sam is reputed to have said, "Sonny, I am a Jew, I believe in the Father, but not the Son."[89] Of Sam and Martha's children, three of them married into other Jewish families: John and Leon Samuel Haas wed Jewish sisters from Opelousas, Jeannette and Mary Roos, daughters of Adolph David Roos originally from Wissembourg, Alsace. Alex Murdock Haas, Jr. took Mattye Loeb, the Jewish daughter of Solomon and Sarah Loeb, also from Opelousas for his wife. But Charlie Haas wed Maccie Rhodes, the Baptist daughter of John T. Rhodes. The latter was not only one of his father, Sam Haas', business associates, but also the spouse of Charlie's uncle Alex Haas' late wife Mary Maccie Marshall's sister, Lucy.

***

Although now a mostly absentee landlord in Avoyelles Parish, due to his wife's distaste for country living, Alex Haas continued to acquire plantation acreage, which was evaluated in a *Times Picayune* article published in 1885:

> *The Alex M. Haas place, rented to John P. Snelling for several years, is a fine piece of property, with open-kettle sugar-house, yielding 200 to 300 hogsheads of sugar, planting 125 acres in cotton. Bunkie Station, on the Texas and Pacific Railroad, is near the Haas place, and is the property of Haas, and receives its name from the beautiful little daughter of Capt. Haas, Miss Bunkie Haas. [...] This is in the tenth ward and Capt. Haas is the member of the Police Jury. He carried the Picayune representative through his ward, where is located some lovely property on Bayou Boeuf. At the junction of the Boeuf and Huffpower, a mile north of Bunkie begins*

a scope of country the equal of any section. Col. Haas's Shirley place, with 800 acres and 500 in cultivation is the first prominent place on the Boeuf in Avoyelles. He also has four other places making him the largest landowner in the Parish. His home place, Haasville Station, on the Morgan Railroad, is the best improved place in the parish in general conveniences. It contains 3000 acres and has a large store on it, where the post office is kept, etc. He has new outhouses, fences, barns, etc. He has just fenced in 1500 acres in wild cane for winter pasture and will enter largely into the cattle and stock business, believing it to be one of the outcomes of the South. He already has some fine cattle and stock. He owns Enterprise near Evergreen, with 400 acres in cultivation. He owns one-half interest in Hopewell with 1000 acres in cultivation.[90]

Hannah Pokorny Haas, the reluctant mistress of Grey Gables, the Alex Haas mansion in Haasville, took every opportunity to return to the social whirl in New Orleans. Furthermore, as a talented singer she was very much in demand for all sorts of events, both religious and secular. In May 1883 she was in New Orleans to be part of the entertainment at the Seaman's Friends' Society at the Upper Bethel, an organization sponsored by Protestant churches for the aid and comfort of seamen visiting the Crescent City. It offered church services, a Sunday School, a library, a boarding house, and cemetery plots in Cypress Grove Cemetery. On that day, Hannah, who sang, and her sister, Rosa, (later the wife of Coleman Adler, the founder of Adler's Jewelry Store, still an iconic business on Canal Street in New Orleans) played the piano. This was just part of the entertainment which accompanied the presentation of the likenesses of Emperor Wilhelm, his son, grandson and great-grandson to a crowd of appreciative Germanophiles, with assurances that Queen Victoria would be honored the following week.[91] On May 4, 1888, Hannah was a featured singer at the Louisiana State Press Convention in Opelousas.[92]

As late as 1887, J.P. Snelling continued to rent and manage Alex Haas' plantation and store on Bayou Boeuf. The *Marksville*

Review dated January 8, 1887, reported on an Avoyelles Parish Police Jury meeting of the previous week where Snelling requested an amount not exceeding $100 to purchase lumber not less than 3 inches thick in order to construct a new floor over the bridge across Bayou Boeuf, opposite the Haas store. Col. Haas was to be appointed commissioner to have the work done.[93] While it is clear from the record that Haas was not at the meeting, it can be assumed that, despite his wife, he would return shortly to manage his business interests, as they could not be left for too long a period in the hands of strangers.

As Alex and Hannah's only daughter, Alice, got older, Hannah was insistent that the couple spend more and more time in New Orleans so that she could not only get a good education, but also, so she could have the proper religious training. Consequently, Alex and Hannah spent much of the 1890s and beyond, separated because of their diverging interests. Alex was happy to return often to Avoyelles Parish to tend to his growing agricultural interests while his wife was constantly drawn back to New Orleans and her family there. He sought, always to compromise with her by renting and furnishing elaborate homes in the city for his family's use. Occasionally he would pay them visits, and she, in turn, would venture to Avoyelles Parish to "visit" him. A curious article in the "Society Column" of the *Daily Picayune*, published in 1894 indicated that Mrs. Alex Haas, and Mrs. John Pokorny (née Nanie Haas, the Colonel's daughter from his first marriage) "spent a few days at the plantation home of Mr. Haas, at Bunkie, returning to the city Thursday evening."[94] In an effort to keep his young wife, Hannah, happy, and with his older children out of the house, the couple spent more time traveling as well. A trip on the Queen and Crescent train to Salem, Virginia is chronicled in the August 1, 1889 Daily Picayune.[95] This journey came fast on the heels of Alex's eldest son, Dr. William David Haas' marriage to his first cousin, Hattie.

The R.G. Dun Credit Report for July 1889 that had been evaluating the credit worthiness and approximate capital of even the smallest businesses in the United States and Canada annually, since June 1841 gave an estimate of the wealth of the Haas brothers at the close of the 1880s. Alex. M. Haas, who was recorded as the owner of a general store and a planter in Haasville, Avoyelles Parish, whose population was 75, had a pecuniary strength of between twenty and forty thousand dollars with "good" general credit. This was, of course, only a tally of his wealth as the proprietor of a mercantile establishment, and not as a plantation owner. Samuel Haas, whose general store was located in Bayou Chicot, St. Landry Parish, population 160, was also listed as a store owner and planter. He had pecuniary strength of between forty and seventy thousand dollars with a "high" credit rating. Included in this tally was a branch store in Lloyd's Bridge, Rapides Parish, population 70, and a "grocery" several miles away in Cheneyville, population 200, which was managed by Roger T. Marshall, one of the many relatives of Alex Haas' first wife, Mary Maccie Marshall. Sam's eldest son, Dr. John A. Haas, was also in business at the time. He had moved to Ville Platte (population 250) in St. Landry Parish to open a medical practice and a drug store. His business was evaluated with pecuniary strength of between ten and twenty thousand dollars with a "good" credit rating.[96] In fact, while a majority of the seven male Haas offspring went on to become very successful and well-to-do businessmen, four of them were also physicians, and one became a lawyer.

In the last decade of the nineteenth century, Alex Haas' older children were all leading independent lives. Seventeen year old Nanie married her step-mother's brother, David Pokorny, and lived at 2113 St. Charles Avenue in New Orleans with the extended Pokorny family, including her mother and father-in-law, Michael and Fannie Singer Pokorny, and her brother and sister-in-law, Coleman and Rosa Pokorny Adler. Although born into Methodism and educated in Christian schools, Nanie converted to Judaism to marry her husband. Dave Pokorny worked with his father in a lucrative shoe and boot business, and ran it after his father's death in 1902, until his own premature demise in 1916. He and Nanie had no children, so she devoted herself to good works and was a board member of the Home for Jewish Children, a charter member of the New Orleans Women's Dispensary. She was also a member of the Era and Orleans Clubs, the National

Council for Jewish Women, and by virtue of her father's service for the South was a member of the United Daughters of the Confederacy. Her entrance into the Spirit of "76" Chapter of the Daughters of the American Revolution was through her mother, Mary Marshall's, ancestors. After Dave's death in 1916 she spent the remaining years of her life alternatively, taking lengthy trips to Europe, South America, and to California, where she died on May 3, 1930, at the San Mateo home of her half-sister, Alice Haas. She left to her brother, A. Marshall Haas, her stock in the Avoyelles Grocery Co., her interest from her father's succession, her stock in the Haas Land Company and $5,000. In addition she left to her two sisters, Maccie Haas Strouse and Alice Haas, $100 a month each for as long as they would live. She left smaller bequests to all of her nieces and nephews, and legacies of $1000 each to the Jewish Widows and Orphans Home, Touro Infirmary, the Jewish Charitable and Educational Fund, the New Orleans Home for the Incurable, the Milne Home, the New Orleans Dispensary for Women and Children, and a lesser amount to the Tulane School of Business. The residue of her estate was to be left to her deceased husband's sisters.[97]

In contrast to her sister's conversion to Judaism, nineteen year old Mary Maccie "Bunkie" Haas wed a noted second generation Methodist Evangelist, Clarence B. Strouse, a native of Salem, Virginia. They were married on November 18, 1890, in Avoyelles Parish, with her uncle, Dr. John A. Haas, acting as a witness.[98] Clarence and "Bunkie" lived primarily with his family in Virginia but also travelled extensively spreading the word of God. The Reverend Strouse was especially popular in Louisiana, but also held revival meetings all over the United States, and abroad, attracting as many as 50,000 people at a time. He and his wife had no children, and after his death on June 13, 1918, "Bunkie" moved back to Louisiana with her brother, W. D. Haas, and his family, living with them until their demise in the 1940s. Nanie and "Bunkie" were widowed two years apart, after which the two sisters traveled together, going to Europe, the Canal Zone, and France. Continuing her husband's good works, on July 30, 1920, "Bunkie" Strouse sailed from the port of Seattle to visit Japan, and

Hong Kong as a delegate to the World Sunday School Convention.[99] Upon her death in New Orleans on November 11, 1959, an obituary carried in the *Bunkie (Louisiana) Record* read: "Mrs. Strouse was a member of the Methodist faith her entire life, and contributed largely toward the support of church work, especially foreign missions. For many years at Christmas time this fine Christian lady mailed a personally selected religious message to friends all over the world, friends she had made while serving with her husband as a missionary in foreign countries." [100]

Col. Alex's son, A. Marshall Haas, married Helen Henrietta Bostick, a Catholic and converted to that faith. When Marshall and Helen came to live in Bunkie in 1896 there was no Catholic Church, so services were held in a private home. In 1904, in honor of his daughter-in-law, Col. Haas donated land for the establishment of a Church. Helen Bostick Haas was given the privilege of naming the new parish by Bishop Cornelius Van De Ven. It was her belief that her husband's conversion shortly before their wedding was due to the intercession of St. Anthony of Padua, so she chose that name out of gratitude to the saint.[101]

At the turn of the century, Alex's daughter, Alice, now a young lady, was immersed in the whirl of New Orleans society. In 1898 when she was sixteen, the family took an extended vacation to California, stopping at San Mateo and San Francisco. They were there to visit relatives of their fellow Alsatian Jewish neighbor, Leopold Goudchaux of Opelousas. Alice Haas was rich, beautiful and eligible, and it was probably decided at that time that she would wed a member of this West Coast family with ties to both New Orleans and San Francisco.

Returning from their west coast trip to a newly furnished house at 4294 St. Charles Avenue (corner of Milan), purchased by Col. Haas in 1897, Alice set about to enjoy all that New Orleans had to offer. In 1899 she was the Queen of the Purim Festival, presiding over a lavish masked ball at the Athenaeum, sponsored by the Young Men's Hebrew Association. Her King was Marion Weis, whose nephew would one day marry Elise Siess Weil, granddaughter of Simon and Fanny Cerf

Siess of Marksville.[102] In February of 1900, Alice portrayed Rebecca at the Well at the annual Jewish Fair where she received much praise:

> *There has been no feature at the fair which has attracted more pleasing attention than Rebecca at the Well. Miss Alice Rosalind Haas is not only a pretty and charming young lady, but has a way of attracting people to her which has made the receipts of that department phenomenal, considering the limited scope of the business, which is confined to the sale of lemonade. She has worn a very strikingly attractive costume consisting of white crepe de chine, panné velvet with pearls, a cap of blue panné velvet with pearls; gilt sandals, mousselin de soie sleeves, a girdle of pearls and a smile of frank cordiality.* [103]

At the close of the festivities, Alice came in second to Miss Beulah Gumbel as the most popular girl at the fair.[104]

Even though Alex Haas' life was now divided between New Orleans, Avoyelles Parish and extended trips to California, his business interests did not seem to suffer, as his trusted son, W.D., was his surrogate. The 1902 edition of the *Merchants, Tradesmen and Manufacturers Financial Condition* revealed that Haasville, as a town had not grown since 1889, still having 75 inhabitants, but Alex Haas' general store now had a pecuniary strength of between $35,000 and $50,000 with a high general credit rating. In addition, the Lone Pine Sawmill and Lumber Company which Alex now co-owned with James Stewart, located both at Haasville, in Avoyelles and at Lone Pine in St. Landry Parish, had a pecuniary strength of between $200,000 and $300,000, also with a high overall credit rating. Stewart and Haas also operated a cotton gin in Cheneyville, which they sold in December 1902 to the Soniat Oil Company for $75,000.[105]

On June 4, 1902, Alice married Arthur Joseph Dannenbaum, a California native whose mother was part of the extended Goudchaux-Loupe-Bier family, in New Orleans. They returned to San Francisco after their honeymoon. In early 1903 Colonel Haas and Hannah made the decision to follow them back to the West Coast to live permanently. The furnishings at 4202 St. Charles Avenue went up for auction on March 3rd, and the house was made available for rent. Offered at that sale were, amongst other things, a six piece parlor set, wicker furniture, an oak and Birdseye maple bedroom set, an oak dining room set, curtains, paintings, lithographs, a gas range and large refrigerator, guilt chairs, an oak china cabinet, rugs and carpets, as well as many well-appointed accessories which one would expect to find in an opulent St. Charles Avenue residence.[106] The announcement of Alex and Hannah Haas' departure for San Francisco was carried in the society column of the same issue of the *Daily Picayune* dated March 1, 1903. Two days later, it was announced in the newspaper that a letter from Col. Haas had been read at the Cavalry Veteran's Association, Camp. # 9, of his removal to California.[107]

The Dannenbaum family lived at 2611 California Street in Pacific Heights in a large but not grandiose home. Newspaper reports indicate that Col. Haas was in San Francisco for the great earthquake of April 18, 1906. Descendants of the Dannenbaum-Haas marriage have in their possession a photo of Alice Haas Dannenbaum and her three year old daughter, Sadie, camping out in front of their home following the earthquake as fears of explosions and fire prevented the residents from staying indoors. An article, which appeared in the *Daily Picayune* in October 1906, shed some light on Col. Haas' residence in San Francisco, and his actions during the disaster:

> *Col. A.M. Haas, the distinguished Louisianian, who established Haasville and Bunkie, naming the latter after his daughter, is in the city on his annual visit. For the past several years Colonel Haas has resided on the Pacific Coast, because of his health, but he comes here once a year to look after his extensive plantation, timber and mercantile interests in this State, which are managed by his sons. Colonel Haas is now at the St. Charles Hotel, but he expects to leave tomorrow to visit Haasville and Bunkie. Colonel Haas was in San Francisco during the earthquake and he was among the first to go to the assistance of those who were made destitute by the catastrophe. He*

was given charge of one of the relief camps, and in appreciation of the good work he did, he was written a letter of congratulations by Captain Benton, the United States Army officer in command of the camps.[108]

Jewish life in San Francisco was centered around Alta Plaza, the tiered park around Pacific Heights. Haas descendant, Brad Fanta, remembers elderly family members recounting that the Colonel rode around the neighborhood on horseback organizing rescues and helping out wherever he could.

With his two sons, W. D. and Alexander Marshall Haas, at the helm of his businesses, Alex Haas continued to travel back and forth between San Francisco and Avoyelles Parish, but remained active to the end. In 1907 his son, W.D., formed the Avoyelles Wholesale Grocery Company, with his father, his cousin Dr. Charles Haas, Charles Cappel and Robert J. Marshall, his relatives by marriage, as well as merchants from other towns on a board of directors. The company was capitalized with $50,000 and Dr. W.D. Haas was elected its first president. It was formed to do a jobbing business with the merchants in the towns of Marksville, Mansura, Hessmer, Long Bridge, Cottonport, Moreauville, Redfish, Simmesport, Woodside, Evergreen, Lecompte, Cheneyville, Bennettville, Haasville, Eola, St. Landry, Ville Platte, Morrow, Rosa, Melville, Fordoche, Grosse Tête, Plaquemine and New Orleans. A local business club, the Mohawk, to which all these men belonged, organized the Mohawk Building Limited for the purpose of erecting a two story building on Main Street in Bunkie. The lower floor housed the Avoyelles Wholesale Grocery Company and the upper floor served as a clubhouse and auditorium with meeting rooms for its members. Robert J. Marshall, the cashier at the Merchants' and Planters' Bank, where W.D. Haas was the president, and Capt. Sam Haas, on the board of directors, was elected president of the Mohawk Building Company to oversee the construction of the wholesale grocery company's headquarters. Alex Haas' first wife's nephew, John T. Rhodes, Jr., an assistant cashier of the same bank, was elected its secretary and treasurer.[109]

Less than a year later, on February 24, 1908, Colonel Alexander M. Haas succumbed to an illness which had confined him to his bed for several weeks at the home of his son, Dr. W.D. Haas in Bunkie. There was a short obituary in the *Daily Picayune* which recognized him as one of the pioneers in Central Louisiana, and one of its leading citizens. His distinguished service to the Confederacy, as well as his membership in the United Confederate Veterans was prominently mentioned. He had, it was said, "been largely identified with planting on Bayou Boeuf, and with his sons W.D. and A.M. Haas had much farm property along that stream." [110] He was interred in the Thomas Douglas Marshall Cemetery, alongside his first wife, Mary Maccie Marshall, in Evergreen, Avoyelles Parish. The cemetery, a private family burying ground for the Marshall-Rhodes-Haas families, is surrounded by farmland and shaded by large oak trees. It is only accessible through a locked gate.

It is noteworthy that for all of the things Colonel Alex Haas would be remembered, it was his knowledge and love of horses which was primary. Several years after his death he was quoted in the *Times Picayune* for having had a sure-fire cure for "charbon" a horse and cattle disease that is today called cutaneous anthrax, an epidemic of which occurred in the summer of 1910.[111] His business acumen, however, would live on in his eldest son, W.D. Haas, who during his own life was one of the most powerful men in Avoyelles Parish.

Alex's widow, Hannah Pokorny Haas, never remarried. She lived, at first, in the Pokorny family mansion. In 1910 John Pokorny and his wife, Clara Markstein, the widow, Hannah Pokorny Haas, her brother, David Pokorny, and his wife, Nanie Haas Pokorny, Rosa Pokorny, and her husband, Coleman Adler, with their children, Milton, Helen and Walter Adler, called 2113 St. Charles Avenue their home.[112] Hannah spent her time doing charitable works and traveled extensively both abroad and to San Mateo, California to see her daughter, Alice Haas Dannenbaum, eventually moving there to live with Alice and Arthur and their three daughters, Sadie, Constance and Carol.

While in California, Alice was introduced to Mary Baker Eddy's Church of Christ, Scientist established in 1879, and became a reader and practitioner.[113] She divorced Arthur Dannenbaum and married a fellow practitioner, Curtis Leroy Coats, who also headed the Church's publication board. Returning to New Orleans, shortly after 1930, with her mother, husband Leroy Coats and children, she devoted her energies and resources to the New Orleans Prison League Board and to her practice of Christian Science. Hannah Pokorny Haas died on April 11, 1935 at her home in New Orleans. Her daughter, Alice, although having been active in Jewish circles in her teen years, and early in her marriage to Arthur Dannenbaum, at the time of her death on June 18, 1963, in New Orleans, she had been a Christian Science practitioner for over 40 years. She was accompanied to her final resting place in Metairie Cemetery by her daughter Carol Dannenbaum's husband and fellow practitioner, Richard Davis.[114]

***

The last decade of the nineteenth century was an eventful one for Captain Sam and his family. He had married his daughter, Hattie, to his brother's son, W.D. Haas, in 1889. Three of his other sons had wed eligible young Jewish girls from Opelousas, and Charlie had married into the Rhodes-Marshall-Cappel clan. With a thriving business and many properties to look after, the Captain was forever on the move, in his buggy with a double team of horses travelling from Chicot to Opelousas, usually to attend the Police Jury meetings of which he was a member, then to Haasville, to visit W.D. and Hattie, and on to Bunkie to attend to his affairs. Unlike his brother Alex, Sam, it was said, "did not care to dress up, and if he got a suit, someone had to get it for him. He usually wore two pair of pants, and would put his roll of money in the pocket of the inside pair."[115] Ever the charitable man, he not only donated to Jewish causes, but carried mortgages, often with only a bit of interest and no principle payment for years so as not to put a poor family out in the cold. Sam, not only saw to it that his children got the best education, he often saw to it that those who could not pay for schooling were given a helping hand. Sam sent David B. Davis, who had been clerking at his store in Chicot for six years, to Haasville to study medicine with his nephew, Dr. W.D. Haas.[116]

Born to Polish immigrants, Abe, Jacob and David Davis lost their father, Benjamin, to tuberculosis in Texas in 1877. Shortly thereafter, their mother sent the boys to live at the Jewish Widows and Orphans Home in New Orleans. David, after finishing McDonough Boy's school at the age of 14, was taken by Capt. Sam Haas, to work in his store at Bayou Chicot. Dave saved his wages in order to go to medical school in Louisville, KY. In 1894 Capt. Sam gave him a horse, and he rode to Kentucky to begin his studies. Each summer he would return to work at the store in Chicot to save for the next year. He graduated in March 1898, and interned at Shreveport Charity Hospital. After W.D. Haas gave up the practice of medicine, Dr. Davis stepped into his shoes, opening a pharmacy on Main Street in Bunkie, and practiced medicine in an office at the back of the store.[117] On October 21, 1900, Haas was the best man at Dave's wedding to Adele, Leopold Goudchaux's youngest daughter with his first wife, Charlotte Eilert.[118]

***

In the final decade of the nineteenth century, Sam and Alex's half-sister, Fanny Haas, her husband, Elias Moch, and their two adult daughters, Bertha (b. 1879) and Laura (b. 1885), emigrated from Ingwiller, Alsace.[119] The Moch family took up residence next door to, Alex Haas' son, Dr. A. Marshall Haas, just outside of Bunkie in Eola where Elias opened a general store. Born in Mertzwiller, Alsace on December 20, 1843, he had undertaken this difficult relocation at an advanced age. The family never would have moved to a small out-of-the-way place like Eola had they not been brought there by the presence of other relatives. The Haas brothers helped finance the move, just as they had done some twenty years earlier for their half-brother, Solomon. Elias Moch's R.G. Dun credit report for 1902 shows that he was doing well in Eola. His store was worth between $2,000 to $3,000 with a fair credit rating.[120]

On March 4, 1904, Elias and Fanny's daughter, Bertha, married less than two years previously to Isaac Silverberg, a jeweller in Alexandria, passed away at the age of twenty-five.[121] Isaac Silverberg followed his wife in death on December 13, 1905, succumbing to typhoid fever in Chicago, at the age of thirty-five.[122]

On November 24, 1908, Laura Moch wed Joseph M. Goldberg, also an Alexandria jeweller, and former partner of the late Ike Silverberg, at the home of Elias and Fanny Moch at Eola. Emma Bostick, A. Marshall Haas' sister-in-law, provided the piano accompaniment at the wedding and sang "Oh Promise Me." Rabbi Leonard Rothstein from Temple Gemiluth Chassodim in Alexandria officiated.[123]

Shortly before Passover in 1910, Elias Moch retired from business after 20 years in Eola, and he and Fanny moved to Alexandria, where they lived with their daughter, Laura, son-in-law Joseph Goldberg, and their grandchildren, Elaine and Beryl. Elias died in Alexandria on February 1, 1928. Fanny followed on May 24, 1930, and both are buried in the Jewish Cemetery in Pineville.[124] Descendants of Elias Moch, now part of the extended Pincus-Rosenthal-Goldberg-Mykoff families still live and work in Alexandria, Louisiana, and attend Temple Gemiluth Chassodim, as did Elias, Fanny and their children.

***

On September 7, 1907, Sam Haas lost his beloved wife of 45 years, Martha Ann Cole. She was buried in the non-sectarian Vandenburg Cemetery in Bayou Chicot, under a large oak tree.[125] After her death, he spent much of his time living with his daughter, Hattie, and her husband at Oak Hall, near Bunkie. After Sam lost his brother, Alex, only six months later, his business affairs were conducted principally by his son-in-law, Dr. W.D. Haas, his sons Dr. John and Leon Haas, and his nephew, Dr. A. Marshall Haas. He also frequently partnered with fellow Alsatian immigrant, Leopold Goudchaux, buying real estate sold at tax sales on the courthouse steps at Marksville. Sam gave Goudchaux power of attorney to conduct the sale of any lands owned either separately or in partnership with him in both Avoyelles and St. Landry parishes.[126] He remained close with the Marshall and Rhodes clans as well. Nowhere are family ties more clear than in an examination of the names of the directors and officers elected to run the Merchants' and Planters' Bank of Bunkie which appeared in the *Daily Picayune* in 1909. Sam Haas, his nephew W.D. Haas, J. P. Snelling, Isaac M. Lichtenstein, Sol Levy and J.T. Rhodes were the bank's directors. R.J. Marshall was its cashier. Thus, five out of the seven members of the bank were Haas family relations, and Snelling was the late Alex Haas' business manager.[127] Lichtenstein was a Summit, MS native, a cotton commission merchant, and the vice-president of two New Orleans banks.

The division of St. Landry Parish into two parts, with the eastern portion being named after the Longfellow poem "Evangeline," occupied much of Sam, John and W.D.'s efforts in 1909-10. The organization of this new parish was not without its problems. Dr. John Haas, Sam's son, who in December 1908, as the president of the St. Landry State Bank, had been instrumental in the development of the town of Mamou, by financing the sale of lots there,[128] was keen on having it as the parish seat of Evangeline. Sam and his son-in-law/nephew, Dr. W.D. Haas, were lobbying for the town of Ville Platte. In October 1909 a "grand demonstration and gumbo dinner" was held at Bayou Chicot to promote Ville Platte's candidacy for parish seat, complete with the Evangeline Brass Band.[129]

Originally there had been ten towns within the newly created Evangeline Parish: Basile, Chataignier, Mamou, Pine Prairie, Bayou Chicot, Turkey Creek, Ville Platte, Lone Pine, St. Landry and Eunice, the most populous. Four of these towns were controlled by Haas family interests. Captain Sam Haas was the heart and soul of Bayou Chicot. His son, Dr. John Haas, developed Mamou. Lone Pine was a lumber company and sawmill controlled by the late Alex Haas' heirs. Pine Prairie was the location of Sam's second eldest son, Charlie's enterprise, who, with his partners Sterling and Curry Cappel, two of Charlie's wife Maccie Rhodes' uncles, had created the Pine Prairie Oil and Mineral Company in July 1909 to search for black gold.[130] Dr. W.D. Haas was also heavily invested in the project. Six months before the inauguration of the new parish, on January 1, 1911, a conference was held in the Governor's mansion where, upon the urging of Sam Haas, the town of Eunice was ceded to St. Landry Parish and Ville Platte was selected as the Evangeline Parish seat. [131]

During the last decade of his life, Sam remained active in politics. Although the late Alex Haas had been a member of the Police Jury from Ward 10 in Avoyelles Parish, Sam Haas had more of a passion for politics. He was an active member of the Democratic Party, and a longtime member of the Police Jury from the Sixth Ward of St. Landry Parish. The year 1910 saw him lend his name and his money to campaign for New Orleans to be chosen as the site of the World Panama Exposition, which was to be held at the completion of the Panama Canal in 1915. Unfortunately, the Crescent City would lose out to San Francisco.[132] In July 1911, Sam headed the Good Government League of Evangeline Parish which was established to reform the state government in Baton Rouge by ousting incumbent Governor Jared Young Sanders, who although a Democrat, had in less than three years incurred the enmity of many voters by his so-called "useless" appointments.[133]

On June 14, 1915, Sam suffered a great loss. His son, Dr. Charles Haas, who had, in addition to pursuing his oil interests with the Pine Prairie Oil and Mineral Company, practiced medicine at Bunkie for over 15 years. He died at the age of 41.[134] Charlie Haas was buried in the Rhodes family plot at the Bayou Rouge Baptist Burying Ground in Evergreen alongside his only child, Stella, who had died in 1907 at the age of 9 years. His wife, Maccie Rhodes, followed on May 1, 1918, ending that branch of the Haas family tree.[135] Despite his loss, two weeks later, Sam Haas accepted the chairmanship of a committee to organize a big celebration to be held in Bunkie on July 3, 1915, which would host three of the candidates for the Louisiana governorship. He arranged special trains from Marksville and Eunice to arrive at Bunkie early enough for the mid-morning meeting to begin. Characterized by the *Daily Picayune* as one of the most "prominent men in Central

Louisiana" Sam Haas had the honor of chairing the affair and was tasked with introducing the Mayor of Bunkie, Dr. E.S. Matthews.[136]

During his last few years Sam Haas saw to it that his first love, his store in Bayou Chicot as well as its Post Office, was kept open for the benefit of its residents who relied on it for supplies of clothing and food though he rarely went there. Heavy rains in December 1911 caused the bridge over Bayou Chicot to collapse under the weight of Capt. Haas' mail wagon, which plunged into the swollen bayou carrying one of the Captain's teams with it. Mail was only delayed a few hours, after a fresh team was found and a wagon procured under the direction of Postmaster Henry Erlich, who sent the cargo on its way in a different direction.[137]

In late 1918 Sam decided to move to his son, Dr. John's home in Opelousas where he died on January 9, 1919, at the age of 82 years, six months and ten days. It was clear from his *St. Landry Clarion* obituary that Sam was a much beloved figure. Known for his democratic ways, his slouch hat, muddy boots, and his ability to drive his buggy pulled by two horses at breakneck speed between Chicot and Opelousas or Bunkie, he was remembered primarily as a charitable man whose last thought was to donate $500 to the Jewish Relief Fund. After a ceremony, held at the home of his son, State Senator Leon Haas, conducted by Rabbi Wise,[138] Sam was laid to rest next to his beloved Martha, at the Vandenburg Cemetery in Bayou Chicot. The graveside ceremony was performed by the Reverend Fox, a Methodist Minister from Bunkie, taking into account the beliefs of the deceased as well as his Jewish and Christian offspring.[139]

In her book, Mabel Alice Thompson reported that Sam's estate was worth three million dollars and that he had one million in the bank. Exaggeration or not, it is noteworthy, perhaps that when an inventory of Maccie Rhodes Haas' estate was made in 1922-23, the various properties that she had inherited from her deceased mother-in-law, Martha Ann Cole Haas through her late husband Dr. Charles Haas, had a total worth of $305,408. This included 201 individual parcels of land in Evangeline Parish, six parcels in Rapides, one parcel in Avoyelles, thirty-six parcels in St. Landry and three parcels in Lafayette. This was only a small part of the total Haas family holdings.[140]

Less than two years later, Sam's second youngest son, Alexander Murdock Haas, Jr., was the victim of a fatal shooting in Opelousas. Haas had been educated as a dentist, but made his living as a farmer and cattle dealer. He had wed Mattye Loeb in 1904, and their only child, Martha Elaine Haas, had been born eight months before the shooting in March 1920.[141] Mattye Loeb Haas was from an observant Jewish family. Her father, Solomon Leob, an immigrant from Gerolsheim in the Rhinepfalz region of Germany, had owned a general store in Opelousas until his death in 1893. One of her elder brothers, Edward Lee Loeb, a cotton and rice factor, had been elected the mayor of Opelousas, in 1918. Edward Loeb lived next door to Leon Haas, and to Alex and Mattye themselves.[142] On November 18, 1920, the *Times Picayune* carried the details of the shooting on page one. The shooter, Roger Dufilho, an employee in Ben Riseman's clothing store, had allegedly repeated a conversation that Alex Haas, Jr. had had with Dufilho's brother-in-law, Hyppolite Robin's wife. Unfortunately, Preston Hollier, another Dufilho brother-in-law, was listening in on the party line to the gossip. Robin questioned Alex Haas, who denied having had the conversation. Subsequently he, Robin, and a friend drove to Opelousas to the Riseman clothing store to confront Dufilho. Haas entered the store and Dufilho fired his gun three times, striking Haas, who died almost immediately, his finger still on the trigger of his unfired weapon. Dufilho, from his jail cell in the Parish prison, claimed self defense.[143] Haas was buried on November 18, 1920, in the Jewish Cemetery in Opelousas. Roger Dufilho was not convicted, living out his life in Opelousas as one of its foremost citizens. Mattye Loeb Haas never remarried, passing away in September 1947. She was buried alongside her husband, as was their unmarried daughter, Martha Elaine, who followed them in June 1970.[144]

***

Capt. Sam's eldest son, Dr. John A. Haas, an 1882 graduate of the Jefferson Medical College, had started his career in Ville Platte as a physician and proprietor of a drugstore. With his marriage, on June 16, 1897, to Jeannette Roos, daughter of a prominent Jewish general store proprietor, he settled down to practice medicine in Opelousas.[145] However, just as his other brothers and cousins, he soon devoted most of his time to business ventures. John and Jeannette had three children, Elise (b.1898), who died at two months of age, Leonard (b. 1899), who died soon after his fourth birthday, and Nathalie (b. 1901). [146]

During the winter of 1902, Dr. John had visited Bayou Chicot to discuss with his father, Capt. Sam Haas, Leon Wolff, and other interested parties in the parish, the development of the Shell Canal at Washington, LA to bring irrigation to the rice farmers of central and southern Louisiana. After studies had been done, St. Landry Parish was chosen as the ideal area to begin the construction of a canal which would have for its source Bayou Courtableau between Opelousas and Washington because of the natural fall of the land which was about 100 feet to the mile. Dr. John Haas was active for two decades promoting this irrigation enterprise, which had a direct effect on the expansion of Evangeline Parish.[147] Ultimately built by the Union Rice and Irrigation Company, the Shell Canal provided irrigation for over ten thousand acres of rice. Both Dr. John Haas and Leon Wolff became directors of the company.[148]

Dr. John Haas began another project in 1910. Along with Thomas and James Lewis, the former an Opelousas merchant, the latter, president of the Eunice State Bank, Haas formed a syndicate to develop the town of Krotz Springs, twenty miles from Opelousas. Originally a turn of the twentieth century saw-mill town, its developer, C.W. Krotz, afflicted by "oil" fever, drilled the first well in St. Landry Parish, only to strike water. Stung by the loss, but not daunted, he began bottling his commodity which became known for its marvellous healing properties, and the little town was put on the map. The Haas-Lewis organization bought the springs from Krotz in 1910 and immediately thereafter raised one hundred thousand dollars to build a "fashionable" hotel and a modern sanitarium. In addition, carbonating plants were proposed both at the Springs and at New Orleans, where, in order to double their output, some non-carbonated water was to be shipped out in railroad tank cars for processing in the Crescent City.[149] Although the water was eventually shipped throughout the country, the project just barely paid for itself.

Devastating floods in northeast Louisiana virtually wiped out St. Landry farmers in 1912, but spared all but the eastern portion of the parish due to the action of a few people including Dr. John A. Haas, who stopped the pull-out of the levee guards near Melville by guaranteeing that the Police Jury would pay them for their service.[150] As the prosperity of bankers like the Haas family and farmers was always intertwined in these small agricultural communities, the agricultural committee of the Louisiana Bankers' Association, of which Dr. Haas was a member, convened in 1915 to develop an education program for farmers. Its aim was to teach farmers how to diversify their crops and extend their growing seasons. The association sponsored free agricultural fairs and the employment of demonstration agents in order to make local farm land more productive.[151]

These efforts must have borne fruit. According to the January 18, 1919 issue of the *St. Landry Clarion*, the St. Landry State Bank, under Dr. John Haas' control was one of the oldest and most substantial institutions in Central Louisiana, paying annual dividends of twenty percent and with assets of over one million dollars. That same year, Dr. Haas was appointed to the State Department of Education by the Governor. He was on the finance committee of the Louisiana Farm Bureau and the Rice growers' co-operative association. In January 1921 he added another five hundred acres to his vast farming interests by purchasing the Golden Plantation near Fordoche, its dwelling and farm implements, from Émile Juge for $15,000.[152]

On September 27, 1922, Dr. Haas, along with another banker friend, J.P. Savant, were standing at the site of a dredging operation in Whiteville, a few miles from Opelousas, where a drainage canal was being dug. A bolt on one of the heavy timber beams broke sending it crashing into the cable, which snapped, striking both men before they could run clear. Several physicians responded, and a special train was chartered to transport the men to a hospital in Opelousas. One of Dr. Haas' legs was amputated near the ankle and the other was badly shattered. Both of Mr. Savant's legs were broken, but only Haas was in critical condition. He rallied, at first, but finally succumbed to his injuries on October 2, 1922. Upon his death it was revealed that he had recently obtained $200,000 to aid the Rice Growers Cooperative Association, and in addition, had been completing arrangements for the construction of a cotton mill at Opelousas.[153]

His funeral was held at 4 o'clock P.M. on the following day, October 3, 1922, with Rabbi Meyerowitz performing the ceremony. Business was suspended and schools closed so that everyone could attend the funeral. The floral wreaths were so numerous that they had to be delivered to the gravesite in a fire truck. Most banking institutions from all around Southwest Louisiana, as well as New Orleans sent representatives. The Opelousas National Guard also paid their last tribute. It was reported that thousands of mourners crowded the small Jewish Cemetery where Haas was laid to rest, clogging many of the surrounding roads. The ecumenical character of the day's activities was highlighted by the *Times Picayune*, in its reporting of the events, noting that Jews and Gentiles, Protestants, and Catholics were brought together for the funeral.[154]

***

Capt. Sam's youngest son, Leon Samuel Haas, had wed his brother John's wife's sister, Mary Roos, on June 11, 1901, in Opelousas. Rabbi Max Heller traveled from New Orleans to officiate at the ceremony.[155] Leon was educated at the University of Virginia Law School, graduating just before his wedding. He returned to Opelousas right away to practice. He and Mary had four sons, Nathan (b. 1902), John (b. 1904), Leon, Jr. (b. 1907) and Jerome (b. 1909). In 1913 he was appointed State Senator from the parishes of Acadia, St. Landry and Evangeline to fill an unexpired term. He held that post, being re-elected many times, until 1934, when he became the postmaster of Opelousas. He was also a vice-president of the People's State Bank of Opelousas, and a member of the Louisiana Woodmen of the World.

His son, John, eventually became the president of the St. Landry Parish Police Jury and was a local Opelousas merchant. Nathan and Leon, Jr. were also merchants, while Jerome, a Tulane graduate and champion middleweight boxer for the University, rose to Captain in the Louisiana State Police. Despite having two observant Jewish parents, the Leon Haas children, their spouses and offspring were all assimilated into Central Louisiana's predominantly Christian culture.

Leon died instantly from heart failure, at the age of sixty-eight, on February 28, 1947 in the bleachers at the local elementary school while watching the Opelousas-Crowley boxing matches with his son John. He was buried on March 2nd at the Jewish Cemetery with Rabbi Brody of Baton Rouge officiating.[156]

Dr. A. Marshall Haas, Alex's son, was the only Haas offspring who did not abandon medicine for a career in business. After his conversion to Catholicism and marriage on June 17, 1896, to Helen Henrietta Bostick at the Immaculate Conception Church in New Orleans, he took his bride back to the Haas family plantation at Haasville. He practiced medicine and kept the U.S. Post Office there, until it closed in 1914. By the time the family moved permanently to Bunkie in 1917, there were seven children: Mary Maccie Haas (b. 1897), Douglas Marshall Haas, (b. 1899), Charles Harold Haas, (b. 1900), Katherine Moore Haas, (b. 1903), Helen Neomi Haas, (b. 1909), Alice Bostick Haas (b. 1913), and Dorothy Haas, (b. 1914). Dr. Haas specialized in gynecology and pediatrics. He was also a Parish and State Medical officer, and at the time of his death on December 13, 1934, he was the Parish Coroner. Dr. A. M. Haas was a member of the Woodmen of the World and the Knights of Columbus, and a founding member, along with his wife, of St. Anthony of Padua Catholic Church. Four of his five daughters were lifelong residents of Bunkie.

Dr. Haas' wife, Helen Bostick Haas, passed away on December 27, 1958 in Bunkie. Not only had she been the driving force behind the foundation of St. Anthony of Padua Church, she had also been the organizer of their Altar Society, a member of the Catholic Daughters of America, and the United Daughters of the Confederacy. She organized

Bunkie's first Parent Teacher Association, and the local chapter of the American Red Cross. She and her husband lie next to one another at the Pythian Cemetery in Bunkie. Also interred there are her son, Charles H. Haas and his wife Maria, and her daughters, Mary Maccie Haas, Katherine Haas and Helen Haas Ducôté.[157]

***

The last surviving Haas brother from Ingwiller, Solomon, lived in New Orleans for almost sixty-four years. He was the proprietor of a livery stable before his retirement in the 1920s.[158] Solomon married Marie Blandin, the widow of Arthur Maillard, in 1895, but their union was without issue. Marie, who immigrated to Louisiana in 1893, was a French Catholic, and mother of Angèle Marie Maillard born September 24, 1887, in Paris.[159] Solomon's step-daughter had a brief marriage to Nicolas Marie Flauss, with whom she had one son, born on July 18, 1909, naming him Émile Haas Nicholas Flauss, in honor of her stepfather. Solomon, despite living in New Orleans where he could have practiced his religion, never had any strong attachment to it. Upon his death in New Orleans on January 12, 1935, he was buried at Evergreen in the Thomas Douglas Marshall family cemetery in the company of his late half-brother, Alex M. Haas, and other members of the Haas, Marshall and Rhodes families.[160] After Solomon's death, Marie Haas lived with her daughter, Angèle, since remarried to George W. Keim, and grandson, Emile, on Bourbon Street in the French Quarter neighborhood that had been her home for many years.[161] Marie Blandin Haas became a costumer, and made Mardi Gras finery for parades and balls until her death on March 28, 1943, at the age of eighty-two. She was buried in St. Roch Catholic Cemetery in New Orleans.[162]

***

When William David, the eldest son of Col. Alex Haas, and Hattie, the eldest daughter of Capt. Sam, were married at Touro Synagogue in 1889 in New Orleans, descendants had been shocked to learn that the couple had had a Jewish ceremony since they had both been raised as Methodists. This first cousin marriage, however, was in keeping with a long-standing Jewish tradition of the merging and protection of assets. William David Haas, or W.D. as he was frequently called, went on to be the richest and most powerful of the Haas brothers' offspring. Although educated as a physician, he only spent twelve years in the profession before turning his practice over to Haas protégé, Dr. David B. Davis, in 1899 in order to take over the Haas family businesses. He conducted his affairs in both Avoyelles and Rapides Parish, living principally at Oak Hall Plantation, situated halfway between Bunkie and Opelousas on State Highway #5.

W.D. and Hattie had five children, all born in Avoyelles Parish: Maccie (b. 1891), Helen (b. 1892), who died in 1895, Samuel (b. 1894), William David, Jr. (b. 1897), and Nanie (b. 1899). They were all raised in the Methodist Church, and would, in turn, marry spouses from Christian denominations. In later years W.D. Haas served as one of the lay members of the Orphanage board of the Methodist Churches of Louisiana.[163]

W.D. Haas was, as was his father and uncle before him, active in politics. In his first foray into that field, he was elected to the Louisiana state constitutional convention in January 1898 as a representative from Avoyelles Parish.[164] After he and his family moved to Bunkie, he advertised one of his enterprises in the weekly newspaper, *The Avoyelles Blade:* "W.D. Haas and Co – Dealer in General Merchandise and Plantation Supplies. We carry a complete stock of Drugs, Paints, Oils, Furniture and Household Furnishings. We always have on hand a full stock of Lumber, Sash, Doors and Blinds, Lime, Bricks and Cement. We are agents for the Celebrated Florence Wagon." In the same edition of the local newspaper, W.D. was mentioned as a member of the Avoyelles Parish Police Jury. At the March 1899 meeting he made ten out of the thirty motions recorded, mostly concerning repairs to roads and bridges, appointments of road commissioners, and the financing of public schools, proving that he was already one of the leading figures in local government.[165]

In 1902 the R.G. Dun *Mercantile Agency Reference Book* evaluated W.D. Haas and Co.'s pecuniary strength at between two and three hundred thousand dollars, with a "#1" credit rating, the highest in Bunkie.[166] That same year the Governor of Louisiana appointed Dr. Haas, to a two year term as one of the eight administrators of the "Colored Insane Asylum" in Alexandria.[167] A 1903 article in the *Daily Picayune,* extolling the virtues of the town of Bunkie, had much to say about the doctor's enterprises. It was reported that he was the president, and his father-in-law, Sam Haas, the Vice-President of the Bunkie Compress and Warehouse Co., one of the largest in the state, equipped to handle as many as a thousand bales of cotton per day. Dr. Haas was, in addition, the president of the Bunkie Brick Works and the Secretary-Treasurer of the Bunkie Carriage Company, Ltd. This enterprise was headed by fellow Alsatian immigrant and family member by marriage, Leon Bloch, whose wife, Mathilde Levy, was the sister of Sol Levy, the vice-president of the Merchants' and Planters' Bank, another Haas enterprise. Dr. Haas was also in partnership with Bunkie Mayor, W.P. Bridenthal, in a recently opened grain and feed business.[168]

In 1906, Dr. Haas formed a company called the Louisiana East and West Railroad, which was constructed from Bunkie, ten miles to the town of St. Landry. In an interview with the *Daily Picayune* in December of that year, Haas predicted that Bunkie would have a population of between five and six thousand people, given that it had grown from nine hundred residents to fifteen hundred in just one year. This growth, he attributed in no small part to the construction of the Louisiana East and West Railroad, which he predicted would be completed through to Eunice during the first part of January 1907. In addition, new sawmills were being constructed along the route to service a Cincinnati consortium controlling some twenty thousand acres of timberland. On January 9, 1907, Dr. Haas gave an update on the railroad's progress which had been delayed due to bad weather. It had been completed to Ville Platte, and within several weeks, grading would be completed to Eunice. The entire thirty-eight miles of track was to be finished by early summer. According to the report, he would not admit that the line was being built for the Texas and Pacific

Railroad, but did say that it would be sold to whoever would pay the highest price for it after its completion.[169]

Dr. Haas was also the Secretary-Treasurer of the Bunkie Ice Company Ltd., which had a capacity, of seventy-five tons of ice daily, selling ice, bottled soda, and coal.[170] He was also involved in the sugar business, not only as a plantation owner, but as the receiver of the Augusta Sugar Company located in St. Mary Parish. In an effort to rescue this company and others, he and other representatives of various Louisiana sugar growers, sued the American Sugar Refining Company in December 1913 for engaging in unlawful practices to depress the prevailing prices on sugar between the years 1898-1912.[171]

Dr. and Mrs. Haas and their family moved from Bunkie to Alexandria, in Rapides Parish in 1914, taking a house at 900 Bolton Avenue. From then on they divided their time between Oak Hall Plantation, used as a summer home, and their new residence in the city.[172] Along with their new location, came a new automobile, an Oakland roadster. According to the *Times Democrat and Daily Picayune*, the cars cost between $1200 and $2500 each, quite a lot for the time.[173]

On April 7, 1914, shortly after his move to Rapides Parish, Dr. Haas was elected president of the Alexandria Chamber of Commerce and on June 3, 1914, his eldest daughter, Maccie Martha Haas, was married to Dr. Roy Bertrand Harrison at the Methodist Church in Alexandria.[174] The couple made their home in New Orleans. Roy became one of the city's leading surgeons, and was for many years president of the Louisiana State Medical Society until his death in 1954.[175]

In October 1914, Dr. Haas divested himself of his interest in the Bunkie Ice Plant, which was now in the business of selling electricity, and planned to expand to twenty-four hour service.[176] When it became clear that America would soon be joining the fight against the Germans in World War I, Dr. Haas supported the effort wholeheartedly, all the while maintaining his vast empire. Even before

America's official entry in April 1917, he encouraged all his employees to join the military:

> Dr. W.D. Haas, of Alexandria who is President of the Commercial Bank and Trust Company, and the Alexandria Compress and Warehouse Company, of Alexandria, the Merchants and Planters Bank, the Avoyelles Wholesale Grocery Company, the Bunkie Compress and Warehouse Company, the Bunkie Brick Works, the Climax Lumber Company, and other farming and industrial enterprises in the vicinity of Bunkie, [...] has announced that any of his employees who desire to join the National Guard will receive full pay during the term of their enlistment and their positions will be open for them on their return. His two sons, W.D. Haas, Jr., and Samuel Haas, Jr., will leave for Fort Oglethorpe, Ga., in a few days to receive military training. [177]

The Haas family's Merchants' and Planters' Bank of Bunkie closed out 1916 giving its investors a 12% dividend with about $235,000 in assets. Later on that same year, less than a decade after building the Louisiana East West Railroad, which was sold to the Texas and Pacific to become its Eunice Branch, Dr. Haas found himself complaining to the Interstate Commerce Commission. He alleged that the carrier was charging him higher rates than it had set on another branch between Opelousas and New Orleans, thereby discriminating in favor of his competitors.[178] Business was business, however, and only months later he purchased 125 acres of land between the Alexandria Cooperage Company and the Willow Glen plantation so that the Texas & Pacific could build a freight switching and storage yard, thereby relieving the problem of having rolling stock blocking city crossings while crews classified freight cars.[179]

In early 1918, Dr. Haas joined with Rabbi Leo Rothstein of Temple Gemiluth Chassodim to petition the Secretary of War to put into effect more stringent regulations concerning alcohol, particularly bootlegging, and the suppression of prostitution around Camp Beauregard. The Rabbi and Dr. Haas travelled to Washington D.C. to appeal to the War Department to close down the saloons in Rapides Parish. Appeals eventually proved ineffective, so a mass meeting was held at the Alexandria City Hall on May 12, 1918, chaired by Dr. Haas, where a resolution was passed making the area within 25 miles surrounding Camp Beauregard a dry zone.[180]

On January 2, 1918, shortly after graduating from Tulane University, Dr. Haas' son, William David, Jr., married Montez Sarah Henning. A Missouri native, she and her family had lived in Kentucky, before moving to Alexandria, where her father was employed as a marble cutter. Several years older than her spouse, the couple had their first child in October 1918, a daughter, that they named Montez Henning Haas. This was the first of Dr. Haas and Hattie's grandchildren. A second child, William David Haas, III, was born in 1923. The couple lived for the first decade of their marriage at 900 Bolton Avenue in Alexandria with Dr. Haas and Hattie, Sam Haas, Jr, Nanie Haas, Maccie Haas Strouse, Nathan Erlich, and six servants.

W.D Haas, Jr. worked for his father as a cotton broker.[181] Eventually though, he and his family moved to Bunkie, where he became a deputy marshal in the town, and later a deputy sheriff of Avoyelles Parish. Sam Haas, Jr., who had attended the Officers' Candidate School at Fort Logan Roots in Arkansas, remained in the army until the close of World War I. Returning, he went to work for his father, W. D. Haas, overseeing various business interests. On July 10, 1920, the Haas family travelled to New York where Sam, Jr. married Lulu Susan Haupt, a New Jersey native. The ceremony was held at the Hotel Pennsylvania by Reverend Elsing of the Dewitt Memorial Church. Sam Jr.'s best man was R.J. Marshall, vice-president of the family bank in Bunkie. The bride and groom returned to Oak Hall Plantation in Bunkie, where they made their home for several months before returning to live in Alexandria where their two children, Samuel Douglas Haas (b. 1923) and Joseph Marshall Haas (b. 1927) completed the family.[182]

In the fall of 1920 a cotton panic took hold all across the South, as the wholesale price dropped to sixteen cents per pound, an amount which did not even cover the cost of growing the commodity. Governor John Parker of Louisiana issued a proclamation on October 27th ordering all gins to be shut down for a period of thirty days, in order to stabilize the price. From his office in Alexandria, Dr. Haas announced that the twelve gins that he owned in Avoyelles and adjoining parishes would close and remain closed as long as necessary. Unfortunately, the Governors of the states of Texas and South Carolina refused to issue a similar proclamation, so the closures never came to pass.[183] In July 1921, Dr. Haas went to the Louisiana Public Service Commission to stop a twenty-one cent per ton increase on sugar cane freight that the Interstate Commerce Commission had declared, in favor of the rail carriers. The following month, he was off to the Hotel Grunewald to meet with others to form the Louisiana Manufacturers' Association, to improve and promote manufacturing in a state which only produced cotton, sugar and lumber. He also sought to create a traffic department to represent manufacturers in freight rate matters, claims and overcharges. Before the meeting was over, Dr. Haas had been elected one of four vice-presidents of the organization.[184] The same month, there was a meeting of the Louisiana State Ginners' Association, of which Dr. Haas was a charter member, Dr. Haas' son, Sam Jr., was elected Secretary-Treasurer for 1921-22. Dr. Haas urged his members to demand more reasonable freight rates, and to request that the Federal Reserve Banks reduce their loan interest rates.[185]

The last of W.D. and Hattie's children to be married was their youngest, Nanie, who wed Franklin Trazevant Mikell. The groom was from a prominent family whose roots were in South Carolina and Georgia. Mikell had been the manager of the Casualty Department of the New Orleans Underwriters Agency.[186] After their wedding in 1922, the couple lived for a time in Atlanta, Georgia. In the summer of 1924, they, Dr. Haas, Hattie and the Roy Harrisons spent several months at the Henning home in Colorado Springs returning to New Orleans, where Nanie's first child, Franklin Haas Mikell, was born in October.[187] Franklin Mikell soon left his job and joined the family firm, moving to Bunkie to become the coal manager and Secretary-Treasurer of the Union Cotton Oil Company, another Haas enterprise.

Mikell replaced Eagan Lisso, a more distant Haas relative through marriage.

In 1925 Dr. and Mrs. Haas decided to take a grand tour of Europe. They left on the *SS. Berengaria* on May 28, 1925, returning on September 11th of the same year. They visited England, France, Belgium, Holland, Germany, Austria, Switzerland and Italy. A postcard sent to Dr. Haas' brother, A. Marshall Haas, mentions that the couple motored to the town of Ingwiller from Strasbourg to look up relatives of Leon Wolff and friends of "Aunt" Fannie Haas Moch. They also visited the cemetery and saw the graves of Sam and Alex Haas' parents. Dr. Haas ended by saying, "Ingwiller is a great old place and has not changed much since Papa and Uncle Sam left there over 70 years ago." [188]

On December 20, 1926, an argument erupted between Dr. Haas and a business associate, Robert Hill Smith, at the office of the Union Cotton Oil Company in Bunkie, which resulted in the latter's death by shooting. A Grand Jury was empanelled at Marksville, and after three days of testimony, Dr. Haas was held without bond. Two witnesses to the death, W.D. Haas, Jr. and Franklin T. Mikell, son and son-in-law of the accused, were cleared of any culpability and were discharged. Dr. Haas claimed self defense. In early January, after being confined to his bed in prison, he was released on $10,000 bail so he could be taken to Oak Hall Plantation for medical treatment.[189]

The trial was delayed over a year, until March 1928, due to his illness, which was characterized as "heart trouble." He was, however, present for its opening in Marksville, with Judge J.P. Gremillion presiding. Testimony by the defendant, his son and son-in-law, as well as J.J. Keller, the day superintendent of the mill, and night watchman J. D. Dubroc took four days. The argument between Dr. Haas and Smith had started over a letter Smith had sent requesting expenses, a retroactive raise of fifty dollars per month, and a 5% commission on $12,000 in profits that the Cotton Oil Company had earned. Haas confronted Smith about the contents of the letter, saying that everything had been settled the previous July at a board meeting. He then asked for

Smith's resignation. When it was not forthcoming, Haas asked his son-in-law to compose a letter convening the Board of Directors with the purpose of demanding that Smith resign. Smith then threatened Dr. Haas' life. During the argument the night watchman came in and put a gun in a desk drawer for safe-keeping, then left. Smith, who had been sitting on a stool, got up and reached for the gun in the drawer, at which time, Dr. Haas pulled his own gun and shot him. Smith's wife, who was called to the office after her husband had been killed, testified that Dr. Haas apologized to her, saying that he had shot him, but that her husband had threatened him. On March 31, 1928, the case was given to the jury, and within forty-five minutes Dr. Haas was acquitted.[190]

"Oil crazy" is the expression that was used during the first half of the twentieth century to characterize the people of Louisiana. Everyone with land, including the Haas family who had thousands of acres in three parishes, went into the oil business. As early as 1909, Dr. Charles Haas, along with other family members, had founded the Lone Pine Oil and Mineral Company. Exploration and production went at a steady pace, but heated up considerably between the two World Wars. In the 1930s the *Times Picayune*, reported daily on the search for black gold. The John Haas heirs had sold interest in their #1 Haas-Hirsch oil well in the Port Barre field to the Pan American Production Company, for development. The Ville Platte oil field, by 1938 had four producing wells, one of which was the #1 Haas.[191]

No one had been successful in finding a real "producer" in Avoyelles Parish until a Texas operator, Sidney Richardson, did a test well on Dr. W.D. Haas' property between Eola and Bunkie on January 17, 1939. The Haas Investment Company was formed to manage the Bunkie-Eola Field. Haas # 2 well showed up a better producer than the discovery well. A third well, Haas # 3, was drilled on March 4, 1939. Its early production was 300 barrels per day. With the Eola Field an established producer, the Haas Investment Company encouraged a wildcat to be drilled on another Haas property, the Shirley Plantation, three miles northwest of Bunkie. By 1941 there were 94 oil wells in Avoyelles Parish. As of April 1941, 306,987 barrels of oil had been produced.[192]

Less than eighteen months after oil was discovered, Dr. Haas expired at his home, Oak Hall Plantation, on August 26, 1940, after a lengthy illness. An article in the *Times Picayune* praised him as one of the founders of Bunkie. If not one of its founders, as that credit properly went to his father and uncle, he had certainly been the most instrumental in its growth. He was also remembered as a founder and leader of the First Methodist Church of Bunkie. Funeral services were conducted at Oak Hall by the Rev. Freeman of Shreveport, the Rev. Bentley, pastor of the First Methodist Church of Bunkie, and Dr. Taylor, pastor of the First Methodist Church of Alexandria. Dr. Haas was interred at Greenwood Memorial Park in Pineville. State police escorted the funeral cortege from Bunkie to the Alexandria city limits, where the city police took over to conduct the mourners to Pineville.[193]

Haas family oil interests continued to develop during World War II. The Old Sam Haas Estate well # 1 at the Pine Prairie Oilfield, held by the heirs of Captain Sam Haas was reactivated, and exploratory drilling to 10,000 feet was contemplated. In November 1942 oil sand was found at a level of 9,000 feet, and the well appeared to be capable of commercial oil production. That same month there was renewed interest in Krotz Springs, an area originally developed as a resort by Dr. John Haas. A test well, #1-E. Haas-Hirsch was at 10,400 feet, but was thought to be a probable success. In early December Sam Haas Estate Well # 1 tested with a satisfactory oil recovery and became a producer for the Pine Prairie Field, but the Haas-Hirsch well at Krotz Springs had, at 10,500 feet, yielded nothing but promise.[194]

On March 8, 1943, Hattie Haas died at the Baptist Hospital in New Orleans where she had been taken for treatment. Her body was returned to Oak Hall where services were held on March 9. She was buried alongside her husband at Greenwood Memorial Park, survived by her children and her six grandchildren. Within three years, however, two of her grandchildren, would die. Second Lieutenant Samuel Douglas Haas, twenty-two year old son of Sam, Jr. and Lulu Haupt was a casualty of war in Germany on March 28, 1945. Then, W.D. Haas, Jr and his wife, Montez Sarah Henning, lost their twenty-three year old son, William David Haas, III, on July 4, 1946.[195] He had been an Air Force pilot in World War II, but crashed his light plane on his parents' property, Mondavia Plantation, returning home for the July 4th holiday. In 1952, W.D Haas, Jr. and his wife [196] gave funds for a new sanctuary for the First Methodist Church of Bunkie, and it was renamed the William David Haas Memorial Methodist Church in his honor.[197]

Montez Henning Haas, W.D., Jr's. only surviving child, spent most of her life in Avoyelle Parish. She married Warren Leroy Constant, a geologist by trade, who was for many years mayor of Bunkie. Constant was also associated with his father-in-law as a director of the Tidelands Insurance Company of Bunkie and a partner in the Haas Oil Leases and Production Company.[198]

While all of the descendants of Alexander Murdock Haas became Christians, Captain Samuel Haas' sons, John, Alexander Murdock Haas, Jr. and Leon Samuel Haas who all married Jewish spouses were able to remain faithful to that religion for another generation. It is noteworthy that, in 1954, Ben Kaplan, who wrote *The Eternal Stranger*, a study of Jewish life in small town Louisiana, was requested by some family members to use a pseudonym when discussing the Haas family, so as not to reveal their Jewish roots. Capt. Sam Haas was referred to as Samuel Blake in the book.[199] Whatever their names, however, there is little doubt that the Haas brothers, two immigrants from Rothbach, Alsace, and their descendants had a profound impact on Avoyelles and surrounding parishes. They were instrumental in the development of Bunkie, Haasville and Eola, as well as Mamou, Pine Prairie, and the parish of Evangeline. They were store owners, politicians, sheriffs, real estate developers, railroad men, and oil barons. That they were Jews seems to have been long forgotten, even by some of their descendants. Just as Maurice Fortlouis, the Frank brothers, and Abe Felsenthal, all who had married into Christian Louisiana, Sam and Alex Haas set themselves and those who would follow on a course which spelled eventual extinction of their Jewish faith.

[1] Rothbach, Bas-Rhin, France, registres de l'état civil (Civil registrations) An VII (1798), Naissances (Births) # 2, Saphel Sender, digital image, Archives départementales du Bas-Rhin, "État civil en ligne," (http://archives.bas-rhin.fr/: accessed 10/ 2010, 4E 415/1). Original in German, translated into French by Daniel Lubrez 03/2006.

[2] Pierre Katz, compiler, *Recueil des déclarations de prise de nom patronymique des Juifs du Bas-Rhin en 1808, - Tome 3 - de Neuwiller-lès-Saverne à Schirrhoffen,* 4th ed. (Paris : Cercle de Généalogie Juive, 1999), unpaginated, Rothbach (1), Aron Haas (formerly Aron Alexander) household.

[3] André Aaron Fraenckel, *Mémoire juive en Alsace: Contrats de marriage au XVIIIème Siècle* (Strasbourg: Éditions du Cédrat, 1997), 151, entry b.

[4] Rothbach, Bas-Rhin, France, registres de l'état civil (Civil registrations) 1829, Mariages (Marriages) # 3, Saphel Sender, new name Alexandre Haas, to Hünel Feist, new name Jeannette Uhri, digital image, Archives départementales du Bas-Rhin, "État civil en ligne," (http://archives.bas-rhin.fr/: accessed 03/ 2012, 4E 415/4).

[5] Rothbach, Bas-Rhin, France, registres de l'état civil (Civil registrations) 1836, Naissances (Births) # 17, Samuel Cerf Haas, digital image, Archives départementales du Bas-Rhin, "État civil en ligne," (http://archives.bas-rhin.fr/: accessed 10/ 2010, 4E 415/2). Also: Vandenburg Cemetery, section 3 (Bayou Chicot, St. Landry Parish, LA), Samuel and Martha Cole Haas markers, personally read, 2009. "Haas, Samuel - 29 Jun 1837 / 9 Jan 1919, Loyal citizen, faithful friend, loving father, devoted husband, a noble & useful life. Haas, Martha Ann Cole, wife of Samuel Haas - 15 Mar 1845 / 7 Sep 1907." Note the discrepancy in the birth year on the tombstone for Sam Haas.

[6] Rothbach, Bas-Rhin, France, registres de l'état civil (Civil registrations) 1838, Naissances (Births) # 19, Alexandre Haas, digital image, Archives départementales du Bas-Rhin, "État civil en ligne," (http://archives.bas-rhin.fr/: accessed 10/2010, 4E 415/2).

[7] Ingwiller, Bas-Rhin, France, registres de l'état civil (Civil registrations) 1841, Décès (Deaths) # 25, Jeanne Uhri, digital image, Archives départementales du Bas-Rhin, "État civil en ligne," (http://archives.bas-

rhin.fr/: accessed 10 / 2010, 4E 221/13). Note: Henriette was enumerated as "Jeanne" Uhri in the 1808 census as well. Her pre-1808 name was "Hunel Samuel."

[8] Weinbourg, Bas-Rhin, France, Registres de l'état civl (Civil registrations), 1843, Mariages, # 6, Haas-Wolff; digital image, Archives départementales du Bas-Rhin, "État civil en ligne," (http://archives.bas-rhin.fr/ : accessed 2/ 2011, 4E 521/5).

[9] Ingwiller, Bas-Rhin, France, registres de l'état civil (Civil registrations) 1844, Naissances (Births) # 68, Sophie Haas; 1846 Naissanaces (Births) # 44, Salomon Haas; 1848 Naissances (Births) # 31, Fanny Haas; 1849 Naissances (Births) #62, Sara Haas, digital images, Archives départementales du Bas-Rhin, "État civil en ligne," (http://archives.bas-rhin.fr/: accessed 10 /2010, 4E 221/4); Ingwiller, Bas-Rhin, France, registres de l'état civil (Civil registrations) 1852, Décès (Deaths) # 23, Sophie Haas; 1865, Décès (Deaths) #9 Sara Haas, digital images, Archives départementales du Bas-Rhin, "État civil en ligne," (http://archives.bas-rhin.fr/: accessed 10 / 2010, 4E 221/4 and 4E 221/14). Originally researched by Daniel and Bettina Lubrez 4/ 2006.

[10] St. Landry Parish Courthouse Records (Opelousas, St. Landry Parish, LA), "Petition for Naturalization, Fifteenth Judicial District Court of the State of Louisiana, # 22, Petition of Samuel Haas," filed 6 October 1860.

[11] St. Landry Parish was divided on January 1, 1911, and its northwest portion became Evangeline Parish, where Bayou Chicot is now located.

[12] "New Orleans Passenger Lists 1820-1945," digital image, *Ancestry.com* (http://www.ancestry.com [hereinafter cited as "A"]: accessed 1/ 2008), citing, NARA microfilm publication M259, roll 42. Manifest of *SS Baden*, 26 June 1855, p 2, line 5 (# 41), Alexandre Haas, age 16.

[13] Ingwiller, Bas-Rhin, France, Dénombrement de la Population (Population Schedule) 1856, 7M 454, House #16, Family #23, (Individuals 111-115), Samuel Haas, digital image, Archives départementales du Bas-Rhin, "Population Bas-Rhin," (http://population.bas-rhin.fr/ellenbach/: accessed 5/ 2011).

[14] 1860 U.S. Census, St. Landry Parish, Louisiana, pop. sch., Opelousas, p. 121 (penned), Dwelling #769, Family #769, Samuel Haas household, digital image, (A: accessed 1/ 2008), citing NARA microfilm publication M653, roll 424. Date of enumeration: 6 August 1860.

[15] 1860 U. S. Census, St. Landry Parish, Louisiana, slave schedule, p. 15 (penned), column 1, lines 9 & 10, Samuel Haas, owner, digital image, (A: accessed 1/2008), citing NARA microfilm publication, M653 (1438 rolls, no roll given). No date of enumeration.

[16] Arthur W. Bergeron, *Guide to Louisiana Confederate Military Units, 1861-1865* (Baton Rouge: Louisiana State University Press, 1996), 43, 44, 178.

[17] *Compiled Service Records of Confederate Soldiers who served in Organizations from the State of Louisiana*, microfilm publication M 320, roll 14 (NARA: Washington D.C, 1960), folder containing 11 records for Samuel Haas, Capt., Co. K, Third (Harrison's) Louisiana Cavalry. (Copies provided by NARA to the author in January 2008).

[18] John Dimitry, "Louisiana," in Clement A. Evans (ed.), *Confederate Military History*, 12 volumes (Atlanta, Ga.: Confederate Publishing Company, 1899), Vol. X, pp. 435-36. (Note: Fortier's *Louisiana: Comprising Sketches of Parishes, Towns, Events, Institutions, and Persons, Arranged in Cyclopedic Form*, Vol. 3, pages 621-622, confuses the two brothers, stating that Alex Haas was a Captain and that he was on the staff of General Richard Taylor, when it was Sam Haas who was in that role.) See also: Arthur Bergeron, *Guide to Louisiana Confederate Military Units, 1861-1865*, Appendix 1, p. 178.

[19] The late Arthur W. Bergeron in email to the author dated 24 January 2008 wrote that this affirmation was illustrated by Special Order # 182, paragraph V, the contents of which is contained in Samuel Haas' combined military service record and reads: "Lieut. S. Haas, Prairie Rangers, will proceed to Harrisonburg taking in the line of couriers now extending from Natchitoches to that point and change it to Alexandria." It was signed by Major Eustace Surget, General Richard Taylor's Assistant Adjutant General.

[20] Rabbi Martin I. Hinchin, D.D., *Fourscore and Eleven, A History of the Jews of Rapides Parish 1828-1919* (Alexandria, LA: McCormick Graphics, 1984),

102. Note: The retreat by Banks from Alexandria was in May 1864, after the Trans-Mississippi Division of the Confederate Army under General Dick Taylor routed the Union forces at Mansfield, thus thwarting Union General Nathaniel P. Banks' attempt to capture Shreveport.

[21] "Louisiana Confederate Soldiers," database, (A: accessed 1/ 2008), citing Andrew B. Booth, *Records of Louisiana Confederate Soldiers & Confederate Commands* (3 vols.), New Orleans, LA, 1920, Vol. 2. "H," 219. Entry for A. Hass (sic).

[22] Howell Carter, *A Cavalryman's Reminiscences of the Civil War* (1900; Reprint, Clearwater, SC: Eastern Digital Resources, 2008), 218. Note: Carter met Alex Haas in October 1902 when the latter, with a rank of Lieutenant Colonel Commissary General, was on the staff of Major General J.B. Levert, commanding the Louisiana Division of the UCV. Howell Carter was one of the historians on the Major General's staff. See "General Levert's Staff," *The (New Orleans, LA) Daily Picayune* (hereinafter cited as *"DP"*), 5 December 1886, p. 11, cols. 5 & 6, digital image, *Genealogybank.com* (http://www.genealogybank.com [hereinafter cited as "GB"]: accessed 8/ 2009).

[23] The Creole Chargers' first commander was Fenelon Cannon, a representative at the Confederate States convention who signed the ordinance of secession on behalf of Avoyelles Parish. See: Randy DeCuir, author and compiler, *Biographical and Historical Memoirs of Avoyelles - 1890-1990*, reprinted & supplemented by Randy DeCuir, (Marksville, Louisiana: Avoyelles Publishing. Co., 1990), 28, 29.

[24] Louisiana State University Libraries On Line Catalog, Special Collections, Louisiana and Lower Mississippi Valley (hereinafter cited as "LLMV"), Microfilm # 5753, *The Avoyelles Pelican*, Marksville, Avoyelles Parish, LA, 5 October 1861, p. 2, col. 1.

[25] *Ibid.*, *The Avoyelles Pelican*, 12 October 1861, p. 2, col. 3.

[26] *Ibid.*, *The Avoyelles Pelican*, 26 October 1861, p. 1, col. 3.

[27] The Southern Publishing Co., editors, *Biographical and Historical Memoirs of Northwest Louisiana* (Greenville, South Carolina: Southern Historical Press, 1976), 635.

[28] See note 17.

[29] "All Favor New Orleans – As Permanent Headquarters of the Confederate Veterans," *DP*, 5 December 1886, p. 8, col. 6, digital image, (GB: accessed 8/ 2009).

[30] "Cavalry Veterans Pledge their Support to the Local Battle Abbey," *DP*, 8 December 1896, p. 8, col. 6, digital image, (GB: accessed 8/2009).

[31] "Jefferson Davis, The Remains of the Southern Leader," *DP*, 29 May 1893, p. 2, col 5; and " The Last Day," *DP*, 3 July 1896, p. 7, col. 2, digital images, (GB: accessed 9/ 2009).

[32] St. Landry Parish Courthouse Records (Opelousas, St. Landry Parish, LA), *Marriage Record # 2318*, "Samuel Haas to Martha Ann Cole." Bond signed 15 March 1862, civil marriage recorded on 27 March 1862.

[33] Avoyelles Parish Courthouse Records (Marksville, Avoyelles Parish, LA), *Family Meetings,* Book B, p. 60, "Estate of Lavinia Hudson deceased," filed 2 November 1859.

[34] Avoyelles Parish Courthouse Records (Marksville, Avoyelles Parish, LA), *Inventories* , Book D, pp. 545-553, "Estate of John Cole, deceased," filed 23 October 1861.

[35] "Jewishgen On-Line Worldwide Burial Registry*,*" database, *Jewishgen.org* (http://www.jewishgen.org: accessed 7/ 2008), entry for John A. Haas. (1863-1922), Cemetery Gemiluth Chassodim, Opelousas, St. Landry Parish, LA.

[36] Greenwood Memorial Park (Pineville, Rapides Parish, Louisiana), Hattie Haas marker, personally read, 2009.

[37] The following appeared in her obituary "Her lines of entrance into the Louisiana Colonials and into D.A.R., 'Spirit of '76' chapter, were through Col. Thomas Marshall and Mary Randolph Keith, Col. Richard Adams and

William Marshall. She was a great-granddaughter of General David Thomas of Cottage Hall, East Feliciana, of Battle of New Orleans fame. Through the service of her father, the late Col. A.M. Haas, in General Wheeler's cavalry, Mrs. Pokorny was a U.D.C." See: "Stroke is fatal to Mrs. Pokorny," *The (New Orleans, LA) Times Picayune* (hereinafter cited as *"TP"*), 4 May 1930, p. 3, cols. 1, 2, digital image, (GB: accessed 8/ 2009).

[38] Greenwood Memorial Park (Pineville, Rapides Parish, Louisiana), W. D. Haas marker, personally read, 2009.

[39] Nanie Haas Pokorny, U.S. Passport application # 144348 , 12 April 1922 (issue date), digital image, (A: accessed 8/ 2009), citing *U.S. Passport Applications 1795-1925*, NARA microfilm publication M1490, roll 2381.

[40] Maccie Strouse, U.S. Passport application # 43786, 27 May 1920 (issue date), digital image, (A: accessed 8/ 2009), citing *U.S. Passport Applications 1795-1925*, NARA microfilm publication M1490, roll 1232.

[41] Leon's parents were Cerf (aka Hirsch) Wolff and Sarah Weil. Cerf Wolff was Zerlina Wolff Haas' brother, their parents being Jonas Wolff of Muelhausen, Alsace and Fradel Blum of Weinbourg, Alsace. Leon was born "Leopold" Wolff on May 18, 1850 in Weinbourg, Alsace, the information on his tombstone having the wrong place of birth, as well as the date which was off by a month. (Source: Weinbourg, Bas-Rhin France, Registres de l'état civl (Civil registrations), Cote 4E 521/3, 1850, Naissances (Births), no 9, Leopold Wolff, digital image, Archives départementales du Bas-Rhin, "État civil en ligne," (http://archives.bas-rhin.fr/ : accessed 2/ 2011).

[42] Mabel Alice Thompson, *Looking Back – A Narrative History of Bayou Chicot* (Ville Platte, LA: Mabel Alice Thompson [Rt. 3, Box 471, Ville Platte, LA], 1983), 149.

[43] "New Orleans, Louisiana Directories, 1890-1891," digital image, (A: accessed 8/ 2009), citing *Soards New Orleans City Directory, 1891,* New Orleans, LA: L. Soards, 1891, p. 506. Entries for Frederick Kuhne and Solomon Haas.

[44] "New Orleans in 1897 – Underwriters Inspection Bureau of New Orleans Street Rate Slips," database, *Nutrias.org* (http://nutrias.org/info/louinfo/1897/bourbonr.htm: accessed 8/ 2009). Entry for S. Haas at 424-428 Bourbon Street.

[45] "Judicial Notice," *DP*, 1 February 1899, p. 5, col. 6, digital image, (GB: accessed 5/ 2009).

[46] Thompson, 240-241.

[47] Avoyelles Parish Courthouse Records (Marksville, Avoyelles Parish, LA), *Inventories*, Book I, pp. 286-288, "Estate of Mary M. Marshall, deceased," filed 29 July 1879.

[48] "Personal," *The New Orleans (LA) Times*, 15 August 1875, p. 8, col. 1, digital image, (GB: accessed 5/ 2009).

[49] Avoyelles Parish Courthouse Records (Marksville, Avoyelles Parish, LA), *Conveyances*, Book 00, pp. 629-630, "Statement of agreement between A.M. Haas and Mrs. Azema Demaret, wife of William Murdock," filed 11 December 1875.

[50] "Closing Out Sale of Horses, Wagons, Etc," *DP*, 2 August 1877, p. 1, col. 4, digital image, (GB: accessed 5/ 2009).

[51] "The City - A Horse Transaction," *DP*, 8 September 1877, p. 1, col. 6, digital image, (GB: accessed 5/ 2009).

[52] "Public Notice, A Card, New Orleans, September 14, 1877," *DP*, 15 September 1877, p. 4, col. 5, digital image, (GB: accessed 5/ 2009).

[53] Alex was not the only Haas to have "horse troubles." In 1877 Captain Sam Haas had horses stolen from his pasture at Bayou Chicot and taken towards Texas. Postcards were sent out offering a one hundred dollar reward for their capture and recovery. The horses were found in Bonham, Texas. Sam Haas and Sheriff Duson of Bayou Chicot rode to Bonham via Morgan City and Galveston to bring them back. They returned making the trip, a distance of between eight and nine hundred miles, in about eighty-five hours. See:

"Southern News – Louisiana," *The New Orleans (LA) Times,* - 8 January 1878, p. 6, col. 1, digital image, (GB: accessed 8/ 2009).

[54] "Marine News, The New Orleans and Mobile RR," *The (New Orleans, LA) Evening Picayune,* 26 March 1878, p. 2, col. 4, and *DP,* 27 March 1878, p. 3, col 7; also "Washington," *DP,* p. 3 col. 5, digital images, (GB: accessed 5/ 2009).

[55] "Jewishgen On-Line Worldwide Burial Registry," database, *Jewishgen.org* (http://www.jewishgen.org: accessed 7/ 2009). Entry for Hannah Haas. Note: The stone is decorated with muscal notes.

[56] *Ibid.* , Entry for David Pokorny (1861-1916).

[57] "M. Pokorny dead," *DP* , 5 June 1903, p. 2, cols. 5, 6 ; also "American Mutual Insurance Association of New Orleans," *DP,* 10 March 1873, p. 7, col. 4, digital images, (GB: accessed 3/ 2012).

[58] "Louisiana Marriages, 1718-1925," database, (A: accessed 8/ 2009), citing a variety of sources including original marriage records located in Family History Library microfilm, microfiche, or books. Marriage of Alexander M. Haas to Hannah Pokorny.

[59] Corinne L. Saucier, *History of Avoyelles Parish* (Gretna, LA: Pelican Publishing Co., 1998), 264.

[60] Saucier, 121.

[61] "Killed by Accident- A Sad affair on Christmas Eve at Tiger Bend ," *DP,* 30 December 1880, p. 2, col. 5, digital image, (GB: accessed 8/ 2009).

[62] Thompson, 242.

[63] St. Landry Parish Courthouse Records (Opelousas, St. Landry Parish, LA), *Donation Book B*, pp. 220, 221, no. 13338, "Samuel C. Haas to Samuel Haas, Senior," filed 28 April 1874.

⁶⁴ "Mississippi Marriages, 1776-1935," database, (A: accessed 8/ 2009), citing Mississippi marriage information taken from county courthouse records. Marriage of Marks L. Erlich and Rosalie Franklin, 30 December 1873.

⁶⁵ 1860 U.S. Census, Yazoo County, Mississippi, pop. sch. Yazoo City, p. 120 (penned), Dwelling #991, Family #885, M.L. Erlich household, digital image, (A: accessed 8/ 2009), citing NARA microfilm publication M653, roll 594. Date of enumeration: 25 September 1860.

⁶⁶ "Died," *The New Orleans (LA) Times,* 10 July 1865, p. 4, col. 4, digital image, (GB: accessed 8/ 2009).

⁶⁷ 1870 U. S. Census, Orleans Parish, Louisiana, pop. sch. New Orleans, Ward 10, p. 277 (penned), Dwelling #1815, Family #1999, inmates of Jewish Widows and Orphans Home: Henry, Nathan and Philip Ehrlich, digital image, (A: accessed 8/ 2009), citing NARA microfilm publication M593, roll 524. Date of enumeration: 28 July 1870.

⁶⁸ "Co-partnerships and Dissolutions," *The New Orleans (LA) Times,* May 1867, p. 9, col. 1, digital image, (GB: accessed 8/ 2009). Note: Newgass worked with Henry Abraham in a company doing business as Lehman, Newgass & Co., of 61 Carondelet Street in New Orleans which was affiliated with both Lehman, Durr and Co, in Montgomery, AL and Lehman Bros. in Manhattan.

⁶⁹ 1880 U.S. Census, St. Landry Parish, Louisiana, pop. sch., Ward 5, ED 43, p. 18B (penned), Dwelling #167, Family #167, L. Wolff household, digital image, (A: accessed 8/ 2009), citing NARA microfilm publication T9, roll 470. Date of enumeration: 1 June 1880.

⁷⁰ 1880 U.S. Census, St. Landry Parish, Louisiana, pop. sch., Ward 5, ED 43, p. 52D (penned), Dwelling #516, Family #515, L. Godcheaux (sic) household, digital image, (A: accessed 8/ 2009), citing NARA microfilm publication T9, roll 470. Date of enumeration: 1 June 1880.

⁷¹ "A Wrecked Life – Which Sam Ehrlich Attempted to Finish but Without Success," *DP,* 11 July 1886, p. 3, col. 7, digital image, (GB: accessed 8/ 2009).

[72] 1880 U.S. Census, St. Landry Parish, Louisiana, pop. sch., Ward 6, ED 45, p. 52D (penned), Village of Chicot, Dwelling #1, Family #1, Sam Haas household, digital image, (A: accessed 8/ 2009), citing NARA microfilm publication T9, roll 470. Date of enumeration: 30 June 1880.

[73] "Louisiana Statewide Death Index, 1900-1949," database, (A: accessed 8/ 2009), citing State of Louisiana, Secretary of State, Division of Archives, Records Management, and History. *Vital Records Indices.* Baton Rouge, LA. Death of Henry L. Erlich.

[74] 1910 U.S. Census, Avoyelles Parish, Louisiana, pop. sch. Bunkie, Ward 10, ED 26, p. 18A (penned), Dwelling #344, Family #394, Nathan L. Erlich household, digital image, (A: accessed 8/ 2009), citing NARA microfilm publication T624, roll 508. Date of enumeration: 17 May 1910.

[75] 1920 U.S. Census, Rapides Parish, Louisiana, pop. sch. Alexandria, Ward 1, ED 58, p. 13B (penned), Dwelling #277, Family #296, William D. Haas household, digital image, (A: accessed 24 August 2009), citing NARA microfilm publication T625, roll 626. Date of enumeration: 12 and 13 January 1920.

[76] "Louisiana Statewide Death Index, 1900-1949," database, (A: accessed 24 August 2009), citing State of Louisiana, Secretary of State, Division of Archives, Records Management, and History. *Vital Records Indices.* Baton Rouge, LA. Death of Nathan L. Erlich.

[77] The Southern Publishing Co., editors, *Biographical and Historical Memoirs of Northwest Louisiana,* 635.

[78] "Hiwassee College, United Methodist Church," *Hiwassee.edu* (http://hiwassee.edu/about-us/history/ : accessed 9/2009).

[79] "Education," *DP,* p.2, col. 4, digital image, (GB: accessed 8/ 2009).

[80] "W.D. Haas, (Haasville, Louisiana) to Miss Lizzie Clark," letter dated 18 June 1885. Privately held by the author.

[81] John O'Shane, "Tiger Bend Dots," *The (New Orleans, LA) Afternoon Picayune,* 21 June 1881, p. 1, col. 4, digital image, (GB: accessed 8/ 2009).

[82] LLMV, Microfilm #5730, "Tiger Bend – Editor Bulletin," *The Marksville Bulletin,* 22 October 1881, p. 1, col. 1.

[83] Avoyelles Parish Courthouse Records (Marksville, Avoyelles Parish, LA), *Conveyances*, Book ZZ, p 313, "Samuel Haas to A.M. Haas, power of attorney," filed 5 October 1886.

[84] "David Haas Memorial United Methodist Church," Historical Register, Louisiana Conference, United Methodist Church, (http://www.iscuo.org/al_bunkie.htm : accessed 9/ 2009).

[85] Mabel Alice Thompson describes "Martha Manor" in this way. "This fine old home was built somewhere around 1880, and had four bedrooms, a large entrance hall, and a parlor downstairs. The kitchen and dining room were built off to the back having a porch to connect them to the main house. [...] On the back porch of Martha Manor there was a large bell mounted up high, and when dinner was ready, Mrs. Haas or a servant rang this bell to let Captain Haas know it was time to come to dinner. He would close his office and invite whoever was there to go to dinner with him. It was told that Mrs. Haas usually prepared a large meal as she never knew how many would be there. His store and house were about the distance of two or three city blocks apart." (pp. 238, 242).

[86] "Hymeneal," *DP,* 12 July 1889, p. 1, col. 4, digital image, (GB: accessed 9/ 2009).

[87] LLMV, Microfilm #137, " Obituary of Samuel Haas," *The St. Landry (LA) Clarion,* 11 Jan 1919, p. 1, col. 4; p. 2, cols. 3, 4.

[88] LLMV, *Samuel Haas Record Books 1881-1915*, Mss.3400, LSU Libraries, Baton Rouge, LA, "Letter from Samuel Haas to Leon Wolff, Washington, LA," Microfilm reel 1, p. 10.

[89] Thompson, 241-242.

[90] "The Parish of Avoyelles – Its Early History and Present and Prospective Condition," *The (New Orleans, LA) Daily Picayune,* 26 October 1885, p. 8, cols. 2, 3, digital image (GB: accessed 8/ 2009).

[91] "The Royal German Family – Their Photographs presented to the Bethel," *DP,* 29 May 1883, p. 8, col. 6, digital image, (GB: accessed 8/ 2009).

[92] "Louisiana – Opelousas," *DP,* 29 May 1883, p. 1, col. 4, digital image, (GB: accessed 8/ 2009).

[93] LLMV, Microfilm #1032, *Marksville Review,* "Police Jury Proceedings," 8 January 1887, p. 1, col 3.

[94] "Society," *DP,* 24 June 1894, p. 13, col. 2, digital image, (GB: accessed 9/ 2009).

[95] "Personal and General Notes," *DP,* 1 August 1889, p. 4, col. 5, digital image, (GB: accessed 9/ 2009).

[96] *Mercantile Agency Reference Book (And Key) Containing Ratings of the Merchants, Manufacturers, and Traders, Throughout the United States and Canada,* Vol. 85, 1889, image reprint, CD-ROM, *The Mercantile Agency Reference Book* (R.G. Dun & Co., 1889), (Pennsylvania, www.pa-genealogy.net, 2009), See Louisiana, Avoyelles and St. Landry parishes.

[97] "Stroke is Fatal to Mrs. Pokorny," *TP,* 4 May 1930, p. 3, col. 1 ; also, "Special Legacies Left Institutions," *TP,*14 May 1930, p. 26, cols. 5, 6, digital images, (GB: accessed 10/ 2009).

[98] Jeraldine DuFour LaCour, *Brides Book of Avoyelles Parish, 1881-1899,* Vol. 3 (Alexandria, LA: Jeraldine DuFour LaCour [P.O. Box 5022, Alexandria, LA], 1986), 70.

[99] See note 40.

[100] Obituary for Maccie Haas Strouse, undated, in the *Bunkie Record,* "Esteemed Lady Died Saturday in New Orleans," , in possession of Alice Ducote Holland.

[101] "Obituary - Helen Henrietta Bostick Haas," *The Bunkie Record,* 28 Dec 1958, in possession of Alice Ducote Holland.

[102] "The Feast of Purim fitly Celebrated by a Magnificent Ball at the Athenaem," *DP,* 8 March 1899, p. 11, col. 3, digital image, (GB: accessed 10/ 2009).

[103] "The Jewish Fair Will Close Tonight," *DP,* 18 February 1900, p. 3, cols. 2, 3, digital image, (GB: accessed 10/ 2009).

[104] "Society," *DP,* 25 February 1900, p. 13, col. 6, digital image, (GB: accessed 10/ 2009).

[105] Jan and Naomi McPeek, *Merchants, Tradesmen and M anufacturers Financial Condition for 1902 Avoyelles Parish Louisiana.* Image reprint. The 1902 R.G. Dun Mercantile Agency Reference Book. (Salem, OH: Aaron's Books), 2005, Bunkie, 5. See also: "Latest News in Louisiana – Cheneyville," *DP,* 29 December 1902 p. 12, col. 3, digital image, (GB: accessed 10/ 2009).

[106] "Auction Sales," *DP,* 1 March 1903, p. 32, col.5, digital image, (GB: accessed 10/ 2009).

[107] "Cavalry Veterans will Ride with Gordon in the Reunion Parade," *DP,* 3 March 1903, p. 4, col. 4, digital image, (GB: accessed 10/2009).

[108] "Captain Haas Here," *DP,* 18 October 1906, p. 5, col. 2, digital image, (GB: accessed 10/ 2009).

[109] "Bunkie – The Avoyelles Wholesale Grocery Company Organized," *DP,* 21 April 1907, p. 41, col. 4, digital image, (GB: accessed 10/ 2009).

[110] "Colonel Alex M. Haas," *DP,* 26 February 1908, p. 16, col. 6, digital image, (GB: accessed 10/ 2009).

[111] "Charbon remedies Revived in View of Recent Reoccurrence," *DP,* 27 June 1910, p. 7, col. 5, digital image, (GB: accessed 10/ 2009).

[112] 1910 U. S. Census, Orleans Parish, Louisiana, pop. sch. New Orleans, Ward 10, ED 165, p. 43B (penned), Dwelling #68, Family #76, John Pokorny household, digital image, (A: accessed 10/ 2009), citing NARA microfilm publication T624, roll 523. Date of enumeration: 19 April 1910.

[113] Christian Science attracted many American Jews, especially women, because membership in the Church was not accompanied by baptism and therefore entailed no apostasy from Judaism. For further study see: Ellen M. Umansky, *From Christian Science to Jewish Science: Spiritual Healing and American Jews* (London and New York: Oxford University Press, 2005).

[114] "Services Held for Mrs. Coats," *TP,* 20 June 1963, p. 5, col 1, digital image, (GB: accessed 10/ 2009).

[115] Thompson, 242.

[116] "Personal," *DP,* 20 May 1894, p. 10, col. 2, digital image, (GB: accessed 11/ 2009).

[117] Dr. David B. Davis, II, "Goudchaux Memories," unpublished manuscript emailed to the author in 8/ 2010. (Dr. David B. Davis, II is the grandson of Dr. David B. Davis, who was mentored by Dr. W.D. Haas.)

[118] "Society," *DP,* 21 October 1900, p. 13 col. 7, digital image, (GB: accessed 1/ 2010).

[119] 1900 U. S. Census, Avoyelles Parish, Louisiana, Bunkie, Ward 10, ED 25, p. 18A (penned), Dwelling #351, Family #351, Eli Moch household, digital image, (A: accessed 11/ 2009), citing NARA microfilm publication T623, roll 558. Date of enumeration: 22 June 1900.

[120] McPeek, *Merchants, Tradesmen and Manufacturers Financial Condition for 1902 Avoyelles Parish Louisiana,* Town of Eola, Eli Moch entry # 5.

[121] Jewish Cemetery (Pineville, Rapides Parish, LA), Bertha Silverberg marker, row 24, personally read, 6/ 2008. "Bertha, beloved wife of Ike Silverberg, Daughter of Fanny and Elie Moch, born in Ingwiller, Alsace Dec. 10, 1875, Died Mar 2, 1904."

[122] Hinchin, 123.

[123] Hinchin, Appendix # 45, A-105-106.

[124] Jewish Cemetery (Pineville, Rapides Parish, LA), Elias and Fannie Haas Moch double marker, row 24, personally read, 6/2008.

[125] Vandenburg Cemetery (Bayou Chicot, Evangeline Parish, LA), Martha Ann Cole marker, personally read, 6/2008.

[126] Avoyelles Parish Courthouse Records (Marksville, Avoyelles Parish, LA), *Conveyances* Book P-1, p. 423, "Samuel Haas to Leopold Goudchaux, Power of Attorney," filed 31 July 1909.

[127] "The Latest News in All Louisiana – Bunkie – Annual Bank Meeting," *DP,* 16 July 1909 p. 17, col. 7, digital image, (GB: accessed 11/ 2009).

[128] "Bayou Chicot," *DP,* 19 December 1908, p. 14, col. 5, digital image, (GB: accessed 11/ 2009).

[129] "Bayou Chicot," *DP,* 15 October 1909, p. 7, col. 2, digital image, (GB: accessed 11/ 2009).

[130] "Bayou Chicot," *DP,* 3 July 1909, p. 16, col. 4, digital image, (GB: accessed 11/2009).

[131] "St. Landry Division," *DP,* 8 June 1910, p. 15, col. 6, digital image, (GB: 11/ 2009).

[132] "Whole Country Rallies to Support of New Orleans," *DP,* 8 June 1910, p. 5, col. 5, digital image, (GB: accessed 11/ 2009).

[133] "Ville Platte Rally," *DP,* 17 July 1911, p. 3, col. 2, digital image, (GB: accessed 11/ 2009).

[134] "C.E. Haas, Bunkie, LA," *DP,* 16 June 1915, p. 9, col. 6, digital image, (GB: accessed 11/ 2009).

[135] Porter and Barbara Wright, *The Old Evergreen Burying Ground* (Rayne, LA: Hébert Publications, 1990), 34.

[136] "Three Candidates for Governorship speak at Bunkie," *DP,* 4 July 1915, p. 11, cols. 2, 3, digital image, (GB: accessed 11/ 2009).

[137] "Bridge Spanning Chicot Bayou Caves In. Roads Impassable," *DP*, "16 December 1911, p. 16, col. 6, digital image, (GB: accessed 11/ 2009). Note: This was not Erlich's only problem with the U.S. Mail. A few years later it was reported in the *Daily Picayune* that, Sam's store had been broken into shortly before Christmas 1914, but only the Post Office was robbed. See: "Post Office Robbed," *DP,* 17 December 1914, p. 10, col. 7, digital image, (GB: accessed 11/ 2009).

[138] This is probably Rabbi Harry Weiss from Alexandria.

[139] LLMV, Microfilm# 137, *St. Landry Clarion,* 10 January 1919, p. 3; also 17 January 1919, p. 1 (with photo) & 3. See also: "Died – HAAS, Samuel," *DP,* 10 January 1919, p. 2, col. 6, digital image, (GB: accessed 12/ 2009).

[140] Avoyelles Parish Courthouse Records (Marksville, Avoyelles Parish, LA), *Inventories,* Book M, pp. 465-497, "Succession of Maccie Haas Dec'd," filed 11 January 1923.

[141] Cemetery Gemiluth Chassodim (Opelousas, St. Landry Parish, LA), Martha Elaine Haas marker, personally read, 5/2007. Note: Monument is one stone with triple inscription, Dr. A.M. Haas (1876 – 1922), Mattye Loeb Haas (1880-1947) and Martha Elaine Haas (1920-1970)

[142] 1920 U.S. Census, St. Landry Parish, Louisiana, Opelousas, Ward 1, ED 89, p. 11B (penned), Dwelling #215, Family #219, Leon Haas household; Dwelling #216, Family# 220, Edward L. Loeb household; Dwelling #217, Family #221, Aaron (sic) Haas household, digital image, (A: accessed 1/ 2010), citing NARA microfilm publication T625, roll 630. Date of enumeration: 17 January 1920. Note: Edward Loeb was not only Alex Haas, Jr.'s brother-in-law, but Loeb's wife, Rosetta Wolff, was Leon and Lena Heyman Wolff's daughter. Leon Wolff was the Haas brothers' step-mother Zerlina Wolff's nephew, who had settled in Washington, LA. Rosetta's Wolff Loeb's sister, Florence Wolff married Charles Abraham Goudchaux, son of Leopold Goudchaux and his wife Charlotte Eilert.

[143] "Misunderstanding Leads to Killing in Opelousas," *DP,* 18 November 1920, p. 1, col. 1, digital image, (GB: accessed 12/ 2009).

[144] See note 141.

[145] "Society – Haas-Roos Wedding," *DP,* 20 June 1897, p. 13, col. 7, digital image, (GB: accessed 1/ 2010).

[146] Cemetery Gemiluth Chassodim (Opelousas, St. Landry Parish, LA), Leonard Haas marker; Morris Aaron Hirsch and Nathalie Haas Hirsch double marker, personally read, 6/ 2008.

[147] "Pennsylvania Party Spends Day Inspecting Rice Industry – Opelousas," *DP,* 25 July 1909, p. 6, col. 3, digital image, (GB: accessed 1/2010).

[148] "More Millions invested in Irrigation for Louisiana's Fast Developing Rice Industry," *DP,* 27 February 1903, p. 8, col. 1; See also, "Agricultural Development – Ten Thousand Acres of Rice on the Shell Canal this Year," *DP,* 8 February 1914, p. 6, col 4, digital images, (GB: accessed 1/ 2010).

[149] "Syndicate of St. Landry People Formed to Take Over Property and Promote Enterprise," *DP,* 30 July 1910, p. 4, col. 5, digital image, (GB: accessed 1/2010).

[150] "Fifteen Million Dollars Loss. Eleven Parishes hit by Floods," *DP,* 26 April 1912, p. 2, col. 3, digital image, (GB: accessed 1/ 2010).

[151] "Bankers Move for More Efficiency Among Farmers," *DP,* 24 October 1915, p. 13a, col. 3, digital image, (GB: accessed 1/2010).

[152] "Plantation Sold for $15,000," *TP,* 22 January 1921, p. 2, col. 2, digital image, (GB: accessed 1/ 2010).

[153] "Two Men Injured When Cable Snaps," *TP,* 28 September 1922, p. 6, col. 2; also, "Injuries Cause Death of Banker," *TP,* 3 October 1922, p. 13, col 6, digital images, (GB: accessed 1/2010).

[154] "All Sects Mourn Death of Dr. Haas – Business is suspended and Schools Closed for Funeral of Civic Leader," *TP,* 4 October 1922, p. 11 cols. 4, 5, digital image, (GB: accessed 1/2010).

[155] . "Hymneal – Haas-Roos," *DP,* 12 June 1901, p. 2, col. 1, digital image, (GB: accessed 1/ 2010).

[156] "Leon Haas Dies of Heart Attack," *TP,* 2 March 1947, p. 9 cols. 1-3, digital image, (GB: accessed 1/ 2010).

[157] All information concerning the A. Marshall Haas family supplied to the author by their granddaughter, Alice Ducote Holland, including obituaries from the *Bunkie Record,* for Dr. A.M. Haas and Helen Henrietta "Nettie" Bostick Haas.

[158] "Obituaries – Solomon Haas," *TP,* 13 January 1935, p. 6 col. 4, digital image, (GB: accessed 1/ 2010).

[159] Louisiana State Board of Health, Bureau of Vital statistics, Certificate of Death # 4962 (1952), Angela Maillard Keim; photocopy obtained from Louisiana Secretary of State, Department of Archives, Records Management and History, Baton Rouge, LA. (Page 4962, Vol. "O").

[160] Thomas Douglas Marshall Cemetery (Evergreen, Avoyelles Parish, LA), Solomon Haas marker, personally read, 6/ 2008. "Sol Haas – Born in Alsace France Sept 25, 1846, Died Jan 13, 1935."

[161] 1930 U. S. Census, Orleans Parish, Louisiana, pop. sch. New Orleans, Ward 4, ED 63, p. 10B (penned), Dwelling #91, Family #91, Marie C. Maillard household, digital image, (A: accessed 12/ 2009), citing NARA microfilm publication T626, roll 803, Date of enumeration: 11 April 1930.

[162] "Obituaries – Marie Blandin Haas," *TP,* 30 March 1943, p. 2 col. 6, digital image, (GB: accessed 1/ 2010).

[163] Biographical information for W.D. Haas children courtesy of Mr. Brad Fanta, great-great grandson of Alexander Murdock Haas. On Methodism see: "Progress Shown as Methodists Open Conference," *TP,* 23 November 1922, p. 17 col. 2, digital image, (GB: accessed 1/ 2010).

[164] "Official returns of the Election," *DP,* 28 January 1898, p. 8, col. 4, digital image, (GB: accessed 1/2010).

[165] LLMV, Microfilm# 5976, "W.D. Hass (sic) & Co., advertisement," *The Avoyelles Blade*, Marksville, Avoyelles Parish, LA, 11 March 1899, p. 1 col 6; also "Police Jury Proceedings," p. 1 col 4.

[166] McPeek, *Merchants, Tradesmen and Manufacturers Financial Condition for 1902 Avoyelles Parish Louisiana.* Town of Bunkie, 5.

[167] "Latest News in Louisiana," *DP,* 22 August 1902, p. 14 col. 4, digital image, (GB: accessed 1/2010).

[168] "Bunkie, LA," *DP,* 23 February 1903, p.8, cols. 4, 5, digital image, (GB: accessed 1/ 2010).

[169] "Bunkie Growing Fast," *DP,* 12 December 1906, p.10, cols. 6, 7; also, " Louisiana East and West," *DP,* 9 January 1907, p. 12, col 3, digital images, (GB: accessed 1/ 2010).

[170] LLMV, Microfilm# 1032, *The Avoyelles Enterprise*, Marksville, Avoyelles Parish, LA, "Bunkie Ice Co., Ltd. – Advertisement," 7 May 1910, p. 3 col. 6.

[171] "64 More Sue Sugar Trust," *DP,* 4 December 1913, p. 4, col. 1, digital image, (GB: accessed 1/ 2010). Note: The Augusta Plantation was operated by August Hamilton deLesseps, and named after his wife, Augusta Story. Upon his death, deLesseps' son operated it, but it and the sugar factory were eventually bought by the Haas Investment Co. William David Haas, Jr. became the General Manager of the Sugar Refinery and held that post for many years until it shut down in the late 1940s.

[172] "Society," *DP,* 07 December 1913, p. 31, col. 4, digital image, (GB: accessed 1/ 2010).

[173] "Oakland, The Car with a Conscience," *The (New Orleans, LA) Times Democrat and Daily Picayune,* 15 April 1914, p. 9, cols. 1-3, digital image, (GB: accessed 1/ 2010).

[174] "Dr. W.D. Haas Heads Commerce Chamber," *The (New Orleans LA) Times Democrat and Daily Picayune,* 8 April 1914, p. 9, cols. 5, 6; also "Wedded in Alexandria," *The (New Orleans, LA)Times Democrat and Daily*

Picayune, 7 June 1914, p. 25, cols. 6, 7, digital images, (GB: accessed 1/ 2010).

175 "Rites Set Today for Dr. Harrison," *TP,* 26 July 1954, p. 1, col. 7 and p. 9, col. 3, digital images, (GB: accessed 1/ 2010).

176 "Will Take over Light Plant," *The (New Orleans, LA) Times Democrat and Daily Picayune,* 15 October 1914, p. 4, col. 4, digital image, (GB: accessed 8 January 2010).

177 "Full Pay For Fighting Men," *TP,* 27 June 1916, p. 13, col. 1, digital image, (GB: accessed 1/2010).

178 "Bunkie Banks Show Prosperity," *TP,* 3 January 1917, p. 10, col. 8; also, "Industries Board Selects Downman Lumber Director," *TP,* 15 November 1917, p. 6, col 3, digital images, (GB: accessed 9/ 2010).

179 "T. & P. Plans Improvements," *TP,* 30 March 1918, p. 16, col. 2, digital image, (GB: accessed 1/ 2010).

180 "U.S. Geologist to Investigate Local Gas Field, " *TP,* 20 January 1918, p. 1, col. 4; also, "Urge Legislature to Pass Dry Zone Bill for Soldiers," *TP,* 3 May 1918, p. 14, col 1, digital images, (GB: accessed 1/ 2010).

181 1920 U. S. Census, Rapides Parish, Louisiana, pop. sch., Alexandria, Ward 1, ED 58, p. 13 B (penned), Dwelling #277, Family #296, William D. Haas household, digital image, (A: accessed 12/ 2009), citing NARA microfilm publication T625, roll 626. Date of enumeration: 12 & 13 January, 1920.

182 "Social Events," *TP,* 24 July 1920, p. 6, col. 2, digital image, (GB: accessed 1/ 2010). Note: Birth dates of the Sam Haas, Jr. children courtesy of Alice Ducote Holland.

183 "Dr. Haas To Close All Gins," *TP,* 28 October 1920, p. 11, cols. 5, 6, digital image, (GB: accessed 1/ 2010).

184 "Sugar Cane Rate Boost is Opposed," *TP,* 28 July 1921, p. 9, cols. 7, 8; also, "Industry Captains Having $700,000,000 Turnover Elect," *TP,* 27 August 1921, p. 1, col. 4; p. 17, col. 3, digital images, (GB: accessed 1/ 2010).

[185] "Ginners Fix Price of 70 cents to 100," *TP,* 21 July 1921, p. 6, col. 1, digital image, (GB: accessed 1/ 2010).

[186] "Advertisement," *TP,* 25 April 1921, p. 12, cols. 6-8, digital image, (GB: accessed 1/2010).

[187] "Extremely Dull Weekend Spent By Stay-At-Homes," *TP,* 8 July 1924, p. 10, col. 3; also "Births," *TP,* 3 October, 1924, p. 14, col. 3, digital images, (GB: accessed 1/ 2010). Note: The Mikells had their second child, Nancy Haas Mikell, in 1927.

[188] William D. Haas U.S. passport application no. 2155, 10 March 1925 (issue date), digital image, (A: accessed 1/ 2010), citing *U.S. Passport Applications, 1795-1925,* NARA microfilm publication M 1490, roll 2722; Also: "W.D. Haas, (Haasville, Louisiana) to A. Marshall Haas," postcard, privately held by Alice D. Holland, Bunkie, Avoyelles Parish, LA, 2008.

[189] "Dr. Haas is held without Bond in Smith Killing," *TP,* 31 December 1926, p. 1, col. 8; p. 2 cols. 2-4, digital images, (GB: accessed 1/ 2010). "Illness Cause of Release of Dr. W.D. Haas," in possession of Alice Ducote Holland.

[190] "Dr. Haas' Trial as Slayer Opens at Marksville," *TP,* 30 March 1928, p. 4 cols. 2, 3; also, "Victim's Widow Cites Admission at Killing Scene," *TP,* 31 March 1928, p. 33, col. 3; also "Haas Acquitted After He Tells of Killing Smith," *TP,* 1 April 1928, p. 1, col. 6 and p. 18, cols. 4-6, digital images, (GB: accessed 1/ 2010).

[191] "Twelve New Oil Wells Completed in State Fields," *TP,* 26 April 1936, p. 13, col. 3; also "Ville Platte Oil Field Chalks Up Fourth Producer," *TP,* 30 March 1938, p. 19, col. 2, digital images, (GB: accessed 1/2010) Note: The Haas-Hirsch oil well was owned by Dr. John Haas' only surviving child, Nathalie Haas Hirsch, wife of Morris Aaron Hirsch, a dry goods merchant in Opelousas.

[192] "Oil Field Opened South of Bunkie By Eola Wildcat," *TP,* 18 January 1939, p. 1, col. 6 and p. 2, col. 3; also, "Sparta Section Reported Good in New Bunkie Test," *TP,* 5 March 1939, p. 16, col. 3, digital images, (GB:

accessed 1/ 2010). See also: Corinne L. Saucier, *History of Avoyelles Parish,* pp. 233-234.

[193] "Dr. W.D. Haas, Sr., Bunkie Business Figure, Expires," *TP,* 27 August 1940, p. 15, col. 1; also "Last Rites Held for Dr. W.D. Haas, Business Leader," *TP* , 29 August 1940, p. 2, col. 4, digital images, (GB: accessed 1/ 2010).

[194] "Union Spuds New Relief Project in Acadia Parish," *TP,* 28 November 1942, p. 21, col. 1; also "Flank Producer At Vinton Field Holds Interest," *TP,* 10 November 1942, p. 31, col. 5; also, "Seven New Oil Wells Brought In During Week," *TP,* 6 December 1942, p. 26, col. 3, digital images, (GB: accessed 1/ 2010).

[195] "Young Dave Haas Killed in Crash," *TP,* 5 July 1946, p. 2, col. 7, digital image, (GB: accessed 1/2010).

[196] "Mrs. H. Haas' Rites Set at Bunkie," *TP,* 9 March 1943, p. 3, col. 1, digital image, (GB: accessed 1/2010). Personal information concerning Haas grandchildren courtesy of Alice Ducote Holland and Brad Fanta.

[197] "David Haas United Memorial Methodist Church," The Historical Register of the Louisiana Conference of The United Methodist Church, database, *Iscuo.org* (http://www.iscuo.org/al_bunkie.htm: accessed 10/2009.

[198] "We Salute Oil Progress Week," *TP,* 14 October 1951, p. 107, cols. 6, 7; also "Tidelands Life Insurance Company- advertisement," *TP* ,1 June 1956, p. 21, digital images, (GB: accessed 1/ 2010).

[199] Benjamin Kaplan, *The Eternal Stranger – A Study of Jewish Life in the Small Community* (New York: Bookman Associates, 1957), 109, Note 1.

Alexander M. Haas, ca. 1861 – Confederate soldier
(*Courtesy of Brad Fanta*)

Grey Gables, Haasville, LA - Home of Alex Haas
(*Courtesy of Brad Fanta*)

Mary Maccie "Bunkie" Haas, ca. 1888
(*Courtesy of Brad Fanta*)

Alex Haas, ca. 1905   (*Courtesy of Brad Fanta*)

Alice Haas, ca. 1887 - (*Courtesy of Brad Fanta*)

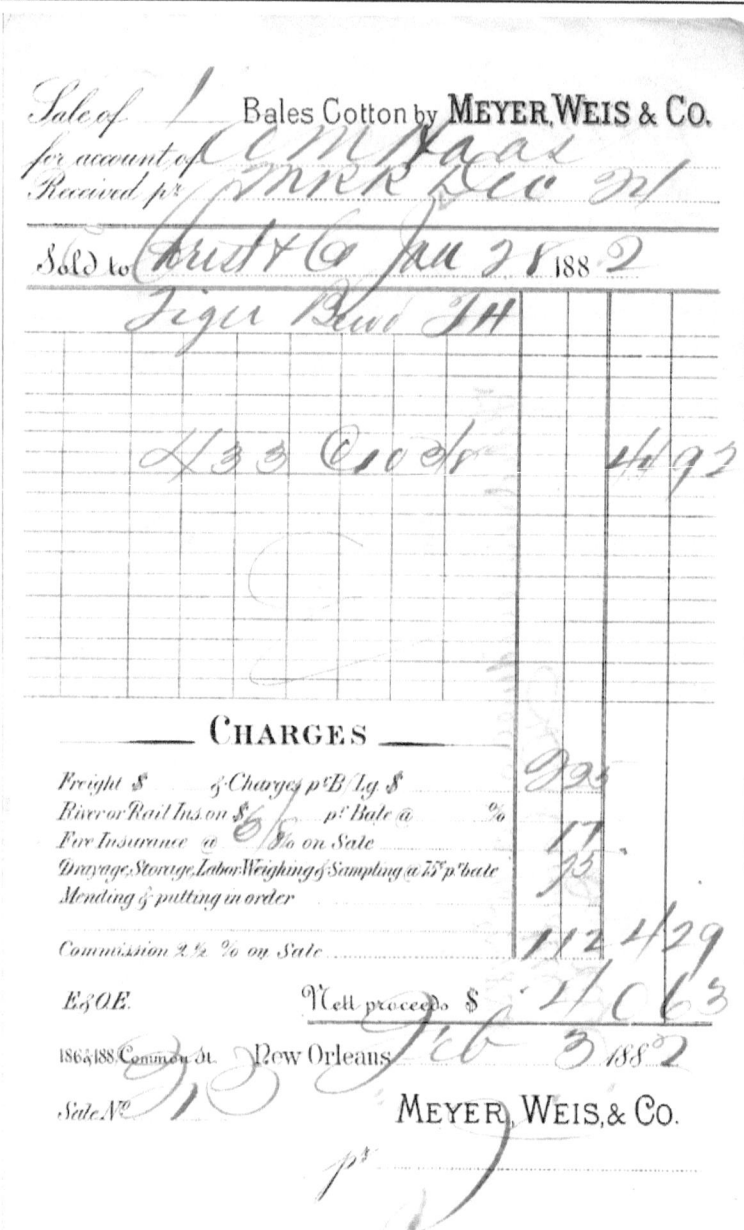

Meyer Weis, bill for shipped cotton from A.M. Haas, 1882

CHAPTER 4
MANSURA BOUND

Simon Siess left Le Havre on October 23, 1852, aboard the American sailing ship, *William Nelson,* arriving in New Orleans on December 22nd of the same year.[1] In April 1853 he headed for Avoyelles Parish.[2] Born in Mühlheim an der Eis in the Rheinland-Pfalz region of Germany on November 28, 1830,[3] he was the first child of Michael Süss, a twenty-nine year old broker and native of nearby Albsheim, and his twenty-four year old wife, Minette Dalsheimer. Minette was born on June 11, 1806, in Heiligenmoschel, near Niederkirchen where her family had eventually settled, and less than 30 miles from Mühlheim where Michael Süss had gone into business.[4] The couple wed on December 1, 1829, in Niederkirchen.[5] Although their marriage had taken place two decades after Jews had been forced by Napoleonic decree to take and formally register surnames, they had used their pre-1808 names, Ayel Süssel and Mundel Löb, on the document.[6] The couple's second child, Leopold, was born at Mühlheim on January 5, 1833. Their last, David, was born on May 31, 1835.[7]

Thirty-six year old, Michael Süss died on February 2, 1837, at his home on the main thoroughfare in Mühlheim, leaving Minette with three young sons to raise.[8] Soon afterwards, she, her boys and her widowed mother, Frommet Raphael, moved sixty miles across the German border into Lembach, Alsace. There Minette met Salomon Lehmann, a thirty-nine year old bachelor and prosperous merchant. The couple had two sons, Isaac (b. 1839) and Abraham (b. 1841), the latter living less than a year, before they finally obtained permission to marry on January 14, 1842.[9] One more child, Michel (b. 1846), lived only eight days. Their surviving children, Simon, Leopold and David Süss, and Isaac Lehmann received a basic education at the local Hebrew primary school, which taught its pupils religion as well as French, Hebrew and German.[10] In the 1851 census of Jews residing in

Lembach, Salomon Lehmann, a fifty year old merchant, was enumerated with his wife Minette, age forty-one, his three stepsons, Simon, age nineteen, Leopold, age eighteen, and David, age fifteen, all merchants, and his son Isaac Lehmann, age twelve.[11] This was the last time the family appeared together in any civil record.

Simon left for New Orleans just a year after that census was taken. He became one more link in a chain of emigrants from Lembach, which had begun in the late 1840s, drawing Jews and Christians alike to America. Louis Kieffer, his wife, Marie Roser, and their two children, Julia and Emanuel, immigrated to Port Gibson, Mississippi around 1848. They were joined by Marie Roser's brothers, Simon and Samuel, and her sister, Rosalie.[12] Another family, Lazarus Sommer, his wife, Thérèse, and their daughter, Rosalie, who were all enumerated in the 1851 Lembach census living near the Lehmann-Siess family, soon left for Port Gibson, as well, where they took up residence next door to Louis and Marie Kieffer.[13]

Immigrants from Lembach had become so successful in their newly adopted country, that they had sent back glowing reports of the many opportunities in the antebellum South to their former neighbors, who, in turn, prepared to make the voyage themselves. The exodus to America had such a profound impact on Lembach that, at the conclusion of the 1856 enumeration of residents, the Mayor made the following notation: "La population a diminué depuis 1846 de 69 habitants, cette diminution doit être attribuée à l'émigration en Amérique." (Since 1846 the population has dropped by 69 inhabitants because of immigration to America.)"[14] Money played a significant part in Simon, his neighbors, and his brothers' decisions to sail to New Orleans instead of elsewhere in America, as it did for many nineteenth century immigrants. After a grueling stagecoach trip from interior points in France to the coastal city of Le Havre where ships awaited their human cargo, the choice between the two major American ports, New York or New Orleans, became a matter of economy. Although the distance from Le Havre to New York was almost twelve hundred miles shorter than the same voyage to New Orleans, the fare to the latter was significantly less. Before the Civil War, New Orleans was the second busiest port in America for agricultural exports to Europe, but the reverse trade from Europe back to the United States was limited mostly to paving stones and French wines. So, not wishing to sail back on empty ships, their Captains often loaded up with immigrants instead, and charged a significantly lower price than those demanded by ships headed for Northern ports in America. Although the voyage could take from forty to sixty-five days under cramped and often difficult and dangerous circumstances, a substantial cash savings was often a great incentive to attract potential customers to this longer voyage. For that reason alone, New Orleans was America's second leading port of entry after New York. Even if the immigrants were headed north or west, steamboat travel up the Mississippi was reasonable and relatively safer than an overland journey from the East Coast. Statistics indicate that 550,000 immigrants passed through the port of New Orleans, between 1820 and 1860, with the heaviest traffic coming in the decade following 1847.[15]

According to his 1857 application for American citizenship, Simon's younger brother Leopold, arrived in New Orleans on May 1, 1854.[16] David, at age nineteen, followed on October 29th of the same year out of Le Havre, arriving in New Orleans on the sailing ship *Suffolk,* which was towed up from the passes to the First District by the *Mary Kingsland* on December 29th.[17] Isaac Lehmann, the only one of Minette's sons to appear in the 1856 Lembach census, made the voyage probably at eighteen years of age in 1858, being enumerated in the 1860 census for Avoyelles parish along with his half-siblings.

On January 21, 1856, the three Süss brothers, whose surname was Americanized to "Siess" purchased four arpents[18] of land between Bayou des Glaises and Cross (now Belsen) Lake near the present day settlement of Big Bend in eastern Avoyelles Parish. The price of the land was $1250 for which the sellers, Edmond Chatelain and his wife Clara Tassin, received $400 with a promise that they would be paid the balance in four installments over the course of the next eighteen months.[19] It was here that the immigrant brothers started their first mercantile establishment.

Their partnership, however, did not last long. Leopold took out a bond and license in Wilkinson County, Mississippi on August 13, 1856, with the intention of marrying Celestine Roz (Roos), a union which his brothers would have certainly approved, and, perhaps even encouraged or arranged. For whatever reason, it never took place and there is no further record of this mysterious Mississippi Jewish bride.[20] Undeterred, he courted eighteen-year old Josette Chatelain Couvillion, the widowed sister of Edmond Chatelain, from whom the brothers had purchased their property near Bayou des Glaises. Josette was born on April 23, 1838, near present-day Mansura, the eighth of the sixteen children of Joseph Belony Chatelain and his wife, Marie Roy.[21] Her ancestors could be traced back to Kaskaskia in the Illinois Territory. Josette's fourth great-grandmother was Marie Rouensa-8cate8a, daughter of Chief Rouensa (Mamaenthoüenta) of the Illini Confederation. Marie, a convert to Catholicism, gave birth to seven children in a second marriage to Michel Philippe, a Lieutenant in the Kaskaskia Militia. One of those, their eldest daughter, Agnès Philippe, married René Roy, the French surgeon at nearby Fort de Chartres. This latter couple, the ancestors of many Louisianans, were Josette's third-great-grandparents.[22]

On November 22, 1853, fifteen year old Josette had been married to Jean-Baptiste Valsain Couvillion,[23] Her husband died five months later leaving her pregnant with a son, Jean-Baptiste Couvillion, who lived just over a year. Leopold had made up his mind to wed Josette, an observant Catholic, but she refused until such time as he would convert to her religion. Several Jewish immigrants had already taken Catholic wives in Avoyelles Parish. Some even had religious ceremonies conducted by the local priest, but none had ever converted to the spouse's faith, until now. Leopold's decision to abjure Judaism in the summer of 1857 fractured the family unit causing the following to appear in the *Villager* newspaper: "DISSOLUTION OF PARTNERSHIP, The public is hereby notified that the partnership hereto existing between the undersigned has been dissolved by mutual consent. The firm will be continued by Simon Siess and David Siess, who will settle all business connected with the former firm." It was signed by all three and dated July 8, 1857, at Bayou des Glaises.[24] Less than two weeks later, Leopold sold his interest in the land and store back to his brothers for $198.61 with a note for $239.39 payable in January 1858.[25]

On August 16, 1857, twenty-four year old Leopold Siess was baptized into the Catholic faith at St. Paul the Apostle Church by Father Henri Durand.[26] A week later he was the first of his brothers to apply for citizenship. On October 28, 1857, he registered his earmark and cattle brand at the Avoyelles Parish Courthouse, and on November 15, 1857, he and Josette were married at St. Paul the Apostle Church, by Father Jules Janeau. The bride's elder brother, Zélien Chatelain, along with two neighbors, Dorsin Mayeux and Espire Ducôté, were witnesses to the ceremony.[27] His brothers did not attend. The couple returned to a piece of land belonging to Josette in Mansura, where Leopold tried his hand at farming.

Not two years later the family was in difficult straits. Josette had given birth to her first child, Auger, on February 10, 1859.[28] Later that same year, in order to protect their few possessions from creditors, she sued her husband for their moveable property including one Creole pony, one small wagon, one cow and calf, one earmark and brand and all the buildings and improvements situated on their land in Mansura. The goods were seized by the Sheriff, auctioned, and sold back to Josette for $220.[29] Leopold then set up shop in the town as a butcher, going into business with his brother-in-law, Ludger Chatelain.

Simon and David Siess relocated to Mansura, buying a tract of land on Léglise Street from Martin Rabalais in July 1858, where they continued their mercantile partnership.[30] On January 10, 1859, they purchased a "mulatto slave named Geneviève" from Adeline Bordelon for $900 payable in three installments.[31] The 1860 census records show that the Leopold Siess family had only $500 invested in real estate and $300 in personal property, however, Simon and David held real estate and personal property worth $9000, and employed their half-brother, Isaac Lehmann, as a clerk in their store.[32]

With their sons in Louisiana, Salomon and Minette Lehmann began making plans to join them in America. Five other Jewish residents from Lembach had made similar arrangements. Leopold Meyer, his wife, Sophie, and their two children, Lienhard and Henriette, were making the trip, as well as Joseph Loeb, the single son of Elias and Rosalie Bloch Loeb.[33] They all booked passage on the *Luna*, a sailing schooner, based out of New Orleans, due to leave Le Havre in early February 1860.

Efforts to trace the origin of this particular ship were challenging because a number of vessels were registered with the same name. It is known that the skipper was Captain John Shannon, and that before setting sail for Le Havre, the schooner had made a two month round-trip to Boston. The New York *Commercial Advertiser* reported that on September 26, 1859, the *Luna*, with Captain Shannon cleared Boston Harbor for New Orleans, arriving on October 19th.[34] From that time on, the ship remained in port until her departure for Le Havre. On November 6th the Captain advertised that his vessel was soon leaving: "For HAVRE – The A-I clipper ship LUNA of small capacity is now loading and will have immediate dispatch. For freight or passage apply to Capt. John Shannon on board. Post 18, First District, or to T.C. Jenkins, 132 Gravier Street."[35] On November 19, 1859, the Luna was towed from her berth by the tugboat, *Ocean*, under Captain Chapman's guidance, through the passes out to sea.[36]

The crossing to France took forty-seven days. It was uneventful until the ship attempted to enter the port of Le Havre on the northern coast of France, just before daylight on January 4, 1860. Even though she had dropped her anchor in the outer harbor, she was caught by a gust of wind from the southwest, causing the chain to part. She then slammed into a floodgate buttress. The stern of the ship was damaged and started to take on water. An attempt was made to dock but had to be put off until the evening tide, so pumps were sent out to keep her afloat.[37] Once docked, she remained in port for just over five weeks where repairs were made. It is doubtful that the passengers, scheduled to board for the trip back to New Orleans, had any idea of the damage she had sustained.

Late in the afternoon, on February 16th, 1860, the *Luna* left Le Havre with her crew of eighteen and between eighty and one hundred passengers, including Salomon and Minette Süss Lehmann. She sailed at the high tide with a strong northeast wind, which ordinarily would have been sufficient to allow her to round the cape at Barfleur and leave the English Channel behind for the relative safety of the open sea. Unfortunately, the winter of 1859-60 had been particularly rough and navigating west around the rocky coast of Normandy was the most treacherous part of the trip. The next morning, on Friday, February 17th, after being forced to trim her sails due to very strong winds, the ship had gone seriously off course and was headed for the reefs near Barfleur. Witnesses at St.-Vaast-la-Hougue reported seeing her dangerously close to the rocks of Tatihou Island, but saw that the Captain had been able to maneuver the vessel clear and sail farther north battling a northeast wind and snow squalls. The ship passed the entrance at Barfleur in safety, but with the tide now against her, she was pushed back towards the rocks at Quilleboeuf, unable to round the northern coast and put out safely to sea. Some of the inhabitants of Barfleur reported seeing the struggling schooner, and moved closer to shore to watch her, praying that she would catch the wind and sail away. Tragically the ship was driven onto the rocks in full view of the horrified witnesses on land. Several of them tried to launch small boats in an effort to try to save some of the *Luna's* passengers, but with the raging storm any rescue was impossible. It was reported that the impact of the wooden ship on the rocks could be heard over the howling winds. A local priest, Father LeBlond, who witnessed the accident, wrote in his journal "A terrible shock shook the vessel from keel to the top of its mainmast. Its masts ripped off by the force of the wind, the disemboweled *Luna*, was in its death throes, water pouring into the ship, and the squalls ripping its sails one by one to shreds." In the storm and confusion, no lifeboats could be launched from the sinking ship.

The *Luna's* ill-fated passengers had never even lost sight of the French coast. Clad in heavy woolen clothes few had any chance to escape from the maelstrom caused by the sinking vessel which was reduced to splinters within an hour. Three crew members from the ship who had clung to a barrel after it had broken apart made it to shore. Battered and half frozen from their wild ride towards the beach, two would survive. The other would die on the way to a hospital in Cherbourg. For several months afterward, debris from the wreck, and the personal possessions of the drowned including a watch, a signet ring, some clothing, a miraculous medal, and a goatskin vest, washed ashore, followed later by the remains of thirty-eight victims. Most were interred at Gatteville-le-Phare. A stele in the cemetery erected to the memory of those lost was unearthed in the graveyard in 1950 and transported to the Sailor's Chapel (Notre Dame du Bon Secours) in town where it is still displayed along with a piece of the splintered wood from the *Luna* which had washed ashore after the storm.[38]

The first report of this tragedy appeared in the press almost a month afterwards, initially in the *London Observer*, then in the *New York Herald,* which on March 15, 1860, published a short account of the marine disaster. At the time, it was said that two sailors had been rescued, and eleven corpses had washed ashore from the wreck of the American vessel, *Luna*. The article explained that she was a "three masted vessel of 625 tons, and belonged to New Orleans; she was bound to Louisiana with 67 emigrants on board and a miscellaneous cargo of wine, spirits, &c."[39] The *Herald* also ran an addendum to the story on the same day reporting that all the American vessels in the port of Havre had flown their flags at half-mast out of respect for the death of Captain Shannon, commander of the *Luna*.[40]

It is not known how long it took for the Siess brothers in Central Louisiana to find out about Salomon and Minette's demise. Searches in the *Daily Picayune* for March 1860 show no reports of that shipwreck, even though she was a New Orleans-based vessel. Perhaps word reached them via mail from friends or relatives in Lembach as the town had lost seven of its Jewish inhabitants in one tragic occurrence. The dream of their parents settling in America having been shattered, the brothers resumed their day-to-day toils, unaware that further tragedy for them and for their fellow Southerners was just around the corner.

***

Leopold Siess and his wife, Josette, welcomed a baby girl into their family on June 20, 1860, and named her Florestine. She was baptized by Father Jules Janeau on August 28th of the same year at St. Paul the Apostle Church in Mansura.[41] Less than six months later, on January 26, 1861, Louisiana was the sixth state to secede from the Union. On February 7, 1861, fearing that he might have to leave for the front, he had Josette purchase two slaves from Zénon St. Romain, thirty-eight year old Elizabeth, and her four year old son, Ben, for $2335 payable in three equal installments using promissory notes that Josette held from her brother and mother as collateral.[42] Two months later, the first shots were fired on Fort Sumter.

In the summer of 1861 the people of Mansura, now part of the Confederate States of America, elected Dr. Jules Desfossés as their mayor, and Charles Dimarquis, Louis Drouin, Victor Prostdame and Simon Siess as aldermen. In early September, the first group of Avoyelles Parish volunteers, sixty-six men known as the Creole Chargers, led by Captain Fénélon Cannon, left for Baton Rouge, where they joined the First Regiment Cavalry as Company G. In order to help the families who were now without husbands, fathers and brothers to support them, the citizens of the Parish formed a "Benevolent Association," and held their first meeting on November 17th to elect officers at the Siess Brothers' store in Mansura.[43]

As the war dragged on, it became apparent that there were divided loyalties in Avoyelles Parish. The French non-citizens were simply hopeful to be able to stay out of the fray and protect their lives and property. Those in the Confederate camp sent their sons to war. On April 10, 1862, *The (New Orleans) Daily True Delta* reported that over four hundred men had arrived from Avoyelles Parish on the steamer *Dr. Batsey*. Captain Joffrion led the Mansura Guards with eighty-two men. Capt. J.J. Ducôté headed the Creole Rebels consisting of eighty-one men. There were seventy-eight volunteers in the Avoyelles Fencibles with Capt. H.W. Verstile. Captain Ludger Barbin commanded the Marksville Guards with an additional eighty soldiers and Captain L. Phillipon was in charge of the eighty Marksville Chasseurs à Pied.[44] Not everyone was as enthusiastic. Other residents, amongst them many "Anglos," were secretly Unionists, whether out of loyalty to the United States or fear that the rebel cause was fruitless. These former practiced the utmost secrecy because earlier in 1861 a draconian sequestration notice required the seizure of any land, chattels, or possessions of enemy aliens residing within the State. There were also stiff penalties for those who, having knowledge of such "traitors," did not turn them in to the authorities.

After the fall of New Orleans, on April 25, 1862, the situation in Avoyelles Parish worsened. The first order issued by military commanders was to stop the shipment of cotton from the interior of the state to any point on the Mississippi River for storage or sale. This, of course, put the local farmers in an impossible economic situation. This news was followed by the Confederate government's adoption of a conscription act in late April of the same year, which required any man between the ages of eighteen and thirty-five to report for military service for three years, or the duration of the war. At this point, non-citizens were exempt from the law.[45] The order affected Leopold Siess, who had filed for citizenship in 1857, but not his brothers, who were still French subjects. Any Confederate conscript who could afford the price could engage a substitute to do his fighting for him. This practice was common in European countries, although Jews had been, until recently, forbidden from engaging substitutes. An article in late June in the French section of the *Avoyelles Pelican,* advertised the availability of replacements for those who had been called up to fight. The purveyors of this service, Paul Michel-Firment of Marksville, Louis Gallemand of Mansura, and Firmin Grégoire of Moreauville, offered non-naturalized substitutes, who were still exempt from conscription, for a very favorable price.[46] Leopold Siess, however, had no means by which to employ someone to do his fighting for him.

Life in the parish became even more complicated at the conclusion of an incident called by journalists of the day the "Masters' Affair." After the fall of New Orleans, the division between Confederate loyalists and Union sympathizers had widened significantly. The acrimony between these factions culminated in the death of several parish residents. William Edwards, a Kentuckian, who had come to Avoyelles Parish in 1830 and subsequently married into the Gaspard-Normand family, was a major player in this drama. The Masters' and Edwards' Union leanings were not a very well-kept secret. According to accounts reported in both the Confederate-leaning *Avoyelles Pelican*, as well as the New Orleans *Daily Delta*, the trouble started because the Edwards and Masters families were thought to be at the heart of a group of one hundred or so who were trying to prepare their friends and neighbors for eventual repatriation into the United States. In order to undermine loyalist morale and enthusiasm for continued hostilities with the North, these local Unionists were allegedly spreading false rumors that Confederate militias would burn their cotton crops rather than allow them to be confiscated and sold by the Union Army. Word had also been spread that the Edwards family had recently received a secret shipment of guns and ammunition at Normand's landing with which they intended to arm themselves.

Everything came to a head on May 11, 1862, the day after Order #25 issued by Brigadier General John G. Pratt calling for the immediate destruction of all cotton stored along the Atchafalaya River in the parishes of St. Landry and Avoyelles, appeared in the local newspaper.[47] A contingent of Confederate militiamen, under the direction of Captain Eloi Joffrion with Scott Gray, Cyriaque Gaspard, and Orfila Normand, went to the house of Céleste Mayeux, the widow of Litchfield, Connecticut native, Frederick Masters, to investigate the arrival of John Deavers from New Orleans, who was also a suspected Unionist. Deavers prevailed upon Captain Joffrion to allow him to finish his breakfast before he was led away for questioning. In the meantime, word of this impending arrest was sent to the residence of William Washington Edwards, Celeste Masters' son-in-law. William Washington Edwards being absent, his brother, Thomas Jefferson Edwards, his elderly father, William Edwards, and friends, William Battell, and Antoine Denis rushed over to the Masters' house. Since both factions were armed, a gunfight ensued which resulted in the wounding of Scott Gray, Thomas Jefferson Edwards and Antoine

Denis. William Edwards and Cyriaque Gaspard were both shot and killed. During the fray, Deavers fled towards Foulk's landing. Thomas Jefferson Edwards took up the rest of the story in the July 15, 1862 edition of the New Orleans *Daily Delta.* Fearing execution, he, Denis, and Battell, aided by his brother, William Washington Edwards, and his uncle, Fielding Edwards, fled down the Red River. Hearing that it was blockaded some miles down to prevent their escape, the party took to the swamps from the Red River towards the Mississippi, where T.J. Edwards, Battell and Denis were taken aboard the Union gunboat *Kino*, and their wounds dressed. They were then transferred to the sloop of war, *Brooklyn*, at Natchez which made its way down the river to New Orleans. As a consequence, some of the Edwards' land in Avoyelles Parish was seized, and friends and relatives were thrown into jail. Others hid in the swamp and their houses and possessions were left, according to Edwards, "to the mercy of the Confederate rabble."[48] T.J. Edwards remained in exile in New Orleans until the end of the war.

The publication of Order # 25 to destroy cotton was followed up by an even more disturbing article in the *Pelican,* a week after the Masters' fiasco. A new directive put some teeth into the original pronouncement, which had simply appealed to farmers to "do the right thing" by burning up their livelihood for the good of country. Two Confederate military officers, Cols. Wren of Adams County, Mississippi and Denis of New Orleans visited Avoyelles Parish and appointed commissioners to see to it that all cotton was destroyed. Speaking to Parish residents through the weekly newspaper, Colonel Wren wrote to the military commissioners urging them "to determine calmly and deliberately, but without hesitation, the time when the patriots of your noble parish shall themselves apply the torch to the product of their labors. I feel convinced that everyone will do it promptly, when you order it, in cheerful obedience to the laws of our Government. A correct account of all cotton destroyed will be kept by you and receipts furnished by me that proper and just reparation may be made by our government at Richmond."[49]

The people of Avoyelles Parish knew that receipts issued to them by the Confederacy could hardly be turned into food for their families. For the small, independent farmer like Leopold and his family, this order would surely bring ruin. For the local merchants like Simon and David Siess who sold supplies on credit to farmers in anticipation of a successful harvest, a destruction of the fall's cotton crop would cause the storekeepers to default on their own debts to New Orleans suppliers. By the first of June the Avoyelles commissioners had ordered that all cotton stored on wharfs along any waterway was to be burned immediately if not removed by the owner and secured in a "safe" place.[50]

In the midst of all the confusion, elections were held again in Mansura for the mayor and Town Council on June 3, 1862. Dr. Desfossés was re-elected mayor, and all the aldermen, including Simon Siess, were given another term in office.[51] On June 26, 1862, in order to control the growing unrest in Central Louisiana, martial law was declared in the parishes of Avoyelles, Natchitoches and Rapides and the writ of habeas corpus was suspended. William F. Cheney was appointed Provost Marshall of Avoyelles Parish.[52] By the end of August a list of laws promulgated by Cheney earlier in the month was published in the *Avoyelles Pelican*. Trading with the enemy, as well as travelling to New Orleans, except under a flag of truce, was prohibited. Conscripts shunning duty were to be treated as public enemies. Spies were to be rooted out and subject to punishment under martial law. Confederate money must be received as legal tender and those failing to accept it would be promptly fined and imprisoned. Citizens having surpluses of corn, bacon, beef, cattle or other provisions were forbidden to sell to persons outside of Avoyelles Parish, except for use by the Confederate army.[53] Two days after martial law was declared it was reported that Simon Siess had resigned as alderman in Mansura and a special election would be held on July 10th to fill the vacancy.[54]

***

During the summer of 1862 there was a public discussion concerning the conscription of non-naturalized residents of Avoyelles Parish. Word had appeared in the *Avoyelles Pelican* dated July 19th that the Confederate government had broadened the scope of those whom they considered to be eligible for military service in order to replace the heavy casualties of the past year. Now included were non-naturalized foreigners who owned slaves, or who had held political office, or who had voted, or who had held rank in the military (on either side). Those foreigners who were married to an American, or owned a home, or had taken out a license to practice a certain trade or open a business were still exempt.[55] Perhaps Simon, by virtue of his having resigned from the Town Council, hoped to avoid his being drafted into Rebel service.

Twenty-nine year old Leopold Siess was finally inducted into the Confederate Army on October 5, 1862. He was sent in a contingent of reinforcements to join the 18th Regiment Infantry, Company I, which had just come back to western Louisiana from Shiloh, TN where it had lost two hundred men. The soldiers reached New Iberia, LA by October 12th. It is probably here that Private Leopold Siess joined them. If this is accurate, he participated in the battle of Labadieville in Assumption Parish where the Confederates lost several hundred men, with about the same number being captured. In retreat, the regiment stayed for some time at Fort Bisland (St. Mary Parish) and spent the winter and early spring of the following year at Camp Qui Vive at Fausse Point (St. Martin Parish), returning to Fort Bisland in March 1863.[56] According to what little remains of his Confederate service record, Leopold was on the muster roll for January and February 1863 and AWOL beginning in March 1863.[57] This absence coincided with the birth of his third child, a daughter, Hermina, who was born on March 7, 1863, at Mansura. His baby daughter was baptized by Father Jules Janeau on May 2, 1863, at St. Paul the Apostle Church.[58] It is doubtful that Leopold attended the baptism because he was reported on the Confederate muster rolls for May, June, July and August 1863, having been paid by Captain Silas T. Grisamore through June of that year.[59] In July, he was at Bayou Lafourche, and then at Vermillionville (present-day Lafayette), where he was on "provost guard." Company "I" was stationed locally in Central Louisiana until November, patrolling between Vermillionville, Simmesport (Avoyelles Parish) and Moundville (St. Landry, Parish).[60]

Despite Simon Siess' best efforts to avoid service, the July 1862 law was clear. Both his and David's names appeared on a list of one hundred twenty-six conscripts for December 29th of that year, for which seven had already provided substitutes under the age of forty. [61] Their twenty-three year old half-brother, Isaac Lehmann, who clerked in the Siess Store, was not called to serve. Captain William Cheney, the enrollment officer for the parish, had the following notice published in the January 3rd, 1863 *Pelican*, "Attention, Conscripts! You are ordered to rendez-vous at Marksville on Wednesday, 14th, inst. at 10:00 A.M. Each man must bring a blanket, knapsack, canteen and a change of clothing, and be prepared to take up the line of march for Camp Pratt."[62] By the time of this notice, the draft age had been raised to fifty years of age, and slaves were now being conscripted to perform non-combat duties. Every plantation owner was expected to give up one-half of his workforce to the cause, and was promised reimbursement of one dollar per man per day, and the appraised value of any slave were he to perish in the service of the Confederacy. The same issue of the newspaper offered a general amnesty for all deserters or those men between the ages of eighteen and thirty-five who had, to this point, evaded the draft, as long as they reported to Camp Pratt by January 25, 1863. [63]

Simon and David did not leave for Camp Pratt on the appointed date. All three Siess brothers were in Avoyelles Parish on March 16, 1863, when Simon and David sold a small tract of land adjacent to theirs in Mansura to their brother Leopold's wife, Josette Chatelain, for one hundred fifty piasters.[64] Soon after that sale, Simon and David answered the call from Lieutenant Colonel Aristide Gérard, who had just been appointed the commander at Fort DeRussy (originally called Fort Taylor) located on the Red River north of Marksville. Gérard had asked for volunteers to defend it in an article which appeared in the March 21,1863 issue of the *Pelican*: "At the hour of danger the Commanding Officer calls upon all volunteers willing to share the glory and dangers of the defenders of Fort DeRussy. The Post Commander and Quarter Master have received instructions, to provide for the feeding and comfort of all those who will report to Major P.E.

Théard, acting officer of Artillery at this Post. Come all. None should be excused! The Commanding officer relies on the assistance of all good citizens." On the same page, a small article in French entitled "Sous la Tente," extolled the virtues of the gallant French residents of Mansura who had already answered his call to arms. Those listed were Alphonse Durand, Louis Roulé, his son Aloys Charles Roulé, Louis Grégoire, Simon and David Siess, Henri Fontanille, Émile Talabardon, Pierre Thomas and Paul Dantain.[65] Although the Commander at Fort DeRussy had feared Union retaliation subsequent to the Confederate capture of the U.S. Ram ship *Queen of the West* a month earlier after she had run aground there, no action was seen until several months later on May 3rd.[66]

Simon Siess stayed on in the parish until the summer of 1863, whereupon he defied martial law and made his way to New Orleans. The brothers were now in serious financial trouble, as was just about everyone in Avoyelles Parish. Simon's whereabouts between 1863 and 1867 was clarified in the testimony given by Thomas Jefferson Edwards in an 1866 suit brought by Martin Rabalais against the Siess brothers for failing to pay the mortgage on the land which they had bought from him in 1858. Edwards, remembered as the "exiled unionist" in the Masters' affair, testified that "Simon Siess went to New Orleans in 1863, returned with the Federal army in 1864, remained a few days and returned with the Army to New Orleans and never again returned to Avoyelles until after the surrender of the Confederates. He first went to New Orleans in the summer of 1863. He still lives in New Orleans. Witness saw him here about a month ago."[67] Once in New Orleans, Simon realized he could not return during the conflict without being prosecuted as a traitor so he found employment at Wells Bros. & Co., commission merchants in the city, with offices at 36 Poydras Street. He took rooms on the corner of Fulton and St. Andrews.[68] David, on the other hand, stayed on in Avoyelles Parish until after the fall of Fort DeRussy in 1864.

***

Union forces led by General Nathaniel P. Banks' XIXth Corps, the Army of the Gulf, had been victorious at the siege of Port Hudson, Louisiana in July 1863. Three other divisions, one from the XIIIth and two from the XVIth Corps were then added. General William Helmsley Emory was given command of the XIXth Corps, and together Banks and Emory planned, with the aid of Union General in Chief, Henry W. Halleck, the ill-fated Red River Campaign, which would be so devastating to the residents of Avoyelles and Rapides Parishes. The Union Army was tasked with the capture of Shreveport, Louisiana in order to cripple the Confederate Trans-Mississippi Department headed by General Dick Taylor (son of former U.S. President Zachary Taylor). The Union also sought to control the Red River, and to occupy east Texas in order to stop supplies coming into the South from Europe via Mexico and Texas, and conversely to stop Confederate cotton shipments out of Louisiana via the same route. The lure of thousands of bales of cotton thought to be sitting on the wharves of the Red and Black Rivers which could be confiscated and shipped back to mills in New England to support the war effort was also an important incentive. General Banks and his thirty-five thousand men, however, were never able to achieve any of the major goals of their campaign, although their opposition, General Dick Taylor's Trans-Mississippi Army, never seemed to amount to more than nineteen thousand soldiers.

Mistakes and delays on both sides plagued the campaign, which started out with a victory for Union General A. J. Smith's Army of the Tennessee, as they overwhelmed Fort DeRussy north of Marksville on March 14, 1864. Banks had been ordered by Ulysses S. Grant, newly appointed General-in-Chief of the Union Army, to send A. J. Smith and his troops to capture Shreveport immediately, as Grant needed Smith back by the middle of April, even if it meant abandoning the Red River campaign. The Union forces, flush with victory in March, eventually found that April would not be as kind to them. They were routed at Pleasant Hill on April 2nd and then again at Mansfield on April 8th, bringing their drive northward towards the capture of Shreveport to a virtual standstill.

With the war unfolding in their back yards, Avoyelles Parish residents were in turmoil. The Union Army was in full retreat from their disastrous attempt to capture Shreveport, and stalled at Alexandria some thirty miles away. Despite these recent southern victories, many Avoyelleans were convinced that the Confederate cause had been lost. Emboldened, a local unit of Union sympathizers dubbed the "Home Guard," was looking for recruits. In mid-to-late March 1864, Private Leopold Siess, formerly of the 18th Louisiana Infantry, deserted in order to defend his family and property. He joined as a lieutenant in the "Home Guard" serving under Captain Frederick William Masters, Jr., son of Celeste Mayeux Masters. Two years earlier Masters had witnessed his sister Clarisse's father-in-law, William Edwards, being fatally shot and his brother-in-law, Thomas Jefferson Edwards, wounded by Confederates, yet these families had never flagged in their support for the Union cause. Lieutenant Siess and the "Home Guard" lived in hiding by day in the woods and swamps of Avoyelles Parish, occasionally visiting the town of Mansura under cover of darkness to visit their loved ones. In a family of well-kept secrets, the memory of Leopold's anger and disillusionment with the Confederate government because of the destruction of his cotton crop, was one of the few memories that was passed down through the generations to Bill Friend, Leopold's great-grandnephew.

On April 14, 1864, being low on arms and ammunition, Captain Masters had made it up through the woods in a light rain to Fort DeRussy, lately captured by the Union army, where the USS *Essex* was moored. Information taken from the deck log of the *Essex*, recorded by S. Johnson, revealed that "From 4 to 6 [PM] Weather clear and pleasant. Wind light from N.W. Furnished Capt. Lee 25 muskets and accoutrements to arm Home Guards Company commanded by Capt. Morters [sic]." The log for the next day reported the return of those same arms and ammunition to the ship, after the capture of 5 guerillas [Confederates] and ten horses by Capt. Lee and his "contrabands."[69]

The "Home Guard's" next known exploit would make national news. Termed the most barbarous act of the war, the *Daily True Delta* reported the story from a private letter sent to the publication, dated April 30, 1864, by the US steamer *Argosy* (Tinclad #27) which was anchored off of Fort DeRussy on the Red River. Various versions of this atrocity were carried in the Houston *Daily Telegraph*, the New Orleans *Bee*, and Alabama's *Mobile Advertiser and Register*, but the *Delta's* account was, by far, the most complete:

> *There has come to us for protection since our arrival some twenty-five Creole citizens, natives of the parish. They have organized themselves into a 'Home Guard' for mutual protection, and have drawn rations from the government to meet their immediate necessities. The organization is in charge of Capt. F.W. Masters and Lieut. Cease, both natives of this parish. On Wednesday last Lieut. Cease started out with 22 mounted men, with 13 U.S. muskets, with the intention of hunting up some more of their members, who had been frightened by the barbarities of the guerillas and had sought concealment in the woods. They hunted about during the day, and at night arrived at the vicinity of a brother of Lieut. Cease, and went into quarters in a vacant house. About three o'clock on he morning of Thursday they were surprised by about forty or fifty rebels and without scarcely a struggle 12 of them were taken prisoners. The Lieutenant was the only one who fired a shot, and he succeeded in making his escape during the morning, and arrived here early in the afternoon. Among the prisoners was the lieutenant's brother, who does not belong to the organization, and two boys. The two latter were allowed to leave, after having been interceded for by a neighbor, who chanced to be present. The balance, nine men, were then stripped to the skin, and at nine o'clock drawn up in a line and deliberately shot. This outrage has cast a gloom over everyone here, and the citizens loudly call for vengeance.* [70]

The homonymic spelling of the name "Cease" in the *Delta* article, and the declaration that he was a native of Avoyelles cast some doubt upon the true identity of this Lieutenant in the "Home Guard."

However, Leopold Siess might well have been mistaken for a native by the Union Army because, like most everyone else in the parish, he spoke French. Did the dead brother refer to Isaac Lehmann, Leopold's half-brother, who disappeared from all records after 1860? His identification remained in question until the discovery of two additional pieces of information.

When researching his book, *Earthen Walls, Iron Men,* its author, Steven Mayeux ordered transcripts of testimony given during the French and American Claims Commission hearings held at the Frank Hotel in Marksville. Claim #250, Ferréol Regard vs. United States, heard on May 9, 1882, contained the evidence needed to confirm the identity of Lieutenant "Cease." The witness, Joseph Laurent, Jr., had been an eye witness to many events that had taken place in April and May 1864 in the town of Mansura. In question was the motive behind the torching of a house owned by Victor Prostdame. It was the United States' position that the place had been burned, not by Federal troops, but by Severe Dupont, who had been one of the two young men spared by the Confederates on April 17, 1864, when nine of his "Home Guard" compatriots had been executed. Laurent, a witness for the United States, when asked the cause of the grudge that Sévère Dupont had against Prostdame stated, "I know from what I was told during the time that Bank's army was at Mansfield or above here, they had a kind of company here they called home guard at which Mr. Leopold Siess was at the head. They came one evening to Mansura and staid [sic] there all night and I heard that a company of Confederate cavalry came and captured a portion of them. That young man [Dupont] was one that escaped. They said it was Mr. Victor Prostdame who had sent for the Confederate soldiers, this was the grudge that he had against him." When asked what had become of the Home Guard members who had been taken that day, Laurent testified: "The Confederates who captured them brought them to Holmesville,[71] and killed them. There were between two and twelve of them killed."[72]

The second piece of evidence came from one of the applications that David Siess made for a Confederate pension. In support of his attempt filed in 1921, Fulgence Z. Lemoine and Henri

Fontanille affirmed "that after the fall of New Orleans, the said David Siess performed the duties of a soldier at Fort DeRussy, in Avoyelles Parish, on the Red River under the command of Col. Gérard and Major Théard; that David Siess was doing duty at Fort DeRussy at the time one of his brothers was killed."[73]

Since both Leopold and Simon were alive at the close of the war, the evidence is conclusive that Isaac Lehmann was the brother executed by Confederate loyalists in the woods near Holmesville on April 17, 1864. It was a severe blow to the family coming just four years after the loss of their parents in the wreck of the *Luna*. It must have been especially difficult for Leopold, who having made his escape through an open window after his capture, had left Isaac behind to fend for himself. This youngest brother's death would cast a long shadow over another household as well. It was recently discovered that he left behind a son, Paul Marius Lehman, born in March 1864 to Marie Charlot, a twenty-four year old person of color, just a month before his murder. After the War, Marie raised Paul, along with another son, Oliver Rabalais, alone, until she married Louis Olivier in 1868. The Olivier family tended a farm in Mansura and had seven children of their own.[74] Paul M. Lehman married Harriet Thompson and raised six children. He became a parish peace officer for the Third Ward, and Harriet was a registered mid-wife.

***

The hardships that would follow during the ensuing months for the inhabitants of Central Louisiana were unimaginable. After the Union defeats at Mansfield and Pleasant Hill, General Banks called for retreat back to Alexandria. When he had marched north through the town earlier in the spring he had convinced many residents that a Union victory was inevitable. To that end, he had set up a Union recruiting station, and promising protection for their wives and children, he had arranged for hundreds of men to take the oath of allegiance to the United States and join up. Many so-called "Jayhawkers" from the surrounding parishes had also taken advantage of this opportunity, coming out of the woods to join Banks' army. Exactly when David

Siess arrived in Alexandria is not known. Perhaps it was as Lemoine and Fontanille had sworn in an affidavit accompanying David's application for a Confederate pension. They wrote that he had followed the 18th Louisiana Infantry up to Alexandria sometime after the fall of Fort DeRussy on March 14, 1864. It is evident, from other facts uncovered, that David did change sides, disgusted with the fighting after the death of Isaac Lehmann. With one brother dead, Leopold on the run, and Simon in New Orleans, he eventually threw his lot in with the Federals after his arrival in Alexandria.

After Banks' defeated Union army retreated back into Rapides Parish in early May, his troops stayed several weeks in Alexandria waiting for the departure of Admiral Porter's fleet, which was marooned at the falls on the Red River due to insufficient spring rains. With Porter's ships finally in the clear, Banks sent his "Jayhawk" force, including David Siess, out of Alexandria on May 12, 1864, as guides for the main Federal troops scheduled to leave the next day. On May 13, 1864, the New York 13th Regiment, commanded by General A. J. Smith, previously charged with keeping the peace in Alexandria, was withdrawn from the town. As the Union regiments marched south towards Mansura, the New York 13th doubled back to set Alexandria afire, burning ninety percent of the town to the ground, to the horror of the defenseless women, children and old men who had seen their husbands, fathers and sons march off the previous day.[75] The former Confederates, who had left with Banks, would not learn of this cruel Union betrayal of their loved ones for quite some time. In 1882 David Siess confirmed his presence with General Banks' Army in the testimony he gave at the French and American Claims Commission in support of the United States against fellow Mansurian, Ferreol Regard. In answer to the question, "Where were you in the month of May 1864?" he answered, "I was with General Banks' Army, [...] I was in front of it as a guide."[76] In another claims commission case David Siess testified: "I was a guide from Alexandria down to Simsport [sic], Atchafalaya River [...] The 16th day of May 1864, at half past eleven in the morning, [...] I was the first man going into that town [Mansura] with General Grover. I was with the advance guard."[77]

The march out of Rapides Parish to Simmesport, where the Federal troops crossed the Atchafalaya River into Pointe Coupée Parish, took several days and cost several hundred lives on both sides. The Confederates under General Dick Taylor did not have a sufficient force to be able to stop the Union retreat, trying unsuccessfully at the Battle of Mansura on May 16, 1864, and the Battle of Yellow Bayou two days later. Contemporaneous accounts of these few days in May when the fighting came to an end in Avoyelles Parish show a land and people impoverished by war and defeated in spirit.

Mother Marie Hyacinthe le Conniat, the Breton superior of the Daughters of the Cross, was an eyewitness to these events. She and several other sisters from the order had arrived in Avoyelles Parish in 1855 to bring Catholic education to the area. On June 14, 1864, Mother Marie Hyacinthe wrote to her parents from the Presentation Convent in Mansura. She explained that, on the way north through the parish earlier in the year the Union general, believing that they would have an easy victory ahead, was most gracious to her and assigned a man to guard the Community. Upon their return, the Federals, she said, "retreated, burning and devastating everything, and they, of course, looted."[78] On May 15, 1864, Mother Hyacinthe was told that Federal troops were within three miles of Mansura. She told the sisters to take their forty or so boarding students into the woods, and she, Father Rebours, the Curé at St. Paul the Apostle, and four other sisters stayed to guard the house. She wrote, concerning the Battle of Mansura, which took place the following day:

> *The Community was between two armies. A bomb exploded above our heads, and destroyed a wooden bed, and created much damage in the convent. Five bombs fell upon our little chapel, broke the statue of St. Joseph, etc. Our animals were enclosed in a little field near the chapel. A bullet killed four: a cow a heifer and two sheep. More than fifty cannon balls and I do not know how many bullets crossed over the Community for three hours while the battle went on. [...] Our soldiers had retreated toward the bayou and the next day at 5 o'clock in the morning, the enemy was in the neighborhood again.*

> *Useless was it to ask for protection this time. They were irritated over their defeat. They were twice as many as our Confederates in number. They revenged themselves upon the country—pillaging, looting and burning! We were not spared! [...] The enemy enjoyed tearing down the fences, burning them, and laying waste to everything. They had 1,500 wagons or carts with them. They came through our enclosure and garden with this train of carts. More than 100 of these brigands made a tour of our enclosure, our grounds. We had to tell them it was against the law for them to steal and destroy such an establishment as ours. They did not care. They took 100 barrels of corn from our storehouse, more than 150 of the poultry, all our animals (horned ones), thirty-six cows and calves in all, a mule worth 1500 francs, or $300 in gold to us. [...] We have made formal complaint, filing a suit, but I do not believe we will get anything, any response to our claim. There is no justice in this country.*[79]

The Bishop of Natchitoches, Auguste Marie Martin, after travelling through the war-torn parishes in August 1864, reported conditions on the ground to the officers of the Society of the Propagation of the Faith. Central Louisiana, he wrote, was: "racked by run-away inflation, harassed by jayhawkers and deserters and stripped of their labor force, the remaining civilian population tried to survive as best they could in a hostile environment. By May, the people in Mansfield were 'almost reduced to starvation.' By the end of June, eggs were $5 per dozen and there was no more meat." [80] He added that in Alexandria, which had been burned to the ground, most people were without clothing, shelter or food. Many were foraging in the woods, living on blackberries.

Significantly, even Union participants in the Battle of Mansura concurred that they were the authors of the revenge that rained down on the hapless residents of Mansura. Henry Shorey, in his history of the Fifteenth Maine Regiment from the town of Bridgton, explained that "furniture was pitched out of windows, soldiers dressed in lace curtains and danced on the wires of pianos after ripping off the tops, libraries and paintings were 'trodden under foot' and three homes were burnt to the ground." [81]

Twenty years later, David Siess, in both the Poret and Regard cases before the French and American Claims Commission, claimed no knowledge of the chaos, devastation, and looting that took place during Banks' march to the Atchafalaya River. He testified that he was in the front of the Army as a guide, and had no idea of what was happening behind him. It is not known why he characterized these events in such a way as to give cover to the destruction wrought by the Union armies. If he was not aware of it at the time, upon his return to Avoyelles Parish his friends and relatives must certainly have told him what had happened. Perhaps he simply did not wish to jeopardize his federal job as the postmaster of Mansura which he occupied at the time of the Commission hearings. When asked if he had lost anything himself, he testified that Confederates had driven everyone's cattle and other livestock into the woods, so that the Federals could not take them. When asked whether he had been singled out because he was a "Union man," he said that he had not. Although still a French citizen during the war, he requested no reparations for himself, nor did his brother, Simon.[82] It is little wonder that most of the claims against the government by the French citizens of Avoyelles Parish were never paid out because the damage and destruction had been successfully blamed on the Confederate troops themselves.

***

When Banks' army, with David Siess and other Jayhawkers acting as guides, reached the Atchafalaya on May 18th, there was no way across the six hundred foot wide river. Lieutenant-Colonel Joseph Bailey, chief engineer of General William Helmsley Emory's XIXth Corps, came through for his Union forces. He had twenty steamboats lined up across the water and fastened to one another by ropes. Planks and timbers were put across their decking, and by the afternoon of May 19th the entire Federal army, men, wagons, horses began crossing the river to relative safety at Morganza in Pointe Coupée Parish. After all the troops were across, the last being the Army of the Tennessee on the twentieth of the month, the bridge "dissolved into boats again, and started for the Mississippi River." [83] David Siess, according to the testimony of Thomas Jefferson Edwards, in "Martin Rabalais vs. David Siess," left with the Federal Army on the 15th or 16th of May 1864, and did not return until after the surrender, sometime in June or early July 1865.[84]

Simon stayed in New Orleans, except for a few brief visits, until 1867. During the war he met Fanny Cerf, a native of Bouxwiller, Alsace, who had come to America on the French Steamer, *Washington*, landing in New York on December 5, 1864.[85] Her destination had been New Orleans, but since the port was blockaded she travelled overland to Louisiana to join her brother, Samson, who had immigrated to America in 1857.[86] Samson and Fanny's father, Léon Cerf, had been the cantor at the local Synagogue in Bouxwiller, and their grandfather, Isaac Cerf, had previously been its Rabbi. Soon after his arrival in New Orleans, Samson was accepted as the cantor for the old Gates of Prayer Synagogue, also often serving as its Rabbi. He was, in addition, a successful shoe merchant. Before her marriage, Fanny worked briefly as a nursemaid. She and Simon were wed on November 15, 1865, in New Orleans. Rabbi James Gutheim of the Hebrew Congregation Shangarai Chassed (Gates of Mercy) conducted the ceremony. Simon's first child, Mathilde, was born there on September 10, 1866.[87]

David Siess reopened his mercantile business after returning to Avoyelles Parish at the close of the Civil War. His brother, Leopold, was attempting to rebuild his farm and to restart his butcher business. Whatever enmity local residents had for one another, given that Unionists and Confederates were living side by side, along with former slaves, seemed not to have been a problem. Of far more serious concern was the heavy hand of Reconstruction which oppressed the defeated population. Louisiana residents, who were struggling just to put food on the table, would ultimately unite in their hatred of Federal authority.

In August 1861 Congress had leveled a direct tax on each state in an effort to raise twenty million dollars needed to fight the Civil War. Louisiana's portion was $386,000, which, during hostilities, was not collected. It was a property tax on all lands and lots of ground with their improvements, including personal dwellings. If not paid, the money owed could be collected by the forced sale of personal goods or chattels. In 1865, Mrs. Leopold Siess paid eighty cents on behalf of herself and her husband. The Mansura mercantile establishment, Simon Siess and Bro., was charged two dollars and thirteen cents.[88] A federal excise tax was also reinstated on certain luxury items. Simon, who was still in New Orleans in 1865, paid a two dollar excise tax for owning a gold watch.[89] In order to force these collections, the United States Government appointed men, usually veterans of the Northern armies, as tax collectors. Many of these Northerners remained in the area and married into Louisiana families.[90] It was in this atmosphere of defeat, with Union soldiers and Northern interlopers firmly in control, that the people of Central Louisiana sought to rebuild their lives.

Emmanuel Siess, Leopold and Josette's fourth child, was born on February 1, 1866. He was baptized on August 7th of the same year.[91] On April 12, 1866, Josette Siess sold a town lot with its improvements to her brother-in-law, David Siess, for one thousand dollars cash in hand. The lot was bounded on the west by Leglise Street in Mansura, being one arpent wide, and five arpents deep, and became the location of the new, larger, Siess Brother's store which would operate almost into the twentieth century.[92] The one thousand dollars Leopold received from his brother helped to support his family as he tried, like everyone else, to recover from the ravages of war. Simon and Fanny Siess remained in New Orleans where he continued working for Wells Bros. & Co. He and his bride did not return to Mansura until 1868.

---

[1] "Arrived," *The (New Orleans) Daily Picayune* (hereinafter cited as "*DP*"), 23 December 1852, p. 3, col 6, digital image, *Genealogybank*.com (http://www.genealogybank.com [hereinafter cited as "GB"]: accessed 7/ 2011). Note: On December 22, 1852, the *Matador*, from Bremen and the *Star Republic*, outbound ships reported passing in the river coming up, the *Wm.*

Nelson. The following day, the *Wm. Nelson*, 60 days from Havre under Captain Cheever arrived First District to William Whitlock.

² Avoyelles Parish Courthouse Records (Marksville, Avoyelles Parish, LA), Civil Docket #5771, Book "O," Folio 355, "Simon Siess for Citizenship," filed 2 October 1872. See also: Simon Siess, U.S. passport application no. 14131, 25 April 1890 (issue date), digital image, *Ancestry.com* (http://www.ancestry.com [hereinafter cited as "A"]: accessed 2/ 2011), *U.S. Passport Applications, 1795-1925,* citing NARA microfilm publication M1372, roll 347.

³ Obrigheim, Rheinland-Pfalz, Germany, Zivilstandsregister [Civil registrations], 1830, Geburtsakten [Birth records], no. 12, Simon Süss; original records on file at the Standesamt [Civil Registry Office] in Obrigheim. The author is indebted to archivist Wolfgang Heiss of Obrigheim for transcribing the Süss family vital records, and to Daniel Lubrez (Lembach, France) for providing French translations of Mr. Heiss's transcriptions.

⁴ Niederkirchen, Rheinland-Pfalz, Germany, Zivilstandsregister [Civil registrations], 1806, Geburten [Births], Entry for Mindel, daughter of Abraham Loeb and Frommet Raphael, 11 June 1806; Standesamt [Civil Registry Office] Niederkirchen; FHL microfilm 489,070.

⁵ Niederkirchen, Rheinland-Pfalz, Germany Zivilstandsregister [Civil Registrations], 1829, Heiraten [Marriages], no. 4, Ayel Süssel and Mundel Löb; Standesamt [Civil Registry Office] Niederkirchen; FHL microfilm 489,072.

⁶ In a name adoption list done on 2 and 3 November 1808 at Niederkirchen, Abraham Löb took "Dalsheimer" as the family's surname, and "Leopold" as his new first name. His youngest daughter, Mindel/Mündel Löb, adopted the name, "Martha," the only time this first name was used in any official document. She used "Amalie Dalsheimer" on her marriage certificate to Salomon Lehmann. "Minette Thalsheimer" was used in the 1851 census of Lembach.

⁷ Obrigheim, Rheinland-Pfalz, Germany, Zivilstandsregister [Civil registrations], 1833 & 1835, Geburtsakten [Births], 1833, no. 1, Leopold Süss;

1835, no. 8, David Süss; original records on file at the Registry Office in Obrigheim. Transcription by Wolfgang Heiss. Translation to French by Daniel Lubrez

[8] Obrigheim, Rheinland-Pfalz, Germany, Zivilstandsregister [Civil registrations], 1837, Sterbeakten [Death records], 1837, no. 2, Michael Süss, formerly Auschel Süssel; original records on file at the Registry Office in Obrigheim. Transcription by Wolfgang Heiss. Translation into French by Daniel Lubrez

[9] Lembach, Bas-Rhin, France, Registres de l'état civil [Civil registrations], Mariages, 4E 263/8, 1842, no. 2 Lehmann-Löb, digital image, Archives départementales du Bas-Rhin, "État civil en ligne" (http://archives.bas-rhin.fr/: accessed 9/ 2010.) Note: In both the 1841 and 1846 censuses of Lembach the three Süss brothers were erroneously enumerated using their stepfather's surname.

[10] For a more complete discussion of the development of the Hebrew primary schools in Alsace, France see: Anny Bloch-Raymond, " Les écoles primaires israélites en Alsace au XIXe siècle," at http://www.anny-bloch.net/#agenda.

[11] Lembach, Bas-Rhin, France, Dénombrement de la Population (Population Schedule) 1851, 7M 495, House #124, Family #162, (Lines 12-17) Salomon Lehmann, digital image, Archives départementales du Bas-Rhin, " Population Bas-Rhin, " (http://population.bas-rhin.fr/ellenbach/: accessed 5/2011). Note : In this census the three Siess brothers were enumerated using their own surname: Süss.

[12] 1850 U.S. Census, Claiborne Co., MS, pop. sch., p. 103B (penned), Port Gibson, Dwelling #24, Family #24, Simon Roser household, digital image, (A: accessed 2/ 2011), citing NARA microfilm publication M432, roll 370. Date of enumeration: 13 August 1850.

[13] 1860 U.S. Census, Claiborne Co., MS, pop. sch., p. 487 (penned), Port Gibson, Dwelling #19, Family #19, Louis Keiffer household; and Dwelling #20, Family #20, L. Summer household, digital image, (A: accessed 2/ 2011), citing NARA microfilm publication M653, roll 580. Date of enumeration: 1 June 1860.

[14] Lembach, Bas-Rhin, France, Récapitulation générale (General review) 1851, 7M 495, General Observations, Mayor's notation, digital image, Archives départementales du Bas-Rhin, "Population Bas-Rhin," (http://population.bas-rhin.fr/ellenbach/:accessed 5/2011). Note: Both the 1846 and 1851 censuses indicated that there were 1949 inhabitants of Lembach. The 1856 census put the population at 1880 persons. In 1851 there were 147 Jewish residents and in 1856 only 126 remained.

[15] M. Mark Stolarik, compiler, *Forgotten Doors – The Other Ports of Entry to the United States* (Philadelphia: Associated University Presses, 1988), 108.

[16] Avoyelles Parish Courthouse Records (Marksville, Avoyelles Parish, LA), Civil Docket #3646, Book J, Folio 456, "Leopold Siess, Declaration of Intention," filed 22 August 1857.

[17] David Süss search, *Castlegarden.org* (http://www.castlegarden.org: accessed June 2011). Also, concerning ship's arrival: "Markets & Marine," *DP*, 29 December 1854, p. 3, col 6, digital image, (GB: accessed 7/2011). The *Suffolk*, commanded by Captain Edwards, was reported to have sailed out of Le Havre on October 29th, in the December 17, 1854 issue of the *Daily Picayune* (p. 3, col 1).

[18] One arpent is approximately 8/10 of an acre, so the lot was about 3.2 acres.

[19] Avoyelles Parish Courthouse Records (Marksville, Avoyelles Parish, LA), *Conveyances*, Book AA, p. 75-77, No. 90804, "Edmond Chatelain to L. & D. Seisse [sic] – Sale of Land," filed 21 January 1856.

[20] Wilkinson County Courthouse (Woodville, Wilkinson County, MS), *Marriage book for Whites 1856*, "Leopold Siess to Celestine Roz – Marriage bond and license," filed 13 August 1856.

[21] Alberta Rousseau Ducôté, compiler and translator, *Early Baptism Records – St. Paul the Apostle Catholic Church 1824-1844 – Avoyelles Parish* (Mansura, Louisiana: St. Paul the Apostle Church [P.O. Box 130, Mansura, LA 71350], 1982), Part II, p. 31, Baptism of Josepha Chatelain.

[22] For further information on Marie Rouensa-8cate8a and Kaskaskia in general see: Natalia Maree Belting, *Kaskaskia Under the French Regime* (Carbondale, Illinois: Southern Illinois University Press, 1948, reprinted 2003).

[23] Avoyelles Parish Courthouse Records (Marksville, Avoyelles Parish, LA), *Marriages,* Book B-2, p. 337, "Jean-Baptiste Couvillion and Josette Chatelain."

[24] "Miscellaneous Notices," Louisiana State University Libraries On Line Catalog – Special Collections – Louisiana and Lower Mississippi Valley (hereinafter cited as "LLMV"), Microfilm # 5964, *Villager,* 18 July, 1857, No. 28, p 1, col 4.

[25] Avoyelles Parish Courthouse Records (Marksville, Avoyelles Parish, LA), *Conveyances,* Book BB, pp. 322-323, No. 9767, "Leopold Siess to Simon & David Siess, Sale of land with mortgage," filed 1 August 1857.

[26] St. Paul the Apostle Catholic Church (Mansura, Louisiana), Baptism Book 6, p. 160, entry 122, Leopold Siess baptism (1857), parish rectory, Mansura.

[27] Avoyelles Parish Courthouse Records (Marksville, Avoyelles Parish, LA), *Marriages,* Book B-3, p. 32, "Leopold Siess and Josette Chatelain."

[28] St. Paul the Apostle Catholic Church (Mansura, Louisiana), Baptism Book 6 (In French), p. 191, entry 75, Auger Siess baptism (1859), parish rectory, Mansura.

[29] Avoyelles Parish Courthouse Records (Marksville, Avoyelles Parish, LA), *Conveyances,* Book CC, pp. 537, 538, No. 10,606, " Sheriff of Avoyelles to Mrs. Josette Chatelain, Sale of Improvements," filed August 11, 1859.

[30] Avoyelles Parish Courthouse Records (Marksville, Avoyelles Parish, LA), *Conveyances,* Book CC, p. 435, No. 10,218, "Martin Rabalais to Simon and David Siess, Sale of land," filed July 27, 1858.

[31] Avoyelles Parish Courthouse Records (Marksville, Avoyelles Parish, LA), *Conveyances*, Book CC, p. 500, No. 10,344, " Adeline Bordelon to Simon and David Siess, Sale of slave," filed January 10, 1859.

[32] 1860 U.S. Census, Avoyelles Parish, LA, pop. sch., p. 329 (penned), Dwelling #236, Family #236,Simon Siess household; and p. 384 (penned), Dwelling #612, Family# 612, Leopold Siess household, digital images, (A: accessed 2/2011), citing NARA microfilm publication M653, roll 407. Dates of enumeration: 20 July 1860 & 27 September 1860.

[33] Marie-Yvonne LeBon, "L'Émigration de l'Arrondissement de Wissembourg Durant le 19ème Siècle," Atelier Généalogique de l'Arrondissement de Wissembourg et Environs (AGAWE), mai 1999, Introduction, p. 1

[34] "Arrivals, New Orleans," *The (New York) Commercial Advertiser*, 19 October 1859, p. 4, col 5, digital image, (GB: accessed 12/ 2010).

[35] "For Havre," *DP*, 6 November, 1859, p. 1, col 1, digital image, (GB: accessed 12/ 2010).

[36] "Towboats," *The (New Orleans) Daily True Delta*, 27 November 1859, p. 7, col. 1, digital image, (GB: accessed 12/ 2010).

[37] "Havre, Jan. 4 – The *Luna* (American ship), Shannon," *The New York Herald*, 24 Jan 1860, p. 8, col. 6, digital image, (GB: accessed 12/ 2010).

[38] CERES (Center for European Underwater Research), *Épaves (Shipwrecks), Luna,* (http://www.ceresm.com/epaves/luna.htm: accessed 12/ 2010), An anonymous description in French of the wreck of the *Luna* written by a member of the Centre Européen de Recherches et d'Etudes Sous-marines (CERES), translated by the author. Transcripts of the autopsies of the victims may be found in French at: http://www.wikimanche.fr/Proc%C3A8s-verbaux_ constatant_les_d%C3%A9couvertes_des-
victimes_du_naufrage_de_la_Luna_(1860). Note: the site of the wreck of the *Luna* is not far from where U.S. troops came ashore on D-Day at Utah Beach.

[39] "The Loss of the American Emigrant Ship Luna," *The New York Herald*, 15 March 1860, p. 1, col. 4, digital image, (G: accessed 12/ 2010).

[40] "Our Paris Correspondence," *Ibid,* , p. 4, col. 3., digital image, (G: accessed 12/ 2010).

[41] St. Paul the Apostle Catholic Church (Mansura, Louisiana), Baptism Book 6 (in French), p. 220, entry 110. Florestine Siess baptism (1860), parish rectory, Mansura.

[42] Avoyelles Parish Courthouse Records (Marksville, Avoyelles Parish, LA), *Conveyances*, Book DD, pp. 240-243, No. 11,369, - " Zénon St. Romain and Mrs. Josephine Chatelain, Sale of slaves with mortgage," filed February 7, 1861.

[43] "Benevolent Association," LLMV, Microfilm # 5753, *Avoyelles Pelican*, 9 November, 1861, Vol. XVIII, no. 28, p. 1, col. 1.

[44] "Arrival of Troops," *The (New Orleans, LA) Daily True Delta*, 10 April 1862, p. 1, col. 5, digital image, (GB: accessed 12/ 2010).

[45] "Headquarters Avoyelles Rt., 27 March 1862 – General Order 15 issued by Pratt and Cheney," LLMV, Microfilm # 5753, *Avoyelles Pelican,* 19 April , 1862, Vol. XVIII, no. 49, p. 1, col. 2; also regarding conscription, see "Summary of News," *Avoyelles Pelican,* 26 April , 1862, Vol. XVIII, no. 50, p. 1, col. 2.

[46] "Remplacements Militaires," [Military replacements,] LLMV, Microfilm # 5753, *Avoyelles Pelican, 21 June* 1862, p. 2, col. 4. Translated from French by the author. Note: Julius Levin, whose daughter Fanny married Auger Siess, Leopold's eldest son, procured a substitute for his brother Herman Levin. He engaged his wife's youngest brother, Stephen Dupuy, age 16, who acted as a courier for the Confederate Army in northeast Louisiana. Stephen Dupuy died at age 104 in 1949, the longest living Confederate veteran from Rapides Parish, LA.

[47] "Ordre Général No. 25 – 30 avril 1862, " LLMV – Microfilm # 5753, *Avoyelles Pelican,* 10 May 1862, p. 2, col 3. Translated from French by the author.

[48] "Letter from an Exiled Unionist – A Painful Story," *The (New Orleans, LA) Daily Delta,* 15 July 1862, p. 2, col. 2, digital image, (GB: accessed 12/ 2011). Note: After the war Edwards returned to Avoyelles, married Irma Moreau and raised a family. His brother William Washington Edwards' great-grandson Edwin Washington Edwards is a former Governor of Louisiana. Most of the Edwards and Masters family members remained in the parish.

[49] "To the Military Commissioners for the Parish of Avoyelles," LLMV, Microfilm # 5753, *Avoyelles Pelican,* 17 May 1862 , Vol. 21, no. 1, p. 1, col. 3. Note: The Avoyelles commissioners appointed were G.P. Voorhies, Dr. T.J. Spurlock, William Mock, Captain Anatole Coco, Joseph Moreau and Dr. J.C. Desfossés, Mayor of Mansura.

[50] "Notice," LLMV, Microfilm # 5753, *Avoyelles Pelican,* 31 May 1862, Vol. 22, no. 2, p. 1, col 4.

[51] " Retours d'Élection, " [Election Returns], LLMV, Microfilm # 5753, *Avoyelles Pelican,* 7 June 1862, Vol. 22, no.4, p. 2, col. 1. Translated from French by the author.

[52] "Proclamation," LLMV, Microfilm # 5753, *Avoyelles Pelican,* 12 July 1862 , Vol. 21, no. 3, p. 1, col. 3.

[53] "Provost Marshall's Office, August 9, 1862," LLMV, Microfilm # 5753, *Avoyelles Pelican,* 30 August 1862 , Vol. 22, no. 10, p. 1, cols. 3, 4.

[54] "Election Notice, " LLMV, Microfilm # 5753, *Avoyelles Pelican,* 28 June 1862, Vol. 22, no. 7, p. 1, col. 1.

[55] " Les Étrangers Non Naturalisés et la Conscription, " [Non-naturalized Foreigners and Conscription,] LLMV, Microfilm # 5753, *Avoyelles Pelican,* 28 June 1862 , Vol. 22, no. 10, p. 2, col. 1. Translated from French by the author.

⁵⁶ Arthur W. Bergeron, Jr., *Guide to Louisiana Confederate Military Units 1861-1865* (Baton Rouge, LA: Louisiana State University Press, 1989), 118.

⁵⁷ "Compiled Service Records of Confederate Soldiers who served in organizations from the State of Louisiana, Roll 296 – Eighteenth Infantry, Pl-Sh," National Archives Microfilm Publications, Microcopy No. 320. Record for L. Seiss, Card Numbers 46942033, 46942127 and 46942222, National Archives, Washington D.C.

⁵⁸ St. Paul the Apostle Catholic Church (Mansura, Louisiana), Baptism Book 6 (in French), p. 258, entry no. 61 Hermina Siess baptism (1863), parish rectory, Mansura.

⁵⁹ See note 57.

⁶⁰ Bergeron, 118.

⁶¹ "Marksville, LA, Dec. 20, 1862, " LLMV, Microfilm # 5753, *Avoyelles Pelican*, 28 June 1862 , Vol. 22, no. 32, p. 2, col. 3.

⁶² "Attention Conscripts," LLMV, Microfilm # 5753, *Avoyelles Pelican*, 3 January 1863 , Vol. 23, no. 34, p. 2, col. 1. Note: Camp Pratt, near New Iberia, Louisiana, was the largest training camp for Confederate recruits.

⁶³ "EXTRA of the Avoyelles Pelican," LLMV, Microfilm # 5753, *Avoyelles Pelican*, 9 January 1863, single flyer, republished from the (Alexandria) *Louisiana Democrat*, col. 2.

⁶⁴ Avoyelles Parish Courthouse Records (Marksville, Avoyelles Parish, LA), *Conveyances*, Book GG, pp. 146-147, No. 11,888, " S. Siess & Bro. to Josephine Chatelain, wife of Leopold Siess, Sale of land," filed March 16, 1863.

⁶⁵ "Volunteers for Home Defense," LLMV, Microfilm # 5753, *Avoyelles Pelican*, 21 March 1863, Vol 23, no. 45, p. 2, col 1; and "Sous la Tente," same page, col. 2. Translated from French by the author.

[66] For an account of the history of Fort DeRussy, please see Steven M. Mayeux, *Earthen Walls, Iron Men – Fort DeRussy, Louisiana and the Defense of the Red River* (Knoxville, TN: University of Tennessee Press, 2007).

[67] Avoyelles Parish Courthouse Records (Marksville, Avoyelles Parish, LA), District Court, Parish of Avoyelles, State of Louisiana, Case # 4614, (Book L, Folio 713), "Martin Rabalais vs. David Siess. Notice of evidence on trial of exception: 6 October 1866 – Plaintiff's Exhibit C, Defendant's Exhibit A."

[68] *Gardner's New Orleans Directory, 1867,* digital image, Fold3.com (www.fold3.com : accessed on 12/2010), p. 364 Entry for S. Siess.

[69] Mayeux, Chapter 14 – "Gunboat Station and Contraband Camp," 211-224. Note: A copy of the Deck Log of the *Essex* taken from Charles J. Drew's diary edited by Tom Baskett, Jr., a transcript of which is in possession of Steven Mayeux, was furnished to the author.

[70] Clipping from *The (New Orleans, LA) Daily True Delta*, dated Thursday Morning May 5, 1864, from the private collection of Steven M. Mayeux.

[71] Holmesville, one mile south of present-day Eola, had previously been known as Shinbone Alley.

[72] Transcript of the hearing furnished to this author by Steven Mayeux in October, 2010. See also: *48th Congress, 2nd Session. House of Representatives, Ex. Doc. No. 235, A Report from the Secretary of State concerning the transactions of the French and American Claims Commission,* ordered to be printed February 17, 1885, (Vol. 27, No. 144, pp. 164, 165), U.S. Government Printing Office.

[73] "Confederate Pension Application for David Siess, Avoyelles Parish, LA, File 12,499," Louisiana State Archives, Reel CP1.127, Microdex 2, Sequence 6, Baton Rouge, Louisiana, 36 pages. Affidavit of Fulgence Lemoine and Eléo Fontanille, dated 13 April 1914.

[74] Paul Marius Lehman's great-great-grandson, Jay Lehman, believes, as does the author, after many years searching for the identity of Paul's father, that

Isaac is the only possible candidate. Paul M. Lehman had passed down that his father was one of a number of brothers who came from Germany to Avoyelles Parish to settle. In the 1900 census, Paul's father was recorded as having been born in Germany. (At that time, Alsace was part of the German Empire). No other person using the surname Lehman has appeared in any census, courthouse record or newspaper article in Avoyelles Parish that can be found either during or after the Civil War.

[75] See Harry G. and Elizabeth Eskew, *Alexandria' Way Down in Dixie* (New Orleans, LA: The Southern Publishing Co., 1950) , 65-72, out of print but excerpted at *Libertychapelcemetery.org* (http://www.libertychapelcemetery.org/files/a_burns.html: accessed 3/ 2011).

[76] See note 72.

[77] Transcript of a portion of the French and American Claims Commission #54, Isidore Poret vs. US, furnished to this author by Steven Mayeux in October, 2010. Note: Poret's claim against the US government for $13,272.50 for damage to his house and the seizure of cotton was disallowed. General Grover was General Cuvier Grover who commanded a portion of Brigadier General William Helmsley Emory's XIXth Corps during the Red River Campaign.

[78] Sister Dorothea Olga McCants, D.C., compiler and translator, *They Came to Louisiana – Letters of a Catholic Mission, 1854-1882* (Baton Rouge: Louisiana State University Press, 1970), 171.

[79] McCants, 172.

[80] Fr. Chad Anthony Partain, *A Tool Pushed by Providence : Bishop Auguste Marie Martin and t he Catholic Church in North Louisiana* (Austin, TX: Persidia Publishing Co., 2010), 180-181.

[81] William Riley Brooksher, *War Along the Bayous, The 1864 R ed River Campaign in Louisiana* (Dulles, VA: Brassey's Books, 1998), 219, citing Henry A. Shorey, *The Story of the Maine Fifteenth; Being a Brief Narrative of the More Important Events in the History of the Fifteenth Maine Regiment, Bridgton, Maine*: Press of the Bridgton News, 1890.

[82] See note 72.

[83] "The Steamboat Bridge at Simmesport, May 18-20, 1864," *Fortderussy.org* (http://www.fortderussy.org/Steamboat%20bridge.htm : accessed 3/2011).

[84] See note 67.

[85] "New York Passenger Lists, 1820-1957," digital image, (A: accessed 3/2010), citing *Passenger lists of Vessels Arriving at New York, New York, 1820-1897*, NARA microfilm publication M 237, roll 248. Manifest of SS *Washington*, 5 December 1864, p. 1 , line 25, Mlle. Fanny Cerf (age 22) from France.

[86] "New York Passenger Lists, 1820-1957," digital image, (A: accessed 3/2010), citing *Passenger lists of Vessels Arriving at New York, New York, 1820-1897*, NARA microfilm publication M 237, roll 178. Manifest of SS *Globe*, 28 August 1857, p. 2 , line 70, Samson Cerf (age 20) from France.

[87] "New Orleans, Louisiana Birth Records Index, *1790-1899,*" database , (A: accessed 1/ 2011), citing State of Louisiana, Secretary of State, Division of Archives, Records, Management and History, *Vital Records Indices* (Vol. 42, P. 333), Baton Rouge, LA, USA. Birth of Mathilde Siess.

[88] John Milton Price, compiler, *The Civil War Tax in Louisiana: 1865* (1891; reprint, New Orleans, LA: Polyanthos Press, 1975), pp. vi, vii, 15.

[89] "U.S. IRS Tax Assessment Lists, 1862-1918," digital image, (A: accessed 3/2010), citing NARA microfilm series M769, roll 2, Louisiana, S. Seiss.

[90] Andrew J. Whittier, a New Hampshire native, was one of these men. After the siege at Port Hudson, Private Whittier accepted a commission as a Second Lieutenant in the First Cavalry Corps d'Afrique commanding African-American troops during the occupation of New Orleans. He was promoted to First Lieutenant in the Fourth U.S. Colored Cavalry. After the war he resigned his commission, remaining in New Orleans as an officer in the U.S. Custom's House. In June 1869 he received a long sought-after sinecure as a Deputy Collector of Internal Revenue for the Second District of Louisiana including

Sabine, Grant, Vernon, Rapides, Avoyelles, Pointe Coupée, East and West Feliciana and West Baton Rouge Parishes.

[91] St. Paul the Apostle Catholic Church (Mansura, Louisiana), Baptism Book 6 (in French), p. 308, entry no. 83, Samuel Siess baptism (1866), parish rectory, Mansura. Note: Father Jules Janeau of St. Paul the Apostle Church erroneously recorded "Samuel," instead of "Emmanuel."

[92] Avoyelles Parish Courthouse Records (Marksville, Avoyelles Parish, LA), *Conveyances*, Book HH, pp. 296-297, No. 343, " Mrs. Leopold Siess to David Siess, Sale of town lot and improvements," filed April 12, 1866.

Leopold Siess, ca. 1884

Simon Siess – Undated photo (*Courtesy of Joseph E. Friend family*)

David Siess at Mansura, LA Post Office/Store, ca. 1922
(*Courtesy of the late Murrell Smith Siess*)

CHAPTER 5
FAMILY FEUDS

On January 13, 1868, David Siess married twenty-four year old Clara Cochrane in a ceremony conducted by Nelson Durand, J.P. in the town of Mansura. [1] The bride was a descendant of one of the largest genealogical families in the world: the Voorhies, whose Louisiana branch may be traced back to Coert Stevense Van Voorhies, a native of the Netherlands and his wife, Marretje Gerretse Van Couvenhoven. After the English defeated the Dutch in 1664, taking over their colony and renaming it New York, many Dutch settlers began their trek westward, including Coert and Marretje's great-grandson, Cornelius Van Voorhies, who made his home near Princeton, New Jersey. Two of the latter's grandchildren, Peter Gorden Voorhies, and his younger brother, Cornelius, moved to Kentucky, from where both eventually made their way further south to Louisiana. Cornelius married Agathe Aimée Gradenigo, daughter of a Venetian immigrant, at Opelousas Post, St. Landry Parish, Louisiana on August 2, 1803, [2] where six of his nine children, including Clara Cochrane's mother, Chrissa Eliza Voorhies, were born. Cornelius, who served in the War of 1812, was, subsequently, Sheriff of St. Landry Parish, being appointed by Governor W.C.C. Claiborne in 1813. Several years thereafter he moved his family to Avoyelles Parish where he became the parish judge then later, the sheriff. Chrissa Voorhies' marriage, at the age of fifteen, to Robert Alexander Cochrane, the parish coroner and a member of the Avoyelles militia, on December 15, 1825,[3] produced nine children, eight of whom, including Clara, survived to marry into prominent local families.

In the spring of 1868 Simon Siess brought his wife, Fanny, and daughter, Mathilde, back to Avoyelles to live and he and his newly-married brother, David, resumed their partnership in the store on Léglise Street in Mansura. David and Clara's first child, Mathilde, was born on October 19, 1868, in Mansura. Although Clara was raised as a Catholic, there is no record of Mathilde having been baptized. On December 9, 1869, David and Simon purchased the plantation and buildings belonging to the estate of Eulalie Dufour. It consisted of 169 arpents of land plus an additional 30 acres for just over five thousand dollars to be paid in two installments.[4] Twenty days later, on December 29, 1869, the brothers purchased an additional forty arpents from Jules Coulon.[5]

In 1870 the three Siess brothers were living in close proximity to one another in Mansura. David, Clara and Mathilde lived in dwelling # 747 with one servant, Eugenie Luneau, and thirteen year old Edmonia Cochrane, the orphaned daughter of the late Edgard E. Cochrane, Clara's brother. David declared $6,500 in assets. Leopold Siess, his wife, Josette, and four children, Auger, Florestine, Hermina and Emmanuel lived in dwelling # 753. He listed no assets, and was working as a butcher. Next door, in dwelling #754, Simon, Fanny and their daughter, Mathilde, lived along with two servants, Estelle Martin and Adolphine Laurent. Simon declared the identical $6,500 in assets as his brother, David.[6]

In July 1870, David Siess was appointed the Mayor of Mansura by Republican Governor Henry C. Warmoth, who had defeated the Democrat, James Talliaferro in a special election in 1868. Warmoth also named five Mansura residents as aldermen: Leandre T. Roy, Jean B. Lavalle (probably Lavallais), Joseph Laurent, Joseph Reynaud, and Clement Pierrot.[7]

During the difficult period of Reconstruction after the close of the Civil War, the store was constantly in financial trouble. David and Simon used every legal trick possible to stay ahead of creditors in New Orleans, while they continued to have great difficulty in collecting debts from the local farmers to whom they sold supplies on credit. On October 13, 1871, Simon turned over his undivided half of all the goods in the Siess Bros. store, including dry goods, clothing, shoes, crockery and hardware, as well as the undivided half of three horses, seven mules, one wagon, one ox cart, one horse cart, one pair of wheels, and three yokes of oxen, and 125 cypress logs, all to David Siess for $4185. It is not known if any money ever changed hands.[8] Seven months later David "sold" the same items back to Simon Siess for $1,000.[9]

While Simon and David were juggling the ownership of the Siess Store back and forth for their own benefit, Leopold was trying to make a go of a family farm with the help of his wife and twelve year old son, Auger. He also earned extra money as the local butcher. On August 30, 1871, his fifth child, Isaac Edouard Siess, was born in Mansura. The baby was baptized on April 1, 1872, by Father Jean Marie Émeric Chauvin of St. Paul the Apostle Church.[10] Simon and Fanny's son, Leon, was born on February 15, 1872, at Mansura.[11] Later that year Simon filed his declaration of intention to become an American citizen which was granted to him two years later, on October 6, 1874.[12] David and Clara's second daughter, Eugénie, was born on December 20, 1872.

In 1873 Leopold Siess was a delinquent taxpayer in Mansura to the tune of $30.80, but he was finally able to pay his debt.[13] His last child, Louis Preston Siess, was born on December 13, 1875. Father Chauvin of St. Paul the Apostle Church baptized him on February 12, 1876.[14] The couple, now the parents of six children, could barely make ends meet. David and Simon, however, were having their own difficulties in a post-war economy. Their financial and personal troubles had come to a head during the spring of 1872. There was an acrimonious parting which resulted in the dissolution of their commercial partnership. The store merchandise was divided up at the end of the year and Simon moved his family to a small cottage on one of the Mansura properties. David remained in the former D. Siess & Bro. store.

Simon, now on his own, was sued in 1873 in "Waddil & Barbin vs. Simon Siess" for non-payment of bills, and Sheriff Pierre Magloire seized all of his property, the plantation, an additional forty acres, his home, cotton gin and saw mill and put it up for sale. In the counter-suit, Simon asked for an injunction based on the fact that the property was his homestead, and thus exempt from seizure. A temporary injunction was granted after the payment of a $300 bond because the Parish Judge was away. The bond was returned and the property was eventually seized. [15]

On November 11, 1873, Fanny Cerf Siess filed suit against her husband alleging that his business affairs were in such a disorderly condition, owing to mismanagement, that she believed him to be insolvent. She petitioned the court for dissolution of the community between them in order to preserve her own acquisitions from her husband's debtors so that she could support her two children. She petitioned the court that she be allowed to manage her own separate affairs and to carry on a separate trade in order to support herself and her children, free from the interference of her husband. In January 1874, Simon was forced to put his Mansura mercantile business, due to his embarrassing financial conditions, under the name of his brother-in-law, Samson Cerf, who then granted Simon his power of attorney to do any and all business on his account. Fanny's complaint was finally heard on March 18, 1874. David Siess testified that if Simon were to pay all his debts he would leave his wife and children destitute. Appended to Fanny's suit was a copy of a legal document showing the brothers' separate indebtedness to Lehman, Abraham & Co. of New Orleans in the amount of $2500 each, payable in two instalments at one and two years from November 20, 1872. As collateral they had mortgaged the land which they had originally purchased from Martin Rabalais in 1858, as well as the land they had acquired from Jules Coulon in 1869, on which the gin and mill were located. On March 19, 1874, Parish Judge James Madison Edwards ruled in Fanny's favor. After the dissolution of community between Fanny and Simon, the latter transferred the business from his brother-in-law, Samson Cerf, to his wife. Fanny was now in charge of the couple's commercial venture, with Simon designated by her as her business agent. To make matters worse, in July 1874 Simon was forced to sell his cotton crop to his brother, David, to whom he was indebted as well.[16] At the end of 1874 Simon and Fanny decided to take their children and move to Marksville so they could get a fresh start.

After much hard work, Simon and Fanny were finally able to settle their outstanding debts, and their property was returned almost a year and a half later. As a consequence of that seizure, Simon sued Sheriff Magloire, Paul Thomas, James Madison Edwards, Arthur Barbin, Victor Reynaud, Eugene Gaspard, Fielding Edwards, Victor Bizé, Jacques Casteran and Henry Clay Edwards alleging that they had sold or bought some of his merchandise for their own profit, and damaged other items. Simon asked for $322.51 as the value of the missing items and an additional two hundred dollars in special damages because the Sheriff had unlawfully begun to dispose of his goods. The defendants countered that they disposed of no more than $50 in goods, and, that if others were damaged or lost it was due to the extended length of time that they were held, some being perishable by nature. Furthermore since Siess owed an unstated amount of money for sheriff and guardian fees, they owed him nothing. Simon eventually recovered $218.01 with five per cent interest from Magloire and the others.[17]

***

On September 27, 1876, a suit entitled Siess vs. Siess was filed by Simon Siess against his brother David, which would bring all family disputes to a head. The details of this court action, however painful for the families at the time, allow the twenty-first century reader a glimpse into the inner workings of a small post-Civil War mercantile and planting partnership. Simon's petition alleged that he and his brother David were owners of a tract of land (the old Coulon place) near Mansura on which there were two dwelling houses, a cotton gin, and a saw mill, which had been under David's sole control during the years 1875 and 1876. Simon further alleged that his brother had earned more than $2300 at the gin and mill, both of which were available to the public. He alleged that David refused to give him any account of his income, or any portion of the revenue arising from their property. Simon also stated that he was a partner with his brother in two hundred acres of swampland, which David had bought in his own name with partnership funds. Simon also disputed the ownership of two mortgages each worth $500, as well as one four horse wagon, one ox cart, one pair of timber wheels, one wheelbarrow, one iron safe, one platform scales, one counter scales, one oil can, a large lot of carpenters and plantation tools, and a lot of valuable belts for the use of the gin and saw mill. Simon sought to be recognized as the joint owner of all the above-named property, that he be given a full and particular account of all revenues from said property, and be reimbursed in the amount of one-half. Simon further asked that all personal property named in the petition be sold and the proceeds be equally divided between them.

David's answer was filed on October 12, 1876. He denied all the allegations except the partnership which was formed between the two of them in 1867 to carry on a mercantile business which was dissolved in 1872, and a planting partnership which was formed in 1870. Simon had been appointed to liquidate the affairs of the firm, Siess & Bro., but there was real and personal property that remained on hand in possession of them both. David also alleged that Simon was indebted to him in the amount of $2878.50 which had been partnership funds that the latter used to pay his individual debts. He alleged that Simon had refused to pay his half of the taxes due on the partnership property in the amount of $237.69 and one half cents. David claimed he was also due one half of $64.18 that he paid to the Sheriff and a printer on behalf of the partnership. He also claimed one half of a debt that Simon collected from Casimir Thomas in the amount of $123, as well as three bales of cotton that Simon sold on his own for at least $150, half of which he never received. Regarding the plantation, David claimed that Simon failed to hire any hands to work the fields in 1876, and abandoned any idea of raising a crop. David, himself, employed hands, and cultivated one half of the field held in common between them, and was therefore in no way responsible for any money owed to Simon. Furthermore he had the fence repaired around the entire field, which had cost him $150. With regards to the income from the gin and sawmill, David testified that he ginned three hundred bales, making $300, pressed 450 bales, making $450, made 135,000 pounds of cotton lint at eight dollars per one thousand pounds, making $1080 and sold cotton seed worth $125 in 1875. His expenses for running the gin were $438.80, including money expended for wood and belt lacing, for some repairs to the coupling and for payment of a salary to the engineer who ran the steam driven ginning apparatus. His profit for 1875 was $766.20. In 1876 he only ginned cotton in the amount of $357 but sawed forty three thousand feet of cypress lumber valued at $860. His expenses, including salaries for a sawyer and an engineer were $480, leaving him a profit of $731. David also alleged that Simon borrowed $25 from him which he never paid back, and retained in his possession a lot of guns belonging to the partnership worth $200, for which he had never accounted. According to David's calculation, Simon owed him $3412.

Before any testimony was taken, the Judge ruled that any discussion of debts, or business transactions during the life of the commercial firm of Siess & Bro. could not be grafted onto this suit, as the defendant, David Siess, had tried to do in his answer, as it would reopen the settlement of an old commercial partnership, which was not part of the case at hand.

The court reporter took down the gist of the testimony in longhand. The complainant, Simon Siess, swore that he and David had purchased 160 acres of cypress land in 1871. When Simon left Mansura in the winter of 1874, David Siess occupied the two pieces of property in Mansura, two store houses, one small cottage dwelling house, the largest store house and the dwelling house. The other store house that Simon had previously occupied as both a residence and his commercial enterprise was rented to Clovis Lemoine. Simon had retained possession of this property until it was relinquished to Lehman Abraham & Co. for outstanding debts. Simon also swore that he paid taxes on the property occupied by him in 1873 and 1874, and that as long as he continued to live in Mansura he and David had split the profits made at the mill and gin. Under cross-examination, Simon admitted that he had a show case belonging to the partnership, a copying press which belonged solely to him, and the guns previously mentioned in the suit, as yet unsold, were still being held to their joint account in Marksville.

Auger Siess, their brother, Leopold's eighteen year old son, was called as the next witness because he had worked for his Uncle

David during 1875 in both the engine and gin house, for which he was paid seventy-five cents per day. Auger testified that David had told him that they had ginned about 425 bales of cotton in 1875 and sold about 325 sacks of seed at about seven or eight dollars a ton, part of which belonged to his Uncle Simon. He elaborated that each sack held about one hundred pounds that he and his father, Leopold, had personally filled. Regarding the sawmill, Auger believed that in 1875 David might have sawed some thirty to forty thousand feet of lumber, half of which he kept for himself. Leaving his Uncle David's employ on October 18, 1876, Auger recalled that, up to that time, about fifty or sixty thousand feet had been sawed, and about 92 bales of cotton had been ginned. When cross-examined, Auger stated that he was now living with his uncle, Simon Siess, in Marksville, and working for him as a clerk in his store. He stated that although not friendly with his Uncle David, he never had any difficulty with him, but they no longer spoke. He also testified that the cotton seed sold in 1875 was from the 1874 crop but did not know whether Simon had been paid for his share of the seed that was sold. He testified that it took two boys and three men to run the gin, and six hands to operate the sawmill.

David Siess took the stand to testify that he paid all taxes due upon the property held with his brother between 1872-1875 out of his personal funds in the amount of $261.94. Simon, he alleged, had abandoned the property, refusing to pay taxes on it, because he thought it could be foreclosed on any day since it was mortgaged. He brought five guns to Marksville, worth about twenty-five dollars apiece, and gave them to Simon to sell as he had no market for them in Mansura, agreeing that they would split the proceeds. David also alleged that he told Simon that if he would pay for half of the gin and mill employees, that he (David) would run both in partnership with him. Simon refused because he thought the property was going to be foreclosed. David explained that he was going to make as much money as possible at the mill and gin because he did not want his share to lay there idle. He also testified that during the two years in question he only ginned about two hundred bales of cotton and sold no seed in 1875 as it was unsalable. He did not get any seed in 1876 as the planters generally carried their own away. In 1875 he sawed very little timber and did not float any logs. When he did saw in 1876 he was usually paid by taking half the lumber, some of which he sold, the rest he used to repair fences, outhouses and other structures on his own property. David also alleged that shelves, worth about $25, were removed from his store on Simon's orders in December when he was away in New Orleans. As for the press, Simon had asked for it and he had given it to him. The showcase in question was bought in New Orleans for $22 not including a four dollar freight bill. David further stated that he attended to the mill, which he described as a circular saw mill, as the engineer, manager and sawyer in order to save the $10 per day it would cost him to run it. As for the gin, he could only work as the engineer, running the engine and managing the gin. He could not, however do any ginning. He had, moreover cut lumber and ginned cotton for his brother, Simon, at no cost to him. David ended his testimony by saying that the two mortgage notes owed the partnership still remained uncollected in the hands of the lawyer, Mr. Edwards.

Under cross-examination David made it clear that he learned by himself how to run and repair the steam engine for the gin. Although he never kept records of how long he worked and when, he would have paid a stranger at least $5 per day. He usually hired a man at a dollar per day to haul wood to the saw mill, using his own wagon and team. Since Simon had left, he spent $41 to have the press and the gin repaired. He also had to pay seven dollars to replace belt lacing and five dollars for new grates. Because his original memorandum of expenses had been lost at the courthouse during the lawsuit he could only estimate that his expenses were $144 and his personal labor for sixty days at five dollars per day was valued at $300. Hired help, five hands for twenty days at one dollar per day, were paid a total of $100.

David Siess' lawyer called several witnesses on his behalf to testify that the defendant had paid for all the repairs to the gin, the press, and the mill. David's brother-in-law, Onil Gremillion, husband of Clara Cochrane Siess' sister, Louise, who lived on the Siess property, about thirty-two yards from the mill, attested to the fact that David acted as both engineer and sawyer at the mill. Onil was only employed at the gin and mill during the summer, but he never knew how much cotton was ginned. He helped make repairs to the pasture fence, using planks and posts from the mill, at the direction of David Siess, who kept his own livestock there. Pierre Durand, who had worked for both brothers as their clerk at Mansura, and then worked for David Siess doing some accounting, testified that the separate Siess stores were on opposite sides of the Mansura property after the breakup of the partnership. After Simon Siess moved to Marksville, his store fell into disrepair, but David's property was well-kept. L.P. Normand, clerk at the parish tax collector's office, testified that David had paid taxes on his own property as well as those due by D. Siess & Bro.

Simon was recalled as a witness to aver that he had never abandoned his property at Mansura, but rented it out until the property was taken over by Lehman, Abraham & Co., in February 1877. He also testified that he had tried several times, unsuccessfully, to get David to agree to an arbitrated settlement concerning the income from the gin and mill in 1875-1876.

Additional witnesses were called to challenge David Siess on exactly how much time he spent at the gin and mill, and how many persons were actually employed there. Blaise Barrière testified that he had worked for David since 1875 at the gin, packing cotton. David, he said, was there on some days, but not on others. Barrière also testified that David employed his nephew, Emmanuel Siess, who was probably 10 years old, taking out lint cotton, while his older nephew, Auger, attended to the engine when David was not there. When not at the engine, Auger was at the gin stand. Barrière added that David also had a grist mill which he opened to the public every two weeks.

Leopold Siess was called by the plaintiff as a witness to refute his brother David's testimony. He testified that in the spring of 1875 he and his son, Auger, put cotton seed in sacks at the Siess gin in Mansura. The seed was from the 1874 crop during which time Simon was still in town. David, he said, had sold the seed to Mr. Staples for $125 and refused to share the proceeds with his brother. Leopold received three cents for each sack of seed he filled. When Leopold worked at the gin, principally at the press, he got a dollar a day. His son, Auger, acted as the engineer, keeping the engine running. Occasionally David would come out of the field to lend a hand. Blaise Barrière put seed cotton in the hopper, and little Emmanuel took the lint cotton to the press, for which he received fifty cents per day. Leopold also testified that he was only employed by David during the spring, and for three weeks in the fall after he returned from working in Big Cane. David, however, used his horse for the entire year, for which he received no money, but David fed the animal. Leopold also worked, from time to time, at the sawmill. He received one dollar per day if he sawed for the public and seventy-five cents per day if he sawed for his brother, David. Leopold thought the lumber might have been worth twenty dollars per thousand feet. He knew that David had sawed for Alfred Sampson and had received about one hundred dollars. When asked if he and his brother David were friends, he answered yes, he was, but perhaps, David was not so friendly with him!

David Siess' attorney called several witnesses to impeach Leopold's testimony. A.J. Ducôté said he had known Leopold for about twenty years, and that he would not believe him under oath. When cross-examined, the witness admitted that he had never known Leopold to swear to a lie, but then, he hardly ever saw him except when he was drunk, which probably affected his memory. Ducôté thought, moreover, that Leopold's testimony could be bought. Clovis Lemoine testified that he thought Leopold would not come into the court to lie. V.L. Mayeux, the last witness in the case, testified that if Leopold was sober he would tell the truth. He said, however, that he saw him quite often, and at least half of the time he was drunk.

The case was ended on that sour note, except for an amendment that the defendant, David Siess, presented in writing to the court on May 8, 1877. In it he alleged that Simon was the liquidator of the commercial partnership and he had disposed of many things without ever rendering any account of his administration, including the show case, the bureau, the letter press and the shelves from the Mansura store all worth $145. David concluded that, since the dissolution of the commercial partnership, he had paid all the taxes on the Mansura properties until forfeited by Simon on February 6, 1877 to Lehman, Abraham & Co., which he (David) bought back from that firm for $3000 ($400 cash in hand with a five year mortgage) eighteen days later on February 24, 1877, making all the property his own! Simon, therefore owed him half of the tax payments for 1873, 1874, 1875 and 1876, as well as half of the ten dollar amount that he had spent having the saw teeth recut at the Siess sawmill. Regarding the plantation that was owned by them separately from the commercial partnership, David explained they had worked together and split the profits in 1874, but the following year, they determined to work separately. Simon, however, could not get people to work for him, so David hired hands for him and Simon oversaw their work and kept all the profits for himself. In 1876, Simon refused to cultivate his half of the plantation, so David planted one half of the field. He did, however, have to keep up all the buildings and fences on the entire plantation and incurred all the expenses in doing so, using his own wagons, horses and mules, and had wood cut to repair the fences, which cost him, at least, $500.

The decision, by Judge John Yoist of the Seventh Judicial District of Louisiana was filed on May 23, 1877, after he had requested an accounting from David in writing as to the proceeds and expenditures of the saw mill and cotton gin during the years 1875 and 1876. In his decision he concluded that from David's calculations, the gross revenue of the mill and gin for the two years had been $1928.75, while the expenses had been $1658. Leaving a profit of $270.41, of which $135.20½ was awarded to the plaintiff, Simon Siess with 5% per annum interest from date until paid, less his half of the cost of the suit which was calculated to be $12.50. It was further ordered that the four guns proven to be in plaintiff's hands be returned by him and sold for the benefit of both plaintiff and defendant, or in default thereof, that plaintiff be charged with the sum of ninety dollars. It was also decreed that the timber wheels, one four horse wagon, one ox cart, one horse cart, one wheel barrow, one iron safe, one platform scales, one counter scales, one show case, one oil can and one large lot of carpenter's and plantation tools, all in possession of the defendant, be sold for the benefit of both plaintiff and defendant. The money portion of the judgment was paid the following day, and Simon Siess signed it over to his nephew, Auger, along with one half of the property ordered to be sold.[18]

On May 29, 1877, David Siess paid a bond to the Deputy Clerk of Court at Marksville in the amount of $205 in order to appeal Justice Yoist's decision. On March 6, 1878, Chief Justice Manning of the Louisiana State Supreme Court delivered the following decree: "The lower court gave the Plaintiff judgment for one hundred and thirty five dollars 20/100 dollars. We shall not disturb it. The parties to this suit are brothers. The result of this unseemly wrangle, in which claims, and counter claims are inferred each against the other, amounting to over two thousand on one side and over three thousand on the other, is an adjudication of a beggarly pittance as the just settlement of their preposterous demands. *Il faut laver votre linge sale en famille*."[19] This protracted haggling amongst the three Siess brothers which culminated in the 1877 decision by Justice Manning had succeeded in poisoning family relationships for several generations to come.

***

Simon remained with his family in Marksville, where, after selling from a stand in town, he finally earned enough money to build a permanent establishment. The editor of the Marksville Bulletin opined on February 17, 1877, "Mr. Simon Siess is having built an elegant brick store and dwelling on Main Street. When the edifice will be completed, it will add much to the appearance of that part of our town. There is room yet in Marksville for a few more enterprising gentlemen such as Mr. Siess," [20] Completed in April of the same year, the same editor announced, "Mr. Siess' new and commodious store, corner Main and Bontemps streets, is now completed, and our friend will soon remove his goods therein." [21] In the meantime, Fanny Cerf Siess threw herself into civic life being appointed as assistant recording secretary for the Marksville United Friends of Temperance, an organization of seventy members, which, the editor of the *Bulletin,* A.J. LaFargue, thought, given the preponderance of French people in town, would never get traction.[22]

David carried on his business in Mansura, working both the mercantile establishment and the plantation. His third child, Caroline, was born on February 17, 1877.[23] A popular man in town, despite having led the Union army through Mansura in 1864, and having been originally appointed mayor in 1870 by a carpetbagger Governor, David was subsequently elected Mayor in 1874, and re-elected in 1879 and 1881,[24] the same year in which the Federal Government had made an agreement with France, to reimburse non-citizens who suffered financial losses during the war. This prospect had temporarily lifted spirits, especially in Avoyelles Parish with its large number of French immigrants. Unfortunately, the only people who profited from these proceedings undertaken by the French and American Claims Commission, other than Father Chauvin and Angélique Brochard,[25] were witnesses such as David, himself, Joseph Laurent, and Jean-Baptiste Lavallais who each received a few dollars for their testimony, and Adolph Frank, at whose hotel the commission was convened. David Siess, who acted as a witness on behalf of the government against his neighbors, Feréole Regard, Louis P. Cayer and Isidore Poret, should have incurred the wrath of his fellow citizens, but he seems not to have. Perhaps the Confederate spirit which remained very strong in other parts of the South, was only lukewarm here, as many people who still considered themselves "foreigners" had been caught up in a fight between two factions for whom they had little sympathy and no interest. David's testimony, in any case, was never held against him. He was elected Mayor of Mansura the very year his testimony was taken, and re-elected in June of 1882, then again in 1884, 1886-92, 1895, and 1905.[26]

His life was not, however without its vicissitudes, and given the litigious nature of his business as a merchant dispensing and receiving credit, was forever suing and being sued. In September 1877, he was brought to court by A.D. Lafargue, the tax collector, and found liable for selling liquor without a license. He was fined $262.[27] On September 2, 1878, his fourth child, Alice, was born in Mansura. She died just two months after her ninth birthday on November 26, 1887, and was buried in the Jewish Cemetery in Pineville, Louisiana.[28] It is significant that Alice, the first of the new generation of Louisiana Siess family members to die, was buried as a Jew. As the daughter of a Catholic mother, she should have been raised in the Church. On the other hand, there is no evidence that David or any member of his family ever attended the Synagogue in Alexandria. David was never associated with any of the Jewish civic or fraternal clubs which often drew other Avoyelles Jews to make the thirty mile journey into Rapides Parish to attend. Attesting, however, to his ecumenical spirit or perhaps even his religious indifference, David donated an empty store on his property for a "grand fair" which was held on January 15, 1879, for the benefit of the Catholic Church.[29]

On January 30, 1878, Leopold and Josette's eldest daughter, eighteen year old Florestine Siess, was married to twenty-one year old Abel Léon Philippe Escudé at St. Paul the Apostle Church by Father Jean Chauvin.[30] The groom had been orphaned at the age of seven, by the death of his father, Philippe Escudé, a French immigrant, who had worked as a baker in Mansura. Florestine's new husband made his living as a carpenter and blacksmith in Mansura. Two children were born in quick succession, Louis Philippe on April 25, 1879, and Henriette Zéline on July 27, 1880.[31] Twelve others would follow.

***

In 1879 Simon Siess got a bit more competition in Marksville, when Elie Hiller and his wife, Helvena Kahn, left New Orleans to open up Hiller's Cheap Store in town.[32] Both Hiller and Siess advertised in the *Marksville Bulletin*. Simon bragged that his clothing and fancy goods came directly from New York, while Elie Hiller claimed that his merchandise was directly from New Orleans. Simon, though, had the imprimatur of the editors of the *Marksville Bulletin*, who published articles, almost weekly about Simon's store. In September 1880 the townspeople of Marksville read: "Elsewhere will be found the advertisement of Mr. Simon Siess, of this town, who offers to our community at a very fair price a large and well-selected assortment of dry goods, groceries, shoes, hats, notions and fancy trimmings. One of the principle features of this magnificent store is the immense assortment of ready-made clothing purchased direct from the City of New York. All sizes, all prices and all kinds of goods. Call and examine." [33] An occasional tip of the hat was given to Hiller, when he stocked, "choice lemons," or got in a lot of furniture. Of course, Adolph Frank's son-in-law, George L. Mayer, who sold dry goods and groceries, advertised each week, as well, and was also a rival. But there seemed to be enough trade for all three. On October 9, 1880, a particularly noteworthy announcement appeared. The Hiller store employed: "a polite and courteous clerk, Mr. Weil, who takes great pleasure in waiting upon all those who call." [34]

Ernest M. Weil, born on April 6, 1861, in Mackenheim, Alsace, arrived in Marksville in 1878.[35] The Weil family, four generations strong in Mackenheim, headed by Samuel Weil and his wife, Fanny Marks, a native of nearby Kutzenhausen, like many Alsatians, considered themselves to be French. Yet, with the stroke of a pen, they had suddenly become subjects of the German Empire at the conclusion of the Franco-Prussian War in 1872. When the German government allowed the residents of the newly formed Reichsland Elsass-Lothringen to "opt" for becoming German citizens, or to move out of the region, thousands left. In 1877, Ernest, soon to be of conscription age, opted to come to New Orleans, leaving his family and friends behind. It is not surprising that he finally chose Marksville as a place to settle. The Alsatian enclave in Avoyelles Parish was growing by the year. With the Siess family from Lembach, the Hillers from Niederroedern, the Haas family from Rothbach and Ingwiller, the Karpe's from Puttelange-lès-Farchviller, the Goudchaux and Kahn clans from Brumath and Riedseltz, Felix Bauer from Romanswiller, and the Levy's from Niederbronn, any new arrival from formerly French Alsace felt immediately at home. The Simon Siess and Elie Hiller families, who lived side by side in Marksville, were prosperous enough to afford paid help in their stores. Since it was customary for young clerks to move in with their employer's family, it is not unusual that the 1880 Avoyelles Parish census enumerated twenty-one year old Auger Siess living with his uncle Simon and eighteen year old Ernest

Weil boarding with Elie and Helvena Hiller and their baby daughter, Hannah. [36]

**

During the 1880s the Leopold Siess family was still living on the edge of poverty. Leopold often hired himself out for various menial jobs. If not working for his brother, David, he travelled to St. Landry Parish to work for the Goudchaux family. With his eldest son, Auger, clerking for Simon at the Marksville store and Emmanuel, the younger boy, working for David as well as for his maternal uncle, Zélien Chatelain, where he was employed as a farm hand, the family struggled to live.[37] In 1880 the Leopold Siess household consisted of its head, age forty-seven, who listed his occupation as "retired merchant," his forty-one year old wife, Josephine, his daughter Mina, age seventeen, Emmanuel, age fourteen, Isaac, age nine, and Louis, age four.[38] The Siess family lived next door to Leon Drouin's widow, Zaïre, whom Leopold, had sued the previous year for failing to pay his wages, causing her bay horse to be sold on the courthouse steps to the highest bidder.[39] His addiction to alcohol, one of the few facts about him that had actually filtered down to present day descendants, did not make matters any better.

**

In the fall of 1881, Mayor David Siess offered his steam engine for sale. He had decided to suspend his ginning operation temporarily because of the scant profit he was making for such a labor intensive job. Moreover, his duties at the store as well as his job as mayor and postmaster left him little time for much else. In September he had made a verbal contract with François Francisco to purchase the engine for $700. Returning to the store several weeks later, Francisco reneged on the deal, although David indicated that he would help him move the engine to his property if the purchase could be concluded. With no money forthcoming, David sued Francisco for breach of contract. The case was decided in David Siess' favor in the amount of seven hundred dollars, but appealed by the defendant in January 1882, to no avail. On

April 1, 1882, the Sheriff seized the engine and made it available for purchase by the public on the courthouse steps. The amount received at auction for the engine was $270.40, which was turned over to Siess, with the defendant Francisco still owing him the balance. As the case dragged on the Sheriff finally seized 134 acres belonging to Francisco which was sold to satisfy the plaintiff's claim as well as court costs for the original case and the appeal. It wasn't until the spring of 1884 that David received the rest of his money.[40]

In 1881, David Siess took a final judicial potshot at his brother, Simon. The latter had gotten a judgment against Nolan T. Waller in which the Parish Sheriff, Léon Gauthier, had been authorized to seize the undivided three-fourths of about seven acres of growing cotton in the field, and three-fourths of three thousand pounds of seed cotton, which sale was to take place on November 5, 1881. David went to court to have a lien put on the money due Simon, alleging that he (David) had advanced provisions and necessary supplies to Nolan Waller in the amount of $199.28 for which he offered a detailed accounting: farm implements including a plow, horse collar, trace chains, a hoe, a riding bridle, milk bucket; clothing, including cloth ticking and calico for dresses, shoes, men's pants; provisions, including flour, corn, bacon, whiskey, coffee, sugar, black pepper, grits and one bottle of pills. Proof given that Waller was indebted to David Siess resulted in the proceeds of the sale being withheld from Simon until such time as Waller's debt to David was satisfied.[41]

Although David Siess had long been the postmaster at Mansura since the close of the Civil War, he was temporarily replaced in January of 1882 by J.O. Domas.[42] The latter's new job evidently interfered with his other employment as a road and bridge contractor for the municipality. In September 1882, having seen that the firm of Coco and Domas had done little or nothing for an entire year, the Council voted to pay Coco and Domas twenty dollars, and authorized Mayor Siess to advertise the contracting job to the last and highest bidder, as long as it did not exceed $300.[43]

***

In 1882, Simon's wife, Fanny Cerf Siess, who was known to everyone as a difficult person, sued Dr. James Ware who kept a steamboat landing on the Red River. Goods shipped out of New Orleans were routinely sent there to be forwarded by wagon to his main depot in Marksville. In January 1882, Fanny, the proprietress of the Siess Store, with Simon acting as her agent, ordered a small fireproof safe from Mosler, Baumann & Co. of Cincinnati, Ohio. Fanny alleged that although the safe arrived sometime in February 1882, Dr. Ware failed to forward it to his warehouse in Marksville, instead, keeping it on the landing where it was submerged by the subsequent flooding of the Red River. The safe remained under water for two or three months, and was damaged so badly that it was useless. When first opened, it was full of sand and water and several of the drawers were rotted. Although it was kept outside on the gallery of her store in an effort to dry it out, it was still unusable. Fanny asked that Dr. Ware be made to provide her with a replacement or pay her the $250 that the safe had cost in the first place.

There was, of course, much more to the story. The first witness for the plaintiff was her nephew and store clerk, Auger Siess. He testified that Dr. Ware brought the bill to his uncle several days after the safe was delivered to the landing. When Simon objected to the freight bill, Dr. Ware agreed, saying he thought it was high and would seek a reduction. But Dr. Ware only delivered the safe several months later, after it had been submerged in the flood waters of the Red River, at which time Simon paid the freight bill under protest. Two additional witnesses for the plaintiff, Adolphe Blanchard and J.A. Riché attested to the safe's condition saying that it was badly damaged, and now worth no more than sixty or seventy dollars.

In his defense, Dr. Ware testified that Simon Siess was irate about the freight bill because the cost to move it from Cincinnati to New Orleans was $18.50, but the captain of the *Yazoo Valley* charged $32.65 from New Orleans to Ware's landing. While Ware agreed that the bill was high, it was the prevailing price, and furthermore the safe weighed 2750 pounds. Ware said the clerk on the *Yazoo Valley* had refused to reduce the delivery charge so he was told to take the safe back. Captain George W. Rea, tried to comply but was never able to get the safe back on board due to its excessive weight. In March the Red River began to rise causing Ware's warehouse to collapse with the safe still in it. The defense attorney took that opportunity to present a letter from the Captain Rea which stated that Dr. Ware was, at the time of the flood, not in possession of the safe, as it had been turned back over to Captain Rea who was unable to get it back on the boat due to technical problems. The letter stated further that Siess, lately a passenger on Captain Rea's steamboat, had agreed to take the safe and pay the charges. Armed with Rea's letter, Ware had confronted Simon Siess, who seeing he had no other choice, had agreed that he would accept the safe as is. On October 4, 1882, Judge W.F. Blackman of the 12th Judicial District, ruled against Fanny, with no other comment except, that she was now liable for payment of the court costs.[44]

***

Auger Siess, Leopold's eldest son, did not stay around long enough to find out the results of his Aunt's lawsuit against Dr. Ware. He had been travelling to Alexandria to court the young daughter of Julius Levin, a prominent Jewish merchant, and his wife, Justine Dupuis. One of his trips north was reported in the local paper: "Several young gentlemen of this town were passengers on the *Jesse K. Bell* [...]. Messrs. Emmanuel Blanchard, Arthur Barbin and Auger Siess had taken occasion to go up the river. The latter gentleman remained for a few days in our beautiful sister town of Alexandria." [45] On Tuesday, September 5, 1882, Rabbi Abraham Meyer married Auger Siess of Marksville to Miss Fannie Levin at the Congregation Gemiluth Chassodim in Alexandria.[46] Auger, who was a baptized Catholic, had, in the end, returned to the Jewish faith. In 1883 and again in 1884 he was elected to the position of Secretary of the Jewish Temple.[47] Once in Alexandria, his fortunes would be inextricably tied to his successful father-in-law, who having started out as a simple grocery merchant, had come to be known as the "lumber king of Rapides Parish."

It is not known what Josette Chatelain Siess, a devout Catholic, thought of her son's conversion but it is probably around this time that Leopold came to live in Rapides Parish, while Josette stayed behind in Avoyelles Parish with the younger children, and a growing brood of grandchildren. Leopold and Josette's daughter, Florestine Siess Escudé, gave birth to twins, Émile and Édouard on April 4, 1882. Edouard, however, died two months later.[48] The very next year, on June 19, 1883, their fifth child, Alice Josephine, named after her grandmother, was born.

The Siess Store in Mansura finally began to prosper in the 1880s. David hired his niece, Florestine's brother-in-law, Alphonse Escudé, as his clerk. Alphonse also lived with the Siess family, including David, his wife Clara, daughters Mathilde, Eugénie, Carrie, Alice and the latest arrival, Harry James Siess, born on July 31, 1882.[49] Vinya Brooks, a fourteen year old African-American girl, worked as a domestic for the couple to help Clara with the children. On September 19, 1882, voter registration was held at the David Siess store for the benefit of the citizens of Mansura.[50] David continued to buy his neighbors' cotton crops in payment for the plantation supplies that he sold them. In 1878 he had bought Jean Baptiste Lavallais' crop, then in 1880 he bought from Celestin François and Charles Smith making a handsome profit. In October 1882 he had the court seize as much of the corn and cotton crop of Jean Baptiste François as necessary to satisfy, François' debt to him in the amount of $156.20.[51] It was by collecting these debts, large and small, that he was able to keep paying off the mortgage for the land which he had bought from Lehman, Abraham & Co. after Simon had defaulted on his payments.

***

In 1882 Elie Hiller sold his stock to Alfred J. Mayer, and left Marksville to set up shop in Jennings in Jefferson Davis Parish, leaving his clerk, Ernest Weil's replacement, Henry Dufour, without employment.[52] Weil had, nine months earlier, moved on to Shreveport to find a better job.[53] With one rival in the retail business gone, Simon and Fanny were still prospering. Simon travelled several times per year to New Orleans to buy merchandise. In 1882 the family had enough money to send their sixteen year old daughter, Mathilde, to school in the Crescent City.[54] Simon was finally able to invest some money, buying up successions from cash-strapped neighbors and acquiring land at Sheriff's sales.

The 1884 business directory published in the *Marksville Bulletin* listed seven retail merchants in Marksville and two in Mansura. Only two were Jewish, Simon in Marksville and his brother, David, in Mansura. While David's only competition was P.D. Roy, Benjamin Franklin Edwards, George Mayer, and A.J. Riché vied with Simon for business. Symphorien Tassin, also a merchant, operated a lunch room out of his Washington Street address, across from the courthouse. A.J. Ducôté kept a bar room and sold liquor and cigars on Marks Street. Mrs. Adolph Blanchard (née Irene Elmire Glasscock) had a millinery and dressmaking business and James McLaughlin was the town barber.[55]

***

In Alexandria, Auger Siess, newly married, had taken over his father-in-law, Julius Levin's Saloon and Oyster House. He advertised all kinds of fish on two days' notice, and sold oysters at one dollar per can.[56] In order to promote his enterprise he had a grandstand at the local baseball field constructed so that fans of the Alexandria Goldens could watch their team free of charge. Leon Weinburg and Henry Thalsheimer, two local Jewish residents and members of the Synagogue where Auger served as Secretary, were team participants as well, the former, a player, and the latter, an umpire.[57] Team meetings were held at the Siess office/saloon. In April 1884 Auger opened up a refreshment stand at the town picnic.[58] That same month, he and Rabbi Marx Klein, a native of Hatten, Alsace, were elected as delegates to the Pacific Fire Company.[59] That fall, Auger renovated his saloon, turning it into a full service restaurant, which the *Louisiana Democrat* observed was going to be a "first class establishment." [60] Auger, under the tutelage of his father-in-law, Julius Levin and the extended Levin family, had, not only become an observant Jew, but had plunged headlong into the Jewish social whirl of the city. In the fall of 1884

Auger joined the Hebrew Benevolent Association where he was immediately elected secretary.

It is not known if Leopold was employed during his time in Alexandria, but evidence suggests that he may have been working as an agent of his son's father-in-law, Julius Levin, who was now in the lumber business. In early January 1885 Leopold travelled to Orange, Texas, on the Sabine River which was the home base for the developing James Lutcher lumber empire. On January 14, 1885, it was reported in the *Louisiana Democrat* that "Mr. A. Siess left by Morgan train on Sunday morning last for Orange, Texas, where he goes in response to a telegram announcing the serious illness of his father." [61] He brought Leopold back home to Alexandria where he expired on Wednesday, February 4th, 1885, at two o'clock in the morning. He was buried, according to newspaper accounts, on the same day, at three in the afternoon, in the Jewish Cemetery at Pineville.[62] His marble marker reads in Hebrew "Jehudah ben Asher Halevi," [63] and continues in English, "Leopold Siess, born in Mulheim, Bavaria, Died Feby. 4, 1885, Aged 52 years." [64] He was buried next to Michael Aaron, Auger's mother-in-law, Justine Dupuis Levin's first husband, who had died from yellow fever in 1853. Josette Chatelain Siess was left in Mansura with four children still at home, trying to make do as she could. On a happier note for her, on March 19, 1885 her daughter Florestine's sixth child, Joseph Leopold Escudé, Sr., was born.

Shortly after Leopold's death, the *Louisiana Democrat* advertised a Grand Purim Ball and Supper to be given in Siess's Hall on February 28th.[65] In early March 1885 the Congregation Gemiluth Chassodim, held a party at Auger's restaurant for all the Synagogue's "Sunday School" students.[66] It was reported in the *Louisiana Democrat* that in May 1885, Auger was now the recorder for a fraternal organization, The Ancient Order of United Workingmen, which had been organized after the Civil War. Originally designed to bring together the conflicting interests of capital and labor, and to settle disputes between them, it evolved into a mutual benefit society, and finally a life insurance company.[67] On September 5, 1885, Auger and Fannie Levin Siess celebrated their third anniversary. "Their spacious and comfortable residence on Murray Street," reported the *Louisiana Democrat* "was crowded and echoed with the subdued sounds of mirth and rejoicing, and many were those who stepped forward under the roof-tree of the happy pair to congratulate them upon the first years of their connubial felicity." [68] On October 1, 1885, Auger Siess closed his restaurant, deciding to follow his father-in-law, Julius Levin, into what had become the very lucrative lumber business.[69] Before returning to work he accompanied his wife on a trip via the Texas and Pacific Railway to visit his Uncle Simon and Aunt Fanny Siess in Marksville.[70]

***

For the David Siess family in Mansura, 1885 was one year in which the head of the household was not the town's mayor. Nevertheless, he was heavily involved in civic affairs. He had been appointed by the Police Jury, along with H.O. Couvillion, Hypolite Ducôté, Eugene Gauthier and Valery Coco, to choose a company to rebuild the Long Bridge across Bayou des Glaises, originally constructed in 1870, but damaged by subsequent flooding. On August 3, 1885, a meeting was held at the Siess store where the contract was given to the Smith Bridge Company of Toledo. Ohio. Under the terms of the contract, the bridge which was to be 2600 feet long, made of 2550 feet of wood and 250 feet of iron, would cost the town $10,000. The *Marksville Bulletin* reported that, "After the award, Mr. Siess and his estimable lady, proverbial for their hospitality, invited a large number of the citizens to partake of a most excellent dinner. The dinner over, the guests were entertained by the Misses Siess [Mathilde, Carrie and Eugénie]. The finale of the bridge award was indeed a pleasurable event and we only regret that there are not oftener bridges for sale. Mr. A.J. Escudé deserves thanks for courtesies." [71] The year 1885 ended, however on a difficult note, when, after having had to mortgage his plantation, one more time in order to bring in his cotton crop and continue the operation of his saw and grist mills, he was sued by Charles Hernandez of New Orleans. In order to liquidate a debt to Hernandez, he had promised to furnish the New Orleans cotton factor at least one hundred bales of cotton, of which he had only been able to supply thirty-seven, due to a poor crop and the subsequent low prices.

This lawsuit extended into the following year and produced negotiations between the two parties to allow David to remain in business.[72]

---

[1] Avoyelles Parish Courthouse Records (Marksville, Avoyelles Parish, LA), *Marriage Book* B-3, p. 424, No. 10,344, "David Siess and Clara Cochrane," filed January 22, 1868.

[2] Rev. Donald G. Hébert, compiler, Southwest Louisiana Records, 1750-1900, CD-Rom 101, database, (Rayne, LA: Hébert Publications, 1975-2001), Original record: Opel. Ch.: v. 1-A, p. 125. Marriage of Cornelius Voorhies and Aimee Gradenigo

[3] *Ibid.,* Original Record: Opel Ch, v. 1-B p. 450. Marriage of Robert A. Corkran (sic) and Eliza Voorhies.

[4] Avoyelles Parish Courthouse Records (Marksville, Avoyelles Parish, LA), *Conveyances,* Book JJ, p. 782, "Succession of Mrs. Eulalie Dufour to David and Simon Siess," filed December 9, 1869.

[5] Avoyelles Parish Courthouse Records (Marksville, Avoyelles Parish, LA), *Conveyances,* Book JJ, p. 809, " Jules Coulon to David and Simon Siess, Sale of Land," filed December 29, 1869.

[6] 1870 U.S. Census, Avoyelles Parish, LA, pop. sch., pp. 93, 94 (penned). Dwellings #747, #753 & #754, families #786, #792 & #793 , David, Leopold and Simon Siess households, digital images, *Ancestry.com* (http://www.ancestry.com [hereinafter cited as "A"]: accessed 3/ 2010), citing NARA microfilm publication M-593, roll 506. Date of enumeration: 15 July 1870.

[7] "Appointments by the Governor," *The (New Orleans) Daily Picayune* (hereinafter cited as *"DP"*), 24 July 1870, p. 2, col 5, digital image, *Genealogybank.com* (http://www.genealogybank.com [hereinafter cited as "GB"]: accessed 1/ 2011). Note: Four out of the five aldermen were persons of color, one of whom, Joseph Laurent, was a witness in the Regard case before the French American Claims Commission.

[8] Avoyelles Parish Courthouse Records (Marksville, Avoyelles Parish, LA), *Conveyances*, Book LL, #2409, pp. 382-384, "Sale of property Simon Siess to David Siess," filed 13 October, 1871.

[9] Avoyelles Parish Courthouse Records (Marksville, Avoyelles Parish, LA), *Conveyances,* Book LL, #2699, pp. 63,64, " Sale of property David Siess to Simon Siess," filed 3 July 1872.

[10] St. Paul the Apostle Church (Mansura, Louisiana), Baptism Book 6, p. 357, entry 8, Isaac Edouard Siess Baptism (1872), parish rectory, Mansura. Isaac, which was not a first name common to the Siess family was, no doubt, in honor of his murdered half-brother, Isaac Lehmann.

[11] Simon Siess, U.S. Passport application # 1413, 25 April 1890 (issue date), digital image, (A: accessed 8/ 2010), citing *U.S. Passport Applications 1795-1905*, NARA microfilm publication M1372, roll 347.

[12] Avoyelles Parish Courthouse Records (Marksville, Avoyelles Parish, LA), Civil Docket #5771, Book "O", Folio 355 "Simon Siess for Citizenship," filed 2 October 1872.

[13] "Delinquent Taxpayers – Corporation of Mansura," Louisiana State University Libraries On Line Catalog – Special Collections – Louisiana and Lower Mississippi Valley (hereinafter cited as "LLMV"), Microfilm # 1032, *The Avoyelles Republican*, 13 September 1873. Vol. 1, no. 16, p. 3, col 4.

[14] St. Paul the Apostle Church (Mansura, Louisiana), Baptism Book 7 , p. 52, entry 9, Louis Siess Baptism (1876), parish rectory, Mansura.

[15] Avoyelles Parish Courthouse Records (Marksville, Avoyelles Parish, LA), Civil Docket #5668, Book "O," "Injunction," filed December 13, 1873.

[16] Avoyelles Parish Courthouse Records (Marksville, Avoyelles Parish, LA), *Conveyances*, Book NN, p. 510, #3328, "Simon Siess to David Siess , Sale of Crop," filed 31 July 1874.

[17] Avoyelles Parish Courthouse Records (Marksville, Avoyelles Parish, LA), Civil Docket #5820, Book "O" pp. 453-456, "Simon Siess vs. Pierre Magloire, sheriff, & Als," filed 21 April 1875.

[18] Avoyelles Parish Courthouse Records (Marksville, Avoyelles Parish, LA), Civil Docket #5888, 75 hand written pages, " Simon Siess vs. David Siess," filed 27 September 1876, (File located in Court House Annex, file drawer for 1876 Civil cases).

[19] Avoyelles Parish Courthouse Records (Marksville, Avoyelles Parish, LA), Supreme Court of the State of Louisiana, Clerks Office, New Orleans, filed March 6, 1878, "Simon Siess vs. David Siess, No. 6900, Appeal from the District Court for the Parish of Avoyelles," (File located in Court Annex, file drawer for 1876 Civil cases, appended to the original action). Chief Justice Manning's last sentence, which was originally written in French is an admonition "not to wash one's dirty linen in public."

[20] "Parochial," LLMV, Microfilm # 1032, *The Marksville Bulletin*, 17 February 1877, Vol. 1, no. 11, p. 4, col. 1.

[21] *Ibid.*, 14 April 1877, Vol. 1, no. 19, p. 4, col. 1.

[22] *Ibid.*, 28 July 1877, Vol. 1, no. 34, p. 3, col. 2.

[23] Forest Park Cemetery (Shreveport, Caddo Parish, LA), Carrie Siess Mausoleum, personally read, 2004.

[24] Avoyelles Parish Courthouse Records (Marksville, Avoyelles Parish, LA), *Oaths of Office*, Book C (1886-1905), Oaths of David Siess for Mayor of Mansura.

[25] See, Chapter 1, pp. 19-20.

[26] See note 24.

[27] "Parochial," LLMV, Microfilm # 1032, *The Marksville Bulletin*, 15 September 1877, Vol. 1, no. 41, p. 3, col. 2.

[28] Jewish Cemetery (Pineville, Rapides Parish, LA), Alice Siess marker, row 15, personally read, 2009.

[29] "Parochial," LLMV, Microfilm # 1032, *The Marksville Bulletin*, 11 January 1879, Vol. 3, no. 5, p. 3, col 2.

[30] Jeraldine DuFour Lacour, *Brides Book of Avoyelles Parish, Vol 2, 1856-1880* (Bunkie: Jeraldine Dufour LaCour [203 South Gayle Boulevard, Bunkie, LA], 1979), 142. Entry for Florestine Siess.

[31] Births of all fourteen of the Siess-Escudé children were supplied by Mrs. Barbara Escudé Lemoine, granddaughter of Florestine Siess.

[32] This family will be more thoroughly discussed in Chapter 9 devoted to the Kahn's half-uncles, Leopold and Lazard Goudchaux and their relations, as well as in Chapter 14, "The Avoyelles Outrage."

[33] "Parochial," LLMV, Microfilm # 1032, *The Marksville Bulletin*, 11 September 1880, p. 3, col. 1.

[34] "Bargains, Bargains at Hiller's Cheap Store," LLMV, Microfilm # 1032, *The Marksville Bulletin*, 9 October 1880, p. 3, col. 6.

[35] Avoyelles Parish Courthouse Records (Marksville, Avoyelles Parish, LA), Civil Docket #8220, "Ernest M. Weil for Citizenship," filed 14 August 1890.

[36] 1880 U.S. Census, Avoyelles Parish, LA, pop. sch., ED. # 1, p. 355A (printed), Dwelling #49, Family #51, Elie Hiller household, and Dwelling #50, Family #52, Simon Siess household, digital image, (A: accessed 6/ 2007), citing FHL Film 1254448, roll 448, Date of enumeration: 15 June 1880.

[37] 1880 U.S. Census, Avoyelles Parish, LA, pop. sch., ED. # 3, p. 412C (printed), Dwelling #414, Family #438, Zélien Chatelain household, digital image, (A: accessed 6/ 2007), citing FHL Film 1254448, roll 448, Date of enumeration: 25 June 1880.

[38] 1880 U.S. Census, Avoyelles Parish, LA, pop. sch. ED. #3, p. 1 (penned), Dwelling # 8, Family #8, Leopold Siess household, digital image, (A:

accessed 6/ 2007), citing FHL Film 1254448, roll 448, Date of enumeration: 3 June 1880.

[39] "Judicial Advertisements – Constable Sale, Leopold Siess vs. Mrs. L.A. Drouin," LLMV, Microfilm # 1032, *The Marksville Bulletin*, 22 March 1879, Vol. 3, no. 15, p. 3, col. 2.

[40] Avoyelles Parish Courthouse Records (Marksville, Avoyelles Parish, LA), Civil Docket #6487, "David Siess vs. François Francisco," filed 8 October 1881.

[41] Avoyelles Parish Courthouse Records (Marksville, Avoyelles Parish, LA), Civil Docket #6545, "David Siess vs. Léon Gauthier, Sheriff," filed 3 November 1881.

[42] "Parochial Items," LLMV, Microfilm # 1032, *The Marksville Bulletin*, 14 January 1882, p. 3, col. 1.

[43] "Town Council Proceedings, Mansura, September 6, 1882," LLMV, Microfilm # 1032, *The Marksville Bulletin*, 23 September 1882, p. 1, col. 4.

[44] Avoyelles Parish Courthouse Records (Marksville, Avoyelles Parish, LA), Civil Docket #6689, "Mrs. Fanny Cerf, wife of Simon Siess vs. James Ware," filed 14 July 1882.

[45] "Parochial Items," LLMV, Microfilm # 1032, *The Marksville Bulletin*, 1 April 1882, p. 3, col. 1.

[46] Rabbi Martin I. Hinchin, D.D., *Fourscore and Eleven, A History of the Jews of Rapides Parish 1828-1919* (Alexandria, Louisiana: McCormick Graphics, 1984), 34.

[47] Hinchin, 40.

[48] Willie J.. Ducôté, compiler and translator, *Avoyelles Parish St. Paul's, Mansura, Louisiana, Burial register 1870-1885, Book IV* (Baton Rouge, LA: self- published, 1998), 24.

⁴⁹ "World War I Draft Registration Cards. 1917-1918," digital image, (A: Accessed 10/ 2007), Harry J. Siess, Serial # 1380, Order # 1998, Draft Board "0" Marksville, Avoyelles Parish, LA, citing NARA microfilm publication M1509, roll 1653580.

⁵⁰ "Notice of Registration," LLMV, Microfilm # 1032, *The Marksville Bulletin*, 16 September 1882, p. 2, col. 3.

⁵¹ Avoyelles Parish Courthouse Records (Marksville, Avoyelles Parish, LA), Civil Docket #6735, "David Siess vs. Jean Baptiste François," filed 6 October 1882.

⁵² "Parochial Items," LLMV, Microfilm # 1032, *The Marksville Bulletin*, 16 September 1882, p. 2, col. 2.

⁵³*Ibid.*, 14 January 1882, p. 3, col. 1.

⁵⁴ *Ibid.*, 1 July 1882, p. 3, col. 1.

⁵⁵ "Parish Directory," LLMV, Microfilm # 1032, *The Marksville Bulletin*, 23 February 1884, Vol. VIII, no. 11, p. 1, col. 2.

⁵⁶ *The (Alexandria) Louisiana Democrat (*hereinafter cited as *"LD"),* 17 January 1883 , p. 3, col. 1, digital image, *Chroniclingamerica.loc.gov* (http://chroniclingamerica.loc.gov/ [hereinafter cited as "CA"]:accessed 3/2011).

⁵⁷ "Base Ball," *LD,* 16 May 1883, p. 3, col. 1, digital image, (CA: accessed 3/ 2011).

⁵⁸ *LD,* 26 April 1884 , p. 3, col. 1, digital image, (CA: accessed 3/ 2011).

⁵⁹ Hinchin, 44.

⁶⁰ "Town and Parish News," *LD,* 2 October 1884 , p. 3, col. 1, digital image, (CA: accessed 3/2011).

[61] "Town and Parish News," *LD,* 14 January 1885, p. 3, col. 1, digital image, (CA: accessed 3/ 2011).

[62] Newspaper clipping furnished by Rabbi Arnie Task, Congregation Gemiluth Chassodim, in 2008 to the author, taken from the *Alexandria (Louisiana) Town Talk* dated 7 February 1885.

[63] "Judah, son of Asher Halevi." Translation from Hebrew courtesy of Rabbi Emeritus Arnold Task, Temple Gemiluth Chassodim (Alexandria, LA).

[64] Jewish Cemetery (Pineville, Rapides Parish, LA), Leopold Siess marker, Row 16, personally read, 2009.

[65] "Town and Parish News," *LD,* 28 February 1885, p. 3, col. 1, digital image, (CA: accessed 3/2011).

[66] Hinchin, 45-46.

[67] "Town and Parish News," *LD,* 27 May 1885, p. 3, col. 2, digital image, (CA: Accessed 3/ 1884).

[68] "Town and Parish News," *LD,* 9 September 1885, p. 3, col. 2, digital image, (CA: Accessed 3/2011).

[69] Hinchin, 47.

[70] "Town and Parish News," *LD,* 17 October 1885 , p. 3, col. 1, digital image, (CA: Accessed 3/ 2011).

[71] "Parochial Items," LLMV, Microfilm # 1032, *The Marksville Bulletin*, 8 August 1885, Vol. IX, No. 36 p. 1, col. 2.

[72] Avoyelles Parish Courthouse Records (Marksville, Avoyelles Parish, LA), Civil Docket #7514, "Charles Hernandez vs. David Siess," filed 11 March 1886.

From top, clockwise, Louis Preston Siess, Dr. Isaac Siess, Philippe Escudé
(husband of Florestine Siess), Auger Siess, ca. 1895
(*Courtesy of Barbara Escudé Lemoine*)

Alice Siess Tombstone at the Jewish Cemetery, Pineville, LA

Emmanuel Siess, standing. Auger Siess, seated –Alexandria, LA ca. 1900 (*Courtesy of Bettye Jo Bango Maki*)

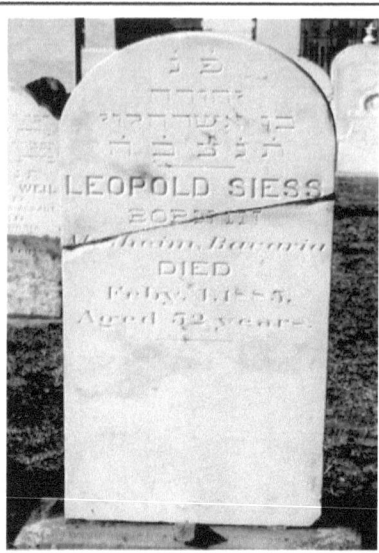

Leopold Siess marker, Jewish Cemetery – Pineville, LA

Florestine Siess Escudé at her home in Mansura, ca. 1930
(*Courtesy of Barbara Escudé Lemoine*)

CHAPTER 6

SIMON SIESS – WORLD TRAVELER

For a period of ten years or so after the death of his younger brother, Leopold, in 1885 Simon Siess lived in Mansura with Fanny and his two children, Mathilde and Leon. Simon had been elected President of the Avoyelles Parish School Board in 1881 and continued in that position until sometime after 1886. It was the Board's job to appoint new teachers, set salaries, and fix the dates for the opening and closing of the schools. Whenever necessary, the board acted upon calls for disciplinary action regarding the staff.[1] In 1887 Simon purchased two town lots from Philibert J. Ducôté, with the thought of an upcoming wedding.

Their twenty year old daughter, Mathilde, was betrothed to Ernest M. Weil, Elie Hiller's former clerk in Marksville. After spending a few months in Shreveport, Ernest was lured westward, ending up in San Francisco. Returning to New Orleans in 1888, he was married to Mathilde at the Congregation Gates of Prayer by Rabbi D. Jacobson on October 17th of that year in front of Simon Siess, Nathan Dreyfus and Edgar M. Cahn.[2] The couple returned to Marksville to begin their married life.

On April 25, 1890, sixty year old Simon Siess applied for a passport on behalf of himself, his fifty-seven year old wife, Fanny Cerf, and his son, Leon, then eighteen. Their great-great grandson, Bill Friend, remembers being told that they planned a tour of the world before they died. They cashed in their savings and headed for New Orleans, where Simon picked up his passport, which had been sent there in care of Simon Gumble & Co.[3] Since Simon had returned to Marksville by September of the same year, it is doubtful that they made anything except a "grand tour" of Europe, probably going back to visit their native towns in Alsace. Ernest and Mathilde were left in charge of the family business during their absence.

Shortly after his in-laws' return from Europe, Ernest Weil made his application for citizenship. Since he had arrived in America at the age of sixteen, a formal waiting period of two years was not necessary. His attorney, William Hall, filed his affidavit of intent on August 14, 1890, at the courthouse in Marksville. His father-in-law, Simon Siess, submitted a letter in support of Ernest's application a few weeks later, on September 3.[rd.] Ernest took the oath of allegiance five days later on September 8th in front of Judge A.V. Coco.[4]

Ernest and Mathilde's first child, Flora, was born on June 17, 1891, in Marksville. It was not much later that Ernest decided to move back out west, this time to Colorado. The plan, it seems, was to sell hats, clothing and supplies to miners. Gold had been discovered in 1890 at Cripple Creek, and within several years there were over five hundred mines in the vicinity. The lure of easy money was irresistible. Ernest, Mathilde, and their young daughter, Flora, set off early in 1893 for Colorado, moving to Florence, a little town about sixty miles south of Cripple Creek, in order to put their plan into action. Their second child, Jeanne, was born there on September 22, 1893.

After Mathilde's departure, Simon and Fanny continued to build up their nest-egg in Avoyelles Parish. They invested in 140 acres of land in Marksville and on the Red River, offered at two different sheriff's sales. In 1894, Simon, leaving Fanny behind, made the trip out to Colorado with his son, Leon, to see what opportunities there might be for him. They set up shop in Denver where Simon was listed in the local directory selling gent's furnishing goods wholesale, with Leon as his clerk at 1413 Larimer Street.[5] Leaving Leon in Denver, Simon joined his daughter, Mathilde, and her family in Florence, Colorado in late 1895 where it was reported in the *Springfield Republican* that on November 9th "C.A. Peavy of the Denver and Rio Grande railway water service was shot and instantly killed on Pike's Peak Avenue, Florence, Col., Saturday night, as he was passing the residence of S. Siess. The theory is that he intercepted burglars there and was shot down by them as they escaped."[6] While in Florence, in February 1896, Ernest invested in the Gismonda Mining and Milling, Co., which was to operate in El Paso and Freemont Counties as well as

Cripple Creek. Along with five other partners (none Jewish), the company was incorporated for a million and a quarter dollars, selling stock at one dollar per share. It was just one of fifteen similar operations started that month in the area and, unfortunately, did not make anyone rich.[7] Disappointing results, coupled with the lawlessness of the area, finally convinced Ernest and Mathilde to leave Florence and take their children one hundred miles away to Denver, Colorado, thus abandoning their attempt to strike it rich. Before they left Florence, their third and last child, Elise, was born on May 2, 1896.

In Denver Ernest Weil was introduced to a relatively new fraternal benefit society, the Woodmen of the World, founded by Joseph Cullen Root in 1890, as a successor to the Modern Woodmen of America which had fallen into difficulty due to internal disputes. The organization provided insurance to hundreds of thousands of subscribers. One of its earlier innovations was the use of tombstones for its members fashioned in the shape of a tree stump, thousands of which may still be seen in cemeteries across the nation. As luck would have it, only a few years before Ernest arrived in Denver, the Woodmen's Pacific Jurisdiction, had been established there, and was looking for employees. Ernest, Mathilde, their children, and brother-in-law, Leon, however, lived only briefly in Denver, moving on to Minneapolis, Minnesota, where Ernest and Leon's new jobs with the Woodmen of the World had taken them. Simon, who had been joined by Fanny, stayed on in Denver and was listed as a "broker" in the 1899 City Directory living now at 1247 South 15th Street.[8] In the 1900 Denver Directory Simon was living at 8 LaVeta Place and his occupation was "mining."[9] At almost seventy years of age it may be assumed that he was selling mining supplies rather than panning for gold!

As of June 1900, Ernest, Mathilde, their three daughters, now eight, six and four years of age, and brother-in-law, Leon Siess, rented a house at 303 15th Street East in Minneapolis, Minnesota. Ernest and Leon continued their work for Woodmen of the World.[10] But Leon would not be there for long. His family had found a bride for him in San Francisco. Jewish marriages in the nineteenth century were usually arranged through business or family connections. Ernest had lived in San Francisco before returning to Louisiana to marry Mathilde. Moreover, the Siess-Weil business in Florence, Colorado had very likely been supplied by San Francisco merchants, so some connection to the prospective bride's family had most likely been forged by Leon's brother-in-law, Ernest. This connection facilitated the introduction of Elizabeth Silverstone to Leon Siess, a young, eligible bachelor. Elizabeth and Leon's engagement was announced in the *San Francisco Call*: "Mrs. C. Silverstone announces the engagement of her daughter, Miss Lizzie, to Leon Siess of Minneapolis, Minn." [11] Leon travelled to San Francisco to get the license which was issued on August 10, 1900. The prospective bride was the youngest daughter of the late Solomon Silverstone, a Russian emigrant who had come to California in the 1850s, and his wife, Charlotte. Solomon had dealt in crockery. The Silverstones had also lived in Oregon, and one son, Emmanuel, became a merchant in Seattle, Washington.[12] Leon and Miss Lizzie's wedding took place on August 12, 1900 and was conducted by Rabbi M.S. Levy.[13] The couple decided to make San Francisco their home, and Leon started looking for work.

Simon and Fanny moved to Minneapolis to join Ernest, Mathilde, and their three daughters in 1902. Both families were enumerated together in the 1905 Minnesota State Census living at 2416 Chicago Avenue. Ernest was now the Minnesota manager for Woodmen of the World, but Simon, at 75, was apparently retired.[14] The following year, Ernest was promoted to the Sovereign Manager of Wisconsin, Minnesota and the two Dakotas.[15] Meanwhile, Leon Siess and his wife Elizabeth lived, first, in San Francisco where he worked as a United States postal clerk in Station #13,[16] but, he soon became involved in an enterprise called the 1-Cent Car Fare Company. In 1909 it was reported that he had moved to Seattle, Washington with Elizabeth and was working as the local manager for this business which was characterized as a "get-rich-quick" operation. It was said to be a type of pyramid scheme whereby a person could ultimately obtain a book containing thirty street car tickets worth $1.20 for twenty-five cents. A customer would buy one coupon for 25¢, then go to Leon's office on the fourth floor of the Arcade Annex building and give him an additional 75¢ for which he would receive three more coupons to sell to his friends at 25¢ each. After those friends brought their tickets to Leon's office and paid their 75¢ for three coupons to sell to their friends the original customer was then eligible to receive the book containing thirty, five cent street car rides. Leon was interviewed and explained that money could only be made if a certain percentage of people who bought a ticket for 25¢ from a friend's book would fail to come to the office to buy a book of coupons themselves. It was profit due to lapses, which according to Leon and a local former prosecuting attorney, was not illegal. [17] Needless to say, he was not in that business for very long.

***

In 1907 the Woodmen of the World transferred Ernest Weil to Louisiana to be its state manager and organizer. Ernest crisscrossed the state, attending meetings, signing up members and giving speeches in an effort to organize as many chapters, or "camps" as they were called. To this end, he and his family moved from Minneapolis to Shreveport, a city in which he had worked as a clerk some twenty years before. In April, 1908, Ernest Weil called a meeting of the council commanders, clerks and bankers of the fifteen camps in the city of New Orleans to plan a great class initiation to be given in July, at which he hoped to have at least two thousand new members. Baton Rouge was willing to try to attract five hundred new subscribers. Ernest announced that, as of the previous month, Louisiana was fourth in membership, with a net increase of 440 men in 458 camps. Statewide the Woodmen of the World had 22,000 members and it was hoped that this would grow to 35,000 by the following year. The nationwide membership had just exceeded 425,000 and had a reserve of six million dollars, which was growing at the rate of two million dollars per year. In 1907 the organization had paid out over four million dollars in death benefits and had erected over fourteen thousand tree stump monuments at the graves of deceased subscribers.[18] Ernest's hard work was rewarded when, in August 1908, the Woodmen of Baton Rouge inducted the largest class in the history of the organization, welcoming eight hundred new men, and hosting an additional two hundred visitors from surrounding towns. Twelve hundred woodmen paraded through the streets of Baton Rouge to the Elk's Theatre, where the induction ceremonies took place. Ernest Weil, Consul Commander and State Manager, was honored by Colonel A.B. Booth, of New Orleans, who presented him with a "gold bonded umbrella" on behalf of the three Baton Rouge Camps and made an eloquent address. Ernest responded, making a speech of his own to the newly inducted members.[19]

On December 2, 1908, *The New Orleans Item* published the charter of "The Woodmen Mutual Health and Casualty Company of Louisiana," notarized by Edouard F. Henriques on October 24th. The organization was set up for the purpose of insuring any person against sickness, bodily injury or death by accident, for a limited sum of five hundred dollars or less, on a single life and to provide a weekly cash benefit of twenty dollars or less for disability caused by sickness or accident, and for which monthly premiums would be charged. Eleven trustees were to be elected by the general membership every four years. Each new board would elect from within itself five officers: a president, vice-president, secretary, treasurer and an attorney. The First Board members named were Ernest M. Weil, Charles de B. Claiborne, Paul B. Alker, Edouard F. Henriques, Otto A. Levy, William E. Dodsworth, A. B. Booth, Charles A. Duchamp, Joseph S. Loeb, Thomas Downey, and Robert Henderson, who were to hold office until January, 1918. The first officers were declared to be Ernest M. Weil, president, A.B. Booth, vice-president, William E. Dodsworth, secretary, Charles de B. Claiborne, treasurer and Charles A. DuChamp, attorney, all of whom would hold office until the first meeting in January 1909.[20]

A joint public installation for new Woodmen inductees was held in New Orleans at the Washington Artillery Hall in January of 1909, which was preceded by a vaudeville show and a company drill in the ballroom. In just nine months national membership had exceeded six hundred thousand, with the development of the "Woodmen Circle" for women, and the "Cadets of Woodcraft," for children. Twenty-two more camps were added in Louisiana. Ernest Weil made a lofty speech on fraternalism and assured the membership that the organization had a reserve of eight million dollars to fulfill its monetary promises to its members.[21]

***

In 1909, Ernest, Mathilde, and their daughters moved from Shreveport to 3543 Chestnut Street in New Orleans. Flora was now seventeen. Her sisters, Jeanne and Elise, were fourteen and twelve, respectively. The move was a business necessity as the main office of the Woodmen Mutual Health and Casualty Company of Louisiana was located in New Orleans. Living with Ernest and his immediate family were, Mathilde's parents, eighty year old Simon Siess and his wife, Fanny Cerf, now seventy, and Ernest's niece, Fanny Kirsch, newly arrived from Alsace.[22]

In the summer of 1910, E.M. Weil Camp 563 was founded in New Orleans, and named after its organizer. Its membership was primarily from the passenger departments of some of the big New Orleans railways. Traditionally it had been impossible for a railroad worker to get any type of death or accident insurance because it was such a dangerous occupation. Some carriers had formed their own mutual beneficial associations. So when the Woodmen of the World were willing to accept rail workers into their midst, it was met with much enthusiasm. The installation of thirty-two new members took place at the Odd Fellows' Hall, and was followed by a banquet at Tujague's restaurant near French Market. Later that month an executive committee meeting was held in order to prepare for the initiation of two thousand new woodmen on September 29th. Ernest, because of the size of the class to be inducted, had prevailed upon the sovereign commander and founder of the Woodmen, J.C. Root, to receive members at six instead of ten dollars per person.[23]

Ernest expanded his influence with fraternal organizations, joining the Benevolent Knights of America which also provided sickness and death benefit insurance. He soon became its national organizer. He was also asked to manage the LaSalle Industrial Life &

Accident Benefit Insurance Company on Carondelet Street.[24] Nor did he neglect his duties as an observant Jew, joining the board of Touro Infirmary, becoming a member of the Young Men's Hebrew Association, and accepting the presidency of the New Orleans B'nai B'rith. He was elected as a trustee of the Jewish Congregation Gates of Prayer in 1916.[25]

Ernest was also an advocate of the public school system. High school education for girl's had been limited to private, mostly religiously affiliated institutions in the previous century. His youngest daughter, Elise, had the privilege of attending Sophie B. Wright High School, the first ever public girls' high school in the city of New Orleans which opened on Napoleon Avenue in 1912. In May, 1913, the Senior class, including Elise, portraying an old man, scored a triumph at the Tulane Theatre, where they presented "Cricket on the Hearth," and bid farewell to their school days. [26]

In early 1915 Ernest moved his family from Chestnut Street to 1712 Soniat, two blocks north of St. Charles Avenue. It was and still is a grand old double house where he lived with Mathilde and the three girls, his elderly in-laws, Simon and Fanny Siess, and his niece, Fanny Kirsch. By this time also, Leon and Elizabeth Siess had moved back from the West Coast. Leon started up a business as a retail merchant.[27] He and Lizzie lived in a series of rented apartments and rooming houses as they never had children. Leon's first enterprise was a gentlemen's ready-to-wear clothing store located at 164 South Rampart Street.

On Friday, December 3, 1916, Ernest Weil died unexpectedly at the age of fifty-five. He had been in the United States for thirty eight-years, and had accomplished much in his career which had been devoted to the development of various fraternal organizations. He was remembered in the *Times Picayune* with a small article and photo, and praised as the state organizer of Woodmen of the World, and a member of a myriad of other organizations.[28] The family continued living together on Soniat Street, along with Ernest's niece, and Mathilde's parents, Simon and Fanny Siess.

After the death of his son-in-law, Simon Siess began to take stock of his assets. According to his great-grandchildren he and Fanny had blown their savings on their trip abroad, as well as speculation out west, never imagining that they would live as long as they did. During their years in New Orleans, they had been supported in large part by Ernest Weil, but with his death, finances in the family were tighter than ever. So in the summer of 1919, Simon redeemed one hundred forty acres of land on Bayou du Lac, in Avoyelles Parish on which he had let the taxes lapse. Upon payment of the full amount of taxes, interest, costs and penalties, he was able to buy it back from the State of Louisiana. On the same day he sold it to his children, Mathilde Siess Weil and Leon Siess, for $300 cash.[29]

***

The first of Mathilde Siess Weil's daughters to marry was also the youngest. Elise Weil had become engaged to the brother of one of her female acquaintances, Kitty Friend. The prospective groom, Julius Weis Friend, was the son of Joseph Emmanuel Friend and his wife, Ida Sophie Weis. Julius's paternal great-grandfather, Loeb Friend, a cattle dealer from Autenhausen, Bavaria, had seen his seven sons and two daughters immigrate to America, in the late 1840s. Several of his sons became prosperous dry goods merchants in Milwaukee, Wisconsin, eventually opening up a successful clothing factory which afforded everyone a comfortable living. One of them, Henry Friend, and his English wife, Frances Samuels, raised ten children in relative luxury in Milwaukee. The 1870 Federal Census recorded that he was in possession of $25,000 in real estate and $100,000 in personal property, a fortune for the time.[30] When their sixth child, Joseph, was fifteen years old, and the baby, Adeline, was just five, Henry and Frances made a trip back to Germany, sailing on the *SS. Schiller* from New York on April 27, 1875. The pride of the German Transatlantic Steam Navigation Line, she was just two years old, when due to an error in navigation she foundered and broke up on the notorious Retarrier ledges in the Isles of Scilly in the English Channel, killing 335 out of the 372 passengers and crew members on board, including Henry and Frances Friend. The disaster was one of the worst in British naval history, and was devastating for the Friend family. Henry and Frances' minor children were split up and sent to live with other relatives.

Despite the tragedy, the family was able to send the deceased couple's son, Joseph Emmanuel Friend, to Yale University in New Haven Connecticut. After graduation in 1882 he went back to the family firm in Milwaukee. With business connections in New Orleans to the most well-known cotton factor of the city, Julius Weis, a marriage was eventually, arranged between Joseph Friend and Julius Weis' daughter, Ida Sophie.[31] The couple married in New Orleans on March 19, 1890,[32] after which Joseph Friend left his family in Milwaukee to join his father-in-law's cotton brokerage firm.

Joseph and Ida's second child, Julius Weis Friend, born on August 20, 1894, in New Orleans, married Elise Siess Weil on April 22, 1922, at the home of the bride's mother, Mathilde, at 1721 Soniat Street.[33] It is worth noting that both the bride's maternal great-grandmother, Minette Siess Lehmann, and the groom's paternal grandparents, Henry and Frances Friend had died in devastating shipwrecks in the English Channel less than fifteen years apart in the previous century. Elise and Julius spent their honeymoon in New York, New Haven, Ct. and in the Berkshire Mountains.[34]

Elise's new husband, also a Yale graduate, enlisted in the U.S. Army in 1916 and served in France with the medical corps throughout the First World War. Unlike his father and grandfather before him, he was not drawn to the business world. After his return from the Army he did put some time in at the family firm, as a clerk for the Julius Weis & Co. cotton brokerage. He was, however, more interested in literature and the arts. In 1921 he and Albert Goldstein founded *The Double Dealer*, a literary magazine which published the early works of Faulkner, Hemingway, Amy Lowell, Robert Penn Warren Sherwood Anderson and Thornton Wilder. It was almost a family affair, with Julius Friend's sister, Lillian Marcuse, recruiting people who would pay ten dollars per month to keep it going, and his Uncle Samuel Weis contributing the use of a downtown New Orleans loft as an editorial office. According Julius Weis Friend's son, Bill, both his father and his

Aunt Lillian appear in an early William Faulkner novel entitled *Mosquitoes*. With generous out of pocket contributions, Julius Weis Friend kept the magazine going for seven years.

Julius never practiced his religion because he thought it useless, so his two sons, Bill and Joe, were not brought up in an observant household. Joe recalled that "my whole extended family was non-observant. We went to Seder dinner at great-aunt Henrietta Godchaux's house until she died, then to grandmother's [Ida Sophie Weis Friend]. Henrietta's daughter, Caroline Godchaux Wolf Mayerson's husband, Hyman, was the only member of the family who could read Hebrew. After he stopped coming to dinner, the whole thing was read in English. But it was never serious….just an excuse to get a lot of people together and remind each other they were Jewish. And the food was good." [35] Joe's older brother, J. W. "Bill" Friend, was never involved in religion but Elise finally convinced her husband to allow Joe to go to Sunday School when he was twelve. Temple Sinai's reform Rabbi Julian Feibelman, did not believe in bar mitzvah, so, at fourteen, Joe was "confirmed." After Elise Weil Friend's husband died she did start going to the synagogue regularly, but her son, Joe, did not think of her as much more than a cultural Jew.

In October 1922, Leon Siess saved enough money to open up a clothing store, moving from South Rampart to 506 Frenchmen Street, specializing in mostly women's fashion and undergarments. He also stocked furs, luggage, and umbrellas. For the men, he sold handkerchiefs, ties, shirts and underwear. He also displayed a full line of boys' clothing, including caps, blouses and knee pants at forty-nine cents each. The grand opening sale was held on Saturday, October 14, 1922. Ernest Weil's niece, Fanny Kirsch, was hired as his saleslady to help his wife, Lizzie, in the store.[36]

Mathilde Siess Weil's daughter, Jeanne, married only months after her younger sister, Élise. Her groom, Ernest Daniel Lopez, came from a family of Sephardic Jewish caterers and confectioners whose ancestors, centuries before, had been expelled from Spain during the Inquisition. Many had settled in Bordeaux, France including Ernest

Lopez's grandfather, Daniel, who was born there on March 22, 1827.[37] He immigrated to New Orleans around 1850 and married Toba Laura Levy, also originally from Bordeaux. Lopez started a confectionery business at the corner of Conti and Chartres Street. In 1864 he moved to 154 Canal Street where he opened a restaurant which was divided into numerous rooms, and included a fine gallery where he served lunch, all sorts of confectionery, biscuits glacés, sherbets and ices.[38] Daniel and Toba were the parents of six children, two of whom, Aristide and Blanche figure prominently in New Orleans author, Frances Parkinson Keyes,' novel *Once on E splanade*. Ms. Keyes paints a wonderful picture of the Lopez family business, their magnificent red and white delivery wagons, the shop on Canal Street with vanilla beans hanging from the ceiling, and a peep hole from the Lopez family's second floor residence down to the selling floor, where the boss could keep an eye on his employees. If important customers came into the shop, Aristide or his brother Arthur, Daniel's two eldest sons, went down to wait on them personally. After Daniel's death on December 2, 1883, and his burial in the Dispersed of Judah Cemetery the following day,[39] his two sons and widow carried on the family business. Arthur Lopez married a German immigrant, Amelia Gebhardt, in New Orleans on May 3, 1888,[40] and their only son, Ernest Daniel, Jeanne's future groom, was born on November 8, 1890.[41] In 1912, after sixty-two years of continuous operation, Arthur Lopez closed the door on his family's confectionery business. The store was a victim of fierce competition and a stubborn recession, which despite a brisk walk-in trade and a successful mail-order business, could not overcome outstanding debts. Although disputed by the Whitman Candy Company, Daniel Lopez claimed to have invented the chocolate bonbon, which had been hand-made and sold for over a half-century in the New Orleans store.[42] Arthur's son, Ernest Lopez, but for the bankruptcy, would have inherited his father's share of the company. As an alternative, he went to work for the Runkel Brothers Chocolate Manufactory. Based in New York City at 447 West 30th Street between 9th and 10th Avenues, their six story brick building had burned completely to the ground in 1901, but had risen from its own ashes. The Runkel's, despite the location of their business in New York, were first generation Louisianans, whose father, Sigismond Runkel, from Frankfort, Germany, and his French born wife, Malzy Levy, had settled in New Orleans in 1850. Moreover, Ernest's aunt, Victoria Rebecca Lopez, was already married to the eldest Runkel brother, Herman, so there was a family connection. Ernest's work for Runkel's had predictably taken him to New York, and Jeanne Weil's studies had taken her to Boston where she had majored in social work. They continued their courtship in the northeast and married on December 7, 1922, at a New York City hotel in a ceremony conducted by Rabbi Hyman G. Enelow of Temple Emanu-El.[43] Their only child, Ernest Weil Lopez, born in 1926, was a lifelong New Yorker.

Flora, Ernest Weil's eldest daughter, was the last to marry. The wedding was celebrated quietly at home in Soniat Street on Thursday October 30, 1924. The groom, Leon Simeon Kahn, whose father, Lazare Kahn, had emigrated from Mommenheim, Alsace, was a native of Jackson, Mississippi. The bride was given away by her Uncle Leon Siess, Her mother, Mathilde Siess Weil, was her matron of honor. Simon and Fanny Siess were in attendance as well. The ceremony was performed by Rabbi Dr. Mendel Silber of the Congregation Gates of Prayer.[44] After a honeymoon in Florida, Flora went to live in Mississippi with her husband who was the vice-president of a Dry Cleaning establishment.

***

Simon and Fanny Cerf Siess celebrated their fifty-ninth year of marriage on November 15, 1924 and nine days later Simon died from bronchial pneumonia at home in his ninety-fourth year. An article in the *Times Picayune* remembered Simon as an Alsatian immigrant who had lived in Louisiana for seventy years. Having come to Marksville as a young man, he had fought for the Confederacy after which he returned to Avoyelles Parish to resume his career. Funeral services were held at home followed by interment at the Gates of Prayer Cemetery on Joseph Street in New Orleans.[45] Simon's wife, Fanny, died from heart failure less than three years later on November 3, 1927 at the age of eighty-seven. She was interred the following day next to

Simon at the Gates of Prayer Cemetery. Fanny was remembered by her son and daughter and three grand-children as a stern and difficult person, just the opposite of her mild-mannered and gentle late husband Simon Siess.[46]

After the death of her parents, Mathilde moved to Jackson, Mississippi to live with her daughter, Flora Weil, Flora's husband, Leon Kahn, and their daughter, Leona. Ernest Weil's niece, Fanny Kirsch, had been married in 1927, at the age of thirty-six, to a fifty-one year old widower, Moise Levy, who sold new and used furniture. Childless, they lived at 621 Royal Street.[47]

***

Although doing a fairly decent business in a store he called the *Emporium*, which handled both men's and women's wear, Leon and Elizabeth Siess, decided to open a specialty shop in the French Quarter selling ladies frocks, suits and coats. It was located at 136 Baronne Street next to the Roosevelt Hotel. Leon named it the Elizabeth Dress Shop in honor of his wife. The grand opening was held on Monday, March 11, 1929.[48] It was the Roaring Twenties, and what could go wrong? Yet it did. Just seven months later, on October 29th, stock prices on the New York Exchange collapsed, ushering in a twelve year depression. On August 25, 1930, Leon went into bankruptcy, and the contents of the Elizabeth Dress Shop, less than a year and a half in existence, were put up for auction. On the block to be sold on September 4, 1930, were "high grade dresses, coats, two electric fans, an awning, an iron safe, mirrors and dressing rooms." [49] His business could not overcome the hard times which had befallen the American public.

Mathilde Weil died at the age of sixty-one, less than four years after her mother, Fanny Siess, on June 22, 1931 in Jackson, Mississippi. She was brought back to New Orleans for services which were held the next day at the home of her daughter, Elise Weil Friend, followed by interment next to her husband, Ernest Weil, at the Congregation Gates of Prayer Cemetery.[50]

Mathilde's brother, Leon, recently bankrupt, took a job as a salesman at the Davis Women's Apparel Shop at 1101 Canal Street. He and Elizabeth lived frugally at a boarding house at 4436 St. Charles Avenue, until her untimely death, at the age of sixty-four, from a coronary occlusion which she suffered on May 26, 1941. Services were held at the home of Leon's niece, Elise Weil Friend, and Lizzie was buried in the Hebrew Rest Cemetery #2 at Frenchmen Street and Gentilly Boulevard, in New Orleans.[51]

After Lizzie's death, Leon led a quiet life moving from one rooming house to another, working, at times, as a salesman. All that was left of the Simon Siess family were three nieces, their husbands, one grand-niece and three grand-nephews. Leon's niece, Elise Friend, looked after his interests as he grew older. His grand-nephew, Joe Friend, remembers his beloved Uncle "Lee" as a great old gentleman who had an eye for the ladies, and apparently did quite well with them. He was also always interested in a bargain, a deal, or any quick money scheme, and was not above pleading poverty with his nieces to get a little extra cash to invest in the stock market. He had, according to his grand-nephew, little interest in Judaism. He died on June 28, 1954 at the age of eighty-two in his rooms at 1312 Broadway, and was remembered in a brief article in the *Times Picayune* which recalled his origins in Marksville and his years as a merchant and salesman in New Orleans. He was buried next to Elizabeth the following day at the Hebrew Rest Cemetery #2 in New Orleans.[52]

Few traces of Judaism remain in the Simon Siess family today despite his being the only brother to marry a Jewish woman. Although his children and grandchildren had all taken Jewish spouses, they never seem to have had any strong connections to the Hebrew faith. This lack of connection to their ancestral religion was, perhaps, because Simon, his wife and children, had spent most of their lives in Avoyelles Parish, in a society whose religious underpinnings were mostly Catholic. When the family moved to New Orleans, they found a Jewish population which was more numerous and diverse but it practiced mostly the reformed rite which taught assimilation and discouraged the old-fashioned customs which had separated the Jewish people from the prevailing Christian culture. The Southern Creole Jewish experience of which they were an integral part was just not vital enough to carry their particular brand of Judaism into the next century.

---

[1] "School Board Proceedings," Louisiana State University Libraries On Line Catalog – Special Collections – Louisiana and Lower Mississippi Valley (hereinafter cited as "LLMV"), Microfilm # 1032, *The Marksville Bulletin*, 27 February 1886, Vol. X, no. 11, p. 1, col. 5.

[2] Louisiana Secretary of State, *Orleans Parish Marriage Records*, Certificate of Marriage, Vol 13, p. 416 (1888), Ernest M. Weil to Mathilda Siess; photocopy obtained from Louisiana Secretary of State, Department of Archives, Records Management and History, Baton Rouge, LA.

[3] Simon Siess, U.S. passport application no. 14131, 25 April 1890 (issue date), digital image, *Ancestry.com* (http://www.ancestry.com [hereinafter cited as "A"]: accessed 2/ 2011), *U.S. Passport Applications, 1795-1925*, citing NARA microfilm publication M1372, roll 347.

[4] Avoyelles Parish Courthouse Records (Marksville, Avoyelles Parish, LA), Civil Docket #8220, "Ernest M. Weil for Citizenship," filed 14 August 1890.

[5] Ballenger & Richards, compilers, *Twenty-second Annual Denver City Directory, 1894*, digital image, (A: accessed 3/ 2011). Entries for Simon and Leon Siess, p. 907.

[6] "News Matters in Brief," *Springfield (Massachusetts) Republican* 12 November 1895, p. 5, col 7, digital image, *Genealogybank.com* (http://www.genealogybank.com [hereinafter cited as "GB"]: accessed 9/ 2010).

[7] "Incorporations," *The Denver (Colorado) Evening Post*, 7 February, 1896, p. 3, col 2, digital image, (GB: accessed 7/2012).

[8] Ballenger & Richards, compilers, *Twenty-eighth Annual Denver City Directory, 1900*, digital image, (A: accessed 3/ 2011). Entry for Simon Siess, p. 1039.

[9] Ballenger & Richards, compilers, *Twenty-seventh Annual Denver City Directory, 1899,* digital image, (A: accessed 3/ 2011). Entry for Simon Siess, p. 1129.

[10] 1900 U.S. Census, Hennepin Co., Minnesota, pop. sch., Minneapolis, Ward 5, ED 60, p. 12B (penned), Dwelling #257, Family #286, Ernest Weil household, digital image, (A: accessed 7/ 2010), citing NARA microfilm publication T623, roll 767. Date of enumeration: 9 June 1900.

[11] "They're Engaged," *San Francisco Call*, 29 April 1900, Vol. 87, no. 160, p. 26, col. 1, digital image, (GB: accessed 10/ 2010).

[12] 1880 U.S. Census, San Francisco Co., California, pop. sch., San Francisco, ED 166, p. 271B (penned), Dwelling #110, Family #126, Solomon Silverstone household, digital image, (A: accessed July 8, 2010), citing FHL Film 1254077, roll 77. Date of enumeration: 5 June 1900.

[13] "Births, Marriages, Deaths," *San Francisco Call*, 18 August 1900, p. 13, col. 2, digital image, (GB: accessed 1 October 2010).

[14] 1905 Minnesota State Census, Hennepin County, pop. sch., Minneapolis, Ward 8, ED 43, p. 15, Dwelling (blank), Family members 64-70, Simon Siess household, digital image, *Familysearch.org* (http://www.familysearch.org: accessed 1/2011), citing State Library and Records Service, St. Paul, MN, FHL microfilm 928785. Date of enumeration: June 7, 1905.

[15] "Observe Second Anniversary," *The Duluth (Minnesota) News-Tribune*, 12 November 1903, p. 8, col. 3, digital image, (GB: accessed 1 October 2010).

[16] "Post Office Promotions," *San Francisco Call*, 8 September 1907, p. 37, col. 5, digital image, (GB: accessed 1 October 2010).

[17] "Car Ticket Plan May Cause Inquiry," *The Seattle (Washington) Times*, 14 February 1909, p. 14, cols. 1, 2, digital image, (GB: accessed 1 October 2010).

[18] "Woodmen of the World," *The (New Orleans) Daily Picayune* (hereinafter cited as *"DP"*), 21 April 1908, p. 6, cols. 5, 6, digital image, (GB: accessed 21 October 2010).

[19] "The Latest News in All Louisiana," *DP*, 31 August 1908, p. 14, col. 3, digital image, (GB: accessed 21 October 2010).

[20] "Charter of The Woodmen Mutual Health and Casualty Company of Louisiana," *The New Orleans (Louisiana) Item*, 2 December 1908, p. 13, cols. 4-6, digital image, (GB: accessed 21 October 2010).

[21] "Woodmen of World Hold Joint Public Installation," *DP*, 30 January 1909, p. 4, cols. 1-4, digital image, (GB: accessed 21 October 2010).

[22] 1910 U.S. Census, Orleans Parish, Louisiana, pop. sch., New Orleans, Ward 12, ED 0197, p. 7B (penned), Dwelling #138, Family #146, Ernest Weil household, digital image, (A: accessed 25 October 2010), citing NARA microfilm publication T624, roll 524. Date of enumeration: 20 April 1910.

[23] "E.M. Weil Camp," *DP*, 18 August 1910, p. 5, cols. 4, 5, digital image, (GB: accessed 21 October 2010).

[24] "Soard's New Orleans City Directory 1916," digital image, *Fold3.com* (http://www.fold3.com [hereinafter cited as "F3"]: accessed 31 January 2011), 1296. Entry for "Weil, Ernest M., M'ngr."

[25] "Officers Elected For Gates of Prayer Synagogue for 1916," *The New Orleans States*, 16 January 1916, p. 6, col. 2, digital image, (GB: accessed 21 October 2010).

[26] "High School Play," *DP*, 23 May 1913, p. 11, col. 6, digital image, (GB: accessed 10/ 2010).

[27] "Soard's New Orleans City Directory 1916," digital image, (F3: accessed 1/2011), 1411. Entry for Leon Siess.

[28] "News of the Fraternities – Fraternity leader Mourned by Many," *The (New Orleans, LA) Times Picayune* (hereinafter cited as *"TP"*), 4 December 1916, p. 11, cols. 1, 2, digital image, (GB: accessed 10/ 2010).

[29] Avoyelles Parish Courthouse Records (Marksville, Avoyelles Parish, LA), *Conveyances*, Book A-17, p. 140, 141 , Nos. 28239 & 28240, 28241, 28242, "Redemption Sale of Land – 140 Acres on Bayou Du Lac, Sec. 2, T1 SR3E," filed June 26, 1919; *Conveyances,* Book A-17, p. 142, No. 28243, "Simon Siess to Leon Siess and Mrs. Mathilda Siess, Sale of Land," filed June 26, 1919.

[30] 1870 U.S. Census, Milwaukee Co., Wisconsin, pop. sch., Milwaukee, Ward 7, p. 16 (penned), Dwelling #101, Family #99, Henry Friend household, digital image, (A: accessed 10/ 2010), citing NARA microfilm publication M593, roll 1728. Date of enumeration: 1 June 1870.

[31] Julius Weis, one of the best known and most philanthropic members of New Orleans Jewish Society, emigrated from Klingen, Germany in 1845. He began his career as a peddler in Mississippi saving enough money after eight years to open a dry goods store in Fayette, MS. He sold that and moved to Jackson, MS, becoming a partner in Meyer, Deutsch & Weis. After the Civil War he was sent by the firm to open up a dry goods store in New Orleans. Before leaving Mississippi he married Caroline Mayer of Natchez. He began buying and reselling cotton and made a fortune in the space of thirteen years. He was a founding member of Temple Sinai in 1870. In 1880 he became the president of Touro Infirmary. He was also founder of Touro Home for the Aged and Infirm. His daughter, Ida Weis Friend, Elise Siess Weil's mother-in-law, carried on his philanthropic and civic contributions.

[32] "Louisiana Marriages, 1718-1925," database, (A: accessed 8/ 2011), citing a variety of sources including original marriage records located in Family History Library microfilm, microfiche, or books. Marriage of Joseph E. Friend to Ida S. Weis.

[33] "Latest Social Events," *TP*, 13 April 1922, p. 10, cols. 2, 3, digital image, (GB: accessed 3/ 2011).

[34] "New Orleans Society," *The New Orleans Item*, 11 May 1922, p. 17, col. 2, digital image, (GB: accessed 3/ 2011).

[35] Personal observations of Joseph Ernest Friend to the author in email dated April 7, 2011.

[36] "Leon Siess, Opening Sale," *The New Orleans Item*, 11 October 1922, p. 22, cols.4-7, digital image, (GB: accessed 10/ 2010).

[37] Dispersed of Judah Cemetery Office (New Orleans, Orleans Parish, LA), Index cards citing persons interred in Daniel Lopez plot: "Daniel Lopez born Bordeaux, France Mar 22, 1827. Died in New Orleans, December 2, 1883."

[38] "D. Lopez, 154 Canal Street," *DP*, 19 June 1869, p. 4, col. 5 digital image, (GB: accessed 3/2011).

[39] See note 37.

[40] "New Orleans, Louisiana Marriage Records Index 1831-1925," database, (A: accessed 7/ 2010), citing State of Louisiana, Secretary of State, Division of Archives, Records Management and History. *Vital Records Indices*. Baton Rouge, LA, USA. Marriage of Arthur Lopez, age 24 and Amelia Gebhardt, age 20 (Vol. 13, p. 143).

[41] "New Orleans, Louisiana Birth Records Index, 1790-1899," database, (A: accessed 3/2011), citing State of Louisiana, Secretary of State, Division of Archives, Records Management, and History, *Vital Records Indices*. Baton Rouge, LA, USA. Birth of Ernest Daniel Lopez, Vol. 90, p. 1007.

[42] "Last of Lopez Confectioners," *DP,* 23 July 1912, p. 4, col. 5, digital image, (GB: accessed 3/ 2011).

[43] "Society," *TP*, 11 March 1923, p. 36, col. 3 digital image, (GB: accessed 3/ 2011). Also: State of New York, Certificate and Record of Marriage, City of New York, Certificate No. 31348 (1922), Ernest Daniel Lopez to Jeanne Seiss Weill (sic); photocopy obtained from The City of New York Municipal Archives, Manhattan, New York.

⁴⁴ "Society," *TP*, 2 November 1924, p. 54, col. 5 digital image, (GB: accessed 3/ 2011).

⁴⁵ "Simon Siess Dies at Age of 94 Years – Retired Merchant, Native of Alsace, Was Confederate Soldier," *TP*, 26 November 1924, p. 26, col. 2, digital image, (GB: accessed 3/ 2011).

⁴⁶ "Died," *TP*, 4 November 1927, p. 2, cols. 1, 8, digital image, (GB: accessed 3/ 2011).

⁴⁷ 1930 U.S. Census, Orleans Parish, Louisiana, pop. sch., New Orleans, Ward 5, p. 16B (penned), Dwelling #312, Family #323, Moise Levy household, digital image, (A: accessed 10/ 2010), citing NARA microfilm publication T626, roll 803. Date of enumeration: 17 April 1930.

⁴⁸ "A Newcomer, Elizabeth Dress Shop, 139 Baronne Street," *TP*, 10 March 1929, p. 50, cols. 6, 7, digital image, (GB: accessed 3/ 2011).

⁴⁹ "Bankrupt Sale. Contents of The Elizabeth Dress Shop," *TP*, 31 August 1930, p. 10, cols. 6-8, digital image, (GB: accessed 3/ 2011).

⁵⁰ "Deaths – M.S. Weil," *TP*, 23 June 1931, p. 2, col. 8, digital image, (GB: accessed 3/ 2011).

⁵¹ "Deaths – Mrs. Elizabeth Silverstone Siess," *TP*, 27 May 1941, p. 2, col. 8, digital image, (GB: accessed 3/ 2011).

⁵² "Leon Siess, 82, Taken by Death," *TP*, 29 June 1954, p. 4, col. 3, digital image, (GB: accessed 3/ 2011).

Wedding Photos – Ernest M. Weil and Mathilde Siess, ca. October 1888 (*Courtesy of Joseph E. Friend family*)

CHAPTER 7

SAW MILLS, GUSHERS, AND BROKEN BONES

In the late 1860s long leaf yellow pine forests in the north had been all but depleted, so after the end of the Civil War, the Federal Government started to offer land grants to northern railroads to build south into the pine forests of northern and central Louisiana in order to harvest the lumber. One of the recipients was New York financier, Jay Gould, who acquired the St. Louis, Iron Mountain and Southern Railroad in 1880 and was given thirty thousand acres of land in Arkansas and Louisiana by the Federal Government as an incentive to extend the railway from Memphis, Tennessee to Alexandria, Louisiana. He and his son, George Jay Gould, thus, became major players in the lumber industry in Central Louisiana. They sold a portion of their granted land to local operators, who, in turn, went into the lumber business, thereby guaranteeing their railroad enough revenue to make it profitable. Julius Levin, having been a grocer in Alexandria since the early 1850's, saw the opportunity to make large sums of money in the lumber business because of the completion of two other railroads into Louisiana in 1882: the Louisiana and Texas Railroad and Steamship Company and the Texas and Pacific Railway. Levin sold some of his holdings in Alexandria, turning others over to various relatives to manage for him, in order to devote his energy to this new industry.

In 1885 Auger Siess followed suit. He sold his restaurant and went into the lumber industry with his father-in-law, Julius Levin. Familiar with the trade, he had already done his apprenticeship with his Uncle David at the latter's saw mill and cotton gin when he was just a teenager. Shortly thereafter, on August 4, 1886, Auger's wife, Fannie, gave birth to their first child, Leo Chester Siess.

By 1887 Julius Levin had become the agent for four of the most important providers of long leaf yellow pine in the area: Waters and Bringhorst, J.M. Nugent and Co., Chittenden E. Ball & Son and F.

O. Nugent and Son.[1] He established a yard and planing mill in Alexandria which was connected to the main line of the Texas and Pacific Railway. At one time it was said that he marketed a million feet of sawed logs per month, the bulk of which went by rail to Texas, Oklahoma and the Midwest.[2] Thereafter he was known as the "lumber king of Rapides Parish." On May 27, 1889, in order to expand his holdings, Auger Siess purchased two parcels of pine land in Grant Parish, one containing 636 acres, the other 159 acres, along with all the buildings and improvements of both, from Chittenden E. Ball. The latter also sold him four pairs of timber wheels, two pair lumber cars, four log wagons, one black smith shop, one engine and boiler, one pump, one endless chain, one cut-off saw, and one well shed for which he was paid $4500.[3] Ball, who was a Kentucky born, former steamboat captain on the Red River, immediately bought another mill about three miles north, and established the Sweet Home Lumber Company, in the town he named after himself, Ball, LA.[4]

Two days after Auger Siess bought the Ball place, the *Louisiana Democrat* reported: "Mr. Auger Siess has purchased the Saw Mill of Captain C.E. Ball on the north side of the river near Rigolette. Mr. Siess will shortly take charge and 'move out' with his family."[5] He and Fannie had buried a two day old infant, the previous year at the Jewish Cemetery in Pineville, and his wife was pregnant with a daughter, Rae Ethel Siess, who was born on July 16, 1889. Soon after her birth, Auger and his family moved out into what the locals called the "piney woods." The same issue of the paper reported that Auger, his brother-in-law Charles Goldenberg, Michael Aaron, and Coleman Greenwood went on a fishing trip to Bayou Flaggon (spelled Bayou Flaquin in older maps), just north of Levin, La.[6] This was, no doubt, also a scouting expedition in search of new sites to develop for their growing lumber empire.

In a short typescript history of the Tioga Community and Tioga Baptist Church, compiled in 1968, by Luthur C. Terrell and J. Randall Deen, it was recalled that : "Mr. Bob Ball sold his mill near Merritt's store to two businessmen in Alexandria, Siess and Levin. They began to ship their lumber to northern cities by rail. They built several houses for their employees and established a post office. They called it Levin, Louisiana." Tioga historian, Jimmie Nelle Adams Lewis gave further details of the Siess and Levin enterprise:

> *The first rough cut by the mill was usually to build the company houses for the workers and their families. These dwellings were built almost entirely of wood,[...] The company did not skimp on quality, and some of its best lumber products went into the construction of its houses, a fact attested to by the many original homes still standing today along Tioga Road, Second and Third Streets. Houses [...] were built from only two or three basic shotgun designs, with some variation in size to accommodate different-sized families. Rent was charged at a nominal rate, usually based on the number of rooms. [...] Water and electricity were furnished to the residents for about $5.00 a month.*[7]

Siess and Levin also built a boarding house for the single men and provided them with three meals a day. Because of the isolation, these communities had to be self-sufficient, providing a physician, a minister, a barber, and clerks to staff the company store. Most mill towns paid their workers in script or brass money that could only be used to purchase items at the commissary and for meals at the boarding house. Although peddlers were allowed in the community, the absence of American money in anyone's hands, assured Siess and Levin that they really had no competition when it came to the purchasing power of their workers. After Auger Siess and family moved to Levin, he opened up the Levin Post Office which was located in the commissary building near the railroad tracks, and became its first postmaster.

He and Fannie soon learned that a saw mill town could be a lawless place. There were not only small families like his who were trying to live a peaceful life, but also many young, single men, who spent their off-hours drinking and carousing in the saloons that sprang up in the town. With the bars, came the women, imported for their pleasure, which made the dusty main street a veritable red light district. Under these circumstances violence was no stranger to the community. In December 1889, the *Louisiana Democrat* reported: "Homicide – At Siess' saw mill in this Parish, on the north side of Red River, about nine miles from Alexandria on Friday last, Steve Yarn killed his cousin, Scipio Yarn, the weapon used (we learn) being a whip handle, with which the dead man was struck on the head and face, the wounds from which caused death. These are the only particulars learned. Scipio Yarn, so reports say, was drunk at the time. Steve Yarn surrendered on Monday and was placed in jail, to await a preliminary trial." [8]

Fannie Levin Siess returned briefly to Alexandria from the Levin lumber mill in 1892 to await the birth of her third child, Eunice Vida Siess, on June 24th. Because Fannie and Auger's eldest child, Leo Chester, was of school age he had had to remain in Alexandria during the academic year. Until 1894 there had been no schools recognized by the Rapides Parish school board in the Levin area, referred to as the Rigolette or Ward 10. In January 1894 that would change. A list of Ward 10 schools appeared in the minutes of the Alexandria Board, including the "Suss Mill School," with Bertie Grayson as the teacher. Nothing further is known about this one room school, except that it was located in Levin and was probably started by Auger Siess for his and the other children living in the piney woods.[9] With some education available, it was now possible for the Siess family to remain together for longer periods of time. Auger and Fannie's fourth child, Lucille Beatrice, was born in Levin on November 4, 1894.

***

Auger's brother, Emmanuel, seven years his junior, had been living in Mansura helping out on the family farm. His mother, Josette, he and his two younger brothers, Isaac and Louis, were the only ones left at home. In 1888 Emmanuel began courting a young lady in Marksville, Rose Henriette Firment. They were married by the Reverend A. Chorin of St. Joseph's Roman Catholic Church in Marksville on January 23, 1889.[10] Their first child, Marie Isabelle, was born on December 3rd of the same year and baptized by Father Chorin on January 18, 1890.[11]

Emmanuel's bride, Henriette, was the youngest of seven children of Paul Michel Firment and his wife, Adele Dieudonné, French immigrants who had settled in Marksville, marrying there on January 13, 1859.[12] Paul Michel Firment was a watchmaker and jeweler in Marksville. He eventually opened a saloon and ran it until his death in 1873 when he fell into a cistern behind his place of business and was drowned. Thereafter his wife, Adele, attended the saloon until her death in 1890. The division of her property caused a family feud between two of her sons, Edmond and Jules, which was so vituperative that the former changed his name, becoming simply Edmond Michel. His brothers, Jules and Alfred, kept the name "Firment," as did Emmanuel's wife, Henriette. The two brothers never spoke to one another again, although Edmond Michel owned a general store on one side of Main Street, while Jules Firment ran the town pharmacy diagonally across from him.

Shortly before his first child's birth, Emmanuel had taken a job as the Deputy Constable of Marksville.[13] On July 31, 1892, the couple's second child, Lenox Leopold Siess, was born. The boy was baptized by Father A. Chorin on September 10th of the same year.[14] As his family grew, Emmanuel, seeing how difficult it was for him to make a living in Marksville, was encouraged by his older brother, Auger, to join him in Alexandria in the lumber business, which was, near the turn of the twentieth century, in its heyday. In May 1891, Julius Levin, his son, Jacob, and two sons-in-law, Charles Goldenberg and Auger Siess, bought a sawmill and 10,876 acres of pine land from Mrs. Mary J. Waters for $29,690 in order to expand their logging empire.[15] Since the family needed help managing their holdings, one by one, Auger Siess' brothers were brought into the business.

In 1894, Auger finally convinced his younger brother, Emmanuel, who had previously invested in timber land in Grant Parish, to move his family to Alexandria. Emmanuel's third child, Elmo Paul, was born there on January 12, 1895.[16] Another brother, Isaac Edouard Siess, was induced to move to Levin in 1895, but in a different capacity. He had graduated from Tulane Medical School in April 1894 and opened an office at the Levin Building on Murray Street in

Alexandria.[17] The *Louisiana Democrat* announced that he had moved up to the Levin lumber camp on February 11, 1895, to practice medicine.[18] The position was lucrative as the Siess /Levin operation deducted $2.00 per month from each employee to pay for any medical attention necessary, the majority of which went to the company physician as a salary. Since Dr. Siess was unmarried, life in a lumber camp was no hardship for him. Five months after his brother's arrival the Auger Siess family was able to move from Levin back to Alexandria to a home that had been previously owned by Jonas Hiller, who had just relocated to Bastrop, LA.[19]

Auger and Emmanuel Siess made their first land purchase together, 165 acres in Grant Parish, on September 21, 1895 from Charles Bringhorst, for $720.[20] In April of the following year Auger and Emmanuel, in business as the Siess Bros., bought at auction two parcels of school land containing approximately 160 acres just across the border in Grant Parish, near Levin, Louisiana, for $520 with $52 down, and the rest in promissory notes.[21] It was around this time that Emmanuel became an elections' commissioner, along with Walter Bell and William Brashear from an area called "Bell's" which was in the Rigolette Ward, or Ward 10 of Rapides Parish.[22] On June 6th, the brothers bought, with another partner, Willis F. Johnson, 160 acres of land and 160 acres of timber rights from Ernest and Henry Hardtner for $340 with a promise to pay off the original mortgage. This property included a sawmill and all the machinery to make it operate. In October of the same year, the Siess Brothers bought another 320 acres of timber land, which included a second sawmill operation from Willis Johnson, for $2500. After a down payment of $500, the brothers were to pay the Hardtner Bros. to whom Johnson was originally indebted, one hundred dollars per month for twenty months.[23] Finally, in November 1896, Julius Levin sold six and two-thirds acres of land on Bayou Rapides north of Alexandria, along with the planing mill, machinery, and fixtures in consideration of a payment of $8,330 to the Siess Bros.[24]

In 1897 Emmanuel and Henriette Siess, now the parents of Edna Louise, born on April 25, 1895, and Nellie Adele, born on June 16, 1897, moved north into Grant Parish, about five miles beyond the town of Pollock, to a place called Sand Spur where he established a sawmill. Gladys Selvidge Brewer, in her book about the town of Pollock, spoke of the little community: "Sand Spur, like Simms, was a large town, having a Post Office called Siess. The Siess Sawmill established in 1897, carried on a large volume of lumber business. Any commodity needed for living could be procured at the commissary, which was located one mile from Antonia. The store which was built near the railroad, boasted of a loading platform which enabled employees to ship supplies to all points." [25] There was a school as well which took pupils up to the seventh grade. Emmanuel Siess was appointed the postmaster at Siess, Louisiana on August 28, 1897.[26] Ella Beth Siess wrote: "Papa, known to his friends as Nell Siess, a very good mixer, had gone to the Piney Woods before he and Mama married and went into partnership with a Mr. Nugent in a sawmill. He also bought land that was known as Flagon Falls, in the deep setting of the Piney Woods, which, Mama, as I remember as a child telling her friends and relatives, was a lovely large log home, with a big front porch, and one could smell the pines for miles around but to her that was a mansion of aching hearts." [27] Ella Beth also remembered that her father distilled corn liquor in the woods, ran around with the "loose" women in the lumber camps, and the prostitutes in the red light district in Alexandria. Henriette, who was a refined city woman from Marksville, never got used to the woods, as she said the women drank heavily so she refused to associate with them. Had it not been for the family of James Monroe Nugent, and her many trips into Alexandria, where she was always warmly welcomed by her Jewish sisters-in-law, she would have lost her mind.

On November 20, 1895, Dr. Isaac Siess married Helena Margery Berger, a native of Woodville in Wilkinson County, Mississippi. Helena was the eldest of the seven children of Marcus Isaac Berger, a native of Georgia, and his German born wife, Johanna Starn Davis, whose first husband, Jacob, had died of yellow fever in 1867 at the Circus Street (later, Rampart Street) Infirmary in New Orleans, leaving her with an infant daughter, Henrietta. [28] Marcus was a gunsmith, who also repaired stoves, sewing machines, umbrellas and sharpened gin and wood saws. Isaac and Helena Berger Siess' first two children, Clotile Margery, born on September 23, 1897, and Guy Edward, born on July 12, 1898, spent their first years in Siess, Louisiana, where Dr, Siess, formerly at Levin, had moved to join his brother, Emmanuel, at the latter's sawmill town. In June 1897, Dr. Siess travelled to Alexandria where he and a group of other physicians founded the Central Louisiana Medical and Surgical Association. He was elected the vice-president from Grant Parish.[29] That same year, while living in Siess, Dr. Siess formed a partnership with James "Uncle Jimmy" Sumerall to open the Portable Mills Lumber Co.[30] Nineteenth century doctors usually diversified their interests because it was so difficult to make a good living as a physician. Throughout his career Dr. Isaac would look for various ways to supplement his income. Shortly before the turn of the century, as the mill's output began to diminish, Dr. Siess moved his family from Siess to Lincecum, another, more productive, lumber camp town in Grant Parish where he, his wife and two children were enumerated in the 1900 Federal Census[31] In August of that year he was appointed to the Grant Parish Board of Health for Ward 4, and tasked with examining all suspected cases of small pox.[32]

On July 1, 1897, the Siess Bros. planing mill in Alexandria, which had been bought the previous year from Julius Levin, burned to the ground, despite the prompt arrival of the local fire department. It was estimated that the loss was, including lumber, at least fourteen thousand dollars. As were most sawmills, whose main danger was always the threat of fire, it was heavily insured for the entire amount.[33] Just a year later Julius and Jacob Levin, Charles Goldenberg, and Auger Siess sold the twenty-five acre tract of land where the planning mill had stood to the Rapides Bank for $17,000. The sale was noted in the *Louisiana Democrat* as one of the largest ever to take place in Alexandria with seventeen dollars' worth of revenue stamps being affixed to the deed.[34]

Auger and Fannie's last child, Gladys Josephine Siess, was born on May 28, 1898, after they had moved back to Alexandria. Auger and Emmanuel sold the Sand Spur (Siess) Saw Mill on October 1,

1898, for $4500 cash to James Monroe Nugent. Included in the transaction was the forty acre tract on which the sawmill was located, the mill itself, including the engine and boiler, and all other fixtures, the dry kiln platforms, as well as 600 acres of timber land, and 240 acres of cut timber.[35] Emmanuel remained at the Siess mill, however, as the manager. Auger travelled back and forth to Levin, Louisiana, on a regular basis, and was still, as of 1899, the postmaster there.

***

Leopold's youngest child, Louis Preston Siess, went straight to work out of high school, clerking in his brother Auger's store in Levin, Louisiana, according to his grandson, Charles Preston Siess, Jr. He later joined Emmanuel in Siess, LA to become the clerk and book keeper in the company store near Antonia, a job he held until the summer of 1897, when he quit to work for James Monroe Nugent. The following story, told by his grandson may have been the reason for his having left. One day a drummer came through selling two shot derringers for $2.00 apiece. Louis asked his brother to buy some and try to resell them in the store, but he refused to do so. So Louis bought ten guns, himself, selling them for $5.00 apiece. The next time the drummer came through, his brother did not allow him buy the guns, instead, purchased them himself. Louis was furious and quit the store.

After Louis Preston Siess left home, Josette Chatelain Siess, moved in with her daughter, Hermina Siess, and her husband Abe Rich, who was a merchant in Bunkie in Avoyelles Parish. Josette subsequently sold her farm and house in Mansura to Teska Roy for eight hundred dollars in 1902.[36] She lived with Abe and Mina until Abe died in 1905, then moved in with her son, Dr. Isaac Siess, and his family. Florestine Siess Escudé and her husband, Leon, who worked side jobs as a carpenter, continued to tend the family farm, along with their eleven surviving children, including the latest additions: Jules Isaac Escudé, (b. 1887), Marie (b. 1889), Rhoda (b. 1891), Marie Belle (b. 1893), Edward Leon (b. 1897), and Anna Leah (b. 1899).[37]

***

In 1900, Auger and Fannie Siess, along with their five children were living in Alexandria with her father, Julius Levin, widowed on February 7th of that year, when his wife of forty-three years, Justine Dupuis, passed away at the age of seventy-two. [38] The household also included the elder Levin's single daughter, Flora (called "Rosa" in this record), his daughter, Johanna (Cricket) Levin Sokolosky, and her husband, Isaac, his step-daughter, Mary Aaron, her husband, Cerf Joseph and their son Julius, his grand-daughter, Ida Goldenberg and her husband, Louis Schilling and their daughter Ruby. With seventeen family members under the same roof, the Levin house on Fifth Street was straining at the rafters.[39]

By 1900, Leopold Siess' three youngest sons were all residents of Grant Parish. Dr. Isaac and his family were in Lincecum, where he was the town physician. Their third child, Estelle Johanna Siess, was born there on May 18, 1901.[40] In August 1902, Dr. Siess invested in one hundred sixty acres of timber land, north of the Emmanuel and Auger Siess holdings, close to Lincecum, which he bought from the Brister Brothers for two hundred dollars.[41] At the same time, Emmanuel and Louis Preston Siess and their families had moved twenty-nine miles away to Pollock. The town was built around the Big Creek Sawmill and Lumber Company, at the time, the largest pine mill in the world, which was founded by Jay Gould and connected by spur to his St. Louis, Iron Mountain and Southern Railway. It was managed by Captain James W. Pollock, according to Jerome Scott, the current (2010) town's mayor, where high quality bridge caps and girders were manufactured out of the long leaf yellow pine in the area. When Jay Gould died in 1890, his son, George Jay Gould, took over the railroad and the mill, and it was operated by him until most of the town and the mill were destroyed by fire in 1906. Emmanuel and Henriette Siess welcomed their next three children while living in Pollock, a son, Camille Nugent Siess (named after their neighbor in Pollock, James Monroe Nugent), born September 13, 1899, and two daughters, Mae Rose Siess, born on January 1, 1901, and Edyne Joan Siess born on July 14, 1902. The Siess Saw Mill at Sand Spur was only a little over three miles from Pollock, so Emmanuel could absent himself from home to run the place. Because Henriette had eight small children, he had built a small house behind theirs in Pollock and engaged a family to come and live there to help her out. Pollock was a "white only" town. There were no African Americans allowed there or in the forests surrounding the area so Emmanuel had to tread lightly. He succeeded in engaging a racially mixed couple who had lived in Marksville to come and stay there. "Nonk" and "Tante Thérèse" had children, so when they moved up to Pollock, to help out Henriette and her family, the Siess children had little friends with whom to play. Ella Beth Siess was told by her siblings that their Papa had engaged the couple, giving them everything that they wanted and more, so they would stay in Pollock and look after his family so he would not be obliged to do it himself. He was free, then, to carouse, drink, and see his women as he pleased.

Business dealings, according to Ella Beth, between James Monroe Nugent and Emmanuel Siess were becoming strained because Nugent was a gentleman, and he and his family were horrified by Emmanuel's conduct. Nugent had sold Emmanuel Siess, another of his mill properties in 1901 for $8,000 mostly in promissory notes, containing almost 800 acres of timber land, as well as a sawmill, seventeen yolk of oxen, five wagons, a lot of chains, fifteen head of mules complete with harness and gear, seven tram cars, with a tram road running from said road to Brewer's spur. It specifically excluded all the lumber stock on hand, but did include the timber contracts with two clients.[42] In June of the following year Emmanuel sold the same property back to Nugent for $7250. Whether these transactions heralded the end of a friendship, or were simply legal machinations to avoid creditors is not known.[43]

As the nineteenth century gave way to the twentieth, all three brothers were heavily invested in the Grant Parish lumber business, which was at its peak, but destructive fires and the eventual denuding of the landscape as the yellow long leaf pine was cut down, ushered in a time of declining production. In 1900 the St. Louis, Iron Mountain and Southern Railway reported to the Railroad Commission of

Louisiana that it had completed the following improvements to Siess connected lumber enterprises: a spur for the Tioga Lumber Co., at Levins (sic) Louisiana, a connecting track at the same location, a spur to the planing mill at Levins, an extension of the J.M. Nugent spur, as well as an extension of the spur to the Sand Spur Lumber Company at Siess, Louisiana.[44] Soon, however, Emmanuel Siess would be gone and most of Levin/Tioga, Louisiana would burn to the ground. Julius Levin was growing older and his son-in-law and other partners were looking for an easier, safer way to make a living.

***

Auger Siess and the others, having made their fortune in the lumber business, were looking to move on to the next opportunity. It came in a big way, when on January 10, 1901 the world went "oil crazy." Formerly Pennsylvania had been the only state with any oil production. But recently Spindletop, the first well in Texas had been discovered. Several business men in Alexandria wasted no time in jumping on the bandwagon. On June 22, 1901, *The New Orleans Item* ran a small story about a new company which had just been organized in both Texas and Louisiana and called itself the Southern Development Company of Alexandria. The partners, Auger Siess, president, A.M. Brasher, vice president, C.A. Lehman, treasurer, Charles Clark, secretary and F.S. Hoyt, all residents of Rapides Parish and several former lumbermen, had put together five hundred thousand dollars and acquired perpetual leases on 102 acres of land near Nacogdoches, Texas. They were to begin drilling in July.[45]

Yet it was not Auger who would become the big-time oil baron in the Siess family, but his youngest brother, Louis Preston Siess, who had just joined a mercantile establishment run by Charles P. Mathis. On December 4, 1898, Louis Siess married Charles Mathis' daughter, Minnie Ann, in Winnfield, LA and the couple returned to Pollock to live.[46] However, in 1901 Louis Siess and Charles Mathis decided to return to Winnfield, some forty miles to the north to open the Mathis & Siess general store. The place was known affectionately as "Siess and Roebuck," by the townspeople, who knew they could find just about anything they needed there. A resident of the town, R.W. Oglesby, remembering in 1932 what early life was like in Winnfield reported that "the largest store in town was that of Mathis and Seiss (sic). It stood right where the Peoples Hardware is now located and was housed in the big warehouse just back of the hardware and now fronting on Bevill Street. The stores around the square all had front galleries just as country stores have and what sidewalks they had were out in the street." [47]

After the birth of his first child, Charles Preston Siess, on July 8, 1901, in Winnfield, Louis sought to put together a group of people to explore for the oil, which he was sure was in the parish. On August 30, 1902, the Winnfield Oil Company, Limited, the first outfit to drill in Winn Parish, with a capital stock of two hundred thousand dollars was incorporated with Louis Preston Siess as its president. P.K. Abel was the vice president, J.T. Durham, treasurer, C.M. Bevill, secretary, and B. W. Bailey, general manager. A well of about 2,000 feet deep was to be drilled because shallower attempts had not produced any significant output.[48] Stock was sold at one dollar per share with 2500 people purchasing what they thought would be their ticket to a wealthy future. Winnfield Oil Well No. 1 was drilled at the Cedar Creek salt lick two miles south east of Winnfield and brought in on July 17, 1903. There was, however, little production, and after other attempts to make a go of it, the company went out of existence in May 1914.[49] Fortunately, Louis Siess had a lucrative general store, and the family prospered. Before they left for greener pastures in Calcasieu Parish, their second child, Robert Edward Siess, was born on September 6, 1903, followed by Helen Louise on August 3, 1910, John Dee on September 15, 1911, and Jack on July 16, 1913.[50]

Following in the footsteps of his youngest brother, Louis, Dr, Isaac Siess moved his family from Lincecum to Winnfield in 1903 to set up a practice in medicine. [51] He also opened up a pharmacy he called the City Drug Company. It had a small soda fountain in the front, and he saw patients in the back of the store, or travelled on horseback to their homes. He employed two clerks and a helper. The move proved to be very profitable for him, and his two school-age children had a better grade school to attend. Although Isaac and his brother, Louis, had been baptized as Catholics, they were not observant. Louis' wife had been raised in the Baptist Church, a Protestant denomination which was particularly strong in Northern Louisiana. Isaac's wife, Helena, who was raised in Woodville, MS, where there was quite a large Hebrew community, found herself, once again, in a small town where she could not practice her faith She made the best of it, however, joining the Presbyterian Ladies' Aid Society, where the ongoing topic was the study of missionary work in Africa undertaken by the church.[52] In March 1904, Dr. Siess called a meeting with seven other physicians in Winn Parish in order to form the Winn Parish Medical Society. Dr. Siess was elected its first president.[53]

In January 1905 Louis Siess, and some of the other merchants in Winnfield found out that the Sulphur Timber and Lumber Company, which owned large tracts of wooded land in Winn and Grant Parishes was considering the establishment of a sawmill in Ruston, Louisiana. Siess and the others immediately opened negotiations with the president of the company, O.E. Hodge, asking him to consider Winnfield. A meeting was held at which fifteen or so interested citizens, including Dr. Isaac Siess and his brother, Louis, met with a representative of Sulphur Lumber. It was agreed that if the town would furnish the building site free of charge, indemnify them from municipal taxes for a period of ten years, assure them the protection of their labor force, some of whom would be African American, that the saw and planning mill would be built there. Sulphur further agreed that it would not build a commissary, but let the merchants of the town profit from increased business brought by their hundreds of workers. The company indicated that it would cut 40,000 board feet of lumber per day, from the sixty million feet of standing timber that it owned, an undertaking which would take from five to eight years. The company agreed additionally, that if for any reason the mill was not constructed that the people who subscribed to pay for the land would be reimbursed for their investment by them. Unfortunately the town was unable to raise enough money from its subscribers to purchase the land.

A second contract was negotiated and signed on March 31, 1905. Louis Siess, H.T. Pye, B. W. Bailey, and O.M. Grisham agreed to make up the difference between what was raised by the townspeople and what it would cost to buy the property for the mill site in consideration of which the lumber company would allow Louis Siess to expand his trade to include the mill employees, as long as the prices charged to them did not exceed prices that were paid by local residents. Louis Siess was to pay the company eight per cent of the profit on his sales to its employees, provided that the company kept the books, and paid Siess two per cent profit on a monthly basis. From this money Siess was to reimburse Pye, Bailey and Grisham, for their additional contributions to the land purchase. Sulphur built the saw and planing mill, as promised, in Winnfield in the summer of 1905 and the town profited greatly from its new population of mill workers. However, in the summer of 1906, Sulphur entered into negotiations with the Grant Timber and Manufacturing Co., to sell its mill and most of its timber, and agreed to close down the Winnfield operation in January 1907. Siess and the other participants in this deal sued the Sulphur Lumber company asking that it be enjoined from selling its interests in Winnfield because it had originally agreed to stay, at least five years. The case went all the way to the Louisiana Supreme Court and was finally decided in April of 1907. The injunction against selling the mill was lifted, and the suit was remanded for further action on the facts of the case. The mill, however, operated in Winnfield through at least 1909, but not under the conditions drawn up in the contract, which had afforded Louis Siess and the others the two per cent commission.[54]

Despite this setback, Dr. Siess and his brother, Louis, continued to promote the welfare of the town. When they arrived in 1903, Winnfield had had only three hundred inhabitants. By April 1907 there were over 3,500 townspeople. Dr. Siess was the president of the Progressive League, who with M.C. Bagwell, vice-president, and J.D. Pace, secretary, sought to bring even more business to the town. While the Sulphur project was not an unqualified success, Winnfield now had an independent planing mill, a retail lumber business and an ice house. The City Hotel, as well as a new two story town hall, were also built.

Because of its location in the yellow pine forest, three railroads had already entered the town: the Louisiana Railway and Navigation Co., the Louisiana and Arkansas, and the Rock Island. In addition, Dr. Siess and J. D. Pace sponsored a short line railway to be built from Winnfield out to the oil field, three miles south of town, and called it the Winnfield Oil Well Railway. It was constructed not only for the convenience of the oil field workers but also for the townspeople, because one of the wells, instead of producing oil, had produced a salt water spring. The Progressive League, wishing to turn a faltering oil business into success, proposed building a bath house with two salt water pools, which would be open winter and summer at a nominal price to the public.[55] Unfortunately, after purchasing the right of way and building some track, the project grew too costly and the Oil Well Railway was scrapped. The bath house was built, however, operating from June to October in 1908, showing a profit of $439.95 of which ten percent was paid in royalties to the Winnfield Oil Company.[56] The town also supported two banks: the Bank of Winnfield, of which Dr. Isaac Siess was one of the two vice-presidents, and the Winnfield Parish Bank. Dr. Siess remained an officer of the bank, finally serving on its board of directors until his departure from Winnfield in 1913. It was there, also, that he joined the Eastern Star Masonic Lodge No. 151.

The Isaac and Louis Siess families were both enumerated in the 1910 federal census in Winnfield. Dr. and Mrs. Siess owned their own home on Front Street and employed a live-in servant. Their children, Clotile, age thirteen, Guy, age eleven, and Estelle, nine years old, attended school in the town. Dr. Isaac's mother, Josette Chatelain Siess, seventy-two years old, had come to live with them.[57] Dr. Siess closed his drugstore in August 1910 and the next month he decided to divest himself of the brick, 45X100 building advertising it for sale.[58] This was a prelude to his final decision in the spring of 1913 to move back to Alexandria with his family to be near to his brother, Auger, Fannie and their children.

In 1910 Louis Preston Siess, his wife Minnie Mathis and his two sons, Charlie and Robert, lived on the outskirts of Winnfield. Minnie was expecting her third child, Helen. His in-laws, Charles and

Rachel Bolton Mathis, both sixty-one years of age, also lived in the household, along with a servant, Della Abney, a young African-American girl. Louis listed his occupation as oil business, and his father-in-law indicated that he was a lumberman.[59] In October 1910 Isaac and Louis Siess filed articles of incorporation for the Jessica Lumber Company, Ltd. to be operated in the town of Winnfield by J.G. Gingrass, president, Dr. Isaac Siess, vice-president, and Louis Siess, secretary and treasurer. The aim of this new corporation was to acquire timber, timber contracts and sawmills in order to conduct a general sawmill business, and would begin operations as soon as they could raise eleven thousand dollars. Gingrass and Louis Siess each bought 109 shares at fifty dollars per share, investing a total of $10,900 in the enterprise. Dr. Isaac Siess, bought two shares as well.[60] The company was in business until 1916, when the Louis Siess family moved to Vinton, LA.

***

Emmanuel Siess and family, in the meantime, had continued to live in Pollock. With eight children already and a ninth on the way, Emmanuel ran his sawmills, spent time in Alexandria with his women friends, and brewed booze in the woods. His last child, Ella Beth, was told by her sisters, that her father had a good friend, "Jake" Gould, who visited the Siess family from time to time. Jake was, in effect, George Jay Gould, who inherited the mill and the Iron Mountain Railway after his father's death in 1890. Gould had a wife who had been a stage actress, with whom he had seven children. But he also had a mistress, with whom he had two daughters and a son. Apparently, he brought his mistress over one day to visit Emmanuel's wife, Henriette, pregnant with Ella Beth, while Emmanuel was away in Alexandria on "business." Emmanuel returned unexpectedly, and flew into a rage seeing that Gould had brought his mistress out to meet his wife. He slapped Gould's companion, and the two had a violent argument which ended their friendship. It was not long after that Emmanuel loaded the family up in a wagon and brought them to Marksville, to Henriette's oldest sister, Eliza Gremillion's house. She and her husband, Alfred, already had seven children of their own, so a visit by a pregnant

Henriette with her eight children in tow must have been a daunting sight. But it was only to be for a few days. Emmanuel kissed his wife, handed her $500 and told her the "first breath he ever breathed would always be for her." He was never heard from again. After a week had passed, two of her brothers drove her and the children back to Pollock. Finding the house abandoned, and the sawmill already sold, they took the family back to Alexandria and put one month's rent down on a small house. The following month, with no more rent forthcoming, Henriette and the children were put out on the street. Her brother-in-law, Alfred Gremillion, returned to Alexandria and brought everyone back to Marksville. On September 4, 1904, the *Daily Picayune* ran two small items, without knowing the back story behind this sorry event. It was reported that "Mr. A. E. Gremillion paid a visit to Alexandria Tuesday," then, in a subsequent article that "Mrs. Emanuel Siess of Alexandria, and her children reached here Wednesday [August 31]. They will make Marksville their future home." [61]

Emmanuel's disappearance was the subject of much family speculation. Some said he must have been robbed of the payroll for his sawmill, murdered and dumped in a bayou. Others saw premeditation in his actions, citing what he had said to his wife, the money he had given her, and the pre-arranged sale of the sawmill, which enabled him to run off with a red-headed prostitute from Alexandria. Emmanuel was one of only two descendants of the Siess brothers to be known to another branch of the family. Simon Siess descendant, Bill Friend, remembered that his great-uncle Leon told stories about a rowdy cousin he called "Nell," who was a brawler, but never used weapons – just a chair, with which he was rather deadly.

Once back in Marksville, Henriette's brother, Edmond Michel, had a three room shack built behind his large white house, where she raised her nine children. Ella Beth remembered the place "with cracks so big, it couldn't keep the cold out. I was born on January 30, 1905, and when I got older the people all discussed it with Mama, and I heard them all saying how awful that was. Even Dr. Sylvan DeNux, who delivered me, said all the neighbors were with Mama, and all filled the cracks with newspapers, as it was snowing while I was being born, and

Mama was in hard labor for over two days." [62] Although the large family was living rent-free on Edmond's property, very little other help was afforded to Henriette by her brothers.

Her eldest son, Lenox Leopold Siess, twelve years old, when his father disappeared, went to work right away shining shoes in Jimmy Couvillion's barber shop. Jimmy took him under his wing, teaching him his trade, so that when the family was enumerated in 1910 in Marksville, he was the only one employed. Absent from that census was Nellie Adele Siess, who at age twelve, was sent to live in Bordelonville with Henriette's brother, Alfred Firment, and his family. Although she was treated as well as the other five Firment children, her Aunt Eunice was a stern taskmaster. Adele worked with her cousins doing gardening and farm work. She always resented being sent away, and never forgave her mother. When Elmo Siess was sixteen he went to live with the Charles Gaspard family, working for them as a handyman. He also took a job at the Cappel and Armitage drugstore, where he was learning to be a pharmacist. Camille, the youngest son, had life the hardest. Just five years old when his father left, he seemed to incite the ire of his Uncle Edmond. As he got older and harder to handle, Edmond often beat the boy with a plank to straighten him out and Henriette was afraid to object because they were living rent-free. When, at age fourteen, Camille, got into trouble for stealing a watch from the drugstore where Elmo was employed, Edmond insisted that the owner press charges, even though Camille had returned the watch. Despite this, he was sent away to a boys' reformatory.

***

Shortly after Emmanuel's disappeared, his partner, Auger, whose finances had been depleted by ill-advised oil investments, moved himself and his family temporarily to New Orleans. He found employment first as a real estate agent, and finally as a clerk at the Lhote Lumber Manufacturing Co, on Carondelet Walk, at the corner of N. Dupre.[63] Fannie and the children boarded on St. Charles Avenue. This enabled their eldest son, Leo Chester Siess, to attend the New Orleans College of Pharmacy, which, much later, became a part of

Loyola University. Leo graduated in May 1909, and because of proficiency in his studies was awarded a certificate of membership to the American Pharmaceutical Association.[64] The Auger Siess family, including the newly graduated pharmacist moved back to Alexandria soon after. Auger worked as a bookkeeper in a lumber company and Leo moved away to take a job as a pharmacist in a drugstore in Iberville Parish, to save enough money to go out on his own. His sister, Rae, worked as a stenographer for a wholesale grocery, and Eunice clerked in a dry goods store. Lucille and Gladys were still in school.[65]

On January 5, 1910, Fannie Levin Siess' father, Julius, died at the age of seventy-seven while collecting rent from tenants in the Levin Quarters.[66] Occupied by African Americans, these little shotgun houses were north of the railroad and west of Monroe Street. Fannie inherited them and it fell to her husband to continue the collections. Auger also owned one-half interest in land, which had been in the name of Siess Bros. With Emmanuel gone, he finally paid taxes on two hundred forty acres of timber in Grant Parish, redeeming it for $28.52.[67]

***

After Dr. Isaac and Helena Siess moved back to Alexandria in 1913, he convinced his mother, Josette, to apply for a Confederate Widow's pension, based on Leopold's service. She filed on September 11th of that year, and mistakenly indicated that her husband had died in 1893 in Alexandria, eight years later than his actual date of death. She added that the cause of death was lung trouble. Josette named two witnesses, Edmond Michel and Adolph Bordelon, who attested to the fact that they had known her for forty years and were aware that Leopold had served in the Confederate Army. Her claim was rejected on February 14, 1914, because the last record they had of his service was in August 1863.[68] Unfortunately, four months later, on June 13, 1914, Josette succumbed, at the age of seventy-six, to a cerebral hemorrhage while in New Orleans for treatment. Her body was brought back to Mansura where she was buried at St. Paul's Cemetery on June 15th.[69]

***

In 1914, Auger's son, Leo, after working five years as a pharmacist elsewhere, finally was able to open the Siess Pharmacy in Alexandria on Monroe Street. On June 13, 1915 he married Miss Adele Liebreich, a Monroe, Louisiana native, daughter of the late Pincus Liebreich from Rogozno, Poland and his wife, Florence Kern, born in Downsville (Union Parish), Louisiana. The ceremony took place at the Y.M.H.A. Club in Monroe with Rabbi J.B. Pollak performing the service. After the luncheon that followed, the couple returned to Alexandria.[70] They had a beautiful brick house built at 1906 Monroe Street, where their only son, Chester Paul Siess, was born on July 28, 1916, delivered by his great-uncle, Dr. Isaac Siess. The family did quite well acquiring several rental properties, where an elderly Auger and Fannie Siess lived towards the end of their lives.

Leo's pharmacy was mainly a prescription business, where the clients paid on credit. Two boys on bicycles delivered the medications to his customers. By 1919 he had taken on a partner and it became the Siess & Campbell drugstore. His business, however, did not survive the depression. He was forced to declare bankruptcy in 1932, just as his son, Chester Paul, had entered Louisiana State University. He sold off all his property to pay his debts, and to be able to continue payments on his son's education. After the bankruptcy, Leo worked as a pharmacist in other drugstores in Alexandria. When the Charity Hospital was built there, he was hired to plan their pharmacy and stock it before it opened, staying on until he retired. Leo died on August 14, 1959, and was buried in the Jewish cemetery in Pineville, Louisiana alongside his wife, Adele, who had predeceased him by one year and one week. [71]

Leo and Adele's son, Chester Paul Siess, graduated from the L.S.U. College of Engineering, as a civil engineer in May 1936. After working in Louisiana as a survey party chief in the Rural Road Inventory program of the Louisiana Highway Commission during the depression, he enrolled at the University of Illinois where he received an M.S. in structural engineering in 1939. Chester met his wife, Helen Kranson, in Chicago and they married on October 5, 1941. That same year he was offered a job as a special research assistant in the Department of Theoretical and Applied mechanics at the University of Illinois and earned a PhD. in civil engineering in 1948. Their only child, Judith Ann Siess, was born in Urbana, Illinois in 1947. Chester Paul Siess went on to become the head of the Department of Civil Engineering, serving in that capacity for five years until his retirement in 1978. It was thanks to his research that many of today's modern building codes and standards were developed. Siess also served on the Nuclear Regulatory Commission, as much of his research was invaluable to the Federal Government, in their quest for safer concrete structures within proposed nuclear facilities.[72] His daughter, Judy, became a librarian, a teacher, author of seven books on library science, and a world traveler. She and her husband, Steve Bremseth, born a Lutheran, attend Synagogue services where he serves occasionally as an usher, as well as the local Lutheran Church.

Auger and Fannie's daughter, Rae Ethel Siess, married Rollo Elmer Harper who was a pressman for the Alexandria *Town Talk* newspaper. The family moved to Shreveport before the birth of their first child, Charmian Fae, and where Rollo worked for the local newspaper. The Harpers were not Jewish.

Rae's sister Eunice, married Leo Felix Lichten, an Alabama native, on April 11, 1916 at her parents' home in Alexandria. Rabbi Leonard Rothstein officiated at the wedding.[73] Leo was a merchandise broker for grocery and produce businesses in town. Their two children, Helen Elaine, delivered on September 29, 1917, by Dr. Isaac Siess, and Leo Joseph, born on November 1, 1919, spent their early years in Alexandria. The family moved to Atlanta, GA during the depression where Leo became a salesman for a flour company. The Lichten descendants remained in the Jewish faith.

Auger's daughter, Lucille Beatrice Siess, graduated from the Louisiana State Normal school at Natchitoches in 1914. She secured a position at the new Tioga high school, which opened in the fall of 1915, where she taught for several semesters before marrying Moise H. Crager on June 17, 1917. The groom, a Texas native, worked as an advertising agent. He took Lucille, his bride, back to Monroe, Louisiana to live. She died, just over a year later, on July 23, 1918, at the Alexandria Sanitarium after an emergency Caesarean section performed by her Uncle, Dr. Isaac Siess, which resulted in hemorrhage and shock.[74] She was only twenty-three years old. Lucille Crager was buried in the Jewish cemetery at Pineville, with William B. Nachman, conducting the service in the absence of Rabbi Rothstein.[75]

Auger and Fannie's youngest daughter, Gladys Josephine, was twice married, first to Chalmers Wysong, then to Hank Simpson, who was in the armed forces. In later years she moved with her second husband to Daly City, California where she died in August 1974. She never had any children or any real connection to Judaism.[76]

Auger spent the last few years of his life with his daughter Rae Siess Harper's family. He died on January 3, 1933, a few months after his fiftieth wedding anniversary, at the Tri-State Sanitarium, from bronchial pneumonia. His remains were brought back to Alexandria, and he was buried that evening at the Jewish Cemetery in Pineville. During the funeral the city bell tolled out of respect for Auger, who was for many years a prominent Alexandria resident.[77] Fannie lived another twenty years, dying on May 31, 1953 in Daly City, California, where she had been staying with her daughter, Gladys Simpson.

***

Florestine Siess Escudé's surviving children married and raised their in the Catholic Church, chosing partners from old Avoyelles families. The eldest, Louis Philippe, wed Marcelline Decuir, whose ancestors had emigrated from Hainaut, Belgium to settle in Pointe Coupée Parish. The couple had nine children, of whom five were also lifelong residents of Avoyelles. Louis owned and operated a retail store in Evergreen. Mary Pearce Hart recalled:

> *He was a very fastidious man with a well-trimmed mustache. [...]He worked in Stamps, Arkansas as a telegraph operator and commenced to learn this trade at the age of nine. [He moved to Evergreen in 1914 and] bought the old Pearce Store [...] and sold everything from guitar strings to coffin nails. He wore many hats as he was secretary-treasurer of the Evergreen Gin in 1918, a notary public, city clerk, and had served as treasurer of the Town of Evergreen. He also recorded births and deaths for the Bureau of Vital Statistics in the elegant handwriting and was an active member of the Woodmen of the World. [. . .] His store was huge and at one time there was a skating rink and theater on the second and third floors. The second floor was also used for church services until the Little Flower Catholic Church was completed in 1928. He built a fine brick home, now occupied by his grandson, Philip Heiman, who is Mayor of Evergreen. His customers called him Mr. Sears, Roebuck, because one could buy almost anything on the premises.* [78]

Florestine's daughter, Alice Josephine Escudé, married Victor Prévot, a third generation Avoyelles Parish resident on September 20, 1905. He made his living in Mansura as a photographer. The couple never had any children, and were lifelong residents of the parish.

Joseph Leopold Escudé, Sr., married Blanche Marie Tassin on December 11, 1912. He originally operated a cotton press, and then became a cotton buyer for the firm of Anderson, Clayton and Co., of Houston and New Orleans. In 1927 he graduated from the Dallas, Texas School of Mortuary Science and established the first Escudé Funeral home in Mansura.[79] Joseph and Blanche Escudé's only son, Joseph, Jr., carried on the family tradition, until his death on March 24, 2009. Joe, Jr.'s children, born to him and his wife, Inez Grayson, Gaon, Priscilla and Ira, continue to operate funeral parlors in Mansura, Cottonport, Moreauville and Simmesport, now the third generation in that business. Joseph L. Escudé, Sr's two daughters, Jocelyn and

Barbara, are lifelong residents of Mansura as well. The Escudés have always been members of St. Paul the Apostle Roman Catholic Church. Barbara Escudé, the widow of John V. Lemoine, and a retired Executive vice-president of the Union Bank of Marksville in her eightieth year, continues her devotion to the faith as an altar server and reader at St. Paul the Apostle Church and has become a Benedictine Oblate, associated with the Mother of the Redeemer Monastery at Plaisance (St. Landry Parish), LA.

Léon and Florestine's son, Jules, who married Annie Ducôté, from another one of Avoyelles Parishes first families, raised his two sons, Gerard and Landry, in Mansura. Jules, following in his great-uncle David's footsteps, was Mayor of Mansura from 1933 to 1937 and from 1943 through 1956. He was the owner of a Shell Distributorship, as well as a banker, in Mansura for twenty-five years.[80] His children and grandchildren, all Catholic, were all lifelong Louisiana residents.

Florestine's daughter, Rhoda Escudé, married Albert Fulgence Coco, great-great-grandson of Dominic Baldony, dit Coco who emigrated from Venice, Italy to Pointe Coupée Parish around 1780. Coco descendants eventually made Avoyelles their home. Albert Coco, a widower with three children, wed Rhoda in 1918. The couple had five children of their own and lived in the village of Voorhies, where they ran a family farm.

Edward Leon Escudé and his wife, Elma Cecilia Lemoine, lived their whole lives in Mansura as well. Edward, a veteran of World War I, farmed and worked at odd jobs. Their son, Edward, Jr., born in 1936, relocated to Metairie, Louisiana as a young man. Florestine's daughter, Leah, never married, living with her mother, until the latter's death. Leah died in Mansura on September 15, 1974, at the age of seventy-five.

Three of Florestine's daughters and two sons moved away from Avoyelles Parish. The daughters, Marie, Marie Belle and Henriette, all married men employed by the Texas and Pacific Railway. Their husbands' jobs took them to other Louisiana parishes. Emile Escudé, whose twin Edouard, died as an infant, married and moved to Slidell in St. Tammany Parish. Benjamin, Florestine's youngest son, married Sephora Laborde, also from one of Avoyelles first families. He tried working in Mansura as an auto mechanic, but by 1930 he, his wife, and daughter, Gloria, had moved to Alexandria, where he worked as a clerk in an ice plant.

Florestine's husband, Leon P. Escudé, died on March 13, 1925, in Mansura, and is buried in St. Paul the Apostle Catholic Church Cemetery. Florestine, who died in Mansura ten years later, on September 29, 1935, is buried alongside of him. All of the Escudé family members remained loyal to their Catholic faith.

***

Emmanuel Siess' wife, Rose Henriette Firment, died on February 19, 1922, and was buried in St. Joseph Catholic Cemetery in Marksville. Henriette Siess' last eighteen years of her life, since the disappearance of her husband, Emmanuel, had been filled with sorrow. She raised her nine children in poverty, in a house without running water or heat. After graduation from high school, her eldest two daughters, Belle (Marie Isabelle) and Edna, moved to Alexandria and lived rent free with their uncle Auger and his wife, Fannie Siess, and later on, with Dr. Isaac and Helena Siess. They got jobs in local department stores and sent money back home to support the other children in Marksville. Both girls met and married men in Alexandria. Belle wed Albert Gallatin Leckie in 1915. Two sons were born to them, one of whom was killed in action in 1945 at Luzon in the Philippines.[81] After the death of Henriette Siess in 1922, Albert and Belle Leckie took the youngest of Emmanuel and Henriette Siess' children, Ella Beth, to live with them in Rapides Parish.

Edna married into the Glasscock family. Her husband was the grandson of steamboat captain Louis Downing Glasscock, a Kentucky native, who moved to Louisiana, married Charlotte Marie Lacour of Pointe Coupée Parish, and settled across the Atchafalaya River in Avoyelles Parish. He was captain of a flat-bottomed side wheeler, the

John Armstrong, which first appeared in January 1844 advertising for passengers and freight out of New Orleans for Bayous Atchafalaya and des Glaises in Avoyelles Parish.[82] By 1858 he was master of the *Silver Moon,* described as a "light draught packet steamer" which left New Orleans for Bayou des Glaises, Simmesport, Old River and all intermediate landings.[83] Louis Downing Glasscock's eldest son, Giles Ambrose Glasscock, followed in his father's footsteps, and both were in charge of boats on Avoyelles waters in the 1870s. Giles was the master of the passenger packet *Rapides* which operated on the Red River from the mouth of the Cane River, to Cotile, Alexandria, and Normand's and Barbin's Landings in Avoyelles Parish,[84] at the same time his father was Captain of the *Creole,* servicing the landings on Bayou des Glaises. His namesake and youngest son, Louis Downing, Jr., met and married Irma Australia Aymond, who was a Mansura resident. They settled in Cottonport, worked a small farm, and raised eleven children, of whom Benning Jerrol Glasscock was the youngest, born on July 18, 1893. When Edna met Benning he was a saloon keeper in Alexandria. They married in 1914, and had two children, Ura Mae, and Benning Jerrol, Jr.

Four years before his mother, Henriette's death, Lenox Leopold Siess, who had been working in a barber shop in Bunkie, left Avoyelles Parish, to work as a barber in Baton Rouge. Postponing any thought of marriage, he was able to send home more money to help his mother and sisters. Several years passed and Lenox moved to New Orleans, to go into partnership with Louis Broussard, establishing the Royal Perfume Company with two showcases of scents which the two men blended themselves. Shortly after his mother's death, Lenox, then almost thirty-one years old, wed twenty-three year old Heloise Marie Navarro, a school teacher whose ancestors were originally from La Mancha, Spain. The couple, married in Baldwin, St. Mary Parish, in 1923, and settled in New Orleans, where their two children, Lenox Leopold, Jr. and Héloïse Marie were born.

The Royal Perfume Company grew out of its quarters and moved to 308 Royal Street. Barber and beauty supplies and equipment were added. In 1936 Broussard bought a four story building at 136

Chartres Street and the Royal Beauty Supply Company, Inc. was organized, with Broussard as the president and general manager. Lenox Siess acted as salesmen, travelling throughout Louisiana, Mississippi, Alabama and Florida, and was its secretary-treasurer.[85] Lenox Sr. was associated with the company until his retirement in 1957. He died in New Orleans at the age of seventy-eight, on December 24, 1970.

Lenox and Héloïse's son, Lenox, Jr., a World War II, Iwo Jima survivor, came out unscathed, but, reported, that he wore out a rosary or two while in the service. Upon his return in 1945 he finished college and became a high school English teacher. He married Nhodymay Julia Demesia in 1956. Their two sons, Philip and Douglas, were born in New Orleans where Lenox, Jr. continued his education, receiving his M.Ed. in 1958. He retired from the local school system as a co-Principal. His sister, Heloise, married Edmond Mastio in 1947 and they had four children, Glen, Jean, James and Deborah.

Both Elmo and Camille Siess were veterans of World War I. Before the war, Elmo worked in Oil City, Louisiana, north of Shreveport and Camille was unemployed. Upon returning from duty, they both left for the oil fields again, first back to Oil City and finally to Texas to work as laborers. Elmo seldom visited his relatives back in Louisiana, only making it back briefly for Henriette's funeral in 1922. He worked in Denver, Colorado, then moved to Arthur City, Texas, where he lived with his wife, Ora. They had no children.

Camille, who had been so badly abused by his Uncle Edmond Michel, had an equally disappointing life. He eventually wound up in Los Angeles selling newspapers at a corner stand for over twenty years. He and his wife, Margie, never had children. Donald Clement, his nephew, remembered him as a person always in such dire straits that it is a wonder he managed to live as long as he did: "You have to understand that Camille dressed just like Dick Tracy, hat, large coat lapels; and he even introduced himself to people as, 'FBI-man Camille!' This uncle of mine carried a fake badge, and had a white envelope (in which he carried his poke) pinned to the inside of his coat

– I had no idea that safety pins were made so large, as his was about 3 inches long." [86] After Camille's wife died he came to live with his younger sister, Mae Rose, but they fought so much that he finally went to live with a friend in Jefferson Parish. He died at the age of seventy-five, on October 26, 1974, in Metairie, Louisiana.

Nellie Adele Siess worked her way through the Louisiana State Normal School at Natchitoches (now Northwestern State University of Louisiana). After graduation in March 1918, she got a job teaching in Echo, Avoyelles Parish, then in Delhi, La, in Richland Parish where she taught the third and fourth grade. She married twice and had one child, Carl Hardy, Jr. from her first marriage. Nellie died of cancer at the age of fifty, on July 30, 1947 at a sanitarium in Shreveport.[87]

Two of Emmanuel Siess' youngest daughters, Edyne and Mae Rose Siess, eventually went to live in New Orleans with their cousin, Mary Rich Cone, who was childless.[88] Mae Rose took a three month secretarial course, and got a job right away. Mary Cone did not charge Mae Rose or Edyne rent, but made them do her housework on the weekends. Mae Rose saved money to send to support her mother in Marksville. After their mother died, Edyne went to Alexandria and worked in the cigar stand at the Hotel Bentley. She eventually moved back to New Orleans, to live with Mae Rose, when the latter's boys were young. She moved out, to her own apartment in the French Quarter in the late 1930s, and worked for many years at the Elmer's Candy Company. Marrying only at the age of fifty-seven, she was widowed the next year. She died in New Orleans on June 17, 1964, of a cerebral hemorrhage as the result of injuries from a mugging she and her sister, Mae Rose, had suffered at the hands of two thugs who had tried to rob them.

Mae Rose married Clay Leopold Clement, Sr. at St. Anthony of Padua Church on July 17, 1922, in New Orleans. The couple separated in early 1928, because Clay was an alcoholic. Mae and Clay's two sons, Clay, Jr. born on January 4, 1925, and Donald Martin, born on June 20, 1927, were raised by a single mother, who worked hard all her life to put food on the table. The family lived in a series of small apartments, for a while living just down the street from cousin, Mary Rich Cone, on South Alexander Street. Donald and his brother both served during World War II, both married, had children, grandchildren and great-grand-children. Donald worked in highway, bridge and drainage construction in Jefferson, Orleans, St. Charles and St. Bernard parishes for decades, spending the last twenty-five years as the head of his own firm. In his spare time Donald and his wife Patsy, their children, and grandchildren, toured the world, making many trips to Europe, South America and Russia. Before leaving for what was then the U.S.S.R., Donald learned Russian. Upon return, local Jewish organizations, who were sponsoring newly arriving Russian Jews into the community asked him to help. He sponsored many families, providing jobs, advice, and sometimes money to help them along. An avid astronomer, at the age of thirty-six he designed his own lens, a model that was featured in the December 1962 issue of *Sky and Telescope* calling it the "Clement Reflector," amazingly built for the princely sum of $43.25. Many of the family trips were planned around the appearances of comets or solar eclipses around the world which he would study and photograph, and his images being treasured by those who have them. Donald's brother, Clay, Jr., a retired employee of the New Orleans Levee Board, and his wife Donna Miller raised seven children: Clay III (b. 1950), Craig (b. 1952), Cheryn (b. 1955) Carl (b.1956), Charlene (b. 1958), Curry (b. 1960), and Curt (b. 1961). Mae Rose Siess passed away on July 30, 1990, in Metairie, LA. She never remarried.

The youngest of Emmanuel and Henriette Siess' children, Ella Beth, who never knew her father, was seventeen when her mother died. After graduating from high school she went to live with her oldest sister, Belle Leckie, in Alexandria, where she met and married Henry Jerome Treadway, a city fireman. The couple had four daughters, Gloria Henriette, Betty Jo, Carmen Elaine and Mary Nell. They were lucky that, during the Depression, Henry's father owned a grocery store and twenty-seven rental houses. Each of his four sons, upon their marriage, was allowed to pick one of the houses and live rent free. Henry and Ella Beth's girls grew up in Alexandria and married there.

They gave her fifteen grandchildren. Unfortunately Henry Treadway was an alcoholic, but Ella Beth kept the marriage going. The couple retired to Lafayette, Lousiana where Henry died in 1969. Ella Beth died on February 17, 1988, in Bourg, Terrebonne Parish, LA. All of the descendants of Emmanuel and Henriette Siess remained faithful to their Christian roots.

***

Dr. Isaac Edouard Siess' children finished their schooling in Alexandria. Their oldest daughter, Clotile, married John Morrill Shaw, a machinist who was working at the Ruston Foundry and Machine Co., in 1915. When first wed, they lived with Dr. Siess and his wife on Holly Street in Alexandria. Two of their children, Helen, born on August 5, 1916, and Morrill Edward, born on December 7, 1917, spent their early childhood there at the family home. In 1922, John and Clotile Shaw moved to Baton Rouge, where he began a long career with Standard Oil Company. In 1928 the family adopted a third child, John Siess Shaw, born in Natchez, MS, that year.

Isaac and Helena's only son, Guy Edward Siess, eloped with Alice Weldon, of Boyce, LA. They were married on June 11, 1921 at the Methodist Parsonage in Alexandria and only informed parents on both sides after the fact.[89] Dr. Siess and his wife, initially upset because Alice was not Jewish, eventually forgave the couple. Alice and Guy, however, later joined the Calvary Baptist Church, where he was ordained as a deacon in 1964. Guy worked as a salesman for Nabisco products, and was active in theater groups in Alexandria. Alice worked as an office nurse at a local clinic. The couple never had children. Guy died on November 26, 1974 in Alexandria. His wife followed in April of 1983.

Dr. Isaac Siess died at his home on Holly Street in Alexandria on December 4, 1923 at the age of fifty-two. Services were conducted at the family residence by Rabbi Myron Meyerovitz. He was buried at the Jewish cemetery in Pineville, where the officers of the Oliver Lodge #84 honored his passing.[90] After his death, his widow, Helena

Berger, continued to live in Alexandria with her daughter, Estelle, who never married. Helena died in Alexandria at the age of ninety, on September 13, 1960 and was buried alongside her husband in the Jewish Cemetery in Pineville, following services conducted by Rabbi Martin Hinchin.[91] Estelle died on June 4, 1989 in her eighty-eighth year at a nursing home in Pineville. She was a lifelong member of Temple Gemiluth Chassodim and is buried next to her parents in the Jewish cemetery in Pineville.[92]

Upon graduation from Louisiana State University in 1938, Dr. Isaac Siess' granddaughter, Helen Shaw, married a high school friend, Henry Leonard Bango, who graduated the same year with a B.S. in Forestry. Henry was a fourth generation Louisianan. His great-grandfather, Juan Manuel Bango, had emigrated from Spain in the early 1850s to New Orleans where his son, John Anthony Bango, was born on December 18 1853.[93] The family was from the small town of Bango, in Asturias on the northern coast of Spain, a place that had been named for an eighth century Hebrew patriot who fought against Muslim invaders. Family tradition indicates that they were "conversos," or "marranos," terms that referred to baptized Jews who were outwardly Christian but continued to practice Judaism in private. Many of these so-called "new Christians" fled Spain during the fourteenth and fifteenth centuries, for fear of being turned in by neighbors, and summarily executed for their religious beliefs. Juan Manuel Bango's son, John Anthony, married Rosa Garcia in New Orleans on April 5, 1872.[94] They raised their children as Catholics on Dauphine Street in the French Quarter. John owned a bar and restaurant which he finally lost to bankruptcy in 1897. Thereafter he worked as a bartender, and sold oysters in the French Quarter. Tony and Rosa Bango's children, Paul Leopold, Celina and Antoinette, were born and raised in New Orleans.

Paul Leopold Bango met his future wife, Sarah Glucksman, whose widowed mother, Mina, owned a second-hand clothing store on Rampart Street in New Orleans. Mina Michelson, a Russian Jewish immigrant had married Alexander Glucksman, who originally settled in Avoyelles Parish. He had served in the Civil War in the First Louisiana

Cavalry, Company G, enrolling at Marksville, in March 1862.[95] After the war he and Mina ran a grocery in Alexandria until 1881, when he was forced to declare bankruptcy. He was adjudged insane in August 1884, and spent the rest of his life at the Louisiana State Asylum in Jackson, dying there on September 11, 1891.[96] After her husband's incarceration, Mina and her five children moved to New Orleans, where her daughter, Sarah, met Paul Bango, who agreed to convert to Judaism in order to marry her. He even underwent the difficult procedure of adult circumcision. They had seven children in just nine years, losing three of them, in quick succession, as infants. Unfortunately when Sarah's two youngest children, Amelia and Henry were four and three respectively, she had a breakdown, and was finally placed at the Louisiana State Asylum in Jackson in 1916, where she lived out the rest of her life, dying there, at the age of sixty-eight, on February 4, 1948. Her remains were brought back to New Orleans where she was interred at the Dispersed of Judah Cemetery.[97]

Her husband, Paul Bango, left with four young children, took his two eldest sons, fourteen year old Alex and twelve year old Harold Bango, and moved to Baton Rouge, where he lived in a boarding house, and invested in a furniture store. He left the two youngest children, Amelia and Henry, at the Jewish Orphans Home in New Orleans.[98] They returned to their family in Baton Rouge twelve years later when they were both in high school. During their years in the State Capital, Paul and his children were members of the local synagogue.

After Henry Bango's marriage to Helen Shaw, the couple remained in Baton Rouge where he became the first consulting forester in the State of Louisiana. Henry and Helen's two daughters, Bettye Jo and Clotile Ann, were born there, just before Henry was transferred to Alexandria in 1943. The marriage did not last and the couple went their own ways. Helen remarried, moved to Michigan, and raised her family in the Christian faith. Her brothers, Morrill Edward and John Siess Shaw, likewise married and raised their children as Christians. Helen Shaw Thompson, now ninety-six and living in Michigan, remembers that, while they knew their grandparents were Jewish, they did not remember them as being particularly observant.

***

Louis Preston Siess, who had been bitten by the oil exploration bug in Winnfield, moved his family to Vinton, near Lake Charles in Calcasieu Parish in 1916. Since Vinton was just forty-six miles east of Beaumont, Texas, where the oil boom had been in full swing since 1901, it seemed a logical place to pursue his dream of striking it rich. In 1918, at forty-one years of age, Louis registered for the draft in Vinton, listing his occupation as farmer and oil producer.[99] He was definitely hedging his bets in order to protect his family while he pursued his other goals. After some measure of success in the oil business, Louis entered into a partnership with William Samuel Green, who had previously developed a one acre plot of ground, formerly a rice field, into a moneymaking oil producer in Vinton. The two men developed oil leases in Calcasieu Parish, first in the Ged fields, located a few miles southwest of Vinton, where they became very successful. Bill Green relocated to Lake Charles in 1923 acquiring a charter for his company, the Green Oil Company in that year with a capitalization of $25,000. Louis Siess and his family followed the next year, attracted by the town, which, by now was a growing metropolis.

There was a record amount of home building the year Louis Siess arrived in Lake Charles, with forty-seven new homes constructed. Moreover, the previous year, a much sought after ship channel, to be twelve feet deep and ninety feet wide to accommodate large vessels and oil tankers, was begun after five years of planning. The channel opened to much fanfare in 1925, when on October 1st oil tankers began arriving in the new port of Lake Charles. In 1926 six oil companies received their charters, the largest being the L. Siess Oil Syndicate, with $87,000 in capital.[100] From that point on Louis Preston Siess was one of the most prominent and successful oil operators in the southwestern United States. His home at 903 Broad Street (Old Highway 90), referred to by family members as the "big house," was one of the finest in town.

Louis and Minnie's son, Charles Preston Siess, did not follow his father into the oil industry. He attended the Georgia Military Academy, where held the rank of Major in the Cadet Battalion.

Returning to Louisiana in 1921, he entered Tulane University to study economics.[101] He graduated from Vanderbilt University with a Bachelor of laws degree, passed the bar and opened up his practice in Lake Charles Louisiana in 1924. The following year he married Mary Burem Henderson from Van Alstyne, Texas. Their children, fraternal twins, Charles Preston Siess, Jr., and Marian Siess, were born in January of the following year.

Robert Edward Siess, who was clerking at his father's oil company, married Gladys Leona Walsh in 1926. His daughter, Gretchen, was born in Lake Charles on May 19, 1927. Another daughter, Carolyn Louise, came on June 10, 1929. Louis Siess purchased property behind his house and built two homes, one each for his two eldest sons and their families. Helen Louise Siess, in the meantime, eight years younger than her brothers, Charlie and Robert, had finished high school in Dallas, and gone off to college. Her younger brothers, John Dee and Jack Siess, attended high school in Lake Charles.

The Louis Preston Siess children, along with their mother, Minnie Mathis, were devout Baptists. Louis Preston Siess also attended the Baptist Church. The family remembers that, although baptized a Catholic, he and Minnie had not been married in the Church. One day a priest came to visit in Lake Charles to welcome him to the community. Upon finding out that Louis and Minnie had not had a Catholic service, the priest told him he was living in sin. Incensed, Louis chased the man away with a cane, and never attended or gave to the Church again.

During the depression, Louis Siess fell on hard times. He was forced to declare bankruptcy and was only able to salvage his home on Broad Street and its furnishings from creditors. In failing health he retired to Hot Springs, Arkansas, first living for a year with his wife, Minnie, at the Majestic Hotel, then moving behind the hotel into the Majestic Apartments at 314 Park Street. Their three youngest children spent their early adulthood in Hot Springs. Minnie died there on October 24, 1953, at the age of eighty. Louis Preston Siess, the youngest of Leopold and Josette Siess' children, died in Hot Springs in

November 1961. The couple are interred at the Bolton-Teagle family cemetery on LA Highway 501 in Winnfield. [102]

The Charles Preston Siess, Sr. family moved into the "big house," after their parents' departure from Lake Charles. Their daughter, Marney, married Thomas Henry Kepner, a Monroe, La, native who was a petroleum geologist. Their son, Charles Preston Siess, Jr, a graduate in chemical engineering, returned to his grandfather's occupation, working for fifty years in the petroleum industry, retiring as the chairman of Cabot Oil and Gas in 1998.[103] Charles Preston Siess, Sr. died on February 17, 1977. He was buried in the Prairie Hill Lutheran cemetery in Brenham, TX. His wife, Burem, died on May 28, 1987, and is buried next to her husband.

Louis Preston Siess' son, Robert, went into business with Robert Leon Coleman, forming the Siess Coleman Cable Company, selling new and used wire rope, used primarily to the oil industry. They later formed the Siess Coleman Trucking Contractors holding permits in Louisiana and Texas for the transportation of petroleum products.[104] Robert and Gladys Walsh Siess lived in Lake Charles, Gladys dying in 1976 and Robert following in January 1990 at the age of eighty-seven. Their daughter, Gretchen Siess, married Ardis Lyndon Tadlock, Sr., a U.S. Navy veteran, in 1948. She and Ardis had eight children, and were members of the Methodist Church. Their eldest son, Ardis. Jr., and his wife, Phyllis Cole, have been missionaries in Uganda and South Africa for many years.[105] Gretchen Siess Tadlock passed away on May 23, 2009, surviving her husband, Ardis by almost ten years.

Louis and Minnie Siess' daughter, Helen Louise Siess married Alexander Keirsey, in Hot Springs, Arkansas on September 24, 1934. The couple never had children. Helen died in Lake Charles on January 6, 1974 and was buried at the Bolton-Teagle Cemetery in Winnfield near her parents.[106]

John Dee and Jack Siess, Louis and Minnie's youngest sons, were both veterans of World War II. John married Alberta Morant, in Hot Springs, on December 15, 1943. She was a native of Edmonton,

Canada.[107] Long time hotel owners in Jacksonville, Florida, the couple had no children. John died in Jacksonville on July 4, 1995 and was buried alongside his parents and siblings at the Bolton-Teagle Cemetery in Winnfield, LA.[108] Thirty-seven year old Jack Siess married Immaculata Maria Orrecchio, originally from Naples, Italy, in Hot Springs, Arkansas before a Justice of the Peace on January 18, 1951.[109] The couple's two daughters, Jacquelin and Terri Lynn Siess, were born in Hot Springs where Jack worked as an auditor for a local hotel. Jack and Tina moved to Jacksonville, Florida, where their marriage ended in divorce in 1969.[110] Jack died three years later on October 24, 1972, at the age of fifty-nine. He is buried in the Bolton-Teagle family cemetery in Winnfield, LA.

The only descendants of Leopold and Josette Siess that still live in Avoyelles Parish are descended from the family of Florestine Siess Escudé. Other family members, however, did not move very far away, locating in other cities and towns in Louisiana, Texas and Arkansas. Judaism, even the memory of once being Jewish, hardly survived across the generations, and was almost never acknowledged. Mae Rose Siess Clement, when questioned about the possibility of being Jewish hotly denied the fact. Her cousin, Raye Rich Coberly, was evasive about her ancestry as well, having to hide both a Jewish father and grandfather, from her descendants.

---

[1] "Advertisement, Julius Levin," *The (Alexandria,) Louisiana Democrat* (hereinafter cited as *"LD"*), 9 February 1887, p. 3, cols. 6,7, digital image, *Chroniclingamerica.loc.gov* (http://chroniclingamerica.loc.gov/ [hereinafter cited as "CA"]: accessed 3/ 2010.)

[2] Frederick M. Spletstoser, *Talk of the Town, The Rise of Alexandria, Louisiana and the Daily Town Talk* (Baton Rouge, LA: Louisiana State University Press, 2005), 81.

[3] Grant Parish Courthouse (Colfax, Grant Parish, Louisiana), *Conveyances*, Book F, pp. 370-371, "C.E. Ball to A. Siess, Cash Sale," filed 27 May 1889.

[4] Jimmie Nelle Adams Lewis, compiler, *Forgotten Sites of Tioga* (Tioga, LA: Tioga Historical Society, Inc., 2008, self-published). Available at the Tioga Commissary), 52.

[5] "Town and Parish News," *LD, 29 May 1889,* p. 3, col. 1, digital image, (CA: accessed 3/ 2010.)

[6] "Personal," *LD, 29 May 1889,* p. 3, col. 2, digital image, (CA: accessed 3/ 2010.) Note: Michael Aaron was Auger's wife, Fannie's, half-brother Robert Aaron's son. Coleman Greenwood was Robert Aaron's wife, Betta Greenwood's brother.

[7] Lewis, compiler, *Forgotten Sites of Tioga,* 1. Note: After Siess and Levin sold their holdings in Levin to Stephen R. Lee in 1903, the town was renamed, Tioga.

[8] "Homicide," *LD,* 18 December 1889, p. 3, col. 2, digital image, (CA: accessed 3/ 2010).

[9] Lewis, compiler, *Forgotten Sites of Tioga,* 17.

[10] Avoyelles Parish Courthouse (Marksville, Avoyelles Parish, LA), *Marriage Book F*, p. 51, "Emmanuel Siess to Henriette Firment," filed 1 February 1889.

[11] St. Joseph's Roman Catholic Church (Marksville, Avoyelles Parish, LA), Baptism Book 2, (1890), entry 52. Baptism of Marie Isabelle Siess, parish rectory, Marksville.

[12] Jeraldine DuFour Lacour, *Brides Book of Avoyelles Parish, Vol 2, 1856-1880* (Bunkie: Jeraldine Dufour LaCour [203 South Gayle Boulevard, Bunkie, LA], 1979), 142. Entry for Adele Dundonné, (sic) and Paul Michel Fiermont (sic).

[13] Avoyelles Parish Courthouse (Marksville, Avoyelles Parish, LA), *Oaths of Office* (1890), "Emmanuel Siess, Oath as deputy Constable of Marksville," filed 30 September, 1889.

[14] St. Joseph's Roman Catholic Church (Marksville, Avoyelles Parish, LA), Baptism Book 2, (1892), entry 99, Baptism of Leopold Lennox (sic) Siess, parish rectory, Marksville.

[15] "Transfers of Real Estate, " *LD,* 27 May 1891, p. 3, col. 2, digital image, (CA: accessed 3/2011.)

[16] "World War I Draft Registration Cards, 1917-1918," digital image, (A: accessed 4/ 2011), Paul Elmo Siess, form 2663, no. 281, Draft Board "O," Caddo Parish, Louisiana, citing *World War I Selective Service System Draft Registration Cards, 1917-1918,* NARA microfilm publication. M1509, FHL roll 1684665.

[17] "Tulane University's Medical Class," *The (New Orleans, LA) Daily Picayune* (hereinafter cited as *"DP"*), 19 April, 1894, p. 1, cols. 5-7, digital image, *Genealogybank.com* (http://www.genealogybank.com [hereinafter cited as "GB"]: accessed 4/ 2011.

[18] "Personal and Society Notes," *LD,* 13 February 1895, p. 3, col. 2, digital image, (CA: accessed 3/ 2011).

[19] "Personal and Society Notes," *LD,* 3 July 1895, p. 3, col. 2, digital image, (CA: accessed 3/ 2011). Note: Jonas Hiller was Elie Hiller's older brother. Elie employed Ernest Weil, the future husband of Simon's daughter Mathilde Siess, during his time in Marksville.

[20] Grant Parish Courthouse (Colfax, Grant Parish, Louisiana), *Conveyances,* Book H, pp. 425-427, "C.W. Bringhorst to Emmanuel Siess and Auger Siess, Land with mortgage," filed 4 October 1895.

[21] Grant Parish Courthouse (Colfax, Grant Parish, Louisiana), *Conveyances*, Book H, pp. 527-528, "H. McKnight, treasurer to E. and A. Siess, Land at verbal sale," filed 3 April 1896.

[22] "Commissioners and Clerks of Election," *LD,* 15 April 1896, p. 3, col. 4, digital image, (CA: accessed 3/ 2011).

[23] Grant Parish Courthouse (Colfax, Grant Parish, Louisiana), *Conveyances*, Book H, pp. 759-761, "E.J. & H.E. Hardtner to Siess Bros. and Johnson, Sale of land with mortgage," filed 15 April 1897, and *Conveyances*, Book H, pp. 761-763, "Willis F. Johnson to Siess Bros., Conveyance," filed 15 April 1897.

[24] "Real Estate Transfers," *LD*, 4 November 1896, p. 3, col. 1, digital image, (CA: accessed 3/ 2011).

[25] Gladys Selvidge Brewer, *Cant Hooks and Dogwood Blossoms – Pollock's Story* (Pollock, LA: Gladys S. Brewer [P.O. Box 216, Pollock, LA 71467], 1987), 16. Note: Antonia was the name of the station stop on the Iron Mountain Railway, a mile or so from Sand Spur. The water tower, emblazoned with the name "Antonia," is still there.

[26] "Forty-three Louisiana Postmasters," *DP*, 28 August, 1897, p. 1, cols. 1, 2, digital image, (GB: accessed 26 April 2011.

[27] Ella Elizabeth Siess Treadway, "Autobiography of My Mother's Life: Mrs. Rose Henriette Firment," unpublished typed correspondence dated 1986 in possession of Mr. Donald Clement, her nephew, p. 7.

[28] "Daily Mortuary Report," *The New Orleans (Louisiana) Times*, 24 September 1867, p. 2, col. 2, digital image, (GB: accessed 11/ 2011). Note: Henrietta "Ettie" Davis Berger married Sigmund Moses Eisendrath, a Chicago tanner. On December 30, 1903, Ettie, and her daughter Natalie Eisendrath, died in the infamous Iroquois Theater fire. Six hundred people lost their lives that day from smoke inhalation or being trampled to death in the panic which ensued.

[29] "Physicians Organize an Association," *LD*, 9 June 1897, p. 2, col. 1, digital image, (CA: accessed 3/ 2011).

[30] "Items from Seiss, Seiss, LA, Feb 5, 1897," *The Colfax (Louisiana) Chronicle*, 13 February 1897, p. 1, col 5, digital image, (CA: accessed 6/2011).

[31] 1900 U.S. Census, Grant Parish, Louisiana, pop. sch., Ward 4, ED 65, p. 14 B (penned), Dwelling #264, Family #264, Isaac Siess household, digital image, (A: accessed 7/2010), citing NARA microfilm publication T623, roll 565. Date of enumeration: 20 June 1900. Note: Lincecum is twelve miles north of Pollock, LA, east of what is now LA 165.

[32] "Official Proceedings Police Jury of Grant Parish," The Colfax (Louisiana) Chronicle, 11 August 1900, p. 1, col 4, digital image, (CA: accessed 6/2011).

[33] "Siess Bros.' Planing Mill Destroyed by Fire," *LD*, 7 July 1897, p. 2, col. 3, digital image, (CA: Accessed 3/2011).

[34] "$17 Worth of Stamps Affixed," *LD*, 23 July 1898, p. 8, col. 1, digital image, (CA: accessed 3/ 2011).

[35] Grant Parish Courthouse (Colfax, Grant Parish, Louisiana), *Conveyances*, Book I, pp. 471-472, "A. & E. Siess to J. M. Nugent, Conveyance," filed 12 October 1898.

[36] Avoyelles Parish Courthouse (Marksville, Avoyelles Parish, Louisiana), *Conveyances*, Book C C, pp. 344-345, # 10,665, "Mrs. Josephine Chatelain, wife of etc. to Tesca R. Roy, Sale of land," filed 27 October 1902.

[37] 1900 U.S. Census, Avoyelles Parish, Louisiana, pop. sch., Mansura, Ward 3, ED 14, p. 2B (penned), Dwelling # 34, Family #34, Leon P. Escudé household, digital image, (A: accessed 7/ 2010), citing NARA microfilm publication T623, roll 558. Date of enumeration: 2 June 1900. Note: Birth and death dates supplied by Mrs. Barbara Escudé Lemoine, granddaughter of Florestine Siess After the turn of the twentieth century Florestine's last two children, Benjamin Leon Escudé, born on October 4, 1900 and David Louis Escudé, born on September 2, 1903 (who lived seven weeks), would join the family.

[38] Rabbi Martin I. Hinchin, D.D., *Fourscore and Eleven, A History of the Jews of Rapides Parish 1828-1919* (Alexandria, Louisiana: McCormick Graphics, 1984), 87.

[39] 1900 U.S. Census, Rapides Parish, Louisiana, pop. sch., Alexandria, Ward 4, ED 124, p. 3A (penned), Dwelling #47, Family #49, Julius Levin household , digital image, (A: accessed 7/ 2010), citing NARA microfilm publication T623, roll 577. Date of enumeration: 4 June 1900.

[40] Social Security Administration, "U.S. Social Security Death Index," database, (A: accessed 10/ 2010), entry for Estelle J. Siess, 1989.

[41] Grant Parish Courthouse (Colfax, Grant Parish, Louisiana), *Conveyances*, Book L-47, pp. 728-729, "R.E. L. Brister and E.L. Brister to Isaac E. Siess, M.D.," filed 14 August 1902.

[42] Grant Parish Courthouse (Colfax, Grant Parish, Louisiana), *Conveyances*, Book K, pp. 229-230, "J.M. Nugent to Emanuel Siess, Sale and mortgage," filed 8 February 1901.

[43] Grant Parish Courthouse (Colfax, Grant Parish, Louisiana), *Conveyances*, Book L-4, p. 628, "Emanuel Siess to J.M. Nugent, Cash sale," filed 13 June 1902.

[44] Railroad Commission of Louisiana, *First Annual Report of the Railroad Commission of Louisiana* (Baton Rouge: Office of the Railroad Commissioner of Louisiana, 1900), 451.

[45] "Alexandria, LA," *The New Orleans (Louisiana) Item*, 22 June, 1901, p. 2, col. 2, digital image, (GB: accessed 4/ 2011).

[46] "Louisiana Marriages 1718-1925," database, (A: accessed 9 July 2010), citing Hunting For Bears, Compiled from a variety of sources including original marriage records located in Family History Library microfilm, microfiche, or books. Original marriage records available from the Clerk of the Court, Winn Parish. Marriage of Minnie Mathis to Louis Siess.

[47] R. W. Oglesby, "Passing in review- This week we have Charlie P. Mathis," *The Winnfield (Louisiana) News-American,* at *Usgenwebarchives.net* (http://files.usgwarchives.net/la/winn/bios/biocpm32.txt: accessed 5/ 2011).

⁴⁸ "Winnfield Oil Company," *DP*, 31 August, 1902, p. 1, col. 6, digital image, (GB: accessed 4/ 2011).

⁴⁹ Greggory E. Davies, "Winnfield Oil Company Well No. 1," *Legacies and Legends of Winn Parish*, (The Winn Genealogical and Historical Association), Vol. 7, no. 2 (Aug. 2003): 114.

⁵⁰ Birth and death dates courtesy of Marney Siess Kepner, daughter of Charles Preston Siess, Sr.

⁵¹ Jerome F. Scott "Pollock, Louisiana - Past, Present, and Future," available at Pollock Town Hall, Pollock, LA, 2.

⁵² "Presbyterian Ladies' Aid Society," *The (Winnfield, LA) Comrade*, 26 August 1910, p. 1, col. 1, digital image, (CA: accessed 4/ 2011).

⁵³ "Winn Parish Medical Society," *Winn Parish (Louisiana) Enterprise,* cited by Greggory E. Davies at *U.S. Genweb Archives* (http://files.usgwarchives.net: accessed 5/ 2011).

⁵⁴ *The Southern Reporter,* Vol. 44, *Containing all the decisions of the Supreme Courts of Alabama, Louisiana, Florida, Mississippi, Permanent Edition, July 6, 1907-January 4, 1908* (St Paul: West Publishing Co., 1908) 307-315, "Milling et.al. v. Sulphur Timber & Lumber Co.," 119La. 585 (1907).

⁵⁵ "Winnfield," *DP*, 21 April, 1907, p. 54, cols. 1-3, digital image, (GB: accessed 4/ 2011).

⁵⁶ Davies, "Winnfield Oil Company Well No. 1," 114.

⁵⁷ 1910 U.S. Census, Winn Parish, Louisiana, pop. sch., Winnfield, Ward 1, ED 123, p. 2A (penned), Dwelling #204, Family #220, Dr. I.E. Siess household, digital image, (A: accessed 7/ 2010), citing NARA microfilm publication T624, roll 535. Date of enumeration: 21 April 1910.

⁵⁸ "For Sale," *The (Winnfield, LA) Comrade*, 30 September 1910, p. 8, col. 1, digital image, (CA: accessed 4/2011).

[59] 1910 U.S. Census, Winn Parish, Louisiana, pop. sch., Winnfield, Ward 1, ED 123, p. 27B (penned), Dwelling #576, Family #593, Louis Siess household, digital image, (A: accessed 7/ 2010), citing NARA microfilm publication T624, roll 535. Date of enumeration: 5 May 1910.

[60] "Articles of Incorporation," *The (Winnfield, LA) Comrade*, 14 October 1910, p. 4, col. 3, digital image, (CA: accessed 4/ 2011).

[61] "Marksville," *DP*, 4 September 1904, p. 21, col. 3, digital image, (GB: accessed 4/ 2011).

[62] Ella Elizabeth Siess Treadway, "Autobiography of My Mother's Life," 5.

[63] "Soards New Orleans Directory, 1906," database, (F3: accessed 12/2010), p. 886. Entry for Auger Siess.

[64] "College of Pharmacy Annual Graduation," *DP*, 12 May 1909, p. 15, cols. 2-6, digital image, (GB: accessed 4/ 2011).

[65] 1910 U.S. Census, Rapides Parish, Louisiana, pop. sch., Alexandria, Ward 1, ED 78, p. 12A (penned), Dwelling #263, Family #264, Auger Siess household, digital image, (A: accessed 7/ 2010), citing NARA microfilm publication T624, roll 535. Date of enumeration: 22 April 1910.

[66] Hinchin, 141-142

[67] Grant Parish Courthouse (Colfax, Grant Parish, Louisiana), *Conveyances*, Book V, p. 163, no. 9857, "State of Louisiana to Siess Bros., Certificate of Redemption," filed 18 September 1913.

[68] Confederate Pension Application for Josephine Chatelain Siess, Avoyelles Parish, LA, Louisiana State Archives, File # 12417, Reel CP1.125, Microdex 3, Sequence 13, Baton Rouge, Louisiana – 5 pages. "Application for widow's pension," dated 11 September 1913.

[69] St. Paul the Apostle Church (Mansura, Louisiana), Burial Register 1914, Mrs. Leopold Siess, parish rectory, Mansura. (Original in Latin).

[70] Marriage of Leo C. Siess and Adele Liebreich, undated clipping from unidentified newspaper, in scrapbook of Estelle Johanna Siess, privately held by Mrs. Bettye Jo Bango Maki, West Bloomfield, MI, 2006.

[71] Chester Paul Siess (Urbana, Illinois), Telephone interview by the author on June 6, 2002.

[72] Chester Paul Siess, telephone interview, June 6, 2002. Note: Chester Paul Siess died in Illinois on January 14, 2004.

[73] Hinchin, 171.

[74] Louisiana Secretary of State, Louisiana State Board of Health, Certificate of Death Vol. 24, p. 10780 (1918), Mrs. Moise Crager; photocopy obtained from Louisiana Secretary of State, Department of Archives, Records Management and History, Baton Rouge, LA.

[75] Hinchin, 184.

[76] Chester Paul Siess, telephone interview, June 6, 2002.

[77] Auger Siess obituary, ca. January 1933, undated clipping from unidentified newspaper in scrapbook of Estelle Johanna Siess.

[78] Mary Pearce Hart, *Evergreen on the Bayou* (Evergreen, LA: Self Published, 1995), 51.

[79] Randy Decuir, author and compiler, *Biographical and Historical Memoirs of Avoyelles – 1890-1990* (Marksville, LA: The Avoyelles Publishing Co., 1990), 148.

[80] Jules Escudé obituary, undated clipping from unidentified newspaper in scrapbook of Estelle Johanna Siess.

[81] "U.S. Veterans Gravesites, ca. 1775-2006." database,. Provo, UT, USA, (A: accessed 5/ 2011), citing National Cemetery Administration. *Nationwide Gravesite Locator*. Record for John G. Leckie, born 13 August 1923, died 2 July 1945.

[82] "Steamboats," *DP*, 9 January 1844, p. 3, col. 5, digital image, (GB: accessed 5/ 2011).

[83] "Steamboats," *DP*, 2 February 1858, p. 8, col. 6, digital image, (GB: accessed 5/ 2011).

[84] "Steamboats," *DP*, 10 September 1872, p. 2, col. 6, digital image, (GB: accessed 5/ 2011).

[85] "Success in Beauty Supply Field," *The (New Orleans, LA) Times Picayune*, (hereinafter cited as *TP*), 16 June 1938, p. 26, cols. 4,5, digital image, (GB: accessed 5/ 2011).

[86] Interview with Donald Clement, nephew of Camille Siess, Metairie, Louisiana on 13 May 2004; transcript privately held by the author.

[87] "Obituary - Hymes, Mrs. Nell Siess," undated clipping from unidentified newspaper in scrapbook of Estelle Johanna Siess.

[88] See chapter 13, pp. 439,440, 446-448 concerning Mary Rich and her husband Robert Cone.

[89] "Siess-Welden," undated clipping from unidentified newspaper in scrapbook of Estelle Johanna Siess.

[90] "Deaths – Siess," undated clipping from unidentified newspaper in scrapbook of Estelle Johanna Siess.

[91] "Funerals – Mrs. Helena Siess," undated clipping from unidentified newspaper in scrapbook of Estelle Johanna Siess.

[92] "Estelle J. Siess," The Alexandria (LA) Town Talk," 5 June 1989, p. 6, col. 2. Copy of obituary furnished by Kramer & Sons. Funeral Home, 2905 Masonic Drive, Alexandria, LA. 71302.

[93] "New Orleans, Louisiana Birth records Index, 1790-1899," database, (A: accessed 7/ 2010), citing State of Louisiana, Secretary of State, Division of

Archives, Records Management, and History. *Vital Records Indices*. Baton Rouge, LA. Record for John Anthony Bango.

[94] "New Orleans, Louisiana Marriage records Index, 1831-1925," database, (A: accessed 7/ 2010), citing State of Louisiana, Secretary of State, Division of Archives, Records Management, and History. *Vital Records Indices*. Baton Rouge, LA. Marriage of John A. Bango and Rosa Garcia (Vol. 3, p. 22).

[95] "Louisiana Confederate Soldiers," database, (A: accessed 5/ 2011), citing Andrew B. Booth, records of Louisiana Confederate Soldiers & Confederate Commands, Vol. II, New Orleans, LA, p. 41, 1920. Glutzeman, Alexander (also on Rolls as Glouckmann, A.; Glootzmann, Alexander; Glouetzmann, Alexander).

[96] "City Archives, register of Patients transported to the State Insane Asylum, 1884," database, *Nutrias.org*, (http://nutrias.org/~nopl/inv/civilsheriff/vf350.htm: accessed 6/ 2010).

[97] "Jewishgen Online Worldwide Burial registry," *Jewishgen.org* (http://www.jewishgen.org: accessed 6/ 2010), entry for Sarah Glucksman Bango (1948), Dispersed of Judah Cemetery, Row 19, Plot 317, New Orleans, LA.

[98] 1920 U.S. Census, Orleans Parish, Louisiana, pop. sch., New Orleans, Ward 13, ED 231, p.13A (penned), Dwelling #243, Family #249, Jewish Orphans' Home, lines 1 & 2, Henry and Amelia Bango, inmates, digital image, (A: accessed 7/ 2010), citing NARA microfilm publication T625, roll 624. Date of enumeration: 19 January 1920.

[99] "World War I Draft Registration Cards, 1917-1918," digital image, (A: accessed 4/ 2011), Louis Siess, form 3559, no. 3596, Draft Board "O", Calcasieu Parish, Louisiana, citing *World War I Selective Service System Draft Registration Cards, 1917-1918*, NARA microfilm publication. M1509, FHL roll 1684667.

[100] Stewart Alfred Ferguson, "The History of Lake Charles," Thesis, 1931, McNeese State University, (http://library.mcneese.edu/depts/archive/FTBooks/ferguson.htm), Chapter 19.

[101] Henry E. Chambers, *A History of Louisiana*, Vol. 2 (Chicago & New York: The American Historical Society, 1925), cited at *Usgwarchives.org* (http:// files.usgwarchives.org/la/calcasieu/bios/seisscp.txt– Charles P. Siess, Calcasieu Parish, LA: accessed 5/2011).

[102] Louis P. Siess and Minnie Mathis Siess markers, Bolton-Teagle Cemetery (Winnfield, Winn Parish, LA), personally read, 5/ 2006. Note: Minnie Mathis Siess' mother was Rachel Bolton. Many of the Boltons, as well as Minnie's parents are buried in the small family cemetery.

[103] Louisiana State University, *Spring 2003 Alumni Newsletter- Chemical Engineering Department*, "Alumnus Inducted into the 2003 Alumni Hall of Distinction," Lsu.edu (http://www.che.lsu.edu/newsletter/fall2003_spring2004/alumni_news.html#top: accessed 5/ 2011).

[104] "U.S. City Directories, Lake Charles, Calcasieu Parish, LA (1943)," digital image, (A: accessed 10/ 2010), citing *Polk's Lake Charles (Calcasieu Parish, LA.) City Directory 1943*, entry for Siess-Coleman Cable Co. and Siess-Coleman Trucking Contractors, 360.

[105] Phyllis Cole Tadlock (Kompala, Uganda), Email interviews by the author in 2004. Privately held by the author.

[106] Greggory E. Davis, compiler, "Obituaries: Helen Louise Siess Keirsey," *The Winnfield (Louisiana) News-American,* at *Usgenwebarchives.net* (http://files.usgwarchives.net/la/winn/obits/k/keirhl74.txt: accessed 5/ 2011).

[107] "Arkansas County Marriage Records, 1887-1957," (1943), marriage license and certificate of John Dee Siess, digital image, *Familysearch.org* (http://www.familysearch.org: accessed 5/2011) Digital Film # 1977384, Folder # 4401632, p. 328.

[108] John Dee Siess marker, Bolton-Teagle Cemetery (Winnfield, Winn Parish, LA), personally read 5/ 2006.

[109] "Arkansas County Marriage Records, 1887-1957," (1951), marriage license and certificate of Jack Siess, digital image, *Familysearch.org* (http://www.familysearch.org: accessed 5/ 2011) Digital Film # 2169921, Folder # 4329542, p. 32.

[110] "Florida Divorce Index 1927-2001," database, (A: accessed 5/2011), citing *Florida Divorce Index, 1927-2001,* Jacksonville, FL, USA: Florida Department of Health. Divorce of Jack and Tina Marie Siess.

Josette Chatelain Siess, widow of Leopold Siess, ca. 1886
(*Courtesy of Betty Jo Bango Maki*)

Dr. Isaac Edouard Siess in buggy in Piney Woods- Grant Parish, LA, ca. 1902 (*Courtesy of Bettye Jo Bango Maki*)

Winnfield, LA., ca. 1903 (Left to right) Clotile Siess, Dr. I.E. Siess, Guy Siess, Helena Berger Siess holding Estelle Siess, unidentified African-American girl (*Courtesy of Bettye Jo Bango Maki*)

Interior of City Drug Co., Winnfield, LA – Owned by Dr. Isaac Siess, (second from right) ca. 1912 (*Courtesy of Bettye Jo Bango Maki*)

Winnfield Oil Co. Well #1 – ca. 1908 – Louis Preston Siess - President
(*Courtesy of Bettye Jo Bango Maki*)

CHAPTER 8

WORDS AND MUSIC - THE DESCENDANTS OF DAVID SIESS

David Siess was elected Mayor of Mansura again in 1886, holding that office through 1892. He and Clara still managed their mercantile interests and worked their small plantation. To that end, on March 5, 1886, Clara "duly separated in her property from said husband, and by him herein duly aided," purchased one sorrel horse, one black horse, one red cow and calf, and one old horse cart for the sum of $145 from Louis David.[1] Shortly thereafter, on March 27, 1886, David and Clara signed a new power of attorney agreement wherein she appointed him as the sole and exclusive manager and administrator of her planting interest, giving him full power as General Manager. However, because both the store and farm were constantly in jeopardy of foreclosure from New Orleans' creditors, the agreement expressly denied him the power or authority to contract debts, or subscribe any note, mortgage or other obligation by which she or her property could be held.[2]

In 1887, the firm of E. Marguez and Company seized one hundred sixty acres of land held by David Siess, for outstanding commercial debts. It was put up for auction and sold, encumbered by four judicial mortgages to Mrs. Clara Cochrane, David's wife, who was the highest bidder at two dollars and fifty cents on a twelve month bond. The first mortgage for $1256.34, dating from 1877 against David Siess and Brother, had never been satisfied in favor of C.J. Hambro & Son of New Orleans. A second, smaller one for $300, dating from 1876 was still owed to L. and J. Weil, of New Orleans. A third, more recent indebtedness, amounting to $435.19 taken on in 1886, was in favor of Schnack & Co., while the last, from the same year was in favor of the Kieffer Bros. for $118.53 It is no wonder that Clara was able to buy back the property for less than three dollars with the intention of being able, at some point, to clear off the encumbrances which amounted to just over twenty-one hundred dollars.[3] This cat and mouse game between David and Clara and their New Orleans lenders would play out until well into the twentieth century. David, at this point, still had three minor children and a wife for which to provide, as well as his twenty-one year old daughter, Mathilde, who was still at home.

In 1891 David Siess made an unsuccessful attempt to get an invalid pension from the Federal Government worth between eight and twelve dollars per month.[4] The act of June 27, 1890, had removed one of the original eligibility requirements which required the recipient to have been wounded in action and thereby disabled. The new rules stipulated only ninety days service, an honorable discharge, and a permanent physical disability not due to "vicious habits." Unfortunately, there were no records of David's service anywhere, a problem which did not prevent him from trying to get a Confederate pension when it became available through the state of Louisiana in 1898.

Mathilde Siess, David and Clara's eldest child, had attended school in New Orleans and was a frequent visitor there. In order to keep an eye on her daughter, and to bring in a bit of extra cash, Clara Cochrane Siess left her family behind in 1893 and opened a boarding house at 241 Baronne Street in New Orleans. She advertised it as being "centrally located and convenient to all places of business. Prices very moderate." [5] She hoped to attract visiting merchants and their families from the outlying parishes. She was still in operation over a year later, but this time at 242 Camp Street. While in New Orleans, Mathilde and her mother met Benjamin Mendelson, who had emigrated from England. He started out in New Orleans in the advertising business. From what is known of the family, he was distantly related to the composer, Felix Mendelssohn, a German of Jewish origin who later became a Lutheran in order to further his music career. The courtship was a long one, but on January 14, 1897, Mathilde Siess wed Ben Mendelson at Marksville in a civil ceremony conducted by Judge E. North Cullum of the Tenth Judicial district.[6] The bride and groom returned to New Orleans where they made their home. On December 14, 1898, Ben and Mathilde Siess Mendelson's only child, Harry, was born.[7]

David Siess was once again appointed Postmaster in Mansura in 1897, and his fifteen year old son, Harry, was enrolled in the newly opened Marksville High School for the 1897-1898 academic year. Harry graduated in the summer of 1899, and months later, on November 6, became a member of the first freshman class of the newly established New Orleans Dental College located on Carondelet Street. There were twenty-two people enrolled, including one female student. This was the first dental school in New Orleans in over thirty years, as its predecessor, of the same name, had opened in 1867 and had closed a few years later.[8] There had been a Louisiana Dental Society, however, which was incorporated on January 16, 1880, and fourteen years later, a statement given at the annual convention, painted a clear picture of the primitive state of the profession in Louisiana. In the annual report it was explained that there were between one hundred ninety and two hundred dentists in the state, of which seventy were located in New Orleans, and the rest in other parishes yet the Dental Society's membership for the year of 1893 consisted of only thirty-four men. Giving this discouraging report was Dr. Charles Eckhardt, who ended by saying that the founding of a dental school was an absolute necessity. When the New Orleans Dental College finally opened in 1899, Eckhardt was one of the seven faculty members.[9] Harry James Siess graduated on May 6, 1902. Although relatively new, the college, which was affiliated with the National Association of Dental Facilities and the National Association of Dental Examiners, awarded diplomas which were recognized in the entire United States.[10] Dr. Harry Siess returned to Mansura to set up his dental practice, just two months shy of his twentieth birthday. He moved back in with his parents, and his older sister, Carrie, who worked as a clerk in the Mansura Post Office for her father.

David and Clara's daughter, Eugenie Siess, who was twenty-eight, at the turn of the twentieth century was pursuing a musical career. She was a contralto, who performed in opera and could accompany herself on the piano. She travelled extensively, studied with the famed vocal coach, Georg Ferguson, of Berlin, Germany, and had given concerts at the Metropolitan Opera House in New York.

Eugenie's sister, Carrie, related that once the two of them had taken a riverboat from Mansura to New Orleans and that Eugenie played the piano and sang for the passengers all during the trip. Eugenie never strayed for long from her home in Avoyelles Parish as long as her parents were alive, investing in property there in 1899, when she bought several hundred acres for taxes from the estate of Jules Desfossés, and purchased forty-eight acres from Jules Moreau on Bayou des Glaises in 1902.[11] .

Seventy year old David Siess was elected Mayor of Mansura once again in 1905, then in 1906. He still worked his plantation and kept the store. The sawmill and gin had burned down in the summer of 1901 but the insurance had helped to pay off some of the mortgages on the various family properties held by New Orleans merchants. Dr. Harry Siess, now making a bit of money as the town dentist, bought three lots with a mortgage in Mansura from his mother in March of 1906, and an additional ten acres of land in December of the same year from Onezime Sampson.[12]

***

In 1900 Ben and Mathilde Siess Mendelson were raising their baby son, Harry, in a rented house at 1437 Amelia Street in New Orleans. Benjamin was attempting to get a foothold in the advertising field. He joined a number of fraternal organizations in the city in order to widen his social contacts in the hopes of growing his business. The first that is known of his involvement is in 1901 with his membership in the Grand Grove of Louisiana, United Ancient Order of Druids, where he held the office of Noble Arch.[13] Druidism was based on the seven precepts of Merlin, said to be the first Druid. The order professed a moral, benevolent and fraternal philosophy. The Druids held an annual May festival which included sporting events for children, a picnic, and musical and dramatic entertainment. He also joined the Supreme Order of the Seven Wise Men (Heptasophs).[14] The order had been founded in New Orleans in 1852, and by the time Ben joined, it had about four thousand members nationwide. The improved order, which split from the original group over whether or not to offer insurance to its members, became less of a fraternity and more of an insurance company in 1917, offering death benefits worth from one to five thousand dollars. Ben had also become a member of the Knights of Pythias, and had quickly risen from a representative to the grand lodge to the post of Grand Vice Chancellor, and finally Grand Chancellor. Founded in 1864 in Washington D.C., the organization accepted men who were at least eighteen years of age. An applicant could not be a professional gambler or engaged in the sale of narcotics or alcohol, and must have a belief in a supreme being. Ben travelled extensively for the organization, going to chapters across the state to promote the fraternal order. He was also involved in the Dramatic Order Knights of Khorassan, which was the social and entertainment arm of the Pythians.

While Ben's ties were to the secular and moral fraternalism that was so pervasive in early twentieth century culture, he seemed not to have any particular affiliation to one religion. All faiths seemed to be equally attracted to these organizations more for their social and financial benefits than anything else. Setting themselves apart from the Masonic Order, these fraternal organizations which nevertheless mimicked the structure and rites set forth in the precepts of freemasonry, were more inclusive, welcoming Catholics, which in New Orleans was a huge asset. Although Ben continued to dabble in advertising he soon turned to publishing, managing his own house at 638 Canal Street, where both *The Louisiana Pythian,* the magazine of that organization as well as the *New Orleans Catholic Monthly* were brought out.[15] And while in 1900 he had listed his occupation as advertising, in 1910 he was a "newspaper publisher," and by 1920, simply a "publisher."

***

With a bit of income from the post office and the farm, as well as son Harry's earnings as a rural dentist, David and Clara continued to live in the family home on Clara Street in Mansura. On September 28, 1908, a set of twins was born to Josephine Olivier, a thirty-two year old single woman of color, whose parents, Louis Olivier and his wife, Marie Charlot, were farmers in the area. Dr Harry J. Siess was the father.[16] Only one of the twins survived the day and he was named Louis André. Louis' daughter, Marjorie Ann Seiss, was told that when the baby was born, David Siess approached the family and offered to support the child as long as he would be given the maternal surname of Olivier instead of Siess. The family refused and Louis André Siess was baptized in the Catholic faith on December 26, 1908, by Father Achille Anseeuw of St. Paul the Apostle Church in Mansura. His godparents were Martin Jean-Baptiste, husband of Josephine Olivier's sister Eunice, and his grandmother, Marie Charlot Olivier.[17] Unfortunately little Louis André lost his mother six months later, when Josephine died on March 3, 1909, at the age of thirty-three. He was raised by his maternal grandmother, Marie Charlot Olivier, until her death on July 29, 1918, along with his half-brother, Charles, Josephine's son by Rodolph Berger. Thereafter, until he married, he lived with his aunt, Eunice Olivier Jean-Baptiste, and her husband, Martin.

Louis' father, Dr. Harry Siess, continued to live with his parents and work in Mansura as a dentist. He, too, was bitten by the fraternal "bug," joining Alexandria Lodge No. 38, the Knights of Pythias. On July 15, 1909 he shared the stage with his brother-in-law, Grand Chancellor Ben Mendelson, both of whom gave rousing speeches to the local membership.[18] Although Harry would travel to Alexandria to attend these fraternal meetings, there is no evidence that he ever joined or even attended any services at Temple Gemiluth Chassodim, nor had his father before him, even when the thirty mile trip was made easier by newly mechanized road and rail travel.

Harry was elected to the Avoyelles Parish Police Jury in 1910. It was he who provided the wording for the publication of certain rules for people driving automobiles in the parish, setting a speed limit of 15 mph on a straight road, 8 mph on a curve or near a bridge, 4 mph crossing a bridge or passing in front of a church or public assemblage of people. When meeting people on horseback, or horse drawn conveyances, the driver, when signaled to do so, had to stop his machine until they had safely passed. His rules also allowed for each car to have a number attached to it which was registered with the local Sheriff, and set a license tax of ten dollars per vehicle.[19] In 1911, Harry succeeded his father, David, as postmaster at Mansura, while continuing his work on the Police Jury and maintaining his dental practice. He was also a popular political speaker, hosting in November, 1911, the Democratic candidate for Governor of Louisiana, John T. Michel, when he visited Avoyelles Parish[20]

In 1913 David Siess, whose attempt at a Federal Invalid Pension had gone nowhere, tried to secure a Confederate pension. The five applications he prepared over the course of nine years are quite puzzling given his previous admission to the French and American Claims Commission that he had been one of Union General Banks' guides through Avoyelles Parish. In his first attempt he stated that he had enlisted early in 1862 in Johnson's Battalion. He added that "on account of being sick was discharged in the latter part of 1862 and returned to Mansura and other places in the state up to the close of the war." Unfortunately there were no muster rolls ever submitted for Johnson's Battalion. Furthermore the company was disbanded on July 25, 1862, and its members ordered to report to the Avoyelles Regiment, Louisiana Militia. In a second submission, David obtained two affidavits from neighbors in Mansura who swore he had been a loyal Confederate soldier. Sévère Laborde, who said he had known David Siess for fifty years, swore that he had served with him in the 18th Louisiana Regiment on its expedition up the Red River in 1862 and again in 1864. This evidence was not helpful because in his initial application Siess never indicated that he had been with this regiment. The affidavit of Fulgence Z. Lemoine was more complete. He wrote that David had been with Johnson's Battalion until the fall of New Orleans in 1862. After returning to Avoyelles Parish, he and David joined the artillery forces at Fort DeRussy in 1863 and 1864. After Fort DeRussy was captured by Union forces, David joined the 18th Louisiana Regiment, but was taken sick at Alexandria and sent home. David was denied, once again, not only because there was no record of his service, but also because men in militia service were not eligible for state pensions unless they had been mustered into Confederate service.[21]

Undeterred, David tried again, filing on August 17, 1915. This time he applied based on service in the 18th Louisiana Regiment, whose commander was Capt. Phillipot, alleging that he remained with them until the Confederate surrender. He declared that he was in Rapides Parish when the war ended and was sent home from there. In this application he wrote that he earned about $300 per year as a farmer, and at age seventy-four, was unable to do enough work to support himself.[22] He declared that his estate was worth about $1500 and that his property was assessed at $2620. He called upon two witnesses, Henry George Fontanille and Fulgence Z. Lemoine, to verify his service, first in Johnson's Battalion, then at Fort De Russy, and later with the 18th Louisiana. In two further affidavits, Sévère Laborde swore that David Siess had been with him when he served in Company B, 1st Louisiana Heavy Artillery, and Fulgence Lemoine swore that he had been a comrade-in-arms in Boone's Battery. The next rejection letter, dated September 13, 1915, stated that militia service still did not count, and that there were no records of David Siess being in either Boone's Battery or Company B, 1st Louisiana Heavy Artillery.[23]

At age thirty-five, Dr. Harry Siess was re-elected to the post of alderman in Mansura. His first cousin, Arthur Jules Escudé, was re-elected as the town's mayor, and his first cousin once removed, Joseph Leopold Escudé, Léon and Florestine Siess Escudé's son, had also won another term as alderman.[24] That same year, Harry decided to tie the knot, becoming engaged to Retta G. Kaffie, one of the ten children of Harris Kaffie, a Prussian immigrant and well-known merchant in Natchitoches, Louisiana. The happy news was announced in both the *New Orleans States* and the *Daily Picayune* on September 9th, 1917.[25] Harry and Retta had met earlier that year when she was employed as a teacher in a school near Mansura. When asking for her hand from her father, Harris Kaffie, Murrell Smith Siess, Harry's daughter-in-law, reported that he had to present all sorts of "papers" to prove he was Jewish. The couple were married in Natchitoches on December 4, 1917, and returned to Mansura to begin their life together. On November 6, 1918, Clara Cochrane Siess sold a portion of her home lot so that Harry and Retta could have their own separate residence. A diagram attached to the act of sale showed the location of the property and the buildings thereon. From the corner of Clara and Léglise streets heading towards Bayou Lacombe and the railroad tracks, the first structure was the David Siess store, with the David Siess residence on Clara Street behind the store. Next door to the Siess store was the dental office belonging to Dr. Harry Siess followed by the "old" Siess store abandoned years earlier. Next to that was Dr. Harry's residence. His plot of land was a square, 110 feet by 110 feet, for which Harry had given his mother $1000.[26] By the time their only child, Harry James Siess, Jr., was born on August 13, 1919, Harry, Sr. and Retta were in their new home.

Early in 1919 Harry's other son, Louis André Siess, age eleven, inherited along with his half-brother, Charles Berger, his mother Josephine Olivier's portion of the estate of his deceased grandmother, Marie Charlot Olivier, which consisted of twenty acres of land. The property was divided into eight equal shares amongst the heirs: Olivier Rabalais, Paul M. Lehman,[27] Ernestine Olivier Fontenot, Estelle Olivier Hébert, Edward Olivier, Léonce Olivier, Eunice Olivier Jean-Baptiste, and the late Josephine Olivier's children Charles Berger and Louis Siess. Louis and Charles received one and 38/100 acres of land to divide between them.[28]

In 1920, David and Clara Siess were still in their home behind the Siess Store on Clara Street in Mansura, with their two unmarried daughters, Eugenie and Carrie. Eugenie was teaching music in town and Carrie was unemployed. Harry Siess, his wife Retta, and their baby, Harry James Siess, Jr., lived down the street, next to the dental office.[29] This, however, was a decade of change for the Siess family. David tried one more time for a Confederate pension, sending in one more application dated September 5, 1922. This time he indicated that he was with DuBecq's Cavalry, then took a transfer to Company B. 1st Louisiana Heavy Artillery, then to Boone's Battery, and finally back to DuBecq's Company. He indicated that he was honorably discharged in Alexandria on June 27th 1865. At the age of eighty-seven, he said he owned no property, having transferred all his holdings to his wife and son. He attached several more supporting affidavits of other

Confederate soldiers, including, once again, Sévère Laborde, who indicated, now, that David had been absent from his company at the surrender, due to illness, in an attempt to explain why David did not have any parole papers. A new affiant, Cléophas Juneau, attested to his presence in DuBecq's Company. David received one more rejection dated September 16, 1924.[30]

On March 7, 1925, Dr. Harry Siess was elected president of the Louisiana State Dental Society at the convention, which took place in New Orleans.[31] Exactly one month later, on April 7th, at twelve fifteen o'clock, A.M. David Siess died from heart failure at his residence in Mansura. He was a month and a half shy of his ninetieth birthday and had outlived his late elder brother, Simon, to whom he not spoken in many years, by less than five months. Services were conducted at the family home by Rabbi Myron M. Meyerovitz of Temple Gemiluth Chassodim. Auger and Fannie Levin Siess, and their son, Leo Chester Siess, with his wife, Adele Liebreich, motored down from Alexandria to attend the services. He was interred in the Jewish Cemetery in Pineville, the following day. Those he left behind remembered him as a man, in whose home French was always spoken in preference to English, and who drank only wine imported from France. His great-grand-nephew, Joseph L. Escudé, Jr., recounted seeing him one day when, as a very elderly man, he was attempting to repair one of his fences, and asked a helper for "un poteau," (a fence post). He was brought instead "un pot d'eau," (a jug of water) much to his annoyance.

***

Ben and Mathilde Siess Mendelson's son, Harry, who was growing up in New Orleans, was a young prodigy. He began studying music at the age of six, taking violin lessons. He also played other various band and orchestra instruments, studied arranging, and musical directing. He eventually received a Master of Music Degree from Frederick Neil Innes Conservatory of Music which had opened in New York City in 1915.[32] What was most extraordinary, however, is that the first of many hundreds of articles profiling Harry's career in New Orleans newspapers was published in February 1915 when, at seventeen years of age, Harry and his symphony orchestra played at the Washington Artillery Hall for the Pythian Lodges' fifty-first anniversary celebration.[33] Granted that his father was the president of the New Orleans Lodges, but this performance was a singular honor, and just the beginning of a brilliant musical career.

Just one year later, the eighteen year old Professor Harry Mendelson was preparing his thirty piece symphony orchestra for a series of winter concerts. The *Times Picayune* reported: "Prof. Mendelson has made a name for himself as a director both in this city and in Texas. Prof. Mendelson says he will have some of the best musicians in the city with him. He will have Achille Baquet and R.G. Decuir, late of the New York Symphony Orchestra as soloists." [34]

Harry disappeared from the concert scene in the city for almost two years at the end of 1916, when he became eighteen years of age. He enlisted and was made a lieutenant and bandmaster in the United States Army.[35] After his return in 1918 he enrolled briefly in the Loyola University Dental School. Unlike his cousin and namesake, Harry James Siess, Sr., he soon found out that he was not cut out for that profession.

In the summer of 1918, Ben and Mathilde Siess Mendelson left on a tour of the United States and Canada. They headed first for Detroit, where Ben, as the supreme representative of the Knights of Pythias, was to address the convention of the Supreme Lodge. Their son, Professor Harry Mendelson, stayed back in New Orleans, "having engaged a suite of rooms in one of the hotels." [36] By the beginning of 1921, Harry was back in the music business, this time for good. In February he was appointed band master of the forty piece orchestra sponsored by the Loolo Temple No. 143, Dramatic Order Knights of Khorassan, the entertainment arm of the Knights of Pythias. It would be an association which would last a lifetime.[37] In that same year, he also became the musical director of the New Orleans City Park Concert Band, holding that post for eighteen consecutive seasons. Every week during the summer, his music program selections were published in the *Times Picayune.* His orchestra played an eclectic mix of waltzes and foxtrots, arias from Italian and German opera, as well as popular tunes.[38]

That same year, his father, Ben Mendelson, branched out, taking on the job of secretary of the finance committee for the Liberty Homestead Association, whose aim was to provide affordable housing in New Orleans. In 1921 its assets were over a million and a half dollars.[39] Eugenie Siess moved to New Orleans in 1922, joining her nephew, Professor Harry Mendelson, on stage at various venues. The first of Eugenie's performances that was reported in the newspaper took place in September of that year. Harry directed the Loolo Temple D.O.K.K. band, and she sang two solos to put a close to the City Park music season.[40] Several weeks later she performed on WGV, the broadcast station sponsored by Interstate Electric and the *New Orleans Item* which reviewed her saying: "Miss. Eugene [sic] Siess, a newcomer in New Orleans musical circles, charmed with splendid contralto solos the numbers offered including 'La Habanera' from 'Carmen,' 'The Fields of Bally Claire,' and 'At Dawning.' Miss Siess furnished her own accompaniment." [41] Three weeks later she was, once again, performing, this time in front of the Loolo Temple at 1750 St. Charles Avenue, as the special attraction in four sidewalk concerts given by Mendelson's Band as a kick-off to the annual fair.[42]

In early 1922, Professor Mendelson organized a fifty piece Elks Band, after joining the New Orleans Elks lodge. His first concert there was held on March 19th of that year. His membership in that organization would also be a lifelong affair.[43] Along with the Elks Band, the Loolo Band, his own Mendelson's Concert Band, in 1924 he organized and led the Southern Pacific Railroad Band, and was the musical director for the Josie Corbera School of Dancing, whose students he used for special presentations in his City Park concerts.[44] In addition he organized and led the Dokey Jazz Band!

In January 1925, the doors of the Alcoyne School of Dancing opened its doors at 1021 Soniat Street, the home of Ben and Mathilde Mendelson, with Professor Harry Mendelson as its musical director, and Miss Adonna Houston, directress of character, buck and wing, soft shoe and clog dancing. The school also prepared its students for a vaudeville career, and held ballroom dancing classes in the afternoon and evenings. [45]

In April 1926, Michel Frédéric and Aimée Dupont Gouazé announced the engagement of their daughter, Marcelle Reine, to Professor Harry Mendelson. The couple's daughter, Musette Mathilde Mendelson, said she thought her parents had met at City Park during one of Harry's band concerts. They were married by the Honorable V.J. Stentz, Judge of the First District City Court, in New Orleans on August 3, 1927. Harry was twenty-eight and Marcelle was twenty-four. The ceremony was followed by a small reception at the bride's home on Alexander Street.[46] The bride's father, Frédéric Gouazé, an immigrant from Ariège, France had arrived in New Orleans in 1891 at the age of twenty-two. He became a butcher, married a local girl, Aimée Dupont, in 1902 and had eight children, of whom Marcelle, born on January 31, 1903 was the eldest. [47]

Shortly after the wedding, the seventh annual banquet of Mendelson's concert band was held at Turci's Italian Garden restaurant, with both the superintendent of City Park, and the chairman of its music committee honoring the band's director, Harry Mendelson. He, his parents Ben and Mathilde Siess Mendelson, and his wife, Marcelle Gouazé Mendelson, were the guests of honor.[48] Less than three months later, on December 14, 1927, Ben Mendelson, died of cardiac arrest at his residence on 2121 Audubon Street. He was sixty-seven years old. A large contingent of members from the Druids, Elks, Pythians, Knights of Khorassan, and Knights of America joined the family at their home two days later, on December 16th, from where the funeral took place. He was interred in the family tomb in St. Louis Cemetery #3 near Bayou St. John in New Orleans. Although Mathilde Siess Mendelson's father, David Siess, had broken all ties with his brother, Simon Siess, the latter's son, Leon, was an honorary pallbearer at Ben's funeral.[49]

***

For quite a while Dr. Harry Siess had been having difficulty making a living in Mansura as a dentist. With his father now deceased and an elderly mother, a wife and a little son to support, finances were stretched to the limit. He had thought, for a time, about moving, urged on by a wife, whose occasional reminder of her husband's dalliance with Josephine Olivier in a town as small as Mansura, was difficult at best. On February 16, 1928, Harry's son, Louis André Siess, who had just turned nineteen years of age, married twenty-one year old Helen Prévot, daughter of Celestin Prévot and Marie Eleonore Berger, at St. Paul the Apostle Catholic Church in Mansura. Newlyweds Louis and Helen soon started a family of their own. They farmed the property on Old River Road that Louis had inherited from his grandmother, Marie Charlot Olivier, which was north and west of the old David Siess homestead.[50] Harry's other son, Harry, Jr., was nine years old that same year.

One of Retta's brothers, Dr. Malcolm Kaffie, who was a dentist practicing in Shreveport, had offered to help the Siess family move north to get Harry started again as his partner. Retta was enthusiastic. Harry, himself, was less anxious, as his mother did not want to leave Mansura, and he was happy in the bosom of his extended Escudé and Cochrane family members in the town of his birth. He was respected, well-known and politically connected. The final linchpin of his resistance fell, when on July 5, 1928, his mother, Clara Cochrane Siess, died in her eighty-fourth year. She had been in failing health for some time. A funeral was held at her residence on July 8th conducted by Rabbi Myron Meyerovitz, after which her remains were taken to the Jewish cemetery in Pineville, where she was laid to rest next to her husband, David Siess.[51] Cochrane relatives insist that Clara never converted to Judaism, although she was buried next to her husband at Pineville. Early in the 1830s the Constitution and By-Laws of the first Jewish congregation in New Orleans, Shanarai-Chasset (Gates of Mercy, now Touro Synagogue) had allowed the burial of non-Jewish spouses along with their husbands in Jewish cemeteries due to the high incidence of intermarriage between Christians and Jews, as long as they were buried according to the "Israelite" custom. Children of mixed marriages were entitled to burial there as well. A special section was set aside for these couples, a condition that was not always followed, especially in small cemeteries. According to Bertram Korn, who wrote extensively on the early Jewish families of New Orleans, "these provisions relating to intermarriage offer vivid testimony of the extent of marriage out of the faith, and demonstrate how strongly the congregational leaders tried to keep these men from feeling alienated from their ancestral faith, and how profoundly they hoped that the children of these marriages might be saved for Judaism." [52]

Clara's succession was filed on August 10, 1928, wherein her property was divided equally amongst her sole heirs, Dr. Harry Siess, Sr., Misses Carrie and Eugenie Siess, and Mrs. Mathilde Siess Mendelson. It consisted solely of land belonging to the "home place." less what had already been disposed of to her son, Harry, to neighbors, Dr. Émil Regard and Wade Glasscock, as well as the right of way and an additional twenty-four arpents of farm land in the vicinity sold to the Texas and Pacific Railway.[53] True to his word, after this tragedy, Dr. Malcolm Kaffie, helped Dr. Harry Siess and his family to move to Shreveport. Murrell Smith Siess, Dr. Harry Siess, Jr's wife, remembered that her father-in-law told her that he was so sad to leave Mansura, that he cried the day he left, having spent almost all of his forty-six years in the little town.

***

Carrie Siess, fifty-one years old when her mother died, moved to New Orleans to live with her sisters, Mathilde Siess Mendelson, and Eugenie Siess, at 2121 Audubon Street. Next door, at 2119 Audubon Street, Professor Harry Mendelson, Mathilde's son, resided with his wife, Marcelle. Their only child, Harry Mendelson, Jr., was born in New Orleans on January 26, 1930[54] where little Harry was introduced to the world of music at an early age. When he was barely ten months old he became the Mendelson Concert Band's mascot, and its youngest member. At the tenth annual banquet and dance to celebrate the occasion at Turci's Italian Garden restaurant in October of 1930, he was introduced to his first audience. Eugenie Siess also attended, performing at the ceremony.[55] Mathilde Siess Mendelson and her sister, Eugenie, were practicing Catholics during their years in New Orleans. Mathilde's son, Harry Mendelson, Sr., was raised as a Catholic as well. The band, however, performed at many different venues. Harry's musicians, as well as his sister, Eugenie, were featured entertainers, along with two Yiddish plays sponsored by the Menorah Institute for the benefit of the Hebrew Immigrant Aid Society on October 30, 1932.[56] Later on that same year, as the French citizens of New Orleans celebrated Bastille Day on July 14th, officials at City Park saw to it that a large evening celebration, complete with music and dancing, and a public ceremony commemorating the fall of the Bastille in 1789, was widely publicized. Professor Harry Mendelson conducted the band and Eugenie Siess sang the French National Anthem, "La Marsaillaise." [57]

Early in 1930, Professor Harry Mendelson opened the first version of his Harry Mendelson School of Music, Singing, Dancing and Dramatic Art at 850 City Park Avenue with a faculty of fourteen teachers. The school had its own band with seventy-five students, who received extra training from the Professor himself free of charge. All pupils were guaranteed weekly public appearances, either at City Park or one of the other venues where Professor Mendelson was a regular performer. These opportunities, plus reasonable tuition, were fine drawing cards, which made the enterprise very popular.[58] As a promotion, Professor Mendelson contracted with the well-known New Orleans department store, D.H. Holmes, on Canal Street, to host vaudeville talent shows for children and adults. Held on the second floor auditorium of the store, the performances were free to all. After each show, Harry presided over auditions for the following performance.[59]

On February 4, 1934, Professor Mendelson moved the Mendelson School to the prime uptown location of St. Charles and Jackson Avenues. His aunt, Eugenie Siess, was in charge of the vocal department. A small paragraph in the *Times Picayune* praised her experience, efficiency and musical education. An assistant, Miss Adrynne Gueymard, was in charge of the "personality singing department." Harry, Sr., and later his son Harry, Jr., were able to teach practically any band or orchestra instrument that a pupil wished to learn. Esther Hall, one of the city's foremost dancing teachers, was in charge of that aspect of the program. Drama coaches were available as well. Professor Mendelson declared that the opening of this school was "a complete realization of my desires for many years." [60] Eugenie's tenure at the school was halted abruptly the next year, when on May 22, 1935, she succumbed to cancer at the age of sixty-three. Services were held for her at St. John the Baptist Catholic Church at the corner of Dryades and Clio Streets, followed by interment in St. Louis Cemetery # 3 in New Orleans.[61]

***

Harry and Retta Kaffie Siess, who had moved to Shreveport in 1928, remained there for the rest of their lives, but Dr. Siess' attachment to Avoyelles Parish was deep-rooted. He always maintained his subscription to the *Marksville Weekly News*. His daughter-in-law, Murrell Smith Siess, remembered that Dad Siess sent clothing and other items at Christmas to needy families in Mansura throughout his life.[62] She added that he was a very charitable man, always trying to help others. He often did dental work for little or no money, would not accept payment from other dentists' families, or from the clergy. When informed that her beloved father-in-law had an illegitimate child and grandchildren in Mansura she remarked that she was not really surprised, because "Dad Siess had been such a handsome Frenchmen." She added that when the Siess family got together, they all spoke French amongst themselves, much to the chagrin of her mother-in-law, Retta Kaffie Siess, who had been raised in a German speaking household. Retta was sure that they were talking about her, when the family spoke the language, as she could not understand any of it.

After Dr. Siess left his partnership with his brother-in-law, Malcolm Kaffie, he joined the Tri-State Clinic in Shreveport, which was an association of five physicians and himself, the only dentist, practicing at 708 Cotton Street. He and his wife and son moved to a comfortable house at 754 Unadilla Street. At the age of nineteen, in 1938, Harry James Siess, Jr., was enrolled at Louisiana State University in Baton Rouge, where he lived in off-campus housing. After graduation he followed in his father's footsteps, enrolling at the Loyola Dental School. Graduating in February 1943, he received a commission in the United States Army, Medical Administrative Reserve, for the duration of World War II.[63]

Upon leaving the service, he returned to practice with his father at their home on Unadilla Street. While on duty with the Army in Arkansas, he had fallen in love with a beautiful young lady, Murrell Smith. They were married in her home town of Benton, Arkansas on February 20, 1947. When interviewed late in life, Mrs. Siess said that she and Harry felt they were soul mates, and had decided never to have children. Harry suffered from diabetes, just as did his first cousin once removed, Harry Mendelson, Jr., a fact which could have also driven that decision. Murrell had offered to convert to Judaism for his sake, but he told her that it was not important to him. Neither Harry, Sr., who had taken so much trouble to convince his father-in-law that he was really Jewish, nor his wife Retta, it seems, had ever been too observant, so their son saw no reason to force a change on his bride, who had been raised in the Methodist Church.

Dr. Harry Siess, Jr. remained in practice with his father until the latter's death on October 9, 1959, at the age of seventy-seven. Funeral services were held at the Osborn Chapel, with burial at Forest Park Cemetery in Shreveport. He was remembered as the past president of the Shreveport Dental Society and the Shreveport Charity Medical Unit. He was a Mason and a member of the International College of Dentists.[64] Retta Kaffie Siess, Harry, Sr.'s wife, died almost twenty years later in May 1979. She was buried alongside her husband. Their son, Dr. Harry Siess, Jr., and his wife Murrell remained in Shreveport, where the former continued to practice dentistry. They took care of his aunt, Carrie Siess, the last of David and Clara's children to die. She had never married, working off and on as a seamstress both in New Orleans when she had lived with her late sister, Eugenie, and after Mathilde Siess Mendelson died on September 3, 1939, at Mercy Hospital in New Orleans,[65] she moved to Shreveport when she resided with Harry and

Retta Siess. She succumbed on April 25, 1970, at the age of ninety-three at a local nursing facility.

After David Siess' children left Avoyelles Parish, Louis André Siess and his family were the only remaining members of the family still living there. Harry and Josephine Olivier's son, Louis, and his wife, Helen Prévot, farmed all their lives in Mansura and raised eight children: Marjorie Ann (b. 1928), Charles Andrew (b. 1931), Carl Anthony (b. 1933), Eugene Daniel (b.1934), Vincent Nathaniel (b. 1938), Juanita Veronica (b. 1940), Barbara Elaine (b. 1942), and Mary Yolanda (b. 1946).[66]

***

Professor Harry and Marcelle Mendelson were doing very well in the years leading up to World War II. Their son Harry, Jr., was a musical prodigy as well. His instrument of choice was the baritone French horn. He attended the prestigious Jesuit High School in New Orleans, and graduated from Tulane University with a B.A. in Music, and an M.A. in music education and band from the University of Michigan. Unfortunately Harry, Jr. suffered from an acute form of diabetes, which took a huge toll on his life. His only sibling, Musette Mathilde Mendelson, was born on November 29, 1943 in New Orleans, just as Harry, Jr. started high school.

Professor Mendelson's association as the Band Master for City Park came to an end with the 1939 season, but he was doubly busy, with his Conservatory of Music School and orchestra, his leadership and instruction of the St. Louis Cathedral, and St. Dominic's High School bands,[67] and a new and costly obsession, Mardi Gras Carnival Krewes. Music, especially marching bands, were a staple of the many carnival parades in New Orleans. The short-lived Krewe of Mendelsonians, founded by Harry, himself, made its first appearance in 1940.[68] This was also the year that he was elected president and business manager of the United Musicians' Local Industrial Union # 983, an affiliate of the C.I.O.[69] Carnival was a family affair. In 1941 Professor Harry Mendelson was King Henry III, and Harry, Jr. was a page in the court of Queen Elizabeth, the theme for that year's Krewe of Eurydice's inaugural ball.[70] As Musette Mendelson grew older, she, too, became a lifelong participant in Carnival. Professor Mendelson also took on the New Orleans Civic Band, composed of fifty professionals from the American Federation of Musicians, Local 174. They gave forty-eight Sunday concerts beginning just before Thanksgiving, 1941.[71]

In 1948, Professor Harry Mendelson organized the first New Orleans Music Festival. Held in City Park over a three day period at the close of school in May, all high schools in the South, regardless of size or enrollment were eligible to participate by sending their bands to the competition.[72] This year also saw Professor Mendelson re-elected as state commander of the Louisiana chapter of the All American Drum and Bugle Corps and Band Association. He was also re-elected as the vice-commander of the national chapter of that organization at the meeting which took place in Miami, Florida.[73] Father and son were very active in the 1949 Carnival season. The elder Mendelson was the chairman of the floor committee for the Krewe of Carthage's second Mardi Gras Ball, while his son was its general chairman. The pair swapped roles for their participation in the Caronis, wife of Cynthius, Greek God of Music's first carnival ball.[74] Along with their carnival duties, fraternal organizations, and band concerts, the Mendelsons continued teaching music in New Orleans.

From the age of twenty-four, Harry, Jr. had been the band director and professor of music at Xavier University. He met his future wife, Bonnie Broel, during the social whirl of Mardi Gras balls. According to Bonnie's autobiography, *House of Broel – The Inside Story,* her mother, Olga Tepper, who was a bit of a social climber, encouraged her friendship with the Mendelson family because of their important connections to the heady world of New Orleans Mardi Gras celebrations. While the season of parades and balls lasts anywhere from six to eight weeks depending upon the liturgical calendar of any given year, the preparation for all the parades, float building and planning for the accompanying festivities is a year round activity in Louisiana.

Harry's fiancée, Bonnie Broel, was born in 1938 in Metairie, Louisiana to Albert Broel-Plater, and his Canadian wife, Olga Tepper. Count Broel-Plater, born to Polish nobility at a time when the country was part of the Russian Empire, according to his daughter, Bonnie, had received a medical degree from Warsaw University then went on to St. Petersburg Imperial Military Academy, from where he was drafted into the Russian Cavalry. Captured in battle during the early days of World War I, his escape was facilitated by the fortuitous meeting of his German commander cousin. He immigrated to America in 1915, where he enlisted in the American army. Discharged when it was found out he was an alien, he worked in Detroit, then Chicago, helping other foreign-speaking immigrants. Since he could not practice medicine in the United States, and money he had counted on from his late father, Count Wilhelm, had disappeared, he attended a non-traditional medical "college" which taught the precepts of naprapathy. This "science" was based on a belief that all disease was caused by connective tissue and ligament disorders and could be cured through massage therapy. Armed with his degree, Dr. Broel-Plater moved to Detroit to set up a practice. Called to the bedside of Olga Tepper's dying father, the couple, after a series of personal tragedies including the death of Albert's first wife in childbirth, and the demise of Olga's father, soon wed. In his spare time, Dr. Albert considered raising frogs, a difficult task in the cold northern climates of Michigan, and on the one hundred acre farm that the couple had managed to buy in Fremont, Ohio. During the depression, however, the family fell on hard times. Dr. Broel-Plater's practice was shut down and he was fined for practicing medicine without a license. Olga, who, with Albert's help, had attempted to set up a mail-order matchmaking venture which they called "The American Friendship Society," ran into trouble in 1931, when a notorious serial killer, Harry Powers, from Clarksburg, West Virginia, had used their services to arrange the killing of five women he had met through Olga's organization. To make matters worse, a Detroit widow with three children had been slain by a man whom she had met and married after corresponding with him through the Friendship Society. An investigation, started by the Michigan attorney general's office cast a harsh spotlight on the couple.[75] This publicity caused the

Broel-Platers to have to seek protection from the Detroit Police Department. Although Postal Inspectors, who also investigated this "mail-order" business said they found no real basis to prosecute the couple, Albert and Olga, decided to leave Detroit and take refuge on their Ohio farm.[76]

After several difficult years Albert concluded that his frog business would fare better in a semi-tropical climate. The family moved to Louisiana in 1933, setting up a frog breeding and canning company in Metairie, just outside of New Orleans, where they had moderate success, and where their only child, Bonnie, was born. After a brief return to Detroit to assuage his wife's homesickness, the family moved back to New Orleans in 1952, settling, once again in Metairie, where Dr. Broel-Plater penned several books on frog breeding and canning. After high school, Bonnie studied art history and theory at both Newcomb College in New Orleans, and later at the Cranbrook Academy of Art in Detroit. To pacify her mother she also graduated from Soulé College as a stenographer in April 1959.

Bonnie and Harry, Jr. were quietly married in the Mendelson family's parish church in December 1958. Their first son, Harry Mendelson, III, was born in December 1959. Albert Broel Mendelson arrived fourteen months later in February 1961. The marriage was doomed to failure, however. Bonnie, disenchanted with Harry Jr.'s emotional outbursts she thought it the lesser of two evils to return to her parents' home. She continued to work as a legal secretary, as she had done during her brief marriage, but gradually turned a hobby, sewing, into a money-making sideline. After opening up a small shop on St. Charles Avenue in 1963, she became the most successful bridal designer in New Orleans. She also designed and sewed costumes for Mardi Gras balls.

After being stricken by a cerebral hemorrhage, Harry Mendelson, Jr. died at Baptist Hospital on May 15, 1964, at the age of thirty-four. Having left Xavier University, he had been employed as a music teacher at the Marrero Junior High School. Before his death, he was also serving as senior vice-commander of the All American Drum and Bugle Corps and Band Association, a member of Local 174 of the American Federation of Musicians, assistant director and baritone horn soloist of the New Orleans Civic Band, and first vice-president of the Order of Louisiana Colonels, Inc. After a Requiem Mass held at St. Raphael's Roman Catholic Church, he was interred in the family tomb at St. Louis Cemetery #3. [77]

Harry's sister, Musette, formerly the junior vice-commander, replaced her late brother as senior vice-commander of the Louisiana Chapter of the All-American Drum and Bugle Corps and Band Association for the 1965 season. Harry, Sr. was also elected as the state commander, and his wife, Marcelle Mendelson, became its quartermaster.[78] Several months later Colonel Harry Mendelson, Sr. was promoted to Brigadier General of the Honorable Order of Louisiana Colonels, Inc.[79] Musette graduated from college, then joined the faculty at Laurel-McDonogh Highschool # 1 in New Orleans. On December 27, 1966, Musette wed Thomas Andrew Gonzales at St. James Major Catholic Church. Her little nephews, Harry III and Albert Broel Mendelson, her late brother's children, served as ring bearers.[80] She wore a gown designed and given to her by her former, sister-in-law, Bonnie Broel, one of the first wedding dresses Bonnie had ever created.[81]

Professor Harry Mendelson. Sr. died on August 4, 1969. The *Times Picayune* devoted two columns to his career in New Orleans. He had organized bands as varied as the New Orleans Municipal Band, the Laundry and Dry Cleaning Service Band, the Consolidated Ice Industries Band, the New Orleans Recreation Department Band, and the Mendelson Concert Band, amongst others. He was a member of the Army National Guard, a State Guard officer, and an honorary Colonel on the staffs of four governors from Earl Long to John McKeithen. He was a great friend of long time Mayor of New Orleans, DeLesseps S. "Chep" Morrison, who had presented him a plaque from the city for his civic work on behalf of Mardi Gras. He also composed band music, and wrote a series of teaching methods used in his own schools. He was member of the Knights of Columbus, the American Legion, and numerous musical and educational associations. At the time of his death, he was the chief judge for the All American Association of Music Contest Judges.[82] A Funeral Mass was celebrated for Harry Mendelson, Sr., grandson of Alsatian Jewish immigrant, David Siess, on August 5, 1969 at St. James Major Catholic Church. He was interred in the Mendelson family tomb in St. Louis Cemetery # 3.

***

David and Clara Siess's grandson, Dr. Harry James Siess, Jr., died suddenly while driving his automobile with his wife at his side on December 24, 1983 in Shreveport. He was buried in the non-sectarian Forest Park Cemetery near his parents. Murrell eventually moved back to Arkansas, dying at the age of eighty-eight, on February 21, 2008. She was interred at the Cato United Methodist Cemetery, in North Little Rock, Arkansas.

Harry, Siess, Jr.'s, half-brother, Louis André Siess died in Mansura at the age of ninety-one on November 17, 1999. He left eight children, thirty-four grandchildren, twenty-four great-grandchildren, and three great-great grandchildren, many of whom still live in Louisiana, although some eventually relocated to California and Nevada. All of his children were raised as Catholics. The only members of the Siess family who still carry the name in Avoyelles Parish are his descendants. Louis André's family adopted the alternative spelling "Seiss," which now appears on the street sign at both ends of "Seiss" Street next to the old Texas and Pacific Railroad tracks, the site of the former David Siess homestead. Many of Louis André's descendants hold or have held positions of importance in the community. His granddaughter, Felicia Seiss, after many years with the Avoyelles Parish Sheriff's department, is the Assistant Secretary/Treasurer of the City of Marksville. Her sister, Lorraine Seiss, has worked her entire life for the Avoyelles Parish School Board. Granddaughter, Beryl Seiss Sykes, is the retired postmistress of Hineston in Rapides Parish, Louisiana. She now devotes herself to poetry and writing. Fabian Barbin, another grandson, is a popular teacher at the Avoyelles High school and its Band Master as well. He leads his own musical group in his spare time. His sister, Arlene, is a clerk at the Avoyelles Parish

Courthouse. Although some of the members of the David Siess family have moved to other parts of the country, they, as well as those who have remained in Avoyelles Parish have been completely absorbed into the social fabric of Christian Central Louisiana. There are no members of the David Siess family who have retained their Jewish faith.

---

[1] Avoyelles Parish Courthouse Records (Marksville, Avoyelles Parish, LA), *Conveyances*, Book TT, File # 8411, p. 747, "Louis David to Mrs. David Siess, Sale of Personal Property," filed March 5, 1886.

[2] Avoyelles Parish Courthouse records (Marksville, Avoyelles Parish, LA), *Conveyances*, Book TT, File #8438, p. 800, "David Siess to Mrs. David Siess, Power of Attorney," filed March 27, 1886.

[3] Avoyelles Parish Courthouse records (Marksville, Avoyelles Parish, LA), *Conveyances*, Book ZZ, File #8894, p. 369, " Sheriff Sale of Land on 12 month bond to Mrs. David Siess," filed February 26, 1887.

[4] "Digested summary and alphabetical list of private claims presented to the House of Representatives from the Forty-Seventh to the Fifty-First Congress, inclusive; exhibiting the action of each claim, with references to the reports, bills, etc., elucidating its progress." Serial Set Vol. No. 3268, Session Vol. No.40; Report: H.Misc.Doc. 213, 28 August 1894, p. 624. Record for pension application of David Siess, 51st Congress, digital image, *Genealogybank.com* (http://www.genealogybank.com [hereinafter cited as "GB"]: accessed 5 April 2011).

[5] "Boarding House Kept by Mrs. David Siess," Louisiana State University Libraries On Line Catalog – Special Collections – Louisiana and Lower Mississippi Valley (hereinafter cited as "LLMV"), Microfilm # 1032, *The Marksville Review*, Vol 13, no. 10, 15 April 1893, p. 3, col. 5.

[6] Jeraldine DuFour LaCour, *Brides Book of Avoyelles Parish, Louisiana Volume 3, 1881-1899* (Alexandria: Jeraldine Dufour LaCour [P.O. Box 5022, Alexandria, LA], 1986), 136.

[7] "New Orleans, Louisiana Birth Records Index, 1790-1899," database, *Ancestry.com* (http://www.ancestry.com [hereinafter cited as "A"]: accessed

2/ 2010), citing State of Louisiana, Secretary of State, Division of Archives, Records Management, and History, *Vital Records Indices*. Baton Rouge, LA, USA. Birth of Harry Mendelson, Vol. 114, p. 689.

[8] "Dental College – The First Freshman Class Elects Its Officers," *The (New Orleans, LA) Daily Picayune* (hereinafter cited as "*DP*"), 10 December 1899, p. 25, col. 2, digital image, (GB: accessed 4/ 2011).

[9] "The Dentists' Society," *DP*, 16 February 1893, p. 6, col. 1, digital image, (GB: accessed 4/ 2011).

[10] "Fourteen graduates - Commencement of the College of Dentistry," *The (New Orleans, LA) Daily Item*, 5 May 1902, p. 7, col. 1, digital image, (GB: accessed 4/ 2011). Note: In 1908 the New Orleans College of Dentistry was taken over by Tulane University, becoming the Tulane College of Dentistry.

[11] Avoyelles Parish Courthouse Records (Marksville, Avoyelles Parish, LA), *Conveyances*, Book QQQ, File # 7231, p. 537, "Tax Collector's Sale of Land to Mrs. Jennie Siess," filed May 19, 1899; and *Conveyances*, Book XXX, File 10,081, p. 55, "Rescission of Land – Jules Moreau to Mrs. Jennie Siess," filed April 25, 1902.

[12] Avoyelles Parish Courthouse Records (Marksville, Avoyelles Parish, LA), *Conveyances*, Book H-1, File # 14,510, p. 363, "Sale of Land with Mortgage – Mrs. David Siess to Harry J. Siess," filed March 3, 1906; and *Conveyances* Book K-1, File 15,366, p. 62, " Sale of Land – 10 acres – Onezime Sampson to Harry J. Siess," filed December 29, 1906.

[13] "Died," *DP*, 15 December 1901, p. 4, col. 6, digital image, (GB: accessed 4/ 2011).

[14] "The Fraternities Active in Louisiana," *DP*, 9 June 1902, p. 3, col. 4, digital image, (GB: accessed 4/ 2011).

[15] "Soard's New Orleans City Directory 1915," Listing for "The Louisiana Pythian (monthly) B. Mendelson, pub 638 Canal," p. 1362; and "Soard's New Orleans City Directory 1920," p. 1232, listing for " New Orleans Catholic Monthly Publishing Co. B. Mendelson mngr. 638 Canal," digital

images, *Fold3.com* (http://www.fold3.com [hereinafter cited as "F3"]: accessed 3/ 2011).

[16] Avoyelles Parish Courthouse records (Marksville, Avoyelles Parish, LA), *Family Meetings*, Book G, p. 22, "Succession of Josephine Olivier, dec'd- Family meeting," filed March 8, 1919. Note: The family meeting was held "in behalf of Charles Berger and Louis Siess, minors, minor children, issue of the illicit sectual (sic) intercourse between Rodolph Berger and Harold Siess, with Josephine Olivier."

[17] Baptismal certificate of Louis André Siess, original in possession of the heirs of Marjorie Ann Seiss.

[18] "Alexandria," *DP,* 17 July 1909, p. 16, col. 7, digital image, (GB: accessed 4/ 2011).

[19] "Police Jury Proceedings," LLMV, Microfilm # 1032, *The Avoyelles Enterprise*, Vol. VIII, no. 50, 7 May 1910, p. 3, cols. 3, 4.

[20] "Michel Addresses Two Good Meetings," *DP,* 12 November 1911, p. 3, col. 1, digital image, (GB: accessed 4/ 2011).

[21] Confederate Pension Application for David Siess, Avoyelles Parish, LA, Louisiana State Archives, File # 12494, Reel CP1.127, Microdex 2, Sequence 6, Baton Rouge, Louisiana – 11 pages. Application for pension dated 31 October 1913.

[22] He was actually eighty years old and born in Germany, but had erroneously indicated that he was born on June 3, 1841 in Alsace, France.

[23] Confederate Pension Application for David Siess. Avoyelles Parish, LA, Louisiana State Archives, File # 12494, Reel CP1.127, Microdex 2, Sequence 6, Baton Rouge, Louisiana – 14 pages. Application for pension dated 17 August 1915.

[24] "News From Louisiana and Mississippi Told in Brief," *The New Orleans States,* 7 June 1917, p. 2, col. 3, digital image, (GB: accessed 4/ 2011).

[25] "Society," *The New Orleans States,* 9 September 1917, p. 20, col. 5, digital image, (GB: accessed 4/ 2011).

[26] Avoyelles Parish Courthouse records (Marksville, Avoyelles Parish, LA), *Conveyances*, Book A-13, File # 27342, p. 280, "Mrs. David Siess to Harry J. Siess, Sale of Land," filed 6 November 1918.

[27] Paul M. Lehman was Marie Charlot's son born to her before the 1864 execution of Isaac Lehmann, originally from Lembach, Alsace. Isaac Lehmann was Dr. Harry Siess, Sr.'s half-uncle. See chapter 4, pp. 160-163.

[28] See note 16. A document, No. 27668, entitled, "Olivier Rabalais and others – Partition," was filed March 8, 1919 and attached to the Family Meeting wherein Edward Olivier had been appointed dative tutor to his nephews Charles Berger and Louis Siess.

[29] 1920 U.S. Census, Avoyelles Parish, LA, pop. sch., Mansura, Ward 3, ED 4, p. 4A (penned), Dwelling #63, Family #66, Harry J. Siess household and Dwelling #64, Family #67, David Siess household, digital image, (A: accessed 4/2010), citing NARA microfilm publication T625, roll 605. Date of enumeration: 3 January 1920.

[30] Confederate Pension Application for David Siess, Avoyelles Parish, LA, Louisiana State Archives, File # 12494, Reel CP1.127, Microdex 2, Sequence 6, Baton Rouge, Louisiana – 8 pages. Application for pension dated 5 September 1922.

[31] "Is Named President of Dental Society," *The (New Orleans, LA) Times Picayune* (herein after cited as "*TP*"), 8 March 1925, p. 13, col. 2, digital image, (GB: accessed 4/ 2011).

[32] Frederick Neil Innes was a British born trombone prodigy, who studied abroad, but came to New York City in 1880 where he became famous playing with Gilmore's Band at Manhattan Beach, Brooklyn.

[33] "Pythian Lodges to Mark Anniversary," *The New Orleans Item,* 15 February 1915, p. 20, col. 6, digital image, (GB: accessed 4/ 2011).

[34] "To Give Series of Concerts," *TP* 25 July 1916, p. 4, col. 4, digital image, (GB: accessed 4/ 2011).

[35] "World War I Draft Registration Cards, 1917-1918," digital image, (A: accessed 2/2011), Harry Mendelson, Serial # 1147, no. 526, Draft Board "12", Avoyelles Parish, Louisiana, citing *World War I Selective Service System Draft Registration Cards, 1917-1918*, NARA microfilm publication. M1509, roll 1684925.

[36] "Society Makes Tiger Day Patriotic and Enjoyable Occasion," *The New Orleans States,* 28 July 1918, p. 3, cols. 4, 5, digital image, (GB: accessed 4/ 2011).

[37] "Knights of Khorassan Organize Concert Band," *The New Orleans States,* 22 February 1921, p. 12, col. 8, digital image, (GB: accessed 4/ 2011).

[38] "City Park Concert Program," *TP,* 29 April 1921, p. 23, col. 2, digital image, (GB: accessed 4/ 2011).

[39] "The Liberty Homestead," *TP,* 20 May 1922, p. 2, col. 2, digital image, (GB: accessed 4/ 2011).

[40] "Fine Music to Close Park Season," *The New Orleans Item,* 10 September 1922, p. 1, col. 7, digital image, (GB: accessed 4/ 2011).

[41] "Entertaining Program of Vocal, Music Number Pleases WGV Audience," *The New Orleans Item,* 1 October 1922, p. 13, col. 1, digital image, (GB: accessed 4/ 2011).

[42] "Two Concerts Arranged by Loolo Temple Band," *The New Orleans States,* 19 March 1922, p. 15, col. 6, digital image, (GB: accessed 4/2011).

[43] "First Concert Elks' Band," *The New Orleans States,* 22 October 1922, p. 9 , cols. 7, 8, digital image, (GB: accessed 4/ 2011).

[44] "Band to Play in City Park," *TP,* 20 August 1924, p. 22, cols. 6-8, digital image, (GB: accessed 4/ 2011).

[45] "Alcoyne School of Dancing," *TP,* 4 January 1925, p. 63, col. 1, digital image, (GB: accessed 4/ 2011).

[46] *Orleans Parish Marriage Records*, Certificate of Marriage, Vol 50, p. 1926 (1927), Harry Mendelson to Marcelle Gouazé; photocopy obtained from Louisiana Secretary of State, Department of Archives, Records Management and History, Baton Rouge, LA. Note: The couple, although Catholic, had a civil ceremony because Professor Mendelson had had a brief previous marriage which ended in divorce in 1925.

[47] Louisiana Secretary of State, *Orleans Parish Birth Records*, Certificate of Birth, Vol. 124, p. 997 (1903), Marcelle Reine Gouazé; photocopy obtained from Louisiana Secretary of State, Department of Archives, Records Management and History, Baton Rouge, LA.

[48] "Mendelson's Band Members Honored," *TP,* 11 September 1927, p. 49, col. 2, digital image, (GB: accessed 4/ 2011).

[49] "Last Rites Today for K. of P. Leader- Benjamin Mendelson Was Supreme Representative of Order for 8 Years," *TP,* 16 December 1927, p. 6, col. 3, digital image, (GB: accessed 4/ 2011).

[50] Avoyelles Parish Courthouse records (Marksville, Avoyelles Parish, LA), *Marriages - 1928*, "Louis André Siess to Helen Prévot - Bond and license," filed February 13, 1928.

[51] Louisiana Secretary of State, *Louisiana Death Records*, Vol. 19, p. 8349 (1928), Clara Cochrane Siess; photocopy obtained from Louisiana Secretary of State, Department of Archives, Records Management and History, Baton Rouge, LA; also, "Died, Siess, Clara Cochrane," *TP,* 7 July 1928, p. 2, col. 8, digital image, (GB: accessed 4/ 2011); also, Jewish Cemetery, (Pineville, Rapides Parish, LA) Clara Cochrane Siess marker, row 11, personally read, 2005. Note: According to some Cochrane descendants her Jewish burial may have been preceded by a Catholic service in Mansura.

[52] Bertram Wallace Korn, *The Early Jews of New Orleans* (Waltham, Massachusetts: The American Jewish Historical Society, 1969), 196, 197.

⁵³ Avoyelles Parish Courthouse Records (Marksville, Avoyelles Parish, LA), *Probate Petitions and Wills*, Book T, p. 20, "Succession of Mrs. Clara Cochrane Siess, Judgment Placing in Possession," filed August 10, 1928.

⁵⁴ 1930 U.S. Census, Orleans Parish, LA, pop. sch., New Orleans, Ward 14, ED 235, p. 21A (penned), Dwelling #253, Family #401, Mathilde S. Mendelson household, and Dwelling #253, Family #402, Harry Mendelson household, digital image, (A: accessed 4/ 2011), citing NARA microfilm publication T626, roll 811. Date of enumeration: 14 April 1930.

⁵⁵ "City Park Band Holds Banquet," *TP,* 12 October 1930, p. 9, col. 4, digital image, (GB: accessed 4// 2011).

⁵⁶ "Menorah Institute to Present Plays," *TP,* 26 October 1932, p. 23, col. 1, digital image, (GB: accessed 4/ 2011).

⁵⁷ "French National Holiday Program Scheduled Today," *TP,* 14 July 1932, p. 13, col. 7, digital image, (GB: accessed 4/2011).

⁵⁸ "Mendelson School Boasts of Fine Band," *TP,* 17 September 1933, p. 97, col. 5, digital image, (GB: accessed 4/ 2011).

⁵⁹ "You're Invited to Holmes Vaudeville Shows," *TP,* 6 May 1933, p. 5, cols. 1, 2, digital image, (GB: accessed 4/2011).

⁶⁰ "Harry Mendelson's New School of Music, Singing, Dancing, and Dramatic Art Opened to Public," *TP,* 11 February 1934, p. 8, cols. 4, 5, digital image, (GB: accessed 4/ 2011).

⁶¹ "Deaths – Eugenie Siess," *TP,* 23 May 1935, p. 2, col. 8, digital image, (GB: accessed 4/ 2011).

⁶² Murrell Smith Siess told the author that her husband, Harry Siess, Jr., was unaware that he had a half-brother in Mansura. Yet his charity throughout his life to a family or families in the town of his birth might tell a different story.

[63] "Loyola Dentists Get Commissions," *The New Orleans States*, 7 February, 1943, p. 24, cols. 6, 7, digital image, (GB: accessed 4/ 2011).

[64] "Dr. Siess Last Rites Are Held," *TP*, 14 October 1959, p. 6, col. 6, digital image, (GB: accessed 4/ 2011).

[65] Mathilde Siess was buried in the Mendelson tomb in St. Louis Cemetery # 3 on September 5th. She had succumbed to heart failure just over a month shy of her seventy-first birthday. See: "Deaths – Mrs. Mathilde Siess Mendelson," *TP*, 5 September 1939, p. 2, col. 8, digital image, (GB: accessed 4/ 2011).

[66] Birth dates of the Louis Seiss children were supplied to the author by the late Marjorie Ann Seiss in 2003.

[67] "Two Band Concerts," *TP*, 28 April 1939, p. 17, col. 7, digital image, (GB: accessed 4/ 2011).

[68] "Miss George Queen of Mendelsonians," *TP*, 25 January 1940, p. 3, col. 7, digital image, (GB: accessed 4/ 2011).

[69] "Officers are Named by United Musicians," *TP*, 11 February 1940, p. 21, col. 1, digital image, (GB: accessed 4/ 2011).

[70] "Eurydice Krewe Depicts Court of Queen Elizabeth," *TP*, 11 January 1941, p. 12, col. 1, digital image, (GB: accessed 4/ 2011).

[71] "Orleans Civic Band Starts Rehearsals," *TP*, 10 October 1941, p. 2, col. 5, digital image, (GB: accessed 4/ 2011).

[72] "Announce Music Festival Judges," *TP*, 25 April 1949, p. 50, col. 2, digital image, (GB: accessed 4/ 2011).

[73] "State Commander of Group Renamed," *TP*, 2 September 1949, p. 31, col. 3, and, "Bandmaster's Group Renames Mendelson," 9 June, 1949, p. 47, col. 8, digital images, (GB: accessed 4/2011).

[74] "Spanish Arena Setting for Krewe of Carthage's 2nd Mardi Gras Ball," *TP*, 12 February 1949, p. 21, cols. 1, 2; and "Goddess Caronis, Wife of

Cynthius Makes Her Bow at New Carnival Ball,", 17 February 1949, p. 13, cols. 7, 8, digital images, (GB: accessed 4/ 2011).

[75] "Evidence Against Powers 'Perfect' Says Prosecutor," and "Prosecutor Would Put Society out of Business," *TP*, 3 September 1931, p. 8, cols. 3, 4, digital image, (GB: accessed 4/ 2011).

[76] "Promoter of Letter Club Given Protection," *TP*, 31 August 1931, p. 12, col. 4, digital image, (GB: accessed 4/2011).

[77] "Rites Saturday For Composer – Harry Mendelson Jr., Band leader, Dies," *TP*, 16 May 1964, p. 5, cols. 3-5, digital image, (GB: accessed 4/2011).

[78] "Harry Mendelson Chosen Delegate," *TP*, 16 September 1964, p. 24, col. 3, digital image, (GB: accessed 4/ 2011).

[79] "Mendelson Named Brigadier General," *TP*, 12 December 1964, p. 23, col. 3, digital image, (GB: accessed 4/ 2011).

[80] "Weddings – Gonzales-Mendelson," *TP*, 25 December 1966, p. 29, col. 6, digital image, (GB: accessed 4/ 2011).

[81] Bonnie Broel, *House of Broel, The Inside Story,* (New Orleans: House of Broel Foundation, LLC, [2220 St. Charles Ave., New Orleans, LA,] 2007), 148.

[82] "N.O. Musician's Last Rites Set," *TP*, 5 August 1969, p. 12, cols. 1, 2 ,7, digital image, (GB: accessed 4/ 2011).

David Siess Store and Post Office, Mansura, LA, ca. 1910. David Siess underneath sign, Dr. Harry James Siess, Sr. to the right
(*Courtesy of the late Murrell Smith Siess*)

Dr. Harry James Siess, Jr., ca. 1946
(*Courtesy of the late Murrell Smith Siess*)

Louis André Seiss (half- brother of Dr. Harry Siess, Sr.) and wife, Helen Prévot (*Courtesy of Felicia and Lorraine Seiss*)

Eugenie Siess in costume, ca. 1899
(*Courtesy of the late Murrell Smith Siess*)

CHAPTER 9
THE GOUDCHAUX NETWORK

The name "Goudchaux" is an adaptation of the Hebrew, *Eliakim*, meaning "whom God will raise up." Because it was originally used as a first name it cannot be automatically assumed, therefore, that Jewish families using it as a family name are necessarily related. The surname might simply have been taken at random in 1808, when Napoleon's *Décret de Bayonne* required every Jewish resident in the Empire to adopt a fixed first and last name. For that reason, the "Goudchaux" family of Brumath, Alsace whose children came to Central Louisiana, are not related in any way to the Leon Godchaux family, originally from Herbeviller, France, who settled in New Orleans, and helped to develop the sugar industry in Louisiana. The spelling of the name has also created problems. In France, variations such as "Gutschuh," "Gutschu," even "Gautsch" have been used. In Louisiana "Goudchaud," "Godcheany," "Goudcheaux," and Gottschalk crop up.

Although many members of the Goudchaux family did not originally settle in Avoyelles Parish, the majority made Louisiana their home, and, through their various intermarriages, they created a network which connected Avoyelles to St. Landry, to Iberville, to Morehouse and finally to Orleans Parishes. These alliances were, not only with fellow Alsatians, such as the Kahn, Hiller, Levy, Heymann and Weill families, but also with newer Eastern European immigrants such as the Weiss and Goldring families. The relationships are complicated, close and confusing, but are really at the heart of the development of the phenomenon that is post-Civil War Southern Jewry. Unlike the first Hebrew citizens, who by circumstance, were forced to marry outside their faith, many in the affluent Goudchaux family had the opportunity to do otherwise. Leopold Goudchaux, who arrived as a child just before the Civil War, stood at the crossroads of this phenomenon.

Leopold's grandfather, Abraham Goudchaux, was born in Bouxwiller, Alsace, France, probably around 1700. By the time his grandson, Jacques, was born in 1792, the family had moved fifteen miles away to Brumath. By all accounts, Jacques Goudchaux must have been an extraordinary man. He lived to be seventy-three years of age, was married three times, and fathered twenty-two children, nine by his first wife, Barbe Levi, twelve by his second wife, Rosette Kahn, and one with his last wife, Marie Metzger. Nine of his twenty-two children came to the United States.

Esther (Estelle) and Fleurette Goudchaux, Jacques' daughters with his first wife, came to New Orleans in the late 1840s and married brothers Samuel and Lippman Kahn, who were Jewish immigrants from Riedseltz, Alsace. Since Riedseltz was only twenty-six miles from Brumath, it is probable that the couples' fathers, Jacques Goudchaux, and Abraham Aryeh Kahn, arranged these matches before their children left for Louisiana. These four young Alsatian immigrants started out their married lives in the town of Plaquemine, in Iberville Parish.

***

Seven of the twelve children Jacques fathered with his second wife, Rosette Kahn, immigrated to the United States. Babette Goudchaux, arriving in New Orleans on April 2, 1851 at the age of fourteen on the ship *Old England*, with her nine year old brother, Henry, in tow, married Joseph Dreyfus in Plaquemine, Louisana two years later.[1] After spending some time in Mississippi, they raised their children in New Orleans where Joseph was a liquor dealer. Maline Goudchaux, who came to join her siblings around 1856, married Abraham Lehmann, a native of Gommersheim, Bavaria in Plaquemine, LA in 1857, but lived in New Orleans, where their twelve children were all born. Abe Lehmann, who started out as a peddler, had been in partnership with several men before the Civil War. His establishment in New Orleans was virtually put out of business during the Union occupation, so he and his brother-in-law, Henry Goudchaux, moved to Brownsville, Texas, where they started a smuggling operation out of

Matamoros, Mexico. They also operated stores from Brownsville as well as from across the Rio Grande in Boca del Rio (Baghdad). Their Mexican dealings during the war helped keep these families and their business afloat and are described in great detail in Elliot Ashkenazi's book entitled *The Business of Jews in Louisiana*.[2] After Henry Goudchaux returned with Abe Lehmann from Texas and Mexico, he moved to New York where he married Pauline Schultz and raised his family in Manhattan.[3]

Henry's sister, Sara Goudchaux, immigrated from Brumath just before the Civil War and wed Calmé (Charles) Lazard, from Metz, France. The groom was thirty-seven at the time of his marriage in New Orleans on May 24, 1864. His bride was eighteen. Calmé and Sara's ten children were all born in the city where he owned several clothing stores. After his eldest daughter Rosa's marriage to Meyer Israel in 1883, the latter became Calmé's partner in the clothing business, which by 1891 had expanded to locations on Prytania Street, Esplanade Avenue, and Canal Street.

Jacques and Rosette Goudchaux's daughter, Adele, emigrated from Brumath at the age of fifteen, accompanied by her brother, Leopold, who was thirteen at the time, on the ship *Gulf Stream*, which landed in New Orleans on June 7, 1858.[4] Adele married Jacob Fies, originally from Trimbach, Alsace, in New Orleans in 1859, shortly before her seventeenth birthday.[5] The Fies family made their home in Pine Bluff, Arkansas, where Jacob was a merchant. Unlike many of his compatriots from Alsace, Jacob did not fight for the Confederacy, but instead, joined the Tennessee Cavalry, where he rose to the rank of First Sergeant.[6] After giving birth to five children, Adele died at the age of thirty. A year later her widower married his late wife's half-niece, Fannie Kahn.[7]

Leopold, who had accompanied his sister, Adele, to America in 1858 was just two months shy of his fourteenth birthday when he arrived. He, along with a younger brother, Lazard, are two of Jacques Goudchaux's children who figured most prominently in the history of Avoyelles Parish. When Leopold arrived in New Orleans, he was first taken in by his sister, Maline, and her husband, Abraham Lehmann. By 1860 he had moved and was living with his half-sister, Esther Goudchaux Kahn, and her husband, Sam, in the town of Plaquemine. Leopold Goudchaux, just seventeen years old, worked as a clerk in the family store.[8] During the difficult years of the Civil War he took to the road and toiled as a peddler in the "back country." As a single man, he was able to save and invest his money in the depressed post-war real estate market. He bought many acres in St. Landry Parish, where forty years later, he would be considered one of the most prosperous land owners in the area.

Lazard Goudchaux, Leopold's younger brother, left France at the age of seventeen in 1866, a year after his father's death in Brumath.[9] He filed for citizenship in 1874 in Avoyelles Parish. His application stated that he had arrived before the age of eighteen, and had resided in the United States for eight years. He became an American citizen on October 6, 1874 in Marksville.[10] He, unlike his older brother, Leopold, who spent most of his days in Big Cane, St. Landry Parish, divided his time between Evergreen, in Avoyelles Parish, and New Orleans.

On July 22, 1868, at the age of twenty-four, Leopold married a local farmer's daughter, Charlotte Eilert, in a civil ceremony in St. Landry Parish.[11] By 1870 both Leopold and Lazard had settled permanently in north central St. Landry Parish, only fifteen miles from Evergreen. Leopold bought property from Hamilton Smith on Bayou Rouge and opened up a general store in Big Cane. Judging from the transactions found in the Avoyelles Parish Courthouse, Leopold was, during his early days, principally a trader in horses and cattle, an occupation that had also been his father's back in Brumath.[12] In 1870, he and his wife, "Lottie," age 20, along with their year old son, Jacob, (who was usually called by his French name, Jacques) were enumerated in Big Cane. Lazard, Leopold's younger brother, who was mistakenly recorded as "Levi" lived with them.[13]

Leopold also sold plantation supplies which he had shipped from New Orleans to his rural neighbors. Because of a lack of liquidity, especially after the Civil War, most of his sales were "on credit", a procedure which was the downfall of many a merchant. Filed in the Avoyelles Parish Courthouse at Marksville on October 18, 1870, is a transaction between Louis Booth, a local Avoyelles Parish farmer and Leopold Goudchaux which reads in part: "For and in consideration of plantation supplies already furnished to me by Leopold Goudchaux of Big Cane, I have and do hereby bargain, sell, transfer, and deliver to him, so much of my cotton in the seed, as will liquidate the debt of two hundred and sixty two dollars and fifty cents (262. 50/100) at the sum of three and a half cents per pound or in other words, seven thousand five hundred pounds of cotton in seed." [14]

There were also other, more creative arrangements to be made in this cash poor, war torn, society. For example in December 1871, Silas McNairy of St. Landry Parish, in consideration of a seven hundred and fifty dollar debt to Leopold Goudchaux, sold him three mules and three horses, each worth one hundred dollars, one four horse wagon, also worth one hundred dollars, and one two horse wagon worth fifty dollars. However, McNairy retained the use of said mules, horses and wagons, by paying Goudchaux a "reasonable" rental fee each year for them, and, further, had the right of first purchase should he be able to raise the necessary cash to redeem them for the original purchase price of seven hundred fifty dollars. [15] In May 1874, Gabriel Carter of Avoyelles Parish received two hundred and fifty dollars from Leopold Goudchaux for the sale of one heavy two horse wagon with harness, one creole pony, one mare mule and two plows, on the condition that he be allowed to use said pony, mule, wagon and plows to bring in his crop, from which he would pay back to Goudchaux the sum of one hundred dollars out of the proceeds of his crop when made. [16]

It was by means of business deals both small and large that Leopold began to amass the fortune that he had made by the time of his death in 1920. By 1880 six more children had been born to Leopold and Lottie: Charles Abraham on February 15, 1871, Rosa on October 10, 1872, Caroline, called Callie, on July 15, 1874, Blanche Mathilde on May 13, 1876, Henry, on August 22, 1878, and Adele, born in 1879.[17]

Leopold's younger brother, Lazard, a "clerk" in his brother's general store also bought and sold goods on his own to save enough money to be able to marry. Anyone with a little cash during these difficult times could find extraordinary deals. On May 30, 1873, Lazard bought from T.R. Warner, a resident of Evergreen, one dark grey American horse "fifteen hands high, all white feet, with white speck on forehead, no brand" for fifty cents. On the same day, Lazard bought from Mr. Warner one eight year old roan mare, fifteen and one half hands high, with "one white front and hind foot and white star on forehead," one six year old sorrel mare about "15 hands high, with a perpendicular stripe on forehead," and one "two horse thimble skein wagon," for seventy-five cents cash.[18]

When he was financially able, Lazard sought out a bride in New Orleans. He chose Harriet Oppenheim, the daughter of Bernard Benjamin Oppenheim, a clothier who had a shop on the corner of Front and Gravier Streets in the city. Though her father was Prussian, her mother, Louisa, had been born in Mobile, Alabama. Harriet had two other younger siblings, Lily, who went on to marry the venerable Marks Isaacs (one of the founders of the Maison Blanche Department Store), and Charles who would later become a merchant and broker of some repute. Lazard and Harriet were married in New Orleans on June 12, 1878, and made it their home.[19] At the age of twenty-nine, he was ten years older than his bride. In New Orleans, Lazard worked as a wholesale grocer, often doing business with his brother, Leopold, who bought merchandise for the store in Big Cane from him.

In 1880 Lazard Goudchaux was enumerated in New Orleans with his wife and baby son, Jacob Oppenheim Goudchaux, born on April 27, 1879. If success can be judged by the number of one's servants, Lazard and his wife, living in a house on North Baronne Street, enjoyed the help of Jane Daly, age fifty-three, from Ireland and her daughter, Mary, age fifteen.[20] During their years in New Orleans, five other children were born to them, Rosa, who died as a child,

Bernard, born on September 12, 1882, Herbert, born on March 4, 1884, a son, Leslie, born on February 6, 1887, and May Louisa, born on January 31, 1891.[21] Lazard, his wife and six children returned to live in Evergreen just before the turn of the twentieth century where he owned a general store, working with his two eldest sons, Jacob and Bernard.[22] The family remained in Avoyelles Parish until shortly before his wife's death in 1905.

During the 1880s Leopold Goudchaux's plantation and store in Big Cane were thriving, and Leopold continued to buy and sell cattle, horses and properties in the area. Many farmers in the neighborhood, however, were still in dire circumstances. Cornelius Hatch sold Leopold one black mare, one buggy and eighty bushels of corn, for one hundred and twenty dollars, with the proviso that he could continue to use the mare for a sum of twenty-five dollars in order to bring in his crop.[23] Business was so brisk at the store, the largest one for miles, that Leopold employed Abraham Kahn[24], his half-nephew, a forty year old bachelor who lived next door to Leopold, along with Sam Erlich, Sam Haas' adopted son from the Jewish Orphans Home, Jacob Kahn, another half-nephew, who was the son of Lippman and Fleurette Goudchaux Kahn, Josiah Scott, age fifty and Lucy Weeks, their servant. Abe, Sam, Jake and Josiah were all clerks in the store in Big Cane.[25]

On December 14, 1881, Leopold and Charlotte's last child, Leon Eilert Goudchaux, was born.[26] Six days later Charlotte died from complications due to child birth, and Leopold was left with seven children under ten years of age.

Leopold often attended auctions, where land, on which state and parish taxes were delinquent, was put on the block. And unlike many Jews he did not shrink from taking in a non-Jewish business partner. In 1882 he joined with Clifton Cannon, a second generation resident of Avoyelles Parish, who was both an attorney and also serving as deputy sheriff of the Parish, to purchase land. Mr. Cannon owned 1500 acres which was cultivated by tenant farmers. He was, according to the *Biographical and Historical Memoirs of Northwest*

Louisiana, a "man of means."²⁷ One of the first properties Cannon and Goudchaux acquired as partners, was on Bayou Jack, an area just north and east of Big Cane in St. Landry Parish. They shared the profits from this land together for five years until April 15, 1887, when Cannon gave Leopold Goudchaux power of attorney to dispose of the property, which was ultimately sold to Hermogene Hooter.²⁸

After the death of his first wife, Charlotte, Leopold was anxious to marry again. This time he chose an arranged match with a Jewish spouse, Flora Marx, whom he brought over from Surbourg, Alsace with her sister, Nanette. Leopold traveled to New Orleans to meet the boat and to marry Flora on May 8, 1883. She was twenty-three and Leopold was thirty-nine.²⁹ Six children were born to the couple: Abraham, on June 19, 1884, Hortense Miriam on June 2, 1885, Sylvan on June 2, 1886, Sarah on March 13, 1891, Julius Joseph on December 31, 1894 and Elsie on September 18, 1897.³⁰ In 1900 Leopold was enumerated living on his plantation in Big Cane with Flora and all six of his children by her, as well as her sister, Nanette Hockwald, an English Engineer, John Park, his African-American cook Winnie Lester, the cook's two children, Lagardy and Dave, and William Johnson, who was Leopold's hostler. John Park, whose occupation was "engineer," was in charge of the steam engine in Leopold's saw mill. John, Winnie and her children, and William Johnson were all "boarders" in the Goudchaux household.³¹ Leopold Goudchaux's half nephew, Abraham Kahn, age sixty-one, and Leopold's son, Leon Eilert Goudchaux, now nineteen, and a clerk in his father's store, lived next door.

***

In addition to the Kahn family members living in St. Landry Parish, three of Samuel and Esther Goudchaux Kahn's eight children, and one son-in-law lived, at one time, in Avoyelles Parish, and did business, with their half-uncle, Leopold Goudchaux. The eldest, Max Kahn, born in Plaquemine on April 11, 1851, lived in Avoyelles Parish in the 1880s working as a merchant.³² He was located somewhere around Simmesport not far from his two younger brothers, Henry (b.

July 1859) and Aaron (b. Dec. 1860), who lived together in a house in Evergreen with two "salesmen," William H. Jackson, and Julius Schwabacher, the former from England and the latter from Wurtemburg, Germany. The Kahn brothers operated a successful general merchandise establishment and employed a cook, Eppy Smooth, age sixty.[33] The brothers lived four houses down from another French Jewish merchant, Simon Karpe, and his family. By the middle of the 1880s they had become very prosperous. Evergreen was a bustling little town, and an important steamboat landing in the parish. Max left Avoyelles Parish after marrying Adele E. Bier in New Orleans on November 27, 1884.[34] He opened up a store in Mansfield in DeSoto Parish where the couple's two children, Sigmund and Estelle, were born in 1892 and 1894 respectively, and where his wife died in 1899. Upon her death, Max Kahn left to join three brothers-in law, Joseph, Charles and Hippolyte Bier, who were already settled in California as prosperous merchants, as well as his brother, Aaron, who had left Louisiana for San Francisco, in 1887 to start a new life, after a chilling anti-Semitic attack in Evergreen.[35]

***

Another Goudchaux in-law, Elie Hiller, who became one of Simon Siess' chief business rivals in Marksville, was an integral part of this family network in Avoyelles Parish during the 1880s. The three Hiller Brothers, Matz (Matthew), Herz (Hatch) and Abraham, had left Niederroedern, Alsace in the 1840s to settle in Mississippi, where they rarely lived more than forty or so miles apart from one another in or near the town of Summit, which boasted of a synagogue, as well as a small Jewish cemetery. Two of Abraham Hiller's sons, Jonas (b. 1849) and Elie (b. 1851), operated stores in Avoyelles and farther north in Morehouse Parishes. Elie Hiller married Samuel and Esther Goudchaux Kahn's, daughter, Helvena Kahn, on December 4, 1878,[36] in New Orleans.

Elie Hiller's older brother, Jonas, married Rosalie Levy of Bastrop, Louisiana on April 11, 1875.[37] Bastrop, in Morehouse Parish, is in the northeast corner of the state just south of where Arkansas and

Mississippi meet with Louisiana. Rosalie had been born there in November 1854 to Michel Levy, an Alsatian immigrant, from Marmoutier, and his German born wife, Eliza Freidheim, from Lamsheim. Rosalie Levy Hiller's father, Michel, who was a passenger on the *J.H. Cooper* that landed in New Orleans on July 20, 1846, [38] spent a few years clerking and peddling in Central Louisiana. He ultimately, however, set up shop in Marksville, in Avoyelles Parish, in 1850 where he and Solomon Zucker both still single were living together and working as merchants.[39] Just before Rosalie was born, Michel Levy and his partner, Solomon Zucker, decided to move north to Bastrop in Morehouse Parish where they established a merchandising business and raised their families.

After Jonas Hiller wed Rosalie Levy they settled in Magnolia, Mississippi, where they operated a store until his widowed mother, Caroline Oppenheimer, passed away on April 13, 1887. [40] Soon after, Jonas moved his family to Bastrop to join his father-in-law, Michel, in his enterprise. After Michel Levy died in Bastrop on June 1st 1895 and was buried in the B'nai Sholom Jewish Cemetery in that town, [41] Jonas took over the family business. Then, a cousin, Daniel Hiller, Matz Hiller's son, who had married Jonas Hiller's wife Rosalie's sister, Julia Levy, moved from Mississippi to Alexandria, Louisiana, where Dan became the manager of Abraham "Bear" Heyman's mercantile establishment. Heyman was also a Goudchaux relative, the son of Jacques and Barbe Levi Goudchaux's daughter, Louise, and her husband, Emmanuel Heyman of Brumath."[42]

So it was no accident that Elie and Helvena Kahn Hiller, with relatives from both sides of their families active in Avoyelles, Morehouse, St. Landry and Rapides Parishes, decided to take up residence in Marksville, with their firstborn daughter, Ida Hannah, to become one of the many merchants there. In 1880 Marksville was a thriving town of approximately 1550 inhabitants. The majority of the twenty-three merchants there were of French descent. Amongst them, nine were selling dry goods, brothers George and Alfred Mayer, Frank Minoret, Fabien Bordelon, Séverin Garrot, Jules Ducôté, Antoine Grandpierre, Elie Hiller and Simon Siess. The Hiller and Siess families were, along with Adolph Frank who ran the Frank Hotel, the only Jewish merchants in town. In addition, A.J. Ducôté sold liquor and Gerand Brouillette, Adèle Michel, and Adolph Blanchard were grocers. Adolph Frank's son, Émile, was a butcher. Rose Couvillon and J.A. Riché kept stores. J.B. Poret was the cabinet maker. Benjamin Franklin Edwards, cousin to former Louisiana Governor Edwin Edwards, and Clifton Cannon were both store keepers. J.N. Randner sold shoes and boots. G.H. Griffin made and repaired watches, and Stefan Chavez was a cigar maker. [43]

Three children were born to Elie and Helvena Hiller, while they were living in Marksville: Arthur Aby Hiller on February 12, 1882, Mabel on May 30 1884, and Edwin Jacob on January 1, 1886. [44] Nine dry goods merchants eventually became too much competition for the Hiller family. They moved to Franklin, St. Mary Parish, in 1887 where their fifth child, Lawrence Estelle Hiller, was born on the October 11th. [45] A sixth and last child, Melvin Errol Hiller, was born in Lecompte, another small town in Rapides Parish, not far from Alexandria where, Jonas, Elie Hiller's brother, and their cousin Dan Hiller, formerly manager of the Heyman Dry Goods Store, had formed a brief partnership. Jonas had become active in the affairs of the Alexandria Synagogue, Gemiluth Chassodim. By joining his brother and cousin up north, Elie hoped to make a better living for his growing family. But Dan left the state in 1889, and Jonas stuck it out in Alexandria only until 1895, when he returned to Bastrop, with Dan and his family finally joining him there by 1900 from Canton, Mississippi. [46]

Divorce in the late nineteenth century was rare and often treated as a shameful event. Whenever Elie and Helvena broke up their family, it was certainly final by the time of the 1900 Census. Helvena was living in New Orleans at 1725 Euterpe Street with her five surviving children. She told the enumerator that she was a widow, living off her investments. Her oldest son Arthur, at eighteen, was working as a collector in a rice mill. [47] At the same time in Jefferson Davis Parish, the "deceased" forty-eight year old Elie Hiller was living in the soon-to-be boom town of Jennings, with his twenty-two year old

French bride, Carrie. There was no occupation listed for either of them, so one can only speculate that the attraction might have been the anticipation of an oil strike. Prospectors had been searching for oil in the area between Beaumont, Texas and Lake Charles, Louisiana for, at least, twenty years. It was known that natural gas often bubbled up to the surface in the swampy land and farmer's fields in the area. There was heightened anticipation with the strike at Spindletop, near Beaumont on January 10, 1901. The first Louisiana oil well was brought in on September 21, 1901 in Acadia Parish, just across Bayou Nezpiqué from Jennings. The Jules Clement # 1, named for the farmer in whose rice field oil was discovered, made Jennings, the closest village to the well, a boom town. If Elie had not gone into the "oil business" he certainly could have made out handily in any merchandising pursuit he might have chosen.[48] Unfortunately, he died only six years later on January 30, 1907 and was buried with other members of the Hiller family in the cemetery in Summit, Mississippi.[49]

The Goudchaux connections to Avoyelles do not, however, stop with the departure of the Hillers, or the Kahn cousins. Leopold's half-sister, Madel, and her husband, Cerf Kahn, who had sent five of their fourteen children from Schirrhoffen, Alsace to the United States, now saw many of their grandchildren emigrate as well. Their daughter Emilie Kahn, born in Schirrhoffen on May 25, 1850,[50] married Charles Weill in 1865. Of Charles and Emilie's thirteen children born between May 1868 and April 1895, eleven of them would eventually come to the United States. Nine of them would settle in Louisiana, and two of those would play a part in the history of Avoyelles Parish. Their first, a daughter, Josephine Weill, born on May 15, 1868, was sent to St. Landry Parish to marry Leopold and Charlotte's first born child, Jacob Lehman Goudchaux, on March 19, 1892.[51] The two young people were half first cousins once removed, a relationship which was, in those days, no impediment to marriage. Their three children were all born before the turn of the century in Big Cane: Lottie in 1893, Callie born on September 3, 1896 and Eugene born on August 24, 1899.[52] Callie died on March 25, 1898 and was buried in the Jewish Cemetery in Opelousas, Louisiana.[53] In 1900, baby Eugene, Lottie, age seven,

Jacob, and his wife, Josephine, were still living near Leopold and Flora Marx Goudchaux in St. Landry Parish where he was a general merchant.[54] Soon, however, the family would be on the move, first to the town of Bunkie, in Avoyelles Parish.

Bunkie, although the youngest town in Avoyelles Parish, would soon eclipse Evergreen, Marksville, Mansura and Cottonport as the premier cotton shipping point thanks to the arrival of the Texas and Pacific Railway. Jacob Lehman Goudchaux, who had already dabbled in several careers, moved there with his wife and two children, just after the turn of the century, to open an insurance agency.[55] However, he and his family were soon on the move again, first to Alexandria, then by 1920 he was the owner/operator of a drugstore in Lake Charles, Louisiana.[56]

Before their move to Lake Charles, Jacob Goudchaux's twenty-two year old daughter Lottie married her second cousin once removed, Albert Kahn, son of Medar and Fleurine Schmulen Kahn at their home in Alexandria, Louisiana on August 20, 1915.[57] Albert's father, Medar, was one of five employees of his first cousin, the "Bear," Abraham Heyman, in the latter's successful Alexandria merchandising establishment.[58] Less than three years after her wedding on October 31, 1918, Lottie succumbed, during the great influenza epidemic in Rayne, leaving her nineteen month old baby girl, Brunette, without a mother.

Jacob and Josephine Goudchaux survived all three of their children. On March 15, 1929, at the age of twenty-nine, their son, Eugene Weill Goudchaux, died in St. Landry Parish.[59] He had been associated with his father as the manager of the Lake Charles drugstore. Jacob Goudchaux died on January 20, 1937, soon after the family relocated, once again, this time back to St. Landry Parish.[60] His wife, Josephine, followed on August 25, 1939.[61] They were buried with their son, Eugene, and daughter, Callie, in the Jewish Cemetery in Opelousas.

***

The Weill–Kahn–Goudchaux connection did not end there either. Josephine's sister, Fanny Weill, born on August 3, 1882, in Schirrhoffen, Alsace, arrived in New York from Le Havre on August 29, 1903, on board the *La Lorraine*. She was accompanied by her brother, Jules, who had returned to France to fetch her, from his home in Napoleonville, Louisiana.[62] She was married to Herman Weiss, an Austro-Hungarian immigrant who had been in the United States since 1885, at her sister Josephine Weill Goudchaux's house in Bunkie. The couple moved to Robeline, not far away in Natchitoches Parish, where their first child, Mervin Weiss, was born on November 28, 1907.[63] A second son, Charles, was born in Robeline on May 20, 1912.[64] Late in the second decade of the twentieth century, Herman, Fanny, and their two children moved to Alexandria, where Herman was an independent merchant, never being employed by either Weiss Bros. or Weiss and Goldring. Eventually however, both sons, Mervin, who had first been employed as a book keeper in a local Alexandria Bank, and his younger brother, Charles, moved to New York to work for Weiss Bros. Stores, Inc., headed by their first cousin, David Weiss. Herman Weiss died in Alexandria on August 31, 1937 and is buried in the Jewish Cemetery in Pineville. His widow, Fanny Weill Weiss, followed her sons to New York and died one month shy of her 82nd birthday in Forest Hills, Queens on July 1, 1964.[65] Their son, Charles, never married, dying in Oceanside, Long Island on June 23, 1995.[66] Mervin, however, who had wed Philadelphia native Annette Somers in 1944 and raised two children, a daughter, Mervine, and a son, Richard, died ten months shy of his 100th birthday on January 24, 2007, in Lynbrook, Long Island.[67]

Seven members of the Weiss family, including Fanny Weill's groom Herman, had emigrated from the area around Ungvar, originally part of the Austro-Hungarian Empire, now called Uzhorod and located in the Ukraine, to Louisiana in the late 1880s. According to the 1900 U.S. Federal Census, sixty year old Martin Weiss and his forty-four year old wife, Sarah Samuel, arrived in the United States in 1888 with their daughter, Rosa. They had been preceded by their sons, Sam in 1884, Joseph and Herman in 1885, and Morris Joseph in 1887.

Everyone, with the exception of Morris Joseph, settled in the growing railroad town of Bunkie in Avoyelles Parish.[68]

Joe Weiss, born on November 10, 1863,[69] in Ungvar, married Annie Roth, also a Hungarian immigrant, on January 29, 1893.[70] Since he was already settled with his brothers and sister in Bunkie, he brought his bride back to the small town, where the family operated a dry goods store. Joe and Annie, however, were the only members of the Weiss family ever to be lifelong residents of Avoyelles Parish. Their three sons and three daughters would make homes in New Orleans and Alexandria, Louisiana, Virginia, Pennsylvania, Nashville, Tennessee and New York City.

Their first child, Meyer Roth Weiss, was born on Joe's thirtieth birthday on November 10, 1893 in Bunkie.[71] Five other children would be born to them between 1893 and 1903 in the fledgling town: David Bernard Weiss on September 10, 1895,[72] Edda (Edith) Weiss in March 1897,[73] Gustave Waldorph Weiss on October 24, 1898,[74] Selma H. Weiss on September 14, 1900[75] and Lillian R. Weiss on August 7, 1903[76].

Meyer Roth Weiss, married into the Jackson family of Alexandria, Louisiana. Selma Jackson, born on March 9, 1896, to Israel and Hannah Rosenthal Jackson, was a second generation Louisianan. The Jackson (originally Jacob) family were Prussian, while the Rosenthal's were Polish, having spent one generation in Oberlauterbach, Alsace, France before arriving in America. Both families had been prominent merchants and residents of Alexandria for many years. Meyer and Selma Jackson Weiss married on December 31, 1916, at Temple Gemiluth Chassodim.[77] After the wedding the couple moved back to Bunkie. Meyer was trained as a book keeper, and worked in his father's store. On August 2, 1919, his only son, Joseph M. (Jack) Weiss II, was born.[78] The family lived in Bunkie until 1928, when they relocated to Atlanta, Georgia so that Meyer could take the helm of a local family-run department store.

Meyer's younger brother, David Bernard Weiss, a World War I veteran, who had left Bunkie to be trained at Fort Logan H. Roots in North Little Rock, Arkansas, struck out on his own, and with the help of two of his sisters, Selma and Lillian, grew the proprietorship of a dress shop located in Philadelphia, Pennsylvania [79] into the Weiss Bros. chain, of which he was the president and general manager. While Meyer was managing a store in Atlanta, Georgia, and a younger brother, Gustave Waldorph Weiss, was at the helm of the Gus Mayer department store in Richmond, Virginia, David and his sisters decided to expand their Philadelphia business. Over the next twenty years, Weiss Bros. would go on to purchase the Gus Mayer store in New Orleans in 1934 and H.P. Selman's in Louisville, Kentucky in 1961. They also developed concessions in existing department stores, thereby creating a chain of high-end women's specialty shops throughout the south and southwest. After the acquisition of the Gus Mayer store in New Orleans, David tapped his brother, Meyer, to become its president. Meyer managed the store, overseeing its renovation in 1948 in the Art Deco style. Meyer had lost his wife, Selma Jackson, on July 10, 1945 while his son, Lt. Jack M. Weiss, was serving in the U.S. Naval Reserve.[80] Meyer, himself, died nine years later on July 16, 1954. He was still at the helm of the Gus Mayer Department Store, overseeing its day to day operations.[81] Selma and Meyer were both buried near her family in the Jewish Cemetery in Pineville, Louisiana.[82] While Meyer had remained in New Orleans until his death, Gustave Waldorph Weiss settled down with his wife, Natalye Reuben, and raised their son Gus, Jr. in Nashville, Tennessee.[83]

The main office of Weiss Bros, Inc. was located at 232 Madison Avenue in New York City. It is in Manhattan that David, his wife, Claire Stolar, and daughter, Claire Weiss Weisman, would spend the rest of their lives, along with his two sisters, Selma and Lillian, who never married. A third sister, Edda (Edith), wed a New Yorker, Victor Steinfeld, and made her home there as well. David Weiss died in New York City on November 14, 1964. He was survived by his daughter Claire, a son-in-law, and two grandchildren.[84] Selma died in Manhattan at the age of ninety, on June 4, 1991.[85] Lillian died at the age of one hundred on March 28, 2004.[86] They had all been members of New York City's Congregation Emanu-El.

Samuel Weiss, Martin and Sarah Weiss' second child, was born in Ungvar on October 21, 1865.[87] Sam took Gisella Elias, a German immigrant, as his bride on February 14, 1895, in New Orleans.[88] Their stay with the family in Bunkie, where Sam was a merchant, was short-lived. There was just too much competition in town, the two Gross brothers, the three other Weiss Brothers, one Haas brother, and Abe Rich, to mention only the ones of Jewish descent in a town of four hundred people. Shortly after 1900 Sam Weiss and his family left Bunkie for Abbeville in Vermillion Parish, then to Palestine Texas, where Sam's health failed. He died at the age of forty-six in Battle Creek, Michigan, on December 11, 1911,[89] where he had gone to seek medical treatment, no doubt at the "San," as it was called, the "medical facility" run by the inventor of the corn flake, Dr. John Harvey Kellogg. Sam left his widow, Gisela, and four sons. The eldest, Seymour, was born September 13, 1896, in Bunkie.[90] At age fifteen, after his father's death, he accepted a position in his Uncle Morris' store, Weiss and Goldring, in Alexandria, but after his mother, Gisela, and brothers decided to make New Orleans their home, he followed them there. His first employment was in the shoe department of the legendary Maison Blanche Department Store on Canal and Dauphine Street.[91]

In 1926, after fourteen years in the retail business, Seymour became the manager of the barber shop at the Roosevelt Hotel in New Orleans. It was during this time that he became the confidant of Huey Pierce Long, a regular at the hotel, who was then seeking the governorship of Louisiana. Promoted from the Barber Shop, Seymour rose to the position of publicity director. His fortunes were linked to Long's ascendancy to power. He was soon appointed to head the Democratic Party in Louisiana, and formed a consortium to buy the Roosevelt Hotel outright, becoming its president and general manager. Seymour, being Governor Long's unofficial treasurer, became the guardian of the infamous "deduct box" and Long became a fixture at the Roosevelt Hotel, financing and having Louisiana Route 61 built from the State Capitol in Baton Rouge to its front door.⁹² Subsequent to Long's assassination, Weiss was convicted of mail fraud in 1939, spending eighteen months in the Federal penitentiary in Atlanta, Georgia, before being released for "good behavior." During his incarceration, his brother, Bernard, took over temporary stewardship of the hotel. Seymour was ultimately given a full and unconditional pardon by President Harry Truman.

Seymour, unlike all his other Weiss relatives, was the only one to marry outside of his religion. He was married twice, first to Notie Fay Turner on April 19 1925, and towards the end of his life, on June 12, 1953, to Elva Mae Lavies, the widow of prominent New York banker, Walter Gardner Kimball. Seymour's time in jail did not tarnish his position as a behind the scenes "player" in Louisiana politics. The Bunkie native continued to wield immense power as owner of the Roosevelt Hotel and acted as the Crescent City's official "host" to celebrities and politicians alike until he sold out in 1965. Ever the "political operative" Seymour died in Baton Rouge on September 17, 1969. At the time, he was vice-chairman of the Board of the Louisiana Department of Commerce and Industry.⁹³ Seymour left no children. Two of his younger brothers, Bernard and Milton, Bunkie natives as well, had been carried along by his success, and, tragically, were doomed by it as well.

Bernard was born in Bunkie on February 28, 1898, and raised in Abbeville.⁹⁴ He started his career in New Orleans as a cotton broker, but soon turned to the retail clothing business. In the 1920s he moved to Shreveport in order to manage his Aunt Rosa Weiss' husband, David Goldring's, department store. Bernard married Natalie Heilperin, daughter of a deceased Shreveport merchant, Louis Heilperin, a native of Russia and his wife, Fannie D. Bluestein. Bernard, his wife Natalie, and their two children, Louise and Barbara Ann, lived with Louis Heilperin's widow, Fanny, on Centenary Boulevard in Shreveport. Fanny listed her occupation as "capitalist". Bernard was the manager of Goldring's, a retail ready-to-wear store.⁹⁵ His younger brother, Milton Eli Weiss, born in 1905, was also destined for the retail business. After a childhood spent in Abbeville and New Orleans, he headed west for

Texas, where he managed Volk's Department Store in Dallas, which included a leased department of the Weiss Bros. chain, and where he was employed until his death. He and his wife, Adelyn Dorothy Loeb, were the parents of one son, William Morris, born on October 13, 1926, in that Texas city.[96]

Tragically, both Bernard and Milton perished on January 11, 1954, as a result of a seaplane accident at Wallace Lake, near Shreveport. Their brother, Seymour, was to have been with them, but cancelled at the last minute, due to a bad cold. The headline in the European edition of the *Stars and Stripes* newspaper the next day read: "Plane Crash Kills 10 Magnates" Two seaplanes had taken off from a fishing camp located south of Lake Charles, which was owned by Bernard Weiss. One of the planes, with six people aboard, made it back to Shreveport, but the other took the lives of not only Bernard and Milton Weiss, but Thomas Braniff, the founder and president of the now defunct Braniff Airways, R.H. Hargrove, president of Texas Eastern Gas Co, which operated the "Big and Little Inch" gas pipelines to the east coast, Chris Abbott, a Nebraska banker and director of the Union Stockyards, Edgar Tobin, head of a serial mapping firm, and brothers, Justin and Randolph Querbes, prominent Shreveport businessmen.[97]

Less than eight months later, Seymour's brother, Julius, who after moving to New Orleans with his mother and brothers, had risen to become vice-president of the Goldring's chain, with more than thirty stores located in Louisiana, Virginia and New England, died of heart failure on August 31, 1954, in New Orleans. He left his second wife, Noella Martinez (his first wife, Anona Picard Weiss, had predeceased him by twenty years), three sons, Samuel Joseph, Seymour II and Johnny Weiss, as well as his mother, Gisella.[98]

Martin and Sarah Weiss' fourth and last son, Morris Joseph, was born on December 15, 1874, in Ungvar, and came to the United States as a thirteen year old boy. Unlike the other Weiss family members, Morris and his wife Hannah Cohen, whom he married in New Orleans on November 14, 1899,[99] did not settle in Bunkie. After brief stays in Alexandria, where their son, Sam Weiss, was born on January 2, 1901,[100] and New Orleans where his daughter, Miriam, was born on March 2, 1903,[101] they established themselves in Sabine Parish, near the Texas border in the small town of Many where Morris opened up a dry goods store.[102] Their daughter, Annette, was born in Many on February 10, 1905.[103] In the town of Zwolle, about fifteen miles to the northwest, Morris Weiss' friend and fellow immigrant, Joseph Mermelstein, also from Ungvar/ Uzhorod opened up a similar establishment.[104] Morris Weiss and Joe Mermelstein forged another connection when on March 12, 1905, Joe travelled to New Orleans to marry Morris Weiss' wife Hannah's youngest sister Henrietta Cohen.[105]

In the meantime, Martin and Sara Weiss' youngest child Rosa Weiss, born in 1884 in Ungvar/Uzhorod, had married David Goldring, a Russian/Polish immigrant. The couple spent a few years in Bunkie, where their first child, Martin S. Goldring, was born on February 14, 1903.[106] They soon joined Morris and Hannah Weiss, and their children, in Many. Dave and Rosa Goldring's second child, Ferdinand, was born on the same date as Morris and Hannah's daughter, Annette Weiss, on February 10, 1905, in Many.[107] The growth of the Weiss and Goldring chain of stores was described in Ferdinand Goldring's obituary: "David Goldring [was] an itinerant merchant, who travelled in his early business years through the Bunkie, Marksville, Big Cane and Cheneyville areas. Permanent stores then were established in Many, Marksville, Cheneyville, Cottonport and Abbeville. David Goldring and his brother-in-law Morris, J. Weiss, later established a store in Alexandria."[108]

In 1907 the three brothers-in-law, Morris Weiss, Joe Mermelstein and David Goldring, decided to move their families to Alexandria, in Rapides Parish, a much larger town not only with many more economic opportunities for the men and their families, but with an established Jewish community, including a synagogue and a Jewish burial ground in nearby Pineville. The local Alexandria newspaper, *The Daily Town Talk* reported in its May 31st, 1907 edition that Dave Goldring and his family had moved from Many to open a "Gent's store" which would be in business by September.[109] The Weiss and Goldring store was finally incorporated on January 22, 1913, with Dave Goldring as president, Joe Mermelstein as vice-president and Morris Weiss as secretary-treasurer.[110] Although the store was a huge success, the partnership did not last. By 1915 Joe Mermelstein had left to run the Hub Dry Goods Company at the corner of Lee Street, which he bought from Morris and Dave in January of 1917.[111]

After the Weiss and Goldring partnership was dissolved in 1927 due to business differences, Dave, Rosa and their children left Alexandria for Shreveport, finally settling on the upper west side of Manhattan first at 240 West 94th Street, then at 300 Central Park West. He achieved his dream of expansion and operated the Goldring chain, one store of which was opened in Shreveport, another in New Orleans, from his Manhattan office,[112] just as his wife Rosa's nephew, David Weiss, did with the Weiss Brother's chain. Morris and his family remained in Alexandria, and true to their word, Weiss and Goldring, remained a single independent store and is, to this day, still in operation. Morris ran the business until his death at the age of 83 on January 23, 1958, with the aid of his son-in-law, Louis J. Levy, a Pennsylvania native who married Morris' daughter, Miriam. The *Daily Town Talk* praised Morris Weiss' many achievements in an extensive obituary. On the board of directors of Temple Gemiluth Chassodim, he had also been active in the founding of St. Francis Cabrini hospital in Alexandria, and was a past president of B'nai B'rith, which eventually changed its name from the Rebecca lodge to the Morris J. Weiss lodge, in his honor. He was also a Mason, a member of the Alexandria Elks and Rotary Clubs, the 4-H Club, and a founder of the Alexandria Garden Club.[113] Less than three months later, on March 12, 1958, his wife, Hannah, died. They were both buried in the Jewish Cemetery in Pineville.[114] Miriam's husband, Louis Levy, carried on in the family firm. Now Louis and Miriam's daughter Marilyn's husband Harry Silver and their son, Ted, continue the Weiss family tradition in Alexandria.

Morris and Hanna's son, Samuel C. Weiss, married another Goudchaux relation, Emelie Weill, his Uncle Herman Weiss' wife

Fanny Weill's niece. Emelie was born to Jacob Weill and his wife Mae Wolff on October 24, 1909, in Abbeville where two of Jacob's brothers, Jules and Jonas, had settled as well.[115] Samuel C. Weiss' sister, Annette, married Mandel Charles Selber in 1925, proprietor of Selber Bros. clothing store, which was founded in Baton Rouge in 1896 and relocated to Shreveport in 1907.[116]

Martin Weiss died on February 2, 1903 in Bunkie and was buried in the Canal Street Cemetery in New Orleans.[117] His widow, Sarah Samuel, went to live with her daughter and son-in-law, Rosa and Dave Goldring, until her death on April 20, 1915, in Alexandria.[118] Sarah was buried in the Jewish Cemetery in Pineville next to her son Samuel.

***

Other members of the Goudchaux family continued to move in and out of Avoyelles Parish. Leopold and Charlotte Eilert's second son, Charles Abraham Goudchaux, married a local girl, Florence Wolff, Mae Wolff Weill's sister, born on September 4, 1883, in Washington, a small town northeast of Opelousas in St. Landry Parish.[119] Her father, Leon Wolff, Sam and Alex Haas' step-mother's nephew, had settled in Washington, St. Landry Parish. Leon not only ran a successful mercantile business, but was also an officer in the local bank, and for a time, the town's mayor.

Charles Goudchaux was trained as a physician, an occupation he practiced at least through 1900 in St. Landry Parish. After he married Florence on November 14, 1906, and welcomed his first daughter, Lottie Eilert Goudchaux, in 1908,[120] he opened a general store in Melville in St. Landry Parish, about twenty miles from his family's home in Big Cane. He and his family remained there for about twenty years as one of Melville's leading merchants. His second daughter, Leona, was born in Big Cane on April 14, 1911.[121] By 1930 he and his wife and daughters had retired to the Alexandria/ Pineville area, where two of his half-sisters, Hortense Goudchaux Weil and Sarah Goudchaux Mayer, were living with their husbands. Not long after, the family decided to relocate permanently to Bunkie, where their daughter, Leona, had settled with her new husband, Moses Rosenthal Firnberg. Dr. Charles Goudchaux lived a quiet retirement in Bunkie, where on June 27, 1940, he died at the family home, leaving a wife and two daughters, five brothers and six sisters. Rabbi Albert G. Baum came from Alexandria to officiate at the service in Bunkie at the Goudchaux residence. The body was then removed to the Jewish Cemetery at Opelousas for burial.[122] Florence, her daughters Lottie and Leona, and Leona's husband, Moses Firnberg, lived together in Bunkie until Lottie married Jerome P. Morrison the following year and the couple moved to Chicago.[123] Florence Wolff Goudchaux survived her husband by twenty-two years and died at the age of 79 on November 18, 1962, in Bunkie where her daughter, Leona, and son-in-law, Moses Firnberg, still lived and worked. She was buried next to her husband in Opelousas.[124]

***

Leopold Goudchaux and his fellow St. Landry Parish resident, Samuel Haas, did extensive business together in neighboring Avoyelles Parish. As was many times the case with the Alsatian Jewish immigrants to Central Louisiana, a business relationship had often turned into a family affair. Such was the case when Sam's adopted son, Dr. David B. Davis, married Leopold and his late wife Charlotte Eilert's daughter, Adele, in 1900.[125] By the turn of the century Goudchaux and Haas partnered in other ways as well, often buying up tracts of land at tax sales. The granting of a "power of attorney" by Samuel Haas on July 31, 1909, to Leopold Goudchaux to be used for sale of lands in both parishes which were owned jointly bears witness to this close partnership. This power of attorney was renewed in September of 1912, upon the completion of purchases made by the two at a sale in Avoyelles Parish.

Perhaps nothing illustrates better the success that Leopold Goudchaux enjoyed in Central Louisiana than a purchase he made less than seven years before his death. In May 1913 he acquired a logging railroad from the Fischer Lumber company for ten thousand dollars, an enormous sum in the day, paid for with one third down in cash. C.B. Fischer held the mortgage for the additional monies, one third of which would be paid on May 30, 1914, with the balance to be paid on May 30 of 1915.[126] This logging railroad ran from the Atchafalaya River at Woodside in the southeast corner of Avoyelles Parish, westward, paralleling more or less, the parish line, between Avoyelles and St. Landry and turning slightly north to connect with Bayou Jack. Included in this purchase was twelve thousand cypress logs, all the cypress sinkers in Bayou Jack at or near the crossing of the Fischer Railroad one mile on each side of said crossing, as well as five and one half miles of standard gauge right of way including its thirty-five pound steel rail, all ties and bridges as well as all the rolling stock including twelve log cars, one locomotive tank car, one hand car, any spare parts and rail fasteners as well as ten thousand chains used to secure logs on cars. Farmer, plantation owner, general store proprietor and owner of a short-line railroad, Leopold Goudchaux had achieved prominence of the highest order in Central Louisiana. Just before his death, Leopold purchased 52 acres of property in Evergreen which was part of the estate of the late Simon and Fanny Karpe at a tax sale for $56.25.[127]

Leopold Goudchaux died on March 24, 1920, while attending to business in Avoyelles Parish.[128] He was buried in the Gemiluth Chassodim Cemetery in Opelousas alongside his first wife, Charlotte Eilert.[129] His surviving spouse, Flora Marx Goudchaux, died on April 26, 1923, and is buried in the Jewish Cemetery in Pineville along with two of her daughters and their husbands.[130] Of his fourteen children, thirteen of whom reached adulthood, only one remained in Avoyelles Parish, his son, Dr. Charles Goudchaux. The latter's obituary located eleven of his siblings and half siblings living in places as close as Big Cane, Alexandria/Pineville, Lake Charles, New Orleans and Ferriday in Louisiana, and as far away as Dallas and Austin Texas, Los Angeles and San Francisco, California and New York City.

Lazard Goudchaux died nine months after his older brother, Leopold, in New Orleans on December 22, 1920.[131] He had moved there from Evergreen after the death of his wife, Harriet Oppenheim, on October 27, 1905,[132] to become a commission broker, and lived with his brother-in-law, Charles Oppenheim. After their initial beginnings in Evergreen, Lazard's children never again lived in Avoyelles Parish. Jacob and Bernard Goudchaux founded the Goudchaux Department store in Baton Rouge, which was sold in 1945 to the Sternberg family who would later buy and operate the Maison Blanche chain in Louisiana and Florida. Herbert manufactured men's work clothing, opening up branch after branch across the country. His younger brother, Leslie, worked for him until, one by one, the great depression forced the closing of all the outlets except the one in Los Angeles. So the two brothers moved out west where they raised their families. Their sister, May Louisa, married Jesse Sigmund Rosenfeld, an executive in a men's clothing manufacturing firm, and made her home in New Orleans.

The Goudchaux family of Brumath remained Jewish even though the patriarch, Leopold had initially married a gentile. Charlotte Eilert, however, did not raise his children. After her death in 1881, his second wife, Flora Marx, whom he brought over from Alsace to marry and to tend to his family, was instrumental in their upbringing. As the family prospered, the Goudchaux family intermarried with their Weill and Kahn cousins living in southern Louisiana, or imported eligible Jewish brides from family members in Alsace. Other relatives chose their mates from nearby Alexandria, or New Orleans. Even though they lived in the agrarian parishes of St. Landry and Avoyelles, their prosperity allowed them to make connections elsewhere to maintain their Jewish identity. St. Landry Parish, unlike Avoyelles, had a synagogue in Opelousas, and Jewish burial grounds both in Opelousas and Washington, two vital necessities for a full religious life.

---

[1] "New Orleans Passenger Lists, 1820-1945," digital image, *Ancestry.com* (http://www.ancestry.com [hereinafter cited as "A"]: accessed 4/ 2011), Manifest of the *Old England*, lines 4, 5, entries for Babette and Henry Goudechaux (sic), ages 14 and 9, arrived 2 April 1851, citing NARA microfilm publication M 259, roll 34.

[2] Elliot Ashkenazi, *The Business of Jews in Louisiana, 1840-1875* Tuscaloosa: The University of Alabama Press, 1988), 93-96, 123.

[3] According to a letter written by Paul M. Kahn to Milton H. Fies in 1964, shared by genealogist Teri Downs Tillman, Henry returned to France to fight for his country during the Franco-Prussian War (1870-71), then returned to New York to his family.

[4] "New Orleans Passenger Lists, 1820-1945," digital image, (A: accessed 4/ 2011), Manifest of the *Gulf Stream*, lines 101, 102, entries for Adele and Leopold Goudechaux (sic), ages 15 and 9, arrived 7 June 1858, citing NARA microfilm publication M 259, roll 46.

[5] Trimbach, Alsace is only thirty-five miles from Brumath, so this was also probably an arranged marriage between the couple.

[6] "U.S Civil War Soldiers, 1861-1865," database, (A: accessed 12/2007), Jacob Feist, Union, Tenth regiment, Tennessee Cavalry, citing " National Park Service, 'Soldiers' Database," *Civil War Soldiers and Sailors System*, on line at (http://www.itd.nps.gov/cwss/).

[7] Fannie Kahn, born in Schirrhoffen, Alsace, was the fifth child of Cerf Kahn and his wife Madel Goudchaux. Madel was Jacques Goudchaux's daughter by his first wife, Barbe Levi, and the elder sister of immigrants Esther and Fleurette Goudchaux.

[8] 1860 U. S. Census, Iberville Parish, Louisiana, pop. sch., Plaquemine, p. 7 (penned), Dwelling # 573, Family # 573, Samuel Kahn household, digital image, (A: accessed 2/2006), citing NARA microfilm publication M-653, roll 411. Date of enumeration: 14 July 1860.

[9] Avoyelles Parish Courthouse (Marksville, Avoyelles Parish, LA), Book 4, Folio 354, # 5772, " L. Goudcheaux (sic) for Citizenship," filed 6 October 1874.

[10] Jeraldine Dufour LaCour, *Avoyelleans of Yesteryear* (Bunkie:Jeraldine Dufour LaCour [P.O. Box 5022, Alexandria, LA], 1983), 125. File #5772 for Lozard (sic) Goudchaux.

[11] Rev. Donald G. Hébert, compiler, *Southwest Louisiana records (1750-1900)*, CD-Rom, database, (Rayne, LA: Hébert Publications, 1975-2001). Entry for marriage of Leopold Goudchaux and Charlotte Eilert (1868).

[12] *Census 1836, Recensement des cantons de Brumath, Schiltigheim & Truchtersheim*. CD-ROM, database, (Fegersheim, France: C. Geyer 2004-2005), entry for Jacques Gutschu family, Rue Schemesgass # 271, Brumath, Alsace, France.

[13] 1870 U.S. Census, St. Landry Parish, Louisiana, pop. sch., Big Cane, Ward 3, p. 140 (stamped), Dwelling #1061, Family # 1079, Levi (sic) and L. Goudchaux household, digital image, (A: accessed 2/2006), citing NARA microfilm publication M593, roll G 29. Date of enumeration: 13 August 1870.

[14] Avoyelles Parish Courthouse Records (Marksville, Avoyelles Parish, LA), *Conveyances,* Book KK, p. 601, " Louis Booth to Leopold Goudchaux, Sale of Cotton," filed 18 October 1870.

[15] Avoyelles Parish Courthouse Records (Marksville, Avoyelles Parish, LA), *Conveyances,* Book LL, p. 477, "Silas McNairy to L. Goudchaux – Sale of Property," filed 21 December 1871.

[16] Avoyelles Parish Courthouse Records (Marksville, Avoyelles Parish, LA), *Conveyances,* Book LL, p. 205, "Gabriel Carter to Leopole (sic) Goudchaux – Sale of Property," filed 11 May 1871.

[17] Birth dates of Leopold Goudchaux's children courtesy of Teri Downs Tillman Natchez, MS.

[18] Avoyelles Parish Courthouse Records (Marksville, Avoyelles Parish, LA), *Conveyances,* Book MM, p. 549, "R.E. Warner to Lazard Goudchaux – Privilege sale," filed 30 May 1873.

[19] "New Orleans, Louisiana Marriage Records Index, 1831-1925," database, (A: accessed 12/2008), citing State of Louisiana, Secretary of State, Division of Archives, Records Management, and History. *Vital Records Indices.* Baton Rouge, LA, USA. Marriage of Lazard Goudchaux and. Harriet Oppenheimer (sic), Vol. 6, p. 784.

[20] 1880 U. S. Census, Orleans Parish, Louisiana, pop. sch., New Orleans, District 72, p. C-418 (stamped), Dwelling # 157, Family # 159, Lagard Godchaux (sic) household, digital image, (A: accessed 2/2006), citing NARA microfilm publication T-9, roll 463. Date of enumeration: 1 June 1800.

[21] "New Orleans, Louisiana Birth Records Index, 1790-1899," database , (A: accessed 6/2008), citing State of Louisiana, Secretary of State, Division of Archives, Records Management, and History. *Vital Records Indices.* Baton Rouge, LA, USA: Birth of Jacob Goudchaux, Vol 73 p. 684; Birth of Rosa Godchaux (sic) Vol. 76, p. 353; Birth of Bernard Goudchaux, Vol. 79, p. 174; Birth of Herbert Goudchaux, Vol. 81, p. 284; Birth of Leslie Goudchaux, Vol. 85, p. 151; Birth of May Louisa Goudchaux, Vol. 91 p. 466.

[22] 1900 U. S. Census, Avoyelles Parish Louisiana, pop. sch., Evergreen, Police Jury Ward 9, ED 23, Sheet # 21B (penned), Dwelling # 380, Family # 386, Lizard Godcheaux (sic) household, digital image, (A: accessed 3/2006), citing NARA microfilm publication: T-623, roll 558. Date of enumeration: 26 June 1900.

[23] Avoyelles Parish Courthouse Records (Marksville, Avoyelles Parish, LA), *Conveyances,* Book TT, p. 571, "Cornelius Hatch to Leopold Goudchaux, Sale of Personal property with privilege," filed 29 March 1881.

[24] Abraham Kahn was born on October 25, 1839, in Schirrhoffen, Alsace to Madel Goudchaux,(daughter of Jacques Goudchaux and his first wife Barbe Levi) and her husband, Cerf Kahn. Five of Madel Goudchaux Kahn's fourteen children immigrated to America: their son Abraham and daughters Pauline, Fannie, Valerie and Delphine.

[25] 1880 U. S. Census, St. Landry Parish, Louisiana, pop. sch., Fifth Ward, District 43, p.52C (penned), Dwelling # 76, Family # 515, L. Godchaux (sic) household, digital image, (A: accessed 2/2006), citing NARA microfilm publication: T-9, roll 470. Date of enumeration: 1 June 1880.

[26] "World War I Draft Registration Cards. 1917-1918," digital image, (A: accessed 10/2007), Leon E. Goudchaux, Serial # 3169, Order # A536, Draft Board "I" Opelousas, St. Landry Parish, LA, citing NARA microfilm publication M1509, roll 1684937.

[27] The Southern Publishing Company, editors, *Biographical and Historical Memoirs of Northwest Louisiana* (1890. Reprint with new index Greenville, SC: Southern Historical press, Inc., 2002), 623.

[28] Avoyelles Parish Courthouse Records (Marksville, Avoyelles Parish, LA), *Conveyances,* Book AAA, p. 125, "Clifton Cannon to Leopold Goudchaux, Power of Attorney," filed 15 April 1887.

[29] "Louisiana Marriages – 1718-1925," database, (A: accessed 12/ 2008), citing a variety of sources including individual marriage records located in Family History Library microfilm, microfiche, or books. Original marriage records are available from the Clerk of Court, Orleans Parish. Marriage of Leopold Goudchaux and Flora Marx.

[30] All birth records researched by genealogist, Teri Downs Tillman, Natchez, Mississippi.

[31] 1900 U. S. Census, St. Landry Parish Louisiana, pop. sch., Big Cane, Police Jury Ward 4, District 58, Sheet # 20B (penned), Dwelling # 375, Family # 382, Leopold Goudchaux household, digital image, (A: accessed 3/2006), citing NARA microfilm publication T-623 , roll 581. Date of enumeration: 28 June 1900.

[32] 1880 U.S. Census, Avoyelles Parish, Louisiana, pop. sch., ED 4, p. 434 A (stamped), No dwelling or family # listed, M. Kahn, household, digital image, (A: accessed 2/ 2006), citing NARA microfilm publication T9, roll 448. Date of enumeration: June 1880 (no day given).

[33] 1880 U. S. Census, Evergreen, Avoyelles Parish, LA, pop. sch. ED 5, p. 488 C (stamped), No dwelling number, Family # 209, Aaron Kahn household, digital image, (A: accessed 2/ 2006), citing NARA microfilm publication T9, roll 448. Date of enumeration: 18 June 1880.

[34] "New Orleans, Louisiana Marriage Records Index, 1831-1925," database, (A: accessed 2/2008), citing State of Louisiana, Secretary of State, Division of Archives, Records Management, and History. *Vital Records Indices.* Baton Rouge, LA, USA. Marriage of Max Kahn, age 33, and Adele Beer, age 21, (Vol. 10, p. 913).

[35] The "Avoyelles Outrage," as it was called in the local and national newspapers, will be treated in full in chapter 14 of this book.

[36] "New Orleans, Louisiana Marriage Records Index, 1831-1925," database, (A: accessed 12/2008), citing State of Louisiana, Secretary of State, Division of Archives, Records Management, and History. *Vital Records Indices.* Baton Rouge, LA, USA. Marriage of Ellie (sic) Hiller and Helvena Kahn (Vol. 7, p. 121).

[37] "Louisiana Marriages – 1718-1925," database, (A: accessed 4/2006), citing a variety of sources including individual marriage records located in Family History Library microfilm, microfiche, or books. Original marriage records are available from the Clerk of Court, Orleans Parish. Marriage of Jonas Hiller and Rosalie Levy (Vol. 5, p. 158).

[38] "New Orleans Passenger Lists, 1820-1945," digital image, (A: accessed 4/ 2006), Manifest of the *J.H. Cooper,* line 40, entry for Michel Levy, age 21, arrived 20 July 1846, citing NARA microfilm publication M 259, roll 25.

[39] 1850 U. S. Census, Avoyelles Parish, Louisiana, pop. sch., p 68 (penned), Dwelling #513, Family # 513, Michel Levi and Salomon Zucker household, digital image, (A: accessed 2/ 2006), citing NARA microfilm publication M 432, roll 229. Note: Solomon Zucker Americanized his name after moving to Bastrop becoming Solomon Sugar.

[40] "Jewishgen On-Line Worldwide Burial Registry," database, *Jewishgen.org* (http://www.jewishgen.org: accessed 5/ 2006), entries for Abraham and Caroline Hiller buried in Hebrew Rest Cemetery # 1 (through Temple Sinai), New Orleans, Orleans Parish, LA.

[41] *Ibid.*, Entry for Michel Levy (1825-1895), B'nai Sholom, Bastrop, Morehouse Parish, LA. Eliza Freidheim is buried next to her husband but there is no date of death indicated.

[42] Rabbi Martin Hinchin, *Fourscore and Eleven, A History of the Jews of Rapides Parish, Louisiana, 1828-1919* (Alexandria, LA: McCormick Graphics, Inc., 1984), 42-50.

[43] 1880 U. S. Census, Marksville, Avoyelles Parish, LA, pop. sch., ED 1 pp. 1-31 (penned), digital images, (A: accessed 5/2006), citing NARA microfilm publication T 9, roll 448. Date of enumeration: 6 June 1880.

[44] Mabel Hiller marker, Jewish Cemetery, Pineville, Rapides Parish, Louisiana, Row 16, personally read: "Our Darling Mabel, Dau. Of Elie and Helvena Hiller, Born May 30, 1884, Died Nov. 24, 1889, Aged 5 yrs. 6 mts. 26 ds."

[45] "World War I Draft Registration Cards, 1917-1918," digital image, (A: accessed 2 June 2006), Lawrence Estelle Hiller, Form 1956, # 7, Draft Board # 13, New Orleans, Orleans Parish, LA, citing *World War I Selective Service System Draft Registration Cards, 1917-1918*. Washington, D.C.: NARA microfilm publication M1509, roll 1684926.

[46] Hinchin, 51, 53, 55, 65.

[47] 1900 U. S. Census, Orleans Parish, Louisiana pop. sch., New Orleans, ED 6, p. 105A (stamped), Dwelling #205, Family #231, Helvena Hiller household, digital image, (A: accessed 6/ 2006), citing NARA microfilm publication T623, roll 570. Date of enumeration: 11 June 1900.

[48] Joshua Lewis, "All Pumped Up," *Louisiana Life*, Vol. 21, # 3, Autumn 2001, 60-64. (This article recounts the story of the Jules Clement # 1, and the growth of Jennings and the oil industry in Louisiana).

[49] "Jewishgen Online Worldwide Burial Registry," database, *Jewishgen.org* (http://www.jewishgen.org: accessed 5/ 2006), entry for Ellie (sic) Hiller (1851-1907), Summit Jewish Cemetery, Summit, Pike Co., Mississippi.

[50] Pierre Katz, compiler, *Les Communautés juives du Bas-Rhin en 1851* (Paris: Cercle de généalogie juive, 2000), Schirrhoffen families, p. 2. Exact birth and death dates courtesy of Teri Downs Tillman.

[51] Rev. Donald G. Hébert, compiler, "Southwest Louisiana records (1750-1900)," CD-Rom, database, (Rayne, LA: Hébert Publications, 1975-2001), Entry for birth of Josephine Goudchaux.

[52] "World War I Draft Registration Cards, 1917-1918," digital image, (A: accessed 6/ 2006), Eugene Weill Goudchaux, Serial # 622, Order # 619, Draft Board O, Lake Charles, Calcasieu Parish, LA, citing NARA microfilm publication M1509, roll 1684666.

[53] Gemiluth Chassodim Jewish Cemetery, (Opelousas, St. Landry Parish, Louisiana), Callie Goudchaux marker, personally read, 2007.

[54] 1900 U.S. Census, St. Landry Parish, LA, pop. sch., Big Cane, ED 58, Ward 4, p. 1B (penned) Dwelling #15, Family #15, J. L. Goudchaux household, digital image, (A: accessed 6/ 2006), citing NARA microfilm publication T623, roll 581. Date of enumeration: 1& 2 June 1900.

[55] 1910 U. S. Census, Avoyelles Parish, LA, pop. sch., Bunkie, ED 26, p. 16 B (penned), Dwelling #320, Family #367, Jacques Goudchaux household, digital image, (A: accessed 6/2006), citing NARA microfilm publication T624, roll 508. Date of enumeration: 16 May 1910.

[56] 1920 U. S. Census, Calcasieu Parish, LA, pop. sch., Lake Charles, ED 41, p. 11A (penned), Dwelling #214, Family #227, Mary Feeney household, Jacques Goudchaux roomer, digital image, (A: accessed 6/ 2006), citing NARA microfilm publication T625, roll 606. Date of enumeration: 8 & 9 January 1920.

[57] A. P. Quebodeaux, compiler, "Acadia Parish Marriage License Index 1887-1999, Incl.," database, *Usgwarchives.net* (http://www.usgwarchives.net/: accessed 6/2007). Marriage of Albert Kahn and Lottie Godchaux (sic).

[58] "Abraham Heyman, whose business exploits had been highly successful, employed quite a number of the Jewish citizenry of Alexandria in the persons of I. Hirschman, B.H. DeSola, Simon Mann, Adolph Baer, and Medar Kahn. He also owned a plantation on Bayou Robert and as the paper pointed out in Heyman's dialect: 'He watches it, too, for he has 'a hye like a heagle' as all will admit.' " (Source: Hinchin, 48).

[59] "Louisiana Statewide Death Index, 1900-1949," database, (A: accessed 6/ 2007), citing State of Louisiana, Secretary of State, Division of Archives, Records Management, and History. *Vital Records Indices.* Baton Rouge, LA, USA. Entry for Eugene Godchaux (sic).

[60] *Ibid.,* (A: accessed 6/2007), entry for Jake L. Goudcheaux (sic).

[61] *Ibid.*, (A: accessed 6/2007), entry for Josephine W. Goudchaux.

[62] "New York Passenger Lists, 1820-1957," digital image, (A: accessed 11/2006), citing *Passenger Lists of Vessels Arriving at New York, New York, 1820-1897,* NARA Microfilm Publication M237, roll 387; Manifest of S.S. *La Lorraine*, August 28, 1903, page 55, line 25 & 26, Jules Weill, age 26, Fanny Weill, age 21.

[63] Social Security Administration. "U.S. Social Security Death Index," database, (A: accessed 10/ 2007), entry for Mervin Weiss (2007).

[64] *Ibid.*, (A: accessed 10/2007), entry for Charles Weiss (1995).

[65] "Historical Newspaper Collection," Obituary of Fanny Weiss, *The New York Times,* 02 July 1964, digital image, (A: accessed 10/2007).

[66] Social Security Administration. "U.S. Social Security Death Index," database, (A: accessed 10/2007), entry for Charles Weiss (1995).

[67] See note 63.

[68] 1900 U.S. Census, Avoyelles Parish, LA, pop. sch., Bunkie, Ward 10, ED 26 , p. 7B (penned), Dwelling #146, Family #153, Martin Weiss household; p. 8B (penned), Dwelling #163, Family #171, Joe Weiss household, and Dwelling #166, Family #174, Sam Weiss household; p.6B (penned) Dwelling #120, Family #126, Herman Weiss household; digital images, (A: accessed 6/2007), citing NARA microfilm publication T623, roll 558. Date of enumeration; 6 June 1900.

[69] Jewish Cemetery (Pineville, Rapides Parish, Louisiana), Joseph M. Weiss marker, Row 24, personally read, 2007.

[70] "New Orleans, Louisiana Marriage Records Index, 1831-1925," database, (A: accessed 6/2007), citing State of Louisiana, Secretary of State, Division of Archives, Records Management, and History. *Vital Records Indices.* Baton

Rouge, LA, USA. Marriage of Joseph Weiss, age 28, and Annie Roth, age 19, (Vol. 16, P. 562).

[71] Jewish Cemetery, (Pineville, Rapides Parish, Louisiana), Meyar R. Weiss marker, row 5, personally read, 2007.

[72] "World War I Draft Registration Cards. 1917-1918," digital image. (A: accessed 7/ 2007), David B. Weiss, form 2769, no. 11. 2nd Precinct, 10th Ward, Avoyelles Parish, LA. Draft Board "O", Registered at Fort Logan H. Roots, Pulaski Co., Arkansas (Student at Training Corps), citing NARA microfilm publication M1509, roll 1653580.

[73] 1900 U.S. Census, Avoyelles Parish, Louisiana, pop. sch., Bunkie, Ward 10, ED 26, p 8B (penned), Dwelling #163, Family #171, Edda Weiss household, digital image, (A: accessed 6/2007), citing NARA microfilm publication T623, roll 558. Date of enumeration: 9 June 1900.

[74] "World War I Draft Registration Cards. 1917-1918," digital image, (A: accessed 7/ 2007), Gus Waldorph Weiss, serial no. 460, order no. 1763, Draft Board "O," Marksville, Avoyelles, Louisiana, citing NARA Microfilm Publication M1509, roll 1653580.

[75] Social Security Administration, "U.S. Social Security Death Index," database, (A: accessed 10/2007), entry for Selma H. Weiss (1991).

[76] *Ibid.*, (A: accessed 10/ 2007), entry for Lillian R. Weiss (2004).

[77] Hinchin, 176.

[78] 1920 U.S. Census, Avoyelles Parish, Louisiana, pop. sch., Bunkie, Ward 10, ED 16, p. 19B (penned), Dwelling #278, Family #285, Joseph M. Weiss, digital image, (A: accessed 10/2007), citing NARA microfilm publication T625, roll 605. Date of enumeration: 21 Jan 1920.

[79] 1930 U.S. Census, Philadelphia City, Pennsylvania, pop. sch., Ward 46, ED 511, p. 15b, Dwelling #238, Family #659, David Weiss household, digital image, (A: accessed 10/2007), citing NARA microfilm publication T626, roll 2140. Date of enumeration: 25 April 1930.

[80] Selma Jackson Weiss obituary, undated clipping from unidentified newspaper, in scrapbook of Estelle Johanna Siess, privately held by Mrs. Bettye Jo Bango Maki, West Bloomfield, MI, 2006.

[81] Mayer (sic) R. Weiss obituary in scrapbook of Estelle Johanna Siess.

[82] Jewish Cemetery (Pineville, Rapides Parish, Louisiana), Meyar (sic) R. Weiss & Selma Jackson Weiss markers, row 5, personally read, 2007.

[83] Gus, Jr. was educated at Vanderbilt and Harvard Universities, finally receiving a doctorate from New York University School of Economics. He was a foreign policy advisor to Presidents Carter, Reagan, Nixon and Ford, and a member of the National Security Council as well as a CIA consultant. His death, on November 25, 2003, after a fall from his apartment window in the Watergate East building in Washington D.C., has become the fodder for many conspiracy theories. His death was ruled a "suicide." He never married. See: Holly Edwards, "Nashville Native Gus Weiss, Advisor to 4 Presidents, Dies" *The Tennessean*, 1 Dec 2003, digital image, (http://alt-f4.org/img/tennesean_2003-12-01_gus weiss.html: accessed 11/ 2007).

[84] "Historical Newspaper Collection," Obituary of David B. Weiss, *The New York Times*, 15, 16 & 17 November 1964, digital image, (A: accessed 10/2007),

[85] "Historical Newspaper Collection," Obituary of Selma H. Weiss, *The New York Times*, 6 June 1991, digital image, (A: accessed 9/ 2007).

[86] Social Security Administration, "U.S. Social Security Death Index," database, (A: accessed 10/ 2007), entry for Lillian R. Weiss (2004).

[87] Hinchin, 149. Note: The grave marker in the Jewish Cemetery in Pineville, Rapides Parish, LA indicates he was born in Oct. 1855. His obituary states that he was 43 at the time of his death in 1911. Since his mother was born in 1844, his likely birth date is October 1865.

[88] Barbara Finney & Paul Chamberlain, compilers, "Alphabetical Orleans Parish Groom's Marriage Index WA-WH," database, *Usgwarchives.net* (http://www.usgwarchives.net/: accessed 10/2007). Marriage of Samuel Weiss to Augusta Elisa (sic), citing Louisiana Archives [Marriages] Vol.18, p. 174.

[89] Hinchin, 149.

[90] Social Security Administration. "U.S. Social Security Death Index," database, (A: accessed 10/ 2007), entry for Seymour Weiss (1969).

[91] "World War I Draft Registration Cards, 1917-1918, " digital image, (A: accessed 11/ 2007, Seymour Weiss, Order # 101, Registration # 31, Draft Board 12, New Orleans, Orleans Parish, LA, citing NARA Microfilm publication M1509, FHL microfilm roll 1684925.

[92] Ronnie Virgets, "Happy Birthday Huey." *Gambit Weekly,* 26 Aug 2003, *Bestofneworleans.com.* (http://www.bestofneworleans.com/dispatch/2003-08-26/views-virgets.html#top : accessed 10/ 2007), paragraphs 4-7, and 17.

[93] Personal knowledge of David Dewitt Lavies, first cousin twice removed of Elva Mae Lavies, second wife of Seymour Weiss in email to the author dated November 10, 2007.

[94] "New Orleans Passenger Lists, 1820-1945," digital image, (A : accessed 11/ 2007), citing NARA Microfilm publication T905, roll 155, Manifest of S.S. *Contessa,* May 22, 1935, page 1, line 1, E. Bernard Weiss, age 37.

[95] 1930 U.S. Census, Caddo Parish, Louisiana, pop. sch., Shreveport, ED 55, p. 171 (stamped), Dwelling #256, Family #261, Mrs. Louis Heilperin, digital image, (A: accessed 11/2007) , citing NARA publication T626, roll 787. Date of enumeration: 11 April 1930.

[96] "Texas Birth Index, 1903-1997," database, (A: accessed 7/2007), citing *Texas Birth Index, 1903-1997.* Texas Department of State Health Services. Microfiche entry for William Morris Weiss, roll number: 1926_0006, (1926 Births. p. 1479).

[97] "Historical Newspaper Collection," "Plane Crash Kills 10 Magnates – Seaplane Smashes House in LA," *The Stars and Stripes, Mediterranean and North Africa Editions,*12 Jan 1954, page 16, cols 1-2; digital image, (A: accessed 10/ 2007).

[98] "Historical Newspaper Collection," Obituary of Julius Weiss, *The New York Times,* 31 Aug 1954, digital image, (A: accessed 10/ 2007).

[99] "New Orleans, Louisiana Marriage Records Index, 1831-1925," database, (A: accessed 7/2007), citing State of Louisiana, Secretary of State, Division of Archives, Records Management, and History. *Vital Records Indices.* Baton Rouge, LA, USA. Marriage of Morris Weiss, age 24 and Hannah Cohen, age 24, (Vol. 21, P. 738).

[100] Social Security Administration. "U.S. Social Security Death Index," database, (A: accessed 7/2007), entry for Samuel C. Weiss, 1998.

[101] Hinchin, 188.

[102] 1900 U.S. Census, Sabine Parish, Louisiana, pop. sch., Many, Ward 4, ED 91, p 50A (stamped), Dwelling #31, Family #33, Morris Weiss household, digital image, (A: accessed 6/2007), citing NARA microfilm publication T623, roll 579. Date of enumeration: 2 June 1900.

[103] "New York Passenger Lists, 1820-1957," digital image, (A: accessed 11/2006), citing *Passenger Lists of Vessels Arriving at New York, New York, 1820-1897*. NARA microfilm publication T715, roll 4807, Manifest of S.S. *Caronia*, July 10,1927, page 185, line 19, Annette W. Selber, born Many, LA, Feb 10, 1905.

[104] Hinchin, 129.

[105] "New Orleans, Louisiana Marriage Records Index, 1831-1925," database, (A: accessed 7/2007), citing State of Louisiana, Secretary of State, Division of Archives, Records Management, and History. *Vital Records Indices.* Baton Rouge, LA, USA. Marriage of Joseph Mermelstein, age 28 and Henrietta Cohen, age 24, (Vol. 26, P. 691).

[106] "New York Passenger Lists, 1820-1957," digital image, (A: accessed 11/2006), citing *Passenger Lists of Vessels Arriving at New York, New York, 1820-1897*. NARA microfilm publication T715, roll 5805, Manifest of S.S. *Conte di Savoia*, May 21, 1936, page 5, line 11, Martin S. Goldring, born Burkee (sic), LA, Feb 14, 1903.

[107] *Ibid.*, (A: accessed 11/2006), citing *Passenger Lists of Vessels Arriving at New York, New York, 1820-1897,* NARA microfilm publication T715, roll

5489, Manifest of S.S. *Veragua,* May 20,1934, page 70, line 13, Ferdie Goldring, born Feb 10, 1905, Many, LA.

[108] "Goldring Rites Slated in New York," *The (New Orleans, Louisiana) Times* Picayune (hereinafter cited as *"TP"*), 19 April 1961, p. 1, col 4, digital image, (GB: accessed 10/ 2010).

[109] Hinchin, 127.

[110] Hinchin, A127-A129.

[111] Hinchin, 176.

[112] See chapter 15, pp. 498-501.

[113] Morris Joseph Weiss obituary, undated clipping from unidentified newspaper, in scrapbook of Estelle Johanna Siess.

[114] Jewish Cemetery (Pineville, Rapides Parish, Louisiana), Morris J. Weiss & Hannah Weiss markers, row 7, personally read, 2007.

[115] Jewish Cemetery (Pineville, Rapides Parish, Louisiana), Emilie Weill Weiss & Hannah Weiss markers, row 6, personally read, 2007.

[116] Eric J. Brock, *Images of America – The Jewish Community of Shreveport* (Charleston, SC: Arcadia Press, 2002), 82.

[117] "Jewishgen Online Worldwide Burial Registry," *Jewishgen.org* (http://www.jewishgen.org: accessed 5/2006), entry for Martin B. Weiss (1828-1903), Canal Street Cemetery, New Orleans, Orleans Parish, Louisiana.

[118] Hinchin, 163.

[119] Gemiluth Chassodim Jewish Cemetery (Opelousas, St. Landry Parish, Louisiana), Florence Wolff Goudchaux marker, personally read, 2007. Note: Mae Wolff Weill was not only Charles Goudchaux's sister-in-law, but also the wife of his half cousin once removed, Jacob Weill.

[120] 1910 U.S. Census, St. Landry Parish, Louisiana, pop. sch., Melville, ED 108, Ward 4, p. 3B (penned), Dwelling #59, Family #60, Charles Goudchaux

household, digital image, (A : accessed 10/2007), citing NARA microfilm publication T624, roll 530. Date of enumeration: 18 April 1910.

[121] Social Security Administration, "U.S. Social Security Death Index," database, (A: accessed 10/ 2007), entry for Leona G. Firnberg (2006).

[122] Charles A. Goudchaux obituary, undated clipping from scrapbook of Estelle Johanna Siess.

[123] Marriage of Lottie Goudchaux and Jerome P. Morrison, undated clipping from scrapbook of Estelle Johanna Siess.

[124] Mrs. Florence Wolff Goudchaux obituary, undated clipping from scrapbook of Estelle Johanna Siess.

[125] See, chapter 3, pp. 95, 96, 107.

[126] Avoyelles Parish Courthouse Records (Marksville, Avoyelles Parish, LA), *Conveyances,* Book A2, p. 39, "The Fischer Lumber Co. to Leopold Goudchaux, Sale of cypress logs, railroads, etc. with mortgage," filed 30 May 1913.

[127] Avoyelles Parish Courthouse Records (Marksville, Avoyelles Parish, LA), *Succession Book* A-17, p. 118, "Sheriff Sale of Property to Sellers & Goudchaux ," filed 3 June 1918.

[128] "Louisiana Statewide Death Index, 1900-1949, database, (A: accessed 8/ 2007) citing State of Louisiana, Secretary of State, Division of Archives, Records Management, and History. *Vital Records Indices.* Baton Rouge, LA, USA. Entry for Leopold Goudchaux, (Certificate #2341, Vol. 6).

[129] Gemiluth Chassodim Jewish Cemetery (Opelousas, St. Landry Parish, Louisiana), Leopold Goudchaux & Charlotte E. Goudchaux markers, personally read, 2007.

[130] Jewish Cemetery (Pineville, Rapides Parish, Louisiana), Flora Marx Goudchaux, marker, row 12, personally read, 2007.

[131] "New Orleans, Louisiana Death Records Index, 1804-1949," database, (A: accessed 8/2007), citing State of Louisiana, Secretary of State, Division of

Archives, Records Management, and History. *Vital Records Indices*. Baton Rouge, LA, USA. Entry for Lazard Goudchaux, (Vol. 180, p. 858).

[132] *Ibid.*, (A: accessed 8/2007) Entry for Harriet Oppenheim Goudchaux, (Vol. 36, p. 276).

Esther (Estelle) Goudchaux Kahn, mother of Max, Henry, and Aaron Kahn and Helvena Kahn Hiller, ca. 1865

(*Courtesy of Brad Fanta*)

CHAPTER 10

THE CURIOUS CASE OF MOSES WOLF

No study of the Jews of Avoyelles Parish would be complete without a giving an honorable mention to Moses Wolf, a Jewish immigrant who with his brother, Joseph, was an itinerant merchant, selling his wares throughout rural Louisiana. His existence would probably have been forgotten were not for Ira S. Couvillon's book, *To Avoyelles With the Couvillons*. In it he told the story of Marie Ophélia Couvillon, one of the nine children of Sainville Couvillon, and his wife, Azelia, born on November 11, 1843 near present day Mansura.[1]

According to the Couvillon family, the patriarch, Sainville was very strict and never let his children participate in any of the frivolities of youth. Ophelia, who was very strong willed, rebelled and set out to make her escape. How she met Moses Wolf is not known, but since he made frequent trips to Avoyelles Parish to sell his wares, it is likely that they had met more than once, prior to and during the Civil War. It was said that a brother, Joseph Wolf, and he had once settled in Hamburg, in Avoyelles Parish, and had opened a store, from where they fanned out through the countryside to sell their goods. However, no reliable trace of Joseph, or their presence in Hamburg, has been found in any records.

Moses was considerably older that Ophelia, by about twenty years, married, and living in St. Helena Parish in the town of Greensburg. Thirty-eight year old Moses Wolf, a merchant from Germany, was enumerated in the 1860 census living with his wife Sabrina, age thirty-six, born in Louisiana. Their children were James Adolph Wolf (b. 1853), Cornelius N. Wolf (b. 1857), and Robert L. Wolf (b. 1858).[2] An additional child, a daughter, Mattie R. Wolf, was born to the couple in October 1862. It is doubtful that Sabrina, by all account born in Louisiana, was Jewish, given her name and the names that were chosen for their children.[3]

367

It was evidently then, sometime during the 1860s, alluded to in Couvillon's account but never pinpointed, that Moses and Ophelia met. By 1862-63, Wolf was most likely a widower, it being quite possible that Sabrina died giving birth to Mattie. The countryside was in turmoil, and Moses, forced to travel to make a living, would have been on the lookout for a prospective second wife and mother to his small children.

The story of their elopement, as told by the family, is one of high drama. Ophelia, with the help of a "negro slave girl," took a canoe and paddled down the bayou as far as Hamburg. There they were met by Wolf, who put Ophelia in a horse and buggy, and they rode to Naples, at the mouth of the Red River, where they boarded a river boat which took them to Galveston, Texas. According, still, to family legend, they were married by the steamboat captain, and after arriving in Galveston, made their way to Houston, where they settled down. There is no record of that marriage, but there is a rather unusual entry for Moses Wolf who wed Marie Bordelon on July 11, 1865 in St. Helena Parish, the groom's home parish according to the 1860 Census. Perhaps the couple feared that the steamboat wedding was not legal, or maybe the whole story was made up in order to placate disapproving parents. If this is, indeed, the record of their wedding, it is not surprising that the bride would have used a pseudonym, for fear of being found out. After all, Ophelia's first name was "Marie" and she had eight cousins whose names were all "Marie Bordelon."[4]

There is no concrete proof that the couple ever lived in Texas. However, it was not unusual for Louisiana merchants to have travelled to and perhaps settled in Texas during the Civil War, as all the European trade that the South could manage was through Texas and Mexico due to the North's blockade of Southern ports. It would not have been impossible either for the couple to have sought refuge, for a time, in Texas for fear that Ophelia's irate family might track them down.[5]

According to the Couvillons, the couple's first child, Joseph Bernard Wolf, was born in Houston, Texas on May 6, 1865.[6] But Joseph's obituary states that he was born on March 6, 1868 in Amite, Tangipahoa Parish, Louisiana.[7] Various census records show his age to be closer to the 1868 date. The 1900 census taker recorded his birth as "March 1868."[8]

As the story goes, no one in Avoyelles Parish really knew what had happened to Ophelia, much less that she had run off with a Jewish peddler, until about twelve years later, when another itinerant salesman stopped at Sainville Couvillon's house and noticed a remarkable resemblance between several of the Couvillon children and a friend's wife back in Houston. He returned a year later to bring them the joyous news that his friend's wife was indeed their daughter. This resulted in the two families being reunited, and soon after that Moses and Ophelia moved back to Louisiana. While this might be true in part, what we do know is that Moses and Mary Ophelia Wolf had moved from either St. Helena Parish, or Houston, Texas to the countryside near the town of Tangipahoa in Tangipahoa Parish, Louisiana where they would live for a good part of their lives. According to the 1870 census, all of Moses' children with Sabrina were living with them: James, age eighteen, who was a railroad employee, Cornelius, age thirteen, Robert, age ten, and Mattie, age eight, all still in school. In addition, there had been three children born to them in Louisiana: Rosalia, age four (who died as a child), Joseph Bernard, age two and Andrew Jackson, age four months. Moses, at age forty-eight, was employed as a store clerk.[9]

There is never any indication that Moses, the Jewish husband of two gentile wives, made any effort to practice his religion or join a community where there were fellow Jews with whom to interact. He and his family were rather just citizens of the defeated South, trying to lead a peaceful existence during the difficult times of Reconstruction. Without other family members as a support group, and not being able to live amongst other Jews, his assimilation into the Christian, mostly Catholic, Louisiana society seems to have been fairly rapid and essentially complete. While not knowing the religion of his first wife, it is known that his second, Ophelia, was a baptized as a Catholic.

In May 1874 the citizens of Tangipahoa Town elected a mayor and four aldermen. The results were forwarded to Louisiana's Secretary of State, but as of September of the following year, the officials elected had not been commissioned. On September 13, 1875, the *New Orleans Times* published a letter dated September 2nd of the same year, authored by Frank Ferris, the Railway Station Agent of the town to Lieutenant Governor C.C. Antoine, along with a petition signed by the voters, one of whom was Moses Wolf. The latter also appears on a list of registered voters in the Parish of Tangipahoa for the year of 1874. Curiously, the *Times* indicated the letter was published to show its readers the "vast intellect of the average station agent, the political force of his arguments, as well as to show that peace reigns at Tangipahoa." Station agent Ferris indicated that he was writing to Antoine, who was a Southern gentleman, instead of Governor Kellogg, who was deemed by the citizenry to be a carpetbagger, to ask him personally to issue the commissions because "there is no fire eaters in this place and the Collerd People are protected in all theyr rights. But theyr is Some White rowdies in town Some times and Gets drunk and act Verry badly but as soon as we get oure Officer commissioned we will soone put a Stop to theyr transactions." The commissions were approved by the end of the month.[10]

The couple's remaining children were all born in Tangipahoa: Nettie, in 1871, followed by another son, Moses Hamilton Wolf on August 6, 1875, and Anna (Annie) Wolf on November 3, 1879.[11] The 1880 Federal Census shows two of Moses' children by his first marriage, James and Robert, were no longer living at home in Tangipahoa. James left railroading to become a farmer and moved with his new wife, Emelia Bergeron, her family, and their two children, Benny and Eva Wolf, to Bayou Bleue near Houma in Terrebonne Parish.[12] Moses' son, Robert, is missing from subsequent census records, but is buried next to his father in the Amite City Cemetery in Tangipahoa Parish, having died on November 18, 1899.[13] In 1880 Cornelius, from Moses' first marriage, was twenty-three and a laborer. Mattie, Joseph and Andrew were eighteen, twelve and ten respectively and in school. Nettie was eight, Moses Hamilton, five and Anna, the baby, was two years old.[14] In January 1880, Moses ran for constable of Ward 1, in Tangipahoa but was beaten by Hughey Dykes 141 to 120.[15] However, before June of that same year, he had been appointed a deputy sheriff.

His daughter, Mattie, married the son of an Alsatian immigrant, John Saal, on June 26, 1888.[16] That same year Saal became the Sheriff of Tangipahoa Parish. Most of the Saal family remained in the area. John, Mattie and their children, including their son, Johnnie Moses Saal, who died at the age of eight, are buried in the Amite City Cemetery.[17]

Far more is known about Moses Wolf's children with his second wife, Ophelia Couvillon, because there is written evidence that the family rift was repaired before the end of 1879. Their second child, Andrew Jackson Wolf, born on January 8, 1870, in Tangipahoa Parish, was baptized, at the age of nine, on December 5, 1879, at the Sacred Heart Catholic Church of Moreauville, Avoyelles Parish, with two of his mother's siblings, Dorsin and Marie Couvillon as his godparents.[18] Several years after Moses and Ophelia made peace with the Couvillon family they relocated to Rapides Parish.

Moses and Ophelia's first child, Joseph Bernard Wolf, was for a number of years employed, as had been his half-brother, James, by the Texas and Pacific Railway as a conductor. His first wife, Emma Whitstine, whom he married in late 1889 died in childbirth in 1891 at Boyce, and he married Mary Gerdes Grant on September 24, 1894, in Alexandria, with whom he had six children.[19] His first business venture in Boyce was a saloon, which, according to R.G. Dun's *Mercantile Agency Reference Book of 1902*, was worth less than $500.[20] He later moved to Alexandria and opened a very successful grocery store and ran it with the assistance of his sons and daughters. When he died on March 2, 1933, his funeral service was held at St. Francis Xavier Cathedral, and he was interred at Greenwood Memorial Park.[21] Many of his descendants still live in the Alexandria-Pineville vicinity.

Andrew Jackson Wolf married Carrie Labertha Whitfield on April 20, 1897, in Alexandria, Rapides Parish. Like Joseph and James he worked for the railroad as a young man, first living in New Orleans with his wife where he became a passenger conductor on the Texas and Pacific Railway, working between New Orleans and Marshall, Texas. He finally moved to Alexandria in 1905 with Carrie and his four children where he engaged in a wholesale liquor business. By 1920 he had opened a general store, but by 1930 he was the proprietor of a large furniture store in partnership with his only son, Andrew Wolf, Jr., and Carl Pearson, who married Andrew's eldest daughter Clara.[22] Andrew, Sr. died on October 14, 1931. Services were conducted for him at the First Methodist Church. He has descendants in the Alexandria area, as well as in the state of Tennessee.[23]

Nettie Wolf was married to William D. Sutton on December 6, 1887, by Fred White, Minister of the Gospel, in Marksville, Avoyelles Parish.[24] Sutton was a locomotive fireman. Their five children were all born in Boyce. At the turn of the twentieth century he was transferred to Marshal, Texas, where he took his family to live.[25]

Moses Hamilton Wolf, the couple's youngest son became a switchman for the Texas and Pacific Railway. He married St. Agnes Loulette Grant, his brother, Joseph's wife's sister, on February 18, 1898, in Rapides Parish.[26] The Grant sisters were born in Natchitoches, Louisiana to Richard Henry Grant and his wife Kate. They were part of the Natchitoches Parish farming community, and members of the Catholic faith. In the early 1890s the family moved to Boyce, where Grant became a steamboat captain. In 1900 Henry Grant, now a widower, lived with his six younger children next to his son-in-law, Joseph Bernard Wolf, Wolf's wife, Mary Gerdes Grant, and their three children, and not far from Moses Hamilton Wolf, Loulette Grant and their first child, Henry Overton Wolf.[27]

Moses and Loulette added four more children to their family: Bessie (b. 1901) who died three years later, Moses, Jr. (b. 1904), Anna (b. 1906), who died at the age of two, and Mary Myrtle (b. 1908) before they left Boyce for Alexandria. Having temporarily abandoned railroading, Moses became a wholesale liquor dealer.[28] However, by 1917, he was back at Boyce, and listed his occupation as "switchman for the Texas and Pacific Railway." By then he was missing three fingers off his left hand, no doubt from a job-related accident which was all too common when working in the railroad industry.[29] Three more sons were born to the family, Joseph Adolph (b. 1912), George Lawrence (b. 1917), and Kingston Grant Wolf (b. 1919). By then, their eldest child, Henry Overton Wolf, was a "call boy"[30] for the Texas and Pacific Railway.[31] Moses Hamilton Wolf ended his railroad career back in Alexandria, as a roundhouse (locomotive) foreman for the Texas and Pacific Railway.

Moses and Ophelia's last child, Anna Wolf, married James Edward Ray of Winnfield, Louisiana. Parents of three girls and a boy, they were, for many years, residents of Rapides Parish, first at Cotile, then at Boyce, where in 1910, the head of the family worked in a saloon, along with one of his wife's distant cousins, Ludger Couvillon.[32] By 1930 he was a salesman for a wholesale grocery company. One of his children, a daughter named Ophelia, born August 11, 1900, was the only one to abandon Rapides Parish, when she married Alton Bettison Blakewood, originally from Big Bend in Avoyelles Parish in 1919. Their two children were raised mostly in Bunkie, although they spent some time in Rapides and Claiborne parishes where their father worked in the petroleum industry for the Standard Oil Company.[33]

Moses Wolf died in Rapides Parish in 1898 and was buried in the Amite (Tangipahoa Parish) City Cemetery. Although his wife, Ophelia, was said to have been buried there as well, her resting place remains unknown and may be simply unmarked. While the story of Moses Wolf and his wife Ophelia Couvillon is certainly an unusual one, in the end, Moses Wolf was just another early Jewish immigrant to Louisiana who, living in an area where there were few Jews, surrendered his faith in order to blend into the rural farming communities where he operated his mercantile business. That he was politically active, running for office, and finally being appointed a deputy sheriff shows the respect with which he was held in his community, not as a stranger with foreign customs, but as an equal. His descendants, some raised as Catholics, others as Protestants, never looked backward, taking spouses of their own or other Christian faiths. That Moses Wolf apparently did not leave instructions to be interred in a Jewish cemetery, also speaks volumes about his complete alienation from his former life as a German Jewish immigrant.

---

[1] Alberta Rousseau Ducoté, G.R.S., compiler and translator, *Early Baptism Records- St. Paul the Apostle Catholic Church – 1824-1844- Avoyelles Parish* (Mansura, Louisiana: St. Paul the Apostle Catholic Church, 1982), Part 2, p. 38. Baptism of Ophelia Couvillon.

[2] 1860 U.S. Census, St. Helena Parish, Louisiana, pop. sch., Greensburg, p. 78 (penned), Dwelling # 696, Family # 696, Moses Wolf household, digital image, *Ancestry.com* (http://www.ancestry.com [hereinafter cited as "A"]: accessed 5/ 2009), citing NARA microfilm publication M 653, roll 423. Date of enumeration: 20 Aug 1860.

[3] Several on-line genealogies indicate that Sabrina's maiden name was "Moore," and that she had been previously married to William Durbin in St. Helena Parish. Lacking, however a marriage document for Sabrina to Moses Wolf, this previous relationship, as well as her maiden name is impossible, as of now, to verify.

[4] "Louisiana Marriages, 1718-1925," database, (A: accessed 5/ 2009), citing "Hunting for Bears" and a variety of sources including original marriage records located in Family History Library microfilm, microfiche, or books. Marriage of Moses Wolf to Marie Brodelon (sic).

[5] Ira S. Couvillon, *To Avoyelles with the Couvillons* (Simmesport, LA: Mardi Gras Publications, 1966), 429.

[6] Couvillon, 430.

[7] Obituary of J.B. Wolf, undated clipping from unidentified newspaper, in scrapbook of Estelle Johanna Siess, privately held by Mrs. Bettye Jo Bango Maki, West Bloomfield, MI, 2006.

[8] 1900 United States Federal Census, Rapides Parish, Louisiana, Boyce, ED 132, p. 4A (penned), Dwelling #58, Family #58, J.B. Wolf household, digital image, (A: accessed 1/ 2010), citing NARA microfilm publication T623, roll 578. Date of enumeration: 3 June 1900.

[9] 1870 United States Federal Census Tangipahoa Parish, Louisiana, pop. sch., Tangipahoa town, Ward 1, p. 5 (penned), dwelling #38, family #39, Moses Wolf household, digital image, (A: accessed 1/ 2010), citing NARA microfilm publication M593, roll 532. Date of enumeration: 4 June 1870.

[10] "The Political Mill," *The New Orleans (Louisiana) Times,* 13 September 1875, single page, col. 1, digital image, *Genealogybank.com* (http://www.genealogybank.com [hereinafter cited as "GB"]: accessed 1/ 2010).

[11] Couvillon, 431, 432.

[12] 1880 United States Federal Census, Terrebonne Parish, Louisiana, Bayou Bleue, ED 187, p. 2B (penned), Dwelling #14, Family #14, J. Bergeron household, digital image, (A: accessed 1/ 2010), citing NARA microfilm publication, T9, roll 472. Date of enumeration: 2nd and 3rd June 1880.

[13] The Amite City Cemetery (Amite, Tangipahoa Parish, LA) Robert L. Wolf marker, personally read 9/ 2007, "Thy Will Be Done – Robert L. Wolf, Died Nov. 18, 1899. Aged 42 years."

[14] 1880 United States Federal Census, Tangipahoa Parish, Louisiana, pop. sch., ED 178, Ward 1, p. 8D (penned), Dwelling #61, Family #61, Moses Wolf household, digital image, (A: accessed 1/ 2010), citing NARA microfilm publication T9, roll 471. Date of enumeration: 4 June 1880.

[15] "Official – Tangipahoa Parish," *The (New Orleans, LA) Daily Picayune,* 4 January 1880, p. 12, col. 5, digital image, (GB: accessed 1/ 2010).

[16] "Louisiana Marriages, 1718-1925," database, (A: accessed 5/ 2009), citing "Hunting for Bears" and a variety of sources including original marriage records located in Family History Library microfilm, microfiche, or books. Marriage of John Saal to Mattie Wolf.

[17] The Amite City Cemetery (Amite, Tangipahoa Parish, LA) John Saal and Jonnie Moses Saal markers, personally read 9/ 2007.

[18] Ellen Dauzat, compiler, *Sacred Heart Catholic Church Baptisms - Book 1,* Unpublished Manuscript, 2009, 64.

[19] Couvillon, 430.

[20] Jan and Naomi McPeek, *Merchants, Tradesmen and Manufacturers Financial Condition for 1902 Rapides Parish Louisiana.* Image reprint from the 1902 R.G. Dun *Mercantile Agency Reference Book* (Salem, OH: Aaron's Books, 2005), Boyce , 6.

[21] Obituary of J.B. Wolf, undated clipping from unidentified newspaper, in scrapbook of Estelle Johanna Siess.

[22] 1930 U. S. Census, Rapides Parish, Louisiana, pop. sch., Alexandria, Ward 5, ED 14, p. 7B (penned), Dwelling #147, Family #158, Andrew J. Wolf household, digital image, (A: accessed 1/ 2010), citing NARA microfilm publication T626, no roll given. Date of enumeration: 8 April 1930.

[23] Obituary of A. J. Wolf, Sr., undated clipping from unidentified newspaper in scrapbook of Estelle Johanna Siess..

[24] Jeraldine DuFour LaCour, *Brides Book of Avoyelles Parish, Louisiana, 1881-1899,* Volume 3, (Alexandria, Jeraldine DuFour LaCour [P.O. Box 5022, 70107], 1986), 156.

[25] 1900 U. S. Census, Harrison County, Texas, pop. sch.,, ED 45, Ward 1, p. 14 A (penned), Dwelling #267, Family #269, William D. Sutton household, digital image, (A: accessed 1/ 2010), citing NARA microfilm publication T623, roll 1643. Date of enumeration: 16 June 1900.

[26] Couvillon, 431.

[27] 1900 U. S. Census, Rapides Parish, Louisiana, pop. sch., Boyce, ED 132, p. 4A (penned), Dwelling #58, Family #59, J.B. Wolf household and dwelling #59, family #60; R.H. Grant household; p. 2B (penned) dwelling #32, family #33, Moses Wolf household, digital images, (A: accessed 1/ 2010), citing

NARA microfilm publication T623, roll 578. Date of enumeration: 1 June 1900.

[28] 1910 U. S. Census, Rapides Parish, Louisiana, pop. sch., Alexandria, Ward 2, ED 79, p. 18A (penned), Dwelling #267, Family # 280, Moses H. Wolff (sic) household, digital image, (A: accessed 1/ 2010), citing NARA microfilm publication T624, roll 527. Date of enumeration: 23 April 1910.

[29] "World War I Draft Registration Cards, 1917-1918," digital image, (A: accessed 1/2010), Moses Hamilton Wolf,, Serial No. 2047, Order No. A3055, Draft Board 2, Alexandria, Rapides Parish, LA, citing *World War I Selective Service System Draft Registration Cards, 1917-1918*, NARA microfilm publication M1509, roll 1684932.

[30] Before the telephone, railroads employed boys as young as twelve years old to take messages on foot or by bicycle from the crew dispatcher to engine and train crews informing them of their next assignment.

[31] "World War I Draft Registration Cards, 1917-1918," digital image, (A: accessed 1/ 2010), Henry Overton Wolf, Serial No. 265, Order No. 3833, Draft Board 2, Alexandria, Rapides Parish, LA, citing, *World War I Selective Service System Draft Registration Cards, 1917-1918*, NARA microfilm publication M1509, roll 1684932.

[32] 1910 U. S. Census, Rapides Parish, Louisiana, pop. sch., Alexandria, Ward 2, ED 79, p. 18A (penned), Dwelling #267, Family #280, Moses H. Wolff (sic) household, digital image, (A: accessed 1/ 2010), citing NARA microfilm publication T624, roll 527. Date of enumeration: 23 April 1910.

[33] Couvillon, 432.

Amite City Cemetery (Tangipahoa Parish, LA) "Sacred to the memory of our father Moses Wolf.
A Native of Europe – Aged 76 Ys. 5 Mo. 4 Ds."

CHAPTER 11
MOÏSE LEVY – EVERGREEN MERCHANT

Moïse Levy, his wife Rosalie Meyer, and their ten children who settled in Evergreen are another example of how postbellum Southern Jewish families that were scattered throughout the Gulf South formed a cohesive network of business and personal relations, in an effort to safeguard their religion and customs. Moïse Levy was born in Niederbronn, Alsace on February 27, 1823.[1] By 1851, both of his parents, Samuel Levi, a second hand dealer, and his mother, Esther Moses, were deceased and Moïse, who was a twenty-eight year old bachelor, lived with his brother Elie, the latter's wife Gittel Netter, and their two children, Samuel and Moïse. The two Levy brothers were cattle dealers *(marchands de génisses)*.[2] Moïse did not take a wife until almost 10 years later, when he travelled to the village of Niederroedern, some 30 miles to the east, to marry Rosalie Meyer. She was the ninth child born on August 30, 1837, to her parents, Samuel Meyer and Madeleine Auscher, and considerably younger than her spouse when they wed in 1861.[3]

Moïse and Rosalie's first three children were born before they left Alsace: Solomon (b. July 1862), Gustave (b. September 1863), and Marx (b. February 1866). The family immigrated to the United States in 1868. Their next two children, twins Estelle and Jacob Levy, were born in Louisiana in December 1868, just after their arrival. After a brief stay in New Orleans they moved on to make their first permanent home in Forest, Mississippi. Located in Scott County in the central part of the state fifty miles from Jackson, the small town was in the heart of plantation country. The 1870 Federal Census records that Moïse (listed as Moses) age forty-seven was living with his wife, "Rosallee" age thirty-two, and their children, Sallomont (sic), Gustave, M.M. (Marx), and the twins, Jacob and Estelle. Mary Myers (sic), Rosalie's sister, lived with them as well. Mary appears in the 1836 census for the town of Niederroedern as Gertrude Meyer, age six, but in every subsequent United States census is enumerated as "Mary."[4] Their sixth child,

Benjamin Franklin Levy, was born on July 26, 1872, in Forest, Mississippi. Moïse was prospering as much as anyone could in the post-Civil War economy of the South He declared himself to be in possession of $1500 in personal property including the items he carried in his store.

After the birth of their son, Benjamin, the family decided to move on, leaving Mississippi, for Evergreen, Avoyelles Parish, almost three hundred miles away. Their relocation may have been the result of competition at home, or the promise of better opportunities in another town, where they had heard of other Alsatian Jewish merchants who were living and prospering. By September 1874, Moïse Levy and his growing family had settled in Evergreen, awaiting the birth of their seventh child, Ernest Aaron, on September 2, 1874, then Matilda (Maude) on June 26, 1876. [5] The couple's last two children, Julius Meyer Levy born on September 20, 1878, and Mary (b. March 1880), spent their youth there as well.[6] At the time of the 1880 census, sixty year old Moïse was supporting himself and twelve other people, his ten children, his wife Rosalie and his wife's sister, Gertrude/Mary, who was self-employed as a milliner. Also enumerated with his immediate family were Melsy Alexander, a twenty-two year old African-American male employed as a "hostler," and two other French immigrants, twenty-two year old Jonas Weil, a book keeper, and nineteen year old Leon Bloch, a dry goods clerk.[7] Bloch and Weil worked in Moïse's general store along with the couple's eldest sons, Solomon and Gustave.

According to the *Marksville Bulletin*, Rosalie's sister passed away on January 22, 1881, at the age of fifty, and was buried in the Jewish Cemetery in Pineville.[8] Moïse Levy died four years later on July 20, 1885. His passing was noted in the Alexandria *Town Talk* newspaper which reported: "The remains of Moses Levy, 65, of Evergreen were brought here for burial. He had been a merchant there."[9] Rosalie followed her husband in death just thirteen months later. The *Town Talk* reported: "On a sad note, three deaths took place in rapid succession. The first was that of Rosalie Myers Levy from Evergreen in Avoyelles Parish, who was brought here for interment after her death on August 10, 1886."[10] Moïse and Rosalie were both buried near her sister in the Jewish Cemetery in Pineville.

After the deaths of their parents, the Levy children stayed on in Evergreen, some of them for over twenty years. This is a testament to the lucrative business the Levy family had built up in the community. The inventory of their combined estates, filed on November 26, 1887, at the Avoyelles Parish Courthouse in Marksville, is very impressive for a small town merchant. Moïse was much more than the owner of a small country store. He dealt widely in commercial paper, specifically mortgages and promissory notes. After a three day inventory, conducted by Leon Bloch, and J.S. Branch, the value of the entire estate was $36,445.60. The total worth, broken down, included the merchandise in his store which amounted to about $7,900. His real estate was appraised at $5,500, including five town lots in Evergreen and one lot in Holmesville, a small town south of Bunkie, which after the railroad passed it up in 1881, was relocated one mile away to become Eola.[11] The rest of the estate was made up of various notes, including eight mortgages, for a total of $6,620.60 and eighty-nine promissory notes worth $5,145. In addition, one hundred seventeen customers at his store maintained open accounts, totalling a whopping $11,280.[12]

By 1887 his oldest surviving son, Solomon, was involved in no less than twelve civil suits in an effort to recover money from his late father's creditors. He was also the first to marry on October 1, 1890, in New Orleans.[13] His bride, Carrie Justine Weil, was born in 1868 in Homer (Claiborne Parish) two hundred miles away to the north. Her father, Alexander Weil, a German immigrant from Albersweiler, had immigrated to Homer, via New Orleans at the age of twenty in 1850, where he operated a general store for over forty years. He fought for the Confederacy as a member of the Claiborne Guards, Second Louisiana Infantry Volunteers.[14] In 1890, after many years in Homer as a merchant, as well as a member of the town council, Alex Weil moved his wife, Henrietta Wolf, and his four surviving daughters, Carrie, Camille, Omega and Blanche, to Annunciation Street in New Orleans.[15] In retirement, he hoped to facilitate the marriages of his four daughters to eligible Jewish gentlemen in the city. After his eldest daughter Carrie's marriage to Solomon Levy, the young couple returned to Evergreen where they spent the next thirty years of their lives.

Five years later, Moïse's second eldest son, Gustave, married Carrie's sister, Omega, who had just turned nineteen. The ceremony took place on April 30, 1895, in New Orleans. Gus and Omega also returned to Evergreen, where he continued in partnership with his brother, Solomon. Carrie and Solomon's only child, Rosalie, was born in Evergreen in July 1891.[16] Gus and Omega's three daughters were all born in Evergreen: Lucille, on July 23, 1896,[17] Lillian, on December 17, 1898,[18] and Helen in 1901.[19]

Gus and Sol's brother, Jacob, married, Fannie Heymann, who was born in New Orleans on July 12, 1876,[20] to Jacob Heymann and his wife Josephine Heidenheim. The elder Heymann was from Germany, but his wife, Josephine, was from a large and prosperous old New Orleans family. She was the second of the nine children of Moses Heidenheim and his wife Babette Feitel, both immigrants from Hesse-Darmstadt, Germany.[21] Josephine's sister, Caroline Heidenheim, had married Samson Cerf, Fannie Siess' brother, so it is not surprising that two Avoyelles Parish families of long standing had decided to fix Jacob up with a Siess in-law. The couple wed on December 7, 1897, in New Orleans.[22] Jake and Fannie also returned to Evergreen to tend to the family business.

Marx Levy married into the local Goudchaux family. Blanche Mathilde, one of Leopold Goudchaux' eight children with his first wife Charlotte Eilert, became Marx Levy's bride on January 29, 1899, in Big Cane, Louisiana at a marriage that was recorded at the St. Landry Parish Courthouse in Opelousas.[23] He and his new wife moved to Provençal, Louisiana, a village then of about 250 people south of Robeline and Natchitoches, in Natchitoches Parish. The only Jewish family in the town, Marx worked as a grocery merchant and Blanche, always called Bonnie, gave birth to their first son, Marion Levy, who died at six weeks of age.[24]

Benjamin, Ernest and Estelle Levy never married, but could be found living with other family members, usually in Avoyelles Parish. Matilda Levy was married to her father's former clerk, Leon Bloch, in Avoyelles Parish by Rabbi Marx Klein on March 6, 1895, with her brother, Marx, a family friend, Isaac Johnson, and Lazard Goudchaux as witnesses.[25] The youngest son, Julius Myer Levy, married Cora Heymann on August 16, 1905 in New Orleans.[26] Cora was Fannie Heymann Levy, Jake's wife's sister, thus another Siess relation. It is believed that Mary Levy, Moïse and Rosalie's last daughter, died as a child.

In 1900, Solomon, Gus, Jacob and their families, as well as Estelle, Ernest and Julius were all still living in Evergreen. Solomon and Gus were in partnership at the store, and Jacob was a salesman. The brothers lived next door to one another. Jake rented a house with his wife, Fannie Heymann, and their daughter, Ruth who was born on September 30, 1898, in New Orleans.[27] Sol, his wife, Carrie, and daughter, Rosalie, as well as Gus, with his wife, Omega, and daughters, Lucille and Lillian, lived in the old Moïse Levy residence, which was owned outright by the family. Two houses down, brothers Julius and Ernest were sharing a dwelling that they owned. Both were salesmen. Thirty-one year old Estelle, still single, roomed with Isaac Johnson, his wife Esther, their three children and his mother, Martha.[28]

An interesting glimpse of Evergreen merchant Sol Levy, based on reminiscences of the son of the Levy Brothers' bookkeeper, Mr. Baudier, appeared in Porter and Barbara Wright's book, *The Old Evergreen Burying Ground*:

> *M. Levy Sons is the sign appearing in the west gable of the store building at the corner of Main and Hill Streets in Evergreen. [Baudier's son] recounted some of the day to day traffic at the place of business, could name names. One planter popped in to purchase one half dozen (6) cotton wagons. The order was filled instantly without comment. The store sold liq-*

uor by the barrel and by the large glass. On a cold, rainy, wintry day a group of the local gentry was gathered around the stove and bar when up rode a cowboy on a muddy, lash ridden horse. The cowboy stomped into the cavernous store, spurs jingling, viewed behind the bar Mr. Sol Levy, small of statue but of much courage, pounded on the counter with his fist and said, "I'm a sonofabitch from Texas, gimmie a drink!" He thought he would intimidate the little man of the Jewish faith. Sol Levy replied, 'I just figured you were a sonofabitch, but I didn't know where you were from!' M. Levy Sons were commission merchants on a par with many in New Orleans. And consequently fell into ownership of properties all about the Parish.[29]

Sol and Gus Levy were both very politically active in Evergreen. Sol's name first appears as secretary of the Town Council, in an article which appeared in a local Marksville paper, *The New Enterprise*. In question was the proposed building of a railroad in Avoyelles Parish. Pursuant to a petition signed by one-third of the taxpayers in the town, an election was to be held to pass a measure to levy a five mill tax on every dollar of assessed value of taxable property for a term of ten years, to aid the St. Louis, Avoyelles and Southwestern Railroad, provided that said railroad passed through and established a depot in the town. Sol, Gus and Marx Levy, as well as Simon Karpe, Karpe's brother-in-law, Charles Carb (an absent land owner, represented by his sister, Fanny Carb Karpe), and Lazard Goudchaux all signed the petition in favor of the railroad.[30] Although the St. Louis, Avoyelles and Southwestern Railroad was incorporated on January 12, 1894, no construction was ever begun. On October 22, 1895, the company was renamed the St. Louis, Avoyelles and South Western Railway Company and in this and the following year, a right of way was constructed, 25.45 miles from Bunkie to Simmesport, with an 8.10 mile spur from a junction point at Simmesport north to Marksville. As promised, the tracks ran right through Evergreen, and the town got its much coveted depot.[31] The road was sold again on April 5, 1899, to the Avoyelles Railroad Company, which in turn, sold it to the Texas and Pacific Railway Company on December 20, 1900. Subsequently, the T. & P. extended the line 22.45 miles from Melville to Simmesport, completing its Avoyelles and Melville Branches.[32] With the decline in river traffic central Louisiana merchants were more and more dependent on rail links in order to move goods to and from major cities.

Sol Levy was re-elected to the Evergreen Town Council in 1899, 1901 and again in 1902, taking the oath of office at the Avoyelles Parish Courthouse on July 8, 1899, May 14, 1901 and again on April 30, 1902. Gus Levy, as well, served one term as alderman for the town of Evergreen, taking the oath of office on April 26, 1911.[33]

In addition to his business in Evergreen, Sol Levy branched out, going into partnership with Dr. William David Haas, son of Jewish immigrant Alexander Haas, becoming vice-president of the Merchants' and Planters' Bank of Bunkie in 1901. Dr. Haas was its president and a member of the board of directors, along with his uncle, Samuel Haas. The bank was housed in a two-story brick building on Main Street, built, no doubt, with bricks from the Bunkie Brick Works, of which Dr. Haas was also the president.[34]

Leon Bloch took his wife, Maude Levy, to live in Bunkie shortly after their marriage in 1895. The fledgling town had been founded in 1882 in conjunction with the arrival of the Texas and Pacific Railway. In 1900 Bunkie was a bustling place with 900 inhabitants including thirty-nine who were Jews or descendants of Jews. There were eight families whose heads were: Leon Bloch, Herman Gross, Abe Rich, Joseph Weiss, Samuel Weiss (Joseph's brother) and Martin Weiss (Joe and Sam's father), Charlie Haas (Sam Haas' son), and William David Haas (Alex Haas' son). There were also five single Jewish men in town: Myer Hurtz, Solomon Gross, Herman Weiss (Martin's son), Sidney Frankel and Benjamin Levy, (Maude Levy Bloch's brother.) Leon Bloch opened up a livery stable in Bunkie employing his brother-in-law, Ben Levy, as his clerk.[35] An article in the *New Orleans Times Picayune* praised the growth of Bunkie, listing Leon Bloch as the president of the Bunkie Carriage Company, with

J.T. Johnson as vice-president, and Dr. William David Haas as its secretary-treasurer.[36] Leon and Maude's first child, Leon, Jr., was born in Bunkie on June 6, 1898, but only lived nine days. He was buried in the Jewish Cemetery in Pineville, Rapides Parish, LA.[37]

The year 1910 saw big changes in Evergreen. The presence of the railroad had not brought the little town back to life after boat traffic on Bayou Rouge declined. Brothers Solomon and Gus Levy who lived together with their families on Front Street were joined by their single sister, Estelle. Louis Lehmann, a seventy-two year old single man working as a salesman in town, had also taken a room with the family.[38] The village, however, could no longer support Jacob, Julius, and their families, as well as the bachelor Levy brothers, Benjamin and Ernest, who all were forced by economic circumstances to move away.

Marx and Bonnie Goudchaux Levy were also on the move. They left Provençal, for Morrow, Louisiana, in St. Landry Parish, ten miles south of Evergreen in the early years of the first decade of the twentieth century. By January 1908, they had relocated once again, this time to Alexandria. Although Bonnie and Marx had lost their first son, Marion G. Levy, who was interred in the Jewish cemetery in Opelousas alongside other Goudchaux family members,[39] the Levy family had three more children: Lottie Rhoda (b. 1901), Victor (b. 1904), and Donald Eilert (b. 1905).[40] Marx rented a house for his family in Alexandria and worked as traveling grocery salesman. They joined Temple Gemiluth Chassodim and the Alexandria chapter of B'nai B'rith. In March 1909 Marx entertained his former Evergreen neighbor, Simon Karpe at his new residence. Simon later accompanied Marx to the annual B'nai B'rith banquet.[41]

Jacob and Fannie Heymann Levy also abandoned Evergreen. They moved to a rented house on Carroll Street in Mandeville, St. Tammany Parish, Louisiana, with daughters Ruth, now almost twelve, and Selma Jeanne born on June 24, 1901.[42] Jacob was a dry goods merchant in town. [43] Julius and his wife, Cora Heymann, moved to New Orleans to live with his father and mother-in-law, Jacob and

Josephine Heidenheim Heymann. Julius worked as a druggist. A daughter, Rhea, was born to Julius and Cora in 1908.[44]

Maude and her husband, Leon Bloch, had found a permanent home in Bunkie, which by now, had supplanted all the other towns as the economic hub of Avoyelles Parish. Although two of their children died as infants, the couple had two daughters, Annette born on October 29, 1902, and Rosalie born on February 8, 1905, who survived to adulthood. In 1910 Maude's brother, Ernest Levy, who was twenty-five and still single, lived with the Bloch family. He worked as a retail grocery salesman. The family also employed one servant, Mattie Benjamin, a twenty year old African-American, born in Texas.[45] Maude's brother, Benjamin Levy, lived in Bunkie until 1905,[46] finally moving on to New Orleans where he boarded at 1208 Magazine Street. He became a clerk in his brother Julius' drugstore on Canal Street.[47]

The Levy store was out of business in Evergreen by the start of World War I. Evergreen had seen its heyday. Fortuitously located on Bayou Rouge which had afforded access by steam boat to the Atchafalaya River, no farmer had to travel very far to get his cotton or cane crop to market. But the invasion of the boll weevil at the turn of the 20th century, as well as serious threats to the sugar cane crop, brought hard times to Avoyelles Parish, and to Evergreen. While in the previous century, overland travel had been almost impossible during the rainy winters, and miserably hot during the dusty summer season, steamboat travel had been the order of the day. Before the Civil War, there had been as many as thirteen daily steamboats plying the waterways of Avoyelles Parish,[48] including Bayou Rouge, Bayou des Glaises, the Red and the Atchafalaya Rivers. With the introduction in 1882 of the railroad and the founding of Bunkie, not more than five miles away, this latter town began to grow, taking a lot of the river traffic, and some of the Jewish merchants with it from smaller towns such as Evergreen. The Levy and Karpe families, along with other Evergreen merchants' concerted attempts to obtain rail service to the town were successful at first, but ultimately short-lived. This failure to compete spelled the end of prosperity for the little town.

After they closed the store in Evergreen, Gus and Sol Levy, followed their brothers, Jacob and Benjamin, to New Orleans. Gus, who went into the coffee import business with Sol, did not live long after that. He died in New Orleans on May 20, 1918, and was buried in the Hebrew Rest Cemetery # 2.[49] Sol and Carrie Levy's daughter, Rosalie, had married Arthur Alexander Katten on January 17, 1912, and the couple lived in New Orleans as well.[50] Simon Katten and Celestine Heidenheim, Arthur's parents, were already Levy relatives by marriage. Celestine's sister Josephine Heymann's children, Fannie and Cora, had married Rosalie Levy's uncles, Jacob and Julius. So it is not surprising that many of Moise Levy's children would choose New Orleans, the Heidenheim family seat, as an alternative to life in Avoyelles Parish.

Rosalie Levy's father-in-law, Simon Katten, a New Orleans native, was born on July 21, 1850,[51] the third of four children born to Herman Katten of Hesse-Cassel, Germany and Henrietta Julia Goldenberg of Hesse-Darmstadt, Germany. Simon had married Celestine Heidenheim on June 7, 1882 in New Orleans.[52] Almost immediately the couple moved to Mexia, Texas (located south of Dallas and east of Waco) where all five of their children were born and where he became the local grocer.[53] Their first child, Alexander Arthur, born on October 7, 1886, met Rosalie Levy in New Orleans, after he and his younger brother, Edwin, had moved back there to stay with their Aunt Caroline Heidenheim Cerf, the widow of Fanny Siess' late brother, Samson Cerf.[54] Remaining in Mexia was probably never an option, as there were few Jewish families to supply brides for the two Katten brothers, and even fewer business opportunities. Caroline Heidenheim Cerf had never had any children and had recently lost her husband, so at age sixty, she was happy to give the boys a home. Alex and Edwin both served their apprenticeships working locally as clerks in a dry-goods store. The elder Kattens eventually moved back from Texas to retire in New Orleans.[55]

By 1920 all of the Moïse Levy family had moved from Evergreen. Ernest Levy and his sister, Maude Levy Bloch, and her husband, Leon, lived in Bunkie, while Marx and his wife, Bonnie, were still in Alexandria, about 40 miles north in Rapides Parish. Sol and Carrie Levy had a house on Robert Street, in uptown New Orleans. At age 57, he was employed as an inspector at a coffee import company. His married daughter, Rosalie, and her husband, Arthur Katten, who was a manufacturer of men's clothing lived with them. The Kattens had three children, Herman (b. 1913), Camille (b. 1914) and Helen (b. 1919). Sol and Arthur were able to bring in enough money in order to afford a servant, who acted as the children's nurse.[56] Not far away, also on Robert Street, Omega lived with two of her daughters, Lillian and Helen.[57] Unusual for the time, Omega had taken over her deceased husband, Gus Levy's place in the family business, and was working as an overseer at a coffee importer with her brother-in-law Sol.

Omega's eldest daughter, Lucille, had married Dr. Jacob Mahne Bodenheimer in New Orleans on November 19, 1919.[58] The Bodenheimer family had lived in northern Louisiana for over 50 years. Jacob's grandfather, and namesake, was born in Niederhochstadt, Germany in 1808. At the age of 14, Jacob stowed away on a ship which landed in New Orleans in 1822.[59] After five years in the Crescent City, he went out into the countryside to work as a peddler. He finally made his home in Bossier Parish, settling near Lake Bisteneau, where he cleared a farm, built a boat and ran a ferry. In 1843, he moved to Bellevue, the parish seat, and opened up a hotel and general store.[60] He was in his forties when he married Eliza Weil in 1849. He had met the young German immigrant from Beschinger on one of his trips to New Orleans. The couple had four children, Harriette (b. 1850), Henry (b. 1853), Emmanuel (b. 1860), and Theresa (b. 1861).[61] Jacob and Eliza's son, Emmanuel, who started out as a clerk in a store in Shreveport, married Bertha Levy, a Shreveport native, on February 20, 1882.[62] Their first son, Jacob Mahne, was born soon after, on January 28, 1883.[63] Jacob went to New Orleans to attend the Louisiana Medical College where he met and married Lucille Levy. He returned to Caddo Parish to practice medicine, taking his bride, Omega's daughter, with him. They remained there their entire lives, raising two daughters. Jake and Lucille are buried in the Hebrew Rest Cemetery # 3 (the Jewish Section of Greenwood Cemetery) in Shreveport.[64]

By 1920, Jacob and Fannie Heymann Levy had left Mandeville to move across Lake Ponchartrain to # 5612 Magazine Street in New Orleans, where the head of the family worked as a dry goods merchant. His two daughters, Ruth, age eleven and Selma, age eight attended school. Jake's sister, Estelle Levy, now fifty-one years of age lived with them.[65] His brother, Julius, and wife, Cora Heymann Levy, lived on Amelia Street with their daughters, Rhea (b. 1908), and a son, Marion (b. 1913). Julius continued his work as a druggist in his own retail drugstore.[66]

Leon Bloch, age fifty-seven, in 1920, his wife Maude Levy, and their two daughters, Annette and Rosalie, lived on Walnut Street in Bunkie. Despite his age, Leon was still dealing in horses.[67] A 1924 advertisement in the *Bunkie Record* for Bloch and Johnson, reads "Mules, Mules. We have always on hand the very best Sugar and Cotton Mules for sale, which will be sold with strict guarantee that they are represented. Come and see."[68] Maude's brother, thirty-five year old, Ernest Levy, had changed occupations. Formerly a retail grocery clerk, after a period of unemployment in 1918, he had become the manager of a local pool room. He rented accommodations a block from his sister's house on Lake Street.[69]

In 1920, Marx and his wife, Blanche Mathilde Goudchaux, were still renting a place in Alexandria, although he was now a traveling salesman for a coffee company. His sons, Victor and Donald, attended school in town.[70] On August 19, 1919, their eldest child, Lottie Rhoda Levy, married Sol D. Riff in the Jewish Temple in Alexandria. Theirs had been a "Camp Beauregard" courtship, as was explained in the Alexandria *Daily Town Talk* newspaper. The groom, serving in the U.S. Army, was a Little Rock, Arkansas native, the son of Austrian immigrants, Henry D. and Molly Erber Riff. He had met and fallen in love with Lottie, who was three days shy of eighteen at the time of the nuptial celebration, which was described in exquisite detail in the local paper. Annette Bloch, Lottie's cousin, was a bridesmaid. A lavish reception was held at the Hotel Bentley in the "Italian" Hall. The couple left on the midnight train out of Union Station for their honeymoon in New Orleans and "other gulf coast resorts."[71] The groom, Sol Riff, was in the retail clothing business and the couple and their two sons, Lloyd and Maury, lived first in Little Rock, where he was employed in his father's store, then in Hot Springs, Arkansas. At the beginning of the Second World War the family moved to Lake Charles, Louisiana, where they owned Riff's Woman's Apparel. It was there that the couple received the news that their twenty-one year old son Lloyd, who was an Army Air Corps fighter pilot, had been killed over the skies of France in June 1944.[72] Sol passed away on October 12, 1966, and his wife on December 29, 1995 in Lake Charles, Louisiana.[73]

Four of Moïse Levy's children died in the 1920s. Jacob was first, at the age of fifty-seven, of kidney disease, in New Orleans, on February 15, 1923. He was buried with his wife's Heymann family in Gates of Prayer Cemetery in New Orleans.[74] Ernest succumbed to a heart attack in Bunkie on August 3, 1927, at age fifty-three.[75] He was buried in the Jewish Cemetery in Pineville. Sol Levy and his sister, Estelle, did not live into the next decade, either, the latter passing on first, from cancer, on March 13 1928, at the Touro Infirmary, and the former on December 21st in the same year, at the age of sixty-six, from heart failure. They were buried in the family plot in the Hebrew Rest Cemetery # 2 in New Orleans.[76]

In 1930, Solomon's widow, Carrie Weil Levy, still lived at 1821 Robert Street with her daughter, Rosalie, and son-in-law, Arthur Katten, who was now a successful clothing manufacturer in New Orleans.[77] Carrie's sister, Omega, Gus Levy's widow, owned a home at 7220 Mobile Street where both of her daughters, their husbands and children resided. This extended family of eight consisted of Lillian Levy and her husband, Henri Wolbrette, their children Henri (b. 1923) and Betty (b. 1926), Helen Levy, and her husband, Joseph Levy, Jr., and their daughter, JoEllyn (b. 1925). Omega, now fifty-five, had retired from the coffee business.[78]

Omega's son-in-law, Henri Wolbrette, was, like the Levy's, from a well-to-do Alsatian immigrant family, the son of David Wolbrette, and his wife, Anna Moyse. David, unwilling to become a

German subject, had opted for Louisiana, leaving his home town of Schwenheim at the conclusion of the Franco-Prussian War in 1872. He met and married Anna Moyse, a native of Nancy, France, also an immigrant, and they settled in Plaquemine, not far down river from some of Anna's siblings who had made Donaldsonville their home. David appeared for the first time in the 1880 United States census with his wife and five month old baby son, Samuel.[79] Seven more children were born between that time and 1898, the year of Anna's death.

By 1900 David Wolbrette was a widower living on Magazine Street in New Orleans with all eight of his children: Samuel, Thérèse, Jules, Sidney Moyse, Bertha, Louise, Henri and Hermance. He was a prosperous shoe manufacturer.[80] David Wolbrette's seventh child, Henri, met and married Lillian Levy, Omega's daughter, in 1921 in New Orleans, after his discharge from the Army as a sergeant in a machine gun company stationed at Camp Beauregard. Upon his return to civilian life, Henri was employed by a candy company, rising to the post of treasurer of the concern by the time he was thirty-eight. His brother-in-law, Joe Levy, Jr., Helen's husband, at age thirty, was a salesman for a motion picture company. The 1930 census found the extended family, Henri Wolbrette, his wife Lillian, son Henri, daughter Betty, his brother and sister-in-law, Joe and Helen Levy, their daughter JoEllyn, and his mother-in-law, Omega, all living at 7321 Mobile Street.[81]

Moise Levy's youngest son Julius Levy, age fifty-one in 1930, was now a successful druggist, and owner of a drug store on Canal Street in New Orleans. He and his family lived uptown at 2231 Jefferson Avenue. His eldest child, Rhea, was employed as a high school teacher. His son, Marion, age seventeen, was still in school.[82] In 1933 his brother, Ben, still single, moved back to Bunkie, where he spent the last ten years of his life employed as a druggist. He died on January 4, 1943, at the age of seventy at the Bunkie Clinic.[83] Julius continued in business until his death from heart failure and lobar pneumonia at the Touro Infirmary at the age of sixty-one, on January 28, 1940.[84]

Marx and Bonnie Levy and their family moved briefly to San Francisco, California from Alexandria. In his sixties, Marx had covered quite a lot of ground over the years. First in Evergreen, then Provençal, then Morrow, and finally Alexandria. The family was enumerated at the Buckingham Apartments in San Francisco California in 1930. Marx worked as a salesman, and his son, Victor, now twenty-six was employed as a window dresser.[85] Very soon, however, he and Bonnie returned to Louisiana, to Lake Charles to be near their daughter, Lottie, and her husband, Sol Riff. Marx died there on October 7, 1937, at St. Patrick's Hospital at the age of seventy-two.[86]

In 1930s Avoyelles Parish, only Marksville and Bunkie were still home to some families where both partners were practicing Jews. The Gross, Weiss and Bloch families had been joined in Bunkie by Solomon Finklestein, a dry goods merchant who had recently moved from Oakdale (Allen Parish), his second wife, Fannie Saer, and sons, Herbert, Israel and Carl. Mayer Arthur Levy, a native of Pointe Coupée Parish, had also relocated to Avoyelles Parish to open a millinery concession in the back of the Haas store.[87] Mayer's wife, Theresa, fashioned the hats and his son, Meyer, Jr., and daughter, Theresa, were in school. Maurice Saltz, a young single dry goods manager living in a boarding house, had also come to the bustling town of Bunkie to make a living. The Louis Elster family owned a store in Marksville. But none of the other towns, where Jews had once lived, Mansura, Evergreen, Cottonport and Eola, had attracted any other Hebrew residents. There were descendants of those first Alsatian and German Jews who had come over in the nineteenth century and who had married into Christian families to be found almost everywhere in the Parish, but their Jewish roots had long been forgotten.

Leon Bloch, who had always been a trader of horses, was forced, by the changing times, to reinvent himself. At age 67, he, his wife, Maude, and daughter, Rosalie, continued to make their home in Bunkie.[88] He became an agent for an oil and gas company. As luck would have it, Avoyelles Parish, hit hard by the depression, was snatched from the jaws of destruction by the discovery of oil. First found in Jennings in 1901, then in Caddo Parish in 1904, it would not be until 1938 that the Eola well,[89] owned by the Haas Investment Company came in, enriching the well-to-do descendants of Sam and Alex Haas.

Fortunately, Leon Bloch was able to profit from this new industry, and the town of Bunkie, situated a mere three miles from the Haas well, would enjoy continued growth. Although both Leon and Maude were practicing Jews, they had lived so long in the isolation of a predominately Christian community, it is little wonder that both daughters married outside the faith. Annette wed Alvin James DeBlieux, a Natchitoches drugstore owner, in 1928. The family, whose immigrant ancestor, Alexandre Louis DeBlieux, had arrived in Natchitoches Parish in the early eighteenth century from Marseilles had, through the years, married into some of the most influential Catholic families in the Parish. Alvin and Annette DeBleiux raised their children in Natchitoches, and are both buried in the non-sectarian Memory Lawn Cemetery.[90] After Annette's sister, Rosalie, graduated from the Natchitoches State Normal school, she taught in the grammar school at Eunice, Louisiana until her marriage to James M. Russell in 1937. The couple, who never had children, lived out their lives in Bunkie. Too young to have participated in the First World War, James became a Captain in the U.S. Army during World War II. Although probably not Jewish, he was buried alongside his wife in the Jewish Cemetery in Pineville, a privilege which had been granted to the spouses of the many mixed marriages between Christians and Jews in Louisiana.

Leon Bloch died in Bunkie at the age of eighty-three on January 8, 1945, from heart failure. The death certificate listed his usual occupation as "livestock trader." [91] His wife followed him in death on March 27, 1947, at the age of sixty-five. She had succumbed to hypertension and heart failure. They were buried side by side in the Jewish Cemetery in Pineville.

The Levy family was typical of those Jewish immigrants who came to Louisiana after the Civil War. They seldom stayed for more than one generation in Central Louisiana. Not only did their children, often better educated than them, seek opportunities elsewhere, but the boll weevil and subsequent crop failures also made opportunities for a second generation of Avoyelles Parish Jewish merchants a virtual impossibility. Many saw better opportunities for themselves and their children and for the survival of their Jewish identity in New Orleans or elsewhere. Consequently the next generation was often able to choose other Jews as life partners. And for those who stayed behind, like the Bloch family, they risked being absorbed, just as had their pre-Civil War, co-religionists, into the Christian mainstream.

---

[1] Niederbronn, Bas-Rhin, France, registres de l'état civil (Civil registrations) 1823 Naissances (Births) # 10, Moyse Levy; digital image, Archives départementales du Bas-Rhin, "Etat Civil en ligne, " (http://archives.bas-rhin.fr/: accessed 10 /2010,) 4E 324/3. (Note discrepancy on tombstone).

[2] Pierre Katz, compiler, *Les Communautés juives du Bas-Rhin en 1851* (Paris: Cercle de généalogie juive, 2000) (unpaginated) Niederbronn families (2) Elie Levy household (Dartenbach 228).

[3] Niederoeddern, Bas-Rhin, France, registres de l'état civil (Civil registrations) 1837 Naissances (Births) # 24, Rosette Meyer; digital image, Archives départementales du Bas-Rhin, "Etat Civil en ligne," (http://archives.bas-rhin.fr/: accessed 10 October 2010), 4E 330/3.

[4] 1870 U.S. Census, Scott Co., MS, pop. sch., Beat #1, Forest P.O., p. 30 (penned), Dwelling #189, Family #189, Moses Levy household, digital image, (A: accessed 7/ 2007), citing NARA microfilm publication M593, roll 748. Date of enumeration: 21 June 1870. Note: "Gertrude" Meyer is referred to as "Mary" in both the 1870 and 1880 U.S. Censuses, but the name "Gertrude," is engraved on her tombstone in the Jewish Cemetery in Pineville, Louisiana. Unfortunately a birth record for her in Niederroedern cannot be located.

[5] Louisiana Secretary of State, Louisiana State Board of Health, Certificate of Death Vol. 4, p. 159 (1947), Mrs. Maude Levy Bloch; photocopy obtained from Louisiana Secretary of State, Department of Archives, Records Management and History, Baton Rouge, LA.

[6] "World War I Draft Registration Cards, 1917-1918," digital image, (A: accessed 6/ 2006), Julius Myer Levy, Serial # 1678, Order # 2073, Draft Board # 11, New Orleans, Orleans Parish, LA, citing *World War I Selective Service System Draft Registration Cards, 1917-1918.* Washington, D.C.: NARA microfilm publication M 1509, FHL roll 1684924.

[7] 1880 U.S. Census, Avoyelles Parish, LA, pop. sch., Evergreen, ED 5, p. 30 (penned), no dwelling number, Family #233, Morris Levy household, digital image, (A: accessed 7/ 2007), citing NARA microfilm publication T9, roll 448. Date of enumeration: 19 June 1880. Note: Leon Bloch arrived in Avoyelles Parish in June 1880 according to his application for U.S. citizenship. See: Jeraldine DuFour LaCour, *Avoyelleans of Yesteryear* (Bunkie, Louisiana: Jeraldine DuFour LaCour [203 South Gayle Blvd. 71322], 1983), 116.

[8] *The Marksville (Louisiana) Bulletin*, 5 February 1881, "Died—At Evergreen on Thursday the 22nd. Ult., Mary Myers, sister-in-law of T. Levy, aged 50 yrs. N. O. papers please copy." (Clipping courtesy of Ellen Dauzat).

[9] Rabbi Martin Hinchin, *Fourscore and Eleven-A History of the Jews of Rapides Parish, 1828-1919* (Alexandria, LA: McCormick Graphics, 1984), 47. Note: A similar article in the *Marksville (Louisiana) Bulletin*, dated July 25, 1885 p. 1, reads: "The remains of Mr. Moses Levy, of Evergreen, were brought here by T. & P. Train on Monday evening for interment in the Hebrew Cemetery. The deceased was merchandizing at the above named place, and at the time of his death was 65 years of age. He leaves a family to mourn after him.—Alexandria Democrat."

[10] Hinchin, 49. See also: *The Marksville (Louisiana) Bulletin* dated 14 August 1886, p. 8: "Mrs. Marie (sic) Levy, died in Evergreen, La., on the morning of the 8th inst [...]" It is supposed that she did die on August 8, 1886 and the 10th, which appears on her tombstone, and in the Alexandria newspaper article, was the date of interment.

[11] Corinne L. Saucier, *History of Avoyelles Parish* (1943; reprint, Gretna, Louisiana: Pelican Publishing Co., 1998), 283.

[12] Avoyelles Parish Courthouse Records (Marksville, Avoyelles Parish, LA), *Inventories* Book I-J, p. 279-309 , "Inventory of estate of Moïse and Rosalie Levy," filed 26 November 1887.

[13] "New Orleans, Louisiana Marriage Records Index 1831-1925," database, (A: accessed 7/2007), citing State of Louisiana, Secretary of State, Division of Archives, Records Management and History. *Vital Records Indices.* Baton Rouge, LA, USA. Marriage of Salomon Levy, age 28 and Carrie Justine Weil, age 21 (Vol. 14, p. 742).

[14] Southern Publishing Company, *Biographical and Historical Memoires of Northwest Louisiana* (1890, reprint, Greenville, SC: Southern Historical Press, Inc., 2002), 459.

[15] 1900 U.S. Census, Orleans Parish, Louisiana, pop. sch., New Orleans, ED 2, p. 11B (penned), Dwelling #171, Family #227, Henrietta Weil household, digital image, (A: accessed 7/ 2007), citing NARA microfilm publication T623, roll 570. Date of enumeration: 6 June 1900.

[16] 1900 U.S. Census, Avoyelles Parish, LA, pop. sch., Evergreen, ED 23, p. 20 B (penned), Dwelling #350, Family #355, Solomon Levy household, digital image, (A: accessed 7/2007), citing NARA microfilm publication T623, roll 558. Date of enumeration: 26 June 1900.

[17] Eric J. Brock, *The Jewish Cemeteries of Shreveport, LA* (Shreveport, Louisiana: J. & W. Enterprises, 1995), 37.

[18] *Ibid.*, 42.

[19] 1910 U.S. Census, Avoyelles Parish, LA, pop. sch., Evergreen , ED 25, p. 1 A (stamped), Dwelling #7, Family #7, Solomon Levy household, digital image, (A: accessed 7/ 2007), citing NARA microfilm publication T624, roll 508. Date of enumeration: 15 April 1910.

[20] "New Orleans, Louisiana Birth Records Index 1790-1899," database, (A: accessed 7/2007), citing State of Louisiana, Secretary of State, Division of Archives, Records Management and History. *Vital Records Indices.* Baton Rouge, LA, USA. Birth of Fannie Heymann (Vol. 66, p. 84??).

[21] 1870 U.S. Census, Orleans Parish, Louisiana, pop. sch, New Orleans, Ward 10, p. 128 (penned), Dwelling #923, Family #931, Moses Heidenheim household, digital image, (A: accessed 7/2007), citing NARA microfilm publication M593, roll 524. Date of enumeration: 18 June 1870.

[22] "New Orleans, Louisiana. Marriage Records Index 1831-1925," database, (A: accessed 7/2007), citing State of Louisiana, Secretary of State, Division of Archives, Records Management and History. *Vital Records Indices.* Baton Rouge, LA, USA. Marriage of Jacob Levy, age 28 and Fannie Heymann, age 21 (Vol. 20, p. 245).

[23] Rev. Donald J. Hébert, compiler, "Southwest Louisiana Records, 1750-1900," CD-ROM, database, (Rayne, Louisiana: Hébert Publications 1975-2001), Marriage of Bonnie M. Goudchaux to Marx M. Levy.

[24] 1900 U.S. Census, Natchitoches Parish, Louisiana, pop. sch., Provençal, Ward 7, ED 77, p. 1 A (penned), Dwelling #8, Family #8, M.M. Levy household, digital image, (A: accessed 7/2007), citing NARA microfilm publication T623, roll 569. Date of enumeration: 1 June 1900.

[25] Jeraldine DuFour LaCour, *Brides Book of Avoyelles Parish Louisiana, 1881-1899*, Volume 3 (Alexandria: Jeraldine DuFour LaCour [P.O. Box 5022, Alexandria, LA], 1986), 98.

[26] "New Orleans, Louisiana Marriage Records Index 1831-1925,"database, (A: accessed 7/2007), citing State of Louisiana, Secretary of State, Division of Archives, Records Management and History. *Vital R ecords Indices.* Baton Rouge, LA, USA. Marriage of Julius Myer Levy, age 26 to Cora Heymann, age 19 (Vol. 27, p. 96).

[27] "New Orleans, Louisiana Birth Records Index 1790-1899," database, (A: accessed 7/2007), citing State of Louisiana, Secretary of State, Division of Archives, Records Management and History. *Vital R ecords Indices.* Baton Rouge, LA, USA. Birth of Ruth Heyman Levy (Vol. 114, p. 154).

[28] 1900 U.S. Census, Avoyelles Parish, Louisiana, pop. sch., Evergreen, Ward 9, ED 23, p. 20 & 22 B (penned), Dwelling #349, Family #355, Jacob Levy household; Dwelling #350, Family #355, Solomon Levy household; Dwelling #350, Family #356; Gus Levy household; Dwelling #352, Family

#358 Julius Levy household; Dwelling #396, Family #402, J.C. Johnson household, Estelle Levy, boarder, digital images, (A: accessed 7/ 2007), citing NARA microfilm publication T623, roll 558. Date of enumeration: 27 June 1900.

[29] Porter and Barbara Wright, *The Old Evergreen Burying Ground* (Rayne, LA, Hébert Publications, 1990), 88, 89.

[30] "Notice To the Hon. Mayor and Town Council of Evergreen," Louisiana State University Libraries On Line Catalog – Special Collections – Louisiana and Lower Mississippi Valley Microfilm #1032, *The New Enterprise,* 30 June 1894, p. 1 col 7.

[31] Saucier, 175.

[32] *Poor's Manual of the Railroads of the United States, 1906* (New York: American Banknote Co., 1906), 528.

[33] Avoyelles Parish Courthouse Records (Marksville, Avoyelles Parish, LA), *Oaths of Office*, Book C: 485, 495, 505, Oaths of Office for Sol Levy, 1899, 1901, 1902 and Gus Levy, 1911.

[34] "Bunkie, Louisiana – One of the Progressive Towns of Central Louisiana," *The (New Orleans, LA) Daily Picayune*, (hereinafter cited as "*DP*"), 23 February 1903, p. 8, col. 1, digital image, *Genealogybank.com*, (http://www.genealogybank.com [hereinafter cited as "GB"]: accessed 1/ 2007).

[35] 1900 U.S. Census, Avoyelles Parish, Louisiana, pop. sch., Bunkie, Ward 10, ED 26, p. 7 B (penned), Dwelling #138, Family #145, Leon Block household, digital image, (A: accessed 7/ 2007), citing NARA microfilm publication T623, roll 558. Date of enumeration: 8 June 1900.

[36] "Bunkie, Louisiana – One of the Progressive Towns of Central Louisiana," *DP*, 23 February 1903, p. 8, col. 2, (GB: accessed 7/ 2007).

[37] Jewish Cemetery (Pineville, Rapides Parish, Louisiana), Leon Bloch, Jr. marker, personally read, 2007.

[38] 1910 U.S. Census, Avoyelles Parish, Louisiana, pop. sch., Evergreen, Ward 9, ED 25, p. 1 A (Penned), Dwelling #7, Family #7, Solomon Levy household, digital image, (A: accessed 7/ 2007), citing NARA microfilm publication T624, roll 508. Date of enumeration: 15 April 1910.

[39] Gemiluth Chassodim Jewish Cemetery (Opelousas, St. Landry Parish, Louisiana), Marion G. Levy marker, personally read, 2007.

[40] 1910 U.S. Census, Rapides Parish, Louisiana, pop. sch., Alexandria, Ward 1, ED 74, p. 6A (penned), Dwelling #88, Family #94, Marx Levy household, digital image, (A: accessed 7/2007), citing NARA microfilm publication T624, roll 527. Date of enumeration: 18 April 1910.

[41] Hinchin, 130, 135.

[42] Social Security Administration, "U.S. Social Security Death Index," database, (A: accessed 7/ 2007), entry for Selma Levy (1966).

[43] 1910 U.S. Census, St. Tammany Parish, Louisiana, pop. sch., Mandeville, Ward 4, ED 98, p. 9 A (penned), Dwelling #144, Family #145, Jacob Levy household, digital image, (A: accessed July 7, 2007), citing NARA microfilm publication T624, roll 531. Date of enumeration: 20 April 1910.

[44] 1910 U. S. Census, Orleans Parish, Louisiana, pop. sch., New Orleans, Precinct 5, ED 160, p. 7 A (penned), Dwelling #106, Family #122, Jacob Heimann household, digital image, (A: accessed July 7, 2007), citing NARA microfilm publication T624, roll 523. Date of enumeration: 20 April 1910.

[45] 1910 U.S. Census, Avoyelles Parish, Louisiana, pop. sch., Bunkie, Ward 10, ED 26, p. 13 A (penned), Dwelling #246, Family #313, Leon Bloch household, digital image, (A: accessed 7/ 2007), citing NARA microfilm publication T624, roll 508. Date of enumeration: 12 May 1910.

[46] Hinchin, 121.

[47] 1910 U.S. Census, Orleans Parish, Louisiana, pop. sch., New Orleans, Ward 2, ED 75, p. 15 B (penned), Dwelling #36 (crossed out) Family #41, Patrick Hanley household, Benjamin Levy, boarder, digital image, (A:

accessed 7/2007), citing NARA microfilm publication T624, roll 519. Date of enumeration: 22 April 1910.

[48] Saucier, 243.

[49] "Jewishgen On-Line Worldwide Burial Registry", database, *Jewishgen.org* (http://www.jewishgen.org: accessed 7/ 2007), entry for Gustave Levy, Hebrew Rest Cemetery #2 (through Temple Sinai), New Orleans, Orleans Parish, LA.

[50] "New Orleans, Louisiana Marriage Records Index 1831-1925," database, (A: accessed 7/2007), citing State of Louisiana, Secretary of State, Division of Archives, Records Management and History. *Vital Records Indices.* Baton Rouge, LA, USA. Marriage of Arthur Alexander Katten, age 23 and Rosalie Weil Levy, age 20 (Vol. 33, p. 996).

[51] "Jewishgen On-Line Worldwide Burial Registry," database, *Jewishgen.org* (http://www.jewishgen.org: accessed 7/ 2007), entry for Simon Katten, Gates of Prayer Cemetery, New Orleans, Orleans Parish, Louisiana.

[52] "New Orleans, Louisiana Marriage Records Index 1831-1925, "database, (A: accessed 7/2007), citing State of Louisiana, Secretary of State, Division of Archives, Records Management and History. *Vital Records Indices.* Baton Rouge, LA, USA. Marriage of Simon Katten, age 30 and Celestine Heidenheim, age 25 (Vol. 9, p. 353).

[53] 1900 U.S. Census, Limestone County, Texas, pop. sch., Mexia, Precinct 4, ED 59, p. 13 A (penned), Dwelling #244, Family #246, Simon Katten household, digital image, (A: accessed 7/ 2007), citing NARA microfilm publication T623, roll 1655. Date of enumeration: 14 June 1900.

[54] 1910 U.S. Census, Orleans Parish, Louisiana, pop. sch., New Orleans, Ward 10, ED 161, p. 7 B(penned), Dwelling #123, Family #125, Carrie Cerf, household, digital image, (A: accessed 7/ 2007), citing NARA microfilm publication T624, roll 523. Date of enumeration: 28 April 1910.

[55] 1920 U. S. Census, Orleans Parish, Louisiana, pop. sch., New Orleans, Ward 12, ED 216, p. 27 B (penned), Dwelling #665, Family #705, Simon Katten

household, digital image, (A: accessed 7/2007), citing NARA microfilm publication T625, roll 623. Date of enumeration: 15 January 1920.

[56] 1920 U. S. Census, Orleans Parish, Louisiana, pop. sch., New Orleans, Ward 13, ED 230, p. 25 A (penned), Dwelling #534, Family #594, Sol Levy household, digital image, (A: accessed 7/ 2007), citing NARA microfilm publication T625, roll 624. Date of enumeration: 19 January 1920.

[57] 1920 U. S. Census, Orleans Parish, Louisiana, pop. sch., New Orleans, Ward 13, ED 230, p. 18 A (penned), Dwelling #358, Family #403, Omega Levy household, digital image, (A: accessed 7/2007), citing NARA microfilm publication T625, roll 624. Date of enumeration: 13 & 14 January, 1920.

[58] "New Orleans, Louisiana Marriage Records Index 1831-1925," database, (A: accessed 7/2007), citing State of Louisiana, Secretary of State, Division of Archives, Records Management and History. *Vital Records Indices.* Baton Rouge, LA, USA. Marriage of Jacob Mahne Bodenheimer, age 36 and Lucile Weil Levy, age 23 (Vol. 43, p. 388).

[59] Eric J. Brock, *The Jewish Community of Shreveport* (Charleston SC: Arcadia Press, 2002), 10.

[60] Bertram Wallace Korn, *The Early Jews of New Orleans* (Waltham, Massachusetts: The American Jewish Historical Society, 1969), 170.

[61] 1860 U.S. Census, Bossier Parish, Louisiana, pop. sch., Orchard Grove, p. 2 (penned), Dwelling #11, Family #11, J. Bordinghamer (sic), digital image, (A: accessed 7/2007), citing NARA microfilm publication M653, roll 408. Date of enumeration: 5 January 1860.

[62] "Louisiana Marriages 1718-1925," database, (A: accessed 7/ 2007), citing Hunting For Bears, Compiled from a variety of sources including original marriage records located in Family History Library microfilm, microfiche, or books. Original marriage records are available from the Clerk of the Court, Caddo Parish. Marriage of Emmanuel Bodenheimer to Bertha Levy.

[63] Brock, *The Jewish Cemeteries of Shreveport*, 37.

[64] *Ibid.*, 37.

[65] 1920 U.S. Census, Orleans Parish, Louisiana, pop. sch., New Orleans, Ward 13, ED 227, p. 13 B (penned), Dwelling #245, Family #255, Jacob Levy household, digital image, (A: accessed 7/2007), citing NARA microfilm publication T625, roll 624. Date of enumeration: 17 January 1920.

[66] 1920 U.S. Census, Orleans Parish, Louisiana, pop. sch., New Orleans, Ward 12, ED 216, p. 28 A (penned), Dwelling #668, Family #708, Julius M. Levy household, digital image, (A: accessed 7/ 2007), citing NARA microfilm publication T625, roll 623. Date of enumeration: 15 January 1920.

[67] 1920 U.S. Census, Avoyelles Parish, Louisiana, pop. sch., Bunkie, Ward 10, ED 16, p. 22 B (penned), Dwelling #348, Family #356, Leon Bloch household, digital image, (A: accessed 7/ 2007), citing NARA microfilm publication T625, roll 606. Date of enumeration: 27 January 1920.

[68] " Mules…Mules," *The Bunkie (Louisiana) Record*, 1 February 1924, Vol. 15, no. 41, p. 4, cols. 5,6. Back issue consulted 12/ 2010 at *Marksville Weekly News* Office, Main Street, Marksville, LA.

[69] 1920 U. S. Census, Avoyelles Parish, Louisiana, pop. sch., Bunkie, Ward 10, ED 16, p. 19 B (penned), Dwelling #287, Family #293, Ernest Levy household, digital image, (A: accessed 7/ 2007), citing NARA microfilm publication T625, roll 606. Date of enumeration: 27 January 1920.

[70] 1920 U. S. Census, Rapides Parish, Louisiana, pop. sch. , Alexandria, Ward 1, ED 57, p. 18 A (penned), Dwelling #262, Family #313, Marx Levy household, digital image, (A: accessed 7/ 2007), citing NARA microfilm publication T625, roll 626. Date of enumeration: 15 January 1920.

[71] Hinchin, A -163, citing the (Alexandria, Louisiana) *Daily Town Talk*, August 19, 1919 "THE RIFF·LEVY NUPTIALS"

[72] "Death of Lieut. Lloyd I. Riff," *Port Arthur News*, Port Arthur, Texas, 11 July 1944, p. 7, col. 4, digital image, *AccessNewspaperArchive.com* (http://access.newspaperarchive.com : accessed 8/ 2007).

[73] Social Security Administration, "U.S. Social Security Death Index," database, (A: accessed 7/ 2007), entries for Sol Riff (1966) and Lottie Riff (1995).

[74] "Jewishgen On-Line Worldwide Burial Registry," database, *Jewishgen.org* (http://www.jewishgen.org: accessed 7/ 2007), entry for Jacob Levy (1923), Gates of Prayer Cemetery, New Orleans, Orleans Parish, Louisiana.

[75] Louisiana State Board of Health, Bureau of Vital statistics, Certificate of Death # 37 (1927), Ernest Aaron Levy; photocopy obtained from Louisiana Secretary of State, Department of Archives, Records Management and History, Baton Rouge, LA.

[76] "Jewishgen On-Line Worldwide Burial Registry," database, *Jewishgen.org* (http://www.jewishgen.org: accessed 7/2007), entries for Sol Levy (1928) and Estelle Levy (1928), Hebrew Rest Cemetery #2 (through Temple Sinai), New Orleans, Orleans Parish, Louisiana.

[77] 1930 U.S. Census, Orleans Parish, Louisiana, pop. sch., New Orleans, Ward 13, ED 217, p. 12A (penned), Dwelling #210, Family #226, Carrie W. Levy household, digital image, (A: accessed 7/ 2007), citing NARA microfilm publication T626, roll 810. Date of enumeration: 15 April 1930.

[78] 1930 U.S. Census, Orleans Parish, Louisiana, pop. sch., New Orleans, Ward 14, ED 235, p. 6A (penned), Dwelling #50, Family #58, Henri Wolbrette household, digital image, (A: accessed 7/ 2007), citing NARA microfilm publication T626, roll 811. Date of enumeration: 7 April 1930.

[79] 1880 U. S. Census, Iberville Parish, Louisiana, pop. sch., Plaquemine, Ward 3, ED 65, p. 93A (penned), Dwelling #347, Family #404, David Wolbrette household, digital image, (A: accessed 7/ 2007), citing NARA microfilm publication T9, roll 454. Date of enumeration: 14 June 1880.

[80] 1900 U.S. Census, Orleans Parish, Louisiana, pop. sch., New Orleans, Ward 1, ED 4, p. 1B (penned), Dwelling #12, Family #12, David Wolbrette household, digital image, (A: accessed 7/ 2007), citing NARA microfilm publication T623, roll 570. Date of enumeration: (no day given) June 1900.

[81] 1930 U.S. Census, Orleans Parish, Louisiana, pop. sch., New Orleans, Ward 14, ED# 235, p. 6A (penned), Dwelling #50, Family #58, Henri Wolbrette household, digital image, (A: accessed 7/ 2007), citing NARA microfilm publication T626, roll 811. Date of enumeration: 7 April 1930.

[82] 1930 U.S. Census, Orleans Parish, Louisiana, pop. sch., New Orleans, Ward 13, ED 216, p. 25 A (penned), Dwelling #396, Family #456, Julius M. Levy household, digital image, (A: accessed 7/ 2007), citing NARA microfilm publication T626, roll 810. Date of enumeration: 14 April 1930.

[83] Louisiana State Board of Health, Bureau of Vital Statistics, Certificate of Death # 57 (1943), Benjamin Franklin Levy; photocopy obtained from Louisiana Secretary of State, Department of Archives, Records Management and History, Baton Rouge, LA.

[84] Louisiana State Board of Health, Bureau of Vital Statistics, Certificate of Death #1841 (1940), Julius Levy; photocopy obtained from Louisiana Secretary of State, Department of Archives, Records Management and History, Baton Rouge, LA.

[85] 1930 U.S. Census, San Francisco County, California, pop. sch., San Francisco, ED 364, p. 4 A (penned), Dwelling #3, Family #66, Marx M. Levy household, digital image, (A: accessed 7/ 2007), citing NARA microfilm publication T626, roll 208. Date of enumeration: 2 April 1930.

[86] Louisiana State Board of Health, Bureau of Vital Statistics, Certificate of Death #12870 (1937), Marx Levy; photocopy obtained from Louisiana Secretary of State, Department of Archives, Records Management and History, Baton Rouge, LA.

[87] "Every Lady likes to Look her Best on Easter Sunday," *The Bunkie (LA) Record,* 2 May 1924, Vol. 16, no.4, p. 4, col. 5. Back issue consulted 12/2010 at the *Marksville Weekly News* Office, Main Street, Marksville, LA. Note: Mayer was the son of Morris Levy, a grocer who started his business first in Pointe Coupée Parish, then moved to Baton Rouge, and finally New Orleans. Mayer Arthur Levy died in Long Beach, CA. where he had gone to live with his son Meyer L. Levy.

[88] "Bunkie, Louisiana, " *The (New Orleans, LA) Times Picayune*, 23 June 1935, p. 36, col 5 (GB: accessed 11/ 2010).

[89] Saucier, 232, 233.

[90] Memory Lawn Cemetery, (Natchitoches, Natchitoches Parish, LA), Alvin J. and Annette Bloch DeBleiux marker, personally read, 2009.

[91] Louisiana State Board of Health, Bureau of Vital Statistics, Certificate of Death #518-72 (1945), Leon Bloch; photocopy obtained from Louisiana Secretary of State, Department of Archives, Records Management and History, Baton Rouge, LA.

Moses Levy tombstone - Jewish Cemetery, Pineville, LA
"Moses Levy, Born in Niederbronn, Alsace, Feby. 8, 1820. Died at Evergreen, La., July 20, 1885. As a husband devoted, As a father, affectionate, As a friend ever kind and true"

CHAPTER 12

SIMON KARPE – A REFUGEE IN LOUISIANA

Simon Karpe arrived in New Orleans on November 10, 1872, having left the French town of his birth, Puttelange-lès Farschviller (now Puttelange-aux-Lacs), in the province of Moselle the previous month.[1] He, like his co-religionist, Ernest Weil, had found that with the stroke of a pen, he was now a German subject, a refugee of France's loss to Germany of the provinces of Alsace and Lorraine at the conclusion of the Franco-Prussian War. Eighteen year old Simon Karpe could now be drafted into the German Army. So it is not surprising that he set out for the American south, where some twenty years earlier, his uncle, Anchel Karpe, had settled.

The Karpe family had been residents of the district of Sarreguemines in the Moselle region of France for many generations. They can been traced back to, at least, 1750, where Simon's great-grandfather, Anchel David, and his wife, Vogel Levi, had raised their family of four sons: Lion, David, Wolff and Samuel, in Loupershouse, a small hamlet several kilometres north and west of Puttelange. Originally these four sons had used the "last" name of "Anchel," which was their father's first name, according to the Jewish naming tradition. The surname "Karpe" was adopted by the family in 1808 pursuant to Napoleon's *Décret de Bayonne*. It is fortunate that, during the transition period, many of the civil records contained both the former names used by these families as well as their new post-1808 surnames.[2]

It was Anchel's son, Lion, and his wife, Agathe Simon, who were the progenitors of the Karpe families who settled in Louisiana and Mississippi. Lion and Agathe were the parents of eight known children, the eldest surviving being Moïse who was born about 1820 in Loupershouse. Moise married Sophie Hesse, born in Puttelange-lès-

Farschviller on May 4, 1822³, travelling to the bride's hometown, on January 23, 1850, for the ceremony.⁴

Moise and Sophie Karpe had six children, Françoise, Simon, Lazard, Pauline, Leon, and Salomon between 1850-1866, all born in Puttelange. Simon was born at 5:00 A.M. on October 11, 1854,⁵ and it was he who left France in 1872 to come to America, following his father's younger brother, Anchel, who had settled in Canton, Mississippi, just north of Jackson, right after the Civil War. Upon landing in New Orleans, Simon got in touch with his uncle who was not only helpful in finding him a job, but was also instrumental in his choice of a bride. On May 18, 1880, Simon married Fanny Carb, born in May 1859⁶ in Hillsboro, Scott Co., Mississippi, less than fifty miles from Anchel's home in Canton.⁷

The Carb family were originally Sephardic Jews from Spain, who had immigrated to the Moselle region of France.⁸ In 1850 thirty-three year old David Charles Carb, born in France, was living in Hillsboro, Scott County, Mississippi in a tavern kept by John Owen, where he listed his occupation as "merchant" with $800 in real estate.⁹ In a fictional account of his family entitled *Sunrise in the West*, his grandson, David Carb, wrote that his namesake had, upon the death of his parents in France, sold their house, and packed up his belongings, in order to make the trip to America. Once there, he had become the foreman on an estate near Shreveport, where he saved enough money to buy a farm at auction in Hillsboro, MS. Sometime afterward, David met Babette Rosenbaum, who was living in New Orleans with her sister, Hannah Rosenbaum Hollander. Information in David's book, published in 1931, indicated that the Rosenbaum sisters, who had emigrated from Sembach, Germany, not far from the border with Alsace, were working as waitresses in New Orleans, when David Carb, met and fell in love with Babette. Hannah married Frederick Hollander at Congregation Shangarai Chessed on February 7, 1850.¹⁰ Babette wed David Charles Carb in New Orleans less than a year later on January 10, 1851.¹¹

Six of Babette and David's seven children were born in Mississippi, including Fanny, their third child, Simon Karpe's future wife. Grandson David Carb wrote that the Civil War had shattered the Carbs' lives in rural Canton. David had gone to fight for the Confederacy, and apparently when he was away, Union soldiers came to the Carb farm and destroyed it. Babette was forced to flee the ruins of her life in a wagon drawn by oxen, taking her five children with her, returning to New Orleans and the relative safety of her Rosenbaum family. Again, according to the Carb's account, Babette's fifth child, Bertha, was born on May 23, 1864 at the farm just preceding this journey. Whether it was the trauma of the pregnancy during these difficult times, or a fall from a window that Babette had suffered shortly before the child came into the world, Bertha was born mentally challenged. Although there is no record of his service to the Confederacy, David was said to have suffered a debilitating wound when a bullet shattered his hip during the war. He returned to New Orleans and his family, after the cessation of hostilities, but was crippled for the rest of his life. In New Orleans, he supported his family as a dry goods merchant, and appears with his family in the 1870 and 1880 census records living on Claiborne Street.[12]

On May 18, 1880, one month before the family was enumerated in the Federal census, David and Babette's daughter, Fanny Carb, married Simon Karpe in New Orleans. By the time the census was taken on June 18, 1880, Fanny and her new husband, Simon, had set down roots in their new home in Evergreen, Avoyelles Parish, Louisiana. It is not surprising to find that a Carb family member, who had ties to Hillsboro, MS, only eight miles from the town of Forest where the Moïse Levy's had first settled, had followed the Levy's to the same small town in Louisiana. Simon was listed as a town merchant, and working with him was his cousin, Leon Karpe, his Uncle Anchel's son. Living in the same household was another very distant relative by marriage, a sixty year old German wheelwright named Valentin Geiger. This latter's son, Jacob, had married Celina Levy, the daughter of Édouard Levy from Lauterbourg, Alsace, one of the earliest Jewish merchants to come to Rapides Parish. Levy had settled in

Alexandria with his Catholic wife, Adilie Hernandez, a native of Natchitoches Parish. Jacob and Celina Levy Geiger remained in Alexandria, but the groom's widowed father, Valentin, had moved on, first, to Evergreen, then to Bunkie, before returning to live with his son back in Alexandria, ten years before his death in 1898.[13]

Evergreen, in the heart of plantation country in Avoyelles Parish, originally called Bayou Rouge, was only chartered in 1869 and incorporated in 1872.[14] Because of its location on the bayou, halfway between Bunkie and Plaucheville, it enjoyed a brisk trade with neighboring towns, especially Cheneyville, in Rapides Parish, where some of its inhabitants had originally lived. This commerce was only interrupted during the Civil War. The town, itself, never had more than a few streets, and at best a population of around 300 people (as it does today in 2012), but the lush countryside around this little hamlet was the home to large plantations owned by the Ewell's as well as the Pearce, Kemper, Frith and Haas families who all prospered both before and after the War between the States, growing sugar cane and cotton.

By the time Simon and Fanny Karpe settled there in 1880, there was enough business to support three Jewish families. Henry and Aaron Kahn were both listed as merchants in the 1880 census. Jules Schwabacher was a salesman. David Friend and his wife, Jeannette Nathan, had also settled there briefly to open a store. Moïse and Rosalie Meyer Levy and their ten children, as well as his sister-in-law, Gertrude, a milliner, were also thriving in the little town. Local stores employed young Jonas Weil and Leon Bloch as clerks. Of the 246 residents who were enumerated in the 1880 Census, twenty-three were Jewish.[15]

While the Karpe and Levy families would stay in Evergreen for over thirty years, all the others had moved on before the turn of the 20th century. As a general merchant, Simon sold supplies to neighboring farmers, either for cash, which was not always in abundant supply, or for a portion of their crop, cotton, sugar cane or whatever, when the harvest was done. It is evident that Simon prospered in Evergreen. By the time of his death in 1911 he was the owner of fifty-two acres of land outside of town, and one improved town lot bounded on the north by Buck Street, the south by Hill Street, east by W.A. Quirk and west by Jackson.[16]

Simon and Fanny soon started a family. Their first child, Stella, was born in Evergreen in July 1880.[17] Their first son, Lester Isidore Karpe, followed on July 29, 1883, then David Leopold on July 2, 1885, Aaron Charles on October 27, 1887 (who lived less than two months, and is buried in the Jewish Cemetery in Pineville), Arnold Blum on July 21, 1888, and the last, Irvin Meredith, on April 24, 1891.[18]

With his business going well, and his family growing, Simon made one final trip back to Puttelange in 1889, which, at the time, was called Püttlingen, part of the recently formed German imperial territory of Elsass-Lothringen. A copy of his passport application issued on October 13, 1888, included his physical description. At the age of thirty-four, Simon was 5 feet 11 inches tall, with brown hair, blue eyes, a round face and a light complexion.[19] He returned to the port of New York on August 12th, 1889 having sailed from Le Havre on the *SS Champagne*.[20] The ship's record listed him as an American citizen, having made his application at the Avoyelles Parish Courthouse on December 4, 1883.[21] Three years after his return, on September 14, 1892, Simon's father, Moise Karpe, died at 2:30 P.M. in Püttlingen at the age of seventy-two.[22]

In 1900 Simon's sons were all still in school. Eighteen year old Stella was single and living at home. Simon had been elected the constable for the Town of Evergreen, taking the oath of office on July 8, 1899. He was subsequently elected as an alderman for the town on May 14, 1901, and again on April 30, 1902.[23] Evergreen, in 1900, had 322 inhabitants and twenty-eight or 8.6% were Jewish, a large percentage for a small town.[24] The Kahn and Friend families had moved on. Moïse and Rosalie Levy were deceased, but their sons were still in business. Lazard and Harriet Oppenheim Goudchaux and their five surviving children had just moved back from New Orleans.[25]

The Jewish residents of Avoyelles Parish, by virtue of their isolation in a mainly Christian environment, even at the dawn of the twentieth century, tried to maintain a tight network of common interests and family relationships throughout Central Louisiana, New Orleans, often extending as far as Texas and Mississippi. Whether it was a business dealing, a fraternal organization, or a marriage, their lives were linked by their Jewish heritage. At this time in the history of the Parish, the Alsatian, French-speaking, Jewish residents were being outnumbered by the Polish and Austro-Hungarian immigrant arrivals of the 1880s. While the earlier Alsatian Jewish settlers had relied on their French heritage to facilitate their acceptance into the predominately French Catholic society of Louisiana, their Eastern European brethren relied mostly on their commonality of religion to forge business and family ties with the older, more established Western European Jewish residents of Louisiana. While there was, at first, much resistance by the French Hebrews to accept their Teutonic Jewish brethren, especially in New Orleans, their religious ties overcame their smoldering resentment at having lost Alsace and Lorraine to the German empire. Business partnerships sprang up and marriages took place. French, German and Austro-Hungarian Jews met at fraternal organizations such as B'nai B'rith and the Hebrew Benevolent Association that had begun to flourish in Alexandria, the nearest town with any significant Jewish population. Simon Karpe joined B'nai B'rith, and was listed as a member on March 14, 1909, when he attended a meeting at the Hotel Bentley in Alexandria.[26] He was, in addition, as were many of his fellow postbellum Avoyelles Parish Jews, a member of the local Masonic lodge, a fellowship not uniquely Jewish, one of which was located at Evergreen. With no hope of being able to organize their co-religionists spread out in the various small communities throughout the parish into a congregation, many Jews, at the turn of the century, had begun to make the thirty mile trip into Rapides Parish on a regular basis to share in the social contacts and religious services that the small, but thriving, Jewish community at Alexandria could offer them. This long trip, which in the early nineteenth century had been an arduous one made on horseback, by steamboat, or by wagon, could now be made more comfortably and quickly by rail.

On September 23, 1909, Fanny Carb Karpe passed away at the Touro Infirmary in New Orleans. She was barely fifty years old.[27] She was buried in New Orleans in the Hebrew Rest Cemetery # 2. After her death the family continued to live in Evergreen, although the 1910 Federal Census shows them residing in two neighboring houses. Lester and David, both in their twenties, lived next door to their widowed father. They worked as salesmen in the family's store. Twenty-eight year old Stella was keeping house for her father and her brothers, Irvin, age eighteen, who was also a salesman in the family business, and Arnold, twenty years old, who would graduate in less than a month from the Tulane School of Dentistry.[28] By this time, the population of Evergreen had decreased to 299 with only sixteen Jews remaining.

Simon Karpe passed away on December 27, 1911 in Evergreen, at the age of 57. He was buried next to his wife, Fanny, in New Orleans. Appended to his obituary, which appeared in *The (New Orleans, LA) Daily Picayune,* a notice appeared from the Louisiana Relief Lodge # 1, F. and A.M., Room A, Masonic Temple, notifying all members to meet at the Temple for the purpose of attending the burial of Brother Simon Karpe, late member of the Evergreen Lodge No. 139.[29]

Simon's son, Lester, remained longer in Avoyelles Parish than the rest of the Karpe children, securing a job as a salesman at S.L. Campbell's general store in Evergreen. Following in his father's footsteps, he, too, was elected alderman for the town of Evergreen, and took the oath of office on January 9, 1911, then again shortly thereafter on April 26th of the same year.[30] He registered for the draft on September 12, 1918, listing his sister, Stella, of Fort Worth, Texas as next of kin[31] but on October 24th of the same year he died, a victim of the worldwide flu epidemic.[32]

The other Karpe siblings followed their brother, Arnold, north to Shreveport in Caddo Parish where they were listed as residents on a document dated November 19, 1918, which they filed in Avoyelles Parish for probate of a portion of their parents, Simon and Fanny, and brother, Lester's estate, all of whom had died intestate. On the next day the remaining children were declared to be the sole heirs of fifty-two acres of farmland outside of Evergreen, and of one improved lot in the town. The land was considered to be of such little worth that no inheritance tax was imposed by the court.[33]

Arnold, having moved from Evergreen shortly before his father's death, set up his dental practice in Shreveport, because he would have been hard pressed to make a living at his profession in such a small rural community. He married twenty-three year old Dorothy Southard, a Newark, Ohio native, in 1912. By 1918, Arnold's brother, David, had secured a position in the Campbell Dental laboratory also in Shreveport, and was living with Arnold, Dorothy, and his brother, Irvin, at 711 Colton Street. Irvin, the youngest Karpe brother was a "route boy" for the *New Orleans Item*.[34] Ten years later the two brothers were still living with Arnold and his wife. Irvin was clerking in a cigar store, and David was still employed at the Dental Lab. Both men were single.[35]

David Karpe married soon after the 1920 Census, and by 1930 he and his wife, Leah Elizabeth Baker, were living in Memphis, Shelby Co., Tennessee, with their six year old son, David Burns Karpe. The records indicated that he was a "mechanic" for dentists (dental technician).[36] David and Leah's children were raised as Christians.[37] Irvin never married. He remained in Shreveport all his life, working as a paper seller.[38] He died there and was buried in the Greenwood Cemetery. He was remembered as a World War I veteran having served as a Private in Company B, 164th Infantry. A cross on his grave marker belies his original Jewish faith.[39]

Stella left Shreveport before World War I in order to live with her maternal aunt, Babette Rosenbaum Carb, in Texas. After the death of her husband, David, on March 11, 1884, Babette and the remaining Carb family members, with the exception of her daughter, Fanny, Simon Karpe's wife, had followed the eldest son, Isidore Carb, to Fort

Worth, Texas.[40] Babette's son, Isidore, was eager to seek out his fortune in the "West." Stella remained in Texas, with various members of the Carb family for the rest of her life. In 1920 she was enumerated with Babette, Babette's daughters, Sarah, Bertha and Annette Carb Veit, and her granddaughter, Gladys Veit. At that time Stella was working as a cashier in a general merchandising store.[41] After Babette's death on April 12, 1921, Stella remained with Annette Veit, and Annette's mentally challenged sister, Bertha. She was still working as a cashier. Stella, who never married, died on May 21, 1939 in Dallas, Texas.[42]

Arnold and Dorothy remained in Shreveport for the rest of their lives. While the 1920 Federal Census does not indicate that the couple had any children, the 1930 Census showed a "Howard" (sic) E. Karpe, their son, age 14, who had been born in Ohio.[43] This child, adopted by the couple, was Harvard Edward Karpe, born July 26, 1915, in Newark, Ohio. The child's father was Edward A. Smith, a railroad brakeman, who was living as a single parent in Newark, Ohio in 1920.[44] Mr. Smith died in 1921, and the boy came to Shreveport to live with the Karpe family. A baffling custody battle erupted between Dorothy Karpe and Mr. and Mrs. George Harner, of Chicago, who claimed to have adopted the boy in Ohio, one day after Dorothy and Arnold had adopted him on March 15, 1921. An Ohio court gave Dorothy Southard Karpe custody of Harvard pending an appeal which was finally settled in her favor.[45] In 1930 Arnold and Dorothy lived at 575 Unadilla Street, just blocks away from another former Avoyelles Parish resident, Dr. Harry Siess, Sr., also a dentist, who resided at 754 Unadilla with his wife, Retta Kaffie.[46] Dorothy passed away on July 11, 1931,[47] and was interred in the Hebrew Rest Cemetery # 2 in Shreveport next to her brother-in-law, Lester Karpe.[48] A year later, Arnold married a young widow, Jeanne Chauvin Beslin. He continued to practice dentistry in Shreveport, raising his son Harvard as well as Jeanne's son, Gustave Joseph Beslin, Jr. Arnold died on May 12, 1949, and was buried in Greenwood Cemetery, after a Baptist graveside service. There was no mention of his Jewish roots.[49] His son, Harvard Karpe, graduated from C.E. Byrd high school in Shreveport and was a football star of some note. He worked in the oil and gas industry and in the late 1950s was transferred with his wife, Bernice Leone, and daughter, Jacquetta, to Houston, Texas.

While there were barely 100 people to count at the 1920 U.S. Census, in Evergreen, there were no Jewish families left at all in the town. World War I, floods, crop failures including the arrival of the boll weevil which attacked the cotton, and the epidemics of mosaic disease and root rot, which devastated the sugar cane harvests, followed by the Great Depression all attributed to the general poverty and hardships in Avoyelles Parish. The 1930s, however, brought an upsurge in Evergreen's population, with almost 300 people in town. Although there were no longer any Jewish residents, it is noteworthy that the principle merchant in town after the departure of the Karpe and Levy families was Louis Philippe Escudé, the first born son of Abel Leon Philippe Escudé and Florestine Siess, the daughter of Alsatian Jewish immigrant, Leopold Siess, and his wife, Josette Chatelain. Philippe bought the old S.S. Pearce General Store after moving to Evergreen in 1914 with his wife, Marcelline DeCuir. The couple's grandson, Philip Heiman, was, for a period of time in the 1980s, the Mayor of Evergreen.

No trace remains of the Jewish religion in the branch of the Karpe family headed by Simon and Fanny Carb Karpe. Only two of their four children who survived to adulthood married, both taking non-Jewish spouses, which put an end to the Alsatian Jewish traditions brought over by their ancestors. The Jewish connections that Simon had tried to forge had been broken by his and his wife's early demise.

---

[1] Jeraldine Dufour LaCour, *Avoyelleans of Yesteryear* (Bunkie:Jeraldine Dufour LaCour [P.O. Box 5022, Alexandria, LA], 1983), 127.

[2] Registres de l'état civil, Loupershouse (Moselle) - Births, Marriages, Deaths –1793-1867- FHL INTL Film #1957077 Items 2-6. Marriage at Loupershouse of David Karpe born at Loupershouse and Magdelaine Koch, born at Niederbronn on February 13, 1810.

[3] Registres de l'état civil, 1792-1892; Puttelange-lès-Farschviller (Moselle). Births, marriages, deaths, June 1849-1871; Births and marriages, 1872-1875; Deaths 1872-1873 : FHL INTL Film 1979581. Birth of Sophie Hesse on May 4, 1822.

[4] Registres de l'état civil, 1792-1892 ; Puttelange-lès-Farschviller (Moselle). Officier de l'état civil, Births, Marriages and Deaths, Deaths : 1849 juin-1871, Births, Marriages 1872-1875; Deaths, 1872-1873 : FHL INTL Film # 1979581. Marriage of Moise Karpe and Sophie Hesse, 23 Jan 1850, at Puttelange- lès Farschviller.

[5] Registres de l'état civil, 1792-1892 ; Puttelange-lès-Farschviller (Moselle). Births, marriages, deaths, June 1849-1871; Births, marriages, 1872-1875; Deaths, 1872-1873 : FHL INTL Film #1979581. Birth of Simon Karpp (sic) at Puttelange, 11 October 1854.

[6] 1900 U.S. Census, Avoyelles Parish, LA, pop. sch., Evergreen, Ward 9, ED 23, p. 21 B (penned), Dwelling #376, Family #382, Simon Karpe household, digital image, *Ancestry.com* (http://www.ancestry.com [hereinafter cited as "A"]: accessed 5/2007), citing NARA microfilm publication T623, roll 558. Date of enumeration: 26 June 1900. Note: The month and year indicated in this census have been used in the absence of a birth certificate for Fanny Carb Karpe.

[7] "New Orleans, Louisiana Marriage Records Index, 1831-1925," database, (A: accessed 1/2006), citing State of Louisiana, Secretary of State, Division of Archives, Records, Management and History, *Vital Records Indices*, Baton Rouge, LA, USA. Marriage of Simon Karpe and Fanny Carb (Vol. 8, p. 66).

[8] Because of variations in spelling it cannot be ascertained whether or not the Karpe and Carb families were one and the same family. In France, Karpe was spelled: "Karp" or even "Carpp." "Carb" may have also been a variant of this family name. Consequently, this may have been a marriage between cousins.

[9] 1850 U.S. Census, Scott County, Mississippi, pop. sch., Hillsboro, p. 260 (stamped), Dwelling #94, Family #94, David Carb household, digital image, (A: accessed 5/2007), citing NARA microfilm publication M 432, roll 381. Date of enumeration: 10 August 1850.

[10] David Carb, *Sunrise in the West* (New York, Brewer, Warren & Putnam, 1931, out of print), 223. Note: This information was provided by fellow researcher Karen Russell Brown, who, while studying her own Rosenbaum ancestors, discovered the Carb-Karpe connection.

[11] Karen Russell Brown, compiler, *Descendants of Levi Hirsch – Rosenbaum Family Tree* (Tarzana, California: privately printed, 2010), 16.

[12] 1880 U.S. Census, Orleans Parish, LA, pop. sch., New Orleans, ED 22, p. 29 (penned), Dwelling #148, Family #201, D. Carb household, digital image, (A: accessed 5/ 2007), citing NARA microfilm publication: T9, roll 459. Date of enumeration: 9 June 1880.

[13] Geiger family information courtesy of Richard Allen Geiger, great-great-grandson of Valentin Geiger.

[14] Mary Pearce Hart, *Evergreen on the Bayou* (Evergreen, LA: privately printed, 1995), 8. See also: Corinne L. Saucier, *History of Avoyelles Parish* (Gretna, LA: Pelican Publishing Co., 1998), 254-255.

[15] 1880 U.S. Census, Avoyelles Parish, LA, pop. sch., Evergreen, ED 5, p. 491A (stamped), no dwelling #, Family #233, Moses Levy household, and S. Karpe, p. 488C (stamped), no dwelling #, Family #213, digital images, (A: accessed 5/2007), citing NARA microfilm publication: T9, roll 448. Date of enumeration: 18 & 19 June 1880,

[16] Avoyelles Parish Courthouse records (Marksville, Avoyelles Parish, LA), *Probate Book* "O", p. 546-547 "Probate of Simon Karpe estate," filed 19 Nov. 1918.

[17] See note 15.

[18] "World War I Draft Registration Cards 1917-1918," digital images, (A: accessed 5/2007), Lester Isidore Karpe Draft Board "O," Draft card K, Serial #682, Avoyelles Parish, LA; David Leopold Karpe, Board "O," Draft Card K, Serial #1067, Shreveport, Caddo, LA; Arnold Blum Karpe, Board "O," Draft Card K # 744, Shreveport, Caddo, LA; Irvin Meredith Karpe, Draft Board "O," Draft Card K, # 1193, Shreveport, Caddo, LA, citing *World War I*

Selective Service System Draft Registration Cards, 1917-1918. Washington DC, NARA microfilm publication M 1509, rolls 1653580 and 1685002.

[19] Simon Karpe, U.S. Passport application #23427, 13 October 1888 (issue date), digital image, (A: accessed 5/2007), citing, *U.S. Passport Applications, 1795-1905,* NARA microfilm publication M1372, roll 316.

[20] "New York Passenger Lists, 1820-1957," digital image, (A : accessed 6/ 2007), citing *Passenger Lists of Vessels Arriving at New York, New York, 1820-1897,* NARA microfilm publication M237, roll 536. Manifest of SS *La Champagne*, August 12, 1889, line 218, entry for Simon Karpe, age 34.

[21] LaCour, *Avoyelleans of Yesteryear,* 127.

[22] Registres de l'état civil, 1792-1892; Puttelange-lès-Farschviller (Moselle). Births, marriages, deaths, 1886-1892; FHL INTL Film 1979583, Item 1. Death of Moses Karp on 14 September, 1892, 72 years old Jewish resident of Püttlingen. Original record in German.

[23] Avoyelles Parish Courthouse records (Marksville, Avoyelles Parish, LA), *Oaths of Office,* Book 3, p. 456, 485, 500. Simon Karpe for constable of Evergreen, oath taken and filed 8 July 1899; Simon Karpe for alderman, oath taken and filed 14 May 1901, and 30 April 1902

[24] See note 6. An examination of the 1900 census of Evergreen yields these statistics.

[25] See Chapter 9.

[26] Rabbi Martin Hinchin, *Fourscore and Eleven, A History of the Jews of Rapides Parish, Louisiana 1828-1919* (Alexandria, LA: McCormick Graphics, Inc., 1984), 135.

[27] "Died," *The (New Orleans, LA) Daily Picayune*, 26 September 1909, p. 8 col.5, digital image, *Genealogybank.com* (http://www.genealogybank.com [hereinafter cited as "GB"]: accessed 9/ 2007).

[28] 1910 U.S. Census, Avoyelles Parish, LA, pop. sch., Evergreen, Ward 9, ED 25, p. 1 A (penned), Dwelling # 2 , Family # 2, Lester I. Karpe

household; Dwelling #3, Family # 3, Simon Karpe household, digital image (A, accessed 6/2007), citing NARA microfilm publication T624, roll 508. Date of enumeration: 15 April 1910.

[29] "Died," *The (New Orleans, LA) Daily Picayune*, 29 December 1911, p. 8, col. 4, digital image, (GB: accessed 9/ 2007).

[30] Avoyelles Parish Courthouse Records (Marksville, Avoyelles Parish, LA), *Oaths of Office*, Book 3, p. 505, 506, Lester Karpe for alderman oath taken and filed 9 Jan and 25 April 1911.

[31] See note 18.

[32] Louisiana State Board of Health, Bureau of Vital statistics, Certificate of Death # 15196 (1918), Vol. 34, Lester I. Karpe; photocopy obtained from Louisiana Secretary of State, Department of Archives, Records Management and History, Baton Rouge, LA.

[33] See note 16.

[34] See note 18.

[35] 1920 U.S. Census, Caddo Parish, LA, pop. sch., Shreveport, Ward 4, ED 46, p. 5B (penned), Dwelling #83, Family #110, Dottie C. Karpe household, digital image, (A: accessed 5/ 2007), citing NARA microfilm publication T625, roll 608. Date of enumeration: 6 & 7 January 1920.

[36] 1930 U.S. Census, Shelby County, TN, pop. sch., Memphis, District 5, ED 76, p. 20A, (penned), Dwelling #205, Family #365, David Karp (sic) household, digital image, (A: accessed 5/2007), citing NARA microfilm publication T626, roll 2275. Date of enumeration: 7 April 1930.

[37] Information concerning the David Leopold Karpe family courtesy of Leah Rebecca Karpe Thomas, David Burns Karpe's eldest daughter.

[38] "Brueggerhoff's Shreveport City Directory, 1952," digital image, (A: accessed 6/2011), entry for Irvin Karp (sic), 293.

[39] Greenwood Cemetery (Shreveport, Caddo Parish, LA), Irvin Meredith Karpe marker, personally read, 7/2006.

[40] 1900 U.S. Census, Tarrant Co., TX, pop. sch., Fort Worth, Ward 9, ED 108, p. 6A (penned), Dwelling #122, Family #131, Isidore Carb household, digital image, (A: accessed 5/ 2007), citing NARA microfilm publication T625, roll 608. Date of enumeration: 6 June 1900.

[41] 1920 U.S. Census, Tarrant County, TX, pop. sch., Fort Worth, ED 137, p. 1A (penned),Dwelling #8, Family #9, Babett Cobb (sic) household , digital image, (A: accessed 6/ 2007), citing NARA microfilm publication T 625, roll 1850. Date of enumeration: January (no day given), 1920.

[42] "Texas Death Index 1903-2000," database, (A: accessed 5/ 2007), citing Texas Department of Health. *Texas Death Indexes, 1903-2000*. Austin, TX, USA: Texas Department of Health, State Vital Statistics Unit. Death of Stella Karpe (1939).

[43] 1930 U.S. Census, Caddo Parish, LA, pop. sch., Shreveport, ED 59, p. 13A (penned), Dwelling #306, Family #318, Arnold B. Karpe household, digital image, (A: accessed 6/2007), citing NARA microfilm publication T 626, Roll 787. Date of enumeration: 11 & 12 April, 1930.

[44] 1920 U.S. Census, Licking County, OH, pop. sch., Newark, Ward 5, ED 168, p. 6 B (penned), Dwelling #18, Family #18, Laura A. Smith household, digital image, (A: accessed 6/2007), citing NARA microfilm publication T 625, roll 1404. Date of enumeration: 19 January 1920.

[45] Historical Newspaper Collection. "Smith Boy is Ward of Ohio*,"* *The Newark (Ohio)Advocate,* 26 March 1921, p. 1, col. 6., digital image, (A: accessed 6/ 2007).

[46] 1930 U.S. Census, Caddo Parish, LA, pop. sch. Shreveport, ED 61, p. 3B (penned), Dwelling #59, Family #70, Harry J. Siess household, digital image, (A: accessed 6/2007), citing NARA microfilm publication T 625, roll 1404. Date of enumeration: 3 April 1930.

[47] Brock, *The Jewish Cemeteries of Shreveport, Louisiana* (Shreveport, LA: J & W Enterprises, 1995), 30.

[48] *Ibid.*, 30.

[49] "Arnold Blum Karpe," *Findagrave.com* (http://www.findagrave.com: accessed 7/2011) Entry for Arnold Blum Karpe Jan. 22, 1889 – May 12, 1949 interred at Greenwood Cemetery, Masonic plot.

Aaron Charles Karpe marker – Jewish Cemetery, Pineville, LA

CHAPTER 13

THE RICH FAMILY – BUNKIE PIONEERS

Abe Rich, who married Hermina Siess in 1886, had always been a complete mystery to his descendants. Although family members knew that he was a merchant from Bunkie, who spoke Spanish and German, not a word was uttered that he was a Polish Jew, or that he had other family in America. A search of the Jewish Cemetery in Pineville, LA revealed the existence of an imposing marble monument, whose inscription read that he was born on May 5, 1854 in Lubranice (sic), Prussia and died on October 26, 1905.

The 1900 Federal Census listed a nephew, Isidore Goldstein, living with the Rich family in Bunkie. Isidore had been born in Boston, however there were no Massachusetts records for him. Information was found much closer to home in New Orleans. David Goldstein, born in Manchester, England, married Minette Rich, daughter of Isidore Rich, in New Orleans in 1907. Birth records revealed similarities in the naming patterns for Abe and Isidore Rich's children. Both had a son named Benjamin, both a daughter named Sadie. One named a son Leon, the other, Leopold. Minette Rich Goldstein's daughter bore the name Sadye Rae. Abe had two daughters named Sadie and Raye. There were similarities in four of the six named children, not insignificant when trying to research Jewish families. It was also puzzling that Abe Rich had told the census taker in 1900 that he had immigrated to the States in 1863. So where had he been for the twenty years before he had shown up in Avoyelles Parish?[1]

An interview with David and Minette Rich Goldstein's grandson, Jerome Winsberg, a retired New Orleans judge, proved only that descendants of Isidore Rich had never known him to have a brother. Isidore's other grandson's widow, Rose Rubel Rich, was similarly in the dark concerning a possible connection with Abe Rich from Bunkie. Contemporary newspaper articles published between

1900-1930, as well as a Google search for Isidore Rich, uncovering a Nevada Supreme court case, shed a lot of light on the family.

Abe, Isidore, and Jacob, doing business as the "Rich Bros." were at the heart of a Nevada Supreme Court appeal entitled, "Jonas Pinschowers *et. al*. versus W.J. Hanks," filed on October 25, 1883. This case revolved around the sheriff's seizure of a stock of clothing originally belonging to the Rich Bros. which had been turned over to Virginia City merchant, Jonas Pinschowers, at the successful conclusion of his action. Sheriff Hanks, on the same day, levied the clothing a second time, upon a new action brought by another set of plaintiffs, the Coleman Bros, wholesalers from San Francisco. Jacob Pinchowers appealed to get the second seizure overturned, but Hanks' lawyers alleged that the original Pinschowers' suit was perpetrated between Pinschowers and the Rich Bros. as a subterfuge to protect the clothing from possible seizure by the Coleman Bros. It was additionally claimed that there was an error by the court in not naming Isidore Rich as a defendant in the original suit, as it had been brought only against A. Rich and J. Rich, while the second action was brought against the Rich Bros being Isidore Rich, (ostensibly a dormant partner) A. Rich and J. Rich.[2]

Since the original case had been heard in Storey County, Nevada, it appeared that the Rich Bros. had been residents there. The earliest record found was from a tax assessor's list for the month of April 1864, where a partnership known as Rich and Warshauer was operating as clothing manufacturers in Virginia City. Tax records from 1864 through 1866 showed them continuing their partnership. This is only the first in a series of records which would reveal a connection between the Rich and Warshauer families.[3] Isidore Rich was found working in Virginia City in 1870 as a clerk in a store run by M. Banner, a twenty-seven year old Prussian merchant. Isidore was twenty-three at the time and listed no assets of his own.[4] The 1880 U.S. Census also listed Jacob Rich, a twenty-one year old Polish clothing merchant, residing in a boarding house in Virginia City, Nevada.[5] Abe Rich, a thirty-two year old Polish merchant, turned up in Bodie, Mono County, California, the same year.[6] Bodie, a scant 100 miles from Virginia City, was put on the map account of a gold strike in 1876 and became a boomtown almost overnight. Its population had swelled from a few hundred hopeful miners in the middle of the 1870s to between five and seven thousand people several years later. The Rich Bros. enterprise, based in Virginia City, had sent Abe, who left his trace in Bodie, CA, to act as an itinerant clothing merchant throughout the territory, supplying miners with the necessities of life.

Later on, their presence in the West was confirmed in information contained in their obituaries. It was reported that Abe had emigrated from Germany at the age of three with his parents and spent his childhood days in California.[7] Isidore was said to have come from a small Prussian village, landing in Memphis, Tennessee when he was eighteen years old. After a short stay in New Orleans he had gone to California where he was associated with both "Mackay and Lucky Baldwin."[8] The two latter men had made their fortunes in the bonanza mines of the Comstock Lode, and both Baldwin and Mackay [9] lived in Virginia City, Nevada during the time Isidore, Jacob and Abe Rich were in the area. So there was more truth than fiction in these accounts.

It seemed extraordinary that three Polish brothers, born near Warsaw, had wound up as merchants in the Comstock territory. Apparently, however, they were more the norm than the exception. John Marschall, in his recently published work, *The Jews in Nevada: A History*, stated that virtually forty percent of the pre-1880 Jewish migration to Cal-Neva was from Polish-Prussia and Slavic Europe, just the opposite of the case in the Northeast and South, where Eastern European immigration had become predominant only after 1880. Moreover, the normal mode of transportation for these early immigrants was either by ship via Cape Horn, around the entire continent of South America or via the Gulf of Mexico, where they would cross the Isthmus of Panama on horseback to board a vessel headed up the Pacific coast. Very few travellers took the overland route across the continental United States because it was even more dangerous. After their journey, many Jewish immigrants settled in either San Francisco or Sacramento, California, and upon establishing a small base, fanned out into the neighboring states to peddle their wares.

The Polish born Rich brothers were, then, a textbook case illustrating Marschall's thesis.[10] The Pinschowers' lawsuit also confirms that they, as did most of the Comstock merchants, got their supplies from San Francisco via the newly established Virginia and Truckee Railway and its Central Pacific connection, as it had been the Coleman Bros. from San Francisco who ended up with their seized merchandise. Finding all three brothers in the Comstock area between 1870-1880 put them there at the height of Jewish immigration into the region. Marschall's research showed that while in 1860 there were only fifteen Jewish residents in Virginia City and the neighboring camps of Gold Hill, Silver City, Dayton and Sutro, by 1870 there were 110. At the height of the rush in 1878, the Jewish population had quadrupled to almost five hundred. As the mines began to peter out, nearly one hundred Jewish residents had gone to other places by 1880 when the general population, then at over ten thousand began a precipitous drop. It is clear from the Pinschowers lawsuit that the Rich Brothers were in financial difficulty by 1883 as the silver rush had come to a sputtering halt draining Virginia City's population until by 1890 the Jewish population had dropped by seventy-five percent to 123, while the total population had dropped by half to 6,433.[11] By then Abe and Isidore were long gone. A similar assumption could be made of Jacob Rich, but unfortunately all trace of him ends in Nevada.

***

At some time before 1883, Isidore Rich had left the area as evidenced in the original Pinschowers' suit in which he was not named. His obituary indicates that he went to New Orleans, and from there, he set out to make his fortune as a merchant in Central America, settling first in Livingston, Guatemala, then, Punta Gorda, British Honduras, and finally Colon, Panama. Abe Rich left Virginia City in the early 1880's to follow his brother to Central America, where he, too, became a merchant there for a short time. Ships' records as well as his obituary bear out this claim. Had the brothers' attraction to Central America been fuelled by a previous trip across the Isthmus of Panama, when as young boys, they had made the arduous trek to San Francisco?

Isidore Rich made at least twenty-five recorded landings at New Orleans from Central America between 1884 and 1912. In the earlier years, his trips were from Bluefields, Nicaragua, Puerto Limon, Costa Rica, Puerto Cortes, Honduras and Livingston, Guatemala. In the later years he made trips back from Puerto Barrios, Guatemala, Savanilla, Columbia, and Colon, Panama. Abe's name appears on only two records leaving Central America, the first on January 9, 1885, when he accompanied his brother's soon to be father-in-law, Leon Levy, from Colon, Panama to New Orleans. The second was when he arrived in New Orleans by himself from Livingston, Guatemala on April 2, 1885.[12]

His and Leon Levy's first trip was, no doubt, to attend Isidore's wedding to Leon's daughter, Ella Levy, on January 18, 1885, celebrated by Rabbi Isaac Leucht.[13] Leon Levy, an immigrant from France, was also a trader and merchant in Central America. His wife, Félicie, who was born a Levy, was the granddaughter of Moses Ries, originally from Shopfloch, Bavaria, and his wife, Eleanor Salomon, originally from Alsace. The parents of six children, Moses married off two of his daughters, Minette and Jeannette, on the same day, April 29, 1835, in a ceremony which he conducted himself in his own home in New Orleans. Minette was married to Benel Levy of Lixheim, Meurthe, France and Jeannette to Jacob Myer Levi of Landau, Rhinepfalz, Germany (later simply John Mayer, of Natchez, MS). One of Minette Ries Levy's ten children, Félicie, married the aforementioned Leon Levy, father of the bride.[14] Contained in the registry of the marriage performed by Rabbi Leucht were the names of Isidore's parents: Benjamin Rich and Rachel Kolsky. Isidore and Ella, soon left New Orleans to start their lives in Livingston, Guatemala.

***

Abe Rich abandoned his business with his brother in Central America and found his way to Avoyelles Parish sometime during the summer of 1885. Why he chose Central Louisiana and not New Orleans is unknown. There was no town in the parish that could match the thriving Jewish community in Virginia City during the gold rush. In this Nevada town, in order to accommodate the hundreds of Slavic Jews in the area, a visiting Rabbi annually officiated at High Holy Day services. A B'nai B'rith organization had been founded in Virginia City around 1875, and annual Purim Balls were well attended by Jews and Gentiles alike.[15] Perhaps Abe was attracted to the opportunities for growth he saw in the little whistle stop on the Texas and Pacific Railway with the improbable name of Bunkie. According to his obituary, Abe was only the second merchant to open up shop there, so, although small, he must have felt that the town had some potential, even if it did not, as yet have any Jewish social support systems in place. With the advent of the railroad, Bunkie would soon supplant Evergreen, with its old fashioned steamboats, as a shipping point for cotton and sugar cane, and the town would grow from a few railroad workers to about three hundred by 1890. In 1887, 7,887 bales of cotton had been shipped by rail from Bunkie. The little town was booming, but not like Abe had seen in the western mining towns of Bodie and Virginia City.[16]

After Abe set up shop in Bunkie, he went about finding a prospective eligible bride. Having lost her husband in February 1885, Josette Chatelain Siess had four children still at home. Hermina, the eldest, now twenty-three was of marriageable age. Josette, a devout Catholic, may have had doubts about marrying her off to a Polish Jewish immigrant, newly arrived in the parish, but Abe, a travelled man of the world, cut a very fine figure and seemed to be well-fixed. Josette's financial footing was now very precarious, as she and three of her young teenage sons struggled to keep the family farm going. She could little afford to hold the faith of her prospective son-in-law against him, as her children's father had been, after all, a Jew. Moreover her eldest son, Auger, had married into a prominent Jewish family from Rapides Parish in 1882. Abe and Hermina's marriage took place on January 3, 1886 at the Avoyelles Parish courthouse. The civil union, conducted by Judge Thomas Overton of the 12th Judicial District, as witnessed by Felix Bauer, a Jewish merchant from Cottonport, who would, a year later, figure prominently in the "Avoyelles Affair," Leon

Levy, Isidore Rich's father-in-law, from New Orleans, Hermina's brother, Auger, and her uncle, Simon Siess.[17]

Abe and Mina's first child, Miriam, was born at Bunkie in July 1887 followed by a son, Benjamin, on January 15, 1889 as Abe struggled to get his business off the ground. The R.G. Dun *Mercantile Agency Reference Book* published in July 1889 showed fourteen merchants in the town, including four saloons, a livery stable and hotel, a blacksmith, a grocery, and seven general stores. At this point Abe's establishment had a pecuniary strength of between one and two thousand dollars, with only fair credit. The Steven Pearce and Son's emporium had vastly more capital, between twenty and forty thousand dollars, with a good credit rating. Their fine standing was no doubt due to the family's long-time presence in Avoyelles Parish, having settled in Evergreen decades before, and to their substantial land ownership as well.[18] The next year a third child, and second son, named Leopold, after Hermina's late father, was born in Bunkie on July 21, 1890.[19]

***

Isidore and Ella Rich's first child, Benjamin Rich, was born on February 7, 1886. His birth was registered in New Orleans, however he died as a child, probably in Central America, because on May 1, 1888 when the Rich-Levy family returned from Belize to New Orleans, the only child travelling with them was Minette, born on December 6, 1887 at Livingston, Guatemala. She was then five months old.[20] Isidore remained behind to tend to his businesses, so Ella had set sail on the *City of Dallas* with Minette in arms, a servant, Sylvania Ochoa, age thirteen, her mother and father, Leon and Felicie Levy, ages fifty-one and forty-three, her sister Ernestine (called Tenie), age nineteen, and Leopold Klein, age twenty-eight, Tenie's fiancé.[21] A native of Ingwiller, Alsace, Klein had started his career in America as a store clerk in Lafourche Parish for Samuel Karger around 1880.[22] He soon returned to New Orleans and was attracted to the Central American trade, where he met the Rich-Levy family. Whether he originally worked for either family is not known, but once he tied the knot with Tenie on May 9, 1888, in New Orleans, he became a member of the family firm.²³ That same afternoon, the newlyweds, along with Leon and Felicie Levy, and Ella and Minette Rich, left on the return trip of the *City of Dallas* for Livingston, Guatemala.²⁴

After ten or more years of steady work, Isidore had a general merchandise establishment in Bluefields, Nicaragua, as well as business houses in Livingston, Guatemala, Punta Gorda and Belize, British Honduras and Colon, Panama. His third child, Sadye Zona Rich was born on February 2, 1890 in Livingston. With help from his staff, his brother-in-law, Leopold Klein, his father-in-law, Leon Levy, and their families, their fortunes had increased greatly, so a determination was made to move back permanently to New Orleans. Ella was pregnant with her last child, and she may have feared delivering another baby in Central America. On April 21, 1891, Isidore, Ella, their two daughters, Minette and Sadye, his mother-in-law, Félicie Levy, and sister-in-law, Tenie Klein, arrived in New Orleans from Belize aboard the SS *Stillwater*. Ordinarily when they traveled back and forth, they carried very little luggage. This time they arrived with eleven trunks, two boxes, three baskets, one valise, two parcels, and four packages of household goods and clothing. Leopold Klein and Leon Levy remained behind to direct the family business.²⁵ Exactly five months later, on September 21, 1891, Ella's only son, Leon Rich, was born in New Orleans.²⁶ From then on, Isidore would travel back and forth, mostly without his family, staying several months every year in Central America to check on his enterprises.

It was probably about this time that Isidore thought about taking one of his sister's children into the family business. Sarah Rich Goldstein, born in 1852 and her husband, Mark, a tailor, had emigrated from Poland to England, where they had their first two children, David, born in Manchester on March 10, 1876,²⁷ and his brother, Benjamin, born in August 1879. Mark Goldstein left Great Britain ahead of his family in 1879²⁸ and settled in Boston, Massachusetts. Sarah, age twenty-seven, her two sons, David, age four, and Benjamin, age eleven months, along with Fanny Goldstein, possibly Mark's sister, age twenty-two, arrived in the port of New York on July 5, 1880 aboard the SS *Vaderland* out of Antwerp, Belgium. The family's country of origin was listed as England.[29] Sarah and Mark's third and last child, Isidore, was born on May 2, 1881 in Boston.[30] Mark Goldstein died in 1882, leaving Sarah alone in a foreign country with three small children to support. While the widow Goldstein disappeared from vital records at this point, her children reappeared some twenty years later when the two oldest were employed by Isidore Rich in his various enterprises in Central America. The first record of David and Benjamin Goldstein's arrival to work for their Uncle Isidore is a ship's manifest from Belize, British Honduras to New Orleans on March 24, 1896. The Goldstein brothers were twenty-one and nineteen respectively and listed on the manifest as merchants.[31] Their presence, now, was essential, as Tenie Levy Klein's husband, Leopold, had died on September 14, 1894, in Livingston, Guatemala,[32] leaving her alone and pregnant with, Leopold, her only child, born only months later in New Orleans on November 26, 1894.[33] Tenie made her home with Isidore and Ella Levy Rich until she wed Joseph Brooks Joseph Hyams in 1904 and moved to San Francisco.[34]

***

In the intervening years, while Isidore was making his fortune in Central America, his brother Abe's business, and his family had grown. Sadie was born in July 1893, Raye, on April 8, 1896, and Aaron, on November 5, 1898. In 1895 Abe had been able to buy at auction a parcel of land for $600 which had been seized from Leon Gauthier by A. Adler & Co. of New Orleans for non-payment of commercial debts. It had a 75 foot frontage with the Texas and Pacific Railway and was 150 feet deep. His brother-in-law, Leon Escudé, husband of Hermina's sister, Florestine Siess, owned property to the east of it. The address was 303 East Main Street and became the location for the expanded Rich store and home.[35]

As Bunkie grew, so did its number of Jewish residents. If Abe had led the way, he was soon followed by two other Jewish families, the Martin Weiss and Herman Gross families who arrived in Bunkie just before the turn of the twentieth century. Herman came with his wife Bella Warshauer in tow. Herman and Bella's arrival in Bunkie was no random choice. Bella was Abe and Isidore's niece born on June 16, 1871 in Wloclawek, Poland.[36] Bella had immigrated to New York in 1892 at the age of twenty. In February 1894 a line in the *Daily Picayune* read: "Miss Bella Warshauer, of New York, is here as the guest of her aunt, Mrs. Isidore Rich, 103 Louisiana Avenue."[37] Almost a year to the day, on February 3, 1895, Bella was married in New Orleans to Herman Gross, by the Rev. L. Silverstein. A copy of the original civil marriage record shows that the bride's parents were Aaron Warshauer and Lena Rich, Abe and Isidore's sister. The groom's parents were Jacob Gross and Fannie Moses.[38] There was, moreover, another interesting link. Records for Kalman Gross, Herman's brother who settled in Brooklyn, New York, revealed that he was born in Ungvar, Hungary (now Uzhorod, Ukraine), the same town from which the Martin Weiss family had emigrated in 1885, before they, too, had settled in Bunkie.[39] No evidence, so far, has come to light to unite the Weiss and Gross families by blood, but their emigration from the same small town in Hungary to the same small town in Louisiana is strong evidence that, once again, family ties had prevailed. Under the tutelage of Bella's uncle, Abe Rich, Herman opened up his own store in Bunkie, where all three Gross children were born: Fannie in February 1896, Aaron on March 18, 1898, and Jacob Samuel on July 16, 1899.[40]

In 1900 the Gross and Rich families lived only three houses apart in Bunkie. Herman lived in a rented house with Bella, his three children and his brother, Solomon Gross, who had joined them in 1897 from Ungvar, while Abe, his wife Mina, their six children, his mother-in-law, Josette Siess, and a niece, Henriette Escudé, (Leon and Florestine Siess Escudé's daughter) lived a few doors down. Isidore Mark Goldstein, Abe's widowed sister Sarah's eighteen year old son, also enumerated in the household, had come to town to be Abe's clerk.[41]

By 1902 Abe Rich was doing very well in Bunkie, whose population had risen to 873 inhabitants. With fifteen general merchandise establishments, Abe's business was the second most prosperous, with a pecuniary strength of between ten and twenty thousand dollars with good credit. His niece's husband, Herman Gross, had a much smaller store, but the latter had also established a branch at Cheneyville, in nearby Rapides Parish, tended by his brother, Sol. Together these two businesses only had worth of between two and three thousand dollars.[42] In 1902 Cheneyville had barely two hundred residents, and the enterprise folded sometime after 1903, sending Sol to the nearby town of Alexandria, where he found employment and a wife.[43] In February 1903, the *Daily Picayune* published a two column article on Bunkie, naming it one of the most progressive towns in Louisiana. Along with the Weiss and Haas establishments, they mentioned Herman Gross, who sold dry goods and notions, but singled out Abe Rich for a few words of praise writing "Mr. Rich is one of the pioneers of Bunkie. Began business in 1885 and has amassed a large fortune."[44]

Although there had been quite a few Jewish families in Avoyelles Parish, throughout the nineteenth century, no attempt had ever been made to organize a congregation, or to buy land for a Hebrew burying ground. An observant Jew could either make the journey to Alexandria or to Opelousas to attend Sabbath services and burial was either in New Orleans or in the Jewish cemeteries in Pineville or Opelousas. However, the first and only attempt to correct this was noted in the Alexandria *Town Talk* newspaper of June 29, 1903. The Jewish men of Bunkie came together from the Gross, Rich, Weiss, Levy, Wolf, and Goudchaux families on June 3rd, and under the auspices of the Rev. Dr. Emile Ellenger, a Hebrew Congregation was formed with sixteen members, and a Sabbath school of twenty-six pupils. "The officers of the Congregation elected to serve one year were: Mr. Abraham Rich, president; Mr. Al Godchaux [probably Lazard Goudchaux], secretary & Mr. Herman Wise [Weiss], treasurer. They were to finance for $1200 and complete a synagogue by Sept. 1st."[45] Unfortunately circumstances would never permit its construction.

***

During this same time Isidore Rich was amassing a small empire in Central America. Along the way he had become a big supporter of the Central American Improvement Company, headquartered in New Orleans. With the approval of the Guatemalan Government, this consortium had undertaken to complete the 180 mile stretch of the Northern railway from Puerto Barrios to Guatemala City, and then through to San José. Isidore depended upon this railway, and had been using the completed portions of it for years to ship his dry goods and crockery inland, and his produce to the coast, for transfer back to the States.[46] He had recently invested in a banana plantation located somewhere between Guatemala City and Livingston. Since his return to permanent residence in New Orleans he had become more reliant on others to manage all his business interests. His nephews, David and Benjamin Goldstein, now both made their homes in Livingston. But reinforcements were needed, so in 1904 he sent for two more relatives, Moritz and Benjamin Anker. A connection between these two families never would have been made, had it not been for a few lines in the "Society" column of the New Orleans *Times Picayune* which ran on February 4, 1906, stating that Mr. and Mrs. Isidore Rich were entertaining their nephew, Moritz Anker, who lived in Punta Gorda, British Honduras.[47] A search of ships' records revealed that in February 1904 the Anker brothers travelled third class from Hamburg, Germany on the Hamburg-America Lines *Croatia* to the British West Indies, with their ultimate destination listed as Livingston, Guatemala. Moritz, at twenty-one, was single, coming from "Wlozlak," probably Wloclawek, listed as a "commis" or traveling salesman. His brother, "Benno," also a "commis" from the same town, was only sixteen.[48]

In January 1905, Abe Rich's name appeared once again in the *Times Picayune*. Having been a successful businessman in Bunkie for more than twenty years he had "a handsome store, well stocked with a complete line of general merchandise."[49] With a wife, three teenagers, three younger children and a mother-in-law to support, a niece and her family down the street, he had finally found some permanence in his life. But in late October of the same year he fell ill and died on Thursday, October 26, 1905. Upon his death two articles appeared in the *Daily Picayune*. The first was accompanied by a photo and reported that he had moved from New Orleans some thirty years ago, but still had many friends and a "number of relatives" in the city. At the time of his death, after a brief illness of several days, he was said to have been a very wealthy merchant at Bunkie. An article which appeared the next day included the announcement of his funeral, which was held on October 27th by the Jewish Congregation in Alexandria, where he had been a member, with interment following at the Hebrew Cemetery in Pineville. His cause of death was explained by the *Daily Picayune* as "a complication of la grippe." A short, but fascinating summary of his life followed: "Mr. Rich was 52 years old. He was a native of Germany, and at the age of 3 years came to America with his parents. He spent his childhood days in California. He was in business in Central America with his brother, Isidore Rich, now agent for the United Fruit Company in New Orleans and settled in Bunkie when there was only one other store here. The year he came here, Mr. Rich married Miss Mena Siess of Marksville. To them have been born six children, all of whom are living." [50] The Alexandria *Town Talk*'s brief obituary indicated that Abe had been ill for three months. It also included a partial list of those who had accompanied his body to Pineville: "F. Karpe [probably Simon Karpe] of Evergreen, Ben Levy, Joe Weiss, Jacob Godchaux (sic) , J. McGinnis and wife, Joe Aldridge, Mary Rich and her brother Ben Rich, all from Bunkie"[51] Ironically, left out of that list was Abe's brother, Isidore, who "went to Bunkie on Thursday evening to attend the funeral of his brother, whose sudden death was a great shock to a large number of friends," a fact only reported in the New Orleans *Daily Picayune*.[52]

It wasn't until June 1907 that Mina Siess Rich petitioned the court to have an inventory of Abe's estate, as well as to be made tutrix to her minor children: Mary, Bennie, Lee, Sadie, Raye and Aaron. The inventory taken on June 25th, 1907, listed 120 acres of land situated in the "Burns," four town lots in Bunkie, two horses, one wagon, three buggies, two cows with calves, farm implements and the contents of the general store and private dwelling worth a total of $24,494.02. Attesting to the family's relative wealth in this small town were, among other household articles, an expensive piano, four clocks, a stove, a parlor set, and five armoires. The general store contained lots of furniture, clothing, trunks, hats, crockery, shoes, dry goods, groceries, notions, hardware, tinware, drugs, glassware, and saddling. Most astonishing for the time was the amount of cash on hand at the time of death: $3,500.[53]

***

Soon after Abe's death, his nephew, Isidore Mark Goldstein, returned to New Orleans to work for Isidore Rich, who was busy expanding his empire into the Isthmus of Panama, originally part of Columbia. For centuries the idea of a canal to connect the Pacific and Atlantic oceans had been the dream of many nations. A French company started the project in 1880, but, after over twenty thousand deaths, construction came to a halt. President Theodore Roosevelt took up the cause in 1903, drawing up a treaty with Columbia, which the Senate confirmed, but which Columbia failed to act upon. Changing tactics, Roosevelt decided to support a Panamanian separatist movement. The U.S. Navy blockaded the sea lanes, preventing Columbia from quelling the insurrection. By the end of 1903, Columbia surrendered Panama, and the U.S, recognizing the new country, signed an agreement to finish the canal and administer it indefinitely. It is known that Isidore was in Colon as early as 1903, having founded the American Trading Company, a very successfully import-export business. Family members indicate that Isidore walked at the bottom of the canal excavation before it was opened, and contemporaneous articles attest to his political support of those who saw the project, not only as a boon to Central America, but also as an important step for New Orleans to be able to regain its pre-eminence as a major U.S. seaport. In early 1907 Isidore financed the construction of the first office building in Colon on a 65X85 foot lot. It housed two stores on the ground floor and forty-four rooms in two stories above, every one of which had been rented by the time the building was completed. An article heralding the opening of the building appeared in the *Kansas City Star* which reported that "Mr. Rich has been trading in the tropics for a lifetime almost, and is thoroughly posted on all matters there so years ago he foresaw the American occupation of the Isthmus of Panama and made a few investments in Colon."[54]

Isidore's nephew, David Goldstein, was now permanently living in Livingston, Guatemala, and only occasionally visited Isidore and Ella in New Orleans. In May 1905 the *Times Picayune* announced that the Sarstoon River Fruit Company, Ltd. was incorporated with $100,000 in capital. The newspaper reported that it was "authorized to buy, lease, cultivate and deal in lands and to operate saw mills, etc. in Guatemala." Listed among its directors were Isidore Rich, David Goldstein, Alfred Levy, and Sam "the banana man" Zemurray.[55]

At the end of May 1907, Isidore Rich and his wife announced the engagement of their twenty year old daughter, Minette, to their nephew, David Goldstein. Because this was a first cousin marriage it could not take place in Louisiana, whose legislature had outlawed the practice in 1902. So Isidore hired a rail car to be put on an eastbound train out of New Orleans departing at 7:30 A.M. on Sunday August 25, 1907, for Mississippi to bring the wedding guests to the Great Southern Hotel in Gulfport. Rabbi Max Heller, who had been vacationing nearby at Bay St. Louis, performed the ceremony.[56] The couple then left on an extended honeymoon trip, which took them to Boston to visit relatives, and then back to their home in Livingston, Guatemala, via Kingston, Jamaica.[57]

During the first decade of the twentieth century, Isidore and Ella Rich, whose children were now much older and could be left with other relatives, spent months at a time in Livingston, travelling back and forth from their home in New Orleans on United Fruit Company vessels. The stays became more frequent after Minette and David's marriage. However, when it was time for Minette Rich Goldstein to give birth to her only child, Sadye Rae, on September 5, 1908, she and her mother came back to New Orleans for the event.[58] Soon after the birth of her niece, twenty year old, Sadye Zona Rich became engaged to Manheim Harry Jacobs of Houston, Texas. They married on January 18, 1909, at the Hotel Dechenaud,[59] living first, according to the 1910 Federal Census, at 1307 Louisiana Avenue with Isidore, Ella and Leon Rich, as well as David, Minette and baby, Sadye Rae Goldstein. Isidore's occupation was listed as an exporter. His son-in-law, David, was the manager of the American, later Pan American

Exporters, and his son, Leon, was a stenographer there. Manny Jacobs was the manager of a rice business.[60]

After Leon Rich graduated from high school, his father, Isidore, started taking him on business to Central America, first in April of 1910 to and from Bocas del Toro, Panama, then for a two month stay starting in October of the same year to Central America.[61] Both father and son were fluent in Spanish, and it was only natural that Leon would begin to take over the family businesses. However, at some time after those trips, a bitter feud developed between Isidore Rich and David Goldstein, due to business differences. One hundred years later neither side of the family remembers exactly how or why it developed. The result was, however, that after Isidore's death in 1913, there was never, and has to this day, ever been any contact between the two branches. The break-up of the family business left Isidore with very few liquid assets. His old business ally, Sam "the Banana Man" Zemurray, hired Isidore to work for his Cuyamel Fruit Company as a Central American representative. By 1912 bad health began to overtake him, and the first mention of it in the *Daily Picayune* attests to a "seriously ill" man improving enough to risk a trip with his wife to the Magnolia Hotel in Pass Christian, MS.[62]

***

In 1910, Mina Rich, Abe's widow, continued to live in Bunkie with her children. Four of the six were now working. Twenty-two year old Miriam (always called Mary) was a grocery clerk in a store. Benny, age twenty-one, was playing minor league baseball. Leopold, now nineteen, was painting houses, and Sadie, age sixteen, was a public stenographer. Raye, age fourteen, and Aaron, age twelve, were still in school. Five houses down from the Rich family, Herman Gross, who ran a general store, rented a place for his wife, Bella Warshauer, Abe's niece, and their children, Fannie, Aaron, and Jacob.[63]

After Abe Rich's death no one in the household followed the Jewish religion. His wife Mina, although born to a Jewish father, was raised in the Catholic faith, but practiced Methodism. None of the children married Jews. Benny, the ball player, was the first to wed on October 27, 1911. His bride, Addie Maxey, had been raised in the sawmill town of Ludington, Calcasieu (now Beauregard) Parish, Louisiana.[64] After the birth of their daughter, Miriam, in 1915, Bennie secured a job as a member of the Bunkie Town police, a post he held until sometime after 1918, when he became a detective for the Texas and Pacific Railway. Mina, Bennie and his daughter were the only members of the Abe Rich family to stick it out in Bunkie. Sadie Rich, according to her daughter-in-law, Marie Thompson Woodson, was admired by James Raymond Woodson, a locomotive engineer, as she stood near her home, opposite the Bunkie railroad station. The couple eloped in 1911 and lived in Gretna, and later Algiers in Jefferson Parish, LA, where their only son, Raymond Rich Woodson, was born on October 3, 1913. Fifteen year old Raye was the next to marry on January 6, 1912. The groom, Richard Franklin Coberly, eleven years her senior, was a section foreman for the Standard Oil Company. Coberly, a native of West Virginia was a descendant of the Chenowith and Coberly families who had settled in Virginia in the 1720s. He had been a witness at Bennie and Addie's wedding a few months before. The Coberly family lived all over Louisiana and Arkansas, following Dick's work to the various drilling sites owned by Standard Oil. Their only child, Sarah Elizabeth, named after her paternal grandmother, Sarah Elizabeth Messenger Coberly, was born on January 9, 1921, in Shreveport, Caddo Parish, LA. Dick Coberly succumbed to typhoid fever in 1932 and Raye took Sarah to live with her sister, Sadie, in New Orleans.

Leopold Rich, known as "Lee" joined the United States Navy and was mustered out as a coxswain in San Francisco in 1917 where he remained.[65] He worked there as a laborer, and later an office clerk, marrying a young lady some time before 1918, known only as Ella, a Utah native. In 1920 the couple was living in a rooming house in San Francisco.[66] Lee was the first of Abe's offspring to die, without issue, on April 1, 1922. His body was shipped back to Avoyelles Parish and he was buried in the non-sectarian Pythian cemetery in Bunkie.[67] Miriam "Mary," Abe's oldest daughter married Robert "Mickey" Cone, a native of New Orleans in 1913. Cone, a veteran of the Spanish American War, was a taxi driver. Mickey and Mary lived most of their lives on South Alexander Street, just down the street from Mae Rose Siess Clement and her boys. The Cones never had any children, but Mary opened her home to her Uncle Emmanuel Siess' daughters, Edyne and Mae Rose, when they were younger, a situation which was not always without conflict. Mary's brother, Aaron, Abe and Hermina's youngest child, moved to New Orleans early on to find employment, and worked first as a taxi driver, and finally as a Terminix exterminator.[68] Aaron never married, living always with his eldest sister, Mary, and her husband, Mickey.

***

Isidore Rich viewed his reversal of fortune with equanimity, and tried to the end to bolster his finances after the family's split. But death overtook him on November 4, 1913. The *Daily Picayune* ran two articles, the first of which announced his demise and summarized his career. He was considered to have been "a pioneer in establishing trade relations with the tropics and among the first to recognize the importance of the Panama Canal. He had a chain of stores in Guatemala and a large establishment in Colon." In the end "he turned over all his property and all his interests to his creditors so that the work of a lifetime was not sacrificed." [69] His funeral arrangements were revealed in the newspaper the following day, along with a short biography the early parts of which, in no way, corresponded to those of his late brother, Abe's. It was said that he was eighteen years old when he landed at Memphis, Tennessee. Later he came to New Orleans, but soon left for California. It was in the 1870s when he went to the tropics, first to Bluefields, Nicaragua, then to Guatemala. The *Picayune* also reported that he had once owned a banana plantation. The maps of those Central American holdings were, until Hurricane Katrina, in the hands of David Winsberg, grandson of Isidore's nephew/son-in-law, David Goldstein. Isidore's funeral was conducted at the family home by Rabbi Max Heller, and he was interred at Hebrew Rest Cemetery # 2 in New Orleans. Absent from the list of pall bearers was his son-in-law, David Goldstein.[70] The Rich family maintains that, upon Isidore's death, Minette Rich and her husband, David Goldstein, were contacted and asked to help pay for the funeral, but refused. Two weeks later the widow of François Tujague, to whom, apparently Isidore Rich was indebted, won a suit for $7,000 which resulted in the Rich family home on Louisiana Avenue at the corner of Chestnut, being advertised for sale by the Civil Sheriff.[71]

On December 8, 1913, in an attempted end-run around the family, Minette Rich Goldstein petitioned the court with the aim of obtaining letters of administration in the succession of Isidore Rich, deceased allegedly without a will.[72] However, the *Daily Picayune,* dated December 10, 1913, reported that Isidore's will, drawn up in New Orleans on October 8, 1912, had been probated the previous day. He left "to his wife the usufruct of his estate and the naked ownership to his children in various proportions. To his daughter Sara Jacobs and his son Leon Rich, he leaves one third of his estate in Louisiana as an extra share and portion, and to them he gives his entire estate in Guatemala, British Honduras and Panama." There was no mention of his daughter, Minette Rich, or of his son-in-law/nephew, David Goldstein.[73]

Just how much of his estate was actually left, after the creditors were satisfied is unclear, but Leon, was forced to look for work elsewhere, as David Goldstein was now in charge of Pan American Exporters, and possibly whatever was left of any of the other businesses in Central America. Leon became the Central and South American representative for the Fostoria Glass Company, whose home offices were located in Moundsville, West Virginia. As a travelling salesman he spent from six to twelve months on the road and at sea with trunks of glassware and glass lamps, visiting the Windward and Leeward Islands, Cuba, Puerto Rico, Santo Domingo, Costa Rica, Columbia, Panama, Peru, Argentina, Brazil, Chile, El Salvador, Trinidad, and Martinique.[74] The state of Isidore Rich's widow Ella's reduced fortunes was made clear in a small announcement which appeared in December 1918 reporting Leon Rich's engagement to Sylvia Tobias. Pauline Markstein Tobias, Sylvia's mother, had an apartment "at Mrs. Mallon's in Amelia Street," a New Orleans pied-àterre for them, as their family home was in Baton Rouge. Ella Rich and her son, Leon, lived in the same building, a far cry from their beautiful house on Louisiana Avenue. Ella and Pauline opened their apartments on the second and fourth Thursdays of December 1918 to receive guests in honor of the betrothal.[75] The wedding took place on April 10, 1919, at the Hotel Grunewald (now Hotel Roosevelt), with Rabbi Max Heller presiding. It was a small affair limited to family members. After a "short honeymoon at a nearby resort," the couple left on a business trip to the tropics. Until the birth of her children, Sylvia accompanied her husband on his lengthy trips to Central America. They stayed off and on in New Orleans, as lodgers with Sylvia's mother and sister.[76] Their two children, Leon Rich, Jr. (b. 1921) and Jack Rich (b. 1924), were born in New Orleans.

Just before 1920, Isidore's widow, Ella, moved in with her son-in-law and daughter, Mannie and Sadye Jacobs, who were renting at 1628 St. Charles Avenue. By then, he was out of the rice business and had become a very successful motion picture theatre owner. Manny's brother, Lawrence, also lived with them, managing the theatre for him.[77] Mannie and Sadye never had any children. Ella lived with them until her death in New Orleans on September 21, 1944.[78] Jack Rich's widow, Rose, remembers that Sadye lamented her loss of two fortunes. She had been born into wealth, which her father lost before his death, then married Manny, who made a fortune in the theatre business but gambled it away. The couple died only months apart, Mannie on July 23, 1967 and Sadye on November 9th of the same year.[79]

***

On the other side of the rift, David and Minette Rich Goldstein, Isidore and Benjamin Goldstein, Ben and Morris Anker and the Gross family of Bunkie remained close. David was the president of Pan American Exporters, Inc. and Ben Anker, his cousin (David and Esther Rich Anker's son), was the secretary-treasurer of the company. In 1919 Anker announced in the *Times Picayune* that the business was expanding its office in Guatemala City, opening a $100,000 wholesale branch house stocked with all kinds of merchandise, which would be sent through the Port of New Orleans.⁸⁰ Morris Anker also worked for the firm, and lived permanently in Guatemala City, where some time before 1917 he married a local resident, Ilda, whose maiden name is not now known. Ships' manifests of the period record that Ilda was a Spanish speaking native of Guatemala City, born in 1893. Their children, Ludwig (b. 1916), and Ana (aka. Anita), born in June 1918, often travelled to New Orleans where they attended school as teenagers.⁸¹ No more is known of the Moritz Anker family as records of them disappear after 1933. Moritz, however, must have predeceased Benjamin whose obituary appeared in the *Times Picayune* in August of 1947, as there was no mention of his brother.

Ben Anker, unlike his brother, spent more time in New Orleans with his family. While in Central America he met Bella Fisher, born on June 19, 1900, in Quezaltenango, Guatemala, of immigrant parents from Kempen, Germany, who first settled in San Francisco around 1885. Her father, Adolph, had been attracted to the possibilities in Guatemala, moving there with his wife in 1896.⁸² Adolph Fisher's 1918 passport application noted that he had established the first "American gents furnishing goods and hat store in the city of Quezaltenango in 1906, [...] importing and introducing American made goods since established." ⁸³ Ben, whose home was at 2006 General Taylor in New Orleans, and Bella, who was living temporarily at 1057 Grand Concourse, Bronx, New York, were married on January 16, 1924 at the latter address by a local Rabbi.⁸⁴ Their marriage certificate gave the groom's parents' names as David Anker and Esther Rich, the sole document that establishes the Rich – Anker blood relationship, and provides the name of another of Abe Rich's sisters. Their first child, Donald Ralph Anker, was born in New York on November 10, 1924. Their daughter, Marilyn, was born on June 24, 1929, in New Orleans.⁸⁵ When Ben Anker filled out his World War I Draft Registration Card as a single man, he had listed Dave Goldstein as his nearest relative, and noted that he suffered from malaria due to many years in the tropics.⁸⁶ Due to his infirmities, the family lived principally in New Orleans, renting at various addresses, first on St. Charles Avenue, then on State Street. Bella often took her children to see her parents who had retired to New York, and where her son, Donald, was eventually enrolled in the Peekskill (Westchester Co.) Military Academy.[87] Ben continued as the secretary-treasurer of Pan American Exporters, which was located at 1000 Queen & Crescent Building, travelling several times a year to Guatemala to oversee its Central American office. It was on one of these trips, on August 14, 1947, that he died.[88]

***

While David Goldstein, president of the Pan American Exporters, employed his brother Benjamin in Central America, his youngest sibling, Isidore Mark Goldstein, worked for the Rice-Stix Dry Goods Company whose home office was in St. Louis, Mo.[89] He was that firm's traveling salesman and spent most of his time in Central America. Both bachelors, Ben and Isidore Goldstein lived off and on with David, Minette, and Sadye Rae on General Taylor in New Orleans. The Dave Goldstein's were also in touch with Herman and Bella Warshauer Gross and their children in Bunkie, visiting them often. Bella, daughter of Lena Rich Warshauer, Abe and Isidore Rich's sister, was their cousin.

Herman and Bella's son, Aaron Gross, was the first of that family to leave Avoyelles Parish, moving to New Orleans a short time after 1920, where he made his home with Dave and Minette Goldstein. There he first met his mother Bella's two Polish immigrant relatives, Morris James Warshauer and Herman Bratman. According to Morris James Warshauer's passport application made in 1919, it is known that he, like Bella Warshauer, was from Wloclawek, Poland, having been born there on June 16, 1878. His father's name was given as Lewin Warshawski.[90] It is believed that Bella's father Aaron Warshauer was either a brother or a cousin of Morris James' father, Lewin. To further complicate matters, the other partner, Herman Bratman, appears to have immigrated to the United States in 1887, at the age of twenty, under the name of Herman Warshauer. Using this name, he married Henrietta Cohen in Manhattan, New York on February 17, 1889. His marriage record indicates that his place of birth was Lubraniec, Poland (Abe Rich's place of birth), and his father's name was Louis (Lewin) Warshauer, his mother's name, Frances.[91] Herman and Henrietta's only child, a daughter Frances, was born on January 20, 1892, in New York City.[92] By 1900 the family had moved to Monroe, Louisiana, where he was using the name Herman Brackman, working as a "drummer" and living with his wife, Henrietta, born in New York in 1869, and his daughter, Frances, born in New York in January 1892. If this is not, actually, Herman and Henrietta Cohen Warshauer, then this is an astonishing coincidence.[93] To add to the mystery, Herman's daughter, Frances Warshauer/ Bratman married Morris James Warshauer, in Wloclawek, Poland, where she had apparently been sent to be party to an arranged marriage with her father's business partner, who may have been, at worst, her uncle, or perhaps, at best her cousin. According to the 1920 U.S. Census, Morris came back with her in 1914, along with their Polish born first child, Sigmund, to live in the same household as Herman and Henrietta Bratman.[94]

In 1921 the Tropical Clothing Manufacturing Company at 206 Chartres Street in the French Quarter was founded by Morris Warshauer (president), Aaron Gross (vice-president) and Herman Bratman (secretary-treasurer). The company was so successful both locally and in Central America, thanks in large part to the Goldstein-Anker connections in Honduras, Panama and Guatemala, that in July 1925, it was announced that the members of the firm were building a $100,000, three story, 36,000 square foot, clothing factory with a frontage of 113 feet on Toulouse Street through to Jefferson, bounded by Decatur and Chartres Streets. The walls of the building were to be as near as possible solid glass with an "employees' playground" consisting of a kitchen and dining room, where lunches were sold at cost. A roof garden, dance floor with an employees' orchestra to furnish music, reading and recreation rooms were also provided.[95] Two years later, Aaron Gross, along with William Haspel, Melville Sternberg, J.S. Rosenfeld, L.E. Schwartz and George M. Carnes formed the Associated Summer Clothing Manufacturers of New Orleans to promote the city as the "home of the wash suit industry."[96]

Aaron's brother, Jacob Gross, had originally gone away to school to study engineering at Tulane University. In January 1924, he secured a job working as a chemist for the Punta Alegre Sugar

Company at Punta San Juan, Cuba, where he spent six months, returning to Bunkie in June. A small article in the *Bunkie Record* indicated that he loved the island and was looking forward to his return in the late fall.[97] In September 1926, after a brief visit to New Orleans to see the Goldstein and Warshauer families and her son Aaron, Bella Warshauer Gross, died on November 5th in Bunkie and was buried in the Jewish Cemetery in Pineville.[98] Herman carried on in the store, with his daughter, Fanny, acting as book keeper. Jacob returned permanently from Cuba to act as his salesman.[99]

In 1930 the various members of the Rich-Warshauer-Gross extended family all were living in New Orleans. Dave and Minette Rich Goldstein, their daughter Sadye Rae and Aaron Gross lived at 933 Broadway. This is the same address that Isidore Goldstein used when he was visiting from Central America. Morris Warshauer, his wife Frances, and three children, Sigmund (b. 1913 in Poland), Erna and Irving born in 1914 and 1920 respectively in New Orleans, and his in-laws, Herman and Henrietta Bratman lived at 1410 Broadway. On the Rich side of the family feud, Leon Rich, his wife Sylvia Tobias and their two sons, Leon, Jr. and Jack, resided at 1211 Broadway. The logistics of avoiding one another must have been interesting.[100]

***

Of Abe Rich's six children, five of whom were still living in 1930, Robert and Mary Rich Cone lived on South Alexander Street in New Orleans, with her younger brother, Aaron Rich. James and Sadie Rich Woodson had a house in Gretna (Jefferson Parish) with their seventeen year old son, Raymond. Dick and Raye Rich Coberly were staying in Jennings, Jefferson Davis Parish, Louisiana, with their nine year old daughter, Sarah Elizabeth.

Bennie Rich, however, was working in Bunkie as a special agent for the Texas and Pacific Railway. He had been divorced from his first wife, Addie Maxey, who had taken her daughter, Miriam, back to Mineola, Texas, and was employed as the manager of a ladies ready-to-wear store.[101] Bennie married his second wife, Marie Johnson

Rooler, on June 17, 1922, in Avoyelles Parish,[102] but the 1930 Census, taken on April 11th of that year showed him to be divorced, once again, and living with his mother, Mina Siess Rich, at 303 East Main Street in Bunkie.[103] Four days after the census enumeration, he tied the knot one more time, marrying Rosa Mae, the eighteen year old daughter of Albert and Avida Chenevert Milligan. Ben and Rosa Mae were also sixth cousins, a situation not that uncommon in Avoyelles Parish.[104]

Bennie's daughter, Miriam, one of Abe Rich's three grandchildren, was married to James Everett Green, a farmer thirteen years her senior, on October 20, 1940, by a Minister of the Gospel in Avoyelles Parish. The Greens had no children.[105] Abe Rich's widow, Hermina Siess Rich, died in Eola, Avoyelles Parish, LA on December 18, 1945. She was buried from the Methodist Church in Bunkie, and interred in the non-denominational Pythian Cemetery in that town.[106] Six days from the date of his mother Mina's death, Bennie died on December 24, 1945, at the age of fifty-six, in Lake Charles, Calcasieu Parish, LA, where he had been living. He was buried alongside his mother and brother, Leopold, in the Pythian Cemetery in Bunkie.[107] Miriam Rich Green died in 1970 and is buried near her grandmother and uncles in the Pythian Cemetery.

After her father's death in 1932, Sarah Elizabeth Coberly, only child of Raye Rich and her husband, Richard F. Coberly, quit school at the age of sixteen to go to work to help support her mother. She attended the Marinello Beauty School in New Orleans and found work in 1937 at the Roosevelt Hotel barber shop, thanks to her mother's old school friend from Bunkie, Seymour Weiss (Governor Huey Long's unofficial "treasurer"), one of the four sons of Sam Weiss, a former Bunkie merchant. At the age of seventeen she married John Thornton Wagner, a pilot working for Chicago and Southern Airways (later Delta Airlines), who had come in for a haircut. They "eloped" to Mississippi with her mother in tow, where they were married in a civil ceremony in 1938.

Of the remaining members of the Abe Rich family, Miriam Rich, widowed by Robert Cone in 1945, died in New Orleans on

January 9, 1961, and was buried in Cypress Grove Cemetery. Her brother Aaron followed on December 24, 1966, also in New Orleans, and Sadie Rich Woodson on May 1, 1972, in Algiers, Jefferson Parish, LA.

***

While all of Abe's descendants chose to affiliate with various Protestant sects, none married other Jews, and all were buried in non-sectarian cemeteries. Not so with the Gross, Isidore Rich, Goldstein and Warshauer families, most of whom were now located in New Orleans, where they were part of a thriving Jewish community and had found partners of their own faith. Their marriages were all to co-religionists. First to the altar, Sadye Rae Goldstein wed Winfred Julius Winsberg, son of Latvian immigrants, Jacob and Sarah Silberman Winsberg, on April 25, 1933, with Rabbi Louis Binstock of Temple Sinai officiating. Aaron Gross was the best man. His brother, Jacob, was a groomsman, and Fannie Gross was one of the bridesmaids.[108] Jacob Winsberg had originally settled in Franklin, St. Mary Parish, LA .[109] In the 1920s he moved his family to New Orleans, where he became a successful shoe merchant. Sadye Rae and Winfred honeymooned in Cuba and Panama and then returned home to New Orleans where they moved in with Dave and Minette Rich Goldstein and Aaron Gross. Their two sons, David Jacob (b. 1936) and Jerome Meyer (b. 1940), were raised in New Orleans.

Jacob was the only one of Herman Gross' children to marry. After Herman retired from business in Bunkie, Jake came to New Orleans to settle near his brother, Aaron, and the Goldstein family. On August 25, 1936 he married Johanna Brandt, daughter of Peter and Regina Gross Brant, Austrian Jewish immigrants to Louisiana. At the Gross-Brandt wedding, which was conducted at the Brandt home on Second Street by Rabbi Nathaniel Share of the Gates of Prayer Synagogue, Fannie Gross was a maid of honor and Aaron Gross was his brother's best man. Among the guests were Rosalie Bloch, daughter of Leon and Matilda Levy Bloch.[110] The groom, Jacob Gross, was for many years the proprietor of the NOLA Tailoring Company at 831 Baronne Street in the French Quarter.

Herman Gross lived in Bunkie until his death on March 14, 1943. He was buried alongside his wife, Bella Warshauer, in the Jewish Cemetery in Pineville, LA.[111] His daughter, Fannie, who never married, continued to live in Bunkie, but often visited her brothers and cousins in New Orleans. In March 1951, she went on a month long grand tour of Europe, returning to New Orleans in the middle of April to finish out her life there.[112] Fannie died on April 23, 1960, in New Orleans and was buried the next day in the Gates of Prayer Jewish Cemetery in New Orleans with other Gross and Warshauer family members.[113] Aaron Gross, vice-president of the Tropical Clothing Manufacturing Company, died seven months after his father, Herman, on October 26, 1943. He was buried the next day at the Gates of Prayer Cemetery on Joseph Street.[114] The family believes that Aaron had always carried a torch for Sadye Rae Goldstein Winsberg, but that they had discouraged a union because it would have been the second close cousin marriage in two generations.

Herman (Warshauer) Bratman had been the first official of the Tropical Clothing Manufacturing Company to pass away. He died at the Touro Infirmary on September 1, 1933 after suffering a heart attack. At the time, he was the president of the Communal Hebrew School on Joseph Street, as well as a former office holder of the local B'nai B'rith lodge. He was buried the next day at the Chevra Thilim (Canal Street) Cemetery, leaving his wife, Henrietta Cohen, daughter Frances Bratman, her husband, Morris James Warshauer, and their children, Sigmund, Erna Juliette and Irving B. Warshauer.[115] Technical Sergeant Irving B. Warshauer, a member of the Army Air Corps, was killed less than ten years later at the age of twenty-three, while participating in a bombing mission over Hanover, Germany on July 26, 1943. He was awarded the purple heart and the Air Medal posthumously. His father, upon hearing the news of his son's death, volunteered to participate in a suicide mission against the Nazi regime, but was turned down.[116] Young Warshauer was interred at the Neuville-En-Condroz Permanent Cemetery in Belgium.[117] On December 31, 1944, Herman

Bratman's widow, Henrietta Cohen, died. She was buried the following day next to her husband in the Chevra Thilim Cemetery on Canal Street.[118] Her son-in-law, Morris James Warshauer, president of the Tropical Clothing Manufacturing Company died in New Orleans on August 12, 1959. He was buried in the Gates of Prayer Jewish Cemetery on Joseph Street.[119] His wife, Frances passed away ten months later on June 19, 1960.[120]

David Goldstein died on March 27, 1952 at the Touro Infirmary. A short article indicated that at death he was president of Pan American Exporters, Inc., which he had founded 45 years previously. He was a member and past master of the George Washington Masonic Lodge # 65 as well as an instructor in the local Masonic school. Listed as his only survivors were his wife, Minette Rich, his daughter, Sadye Rae Winsberg, his brother, Isidore Mark Goldstein, and his two grandchildren. David Goldstein was buried the next day at the Hebrew Rest Cemetery # 2 in New Orleans.[121] Minette Rich Goldstein died seven years later on April 7, 1959. Only her late husband, her daughter, Sadye Rae Winsberg, and her grandchildren, David and Jerome Winsberg, were mentioned in the obituary.[122] She was buried next to her husband in Hebrew Rest Cemetery # 2 in New Orleans.[123] Four years later on July 31, 1956, Isidore Mark Goldstein passed away at the age of seventy-five in New Orleans. He, too, was buried at the Hebrew Rest Cemetery # 2.[124] He never married, but apparently had a child born to him while in Guatemala, who briefly contacted the family years later, after his death.

Sadye Rae Goldstein Winsberg, died at Touro Infirmary, after a long illness on May 23, 1972, survived by her husband, two children and two grandchildren. A member of the Council of Jewish Women, and the Temple Sisterhood, she was interred at the Gates of Prayer Cemetery on Joseph Street.[125]

***

Isidore Rich's only son, Leon, died on March 18, 1957, and was interred at the Hebrew Rest Cemetery # 2 in New Orleans.[126] Leon and Sylvia's children, Leon, Jr. and Jack, both took Jewish spouses. The former married Joan Goodman on June 28, 1949, a New Yorker, whom he met while she was attending Newcomb College in New Orleans. Leon spent four years in the United States Coast Guard after attending Louisiana State University.[127] The couple had two children, Leon, III (b. 1951) and Carol (b. 1954). Leon, Jr. was the first of the Isidore Rich family to leave New Orleans, moving his family to Memphis, TN to better his business prospects. Leon, Jr. died on December 19, 1999, in Memphis.

On August 2, 1951, Jack Rich married Rose Rubel in Okolona, MS, her home town. Rose met Jack while she was attending Newcomb College. Jack served as an ensign in the United States Naval Reserve and was a graduate of Tulane University.[128] Jack and Rose had two children as well, Jack, Jr. (b. 1953) and Nancy Rose (b. 1955). Jack Rich passed away on October 10, 2000 in New Orleans.

Though many of Abe Rich's descendants lived in New Orleans, they never communicated either with the Isidore Rich descendants, or members of the Warshauer, Gross, Goldstein or Anker families. They seem to have been unknown to one another. Moreover, the Isidore Rich and David Goldstein branches, although they were certainly aware of one another living in the same city, never spoke to one another again. Yet, living in New Orleans, both branches of the Isidore Rich family were able to carry on a Hebrew tradition, supported by a thriving Jewish community, while the Abe Rich family's Jewish tradition in Bunkie, died with Abe in 1905.

---

[1] 1900 U.S. Census, Avoyelles Parish, Louisiana, pop. sch., Bunkie, Ward 10, ED 26, p. 5A (penned), Dwelling # 92, Family #96, Abe Rich household, digital image, *Ancestry.com* (http://www.ancestry.com [hereinafter cited as "A"]: accessed 7/ 2007), citing NARA microfilm publication T623, roll 558. Date of enumeration: 6 June 1900.

[2] The Pacific Reporter Vol. 1 –containing all the decisions of the Supreme Courts of California, Colorado, Kansas, Oregon, Nevada, Arizona , Idaho, Montana, Washington, Wyoming, Utah and New Mexico, Dec. 27, 1883-

January 31, 1884, (St. Paul, MN: West Publishing Co., 1884) p. 454 – 459 Jonas Pinschowers and others v. W.J. Hanks, filed October 25, 1883 (http://books.google.com/books: accessed 2/ 2009). Note: The original verdict was not overturned by the Nevada Supreme Court.

[3] "U.S. IRS Tax Assessment Lists, 1862-1918," digital image, (A: accessed 5/ 2010), citing NARA microfilm publication M-779, roll 1 (April 1864, lines 36 & 37).

[4] 1870 U.S. Census, Storey Co., Nevada, pop. sch., Virginia City, p 170 (penned), Dwelling # 10, Family #10, M. Banner household, digital image, (A: accessed 2/ 2007), citing NARA microfilm publication M593, roll 835. Date of enumeration: 26 September 1870.

[5] 1880 U.S. Census, Storey Co., Nevada, Virginia City, ED 48, p. 230A (stamped), Dwelling #2, Family #2, Hotel at # 6 "C" Street, Jacob Rich – Lodger, digital image, (A: accessed 7/ 2008), citing NARA microfilm publication: T9, roll 759. Date of enumeration: 14 June 1880.

[6] 1880 U.S. Census, Mono Co., California, Bodie, ED 48, p. 111A (stamped), No dwelling or family numbers, Abe Rich (Line 2), digital image, (A: accessed 7/2007), citing NARA microfilm publication: T9, roll 69. Date of enumeration: 15 June 1880.

[7] "Necrology, Death of Abe Rich," *The (New Orleans, LA) Daily Picayune*, (hereinafter cited as "*DP* "), 28 October 1905, p. 2, col. 4, digital image, *Genealogybank.com* (http://www.genealogybank.com [hereinafter cited as "GB"]: accessed 5/ 2009).

[8] "Mr. Rich's Death," *DP,* 6 November 1913, p. 7, cols. 2, 3, digital image, (GB: accessed 5/ 2009).

[9] Mackay's daughter Ellin Mackay was Irving Berlin's second wife.

[10] John P. Marschall, *Jews in Nevada: A History* (Reno, Nevada: University of Nevada Press, 2008), xiv.

[11] Marschall, 52.

[12] "New Orleans Passenger Lists, 1820-1945," digital image, (A: accessed 7/2008), Manifest of the *Ellie Knight*, 2 April 1885, page 1, line 6, Abe Rich; and Manifest of the SS *Discoverer*, 10 January 1885, p. 1, line 1, A. Rich, citing NARA microfilm publication M259.RG036, roll 67.

[13] *Orleans Parish, Louisiana Marriage Records*, Vol. 11, p. 28, Isidore Rich and Ella Levy, 18 January 1885; photocopy obtained from Louisiana Secretary of State, Department of Archives, Records Management and History, Baton Rouge, LA.

[14] "Married," *New Orleans Bee (L'Abeille de la Nouvelle Orléans)*, 5 May 1835, p. 2, col. 3 (in English), p. 3, col. 2 (in French), digital images, *Jefferson Parish Library*, (http://nobee.jefferson.lib.la.us/Vol-011/index.html, accessed 2/2010). Note: Minette Ries Levy's sister, Jeanette Ries Mayer's daughter, Caroline married Julius Weis. The latter couple's daughter, Ida Sophie Weis wed Joseph Emmanuel Friend, whose son, Julius Weis Friend, married Mathilde Siess Weil's daughter, Elise, thereby cementing another Siess-Weis-Rich family connection.

[15] Marschall, 74, 86.

[16] Corinne L. Saucier, *History of Avoyelles Parish* (Gretna, LA: Pelican Publishing Co, 1998), 262.

[17] Avoyelles Parish Courthouse Records (Marksville, Avoyelles Parish, LA), Marriage Book E, p. 513, "Marriage of Abe Rich and Ermina (sic) Siess," filed 4 January, 1886.

[18] R.G. Dun & Co. *The Mercantile Agency Reference Book, 1889* (Vol. 85) Image Reprint (CD-ROM), PA-Genealogy.net (http://www.pa-genealogy.net, 2009), 7.

[19] "World War I Draft Registration Cards, 1917-1918," digital image, (A : accessed 2/ 2010), Ben Rich, form 1853, no. 7, Draft Board "O," Avoyelles Parish, Louisiana, citing *World War I Selective Service System Draft Registration Cards, 1917-1918*, NARA microfilm publication. M1509, roll 1653580.

[20] "New Orleans, Louisiana Birth Records Index, 1790-1899," database, (A: accessed 2/ 2010), citing State of Louisiana, Secretary of State, Division of Archives, Records Management, and History, *Vital Records Indices*. Baton Rouge, LA, USA. Birth of Benjamin Rich, Vol. 84, p. 16 and birth of Minette Rich, Vol. 86, p. 625.

[21] "New Orleans Passenger lists, 1820-1945," digital image, (A: accessed 7/2008), citing NARA microfilm publication M259.RG036, roll 71. Manifest of the *City of Dallas*, 1 May 1888, p. 2, lines 4-11, Ella Rich.

[22] 1880 U.S. Census, Lafourche Parish, Louisiana, Ward 7, ED 133, p. D 24 (penned), Dwelling #187, Family #228, Samuel Karger household, digital image, (A: accessed 2/2009), citing NARA microfilm publication: T9, roll 455. Date of enumeration: 14 June 1880.

[23] *Orleans Parish, Louisiana Marriage Records*, Vol. 13, p. 142, Marriage of Leopold Klein and Tinie Levy, 9 May 1888; photocopy obtained from Louisiana Secretary of State, Department of Archives, Records Management and History, Baton Rouge, LA.

[24] "Nautical News," *DP,* 10 May 1888, p. 6, col. 2, digital image, (GB: accessed 2/ 2010).

[25] "New Orleans Passenger Lists, 1820-1945," digital image, (A: accessed 2/2010), citing NARA microfilm publication M259.RG036, roll 75. Manifest of SS *Stillwater*, 21 April 1891, p. 2, lines 1-6, Isidor Rich family.

[26] Leon Rich, U.S. passport application no. 11543, 22 November 1916 (issue date), digital image, (A: accessed 9/ 2010), citing *U.S. Passport Applications, 1795-1925,* NARA microfilm publication M1372, roll 277.

[27] "Head of Export Concern is Dead," *The (New Orleans, LA) Times Picayune* (hereinafter cited as "*TP*"), 28 March 1952, p. 2, cols. 6 & 7, digital image, (GB: accessed 10/ 2009).

[28] Isidor M. Goldstein, U.S. passport application no. 43726, 6 November 1918 (issue date), digital image, (A: accessed 3/2010), citing *U.S. Passport Applications, 1795-1925*, NARA microfilm publication M1372, roll 621.

[29] "New York Passenger Lists, 1820-1957," digital image, (A: accessed 3/2010), citing *Passenger lists of Vessels Arriving at New York, 1820-1897*, NARA microfilm publication M 237, roll 428. Manifest of SS *Vaderland*, 5 July 1880, p. 2, lines 18-20; Sarah Goldstein (age 27), David Goldstein (age 4), Benjamin Goldstein (age 11 months).

[30] See note 28.

[31] "New Orleans Passenger Lists, 1820-1945," digital image, (A: accessed 3/2010), citing NARA microfilm publication M259.RG036, roll 82. Manifest of SS *Breakwater*, 24 March 1896, p. 3, lines 8 & 9, Benjamin (age 19) and David (age 21) Goldstein.

[32] "Died – Klein," *DP*, 20 September 1894, p. 4, col. 7, digital image, (GB: accessed 5/2010).

[33] See note 23.

[34] Joseph Brooks Joseph Hyams was a descendant of the famous Hyams family. Polish immigrants to the British Isles in the 1750s, they came to America at the beginning of the 18th century, settling in South Carolina and Louisiana. Joseph Brooks Joseph Hyams was named after his maternal uncle, Joseph Brooks Joseph, from a prominent South Carolina Sephardic Jewish family, who was killed at the Battle of Shiloh in 1862. Joseph Brook Joseph Hyams was a first cousin twice removed to Henry Hyams, who served as Lieutenant Governor of Louisiana from 1859-1864 and both were distant cousins of Judah P. Benjamin, Treasurer of the Confederate States of America.

[35] Avoyelles Parish Courthouse Records (Marksville, Avoyelles Parish, LA), *Conveyances,* Book D, p. 303, "Sheriff's Sale of Land," filed 6 March 1895.

[36] Wloclawek is only ten miles from Lubraniec, and approximately 90 miles from Warsaw, Poland.

[37] "Society," *DP*, New Orleans, La., 4 February 1894, p. 9, col. 1, digital image, (GB: accessed 5/2010).

[38] *Orleans Parish, Louisiana Marriage Records*, Vol 18, p. 161, Hermann Gross and Bella Warshauer, 3 February 1895; photocopy obtained from

Louisiana Secretary of State, Department of Archives, Records Management and History, Baton Rouge, LA.

[39] Pittsburgh, Allegheny Co., Pennsylvania Marriage record return, Kalman Gross to Karolin Kohn, 30 May 1909, Family History Library, Salt Lake City, Utah, Film Batch # M748705 (Source Call # 1299366).

[40] "World War I Draft Registration Cards, 1917-1918 ," digital image, (A: accessed 24 May 2010), Aaron Gross, Serial # 435, Order #2438, Draft Board "O," Avoyelles Parish, LA; Jacob Samuel Gross, Serial # 449, Order #581, Draft Board "O," Avoyelles Parish, LA; citing *World War I Selective Service System Draft Registration Cards, 1917-1918*, NARA microfilm publication. M1509, roll 1653580.

[41] 1900 U.S. Census, Avoyelles Parish, Louisiana, pop. sch., p. 5A (penned), Dwelling # 92, Family #96, Abe Rich household , and Dwelling #95, Family #100, Herman Gross household, digital image, (A: accessed 7/ 2007), citing NARA microfilm publication T623, roll 558. Date of enumeration: 6 June 1900.

[42] Jan and Naomi McPeek, *Merchants, Tradesmen and Manufacturers Financial Condition for 1902 Avoyelles Parish Louisiana.* Image reprint. 1902 R.G. Dun Mercantile Agency Reference Book. (Salem, OH: Aaron's Books, 2005), Bunkie, 5, and Rapides Parish, Cheneyville, 6.

[43] Rabbi Martin I. Hinchin, D.D., *Fourscore and Eleven, A History of the Jews of Rapides Parish 1828-1919* (Alexandria, Louisiana: McCormick Graphics, 1984), 111, "[June 1903] S. Gross was living in Cheneyville". Note: Solomon Gross married Emma Feitel and relocated to Kaplan, Vermillion Parish, LA.

[44] "Bunkie, LA – One of the Progressive Towns of Central Louisiana," *DP*, 23 February 1903, p. 8, col. 5, digital image, (GB: accessed 5/ 2010).

[45] Hinchin, 111.

[46] "Guatemala Road Being Hurried," *DP*., 6 June 1901, p. 16, cols. 1, 2, digital image, (GB: accessed 5/2010).

[47] "Society," *DP*, 4 February 1906, p. 19, col. 4, digital image, (GB: accessed 6/2010).

[48] "Hamburg Passenger Lists, 1850-1934," digital image, (A: accessed 9/2007), citing, *Staatsarchive Hamburg*, *373-7 I, VIII A 1 B and 152, Seite 175* (Mikrofilm Nr. *K_1782)*, Manifest of the *SS Croatia*, 8 February 1904, p. 34, lines 6 &7 (2nd Class), Moritz and Benno Anker.

[49] "Snapshots," *DP*, 9 January 1905, p. 6, col. 4, digital image, (GB: accessed 6/2010).

[50] "Necrology – Abe Rich," *DP*, 27 October 1905, p. 9, col. 4, and 28 October 1905, p. 2, col. 4, digital images, (GB: accessed 6/2010).

[51] Hinchin, 121.

[52] [No headline], *DP*, 29 October 1905, p. 19, col. 3, digital image, (GB: accessed 6/2010).

[53] Avoyelles Parish Courthouse Records (Marksville, Avoyelles Parish, LA), *Probate Petitions and Wills*, Book L, pp. 388,389, "Succession of Abe Rich, deceased," filed 22 June, 1907; and Book M, pp. 10-13, "Succession of Abe Rich deceased, Inventory," filed 25 June 1907.

[54] "Colon's New Office Building," *The Kansas City (Missouri) Star*, 7 May 1907, p. 3, col. 5, digital image, (GB: accessed 6/2010).

[55] "Other New Companies," *DP*, 20 May 1905, p. 4, col. 5, digital image, (GB: accessed 6/2010). Note: Samuel Zemurray was called Sam "the banana man", because, as a young Russian Jewish immigrant, he made a fortune buying ripe bananas right off boats landing from Central America on the Gulf Coast. He then sold them locally before they could spoil. With the $100,000 he made from this enterprise, he went into partnership with a Mobile, AL businessman, forming what eventually became the United Fruit Company. He went on to make a fortune. He also instigated and funded a successful revolution using American mercenaries in Honduras when the existing government refused to give him favorable business concessions. See: Rich Cohen, *The Fish that Ate the Whale: The Life and Times of America's Banana King*, (Farrar, Strauss & Giroux: New York, 2012).

⁵⁶ "Society," *DP*, 25 August 1907, p. 31, cols. 4,5, digital image, (GB: accessed 6/ 2010).

⁵⁷ "Society," *DP*, 15 September 1907, p. 18, cols. 4, 5, digital image, (GB: accessed 6/2010).

⁵⁸ *Orleans Parish, Louisiana Birth Records*, Vol. 137, p. 194, Sadye Rae Goldstein born September 5, 1908; photocopy obtained from Louisiana Secretary of State, Department of Archives, Records Management and History, Baton Rouge, LA.

⁵⁹ [No headline], *DP*, 16 January 1910, p. 18, cols. 3, 4, digital image, (GB: accessed 6/ 2010).

⁶⁰ 1910 U. S. Census, Orleans Parish, Louisiana, pop. sch., New Orleans, Ward 12, ED 194, p. 3A (penned), Dwelling #53, Family #55, Isadore Rich household, digital image, (A: accessed 6/ 2010), citing NARA microfilm publication T624, roll 524. Date of enumeration: 16 April 1910.

⁶¹ "Society," *DP*, 25 December 1910, p. 14, col. 3, digital image, (GB: accessed 6/2010). Also: "New Orleans Passenger Lists, 1820-1945," digital image, (A: accessed 6/2010), citing NARA microfilm publication T905. RG085, roll 29. Manifest of *SS. Joseph Vaccaro*, 14 December 1910, p. 3, lines 9 & 10, Isidor and Leon Rich.

⁶² "Society," *DP*, 15 September 1912, p. 18, col. 1, digital image, (GB: accessed 6/2010).

⁶³ 1910 U. S. Census, Avoyelles Parish, Louisiana, pop. sch., Bunkie, Ward 10, ED 26, p. 8B (penned), Dwelling #161, Family #194, Mina Rich household, digital image, (A: accessed 6/2010), citing NARA microfilm publication T624, roll 508: Date of enumeration: 10 May 1910.

⁶⁴ Avoyelles Parish Courthouse Records (Marksville, Avoyelles Parish, LA), *Marriage Book M,* p. 277, "Ben Rich to Addie Maxie," filed November 10, 1911.

[65] "World War I Draft Registration Cards, 1917-1918," digital image, (A: accessed 6/2010), Leopold Rich, Serial # 7745, No. 302, Draft Board 13, San Francisco, California, citing *World War I Selective Service System Draft Registration Cards, 1917-1918*, NARA microfilm publication M1509, no roll given, (FHL roll #1544266).

[66] 1920 U. S. Census, San Francisco, California, pop. sch., San Francisco, Assembly Dist. 33, ED 261, p. 12B (penned), Dwelling #7, Family #53, Louis (sic) Rich, lodger, digital image, (A: accessed 6/2010), citing NARA microfilm publication T625, roll 140. No date of enumeration.

[67] Pythian Cemetery (Bunkie, Avoyelles Parish, LA), Leopold Rich marker, personally read 7/2002.

[68] 1920 U. S. Census, Orleans Parish, Louisiana, pop. sch. New Orleans, Ward 11, ED 183, p. 4A (penned), Dwelling #1, Family #1, Robert Cone household, digital image, (A: accessed 6/ 2010), citing NARA microfilm publication T625, roll 622. Date of enumeration: 5 January 1920.

[69] "Isidore Rich, Pioneer in the Tropical Trade, Defeated by Illness," *DP*, 5 November 1913, p. 7, col. 4, digital image, (GB: accessed 6/ 2010).

[70] "Mr. Rich's Death," *DP*, 6 November 1913, p. 7, cols. 2, 3, digital image, (GB: accessed 6/2010).

[71] "Judicial Advertisement: Widow Francis Tujague VS. Isidor Rich," *DP*, 21 November 1913, p. 10, col. 7, digital image, (GB: accessed 6/ 2010).

[72] "Avis de Successions (Succession notices): Succession d'Isidore Rich, " *L'Abeille de la Nouvelle Orleans*, 8 December 1913, p. 2 col 4, digital image, *Jefferson.lib.la.us* (http://www.jefferson.lib.la.us/genealogy/NewOrleansBeeMain.htm: accessed 6/2010). Note: While this notice appeared in French in the *Abeille*, (New Orleans Bee) it could not be found in the *Picayune* or any other New Orleans newspaper in English.

[73] "The Probate Docket," *DP,* 10 December 1913, p. 9, col. 2, digital image, (GB: accessed 6/2010).

[74] Leon and Sylvia Tobias Rich, U.S. passport application no. 74446, 8 April 1919 (issue date), digital image, (A: accessed 6/2010), citing *US Passport Applications, 1795 - 1925,* NARA Microfilm Publication M1490, roll 743.

[75] "Society," *TP*, 8 December 1918, p. 46, col. 3, digital image, (GB: accessed 6/2010).

[76] "Society," *TP*, 13 April 1919, p. 41, cols. 2, 3, digital image, (GB: accessed 6/2010).

[77] 1920 U.S. Census, Orleans Parish, LA pop. sch., New Orleans, Ward 1, ED 8, p. 13 B (penned), Dwelling #163, Family #185, Mannie H. Jacobs household, digital image, (A: accessed 6/1910), citing NARA microfilm publication T625, roll 618. Date of enumeration: 13 January 1920.

[78] "Deaths," *TP*, 22 September 1944, p. 2, col. 8, digital image, (GB: accessed 6/2010).

[79] "Deaths," *TP*, 24 July 1967, p. 2, col. 6 and 11 November, 1967, p. 2. col. 5, digital images, (GB: accessed 6/2010).

[80] "New Orleans Firm to Open Branch at Guatemala," *TP*, 20 April 1919, p. 10, col. 4, digital image, (GB: accessed 6/2010).

[81] "New Orleans Passenger Lists, 1820-1945," digital image, (A: accessed 6/2010), citing NARA microfilm publication T905, roll 144, Manifest of SS *Turrialba,* 1 May 1932, page 1, lines 1, 2, Ilda de Anker and daughter Ana; NARA microfilm publication T905, roll 153, Manifest of SS *Metapan,* p. 9, lines 1, 2, Ludwig and Anita Anker.

[82] Bella Fisher, U.S. passport application no. 99550, 17 July 1919 (issue date), digital image, (A: accessed 6/ 2010), citing *U.S. Passport Applications, 1795-1925,* NARA microfilm publication M1490, no roll given.

[83] Adolph Fisher U.S. passport application no. 55070, 6 January 1919 (issue date), digital image, (A: accessed 6/2010), citing *U.S. Passport Applications, January 2, 1906-March 31, 1925,* NARA microfilm publication M1490, no roll given.

[84] Borough of Bronx, City of New York, Certificate and record of Marriage # 436, Benjamin Anker to Bella Fisher, 16 January 1932, Family History Library, Salt Lake City, Utah Microfilm # 1954510.

[85] "New Orleans Passenger Lists, 1820-1945," digital image, (A: accessed 6/2010), citing NARA microfilm publication T905, roll 145, Manifest of SS *Castilla*, page 6, lines 5,6, & 7, Bella, Donald and Marilyn Anker.

[86] "World War I Draft Registration Cards, 1917-1918," digital image, (A: accessed 6/2010), Benjamin Anker, Serial No. 1452, order No. 994, Draft Board "1," New Orleans, Orleans Parish, Louisiana, citing *World War I Selective Service System Draft Registration Cards, 1917-1918*, NARA microfilm publication. M1509. (FHL microfilm roll # 1684817).

[87] "New York Passenger Lists, 1820-1957," digital image, (A: accessed 6/2010), citing NARA microfilm publication T715, roll 5874, Manifest of SS *Platano*, September 18, 1936, p. 90, lines 4,5. Donald Anker, age 11, and Juana Fisher, age 60.

[88] "Deaths," *TP*, 26 April 1947, p. 2, col. 5, digital image, (GB: accessed 6/2010).

[89] "World War I Draft Registration Cards, 1917-1918," digital image, (A: accessed 6/2010), Isidore Mark Goldstein, Serial No. 552, Order No. 849, Draft Board 11, New Orleans, Orleans Parish, LA, citing *World War I Selective Service System Draft Registration Cards, 1917-1918*, NARA microfilm publication. M1509, FHL roll # 168492.

[90] Morris James Warshauer. U.S. passport application # 109740, 25 August 1919 (issue date), digital image, (A: accessed 6/ 2010), citing *U.S. Passport Applications, 1795-1925*, NARA microfilm publication M 1490, roll 883.

[91] "New York Marriages, 1686-1980," database, *Familysearch.org* (https://familysearch.org: accessed 5/2011), Source File # 1558517. Marriage of Herman Warshauer to Henrietta Cohen, 17 February 1889. Note: Warshauer is the German spelling of the Polish name Warshawski, both meaning a resident of Warsaw. There is, therefore, good reason to suspect that Lewin (Louis) Warshauer and Lewin (Louis) Warshawski are one and the

same person. May we conclude that Herman Bratman and Morris James Warshauer were brothers or cousins?

⁹² "New York Births and Christenings, 1640-1962," database, F*amilysearch*.org (https://familysearch.org: accessed 5/2011), Source File # 1322260. Birth of Frances Warschauen (sic), daughter of Herman and Henrietta Cohen Warschauen (sic), 20 January 1892.

⁹³ 1900 U.S. Census, Ouachita Parish, Louisiana pop. sch. Monroe, Ward 2, ED 87, p. 15A (penned), Dwelling #304, Family #305, Herman Brackman household, digital image, (A: accessed 6/ 2010), citing NARA microfilm publication T623, roll 576. Date of enumeration: 15 June 1900.

⁹⁴ 1920 U. S. Census, Orleans Parish, Louisiana, pop. sch. New Orleans, Ward 13, ED 227, p. 12 A (penned), Dwelling #229, Family #239, Morris Warschauer household, digital image, (A: accessed 6/2010), citing NARA microfilm publication T625, roll 624. Date of enumeration: 16 (no month given), 1920.

⁹⁵ "$100,000 Clothing Factory to Arise in Vieux Carré," *TP*, 15 July 1925, p. 15, col. 2, digital image, (GB: accessed 6/2010).

⁹⁶ "Wash Suit Firms Form Local Body," *TP*, 1 February 1927, p. 5, col. 3, digital image, (GB: accessed 6/2010).

⁹⁷ "Back from Cuba," The Bunkie (Louisiana) Record, 20 June 1924, Vol. 16, no. 11, p. 1. col 7. Back issue consulted 12/ 2010 at the *Marksville Weekly News* Office, Main Street, Marksville, LA.

⁹⁸ Jewish Cemetery, Row 8, Pineville, (Rapides Parish,) LA, Bella Warshauer Gross marker, personally read 5/2007.

⁹⁹ 1930 U S Census, Avoyelles Parish, Louisiana pop. sch. Bunkie, Ward 10, ED 26, p. 10B (penned), Dwelling #218, Family #232, Herman Gross household, digital image, (A: accessed 6/ 2010), citing NARA microfilm publication T626, roll 784. Date of enumeration: 9 April 1930.

¹⁰⁰ 1930 U. S. Census, Orleans Parish, Louisiana, pop. sch. New Orleans, ED 236, p. 38A (penned), Dwelling #547, Family #551, David Goldstein

household; p. 8B (penned) Dwelling #124, Family #129, Herman Bratman household; ED235, p. 17A, Dwelling #187, Family #225, Leon Rich household, digital images, (A: accessed 6/ 2010), citing NARA microfilm publication T626, roll 811: Date of enumeration: 11 April 1930.

[101] 1930 U. S. Census, Wood County, Texas, pop. sch. Mineola, ED 5, p. 13A (penned), Dwelling #247, Family #321, Addie Rich household, digital image, (A: 6/2010), citing NARA microfilm publication T626, roll 2412. Date of enumeration: 11 April 1930.

[102] Avoyelles Parish Courthouse Records (Marksville, Avoyelles Parish, LA), *Marriage Book I,* p. 640, "Marriage of Bennie Rich to Marie Johnson, the Widow Rooler," filed 19 June, 1922.

[103] 1930 U. S. Census, Avoyelles Parish, LA, pop. sch. Bunkie, Ward 10, ED 26, p. 14A (penned), Dwelling #303, Family #323, Mina S. Rich household, digital image, (A: 6/2010), citing NARA microfilm publication T626, roll 784. Date of enumeration: 11 April 1930.

[104] Avoyelles Parish Courthouse Records (Marksville, Avoyelles Parish, LA), *Marriage Book K*, p. 288, "Marriage of Bennie Rich to Rosa Mae Milligan," filed 15 April, 1930.

[105] Avoyelles Parish Courthouse Records, (Marksville, Avoyelles Parish, LA), *Marriage Book K,* p. 276, "Marriage of James Everett Green to Miriam Rich," filed 22 October, 1940.

[106] Pythian Cemetery, section C, row 44, plot 1, Bunkie (Avoyelles Parish), LA, Mina Siess Rich marker, personally read 7/2002.

[107] Pythian Cemetery (Bunkie, Avoyelles Parish, LA), section C, row 43, plot 3, Bennie Rich marker, personally read 7/2002.

[108] "Society," *TP*, 30 April 1933, p. 32, cols. 3, 4, digital image, (GB: accessed 6/2010).

[109] "Franklin Flourishes," *DP*, 22 August 1900, p. 1, col. 7, digital image, (GB: accessed 6/2010).

[110] "Society, Weddings and Engagements," *TP*, 30 August 1936, p. 4, col. 1, p. 5, col 1, digital images, (GB: accessed 6/2010).

[111] Jewish Cemetery (Pineville, Rapides Parish, LA), row 8, Herman Gross marker, personally read 5/ 2007.

[112] "Society," *TP*, 31 October 1933, p. 3, col. 4, digital image, (GB: accessed 6/2010).

[113] "Deaths," *TP*, 25 April 1960, p. 2, col. 6, digital image, (GB: accessed 6/2010).

[114] "Deaths," *TP*, 27 October 1943, p. 2, col. 6, digital image, (GB: accessed 6/2010).

[115] "Communal Hebrew School Head Dead," *TP*, 2 September 1933, p. 5, cols. 3, 4, digital image, (GB: accessed 6/2010).

[116] "Honor Accorded Flier Who Died," *TP*, 30 October 1943, p. 3, col. 5, digital image, (GB: accessed 6/2010).

[117] "U.S. Rosters of World War II Dead, 1939-1945," database, (A: accessed 6/2010), citing *United States Army. Quartermaster General's Office. Rosters of World War II Dead (all services)*, Warshauer, Irving B., T. SG. # 38308473.

[118] "Deaths," *TP*, 1 January 1945, p. 2, col. 7, digital image, (GB: accessed 6/2010).

[119] "Deaths," *TP*, 14 August 1959, p. 2, col. 8, digital image, (GB: accessed 6/ 2010).

[120] "Deaths," *TP*, 20 June 1960, p. 3, col.8, digital image, (GB : accessed 6/2010).

[121] "Deaths," *TP*, 28 March 1952, p. 2, cols. 6, 7, digital image, (GB: accessed 6/2010).

[122] David Goldstein's grandson, Jerome Winsberg, was married on July 31, 1960 at the Congregation Gates of Prayer to his Fortier high school sweetheart, Isabel Herzog. Jerry went on to become a successful lawyer and has long been a respected jurist in New Orleans. David Jacob Winsberg, the rebel in the family, had a brief marriage, solemnized by Rabbi Nathaniel Share, to Kay Simkin, which took place at the bride's home on November 13, 1960. Following in his father Winfred's footsteps as a proprietor of a shoe store was, however, not for him. David spent years in the Bahamas and the Florida Keys, and became, among other things, a charter boat captain.

[123] "Deaths," *TP*, 7 April 1959, p. 3, col. 2, digital image, (GB: accessed 6/2010).

[124] "Deaths," *TP*, 1 August 1956, p. 2, col. 7, digital image, (GB: accessed 6/2010).

[125] "Deaths," *TP*, 25 May 1972, p. 16, col. 2, digital image, (GB: accessed 6/2010).

[126] "Deaths," *TP*, 19 March 1957, p. 2, col.7, digital image, (GB: accessed 6/2010).

[127] "Society," *TP*, 2 July 1949, p. 12, col. 8, and p. 13, col. 3, digital images, (GB: accessed 6/2010).

[128] "Society," *TP*, 18 April 1951, p. 31, col. 8 and p. 32 cols.1-3, digital images, (GB: accessed 6/2010).

Abe Rich, ca. 1890

Aaron Gross and Sadye Rae Goldstein, Louisiana ca. 1939
(*Courtesy of David Winsberg*)

Aaron Gross and Sadye Rae Goldstein, ca. 1928 Guatemala
(*Courtesy of David Winsberg*)

Sarah Coberly, her grandmother, Hermina Siess Rich (in Cajun bonnet) and mother, Raye Rich Coberly, ca. 1926, in Bunkie, LA

David & Minette Rich Goldstein, ca. 1926 en route to Central America
(Courtesy of David Winsberg)

CHAPTER 14

THE AVOYELLES OUTRAGE

Louisiana saw an outbreak of anti-Semitic attacks during the two decades following the Civil War which alarmed Jews all over the South. The occupation of southern soil by federal agents and carpetbaggers alike, who swarmed to the area to participate in Reconstruction only exacerbated the population's general misery. These northern newcomers not only governed with a determined ruthlessness, but many cashed in on their positions of power to the detriment of the local population still suffering from the impoverishment that four years of fighting had left in its wake. This unrelenting social upheaval and political unrest also laid the groundwork for the rise of the infamous Ku-Klux Klan whose main target was the recently freed African Americans, but who occasionally singled out Jewish merchants as their victims. While the Civil Rights Act of 1871, also known as the Ku-Klux Klan Act, did much to curb the organization's activities, occasional outbreaks of lawlessness and intimidation made news in the local papers.

The senseless violence perpetrated on several Jewish merchants in Cottonport and Evergreen in March 1887 had been preceded by an alarming series of events which had occurred in other rural parishes of Louisiana. In June 1875, arrests had been made under the enforcement arm of the Klan Act of a number of residents of Paincourtville, in Assumption Parish, for an attack on Solomon Klotz, a local Jewish merchant, who had emigrated from Alsace after the Franco-Prussian War. It was said that "by force of arms and by threats and intimidation, [they] compelled deponent for his safety to abandon his home and business and escape to New Orleans." [1] A deputy U. S. Marshall was dispatched to the parish, where the case was summarily, and somewhat inexplicably, dismissed for want of jurisdiction. Solomon, however, eventually returned, settling in nearby Napoleonville, where he raised a family and tended to his store, eventually becoming the town's mayor. He died there at the age of seventy-three in 1931.

Not all of these incidents had such a fortunate outcome. Serious trouble began brewing in West Carroll Parish shortly after the attack on Klotz, the details of which were so shocking that they were carried for months in both local and national newspapers. The residents of this northern Louisiana parish had first risen up against Simon Witkowski in 1879. A Polish-born Jewish immigrant, Simon and his younger brother, Julius, had come to Louisiana in 1856. A year later, at the age of twenty-one, Simon married Adeliza Victoria Davis, the fifteen-year old daughter of Thomas Davis, a wealthy landowner. Upon the death of his father-in-law in 1859, Simon and his wife inherited one sixth of Caledonia plantation, the whole of which contained fifteen hundred acres of land, seventy slaves, a steam gin and saw mill, mules, hogs, oxen, wagons, carts, a dwelling house and slave quarters.[2] In the 1860 Census, Simon Witkowski, enumerated as a planter and merchant, reported $12,800 invested in real estate and personal property totalling $40,000.[3]

The Witkowski family spent the war years in Mexico where their second child, Eugenia Florence, was born in 1865. Simon was just one of the many merchants who had taken up residence outside the United States, in order to keep the blockaded South supplied with European goods which had to be shipped through Mexican ports via Texas. After the end of the conflict they returned to Caledonia plantation. In the 1870 census, Witkowski's net worth had diminished considerably with real estate valued at $3,000 and only $11,845 in personal property.[4] After an unsuccessful bid for the state legislature in 1878, he was, only a year later, at the center of a bloody controversy when his bookkeeper and principle debt collector, Squire Lusk, provoked an altercation with S. L. Austin, the postmaster of Lake Providence, LA. Lusk shot Austin dead on the spot. When Austin's son, the newly elected parish judge, came to his father's defense, he, too, was mortally wounded. A third person became collateral damage during the shoot-out. It was reported in the newspaper that the underlying cause of the tragedy had been the political rivalry between Witkowski and Austin.[5]

In August 1884, however, Witkowski managed to engineer his own election to the Louisiana State Legislature as the representative from West Carroll Parish, serving until 1888.[6] It was alleged that he had bought his seat by cancelling the debts of certain people after they had cast their ballots for him. This rumor, as well as the ruthless way in which he wielded his new-found political power, kept the parishes of East and West Carroll in turmoil for years. Newspaper articles in the New Orleans *Daily Picayune* appeared periodically which fanned the flames of the growing enmity against this Jewish immigrant.[7] Witkowski's shady dealings finally got the best of him when, on November 27, 1886, he and his family were forced to flee Caledonia plantation for Lake Providence when a mob set fire to his store killing his bookkeeper, John McKay, and an unidentified African-American woman, doing untold damage to other property. There was no mention of Simon being Jewish in the *Daily Picayune*. There was, however, general skepticism about his having declared it was simply a robbery. The article's author characterized him as a corrupt politician with an unsavoury past, given the enmity with which he was held in his own district.[8] A follow-up piece excoriated him as the "King of West Carroll, the pet of the Ring, and the dispenser of State patronage," who was unlawfully holding a federal office as a postmaster while also being a member of the Louisiana legislature.[9] Fearful of returning to his plantation in person, Witkowski sent several overseers in his stead. His daughter Eugenia's husband, James Heiner Semple, and a business associate, Virgil H. Tillery, who was, in fact, Simon's enforcer, carried on his business at Caledonia. In June 1887 Tillery was shot dead by persons unknown as he rode along the road near Floyd in East Carroll Parish.[10] However, when all was said and done, despite the arson and murder, no one was ever arrested or charged in connection with any of these incidents. After Simon was voted out of office, his power gone, the family faded into a quiet obscurity. As far as the local press was concerned, this violence was never overtly attributed to Simon's ethnicity, nor was the Klan ever mentioned as having been responsible for the lawlessness which plagued the parish for over a decade. The Witkowski family continued living near Lake Providence for the rest of their lives. Simon died at his home on December 20, 1901, two years after his wife Victoria's passing. He was remembered, in his brief obituary in the *Daily Picayune* only as having been prominent in politics as a member of the Louisiana legislature from West Carroll Parish.[11]

The flames of anti-Semitism finally reached the residents of Avoyelles Parish in October 1884 when the newly-opened firm of Koch and Meyer was attacked. The partners immediately announced their departure, closing their general merchandise store on October 20.th The *Marksville Review* reported: "The fact that Messrs. Koch and Meyer of Moreauville are going to leave this town and the parish of Avoyelles because they do not consider that they are protected by their lives and property has been a serious blow to the community. [...] The Commissioner for Avoyelles [...] ever were he to show that this parish is a land flowing with milk and honey, a perfect garden of Eden, it would amount to nothing were it known that strangers were not accorded protection under the laws."[12] It would seem that self-interest, rather than actual outrage at the treatment of Jews, motivated the author of this article to warn the townspeople that continued violence against "strangers" would have a negative impact on the growth of the parish. Whatever violence had transpired here, the facts of which had been judiciously kept out of print, the two merchants did not think it worth their while to remain in Moreauville. After all, no one had ever been prosecuted in the Klotz or Witkowski cases, so Koch and Meyer had no reason to think that their appeal for justice would bring a better result.

The next incident in Avoyelles Parish took place in the early morning hours of March 7, 1887, when the premises belonging to two Jewish storekeepers were attacked and vandalized, first in Evergreen, and then, five miles away, in Cottonport. The four victims were brothers Henry and Aaron Kahn of Evergreen and Felix Bauer and his nephew, George, of Cottonport.

Although Jews had lived in the parish since the late 1830s, the early Hebrew immigrants had, for the most part, been assimilated by marriage into the prevailing French Catholic culture. Long-time residents, Adolph and Charles Frank, Leopold and David Siess, Abe

Felsenthal, Sam and Alex Haas had all married Christian women most of whose children did not practice the Jewish faith. By 1880, other Jewish immigrants had also been attracted to the commerce in Avoyelles Parish. Proportionately, the little town of Evergreen had the largest concentration.[13] The Karpe, Goudchaux and Levy families, Col. Alex Haas, and the Kahn brothers did business there. In Marksville, Simon Siess and Eli Hiller, with his clerk Ernest Weil, were dry goods merchants. Adolph Frank owned the local hotel. In Mansura, David Siess was the mayor and postmaster. His brother Leopold had been a farmer there until his death in 1885. Some of the Felsenthal descendants still lived in Pointe Maigre, although Abe had passed away in 1877. In Bunkie, a Jew from Poland, Abe Rich, had just married one of Leopold Siess' daughters, Mina, opening the second retail establishment in the newly-founded town.

Why the Kahn brothers, both native Louisianans from Plaquemine in Iberville Parish, were singled out for attack in Evergreen, while the other Jewish merchants in the same town were not, may never be known.[14] The reason for the violence perpetrated on Cottonport residents, Felix and George Bauer, French speaking natives of Romanswiller, Alsace, remains a mystery as well. The incidents, however, received national attention in the newspapers. The first article appeared in the New Orleans *Daily Picayune* three days after the initial attacks. Felix Bauer reported that at three o'clock in the morning on March 7, 1887, a large band of armed men appeared in front of his store in Cottonport and opened fire. Although he estimated there were some forty to fifty shots fired, they were all aimed at or in the building and no one was injured. Some of his stock, however, was damaged. The marauders finally departed after posting a notice on the building which read: "To F. Bauer and his clerk: A warning. If found here after April 1, death to all." [15] Initially Bauer intended to fight back. After contacting the authorities, he wrote to one of his major suppliers in New Orleans, the firm of V. and A. Meyer, cotton factors, headed by General Adolph Meyer.[16] He also informed his cousin, Felix Loeb, from the firm of Loeb and Bro. who were wholesale liquor merchants. Meyer and Loeb met with Louisiana Governor Samuel D. McEnery at the St. Charles Hotel on March 9th in order to deal with the situation. Bauer also reported to the *Picayune* that Aaron and Henry Kahn, two of several Jewish merchants in Evergreen, had been similarly treated, and had also been recipients of a notice to leave. The Kahn brothers wrote to their parents, Samuel and Esther Goudchaux Kahn, and asked that they send them a number of Winchester repeating rifles. Guns and ammunition were also sent to Felix Bauer, as the Jewish merchants said they would stay and resist the pressure to leave. In the meantime, Governor McEnery authorized that a reward be posted for the perpetrators. Felix Loeb, Bauer's cousin, stated optimistically that the attack must have been the result of jealousy rather than anti-Semitism. Both the Kahn Brothers and Bauer carried on very lucrative business dealings for cash and on credit. Dr. Patrick Q. Mason echoed Loeb's views, first expressed over a century ago, in his recent article on anti-Jewish violence in the New South. "The violence," he stated, "frequently took on an anti-Semitic character, but more often than not, Jews' assailants primarily targeted them not because of their religious identity per se, but rather because they had cash in their pockets, wares in their carts, or credit extended to hopelessly indebted farmers." [17]

On March 11th the Merchants and Manufacturers' Association of New Orleans sent a letter to the Governor, which was published two days later in the *Daily Picayune*. Its members requested him to use any and all means necessary to have the guilty parties punished to the full extent of the law, adding that doing nothing would have a negative impact on immigration and capital investment in the state. Of the fourteen members who signed the letter four were prosperous New Orleans Jewish merchants: Selim Barnett of Katz & Barnett, Isidore Hernsheim of S. Hernsheim, Bros. & Co, Gustav Lehmann of A. Lehmann & Co., and Max Schwabacher of J. and M. Schwabacher. [18]

In the meantime, an urgent message was sent out to five hundred voters in Avoyelles Parish to attend a March 12th mass meeting in Evergreen. The editor of the Alexandria *Louisiana Democrat*, reported that almost six hundred had actually showed up, adding, "Alexandrians are loud in their denunciation of this barbarous proceeding, and well might any civilized community be." [19] Thirty-eight citizens of Marksville and Mansura, including Simon and David Siess, signed a letter which expressed their disapproval of the outrage, but were not able to attend. At the meeting, John Ewell, the head of the Avoyelles Parish Police Jury, was elected president, and Dr. Daniel Bester Hudson was voted in as secretary. A committee on resolutions was formed which included Stephen Samuel Pearce, William Haygood, Landry L. Bordelon, Eloi Joseph Joffrion, Cléophas Joseph Ducôté, M.D., Dr. Hudson, and Henry Clay Kemper, all local leading citizens. Speeches were then given by District Attorney Col. John Wickliffe, as well as the Rev. John O'Quinn, Rev. H. Bennett, and Col. Alex Haas. The following resolution was unanimously adopted:

> *Whereas, on Sunday night, 13 inst. the storehouse of the Messrs. Kahn at Evergreen, and that of Mr. F. Bauer, at Cottonport were fired into by unknown parties with arms of heavy calibre, perforating the walls, merchandise and showcases with many shots, also anonymous notices were left in conspicuous places that they must leave the country by April 1 proximo, or death would be the penalty to all Jews. This brings the community of this parish face to face with a grave public emergency. The proprietors and employees of these two establishments number fifteen or twenty people. While in the deep sleep of the after midnight hours their lives were put in jeopardy by this band of lawless individuals. Thus life becomes insecure in our midst, and merchandise and commerce destroyed in a manner becoming the vandal. Valuable property in the parish has been dealt a paralyzing blow; the fair name of the community has been assailed and injured, and the minds of citizens have been unsettled; the rights guaranteed by the laws of this free government have been threatened and trampled upon. [...] When the Jew is driven away, who will next be banished or murdered! Where would such unbridled lawlessness lead to? A little prosperity attaching to a citizen would be a seal of his doom. Therefore, be it resolved, by the citizens of the parish of Avoyelles in mass meeting assembled, that they desire to express, in this public place, in the most*

severe and emphatic manner, their condemnation and abhorrence and detestation of the outrage that has been perpetrated and threatened; and that they call upon the law officers of the parish to put forth every energy to apprehend and bring to justice the guilty parties, and that the citizens themselves in every way possible give their aid to accomplish this object; and that we publicly declare that the merchants assailed have pursued their calling in a business-like and honourable way. Be it further resolved that the law-abiding and order-loving citizens of Avoyelles do pledge their protection and moral support to all men of whatever creed or nation, who seek to make their homes in this parish, so long as they conduct themselves as honourable and peaceable men. [20]

Copies of this resolution were forwarded to the *Marksville Review*, the *Marksville Bulletin*, the *New Orleans Times-Democrat*, and the *Daily Picayune* for publication. At that same meeting it was revealed that Sheriff Louis A. Joffrion had received a communiqué from the Governor, authorizing a three hundred dollar reward for information leading to the arrest of the perpetrators. Sheriff Joffrion and District Attorney Wickliffe replied to the Governor that they had discovered the disguises of the midnight marauders and questioned two witnesses who had seen the men up close, having recognized the horse belonging to one and the "track" of another. This allusion to "disguises" was the only time it was ever intimated that the attack might have been Klan related. Five suspects were interrogated and made to explain their whereabouts during the time of the attacks. Witnesses alleged that the men who engineered the assault and those who had carried it out were well known. In fact, since most people in the parish were related to one another in one or more ways, it is little wonder that the identity of the perpetrators was no real secret. Wickliffe explained that no money would be spared in this investigation, since one of the richest men in the parish, Col. Alex Haas, would foot the bill. A closed-door hearing was to take place the following week at Evergreen to depose the witnesses and further the investigation. Wickliffe offered immunity to any one, two or three of the participants who would turn state's evidence.

The District Attorney also corresponded with the Parish Sheriff to tell him that he had investigated the victims of this attack and found that they were honorable merchants who sold mostly for cash, and it could not be said that they used high-handed tactics to collect debts themselves or by parish seizures. This was an attempt, no doubt, to reassure everyone, including himself, that this case was unlike Simon Witkowski's predicament in West Carroll Parish, as well as to erase any stereotypical anti-Semitic images or prejudices harbored in the community. Wickliffe's investigation concluded that these Avoyelles Jewish residents sold their goods cheaply and fairly and always gave liberally to any charity. Bauer had been in Cottonport for eight years, having come from Kennerville, and the Kahn brothers had been in Evergreen for over a decade. Wickliffe recalled that two years previously a similar incident had occurred in Moreauville, when Koch and Meyer had been attacked causing them to sell out and return to New Orleans. He observed that their flight had probably emboldened the present perpetrators to think that "the shroud of midnight would shield them from prosecution, as it did their successful predecessors." [21]

On March 14th Wickliffe wrote another letter, this time to the *Daily Picayune*, to reassure its readers that the people in Avoyelles Parish were moving with all haste to protect its citizens, and with practically unlimited funds would soon "ferret out the perpetrators." [22]

Not everyone was pleased with the reaction of the local populace or the coverage given the attacks on the four Jewish merchants. On March 19, 1887, an article entitled "It Don't Work Both Ways," appeared in the New Orleans based African-American newspaper, *The Weekly Pelican,* which took the local press to task for ignoring outrages committed against blacks reading in part, "There is something remarkable in the unanimity with which our daily press condemns the recent outrages in Avoyelles Parish. For years just such crimes have been perpetrated upon colored men and no notice taken of them whatsoever. But when white men have outrages of the same nature practiced on them, special press reporters, mass meetings and condemnatory editorials appear with a regularity quite surprising." The article ended by saying, "Verily the democratic press of the South exhibits the meanest and most contemptible spirit of that of any section of the Union." [23] If the reporter from the *Weekly Pelican* envied all the rhetoric put forth by the news media to defend its Jewish citizens, time would tell whether he would be jealous of the results.

Beginning on March 18th out-of-state newspapers started to carry the story. The *Augusta (Georgia) Chronicle* reported Governor McEnery's offer of a reward and clemency for anyone who would turn state's evidence. There was, however, no mention of anti-Semitism or Klan activity, and no reporting of what was actually written in the notices posted on their premises.[24] A similar article appeared on the same day in the *Macon (Georgia) Weekly Telegraph.*[25]

On March 22nd a reporter for the *Dallas (Texas) Morning News*, however, pulled no punches, entitling his story "Religious Persecution – Armed Anti-Semitic Feeling in Avoyelles Parish, Louisiana, to be Squelched." After a brief description of the event it was characterized as "business jealousy, coupled probably with some of that anti-Semitic feeling which so often shows itself in rural districts." [26] In 2005, Dr. Patrick Q. Mason wrote after analyzing attacks against Jews in the postbellum South, that a "class component" caused "respectable citizens" of the New South to condemn "anti-Jewish violence performed by disgruntled farmers or simple ruffians." [27] In this case, a big city reporter took the opportunity to take the backward people of rural Louisiana to task for their intolerance. This article did, however, expand on the notice posted ordering the men to leave the parish by the first of April, writing that it was a general warning to all Jews to leave by that time under penalty of death. The public was assured that a large number of arrests would soon be made.

A similar article was carried in the *San Francisco Bulletin* entitled "Persecuting Jewish Merchants." It was pointed out that this particular outrage was having a different effect than former ones, a reference, no doubt, to the Witkowski affair.[28] The identical story was carried in the *Cleveland (Ohio) Plain Dealer* the following day, but the Witkowski case was prominently mentioned. While all the out-of-town newspaper accounts indicated that the proclamation posted by the midnight marauders included the fact that the "people of Avoyelles" did not want any more Jews in their parish, and gave them all until April to clear out, the *Daily Picayune* had never reported this version.[29] There was continuing concern that these events which, now, had been reported nationwide would cripple the growth of Louisiana's economy and discourage immigration into the state. However, at least one reporter for the Alexandria, *Louisiana Democrat* expressed actual outrage at the religious prejudice:

> *No boisterous rowdy element will be permitted to disturb the good will and order; no jealous person to warn away any one pursuing a legal and honest business. Louisiana throws itself open to the whole world and invites here people from every portion of the Union or of Europe. It makes no distinction of race, religion or politics, and it will permit no one to arouse religious or political prejudices or jealousies. Immigration is pouring in and capital coming in abundance, and these are bringing prosperity with them. Not on this account alone, but from innate justice and honesty, the State of Louisiana stands ready to protect every person, stranger or foreigner, who makes his home here, in all his rights and privileges. It has given its word for this, and it will keep it.* [30]

On March 23rd the *Louisiana Democrat* reported that an investigation before Isaac C. Johnson, J.P., at Evergreen, was to be held behind closed doors several days hence. District Attorney Wickliffe reiterated his offer of immunity to any one, two or three of the actual participants who would turn state's evidence. He concluded that the men who instigated the attack and those who actually carried it out were well known in the community.[31]

Finally, on March 25th the *Daily Picayune* carried the announcement of an arrest in the case on its front page. Datelined

Bunkie, La., the previous day, a detailed description was given of the combined efforts of District Attorney Wickliffe and Justice of the Peace Johnson, along with Deputy Sheriffs Marshall and Tailleure. It was said that eighty-three witnesses had been examined, which had led to the apprehension of Athanase Armand at Cottonport:

> *He was brought to Evergreen and carried into the room where the Justice and District Attorney are holding the investigation and was closeted with them for nearly an hour; not even the deputy sheriffs were permitted to be present. Immediately afterward he was sent to the Marksville jail in the custody of the two deputies. It was noticed that while Armand appeared very much frightened when brought in, when he left he was perfectly composed, and even light-hearted. One of the deputies was heard to say of him as they rode off: 'You have done the best thing you could have done for yourself.' It is known that the warrant upon which he was arrested charged him with complicity in the late outrage.* [32]

Because the examination was private, it could only be surmised that Armand must have "squealed" on his associates, and had received immunity, being sent to jail only for his own protection. If Athanase, born in 1852 to Dorsineau Armand and Eulalie Dufour, was, indeed, one of the perpetrators, it is not without irony to note that his second cousin, Josette Chatelain,[33] was the widow of Alsatian Jew, Leopold Siess, whose brothers David, the Mayor of Mansura, and Simon, the president of the Avoyelles School Board, were also local merchants. In a burst of enthusiasm the article ended by saying that the Sheriff had sent out every deputy he could to Evergreen and had made inquiries about rounding up more handcuffs. However this momentum apparently stalled when there was no more news of additional arrests forthcoming in the newspaper.

Despite Armand's detention, an article appeared in the April 11th edition of the *Daily Picayune* which reported a startling development. The dispatch, dated from Bunkie on the previous day, revealed that Henry and Aaron Kahn of Evergreen had found the following message on their gallery that very morning which read: "H. and A. Kahn – The 1st of April is at hand. We see no appearance of your removal. We hope you will not force us to extreme measures." Attached to the message were two 44 calibre Winchester rifle cartridges, one each for Henry and Aaron, as well as four matches.[34]

On April 16th the *Daily Picayune* reported that Felix and George Bauer had given up their business in Cottonport and transferred most of their merchandise to Alexandria. When asked if he would stay in neighboring Rapides Parish, Felix Bauer indicated that he could no longer remain in Cottonport where he not only had to work all day, but was forced to stand guard at night for fear of another attack. It was apparent from the tone of the article that the second notice to the Kahn Brothers had been sufficient to convince Bauer that he might be in for the same treatment if he did not leave. The *Daily Picayune* encouraged Bauer to remain in Alexandria assuring him that his "nocturnal bliss would not be disturbed." [35] Several weeks later, District Attorney John C. Wickliffe was called back to the area on account of "new developments in trying to bring to justice the participants in the Kahn and Bauer outrage." But he refused further comment on the case.[36]

No additional information was forthcoming in the press until May 23rd when Henry Kahn, visiting Alexandria on business, gave an interview to the *Daily Picayune*. Henry affirmed that he had not been threatened again to vacate the parish. Moreover, he added that he and his partner, Aaron, along with some influential planters and merchants of Avoyelles, and nineteen leading merchants of New Orleans (none of them named in the article), had formed an association known as the Avoyelles Planters' Trading Company. It is significant to note that John Ewell, President of the Avoyelles Police Jury, was the Chairman and Landry Bordelon, Dr. C.J. Ducôté, Frank Haygood and J.T. Johnson were directors. Their goal was to have one hundred thousand dollars in stock subscribed. As of the date of the report, over eighty-five thousand dollars had already been paid in full. The Kahn Brothers had been afforded further protection from violence when the United States Post Office was moved to their store, thereby making any further attacks a federal offense. It was also noted that the Criminal District

Court would be convened in Marksville on May 23rd, and the outrage would soon be investigated more thoroughly.[37] Henry's positive attitude was no doubt bolstered by an event which had occurred a month before. In a hotly contested local election, Judge Isaac C. Johnson had been re-elected Mayor of Evergreen, and Henry Kahn had been chosen as one of the town's five aldermen.[38]

Even after three months of newspaper coverage, the several official inquiries, the mass meetings, and letters of support, no records of any investigation, and no transcripts of any trial, if, indeed there was one, can be found in the Avoyelles Parish courthouse. While it is clear that justice may never have been served, the Levy, Karpe, Siess, Bloch, Frank, Felsenthal, Haas and Rich families, undeterred by the violence, stayed in the parish well into the 20th century. Moreover, they were joined by a new wave of Jewish families coming from Central Europe in the 1890s: the Weiss and Gross families of Bunkie, and the Schreiber, Elster, Schlessinger and Abramson families of Marksville. The victims of the previous attacks, however, did not remain in Avoyelles Parish.

Felix and George Bauer relocated almost immediately to Alexandria. Felix formed a partnership with Bertrand (Bat) Weil, an Alexandria native. The April 27, 1887 edition of the *Louisiana Democrat* announced that in the first days of May, Bauer and Weil would open a new emporium, at the sign of the Great Plow, corner of Second and Jackson, replacing Hustmyre's former stand.[39] George Bauer became the firm's chief clerk, and, eventually, its buyer. Felix Bauer remained in the United States until 1896, whereupon he returned to France for good.[40] George, who married Bat's sister, Rosa, in 1893, stayed with the firm and became the "Bauer" when the store's name was changed to Weil Bros. & Bauer upon his Uncle Felix's departure for Europe. Bat's brother, Samuel Weil, also joined the business, after another brother, Conrad, died at the age of twenty-five. Weil Bros. and Bauer sold dry goods, groceries, liquors, saddlery, carpets, buggies, surreys, in fact, just about anything, and was reputed, at the time, to be the largest department store in Central Louisiana.[41]

Notwithstanding their vow to stay on and fight, Henry and Aaron Kahn left Evergreen in the fall of 1887. Henry had been a frequent visitor to New Orleans, where his parents, who had supported him during the trouble in Avoyelles Parish, still lived. After his mother, Esther Goudchaux Kahn, died on October 10, 1887, Henry moved permanently to New Orleans to be with his elderly father, Samuel.[42] On December 5, 1888 he married Isabelle Stern, whose mother, Annette, was Isidore Newman's first cousin.[43] Henry was immediately introduced to the rice business, and in the spring of 1895 was promoted to the office of vice-president and assistant manager of the National Rice Milling Company.[44] When he succumbed to a year-long illness on March 16, 1911, Henry was the company president, as well as secretary of the Louisiana Life Assurance Society.[45]

Aaron Kahn moved to California, to join relatives of the extended Goudchaux-Weil-Kahn-Bier families, some of whom had begun a westward migration out of New Orleans several years earlier. He married Seraphina "Phina" Loupe, daughter of Samuel and Rachel Weill Loupe, on September 14, 1887. Phina, born in New York, was raised in Gilroy, Santa Clara Co., California, where her father was a dry goods merchant.[46] Aaron and Phina Kahn were childless. Aaron, who had left the occupation of ladies tailor for a career in real estate died, at the age of fifty-nine, in San Francisco on March 2, 1919.[47]

After the turbulent 1880s there were no further reports of any anti-Semitic incidents in Avoyelles Parish. While the attack on Simon Witkowski had been fueled by his unscrupulous dealings as a merchant, and exacerbated by his political power, the attacks on Koch and Meyer, Henry and Aaron Kahn, and Felix and George Bauer were the result of difficult economic circumstances in Avoyelles Parish, and, most likely, the personal indebtedness of some of the perpetrators. The other Jewish merchants in the parish were never targeted, and would continue to be a small but influential part of Avoyelles Parish's economic underpinnings for another fifty years. It was not anti-Semitism that drove Avoyelles Jewish inhabitants away from the parish, but lack of opportunity. The children of the original Hebrew merchants and planters moved away seeking better educational opportunities and more lucrative occupations than this mostly agrarian community could offer.

---

[1] "Ku Klux, An Arrest Under the Enforcement Act," *The New Orleans (LA) Times,* 22 June 1875, p. 2, col. 1, digital image, *Genealogybank.com* (http:www.genealogybank.com hereinafter cited as "GB"]: accessed 10/2011).

[2] "Succession Sale," *The(New Orleans, LA) Daily True Delta,* 22 November 1859, p. 3, col. 1, digital image, (GB: accessed 7/ 2009) . Note: Julius Witkowski, who was 27, married 47 year old Mary Ann Davis, Thomas Davis' widow, becoming the administrator, of her deceased husband's estate. He inherited through Mary Ann, one-half of Caledonia Plantation. Thus, Simon Witkowski, married to Mary Ann's daughter, became his brother Julius' son-in-law!

[3] 1860 U.S. Census, Carroll Parish, Louisiana, pop. sch. Ward 5, p. 61 (penned), Dwelling #583, Family #566, Simon Witkowski household, digital image, *Ancestry.com* (http://www.ancestry.com [hereinafter cited as "A"]: accessed 7/2009), citing NARA microfilm publication M653, roll 409. Date of enumeration: 7 August 1860.

[4] 1870 U.S. Census, Carroll Parish, Louisiana, pop. sch., Ward 5, p. 9 (penned), Dwelling #84, Family #84, Simon Witkowski household, digital image, A: accessed 7/2009), citing NARA microfilm publication M593, roll 509. Date of enumeration: 15 July 1870.

[5] "First Edition. A Terrible Crime." *The New Haven (Connecticut) Evening Register,* 15 July 1879, p.1, col. 2, digital image, (GB: accessed 7/ 2009).

[6] "Election Results," *The (New Orleans, LA) Daily Picayune,* (hereinafter cited as *"DP"*), 22 August 1884, p. 2, col. 4, digital image, (GB: accessed 7/ 2009).

[7] "Simon Witkowski. The West Carroll Boss. More about his career, his men and his methods," *DP,* 30 December 1886, p. 8, cols. 1- 3, digital image, (GB: accessed 7/2009).

[8] "The Witkowski Affair," *DP,* 5 December 1886, p. 6, cols. 3 & 4, digital image, (GB: accessed 7/ 2009).

[9] "Witkowski in a new role," *DP,* 22 December 1886, p. 4, col. 3, digital image (GB: accessed 7/ 2009).

[10] "Witkowski. More Trouble in East Carroll. Semple, son-in-law of Witkowski, returns to scene of trouble and is ordered away. Bloodshed likely at any moment," *DP,* 31 October 1887, p. 3, cols. 1 & 2, digital image, (GB: accessed 7/ 2009).

[11] "Necrology - Simon Witkowski," *DP,* 20 December 1901, p. 4, col.7, digital image, (GB: accessed 7/2009).

[12] " Moreauville Items," Louisana State University Libraries On Line Catalog – Special Collections – Louisiana and Lower Mississippi Valley (hereinafter cited as "LLMV"), Microfilm # 1032, *The Marksville Review*, 18 October 1884, Vol. V, no. 6, p.3, cols. 1 & 4 .

[13] In 1880 twenty-three of a total 246 residents, or almost nine percent of Evergreen town, were Jewish, not including Alex Haas who lived nearby on the family plantation. See: 1880 U. S. Census, Avoyelles Parish, LA, pop. sch. ED 5 , p. 487A- 491-B (stamped), digital images, (A: accessed 2/2006), citing Family History Film 1254448, roll 448. Date of enumeration: 18 June 1880.

[14] It must be reported, however, that another brother, Max Kahn, who had lived in Evergreen for several years previous to the incident, was said to have co-habited with a woman of color, leading some to speculate that his relationship had caused friction between the townspeople and the Kahn family.

[15] "Bulldozing in Avoyelles," *DP,* 10 March 1887, p. 6, col. 2, digital image, (GB: accessed 7/2009).

[16] Adolph Meyer, born to a Jewish family in Natchez, MS, served on the staff of Brigadier General John Stuart Williams of Kentucky during the Civil War, attaining the rank of assistant adjutant general. He was elected to the U.S. House of Representatives from Louisiana in 1891, serving eight terms, until his death in office in 1908.

[17] Patrick Q. Mason, "Anti-Jewish Violence in the New South," *Southern Jewish History, Journal of the Southern Jewish Historical Society* 8 (2005): 77-119, specifically 79.

[18] "The Avoyelles Outrage," *DP,* 13 March 1887, p. 2, col. 7, digital image, (GB: accessed 7/ 2009). Note: Max Schwabacher's older brother, Julius, had been a resident of Evergreen in 1880, living with the Kahn brothers.

[19] "Town and Parish News," *The (Alexandria,) Louisiana Democrat*, (hereinafter cited as "*LD*"), 16 March 1887, p. 3, col. 2, digital image, *Chroniclingamerica.loc.gov* (http://chroniclingamerica.loc.gov ^ [hereinafter cited as" CA"]: accessed 3/ 2011).

[20] H.H. Hargrove, "The Rebuke Coming to the People of Avoyelles," *DP,* 16 March 1887, p. 1, cols. 3 & 4, digital image, (GB: accessed 7/ 2009).

[21] Hargrove, "The Rebuke Coming to the People of Avoyelles," col. 4.

[22] John O. Wickliffe, "Avoyelles People Moving," *DP,* 17 March, 1887, p. 4, col. 4, digital image, (GB: accessed 7/ 2009).

[23] "It Don't Work Both Ways," *The (New Orleans) Weekly Pelican*, 19 March 1887, p. 2, col. 3, digital image, (GB: accessed 7/2011).

[24] "General Notes," *The Augusta (Georgia) Chronicle*, 18 March 1887, Sec. A, p. 3, col. 1, digital image, (GB: accessed 7/2009).

[25] "Outrages in Louisiana," *The Macon (Georgia) Weekly Telegraph*, 18 March 1887, p. 1, col. 6, digital image, (GB: accessed 7/ 2009).

[26] "Religious Persecution – Armed Anti-Semitic Feeling in Avoyelles Parish, Louisiana to be Squelched," *Dallas (Texas) Morning News*, 22 March 1887, p.1, col. 5, digital image, (GB: accessed 7/ 2009).

[27] Mason, "Anti-Jewish Violence in the New South," 79.

[28] "Persecuting Jewish Merchants – An Anti-Semitic Feeling Breaks Out in Louisiana," *San Francisco (California) Bulletin*, 22 March 1887, p. 4, col. 1, digital image, (GB: accessed 7/ 2009).

[29] " Race Hatred in Louisiana – Two Jewish Merchants ordered by Regulators to Leave a Parish," *The Cleveland (Ohio) Plain Dealer*, 23 March 1887, p. 5, col. 3, digital image, (GB: accessed 7/2009).

[30] "The Avoyelles Outrage," *LD,* 23 March 1887, p. 2, col. 3, digital image, (CA: accessed 3/ 2011).

[31] "They Will Be Caught," *LD,* 23 March 1887, p. 2, col. 2, digital image, (CA: accessed 3/ 2011).

[32] "Bunkie – The Efficient District Attorney of Avoyelles Working Up Evidence Against the Bulldozers," *DP*, 25 March 1887, p. 1, col. 4, digital image, (GB: accessed 7/ 2009).

[33] Athanase and Josette shared a set of great-grandparents, Guillaume René Gauthier, born in Natchitoches Post, Louisiana in 1750, and Elizabeth Hennet (Enet), born in 1752, at Fort de Chartres, Illinois.

[34] "Bunkie – The Kahns again notified to Leave. – The People Indignant," *DP*, 11 April 1887, p. 1, col. 3, digital image, (GB: accessed 7/ 2009).

[35] "Louisiana – Alexandria – Arrival of the Expelled Avoyelles Merchants, " *DP*, 17 April 1887, p. 1, col. 2, digital image, (GB: accessed 7/ 2009).

[36] "Louisiana – Alexandria – District Attorney Wickliffe Called to Avoyelles in the Bauer and Kahn Matter," *DP*, 30 April 1887, p. 2, col. 2, digital image, (GB: accessed 7/2009).

[37] "Louisiana – Evergreen – An Interview with One of the Kahn Brothers- The Avoyelles District Court," *DP*, 23 May 1887, p. 1, col. 6, digital image, (GB: accessed 7/2009).

[38] "Judge Isaac C. Johnson," *LD,* 13 April 1887, p. 2, col. 1, digital image, (CA: accessed 3/2011).

[39] "Something New in Town," *LD,* 27 April 1887, p. 2, col. 4, digital image, (CA: accessed 3/ 2011).

[40] Rabbi Martin I. Hinchin, D.D., *Fourscore and Eleven, A History of the Jews of Rapides Parish 1828-1919* (Alexandria, Louisiana: McCormick Graphics, 1984), 107.

[41] Hinchin, 106.

[42] "Mortuary Notice - Estelle Goudchaux Kahn," *DP*, 11 October 1887, p. 4, col. 4, digital image, (GB: accessed 8/ 2009).

[43] "Louisiana Marriages, 1718-1925," database, (A: accessed 8/2009), citing a variety of sources including original marriage records located in Family History Library microfilm, microfiche, "Hunting for Bears" and various books. Marriage of Henry Kahn and Isabella Stern.

[44] "Henry Kahn – Elected Vice-President of the National Rice Milling Company," *DP*, 23 May 1887, p. 9, col. 2, digital image, (GB: accessed 8/ 2009).

[45] "Mortuary Notice - Henry Kahn," *The Montgomery (Alabama) Advertiser*, 17 March 1911, p. 2, col. 5, digital image, (GB: accessed 8/2009).

[46] 1880 U. S. Census, Gilroy, Santa Clara Co. California, pop. sch. ED 257, p. 383 A (stamped), No dwelling number, Family # 109, Samuel Loupe household, digital image, (A : accessed 2/2006), citing NARA microfilm publication: T9, roll 82. Date of enumeration: 5 June 1880.

[47] "San Francisco Deaths," *The Oakland (California) Tribune,* 4 March 1919, digital image, (A : accessed 7/2009). Note: Seraphina (Phina) Loupe's father shortened the name from Laupheimer to Loupe, after immigrating to the USA from Osterberg, Germany.

Aaron Kahn   ca. 1885   (*Courtesy of Brad Fanta*)

CHAPTER 15

THE LAST WAVE OF JEWISH IMMIGRANTS

In late nineteenth century Louisiana the predominately Judeo-Alsatian immigrants to Avoyelles Parish who came before the Civil War, and after the Franco-Prussian War in Europe were being replaced by a wave of Jewish families from the Austro-Hungarian and Russian empires. Unlike the earliest immigrants, these post-Civil War arrivals, more often than not, sought out co-religionists with whom to form business and family relationships. At the very beginning of the twentieth century the Goudchaux-Weill family had forged a bond with another group of newcomers when Fanny Weill Weiss' sister-in-law, Rosa Weiss, married David Goldring on March 7, 1902, in Bunkie.[1] But a different connection explains why some Goldring family members had chosen Louisiana in the first place. David's sister, Libbie Goldring, had married Thomas Elster in Buffalo, New York in 1892. Elster, from Tarnów, Austria,[2] arrived in New York City on February 26, 1888, travelling immediately to Buffalo where he joined his brother, Joseph, who had settled there three years previously. The patriarch of the Goldring family, Kalman, immigrated to the USA aboard the *SS Suevia* from Le Havre arriving in New York on May 31, 1887. He listed his last address as Strassburg, Russia.[3] He, too, settled in Buffalo. A tailor by profession and already forty years old,[4] he sent for his wife, Minnie, and all eight children three years later. They landed in New York on July 16, 1890, from Antwerp, Belgium aboard the *SS Westernland*. A small notation indicated that they were coming to New York to "go to husband."[5]

Erie County in upstate New York, and Buffalo in particular, had become the destination of choice for tens of thousands of eastern European immigrants in the late nineteenth century. Textile mills along the Niagara River offered ample employment. The extreme cold and snowy weather during the long winters in the region did not deter these hardy immigrants from Central and Eastern Europe as they were, in fact, quite used to it. The 1892 New York State Census for the Goldring family found forty-five year old Carlman (Kalman), from Poland, his forty year old wife, Minnie, and eight children: twenty year old Libbie, a tailoress, eighteen year old, David, a tailor, and the younger ones, Molly (12), Abram (11), Anna (10), Henry (8), Louis (9), and Tilly (4) all living in Buffalo. Tom and Libbie Goldring Elster moved from upstate New York to Louisiana in 1893 where he filed his intention for citizenship on November 6, 1895, and become a citizen on September 13, 1899, in Avoyelles Parish.[6]

In the meantime, opportunities were such that Joseph Elster, who remained in Buffalo for the time being, was soon joined by another brother, Louis, and two sisters, Minnie and Annie. All, with the exception of Annie, would make their homes, at one time or another, in Avoyelles Parish. The Goldring and Elster families would continue to have close connections to Buffalo, New York as well as to the downstate metropolitan area.

Joseph Elster, according to census records, arrived in the United States in 1885. He married Mary Cohen in 1890 in Buffalo, where they appeared together in the 1892 New York State census. Joseph was employed in the retail business.[7] He and Mary's first two children, Samuel (b. 1892) and Bertha (b. 1894), were born in Buffalo.[8] Tom Elster left Buffalo for Avoyelles Parish in 1893, yet he would return to New York periodically, as his first two children, daughters Freida (b. 1895), and Gertrude (b. 1897), were born there. By 1899 Elster Bros. & Co., "The New York Bargain Store," with both Tom and Joe in charge, was going full swing in Marksville. Advertising in the *Avoyelles Blade,* they proclaimed, "We are leaders in Ready Made Clothing, Dry Goods, Shoes, Ladies and Gents Goods, Hats, Caps, Etc., Etc. Come one Come All! Price our Goods and see if we do not sell as cheap as New Orleans prices." [9] Both brothers and their respective families appeared in the 1900 census for Avoyelles Parish living next door to one another in Marksville. Joe and Mary's third child, Sadie, was born in Louisiana in 1898, and Mary was expecting another daughter, Harriet, who was born just after the census was taken. [10]

Rooming with the Elster family were Jules Lemoine, an eighteen year old salesman in their store, and Joseph Laff, a Russian Jewish immigrant, who was the local ice dealer. Living with Tom and Libbie Elster, was Libbie's seventeen year old brother, Herman Goldring, who had opened a confectionery shop, and Simon Goldsmith, another Russian immigrant who had started a business in Louisville, Kentucky, but was visiting in the parish to explore his prospects. Goldsmith soon moved his wife, Rosa Schlessinger, and family to Avoyelles Parish, and opened another mercantile establishment in Marksville. His brother-in-law, Moses Schlessinger, was already living close by in rented rooms, a thirty-eight year old peddler of dry goods.[11]

The Schlessinger family had recently immigrated from Mitau, Russia to Louisville Kentucky. Twenty-nine year old Simon was first to arrive in 1885. His eighteen year old brother, Morris, came in 1888, and twenty-one year old sister, Rosa, accompanied by their parents, Jacob, age fifty-five and Sarah, age fifty, had followed in 1890. By the time of the 1900 Census, Jacob and Sarah Schlessinger were living in Louisville with their daughter, Rosa, her husband of eight years, Simon Goldsmith (who was enumerated in both the 1900 Kentucky and Louisiana censuses), and their four children Sam, Julius, Jennie and Freida.[12] Jacob Schlessinger died in Louisville on February 22, 1903.[13] Henceforth Sarah, his widow, lived with the Goldsmiths in Marksville, in Baltimore and finally back in Louisville, where she passed away on March 17, 1912.[14]

There was yet another family of Austrian immigrants, who had first settled in Buffalo, before they chose Avoyelles Parish as their home. Harry Schreiber had emigrated from Rymanów (now in Southern Poland) to New York in 1884, bring his wife, Carrie Cohen, over four years later. The couple had three children, Rosie (b. April 1893) in Austria, Emmanuel Martie Schreiber born in Buffalo, New York on January 10, 1895, [15] and Julius born on July 20, 1899 in Brooklyn.[16] At the time of the 1900 U.S. census the family was living on the Lower East Side of Manhattan on Pitt Street where Harry worked in the garment district.[17] It is not known why they chose Marksville in Central Louisiana. It might be assumed, however, that within the Austrian immigrant community of Buffalo, they had become acquainted with either the Goldring or Elster families who had told them of the business opportunities in the South. Their three or four years in Manhattan, then, had just been a brief stopover, a time to earn enough money to set themselves up in business elsewhere. By 1902, Mrs. Carrie Schriever (sic) and her family were running a clothing, dry goods and cap store in Marksville.[18]

Louis Elster, born December 7, 1878, in Tarnów, Austria, arrived on February 17, 1893, at the Port of New York. Like his brothers before him, he traveled back and forth between New York and Louisiana. His older sister, Annie Elster, marrying in 1894 in Buffalo, New York, had started a family with her husband, Meyer Greenfield, who made his living as a tailor.[19] Louis met his future wife, Annie E. Kurtz, in Buffalo. Born on March 17, 1887, she was an Erie County, New York native, the daughter of German immigrants, David and Sara Davis Kurtz.[20] The couple married in New York in 1905, where their first child, Claire Ruth, was born on September 8, 1908.[21] Louis soon took his family to Marksville to take over the Elster Bros' New York Bargain Store, replacing Tom. The latter, his wife Libbie Goldring, and family had already relocated back to Buffalo, where they were enumerated in the 1905 New York State Census.[22] Tom remained in Erie County becoming a produce commission merchant, at the Niagara Frontier Food Terminal. Eventually his son, Robert Elster, inherited the wholesale produce business which he ran well into the 1950s.[23]

By the time Louis and Annie Kurtz Elster arrived in Marksville with their daughter, Ruth, Joseph Elster, and his wife, Mary had added two more children to their family, Martin born on July 25, 1903,[24] and Rheuben, born on September 9, 1905.[25] Their last child, a daughter Dorothy, was born in New York on December 21, 1909, on one of Mary's trips to the Empire State. Joseph was, however, after a decade in Avoyelles Parish, eager to explore new territory. Several scouting trips around the state brought him to Houma where he saw new opportunities. He soon moved his family to Terrebonne Parish, leaving his brother, Louis, in charge of the store in Marksville.

The Joseph Elster family would become fixtures in Houma, operating "Elster's Store," there for more than sixty years. Widowed on November 13, 1935, when his wife, Mary, passed on, he and his sons, Martin and Rheubin, continued to run the mercantile establishment,[26] until Rheubin's marriage in 1937 and subsequent relocation to Texas. Upon Joseph's death on April 25, 1950,[27] Martin, who married Frances Stern in New York in May 1934, took over the family business and ran it along with his wife until his death in Houma on October 26, 1989.[28] Joseph and Mary Elster's children, Harriet, Sam and Dorothy, none of whom ever married, lived and worked in New Orleans.

Of all the members of the Elster family, only Louis, his wife, Annie, and his daughters, Claire Ruth and Rae, the latter born January 29, 1910, in Marksville, were lifelong residents of Avoyelles Parish.[29] The roster of mercantile establishments now run by Eastern European immigrants in Marksville in 1910 included, the Elster New York Bargain store, with Louis Elster at the helm, Schreiber's, run by Harry and Carrie Schreiber, and Schlessinger's This last store had formerly been run by Rosa Schlessinger's husband, Simon Goldsmith. As late as 1906, Simon Goldsmith, upon leaving for a thirty day buying trip to New York, had been heralded as "one of Marksville's most enterprising businessmen."[30] Yet, just over a year later, Goldsmith, had moved to Baltimore, MD and was just "visiting Marksville on business."[31] His brother-in-law, Simon Schlessinger, had moved his family down from Louisville, Kentucky to take over the Marksville store. Morris Schlessinger, Simon's younger brother, had previously relocated from the bluegrass state to Louisiana. The 1910 Avoyelles Parish Census showed the two Schlessinger families and the Harry Schreibers as neighbors in downtown Marksville. Morris, listed as Maurice, and his wife, Pauline Kassel, also a Russian immigrant whom he had met in Louisville, were living with their four children, Annie (b. 1896), Sarah (b. 1898), Nathan (b. 1900) and Daniel (b. 1905), all born in Kentucky. Morris worked as a commercial traveler.

Harry Schreiber and his wife, Carrie, lived next door to the Morris Schlessinger family. His sons, Martie and Julius, were attending school. His daughters, Sylvia Dora (b. 1908), and Helena Naomi (b. 1910), were both born after the family moved to Marksville.

Simon Schlessinger and his wife, Libby Siegel, were the Schreiber's neighbors. The oldest of the three couples, all of their children had likewise been born in Louisville, Kentucky. Their eldest, Benjamin (b. 1882), was already working in his father's clothing store. Jacob (b. 1889) was twenty-one. Their daughter, Mary (b. 1891), was a teacher and Esther (b. 1894) was still in school. In addition, the family had adopted an "orphan," a little boy, Francis, who was eight years old. Simon was doing well enough in his business to employ a cook, Emma, age fourteen.[32]

Like the previous generation of Jewish immigrants to Avoyelles Parish, these twentieth century inhabitants of Marksville were just as interested in their town's welfare. Attracting better rail service to Avoyelles Parish, and to Marksville in particular, had, in 1910, become of paramount importance. The Texas and Pacific RR had already constructed a branch from Melville to Simmesport. In May of 1910, having been solicited by the newly chartered Avoyelles, Palmetto and Gulf Railroad, a branch line was proposed from Opelousas in St. Landry Parish, via Port Barré, by way of Palmetto through the Eighth Ward to Plaucheville and finally to Marksville. One third of the qualified, property tax paying voters of the town proposed that the Mayor and Town Council levy a tax not to exceed five mills for a period of ten years (1913-1922) to help defray the cost of its being built, provided that the railroad be completed and operational into the corporate limits of Marksville on or before March 1913. Amongst the signers were Simon and Benjamin Schlessinger, Louis Elster, and Harry Schreiber.[33] As Marksville grew, so did its government, and its need for modern services. In 1919, after the town had started to lay water lines in order to establish public water service, the Marksville Volunteer Fire Department was founded. Ben Schlessinger and Harry's son, Martie Schreiber, were two of the original nine volunteers.[34]

In 1910 Simon Schlessinger's daughter, Mary, was teaching in the Marksville school system having graduated from the Avoyelles

High School on May 27, 1908. A picture of the seven graduates, including Mary Schlessinger, appeared in the *Daily Picayune,* along with an article describing the two day festivities which marked the end of the term. Included in the piece was praise for Mary's fifteen year old sister, Esther, who had been the winner of the school debate.[35] Mary soon gave up teaching to marry Bernard Bach in New Orleans on September 8, 1914. The groom was a thirty year old Russian immigrant who had come to the United States with his parents in 1905.[36] He took Mary back to Chicago, where he became a successful real estate broker. They had no children.[37]

On September 12, 1912, Morris Schlessinger died at the age of forty-two. The circumstances of his death were reported in *The (Alexandria, LA,) Town Talk:* "Morris Schlessinger of Louisville, Kentucky who was merchandising in this country, died suddenly at Clear Creek at the home of Mr. Squyres at one p.m. Friday. His brother, Mr. S. Schlessinger of Marksville, was notified, and he came to have the body brought to Pineville this evening at 7 o'clock for interment in the Jewish Cemetery. The deceased also leaves a sister, Mrs. Goldsmith, who resides in Baltimore."[38] Morris' widow, Pauline, and her children soon left Louisiana to return to Louisville, Kentucky.[39]

Morris' death was followed, not long after, by Harry Schreiber, who passed away on February 25, 1915, after a three week illness during a visit to Covington in St. Tammany Parish, Louisiana. The cause of death was listed as a "gastric ulcer." Harry was forty-seven years old.[40] His body was taken to the Dispersed of Judah Cemetery in New Orleans, where he was buried the next day.[41] Harry's wife, Carrie, assisted by her sons, continued in business in Avoyelles Parish for several years thereafter.

During these early days of the twentieth century, the Jewish residents of Marksville were easily accepted in Avoyelles Parish. They appeared often in the society column of the *Daily Picayune.* Esther Schlessinger, for example, was featured in a lengthy article describing the wedding of her school friend and neighbor, Olive Ruth Blanchard to Sydney Pierre Sanchez in May of 1915.[42] After her graduation from Avoyelles High School, Esther completed a secretarial course, and was hired in the law office of Adolph Valery Coco. On April 18, 1916, he was elected Attorney General of Louisiana on the Democrat ticket headed by Colonel Ruffin Pleasant, who became the thirty-sixth Governor of the state. Coco took Esther along with him to New Orleans to be the stenographer in the Attorney General's office.[43] Unfortunately for Esther, her tenure in Coco's office would not survive his term. Early in 1919 she was stricken with tuberculosis. She succumbed to her illness in St. Joseph's Sanitarium, in Asheville North Carolina on September 23rd at the age of twenty-nine. She was buried the next day in the West Asheville Jewish Cemetery.[44]

Jacob Schlessinger, Simon and Libby's eldest son, followed an entirely different path in life which, like so many, took him away from Avoyelles Parish at a young age. Trained as a civil engineer, he joined the Army less than a month after America declared war on Germany, on April 6, 1917. After Officer's training at both Fort Myer, and Fort Belvoir, Virginia, followed by a month at the American University in Washington DC, he was assigned to the 305th Engineers Regiment, 80th Division of the Third Army Corps on August 27, 1917 as a Captain. He arrived in Europe on July 9, 1918 and was appointed Topographical Officer for the Second Batallion. He served in France in the Meuse-Argonne Forest offensive and was wounded on June 11, 1919. He was honorably discharged as a Major on June 30th of the same year.[45] Jacob Schlessinger was employed by the United States Government after the war as a civil engineer in charge of dredging operations. He made his home in Baltimore, Maryland, where he boarded for years in the home of Isadore and Fanny Sachs, Russian immigrants from Mitau, his own parents town of origin.[46]

**

The Goudchaux-Weill-Weiss-Goldring connection amongst these families, explored briefly in Chapter 9, merits further explanation here, given its added "Elster" component. Libbie Goldring Elster's brother David and his wife, Rosa Weiss, and children left Many, in Sabine Parish, in 1907 to live permanently in Alexandria (Rapides

Parish), where with his wife Rosa's brothers Joseph and Morris, he had founded the Weiss and Goldring "Gent's Store" in that same year. The Goldrings lived in Alexandria for almost twenty years before relocating to Shreveport where David opened a women's specialty shop. He had left Alexandria because his brother-in-law, Morris Weiss, was against any expansion. In 1927 Dave Goldring and Morris Weiss dissolved their partnership amicably, according to Weiss descendant Harry Silver, because Dave wished to expand the business throughout the South, and Morris wanted Weiss and Goldring to remain a single independent store.[47]

The amicable dissolution of the partnership allowed David, in a most innovative way, to expand the Goldring brand throughout the South. It was at his Shreveport store that he had the idea of opening women's clothing shops as concessions in high-end men's clothing stores. In the 1920s, women either frequented large department stores or employed their own dressmaker. After World War I, many men's shops found that they had room to spare and looked to make a profit from their underutilized real estate. Enter David Goldring who leased his first space in Atlanta at the George Muse Clothing Company in 1920.[48] By the 1950s Goldring's had leased spaces in thirty-three stores in thirty cities. This growth would not have been possible were it not for David and Rosa's two sons, Martin, who was educated at the University of Michigan, and Ferdinand, who went to Oglethorpe University in Atlanta, and the New York University Graduate School of Business. Beginning in 1923 Martin managed one of the first concessions at J. Black and Sons in Birmingham, Alabama, and then moved to the Goldring location at Godchaux's in New Orleans. At this latter store he was assisted by his mother, Rosa Weiss' nephew, Julius.[49] The David Goldring family permanently relocated to New York around 1928 where Ferdinand supervised the central buying office for all the Goldring stores in Manhattan at 1441 Broadway. David and Rosa shared an apartment at 250 West 94th Street. Ferdinand and his wife, Florence Nanette Ginsburg, and their two children, Rona and Frederick, lived in Mount Vernon in Westchester County, New York.[50] Martin and his wife, Gertrude Lieb, lived in Greenwich,

Connecticut, with their two children, David Leslie and Stephen Goldring. From this time on the heart of the Goldring operation would always be in Manhattan, the fashion capital of the United States.

David and Rosa Goldring retired to their home in Miami, Florida in the 1940s. David was the first of the eight children of Kalman and Minnie Goldring to die on February 8, 1943, in Miami. He was sixty-eight years old.[51] Martin succeeded his father as Chairman of the Board of Goldring, Inc., and Ferdinand became the Company president. In 1955, the business, which was reported to be a twenty-one million dollar a year retail women's fashion empire, finally expanded out of the shadows of the franchise business, to open a store under its own name on Canal Street in New Orleans. A second store was opened in Gentilly Woods, and a third on Airline Highway, barely a year before Martin Goldring's death on July 21, 1958, at his home in Greenwich, Connecticut.[52] Less than three years later, Ferdinand Goldring, would be gone as well, expiring at Beth Israel Hospital in Manhattan on April 18, 1961. However, before that date, Goldring stores had been opened in Baton Rouge and Shreveport.[53] Charles Weiss, formerly the executive vice-president and general merchandiser of the Goldring firm, succeeded Ferdinand as president. Charles was the son of Herman and Fanny Weill Weiss and Rosa Weiss Goldring's nephew.[54] Rosa survived the death of her second son, Ferdinand, by less than a year, succumbing at the age of seventy-eight in March 1962 at her home in Miami.[55] The Goldring chain continued in operation another two decades. Filing for bankruptcy in 1975, unprofitable stores and concessions were closed, and others were opened in different locations, including Staten Island, Philadelphia, Roanoke, Virginia and Providence, Rhode Island. At the time of this 1975 reorganization, Goldring had fifty-nine stores and leased departments.[56] The franchise, however, did not last another decade. The Canal Street Store closed in New Orleans in 1980.[57] Other stores and concessions soon followed. But the original Weiss and Goldring store in Alexandria founded one hundred three years ago by Morris J. Weiss and Dave Goldring, is, still to this day, in operation. The Goldring family enjoyed an unparalleled success, which, unfortunately was not the case with most small town merchants. Soon misfortune and death would hasten the demise of many of the Jewish mercantile establishments in Avoyelles Parish. Daughters would grow up and leave town with their husbands. The sons might stay on for a time to run the family business, but often would follow other relatives to larger cities where opportunities were more available.

***

The number of Jewish residents in Avoyelles Parish was declining by the time of the 1920 Federal Census. In Bunkie the Gross, Levy, Haas and Bloch families were still in town. Abe Rich's widow, Mina, and some of her children were still there as well. Of these Bunkie residents, only the Gross, Levy and Bloch families were observant Jews. David Siess, advanced in age, was no longer a merchant, but his son, Harry, a dentist, and his extended family still lived in Mansura. Several of the descendants of Leopold Siess, as well as of the Adolph and Charles Frank families, were living in Marksville, but none followed the Jewish religion. Schlessinger's store was still open in Marksville, with Simon now sixty-two, as the owner. With his daughter, Mary, now married and living in Chicago, Esther, deceased and Jacob working in Baltimore, only Ben, still single at age thirty-five, and Simon's wife, Libby, age fifty-seven, were at home in Marksville.[58] One block over, on Monroe Street, the widow Carrie Schreiber took care of her two young daughters, Sylvia Dora and Naomi, while her sons, Martie, age twenty-four and Julius, age twenty, ran the family store.[59] The Elster New York Bargain Store was still in business, run by Louis Elster. Annie Elster not only looked after the children, Claire Ruth, age eleven, and Rae, age nine, but she was the milliner at her husband's store, fashioning her hats at home.[60] The Elster girls were much sought after in the Marksville social whirl. As they grew to be teenagers in the second decade of the twentieth century, Rae, especially, who was an accomplished pianist, was often called on to perform locally. She was, notably, the piano accompanist for the exercises held in 1926 for the girls graduating both grammar and high school at the Presentation Convent, run by the Daughters of the Cross.[61]

Each year merchants from all over Louisiana attended a convention in New Orleans, run by the merchants' and manufacturers' division of the Association of Commerce. In August 1913 the *Daily Picayune* devoted several columns to this event, listing amongst the hundreds of others, "Louis Elster, general merchandise, Marksville," and further on, "Mrs. Louis Elster, millinery, Marksville." Another name cropped up in that article, that of Joseph B. Rosenberg, a merchant in Cottonport. [62] This Austrian immigrant, and former Brooklyn, New York resident, was Louis Elster's brother-in-law, married to Minnie Elster, Louis' youngest sister.

Joe, born according to his naturalization record on May 5, 1883, in the Austro-Hungarian Empire, arrived in New York in August 1892 at nine years of age. He became a citizen on October 9, 1905, and was employed in a factory as a cutter.[63] He married Minnie Elster on August 23, 1908, in Brooklyn, New York[64] where their first two children, Louis (b. 1910) and Saul (b. 1911), were born. Their arrival in Louisiana was announced in the *Daily Picayune*, which read "Mr. and Mrs. Joseph Rosenberg and children of New York arrived Tuesday," [65] They settled in Cottonport, where they bought a home and Joe opened up a dry goods store. Their last child, Ruth, was born there in 1919. In 1920 the family was prosperous enough that Joe had brought sixteen year old Edward Gueresko from New York to be his clerk, and he also employed Rose Russell, a black female, as a maid in his home.[66] He and his family, however, did not stay in Avoyelles Parish. After over a decade in Cottonport, by 1930 they had relocated back to New York. Joe opened a retail clothing store in Woodmere, Long Island, and the family rented a house in town.[67]

The first quarter of the twentieth century had been very difficult for the farmers and merchants of Avoyelles Parish, as cotton crops fell to the boll weevil plague throughout the south. In reporting the attendance to the August 1915 Merchants' and Manufacturers' Bureau buyers' convention, *The (New Orleans,) LA Daily Item* reported "For nearly a year the country merchant has been stocking up with only enough to get him through. The uncertainty of business conditions, the cotton situation, and other things that have kept him from buying any more than he actually had to. Now his shelves are pretty near empty. Fine crop prospects and the prospects of good prices for everything, except cotton, have put a little optimism into him." All in all, two hundred fifty merchants attended this convention, with fifty of them being women. The *Item* illustrated its piece with a large photo of seven year old Claire Ruth Elster and her five year old sister Rae, calling them the youngest buyers at the convention, who have "shrewd business judgment and could be counted on to drive hard bargains." [68]

During these hard times the Elster family sought to further bolster their income. Sporadic electric power had come to Marksville in 1903, with the charter of the Marksville Light and Ice Company. The first generating plant was powered by a steam boiler which burned cypress. In 1912 an oil engine plant was put into operation and Louis Elster became its manager for a short time. Interviewed before his death he described an undependable operation with only a few customers. There were times when the service was entirely satisfactory, and others when it would last for only an hour or so. Fuel oil was purchased by the barrel instead of in larger quantities. When the plant ran dry, the lights went out, until such time as, more oil could be bought, usually from the nearest cotton gin. The City of Marksville took over the operation in 1919 after a period of one or two years of no service at all. [69]

On Friday, December 30, 1921, the Elster store and residence burned to the ground, in a fire which, it was reported, had been started by sparks from an open fireplace. The amount of the loss was calculated to be, at least, $30,000. [70] The family, however, would not be deterred. They had both structures rebuilt and were back in business by the end of the next year. The Schlessinger family suffered a terrible loss, as well, when on October 26, 1922, Simon had a cerebral hemorrhage at his home at the age of sixty-five years, eleven months and fifteen days. Fellow merchant, and friend, Louis Elster, was listed as the "informant" on his death certificate. [71] An obituary in the local paper described Simon as "a prominent merchant [...] who had a large trade. He was known all over the parish, and he numbered his friends by the thousands." [72] He was buried the next day in the Jewish

Cemetery belonging to the Congregation B'nai Israel in nearby Pineville. This new Orthodox Jewish congregation has been founded in October 1913 in Rapides Parish because many Eastern European Jews who had settled in Central Louisiana had been unhappy with the liberal views of the older Temple Gemiluth Chassodim, located in Alexandria. None of the other Austro-Hungarian Jews who lived in Avoyelles Parish seem to have been associated with B'nai Israel as Simon was the only one of its Jewish citizens to have been buried there.[73]

Simon's succession was filed on November 2, 1922 on behalf of his widow, Libby Siegel, and his surviving children, Benjamin Schlessinger of Avoyelles Parish, Jacob Schlessinger of Baltimore, Maryland, and Mrs. Mary Schlessinger Bach, of Chicago, Illinois. The estate was valued at just over thirty-five thousand dollars (of which the ten thousand dollar value of one half of the commercial business owned by Simon's partner, his son, Benjamin, had already been subtracted.) In addition to the store, its stock, promissory notes, judgments and open accounts, there were three town lots in Marksville valued at $10,000, mortgage notes in the amount of over $6,000, twenty-four shares of stock in the Union Bank, fourteen shares of stock in the Avoyelles Bank and Trust, and lumber on hand worth $4,000. Subtracted from that amount was $3,400 which was to be returned to Jacob Schlessinger, who had lent money to his father for the family business and for safe keeping for himself.[74] The surviving Schlessinger family members did not remain in Avoyelles Parish.

***

A July 1923 advertisement for Big Yank work shirts in the *Times Picayune* is a good indication of which Jewish merchants were still open in Marksville and the surrounding towns. Ben Schlessinger who was still operating his late father's dry goods emporium in Marksville, would, before year's end, move away. The Herman Gross and Joe Weiss stores sold Big Yank shirts in Bunkie, as did Weiss and Goldring in nearby Alexandria. Simon Goldsmith, Ben Schlessinger's uncle by marriage, back in Louisiana from Baltimore, was listed as the merchant in Welsh, Louisiana who stocked this clothing line as well.[75]

In 1923, the Schreiber family attempted to sell their store, negotiating with a third party who ultimately could not come up with the cash. In January 1924 they took a notice in the local paper indicating that they would remain in business because so many of their friends had asked them not to close. They signed a contract with the American Service Corporation of New York City, a million dollar conglomerate, whose purpose was to keep the store stocked with merchandise to make sure that the people of the parish could have access to the latest fashions.[76]

Always strapped for cash in a poor economy, the Schreiber brothers came up with several clever schemes. They were not only trying to support a widowed mother, but were paying their little sister, Sylvia's tuition and board, at Newcomb College in New Orleans. In 1924 they raffled off several Ford Touring cars to bolster their business. A customer was given one ticket for each dollar of purchase and every dollar paid on account.[77] In 1926 Martie and Julius, faced with a downward spiraling economy both locally and nationally, attempted several large door-busting sales, in order to take the sting out of a new policy, which took effect on February 1, 1926. They no longer offered credit, or charge accounts, becoming a cash-only store. Prices were slashed accordingly to show the customer that this policy would be of benefit to everyone.[78] They took full page advertisements in the *Marksville Weekly News* to showcase their Hart Schaffner and Marx fall suits for $24.95, I. Miller slippers for $8.50, ladies hosiery at ten cents a pair, voile dresses for $3.75, and Stetson hats at $5.50 each, all of which had been personally selected by Carrie Schreiber who now lived in New York, and who " had her hand on the pulse of the fashion world." [79] On July 25, 1926, at the conclusion of the sale, the Schreiber brothers organized a huge picnic to thank their patrons. It was held on the banks of Bayou Bouté. They provided a truck load of food catered by Miss Bella Gremillion. With great food, swimming in the bayou, and iced watermelon and brick ice cream to finish off the party, the Schreiber's declared their appreciation to everyone for their patronage. A list of the attendees included members of the Bordelon, Barbin, Edwards, Ducôté, Guillot, Decuir, Roy, Couvillion, Coco Bernes,

Gosselin and Bergeron families.[80] Nevertheless, by the time of the stock market crash of 1929, the family had closed up the Louisiana store for good and moved to New York.

***

An examination of the 1930 census shows that the Louis Elster's were the only Jewish family remaining in Marksville. An article in a September 1931 issue of *The Marksville Weekly News* wished all the Jewish citizens of the area "Best Wishes" during the season of Yom Kippur, noting that the Elster family of Marksville's store, the "Elster's Quality Shop," would be closed on September 21st, the Day of Atonement.[81] There was no mention of anyone else as both the Schlessingers and the Schreibers had left the area. Simon's widow, Libby Schlessinger moved to Chicago in 1923 to live with her son-in-law and daughter, Bernard and Mary Schlessinger Bach, until her death on March 25, 1940. Libby was buried at Kanesses Israel in Forest Park, Cook Co., IL on March 27 1940.[82] Ben Schlessinger closed up the store in Marksville the same year and moved north as well. He and his family, Jeannette Feinberg, his wife of seven years, and his daughter, Shirley (b. 1924), were enumerated in the 1930 U.S. Census in Chicago, Illinois, where they rented an apartment. Ben worked as a real estate agent, for Gordon Strong, and Co., commercial realtors in South Central Chicago.[83] His phenomenal success up north was noted in a 1931 newspaper article in the *Marksville Weekly News*. He was the only broker in a deal which leased a vacant building with a total area of 58,000 square feet owned by the estate of N.K. Fairbank to the Kroll Baby Carriage manufacturers for a length of twelve years at a term rental of $153,000. Schlessinger also reported that three other real estate transactions completed by him pointed to a change in tenancy in the district which had been principally motor industries to miscellaneous businesses.[84]

The Schreiber family reassembled back in New York. Harry's widow, Carrie Schreiber, died there on August 28, 1934 at the age of fifty-seven. She was buried in the Schreiber family plot at the Union Field Jewish Cemetery in Ridgewood, Queens.[85] Her two sons, Julius and Martie, founded the Milmar Shops, Inc., a women's hosiery chain, whose offices were located in the Empire State Building in Manhattan. Martie was president of the firm, and Julius, its secretary-treasurer. Julius married Emily Hildenbrand and moved to New Jersey, where their daughter, Lynn Carol, and son, J. H Schreiber, were born. Julius was the first of Harry and Carrie's children to die, succumbing on August 6, 1948, while vacationing in Maine.[86]

Martie continued as President of the hosiery firm after his brother's death. He had, at the age of forty-seven, married Maurine Kaufman Raiff, a widow with two children, on February 10, 1944. The wedding took place at the Hotel Pierre in Manhattan and was conducted by Rabbi Nathan A. Perleman of Temple Emanu-El.[87] Maurine was the daughter of a small town southern merchant, Jacob Marcus Kaufman, of Columbus, Mississippi, and his wife, Estelle Levy, of Carroll County, Missouri. Jacob, born on January 17, 1874, was the second generation owner of the dry goods store founded by his father, Herman Kaufman[88] who had immigrated to the United States from Wachenheim, Bavaria, at the end of the Civil War, settling first in Mobile, Alabama where his eight children, including Jake, had been born.[89] Jake and Estelle had two daughters, both born in Columbus, Maurine in 1907 and Rosalyn in 1910.[90] Maurine had made an advantageous first marriage to Isidore Raiff, a Polish immigrant who was president of the Raylass Department Stores, a chain of low-priced variety establishments, which were located throughout the South. Several years after Maurine's marriage to Martie Schreiber, he was elected to the Board of Directors of Raylass, whose current president was Frederick Raiff, his stepson.[91] Martie and Maurine were married at least through the 1950s. When Martie died at the age of seventy-four on May 13, 1969, in New York City, the only next of kin listed was his sister, Sylvia Bensinger. He had been retired from Milmar Shops, and was buried in the family plot at the Union Field Jewish Cemetery.[92]

The Schreiber's youngest daughter, Naomi, studied at the University of California at Berkeley, as well as the University of Wisconsin. Upon returning to New York she had a brief marriage to

Julius (Jack) J. Spring, which was childless and ended in divorce. Naomi worked for many years at the New York Lighthouse for the Blind. Although the youngest, she was the first of the Schreiber children to die at the age of fifty-one on March 29, 1960, while on a trip to Dallas to visit her sister, Sylvia. Her remains were returned to New York for burial on April 1st in the family plot at Union Field Jewish Cemetery in Ridgewood, Queens.[93]

Sylvia Dora, the eldest Schreiber daughter, after graduation from Newcomb College in New Orleans, continued her education at the University of California. Returning to New York City where her mother and brothers were living, she became the assistant society editor for the *New York American*. At the age of thirty-five she married Edwin Milton Bensinger, a graduate of Northwestern University, who was employed in Dallas, Texas.[94] They were wed on February 6, 1941, in Dallas.[95] The Bensingers had one child, a daughter, Wendy Karen (b. 1943), who went on to marry F. Mitchell Dana in 1968.[96] Sylvia Dora was the last of the Schreiber siblings to die, passing away in Dallas on January 31, 1975, at the age of sixty-nine. She was also interred in the family plot at Union Field Jewish Cemetery in Ridgewood, Queens.[97]

***

Claire Ruth Elster was the first of Louis Elster's daughters to marry. She wed Bernard Joseph Averbach, an attorney from Pittsburgh, PA in 1929 and went there to live. Suzanne, their only child, was born in Pittsburgh in 1937.[98] Her sister, Rae, was married six years later on August 4, 1935, in New Orleans to Dr. Albert Moses Abramson, a Tulane University graduate in medicine, who had interned at the Touro Infirmary.[99] He and his brother, Samuel Ralph Abramson, seven years his junior, a 1938 graduate of Tulane, who also interned at Touro, had a profound effect on medicine in the Marksville area.

Samuel Abramson, Albert's grandfather, had emigrated in 1860, at the age of twenty-three, from Zurawie, Poland, northeast of Warsaw to Louisiana where he married Bertha Solomon, a Prussian immigrant. Sam became a dry goods merchant in Baton Rouge where five of his six children were born.[100] Before the birth of their last child, Nathan, on June 17, 1872,[101] Samuel moved his family to Arbroth in West Baton Rouge Parish where he became a retail grocer and prosperous planter. Arbroth, fifteen miles north of Port Allen, just on the other side of the Mississippi River from Baton Rouge had been, before the Civil War, the site of a large sugar and cotton plantation owned by the Sterling family, originally from Scotland. The Abramson children, Rosa, Abe, Daniel, Annie, Louis and Nathan and their families would continue to live and prosper in Louisiana.

Louis Abramson (b. 1868), in whose footsteps, his nephews, Albert and Samuel Ralph, would follow, worked until the age of twenty-three in stores and on plantations in and around Arbroth, until he was financially able to enter Tulane University to study medicine. Interning at both Shreveport and New Orleans Charity Hospitals, he opened his first office in New Orleans in 1898. He soon moved permanently to Shreveport where, in 1907, he founded the North Louisiana Sanitarium.[102] He and his wife, Bella Lowenstein, whom he married on October 14, 1902, in Waco, Texas, were lifelong residents of Shreveport.[103]

During the summer of 1897, Louis' youngest brother, Nathan (b. 1872), was on his own, living in Pointe Coupée Parish working as a merchant.[104] Because opportunities were scarce in this mostly agrarian parish, Nathan moved, just at the turn of the century, to Lafayette where he met and married Ula Coronna, the eldest daughter of Bruno Coronna, a native Missourian and his wife Jeannette Brown. The wedding took place on June 2, 1904, at the Crescent News Hotel in Lafayette under the direction of Rabbi Max Heller. Nathan's brother, Dr. Louis Abramson, was the best man.[105] Six children were born to Nathan and Ula, the eldest, Albert Moses on September 19, 1908, in Lafayette. Three sisters followed: Jeane in 1912, who died at the age of seven in 1919, Natalie, who was born on April 5, 1914, and Bertha, who joined the family on October 2, 1915.[106] Samuel Ralph Abramson, always called "Dr. Pete" by his friends and neighbors in Marksville, was born in Lafayette on March 12, 1917.[107] Nathan and Ula's last child, Janet Lucille Abramson, was born two years later.

Nathan and Ula's son, Albert, followed his Uncle Louis into the medical profession. He graduated from Lafayette High School in 1925 and went on to study at Tulane in New Orleans, graduating from their medical school in June 1932.[108] The following month he started his internship at Touro Infirmary.[109] After completing his studies, Dr. Abramson moved to Marksville and set up an office. Once in town, a young lady, some fifteen months his junior attracted his attention. Louis and Annie Elster's daughter, Rae, had returned from school in Pennsylvania, where she had been living with her sister, Claire Averbach. By this time the Elster family had been residents of Avoyelles Parish for more than thirty years, and their store was a fixture on Main Street. Albert and Rae were married on August 4, 1935, in New Orleans at the home of the groom's mother's sister and her husband, Isidore and Rosalie Coronna Gainsburgh. The ceremony was conducted by Rabbi Louis Binstock of Temple Sinai.[110]

Returning to Marksville to live, Albert and Rae Abramson welcomed two children, Steven Nathan (b. 1938), and Sara Jane (b. 1945). Albert had dreams of setting up a hospital/sanitorium much like his late uncle, Dr. Louis Abramson, had established in Shreveport, then being run by the latter's son, Dr. Paul Dowling Abramson. Moreover, Albert's brother, Ralph "Pete" Abramson, a medical student at Tulane would, he thought, soon be available to come in as a partner in the venture.

In 1938 Dr. Albert Abramson opened the first Marksville Hospital in a wooden building at the corner of Washington and Cappel.[111] In August 1939, Dr. S.R. "Pete" Abramson accepted, along with twenty other New Orleans physicians, an appointment in the Officers' Reserve Corps as first lieutenant in the medical reserve.[112] Upon graduation from Tulane Medical School, he was awarded an internship at the Touro Infirmary for the years 1940-41.[113] After his internship, he joined the U.S. Army as a Captain with the 64th General Hospital Portable Surgical Unit. Trained in anesthesiology at the Mayo Clinic in Rochester, MN, he was sent overseas to care for troops in North Africa and Italy. A partnership with his brother in Marksville was put on hold for the duration of the War.

On April 26, 1941, Louis Elster suffered a heart attack at his residence. His son-in-law, Dr. Albert Abramson, signed the death certificate. The next day Louis, the first of Samuel and Sarah Elster's children to die, was buried at the Jewish Cemetery in Lafayette.[114] Annie Kurtz Elster, his wife, retired from business, living out the rest of her life in Marksville. The era of the Jewish Mom and Pop operated dry goods and clothing stores had finally come to an end in the parish seat. The sole remaining Jewish-owned establishment was Rae Elster Abramson's husband's medical facility. In the spring of 1942, after four years of operation, Dr. Albert was able to move his Marksville Hospital to a brand new one story brick building north of the courthouse on Washington Street.[115] It was only open for a short time, because, following in his younger brother's footsteps, he was called to duty, joining the Army Medical Corps as a First Lieutenant in late 1942. He and his family moved, first to Fort Thomas, Kentucky, and later on to Camp Forrest, Tennessee, where he was promoted to Captain in July 1943. During his stint in the Army the Marksville Hospital was forced to close its doors for almost two years, finally reopening in 1945.[116] From that time on, the Abramson Brothers would dominate the medical scene in Avoyelles Parish.

In August 1946, Drs. Albert and Pete Abramson's father, Nathan, was brought from his home in Lafayette to the Marksville Hospital, where twenty-one days later, on September 21st he succumbed to pneumonia. Dr. Pete had the sad task of filling out his father's death certificate. The deceased's remains were brought back to Lafayette for burial in the Jewish Cemetery.[117]

***

The Second World War brought an end to Claire Ruth Elster Averbach's marriage. Ruth, the name she was always known by in Avoyelles Parish, and her daughter, Suzanne, moved temporarily to Marksville to be with her widowed mother. After her divorce from Bernard Averbach was final, she moved to New Orleans and went back to school at Soulé Business College where she graduated in July 1946 with a degree in shorthand.[118] Ruth remained in New Orleans, after her graduation from Soulé, where she met and married Maurice Pailet, a second generation real estate broker. His parents, Aron Louis Pailet and Rosine Sofnas, had emigrated from Vilna, Russia/Poland, he in 1900 and she in 1903, with their first born child, Albert.[119] Five other children were born in New Orleans where the couple settled, including Maurice on August 13, 1904.[120] Aron Pailet worked first as a peddler, then as a dry goods merchant. In the 1920s after several bad seasons, he left merchandising to try his hand at real estate. Maurice took over the now moderately successful business after his father's death on June 29, 1932.[121] Maurice was forty-three, and Ruth, thirty-nine, when they wed. Two daughters, Luise Adrienne (b. 1948), and Andrée Margot (b. 1949), were born to the couple in New Orleans. In addition, Suzanne Averbach, Ruth's daughter from her first marriage, adopted the Pailet surname.

On the February 21, 1951, Annie Kurtz Elster was taken to the Ochsner Foundation Hospital in Jefferson Parish, by her daughter, Claire Ruth Pailet. Suffering from hypertension and cardio vascular disease, she passed away just one month shy of her sixty-fourth birthday. She was buried the next day in the Hebrew Rest Cemetery #2 in New Orleans[122]

***

The Abramson brother's youngest sister, Janet Lucille Abramson, married John Leigh Dardenne, a fourth generation resident of Plaquemine (Iberville Parish), Louisiana, on December 9, 1950, at the Synagogue in Lafayette.[123] In the nineteenth century, the Dardenne family had been prosperous sugar cane and cotton planters. Two of John Arvilien Dardenne and his wife, Frances Clementine Desobry's ten children, had married into the family of Russian Jewish immigrant, and local store owner, Morris Marx, whose surname was always spelled "Marix" in the parish. Morris' wife, Azéma, was the Catholic daughter of one of the many "Comeaux" families that populated the area. Several of the Marix offspring followed the Jewish religion, while others took the religion of their Catholic mother. Morris' daughter, Cecilia Aline Marix, born in 1851, married John and Frances Desobre

Dardenne's eldest son, John, in 1872.[124] In turn, John and Cecilia's son, Teakle Wallis Dardenne, born on November 14, 1876,[125] wed Esther Cohn, daughter of Jewish immigrants, Meyer Cohn and his wife, Rosa Stern, who had emigrated from Warsaw, Poland. The Cohn's, like the Marix family before them, were dry goods merchants in Plaquemine, Louisiana. This series of interfaith marriages ultimately resulted in Teakle and Esther's son John Leigh Dardenne's marriage to Janet Abramson, and a strengthening of the Jewish line in the Dardenne family. John and Janet had two sons, Richard James and John Leigh Dardenne, Jr. The latter, known to Louisianans as "Jay" Dardenne, was elected to the office of Lieutenant Governor on November 2, 2010. He became the first person of Jewish faith to have held a statewide office since the nineteenth century. Although they never lived in Avoyelles Parish, the Dardenne family frequently visited Janet Abramson's brothers and their families in Marksville.

Nathan and Ula's youngest son, S.R. "Pete" Abramson, finally tied the knot on October 19, 1953, at the age of thirty-six. His bride was Gwendolyn Marguerite Daly, of Lafayette. She was thirty-one. They were married at Temple Sinai in New Orleans, by Rabbi Julian B. Feibelman. After honeymooning in Europe, the couple returned to Marksville, where Pete and Albert continued their stewardship of the Marksville Hospital for another two decades.[126]

Like the Jewish residents before them, the Abramson brothers were civic minded residents of Avoyelles Parish, involved in every aspect of their community. In 1936, both, for example, were elected to positions as directors of the Union Bank, and Dr. Albert was Chairman of the Board until shortly before his death in 1987. In appreciation for their development of the Marksville Hospital, Dr. Albert was made the grand marshal of the Sesquicentennial Parade celebrating the founding of the Parish seat in 1809. The parade, which took place on August 30, 1959, at the conclusion of a weeklong celebration, featured conveyances of all types, surreys, pony carts, covered wagons and even a black horse-drawn hearse. At its head was Dr. Albert Abramson, astride a large brown horse, dressed in a gold costume. [127]

Dr. Pete and his wife, Gwynn, who taught in the parish school system, became the parents of three children, Ralph Keith, Robert Coronna, and Suzanne Denise. Years older than his young cousins, Dr. Albert's son, Steven, a student at Tulane Medical School, soon followed in his father's and uncle's footsteps. After his internship at Touro Infirmary ended in June of 1963, Dr. Steven Abramson accompanied by his bride, Mathile Watsky, returned to Marksville to work in the hospital.[128] He and Mathile, a native of New Orleans and Hammond, Louisiana, had married the year before on June 2, 1962, in New Orleans in a ceremony conducted by Rabbi Julian Feibelman of Temple Sinai.[129] The future of the hospital seemed assured, as now there was a second generation Abramson on the staff.

Dr. Pete, always the more outgoing of the two Abramson brothers, and the father of three school age children, became a member of the Avoyelles Parish School Board. He was elected as its president in 1961, where in the wake of the strong anti-communist feelings of the cold war era, he advocated teaching civics and "patriotism" in school.[130] He also organized the first Chamber of Commerce. Active at the American Legion, he was chairman of its un-American activities committee. He eventually became its Eight District Commander.[131] Very conservative in his political views, he ran several times for public office, first for state representative in 1967, then for Congress in 1968 under the banner of the American Party headed by Presidential Candidate George Wallace and his running mate General Curtis LeMay.[132] As chairman of the American Party in Louisiana, and, after Wallace's defeat in 1968, he was also active in the short-lived attempt at organizing school boycotts in Avoyelles Parish during the turbulent days of desegregation. Dr. Pete tried one more run for Congress in 1972, as the American Party candidate for the Eighth District, but was defeated by Gillis Long.[133]

After almost thirty years of operation, the Abramsons sold the hospital to a national chain in 1969.[134] Dr. Albert's son, Dr. Steven Abramson, moved his family to Gonzales, Louisiana, where he practiced medicine for many years. Dr. Albert, though he retired from medicine in 1971, remained active in banking, living in Marksville for the rest of his life. Unfortunately his more than thirty year marriage to Rae Elster came to a painful end. With his son in Gonzales, and daughter, Dr. Sara Jane Abramson, living in Kansas City, Kansas with her husband, Allan Block, he remarried a seventh generation Avoyellean, Emma Rita Lemoine, a Catholic divorcee with four daughters.

Rae Elster Abramson died on June 4, 1979, after suffering a massive stroke at her home in Marksville. Her son, Dr. Steven Abramson, and daughter, Dr. Sara Jane Abramson, were at her side, along with her sister, Ruth Pailet, now divorced from Maurice, who had been living with her sister in Marksville. Rae was interred next to her parents, Louis and Annie Kurtz Elster, at Hebrew Rest # 2 Cemetery in New Orleans. Her eulogy, which was written by her children and read by her son-in-law, Allan Block, celebrated her Jewish roots. "We feel," her son and daughter said, "that we came from a very Jewish home. She instilled in us a very deep sense of Jewish identity and stressed not only the religious and cultural aspects of our heritage, but the moral ones as well. She also taught us to respect those whose beliefs are different from our own." [135] Rae Elster was sixty-nine years old. Ruth Pailet subsequently moved west to Phoenix, Arizona, to be near her daughter, Luise Adrienne Pailet Tovar. Ruth died at the age of seventy-seven in Maricopa County in 1984.[136]

After many years in predominately Christian Avoyelles Parish, Dr. Pete had often told friends that he was considering joining the Catholic Church, but didn't dare make a move as long as his mother was still living. Others tell the story that stricken with a malignant tumor, he was saved by the fervent prayers of the community he loved so much. The residents of Avoyelles Parish filled the churches and lit candles for his recovery. When the tumor disappeared, he considered it a miracle and a sign which, at the appropriate time, would lead to his conversion. He loved the holiday season, and decorating was definitely part of it. Each year his and Gwenn's home had been decked out for Christmas. In fact, in 1965 he and his family had won the grand prize in the town's annual Christmas lighting contest sponsored by the Marksville Garden Club.[137] But it was not until after Ula Coronna

Abramson's death on October 2, 1975, in Lafayette, that Dr. Pete finally took the step to embrace the Catholic faith.[138] During his retirement in the 1970s until he finally left Avoyelles Parish in 1984 he wrote a weekly political column in the *Avoyelles Journal*, entitled "Out of Pete's Pistol." His son, Robert, graduated from Louisiana State University Medical School, and took his residency training in neurosurgery at the University of Alabama in Birmingham. Robert married Dana Margaret Wilhelmi in 1984 at a Catholic service at St. Mary's on the Hill Church, and the couple remained in Birmingham where he became a successful neurosurgeon.[139] His son, Ralph, who changed his name to Daryl S. Turk, left Avoyelles Parish and began working in Baton Rouge. His daughter, Suzanne, also left the Parish to wed. Just as Albert and Rae's marriage had foundered, his and Gwen's did as well. She stayed on in the house on South Washington Street in Marksville, and Pete returned to live in Lafayette, where he married Bella Nickerson, widow of Colonel Richard D. Chappuis, Sr. in 1985. Bella, a Lafayette native, was a member of the Judice family, southwest Louisiana pioneers. The Abramsons resided in the Nickerson family home in Sterling Grove. Both devout Catholics, they were staunch supporters of the Church and Catholic education. They were also active participants in the Southwest Louisiana Mardi Gras Association.[140]

  Dr. Albert died in Marksville at the family residence on Monday October 19, 1987. He was seventy-nine years old. Surviving were his second wife, Emma Lemoine Abramson, his two children, six grandchildren, his brother, Dr. Pete and three sisters. He was waked at Hixson Bros. Funeral Home in town and buried in the Jewish Cemetery at Lafayette.[141] Emma died nine months later on July 8, 1988. Father Gerald Bordelon officiated at the service in Hixson Brother's chapel, followed by burial alongside her husband in the Jewish Cemetery in Lafayette.[142] Dr. Pete died ten years later on December 31, 1997, at Our Lady of Lourdes Regional Medical Center in Lafayette, at the age of eighty. A Mass of Christian burial was held on January 2, 1998, in St. Geneviève Catholic Church, with interment at the Cavalry Mausoleum of the Resurrection. He was remembered as a devoted physician who had treated tens of thousands of people in Avoyelles parish, and had delivered almost five thousand babies. He was especially beloved for his devotion to Marksville, and to the promotion of its welfare, and as the originator of the biggest Fourth of July Parade that the town had ever had.[143]

The small medical facility that Dr. Albert started in 1938 on the site of the old Adolph Frank hotel, staffed by himself, his brother, Pete, his son, Steven, and others throughout the years evolved into the modern Avoyelles Hospital which is now located just outside of Marksville off State Highway 107 on the Blue Town Road. It is a monument to the continuing influence that the Abramson brothers had and continue to have in this community.

Today in Avoyelles Parish there are many descendants of the original antebellum Jewish immigrants, the Siess and Haas Brothers, the Goudchaux family, Abe Felsenthal, and Charles and Adolph Frank. But none of them follow the Jewish religion, and many do not even know about this part of their heritage. The link to Judaism was lost with the first immigrant generation who married into the prominent Catholic families in the area. The post-Civil War Jewish residents, including those who came in the early twentieth century, the Karpe and Levy families of Evergreen, the Bloch, Weiss, and Rich families of Bunkie, the Schreiber, Elster, Schlessinger and Abramson families of Marksville, the Rosenberg's of Cottonport prospered, but most did not stay. They moved on, or if they stayed, their children moved on to other towns in Louisiana, or other cities in America. They sought out co-religionists with whom to marry, and held on for a generation or perhaps longer to their Jewish heritage and identity.

After World War II several of the members of the Goudchaux family still lived in Avoyelles Parish. Leona, grand-daughter of Leopold and Charlotte Eilert Goudchaux, married Moses Rosenthal Firnberg a descendant of two nineteenth century Rapides Parish Jewish families. The couple, childless, were longtime Bunkie merchants, before moving to Alexandria. Moses ran for mayor of Bunkie in 1958 and only lost by one vote. Another Goudchaux descendant, Sarah, daughter of Leopold Goudchaux and his second wife, Flora Marx, married Sol B. Mayer. Their only son, Solly B. Mayer, born in Big Cane on July 4, 1918, though Jewish, married Ruth Angerer, who followed the Methodist religion. Solly, who died in 2005, was a retired Lieutenant Colonel in the U.S. Marine Corps, and a decorated veteran of both World War II, and the Korean conflict He owned and operated Hoover's Café on Main Street in Bunkie from 1953-1965, where his catfish won first prize for many years.[144] Solly B. and Ruth's three sons were raised as Christians. The youngest, Guy Andrew Mayer, still lives in the Parish with his wife, Regina, née Kojis.

As of the writing of this book, there is but one practicing Jew in Avoyelles Parish. James Roy Levy came to Bunkie in 1962 as the owner and publisher of the *Bunkie Record.* Jim is a third generation Louisianan, whose great grandparents Lazarus Levy and his wife, Frimmit Plonsky, had emigrated separately from Russia/Poland at the close of the Civil War. They met and married in New Orleans, settling first in Abbeville, then Lafayette, Louisiana. The seven Plonsky siblings were from Golub, Poland. Frimmit's brothers and sister, Edward, Hannah and Jacob were lifelong residents of Washington, Louisiana, in nearby St. Landry Parish. Joseph, Mary and Leon Plonsky settled in Lafayette near the Lazarus Levy family. Jim's grandparents, Armand Levy, Lazarus and Frimmit's first born son, and his wife Lena Bendel, settled in Lake Charles, where Jim's father, Florian Levy, was born in 1895. Florian married a young woman from Texas, who despite the unlikely name of Minnie Pearl Williams, was the Jewish daughter of Russian immigrant, Barney Williams, who birth name was Sheftelowitz. Florian and Minnie's son, James Roy Levy, was born in 1934 in Lake Charles where his father was first a clothing merchant, then the owner/operator of a rice farm, and finally the proprietor of an office supply house. Jim, who attended L.S.U. and graduated in journalism, met and married Lois David, daughter of an old established Catholic family from Rayne, Louisiana. After college he joined the Army, where he became the editor of the *Fort Bliss News*. Reentering civilian life, Jim and his family moved from Baton Rouge, where he was a sports writer for *The Advocate*. After a stint in New Iberia, his editor, who knew he had always wanted to own a small town newspaper, received word that the *Bunkie Record* was for sale. Financing for the paper was through private and bank sources which together provided the down payment for the $48,000 purchase in 1962. Jim owned and operated the newspaper until his retirement in 1987. In an interview conducted at the close of 2010, Jim was asked what he considered to be his most important contribution to the future of Avoyelles Parish. He explained that as he got to know his neighbors he realized that he was far more liberal than most, in what is considered to be a very conservative Central Louisiana parish. Yet his editorial views had, over the years, never put him in direct conflict with the local populace. Even during the turbulent years of desegregation, when Bunkie town leaders had vowed to set up a private school in order to circumvent the new Federal law, Jim and his paper sought to change public opinion. The *Bunkie Record* started running a series of twenty different endorsements of the new school integration policy, starting with himself (as editor), followed by the president of the local Bank. With photos ablaze on the front page of each issue, along with the written endorsements from eighteen other prominent businessmen, the Bunkie schools integrated with no trouble. As for the most amusing story, Jim recounted that his friendship with Democrat Sheriff of Avoyelles Parish, F.O. "Potch" Didier, gave him a front row seat at a feud between Didier and District Attorney Charles Riddle, Sr., which culminated in the former's trial for malfeasance in office pursuant to charges brought by Riddle. After a spectacular trial which made the front page of every local paper for a week, Didier was convicted and sentenced to 90 days, seven of which he actually served in his own jail in Marksville. On the first night Didier prepared an andouille gumbo in his cell, which he and his friends, including Jim shared. Didier was subsequently elected twice more as the Sheriff of Avoyelles Parish.

After almost fifty years in Avoyelles Parish, Jim Levy and his wife, Lois, who raised five children in the Parish vow never to leave. As a Jew he has never suffered any significant anti-Semitic treatment. Although there has never been a near-by synagogue, or a Jewish burial ground in the Parish, he is content to travel, as did others before him to

Rapides, St. Landry or Lafayette parishes to follow the precepts of his religion.

---

[1] "Society," *The New Orleans (Louisiana) Item*, 16 March 1902, p. 2, col 2, digital image, *Genealogybank.com* (http://www.genealogybank.com [hereinafter cited as "GB"]: accessed 10/ 2010).

[2] Tarnów was part of the Polish Empire until 1772 when it was annexed by Hapsburg Austria. It remained under Austrian control until after World War I, when it was returned to Poland in 1918.

[3] Some Franco/German families emigrated eastward during the Napoleonic wars to escape the fighting, naming towns in Russia, Strassburg, Seltz, and Baden, after places they had left behind in Alsace and Germany. Many were Catholic, but some were Jewish such as Kalman Goldring and his wife from Strassburg.

[4] "New York Passenger Lists, 1820-1957," digital image, *Ancestry.com* (http://www.ancestry.com [hereinafter cited as "A"]: accessed 9/ 2010), citing NARA microfilm publication M237, roll 507. Manifest of *SS Suevia*, 31 May 1887, p. 4, line 212. Kallman Goldring, age 40.

[5] "New York Passenger Lists, 1820-1957, " digital image, (A: accessed 9/ 2010), citing NARA microfilm publication M237, roll 551. Manifest of *SS Westernland*, 16 July 1890, p. 11, lines 377-385. Mina Goldring (35), Libe (20), David (11), Abraham (9), Malke (8), Josef (7), Ilte (6), Louis (3), Alte (1).

[6] Jeraldine DuFour LaCour, *Avoylleans of Yesteryear* (Alexandria, Louisiana: Jeraldine DuFour LaCour, [P.O. Box 5022, Alexandria, LA], 1983), 122.

[7] 1892 New York State Census, Erie County, pop. sch., Buffalo, Ward 7, ED 2, p. 8 (penned), Dwelling (blank), Family (blank), Joseph Elster household, *Familysearch.org* (http://www.familysearch.org [hereinafter cited as "F"]: accessed 9/ 2010), citing FHL microfilm 0825693. Date of enumeration: 16 February 1892.

[8] "World War I Draft Registration Cards, 1917-1918," digital image, (A: accessed 10/ 2010), Samuel Elster, No. 24, Draft Board 3, New Orleans, Orleans Parish, Louisiana, citing NARA microfilm publication M 1509, no roll given, FHL microfilm roll 1684916.

[9] Louisiana State University Libraries On Line Catalog, Special Collections, Louisiana and Lower Mississippi Valley, (hereinafter cited as "LLMV"), Microfilm, # 5976, "Elster Bros. Advertisement," *The Avoyelles Blade*, 11 March 1899, Vol. 9, no. 11, p. 2 cols. 6, 7.

[10] 1900 U.S. Census, Avoyelles Parish, Louisiana, pop. sch., Marksville, Ward 2, ED 13, p. 36 A (penned), Dwelling #640, Family #640, Joseph Elster household, digital image, (A: accessed 10/ 2010), citing NARA microfilm publication T623, roll 558. Date of enumeration: 29 June 1900.

[11] *Ibid.*, Dwelling and Family #641, Thomas Elster household; and p. 36B (penned), Dwelling and Family #648, Moses Slesinger (sic), digital images (A: accessed 10/2010), citing NARA microfilm publication T623, roll 558. Date of enumeration: 29 June 1900.

[12] 1900 U.S. Census, Jefferson Co., Kentucky, pop. sch., Louisville, Ward 5, ED 49, p. 12B (penned), Dwelling #127, Family #307, Simon Goldsmith household, digital image, (A: accessed 10/ 2010), citing NARA microfilm publication T623, roll 530. Date of enumeration: 12 June 1900.

[13] "Kentucky Death records, 1852-1923," digital image, (A: accessed 10/ 2010), citing *Kentucky Birth and D eath Records: Covington, Lexington, Louisville and Newport Microfilm (Before 1911)*, No roll stated. Kentucky Department for Libraries and Archives, Frankfort, Kentucky. Certificate for Jacob Schlesinger (1903).

[14] *Ibid.*, Certificate of Sarah Schlesinger (sic), 1912.

[15] "World War I Draft Registration Cards, 1917-1918," digital image, (A: accessed 10/2010), Emanuel Martie Schreiber, No. 111, Draft Board "O," Avoyelles Parish, Louisiana, citing NARA microfilm publication M 1509, no roll given, FHL microfilm roll 1653580.

[16] State of New York, Certificate and Record of Birth, City of New York, Certificate No. 12146 (1899), Jules Schrieber (sic); photocopy obtained from The City of New York Municipal Archives, Manhattan, New York.

[17] 1900 U.S. Census, New York, New York, pop. sch., Manhattan, ED 371, p. B-5 (penned), Dwelling #11, Family #88, Harry Schreiber household, digital image, (A: accessed 10/ 2010), citing NARA microfilm publication T623, roll 1098. Date of enumeration: 2 June 1900.

[18] Jan and Naomi McPeek, *Merchants, Tradesmen and Manufacturers Financial Condition for 1902 Avoyelles Parish Louisiana.* Image reprint. The 1902 R.G. Dun Mercantile Agency Reference Book, (Salem, OH: Aaron's Books, 2005), Marksville, 6.

[19] 1905 New York State Census, Erie County, pop. sch., Buffalo, Ward 13, ED 1, p. 56 (penned), Dwelling and Family (blank), Meyer Greenfield household, (F: accessed 7/2010), citing FHL microfilm 0825698. Date of enumeration: 1 June 1905.

[20] Louisiana State Board of Health, Bureau of Vital statistics, Certificate of Death #2023 (1951), Anne E. Kurtz Elster; photocopy obtained from Louisiana Secretary of State, Department of Archives, Records Management and History, Baton Rouge, LA.

[21] Social Security Administration, "U.S. Social Security Death Index," database, (A: accessed 10/ 2010), entry for Ruth Pailet, (1984).

[22] 1905 New York State Census, Erie County, pop. sch., Buffalo, Ward 13, ED 2, p. 9 (penned), Dwelling and Family (blank), Thomas Elster household, (F:accessed 10/ 2010), citing FHL microfilm 0825698. Date of enumeration: 1 June 1905. (Note: Freida and Bertha Elster are located on page 10, which was microfilmed out of order. The address for the family was 65 Brown Street)

[23] "U.S. City Directories, Buffalo, Erie County, New York (1956)," digital image, (A: accessed 10/ 2010), citing *Polk's Buffalo (Erie County, N.Y.) City Directory 1956, Including Kenmore*, entry for Thos. Elster Co. (Robert S. Elster), p. 283.

[24] Social Security Administration. "U.S. Social Security Death Index," database, (A: accessed 10/ 2010), entry for Martin Elster (1989).

[25] Social Security Administration. "U.S. Social Security Death Index," database, (A: accessed 10/ 2010), entry for Rheuben Elster (1984).

[26] "Louisiana Statewide Death Index 1900-1949," database , (A: accessed 10/ 2010), citing State of Louisiana, Secretary of State, Division of Archives, Records Management, and History. *Vital Records Indices*. Baton Rouge, LA. Death of Mary Elster (1935).

[27] "Retired Merchant of Houma Expires," *TP*, 27 April 1950, p. 2, col 6, digital image, (GB: accessed 10/ 2010). Note: Regarding Joseph's other children: Bertha married Sam Burglass, an Austrian immigrant who worked in a family furniture business in New Orleans. She died on December 17, 1940 leaving three children, Irving, Nathan and Sarah Rae. Sadie Elster married Charles Davis, also an Austrian immigrant. Charles, a jewelry salesman, Sadie and their children, Faye Ann and Beverly, were living in Buffalo, New York in 1930. Sadie Elster Davis died on May 12, 1939 at Houma, LA.

[28] Social Security Administration. "U.S. Social Security Death Index," database, (A: accessed 10/ 2010), entry for Martin Elster (1989).

[29] Social Security Administration. "U.S. Social Security Death Index," database, (A: accessed 10/ 2010), entry for Rae Abramson (1979).

[30] "Marksville," *The (New Orleans, LA) Daily Picayune* (hereinafter cited as "*DP*"), 22 July 1906, p. 19, col 7, digital image, (GB: accessed 10/ 2010).

[31] "Marksville," *DP*, 29 December 1907, p. 39, col 7, digital image, (GB: accessed 10/2010). Note: Simon and Rosa Schlessinger Goldsmith moved from Baltimore to Welsh, Jefferson Davis Parish, LA and appear in the 1920 and 1930 censuses.

[32] 1910 U.S. Census, Avoyelles Parish, Louisiana, pop. sch. Marksville, Ward 2, ED 14, p. 24 B (penned), Dwelling #388, Family #389, Maurice Schlessinger household; Dwelling #389, Family #390, Harry Schreiber

household; Dwelling #390, Family #391, Simon Schlessinger household, digital image, (A: accessed 10/ 2010), citing NARA microfilm publication T624, roll 508. Date of Enumeration: 4 May 1910. Note: Francis, the Schlessinger's adopted orphan, may have been one of the children who came to Avoyelles Parish on the 1907 Orphan Train from the New York Foundling Home.

[33] LLMV, Microfilm #1032, *Avoyelles Enterprise*, Marksville, Avoyelles Parish, Louisiana, Vol. VIII, no. 50, 7 May 1910, p. 2, cols. 1, 2.

[34] Randy DeCuir, *Marc's Government, Town Government 1843-2009,* Volume II (Marksville, Louisiana: Avoyelles Publications, 2009), 86.

[35] "Graduates of Avoyelles High School," *DP*, 31 May 1908, p. 26, cols. 3-5, digital image, (GB: accessed 10/ 2010).

[36] "New Orleans, Louisiana Marriage Records Index 1831-1925," database, (A: accessed 11/ 2010), citing State of Louisiana, Secretary of State, Division of Archives, Records Management and History. *Vital Records Indices*. Baton Rouge, LA. Entry for Rita Mary Schlessinger and Bernard Bach.

[37] 1930 U.S. Census, Cook County, Illinois, pop. sch. Chicago, ED 184, p. 10 B (penned), No dwelling stated, Family #230, Bernard Bach household, digital image, (A: accessed 11/2010), citing NARA microfilm publication T626, roll 422. Date of enumeration: 9 April 1930.

[38] Rabbi Martin I. Hinchin, D.D., *Fourscore and Eleven, A History of the Jews of Rapides Parish 1828-1919* (Alexandria, Louisiana: McCormick Graphics, 1984,) 152. Although there are several towns of that name in Louisiana, this is probably Clear Creek in Grant Parish, about eight miles southwest of Pollock. M. Schlessinger is buried in Row 12 at the Jewish Cemetery, Pineville, Rapides Parish, LA.

[39] "World War I Draft Registration Cards, 1917-1918," digital image, (A: accessed 10/2010), Nathan Schlessinger, Serial No. 318, Order No., A2493, Draft Board "3," Jefferson Co. Kentucky, citing NARA microfilm publication M 1509, no roll given, FHL Roll #1653508.

⁴⁰ Louisiana State Board of Health, Bureau of Vital statistics, Certificate of Death #18350 (1915), Harry Schreiber; photocopy obtained from Louisiana Secretary of State, Department of Archives, Records Management and History, Baton Rouge, LA. Note: Schreiber's parents are listed as Rafael Schreiber and B. Singer, both born in Austria.

⁴¹ "Jewishgen Online Worldwide Burial Registry," database , *Jewishgen.org* (http://www.jewishgen.org: accessed 10/ 2010), entry for Harry Schreiber (1915), Dispersed of Judah Cemetery, Row 10, Plot 222A, New Orleans, Orleans Parish, LA. Note: Schreiber's place of birth is indicated as Bymanów, Galicia, Austria. This is, most likely, Rymanów, an understandable spelling error.

⁴² "Society News - Notes," *The New Orleans (Louisiana) Item*, 3 May 1915, p. 7, col. 6, digital image, (GB: accessed 10/ 2010).

⁴³ "Judge Coco will Appoint His Son," *The (New Orleans, LA) Daily States*, 2 May 1916, p. 14, col. 1, digital image, (GB: accessed 10/ 2010).

⁴⁴ State of North Carolina, Buncombe County, North Caroline Standard Certificate of Death #19793 (1919), death certificate of Esther Schlessinger, digital image, (F: accessed 10/2010), Digital Film # 1892498.

⁴⁵ "Maryland Military Men, 1917-1919," database, (A: accessed 11/ 2010), citing *Maryland in the World War, 1917-1919; Military and Naval Service Records*. Vol. I – II, Baltimore, MD; Twentieth Century Press, 1933. Record for Jacob Schlessinger born May 10, 1889, Louisville, KY; Also, "Casualties of World War I from Pittsylvania County & Danville 305th Engineers Regimental History – 1918," *Rootsweb.com* (http://www.rootsweb.ancestry.com./ - vapittsy/320.html: accessed 11/ 2010). Transcription of papers handed down to his grandson by Richard Dewitt Gardner.

⁴⁶ 1930 U.S. Census, Baltimore County, Maryland, pop. sch. Baltimore City, ED 251, p. 2B (penned), Dwelling #36, Family #42, Isadore Sachs household, digital image, (A: accessed 11/2010), citing NARA microfilm publication T626, roll 860. Date of enumeration: 3 April 1930.

[47] Mr. Harry Silver, Miriam Weiss Levy's daughter Marilyn's husband, is the current chairman of the board of Weiss and Goldring. He consented to a short interview with the author by telephone on the morning of November 7, 2007, where he explained the reasons for the amicable dissolution of the partnership. See Chapter 9, pp. 340-348 of this book concerning the Weiss family and the Weiss and Goldring store.

[48] "Goldring to Open Under Own Name," *The New York Times*, 14 September 1955, digital image, *Nytimes.com* (http:// www.nytimes.com: accessed 11/ 2010)

[49] "Goldring Rites Set for Today," *TP*, 23 July 1958 , p. 5, col 4, See also: "Hour-Glass Mode Shown In Parade; Living Mannequins Display New Creations in Exhibit at Godchaux's," *TP*, 27 September 1932, p. 16, col. 6, digital images, (GB: accessed 10/ 2010). Note: Julius was Sam and Gisela Elias Weiss' son.

[50] "Goldring Rites Slated in New York," *TP*, 19 April 1961, p. 1, col. 4, digital image, (GB: accessed 10/ 2010).

[51] "David Goldring – Founder of Women's Clothing Shop Chain is Dead in Florida," *The New York Times*, 9 February 1943, digital image, *Nytimes.com* (http://www.nytimes.com: accessed 2/ 2010).

[52] See note 49.

[53] See note 50.

[54] "Goldstein Will Join N. O. Store," *TP*, 7 July 1961, p. 36, cols. 2, 3, digital image, (GB: accessed 10/ 2010).

[55] Social Security Administration. "U.S. Social Security Death Index," database, (A: accessed 10/ 2010), entry for Rosa Goldring (1962).

[56] "Goldring on Road to Recovery," *TP*, 22 October 1975, p. 22, col. 6, digital image, (GB: accessed 10/ 2010).

[57] "A Final Message from Goldring's Canal Street Store," *TP*, January 1980, p. 73, cols.4-6, digital image, (GB: accessed 10/ 2010).

[58] 1920 U.S. Census, Avoyelles Parish, Louisiana, pop. sch. Marksville, Ward 2, ED 2, p. 2 A (penned), Dwelling #20, Family #24, Simon Slessinger household, digital image, (A: accessed 11/ 2010), citing NARA microfilm publication T625, roll 605. Date of enumeration: 2 January 1920.

[59] 1920 U.S. Census, Avoyelles Parish, Louisiana, pop. sch. Marksville, Ward 2, ED 2, p. 5B (penned), Dwelling #96, Family #110, Carrie Schreiber household, digital image, (A: accessed 11/ 2010), citing NARA microfilm publication T625, roll 605. Date of enumeration: 2 January 1920.

[60] 1920 U.S. Census, Avoyelles Parish, Louisiana, pop. sch. Marksville, Ward 2, ED 2, p. 3B (penned), Dwelling #59, Family #66, Louis Elster household, digital image, (A: accessed 11/ 2010), citing NARA microfilm publication T625, roll 605. Date of enumeration: 2 January 1920.

[61] "Commencement Exercises of Local Convent," *The Marksville (Louisiana) Weekly News*, 29 May 1926, Vol. 23, no. 18, p.1, col 6. Back issue consulted 12/2010, at *Marksville Weekly News* Office, Main Street, Marksville, LA.

[62] "Merchants Crowd to Buy Fall Goods in the Best Place," *DP*, 19 August 1913, p. 1, col 7 and p. 3, cols. 1-3, digital images, (GB: accessed 9/2010).

[63] "Index to Petitions for Naturalization filed in New York City, 1792-1989," database, (A: accessed 9/2010), citing *Soundex Index to Petitions for Naturalization filed in Federal, State, and Local Courts located in New York City, 1792-1989*. New York, NY, USA: NARA, Northeast Region. Index card # R251 for Joseph B. Rosenberg, naturalized on October 9, 1905, Vol. 75, record no. 144.

[64] "Vital records: New York City Groom," database, *Italiengen.org* (http://www.italiangen.org: accessed # 9/ 2010), Joseph Rosenberg entry. (Certificate # 6571).

[65] "Cottonport," *DP*, 8 December 1912, p. 48, col. 1, digital image, (GB: accessed 9/ 2010).

[66] 1920 U.S. Census, Avoyelles Parish, Louisiana, pop. sch. Cottonport, Ward 9, ED 14, p. 15B (penned), Dwelling #291, Family #291, Joe B. Rosenberg household, digital image, (A: accessed 11/ 2010), citing NARA microfilm publication T625, roll 605. Date of enumeration: 22 January 1920.

[67] 1930 U.S. Census, Nassau County, pop. sch. Hempstead Township, Woodmere, ED 116, p. 11B (penned), Dwelling #215, Family #259, Joseph B. Rosenberg household, digital image, (A: accessed 11/ 2010), citing NARA microfilm publication T626, roll 1460. Date of enumeration: 15 April 1930.

[68] "Local Merchants and Manufacturers Cashing In on Buyers' Convention," *The (New Orleans, LA) Daily Item*, 24 August 1915, p. 2, cols. 2-4, digital image, (GB: accessed 9/ 2010).

[69] Randy DeCuir, *Marc's Government, Town Government 1843-2009*, Volume II, 97.

[70] "Killing of Intruder Justified at Alexandria," *TP*, 1 January 1922, p. 49, col. 6, digital image, (GB: accessed 9/ 2010).

[71] Louisiana State Board of Health, Bureau of Vital statistics, Certificate of Death #11182 (1922), Simon Schlessinger; photocopy obtained from Louisiana Secretary of State, Department of Archives, Records Management and History, Baton Rouge, LA. Note: Simon's parents are listed as Gedalia Schlessinger from Russia and Sarah (last name unknown), also from Russia.

[72] Undated clipping from unknown newspaper attached to death certificate for Simon Schlessinger. See note 71.

[73] "B'nai Israel Jewish Cemetery in Pineville, Rapides Parish," database, *Rootsweb.com* (http://www.rootsweb.com/~usgenweb/la/rapides.htm: accessed 9/ 2010). Entry for Schlessinger (1856-1922).

[74] Avoyelles Parish Courthouse Records, (Marksville, Avoyelles Parish, LA), *Probates*, Book Q, p. 210-216, "Succession of Simon Schlessinger," filed 2 November 1922.

[75] "Big Yank Work Shirts," *TP*, 22 July 1923, p. 22, cols. 3-7, digital image, (GB: accessed 9/ 2010).

[76] "To Our Friends and Patrons," *The Marksville (Louisiana) Weekly News*, 18 January 1924, Vol. 15, no. 39, p. 4, cols. 4-6. Back issue consulted 12/2010, at *Marksville Weekly News Office*, Main Street, Marksville, LA.

[77] "Schreiber and Son's First Fall Sale," *The Marksville (Louisiana) Weekly News*, 5 September 1924, Vol. 16, no. 22, p.7, cols. 4-6. Back issue consulted 12/2010, at *Marksville Weekly News Office*, Main Street, Marksville, LA.

[78] "Schreiber and Son's – Cash Only," *The Marksville (Louisiana) Weekly News,* 30 January 1926, Vol. 23, no. 3, p.1, cols. 2- 5. Back issue consulted 12/2010, at *Marksville Weekly News* Office, Main Street, Marksville, LA.

[79] "Schreiber's Greatest Sale," *The Marksville (Louisiana) Weekly News*, 17 July 1926, Vol. 23, no. 24, p.4. Back issue consulted 12/2010, at *Marksville Weekly News* Office, Main Street, Marksville, LA.

[80] " S. G. S. Picnic," *The Marksville (Louisiana) Weekly News*, 30 July 1926, Vol. 23, no. 26, p.4, col 1. Back issue consulted 12/2010, at *Marksville Weekly News* Office, Main Street, Marksville, LA.

[81] " New Year celebrated By Jewish Population," *The Marksville (Louisiana) Weekly News*, 19 September 1931, Vol. 28, no. 30, p. 1, col 4. Back issue consulted 12/2010, at *Marksville Weekly News* Office, Main Street, Marksville, LA.

[82] "Illinois Deaths and Stilbirths 1916-1947," database, Certificate No. m9333, (1940), death certificate of Libby Schlessinger, (F: accessed 10/2010) Digital Film # 1953576.

[83] 1930 U.S. Census, Cook County, pop. sch. Chicago, Ward 35, ED 1201, p. 23A (penned), Dwelling #290, Family #482, Benjamin Schlessinger household, digital image, (A: accessed 11/ 2010), citing NARA microfilm publication T626, roll 468. Date of enumeration: 18 April 1930.

[84] "Read a Few Words about Ben Schlessinger," *The Marksville (Louisiana) Weekly News*, 21 February 1931, Vol. 28, no. 8, p.4, col 2. Back issue consulted 12/2010, at *Marksville Weekly News* Office, Main Street, Marksville, LA.

[85] "Deaths - Schreiber, Carrie," *The New York Times*, 28 August 1934, digital image, *Nytimes.com* (http:// www.nytimes.com: accessed 11/ 2010).

[86] "Julius Schreiber," *The New York Times*, 9 August 1948, digital image, *Nytimes.com* (http://www.nytimes.com: accessed 11/ 2010).

[87] "Mrs. Maurine K. Raiff is Wed," *The New York Times*, 11 February 1944, digital image, *Nytimes.com* (http://www.nytimes.com: accessed 11/ 2010).

[88] "Friendship Cemetery, Jewish Section, Columbus, Lowndes Co., MS," database, *Usgwarchives.net* (http://files.usgwarchives.net: accessed 9/2010), entry for Herman Kaufman (1834-1893).

[89] 1880 U.S. Census, Lowndes County, Mississippi, pop. sch., Columbus, p. 206A (stamped), Dwelling #44, Family #52, H. Kupman (sic) household, digital image, (A: accessed 11/ 2010), citing NARA microfilm publication T9, roll 655. Date of enumeration: 2 June 1880.

[90] 1920 U.S. Census, Lowndes County, Mississippi, pop. sch. Columbus, Ward 1, ED 37 p. 9A (penned), Dwelling #173, Family #181, Jake Kaufman household, digital image, (A: accessed 11/ 2010), citing NARA microfilm publication T625, roll 885. Date of enumeration: 8 January 1920.

[91] "Executive Elections," *The New York Times*, 1 October 1947, digital image, *Nytimes.com* (http:// www.nytimes.com: accessed 11/ 2010).

[92] "E. Martie Schreiber," *The Dallas (Texas) Morning News*, 15 May 1969, p. 6, col. 2, digital image, (GB: accessed 11/ 2010).

[93] "Mrs. Naomi Spring," *The Dallas (Texas) Morning News*, 31 March 1960, p. 7, col. 2, digital image, (GB: accessed 10/ 2010).

[94] "Sylvia Schreiber Engaged to Wed E.M. Bensinger," *The Dallas (Texas) Morning News*, 20 January 1941, p. 6, col. 4, digital image, (GB: accessed 9/ 2010).

[95] "Sylvia Schreiber Becomes Bride of Edwin Bensinger," *The Dallas (Texas) Morning News*, 7 February 1941, p. 12, cols. 2, 3, digital image, (GB: accessed 9/ 2010).

[96] "January Wedding Planned," *The Dallas (Texas) Morning News*, 29 October 1967, p. 5, col. 5, digital image,(GB: accessed 9/ 2010).

[97] "Death and Funeral Announcements – Bensinger," *The Dallas (Texas) Morning News*, 2 February 1975, p. 34, col. 4, digital image, (GB: accessed 10/2010).

[98] 1930 U.S. Census, Allegheny County, Pennsylvania, pop. sch. Pittsburgh, ED 45, p. 6A (penned), Dwelling #35, Family #35, Bernard Averbach household, digital image, (A: accessed 11/2010), citing NARA microfilm publication T626, Penna. roll 1970. Date of enumeration: 5 April 1930.

[99] "Society," *TP*, 5 August 1935, p. 19, col. 4; p. 20, col. 3, digital images, (GB: accessed 9/ 2010).

[100] 1870 U.S. Census, East Baton Rouge Parish, LA, pop. sch. Baton Rouge, Ward I, p. 9 (penned), Dwelling #71, Family #69, Simon (sic) Abramson household, digital image, (A: accessed 10/2010), citing NARA microfilm publication M593, roll 512. Date of enumeration: 4 & 6 June, 1870.

[101] Louisiana State Board of Health, Bureau of Vital statistics, Certificate of Death #10 097 (1922), Nathan Abramson; photocopy obtained from Louisiana Secretary of State, Department of Archives, Records Management and History, Baton Rouge, LA.

[102] "Abramson, Louis, M.D., East Baton Rouge Parish, Louisiana," database, *Rootsweb.com* (http://files.usgwarchives.net: accessed 9/2010), citing Alcée Fortier, Editor, *Louisiana: Comprising Sketches of Parishes, Towns, Events, Institutions, and Persons, Arranged in Cyclopedic Form* (volume 3), pp. 27-28, Century Historical Association, 1914.

[103] "Waco, Texas," *The Dallas (Texas) Morning News*, 4 October 1902, p. 11, col. 1, digital image, (GB: accessed 9/ 2010).

[104] "Society," *DP*, 6 September 1897, p. 13, col. 6, digital image, (GB: accessed 9/ 2010).

[105] "Lafayette," *DP*, 5 June 1904, p. 22, col 7, digital image, (GB: accessed 9/ 2010).

[106] "Louisiana Deaths, 1850-1875; 1894-1954," (F: accessed 10/ 2010), citing FHL microfilm 2365252, Death of Jeane Abramson (1919) ; also, Social Security Administration, "U.S. Social Security Death Index," database, (A: accessed 10/ 2010), entries for Natalie Weill (1989) and Bertha A. McCowan (1987)

[107] Social Security Administration, "U.S. Social Security Death Index," database, (A: accessed 10/ 2010), entry for S. R. Abramson (1997).

[108] "Ducharme Elected Lafayette Captain," *TP*, 17 December 1924, p. 14, col. 6, digital image, (*GB*: accessed 9/ 2010).

[109] "Society," *TP*, 15 June 1932, p. 17, col. 2, also "Resident Doctors Chosen for Touro," *TP*, 1 Jan 1932, p. 21, col. 2, digital images, (GB: accessed 9/ 2010).

[110] "Society," *TP*, 5 August 1935, p. 19, col. 4; p. 20, col. 3, digital image, (GB: accessed 9/ 2010).

[111] Randy DeCuir, *Marc's Town – Two Centuries on the Prairie,* Vol. I (Marksville, Louisiana: Avoyelles Publications, 2008), 78, 79.

[112] "New Orleanians Accept Medical Reserve Places," *TP,* 10 August 1939, p.19, col. 6, digital image, (GB: accessed 9/ 2010).

[113] "19 Interns Chosen at Touro Infirmary," *TP*, 17 December 1938, p. 6, col. 3, digital image, (GB: accessed 9/ 2010).

[114] Louisiana State Board of Health, Bureau of Vital statistics, Certificate of Death #4663 (1941), Louis Elster; photocopy obtained from Louisiana Secretary of State, Department of Archives, Records Management and History, Baton Rouge, LA.

[115] Randy DeCuir, *Marc's Town – Two Centuries on the Prairie,* Vol. I, 79.

[116] "Three Louisianans Given Promotions," *TP,* 12 July 1943, p. 9, cols. 4, 5, digital image, (GB: accessed 9/ 2010); also, Randy DeCuir, *Marc's Town – Two Centuries on the Prairie,* Vol. I, 79.

[117] Louisiana State Board of Health, Bureau of Vital statistics, Certificate of Death #10 097 (1946), Nathan Abramson; photocopy obtained from Louisiana Secretary of State, Department of Archives, Records Management and History, Baton Rouge, LA.

[118] "Diplomas Given to 135 Students," *TP,* 20 July 1946, p. 19, col. 4; p. 13, col. 2, digital images, (GB: accessed 12/2010).

[119] 1920 U.S. Census, Orleans Parish, Louisiana, pop. sch. New Orleans, Ward 3, ED 32, p. 3A (penned), Dwelling #42, Family #54, Aron L. Pailet household, digital image, (A: accessed 12/2010), citing NARA microfilm publication T625, roll 618. Date of enumeration: 3 January 1920.

[120] Social Security Administration, "U.S. Social Security Death Index," database, (A: accessed 12/2010), entry for Maurice Pailet (1980).

[121] "Funeral Rites Held for Louis H. Pailet – Widely known New Orleans Real Estate Man Dies at Residence," *TP*, 30 June 1932, p. 11, cols. 6, 7, digital image, (GB: accessed 12/2010.)

[122] Louisiana State Board of Health, Bureau of Vital statistics, Certificate of Death # 2 023 (1951), Anne E. Kurtz Elster; photocopy obtained from Louisiana Secretary of State, Department of Archives, Records Management and History, Baton Rouge, LA.

[123] "Society," *TP*, 8 November 1950, p. 37, col. 4, digital image, (GB: accessed 12/ 2010).

[124] 1880 U.S. Census, Iberville Parish, Louisiana, pop. sch. Plaquemine, Ward 2, ED 64, p. 45A (penned), Dwelling 4, Family 4, John L. Dardenne household, digital image, (A: accessed 12/2010), citing NARA microfilm publication T9, roll 454. Date of enumeration: 1 June 1880.

[125] "World War I Draft Registration Cards, 1917-1918," digital image, (A: accessed 12/2010), Teakle Wallis Dardenne, No. 2211, Draft Board "O," Iberville Parish, Louisiana, citing NARA microfilm publication M 1509, no roll given, FHL Roll #1684690.

[126] "Society," *TP*, 3 November 1953, p. 29, col. 1, digital image, (GB: accessed 12/ 2010).

[127] "Parade Through Streets Ends Marksville Event," *TP*, 31 August 1959, p. 57, cols. 5, 6, digital image, (GB: accessed 12/ 2010).

[128] "Touro Interns Cited at Dinner," *TP*, 25 June 1963, p. 2, col. 2, digital image, (GB: accessed 12/ 2010).

[129] "Society," *TP*, 20 June 1962, p. 37, cols. 2, 3, digital image, (GB: accessed 12/ 2010).

[130] "Studies Urged on Americanism," *TP* , 15 October 1961, p. 26, col. 8, digital image, (GB: accessed 12/2010).

[131] "LPA Will Stage Seminar on Reds," *TP* , 6 January 1963, p. 12, col. 6, digital image, (GB: accessed 12/ 2010).

[132] "To Vote for Wallace...," *TP* , 5 November 1968, p. 17, cols. 7, 8, digital image, (GB: accessed 12/ 2010).

[133] "Johnston Wins," *TP*, 9 November 1972, p. 6, col. 1, digital image, (GB: accessed 12/ 2010).

[134] Randy DeCuir, *Marc's Town – Two Centuries on the Prairie,* Vol. I, 88.

[135] Blanche Swan, "Mrs. Rae Elster Abramson to God,", *The Marksville (LA) Weekly News*, 14 June 1979, Vol. 136, no. 44, p. 2, cols. 4, 5. Back issue consulted 12/2010 at *Marksville Weekly News* Office, Main Street, Marksville, LA. Note: Dr. Sara Abramson later divorced Allan Block and married Harrison Squire. Dr. Abramson is a pediatric radiologist practicing in New York City.

[136] See note 21.

[137] "Yule Decoration Victors Reviewed," *TP*, 18 December 1965, p. 69, cols. 1, 2, digital image, (GB: accessed 12/ 2010).

[138] "Out of Town Deaths, Abramson," *TP*, 5 October 1975, p. 16, col. 4, digital image, (GB: accessed 12/ 2010).

[139] "Wilhelmi-Abramson," *The Augusta (Georgia) Chronicle*, 14 October 1984, Section F, p. 9, col. 1, digital image, (GB: accessed 12/ 2010).

[140] "Obituary – Bella Nickerson Chappuis Abramson," *The Lafayette (Louisiana) Daily Advertiser*, 31 May 2005, United States Obituary Collection, database, (A: accessed 12/ 2010).

[141] "Noted Marksville Physician Dies," *The Marksville (LA) Weekly News*, 22 October 1987, Vol. 142 no. 43, p. 1, cols 2, 3, & p. 2, col 1. Back issue consulted 12/2010 at *Marksville Weekly News* Office, Main Street, Marksville, LA.

[142] "Obituaries – Emma Abramson," *Avoyelles Ad-Vantage*, 20 July 1988, Second Year, no. 7, p. 2A, col. 2. Back issue consulted 12/ 2010 at *Marksville Weekly News* Office, Main Street, Marksville, LA.

[143] "Former Marksville physician: Rites held for Dr. S. R. "Pete" Abramson ," *The Marksville (LA) Weekly News*, 8 January 1998, Vol. 155 no. 21, p. 1, cols. 2, 3, & p. 1, cols. 3-6. Back issue consulted 12/ 2010 at *Marksville Weekly News* Office, Main Street, Marksville, LA.

[144] "Obituary, Sol Bernard Mayer ," *The Baton Rouge (Louisiana) Advocate*, 2 December 2005, p. 16 A, digital image, (GB: accessed 12/ 2010).

Elster's Sale – Main Street Marksville, ca. 1925
(*Courtesy of Randy Decuir*)

Schreiber & Sons – Main Street Marksville, ca. 1930
(*Courtesy of Randy Decuir*)

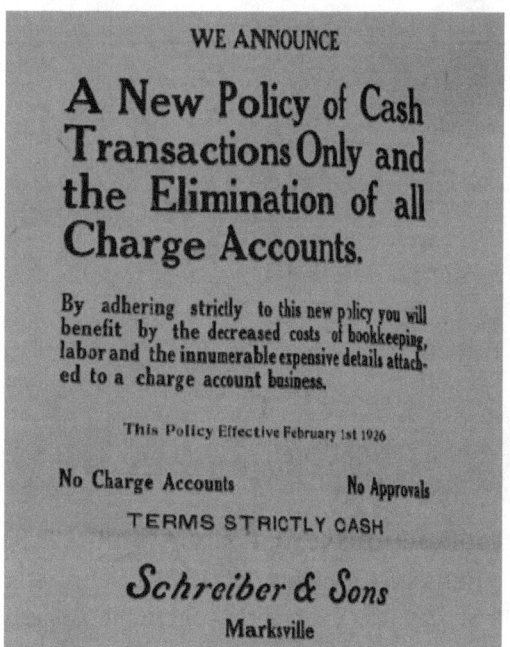

Marksville Weekly News - 1 Feb. 1926   (*Courtesy of Randy Decuir*)

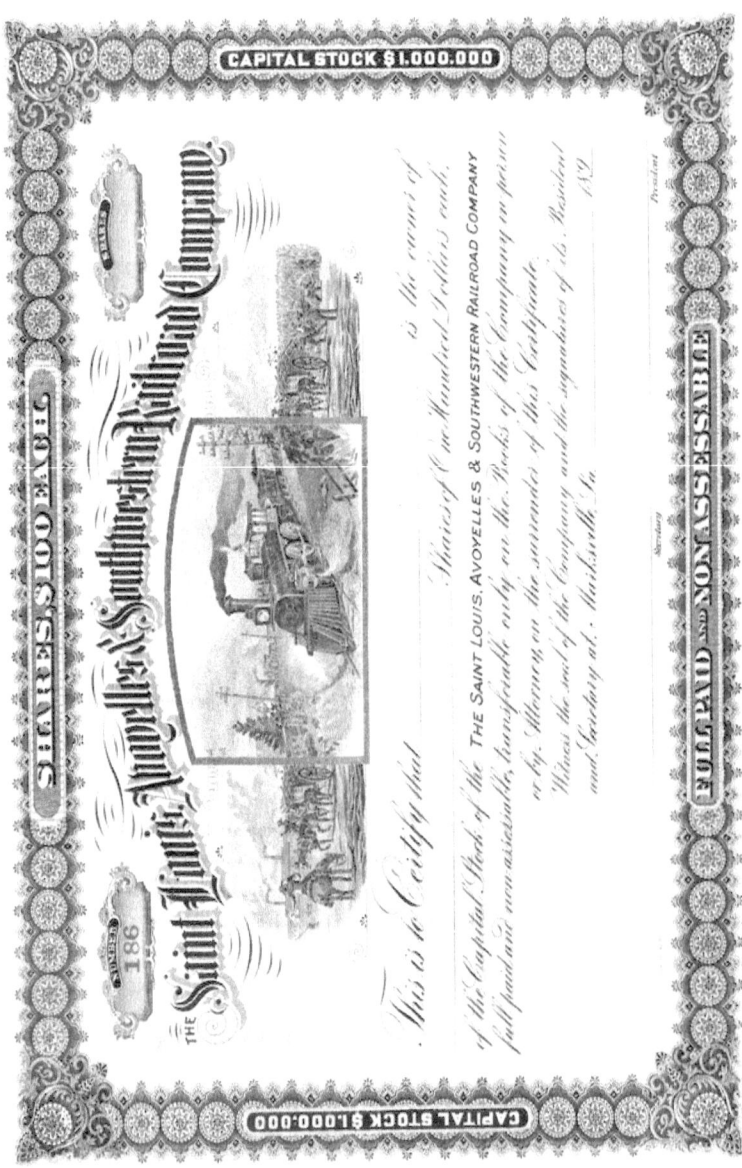

Stock Certificate of The St. Louis, Avoyelles & Southwestern
Railroad Company, ca. 1894 - Never issued
(The right of way was eventually sold to the Texas & Pacific RR
becoming part of its Avoyelles and Melville Branches.)

BIBLIOGRAPY

Ancestry.com (http.//www.ancestry.com).

Archives départementales du Bas-Rhin. État civil en ligne. [On-line Civil records for Alsace, France] (http://archives.bas-rhin.fr/).

Archives départementales du Bas-Rhin – Population du Bas-Rhin [On-line Census records for Alsace, France] (http://population.bas-rhin.fr/ellenbach/).

Ashkenazi, Elliott. *The Business of Jews in Louisiana, 1840-1875*. Tuscaloosa : The University of Alabama Press, 1988.

Belting, Natalia Maree. *Kaskaskia Under the French Regime*. Carbondale, Illinois: Southern Illinois University Press, 1948, reprinted 2003.

Bergeron, Arthur W. *Guide to Louisiana Confederate Military Units, 1861-1865*. Baton Rouge: Louisiana State University Press, 1989.

Bloch-Raymond, Anny. *Des berges du Rhin aux rives du Mississippi – Histoire et récits de migrants juifs*. Paris, France: Michel Houdiard, éditeur, 2009.

Bloch-Raymond, Anny "Mercy on Rude Streams; Jewish Emigrants from Alsace-Lorraine to the Lower Mississippi region and the Concept of Fidelity." *Southern Jewish History*, Journal of the Southern Jewish Historical Society 2 (1999): 81 – 110.

Brewer, Gladys Selvidge. *Cant Hooks and Dogwood Blossoms – Pollock's Story*. Pollock: Gladys S. Brewer [P.O. Box 216, Pollock LA 71467], 1987.

Brock, Eric J. *Images of America The Jewish Community of Shreveport.* Charleston, SC: Arcadia Press, 2002.

Brock, Eric J. *The Jewish Cemeteries of Shreveport, Louisiana.* Shreveport, LA: J. & W. Enterprises, 1995.

Broel, Bonnie. *House of Broel, The Inside Story.* New Orleans: House of Broel Foundation, LLC, [2220 St. Charles Avenue, New Orleans, LA], 2007.

Brooksher, William Riley. *War Along the Bayous, The 1864 Red River Campaign in Louisiana.* Dulles, VA: Brassey's Books, 1998.

Brown, Karen Russell. *Descendants of Levi Hirsch – Rosenbaum Family Tree*, 3 vols. Tarzana, CA: privately printed and distributed to family, 2010.

Carb, David. *Sunrise in the West.* New York: Brewer, Warren & Putnam, 1931 (out of print).

Carter, Howell. *A Cavalryman's Reminiscences of the Civil War.* 1900. Reprint, Clearwater, SC: Eastern Digital Resources, 2008.

Castlegarden.org (http://www.castlegarden.org).

Census 1836. Recensement des cantons de Brumath, Schiltigheim & Truchtersheim. CD-ROM, database, Fegersheim, France : Chantal Geyer, 2004-2005.

Cohen, Rich. *The Fish that Ate the Whale: The Life and Times of America's Banana King.* New York: Farrar, Strauss & Giroux, 2012.

Costello, Brian J. *A History of Pointe Coupée Parish, Louisiana.* Donaldsonville, LA: Margaret Media, Inc. 2010.

Couvillon, Ira S. *To Avoyelles with the Couvillons.* Simmesport, LA: Mardi Gras Publications, 1966 (out of print).

Davies, Greggory E., "Winnfield Oil Company Well No. 1," *Legacies and Legends of Winn Parish*, The Winn Genealogical and Historical Association, Vol. 7, No. 2 (August 2003): 114.

DeCuir, Randy, author and compiler. *Biographical and Historical Memoirs of Avoyelles - 1890-1990*. Reprinted & supplemented by Randy DeCuir. Marksville, LA: Avoyelles Publishing Company, 1990.

DeCuir, Randy. *Marc's Government, Town Government 1843-2009 - Volume II*. Marksville, LA: Avoyelles Publications, 2009.

DeCuir, Randy. *Marc's Town – Two Centuries on the Prairie* Volume I. Marksville, LA: Avoyelles Publications, 2008.

Dénombrement des Juifs d'Alsace – 1784. Paris, France: Cercle de Généalogie Juive, 1999.

Ducôté, Alberta Rousseau, compiler and translator. *Early Baptism Records : St. Paul the Apostle Catholic Church, 1824-1844, Avoyelles Parish*. Mansura, LA: St. Paul the Apostle Catholic Church, 1982.

Ducôté, Alberta Rousseau, compiler and translator. *St. Paul the Apostle Church, Mansura, Louisiana – Baptism Book #5, 1845-1850*. Marksville, LA: Avoyelles Publishing Company, 1994.

Ducôté, Alberta Rouseau, compiler and translator. *St. Paul the Apostle Church, Mansura, Louisiana – Baptism Books #6 & #7, 1850-1872*. Marksville, LA: Avoyelles Publishing Company, 1994.

Ducôté, Willie J., compiler and translator. *Avoyelles Parish, St. Paul's Mansura, Louisiana Burial register 1870-1885, Book I.* Baton Rouge, LA: privately printed, 1998.

Ducôté, Willie J., compiler and translator. *Burial register of St. Paul's Church Mansura, Louisiana, Parish of Avoyelles, Book II – Entries recorded April 1850-December 1859.* Baton Rouge, LA: privately printed, 1997.

Elon, Amos. *The Pity of it All: A History of the Jews in Germany, 1743-1933.* New York: Metropolitan Books, 2002.

Evans, Clement A, editor. *Confederate Military History.* 12 volumes. Atlanta, GA: Confederate Publishing Company, 1899.

Executive Documents of the House of Representatives for the Second Session of the Forty-eighth Congress 1884-1885. Washington DC: U.S. Government Printing Office, 1885.

Familysearch.org (http://www.familysearch.org).

Felsenthal, Emma. *Bernhard Felsenthal Teacher in Israel.* New York: Oxford University Press, 1924.

Ferguson, Stewart Alfred. "The History of Lake Charles," Thesis, 1931, McNeese State University Library On-Line. http://library.mcneese.edu/depts/archive/FTBooks/ferguson.htm,

Fleury, Jean. *Contrats de mariage juifs en Moselle avant 1792.* Paris, France: Cercle de généalogie juive, 1999.

Fold3.com (http://www.fold3.com).

Fortderussy.org (http://www.fortderussy.org).

Fortier, Alcie, Lit.D., Editor. *Louisiana: Comprising Sketches of Parishes, Towns, Events, Institutions, and Persons, Arranged in Cyclopedic Form,* Vol. 3. Century Historical Association, 1914.

Fraenckel, André Aaron. *Mémoire juive en Alsace: Contrats de mariage au XVIIIème Siècle.* Strasbourg, France: Éditions du Cédrat, 1997.

Genealogybank.com (http://www.genealogybank.com).

Greene, William Lemuel. *Antoine Blanc 1792-1860.* Baton Rouge, LA: Claitor's Publishing Division, 2008.

Gremillion, Nelson. *Company G 1st Regiment Louisiana Cavalry CSA – A Narrative.* Lafayette: Center for Louisiana Studies: University of Southwestern Louisiana, 1986.

Hart, Mary Pearce. *Evergreen on the Bayou.* Evergreen, LA: privately printed, 1995.

Hébert, Rev. Donald G, compiler. *Southwest Louisiana Records (1750-1900)* CD-ROM, database, Rayne, LA: Hébert Publications, 1975-2001.

Hinchin, Rabbi Martin, D.D. *Fourscore and Eleven, A History of the Jews of Rapides Parish 1828-1919.* Alexandria, LA: McCormick Graphics, Inc. for Congregation Gemiluth Chassodim, 1984.

Italiangen.org (http://www.italiangen.org).

Janowski, Diane. *In Their Honor: Soldiers of the Confederacy. The Elmira Prison Camp.* Elmira: New York History Review Press, 2009.

Jewishgen.org (http://www.jewishgen.org).

Kaplan, Benjamin. *The Eternal Stranger.* New York: Bookman Associates, 1957.

Katz, Pierre, compiler. *Les Communautés juives du Bas-Rhin en 1851.* Paris: Cercle de généalogie juive, 2000.

Korn, Bertram Wallace. *The Early Jews of New Orleans.* Waltham, MA: American Jewish Historical Society, 1969.

LaCour, Jeraldine DuFour. *Avoyelleans of Yesteryear.* Alexandria, LA: Jeraldine DuFour LaCour [P.O. Box 5022, Alexandria, LA], 1983.

LaCour, Jeraldine DuFour. *Brides Book of Avoyelles Parish Louisiana, 1808-1855,* Volume I. Bunkie: Jeraldine DuFour LaCour [203 South Gayle Boulevard, Bunkie, LA], 1979.

LaCour, Jeraldine DuFour. *Brides Book of Avoyelles Parish Louisiana,1856-1880,* Volume 2. Bunkie: Jeraldine DuFour LaCour [203 South Gayle Boulevard, Bunkie, LA], 1983.

LaCour, Jeraldine DuFour. *Brides Book of Avoyelles Parish Louisiana, 1881-1899,* Volume 3. Alexandria: Jeraldine DuFour LaCour [P.O. Box 5022, Alexandria, LA], 1986.

LeBon, Marie-Yvonne "L'Émigration de l'Arrondissement de Wissembourg Durant le 19ème Siècle," *Atelier Généalogique de l'Arrondissement de Wissembourg et Environs* (AGAWE), mai 1999: Introduction, p. 1.

LeMaster, Carolyn Gray. *A Corner of the Tapestry – A History of the Jewish Experience in Arkansas, 1820s-1990s.* Fayetteville: University of Arkansas Press, 1994.

Leumas, Emilie G., Editor. *Diocese of Baton Rouge Catholic Church Records – Pointe Coupée Records 1722-1769,* Vol. 1b. Catholic Diocese of Baton Rouge, Department of Archives [1800 South Acadian Thruway, P.O. Box 2028, Baton Rouge, LA], 2002.

Lewis, Jimmie Nellie Adams, compiler. *Forgotten Sites of Tioga.* Tioga, LA: Tioga Historical Society, Inc., 2008.

Lewis, Joshua. "All Pumped Up," *Louisiana Life,* Vol. 21, no. 3, (Autumn, 2001): 60-64.

Marschall, John P. *Jews in Nevada: A History.* Reno: University of Nevada Press, 2008.

Mason, Patrick Q. "Anti-Jewish Violence in the New South." *Southern Jewish History, Journal of the Southern Jewish Historical Society* 8 (2005): 77-119.

Mayeux, Steven M. *Earthen Walls, Iron Men – Fort DeRussy, Louisiana and the Defense of the Red River.* Knoxville: The University of Tennessee Press, 2007.

McCants, Sister Dorothea Olga, DC, compiler and translator. *They Came to Louisiana: Letters of a Catholic Mission 1854-1882.* Baton Rouge: Louisiana State University Press, 1970.

McPeek, Jan & Naomi. *Merchants, Tradesmen and Manufacturers Financial Condition for 1902 Avoyelles Parish Louisiana.* Image reprint from the 1902 R.G. Dun *Mercantile Agency Reference Book.* Salem, OH: Aaron's Books, 2005.

McPeek, Jan & Naomi. *Merchants, Tradesmen and Manufacturers Financial Condition for 1902 Rapides Parish Louisiana.* Image reprint from the 1902 R.G. Dun *Mercantile Agency Reference Book.* Salem, OH: Aaron's Books, 2005.

National Archives and Records Administration (NARA). *Compiled Service Records of Confederate Soldiers who served in Organizations from the State of Louisiana.* (Microfilm publication M320, Roll 14.) Washington, D.C., 1960.

Nutrias.org (http://nutrias.org).

Partain, Fr. Chad Anthony. *A Tool Pushed by Providence: Bishop Auguste Marie Martin and the Catholic Church in North Louisiana.* Austin, TX: Persidia Publishing Co., 2010.

Perrin, William Henry, editor. *Southwest Louisiana Biographical and Historical.* New Orleans, LA: The Gulf Publishing Company, 1891.

Poor's Railroad Manual Co. *Poor's Manual of the Railroads of the United States*, 1906. New York: American Banknote Co., 1906.

Poret, Dr. George C. *St. Paul the Apostle Church.* New York: Carlton Press, Inc., 1979.

Price, John Milton, compiler. *The Civil War Tax in Louisiana: 1865,* 1891. Reprint, New Orleans, LA: Polyanthos Press, 1975.

Prichard, Walter, ed. "A Tourists Description of Louisiana in 1860," by J.W. Dorr, *Louisiana Historical Quarterly* Vol. 21 (Oct. 1938):1110-1214.

Railroad Commission of Louisiana. *First Annual Report of the Railroad Commission of Louisiana.* Baton Rouge: Office of the Railroad Commissioner of Louisiana, 1900.

R.G. Dun & Co. *The Mercantile Agency Reference Book, 1889.* (Vol. 85) Image Reprint (CD-ROM). PA-Genealogy.net (http://www.pa-genealogy.net), 2009.

Rootsweb.com (http//www.rootsweb.com).

Saucier, Corinne L. *History of Avoyelles Parish.* 1943. Reprint, Gretna, LA: Pelican Publishing Co., 1998.

Spletstoser, Frederick. *Talk of the Town, The Rise of Alexandria, Louisiana and the "Daily Town Talk."* Baton Rouge: Louisiana State University Press, 2005.

Stolarik, M. Mark, compiler. *Forgotten Doors – The Other Ports of Entry to the United States.* Philadelphia, PA: Associated University Presses, 1988.

The Southern Publishing Co., editors. *Biographical and Historical Memoirs of Northwest Louisiana.* 1890. Reprint with new index. Greenville, SC: Southern Historical Press, Inc., 2002.

The Southern Reporter, Vol. 44, *Containing all the decisions of the Supreme Courts of Alabama, Louisiana, Florida, Mississippi, Permanent Edition, July 6, 1907-January 4, 1908.* St Paul, MN: West Publishing Co., 1908.

Thompson, Mabel Alice. *Looking Back – A Narrative History of Bayou Chicot.* Ville Platte: Mabel Alice Thompson [Rt. 3, Box 471, Ville Platte, LA], 1983.

Turitz, Rabbi Leo & Evelyn Turitz. *Jews in Early Mississippi*. Jackson: University Press of Mississippi, 1995.

Umansky, Ellen M. *From Christian Science to Jewish Science: Spiritual Healing and American Jews.* London and New York: Oxford University Press, 2005.

USGenNet.org (http://www.usgennet.org).

USGwarchives.net (http://www.usgwarchives.net).

Virgets, Ronnie. "Happy Birthday Huey." *Gambit Weekly,* 26 Aug 2003. Online archives: http://bestofneworleans.com: 2007.

Weissbach, Lee Shai. *Jewish Life in Small-Town America.* New Haven CT: Yale University Press, 2005.

Wright, Porter and Barbara Wright. *The Old Evergreen Burying Ground.* Rayne, LA: Hébert Publications, 1990.

INDEX

Aaron, Edwin, 23
----, Henry, 23
----, Mary (Joseph), 248
----, Michael, 23, 240
----, Robert, 23

Abbeville (Vermillion), LA, 343, 344, 346, 348, 518, 549

Abney, Della, 255

Abramson, Abraham, 509
----, Annie, 509
----, Albert Moses, 508, 509, 510, 511, 513, 514, 516, 517
----, Bertha, 509
----, Daniel, 509
----, Janet Lucille (Dardenne), 509, 512, 513
----, Jeane, 509
----, Louis, 509
----, Natalie, 509
----, Nathan, 509, 510, 511
----, Paul Dowling, 510
----, Ralph Keith, 514
----, Robert Coronna, 514
----, Rosa, 509
----, Samuel, 508
----, Samuel Ralph "Pete," 508, 509, 510, 511, 513, 514, 515, 516, 517, 517, 525
----, Sara Jane (Block), 510, 515
----, Steven Nathan, 510, 514, 515, 517
----, Suzanne Denise, 514

Acacia Park Masonic Cemetery, Chicago, IL, 48

Adler, Coleman, 85, 87, 93
----, Helen, 94
----, Milton, 93
----, Walter, 94
Aguillard, Adele (Carmouche), 8, 14
----, Charles, 8, 14,
----, Lucien, 8
----, Paul, 8, 12

Albersweiler (Germany), 381

Alcoyne School of Dancing, 302

Alexander, Melsy, 380

Alexandria (Rapides), LA, 11, 21, 46, 50-52, 68, 69, 71, 79, 96, 107, 108-111, 114, 160, 163, 164, 166, 197, 202, 204, 205, 239, 240, 242, 243, 246- 248, 250, 255, 256, 258- 261, 264, 265, 267, 268-271, 296, 297, 299, 300 , 336, 337, 339-341, 343, 346- 351, 371-373 386-388, 390, 393,410, 412, 433, 435, 474, 479, 481, 482, 497-500, 504, 517

Alexandria Compress & Warehouse Co., 109

All American Drum & Bugle Corps & Band Assn., 310, 312, 313

American Friendship Society, 311-312

American Party, 514

American Trading Co., 436

Amite (Tangipahoa), LA, 369

Amite City Cemetery (Amite, LA), 370, 371, 373

Ancient Order of United Workingmen, 205

Angerer, Ruth (Mayer), 518

Anker, Ana "Anita" (Schwartz), 443
----, Benjamin (Benno), 434, 442, 443, 444
----, David, 443
----, Donald Ralph, 443
----, Ilda de, 443
----, Ludwig, 443
----, Marilyn, 443
----, Moritz (aka Morris), 434, 442, 443

Anseeuw, Fr. Achille, 296

Antonia (Grant), LA, 245, 247

Arbroth (West Baton Rouge), LA, 509

Argosy, USS, 161

Armand, Athanase, 480
----, Dorsineau, 480

Armitage, David L., 48, 49
----, Audrey, 49

Asheville (Buncombe), NC, 498

Associated Summer Clothing Manufacturers of New Orleans, 445

Atchafalaya River, 3, 13, 153, 164, 165,167, 265, 350, 387

Atlanta (Fulton), GA, 111, 260, 341, 342, 344, 499

Aucher, Madeleine (Meyer), 379

Auerbach, Minette (Fortlouis), 3

Augusta Sugar Co.(St. Mary) LA, 108

Autenhausen, (Germany), 225

Averbach, Bernard Joseph, 508, 511
----,Suzanne, 508 , 511, 512

Avoyelles Bank & Trust (Marksville, LA), 504

Avoyelles Hospital, 517

Avoyelles Planters' Trading Co., 481

Avoyelles Wholesale Grocery Co., 92, 93, 109, 128

Aymond, Irma Australia (Glasscock), 265
----, I, Jean-Baptiste, 40
----, II, Jean-Baptiste, 40
----, Selena (Felsenthal), 40, 44

Bach, Bernard, 497, 506

Baden, Duke of, 1

Bailey, US Lieut. Col., Joseph, 167

Baker, Leah Elizabeth (Karpe), 414

Ball (Grant), LA, 240

Ball, Chittenden E., & Son, 240

Bango (Asturias) Spain, 270

Baltimore (Independent City), MD, 493,495, 497, 498, 501, 504

Bango, Alexander, 271
----, Amelia (Reed), 271
----, Antoinette (Dietrich), 270
----, Bettye Jo (Maki), 271
----, Celina (Dussard), 270
----, Clotile Ann (Fox), 271
----, Harold, 271
----, Henry Leonard, 270, 271
----, John Anthony, 270
----, Juan Manuel, 270
----, Paul Leopold, 270, 271

Banks, U.S. General Nathaniel P. 13, 19, 69, 159, 163, 164, 167, 297

Barbin, Arlene, 314
----, Fabian, 314

Barnett, Selim, 474

Barrière, Blaise, 192, 193

Bastrop (Morehouse), LA, 244, 335, 336, 337

Baton Rouge (East Baton Rouge), LA, 13, 69, 70, 98, 104, 151, 221, 222, 265, 269, 271, 307, 344, 348, 351, 442, 500, 508, 509, 516, 518

Bauer & Weil, 482

Bauer, Felix, 198, 428, 472, 473, 474, 481, 482, 483
----, George, 472, 473, 481, 482, 483

Bayou Bleue (Terrebonne), 370

Bayou Bœuf (Avoyelles) LA, 40, 81, 85, 86, 93

Bayou Chicot (St. Landry), LA, 66, 69, 72-74, 76, 77, 79, 83, 84, 87, 94-97, 99, 101

Bayou des Glaises (Avoyelles) LA, 145-147, 206, 265. 294, 387

Bayou Flaggon (Rapides) LA, 240

Bayou Huffpower (Avoyelles LA), 85

Bayou Jack, 334, 350

Bayou Rouge (Avoyelles) LA, 54, 71, 72, 74, 330, 386, 387, 410

Bayou Rouge Baptist Burying Ground (Evergreen, LA), 98

Bayou Wiggins (Avoyelles) LA, 41

Belize (British Honduras, now independent), 429, 430, 431

Bellevue (Bossier), LA, 389

Belmont, KY, Battle of, 12

Bendel, Lena (Levy), 518

Benevolent Knights of America, 223

Bensinger, Edwin Milton, 508
----, Wendy Karen (Dana), 508

Berger, Charles, 299
----, Marie Éléonore (Prévot), 304
----, Helena Margery (Siess), 245, 246, 252, 258, 264, 270
----, Marcus Isaac, 245-246

Bergeron, Emelia (Wolf), 370

Beschinger, (Germany), 389

Bier, Adele E. (Kahn), 335
----, Charles, 335
----, Hippolyte, 335

551

Big Bend (Avoyelles), LA, 145, 373

Big Cane (St. Landry), LA, 193, 330, 331- 334, 338, 346, 348, 350, 382, 518

Big Creek Sawmill & Lumber Co., 248

Big Yank Work shirts, 504

Binstock, Rabbi Louis, 448, 510

Birkenstein, Sigmund, 45, 48

Blakewood, Alton Bettison, 373

Blanc, Bishop Antoine, 3

Blanchard, Adolphe, 201, 337

Bloch, Annette (DeBlieux), 387, 390, 394
----, Leon, 107, 380, 381, 383, 385, 387, 388, 390, 393-394, 410
----, Leon, Jr., 386
----, Rosalie (Loeb), 148
----, Rosalie (Russell), 387, 390, 393, 394, 448

Block, Allan, 515

Blandin, Marie (Maillard, Haas), 105

Bluefields, (Nicaragua), 427, 430, 440

Bluestein, Fanny (Heilperin), 344

Blunt, Alexander, 44, 46
----, Mary Ann Eleanor (Felsenthal, Richey), 44, 46

B'nai Brith (Alexandria, LA), 347, 386, 412

B'nai Israel Congregation & Cemetery (Pineville, LA), 503, 504

Bocas del Toro, (Panama), 438

Bodenheimer, Emmanuel, 389
----, Harriette (Levy), 389
----, Henry, 389
----, Jacob Mahne, 389
----, Theresa, 389

Bodie (Mono), CA, 424, 425, 428

Boll Weevil, 51, 387, 395, 416, 502

Bolton, Rachel (Mathis), 255

Bolton-Teagle Cemetery (Winnfield, LA), 274, 275

Booth, Col. A.B., 222
----, Louis, 331

Bordeaux (France), 227, 228

Bordelon, Adolph, 258
----, Camille A. 50
----, Fabien, 336
----, Pauline (Frank), 7,8

Boston (Suffolk), MA, 148, 229, 423, 430, 431, 437

Bostick, Emma, 96
----, Helen Henrietta (Haas), 89, 104, 105

Bouanchaud, Capt. Alcide, 12

Bouxwiller (Alsace), 168, 328

Boyce (Rapides), LA, 269, 371-374

Brandt, Johanna (Gross), 448
----, Peter, 448

Braniff, Thomas, 345

Bratman, Frances (Warshauer), 444, 445, 449
----, Herman, See Herman Warshauer

Bringhorst, Charles, 244

Brochard, Angélique, 19, 196

Broel-Plater, Albert, 310-12
Broel, Bonnie (Mendelson), 310-312, 313

Brooklyn (Kings), NY, 432, 493, 502

Brooks, Vinya, 203

Brown, Jeannette (Coronna), 509

Brouillette, Caroline (Didier), 18
----, Gerand, 337

Broussard, Louis, 265, 266

Brownsville, TX, 328, 329

Brumath (Alsace), 198, 327- 329, 330, 336, 351

Buffalo (Erie), NY, 491- 494

Bunkie (Avoyelles), LA, 20, 22, 70, 76, 79, 82-86, 88, 89, 91-99 104-110, 112- 115, 247, 265, 339-349, 373, 381, 384-388, 390-394, 410, 423, 428, 429, 431- 435, 438, 439, 442, 444- 449, 451, 473, 479, 491, 501, 517- 519

Bunkie Brick Works, 107, 109, 385

Bunkie Carriage Co., Ltd. 107, 386

Bunkie Compress, 107, 109

Bunkie Ice Company, 108

Bunkie Record, 390, 445, 518, 519

Burials, Jewish of non-Jewish spouses, 304-305

Cahn, Edgar M., 217

Caledonia Plantation, 470, 471

Camp Moore (LA), 70

Camp Pratt (LA), 157

Cannon, Clifton, 333, 334, 337
----, Capt. Fénélon, 70, 119, 151

Canton (Madison), MS, 337, 408, 409

Cappel, Charles, 92
----, Curry, 98
----, Sterling, 98

Carb, Annette (Veit), 415
----, Bertha, 409, 415
----, David Charles, 384, 408, 409
----, Fanny (Karpe), 384, 408-411, 413, 414, 416
----, Isidore, 415
----, Sarah, 415

Carmouche, Louis, 15
----, Numa, 14

Carter, Gabriel, 331

Cassandria (Avoyelles) LA, 40-42, 43, 45

Catahoula Lake (Rapides, LA), 69

Cayer, Louis P. 56, 196

Center Point (Avoyelles) LA, 40

Central American Improvement Co., 434

Central LA Medical & Surgical Assn., 246

Cerf, Fanny (Siess), 90, 168, 169, 184, 186, 187, 195, 201, 202, 217-220, 223, 224, 229, 230, 382
----, Isaac, 168
----, Léon, 168
----, Samson, 168, 186, 382, 388

Chamberlin-Hunt Academy, 80

Charlot, Marie (Olivier), 163, 295, 296, 299, 304

Chatelain, Edmond, 145, 146
----, Joseph Belony, 146
----, Josette (Couvillion, Siess), 146, 147, 151, 157, 169, 184, 202, 203, 205, 242, 247, 254, 258, 259, 275, 287, 416, 428, 432, 480
----, Ludger, 147
----, Zélien, 147, 199

Chauvin, Fr. Jean E., 18, 19, 185, 196, 197
----, Jeanne (Beslin, Karpe), 415

Chenevert, Avida (Milligan), 447,

Cheney, William F., 155, 157

Cheneyville (Rapides), LA, 72, 87, 91, 92, 346, 410, 433

Chevra Thilim - Canal Street Cemetery (New Orleans, LA), 348, 449

Chicago (Cook), IL, 21, 39, 42, 45, 47-49, 52, 96, 220, 260, 311, 349, 415, 497, 501, 504, 506,

Chicago & Southern Airways, 447

Chorin, Fr. A., 20, 242, 243

Church of Christ, Scientist, 94

Chust, Alexander, 12

City Drug Co. (Winnfield, LA), 252, 289

Civil War, 14, 15, 19, 20, 42, 43, 46, 51, 66-71, 78, 145, 151-169, 184, 271, 328-331, 367, 368, 387, 394, 409, 469, 507, 507, 518

Civil War Conscription, Avoyelles Parish, 42, 43, 66, 152, 155-157

Civil War, union sympathizers, 42, 152, 160-164

Clark, Lizzie, 81, 83

Claverie, Jean-Baptiste, 16, 18
-------, Jean-Marie, 16, 22

Clement, Carl, 268
----, Charlene, 268
----, Cheryn, 268
----, Clay Leopold, Sr., 268
----, Clay Leopold, Jr, 268
----, Clay Leopold III, 268
----, Craig, 268
----, Curry, 268

554

----, Curt, 268
----, Donald Martin, 266-268

Coats, Curtis Leroy, 94

Coberly, Richard Franklin, 439, 446, 447
----, Sarah Elizabeth, 439, 446, 447, 468

Cochrane, Clara (Siess), 183, 191, 203, 291, 292, 295, 298, 299, 304, 305
----, Edmonia, 184
----, Robert Alexander, 183

Coco, Adolph Valéry, 498
----, Albert Fulgence, 263
----, Dominic Baldony, dit, 263
----, Judge A.V., 218

Cocoville (Avoyelles), La , 3

Code Noir, 1

Cohen, Carrie (Schreiber), 493-497, 501, 505
----, Hannah (Weiss), 345-347
----, Henrietta (Mermelstein), 346
----, Henrietta Warshauer/Bratman), 444, 445, 446, 449
----, Mary (Elster), 492, 494, 495

Cohn, Esther (Dardenne), 513
----, Meyer, 513

Cole, Charles Carroll, 71
----, John, 71
----, Martha Ann (Haas), 71- 74, 77, 79, 80, 83, 96, 100
----, Millard Ludger, 71
----, Phyllis (Tadlock), 274

Colon (Panama), 426, 427, 430, 436, 440

Comeaux, Azéma (Marix), 512

Comstock Lode, 425

Cone, Robert "Mickey," 439, 440, 446, 447

Confederate Military Units, Louisiana
----, Avoyelles Fencibles, 151
----, Avoyelles Riflemen, 42
----, Boone's Battery, 298, 299
----, Creole Chargers (First LA Cavalry, Co. G), 46, 69, 70, 151, 271
----, Creole Rebels, 151
----, Dubecq's Cavalry, 11, 299, 300
----, 18th Regiment Infantry, Co. I, 156, 164, 297, 298
----, First LA. Heavy Artillery, Company B, 298, 299
----, Harrison's Regiment – See Prairie Rangers
----, Johnson's Batallion, 297, 298
----, Louisiana Swamp Rifles (10th LA Infantry, Company E), 69
----, Mansura Guards, 151
----, Marksville Chasseurs à pied, 151
----, Marksville Guards, 151
----, Prairie Rangers (Third LA Cavalry,Company K), 67, 68, 69
----, Second Louisiana Infantry (Claiborne Guards), 381
----, Todd's Independent Co. Cavalry, 67

Conlan, Margaret (Felsenthal), 47

Constant, Warren Leroy, 115

Corinth, MS, Battle of, 12

Coronna, Bruno, 509

----, Rosalie (Gainsburgh), 510
----, Ula (Abramson), 509, 510, 515, 516

Costello, Brian, 2, 14

Cottonport (Avoyelles) LA , 92, 263, 265, 339, 346, 393, 428, 469, 472, 473,475, 477, 480, 481, 502, 517

Couget, Jean Marie, 17

Couvillion, Anna Florence (Felsenthal), 51
----, Azelia (Couvillion), 367
----, Dorsin, 371
----, Jean-Baptiste, 146
----, Jean-Baptiste Valsain, 146
----, Jimmy, 257
----, Marie Ophélia (Wolf), 367-369-371, 373
----, Rose, 337
----, Sainville, 367

Covington (St. Tammany), LA, 497

Crager, Moïse H., 261

Cripple Creek (Teller), CO, 218, 219

Cullum, E. North, 292

Cuyamel Fruit Company, 438

Cypress Grove Cemetery (New Orleans, LA), 85, 447

Dallas (Dallas), TX, 273, 345, 350, 415, 508,

Dalloz, Fr. Charles, 7, 8

Dalsheimer, Minette, See Mundel Löb

Daly City (San Mateo), CA, 261

Daly, Gwendolyn Marguerite (Abramson), 513, 515

Dana, F. Mitchell, 508

Dannenbaum, Arthur Joseph, 90, 91, 94
----, Carol (Davis), 93,94
----, Constance (Levey), 93
----, Sadie (Levey), 93

Dardenne, John Arvilien, 512
----, John L. 512
----, John Leigh, 512, 513
----, John Leigh, Jr. (aka Jay), 513
----, Richard James, 513
----, Teakle Wallis, 513

David, Anchel, 407
----, Lois (Levy), 518

Davis, Abe, 95
----, Adeliza Victoria (Witkowski), 470, 472
----, Benjamin, 95
----, David B., 94, 95, 106, 349
----, Henrietta (Eisendrath), 246
----, Jacob, 95
----, Jefferson, 71
----, Sara (Kurtz), 494
----, Thomas, 470

Deavers, John, 153, 154

DeBlieux, Alexandre Louis, 394
----, Alvin James, 394

Décret de Bayonne, 327, 407

Decuir, Marcelline (Escudé), 261,262, 416

Delaune, Odette, 51

Delhoste, Mary Virginia (Frank), 18

DeNeckere, Fr. Leon, 5

DeNux, Dr. Sylvan, 257

Denver (Colorado), 218, 219

Desfossés, Dr. Jules, 151, 155, 294

Desobry, Francis Clementine (Dardenne), 512

D.H. Holmes Department Store (New Orleans, LA), 306

Didier, F.O. " Potch, " 519
----, Jean Pierre, 18
----, Jules Émile, 18, 20

Dieudonné, Adèle (Michel), 243, 337

Dimarquis, Charles, 151

Dispersed of Judah Cemetery (New Orleans, LA), 79, 228, 271, 497

Dixon, George L., 50
----, George L., Jr., 50

Domas, J. O., 200

Dorr, J.W., 9, 10

Double Dealer, 226

Dreyfus, Joseph, 328
----, Nathan, 217

Drouin, Léon, 199
----, Louis, 151

----, Zaïre, 199

Druids, United Ancient Order of, 294, 303

Duckhill River Bridge (TN), 70

Ducôté, A.J., 193, 204, 337
----, Annie (Escudé), 263
----, Henriette (Frank), 22
----, Jules, 336

Dufilho, Roger, 100

Dufour, Eulalie (Armand), 184, 480

Dufour, Henry, 203

Dupont, Aimée (Gouazé), 303
Dupont, Sévère, 162

Dupuis, Justine (Aaron, Levin), 202, 205, 248

Durand, Fr. Henri, 147
----, Nelson, J.P., 183
----, Pierre, 192

Eastern Star Masonic Lodge, 254

Edwards, Benjamin Franklin, 204, 337
-----, Camille Henriette (Claverie), 22
-----, Edwin Washington, 22, 337
-----, Fielding, 154, 187
-----, Henry Clay, 22, 187
-----, James Madison, 186, 187
-----, Thomas Jefferson, 153, 154, 158, 160, 168
-----, William, 153, 154, 160
-----, William Washington, 153, 154, 176

Effie (Avoyelles) LA, 40

Egg Bend (Avoyelles), LA, 50, 51

Eilert, Charlotte (Goudchaux), 95, 330, 333, 350, 351, 382, 517

Elias, Gisella (Weiss, Kaplan), 343, 345

Ellenger, Emile, Rabbi, 433

Elmira (Chemung), NY Prison Camp, 13,

Elster, Annie (Greenfield), 492, 494
----, Bertha (Burglass), 492
----, Claire Ruth (Averbach, Pailet), 494, 495, 501, 503, 508, 510, 511, 512, 515
----, Dorothy, 494, 495
----, Freida, 492
----, Gertrude, 492
----, Harriet, 492, 495
----, Joseph, 492, 494, 495
----, Louis, 393, 494, 495, 496, 501, 502, 503, 506, 510, 511
----, Martin, 494, 495
----, Minnie (Rosenberg), 492, 502
----, Rae (Abramson), 495, 501, 503, 510, 511, 515
----, Rheuben, 494, 495
----, Robert, 494
----, Sadie (Davis), 492
----, Samuel, 492, 495
----, Thomas, 491, 492, 493, 494

Elster Bros. New York Bargain Store (Marksville, LA), 492, 494, 495, 503

Elster's Store (Houma, LA), 495

Emory, U.S. Gen. William Helmsley, 159, 167

Enterprise Plantation, 85

Eola (Avoyelles)LA, 76, 82, 92, 95, 96, 113, 115, 381, 393, 394, 447

Erber, Mollie (Riff), 390

Erlich, Henry, 78, 79, 99
----, Marks, 78
----, Nathan, 78, 79, 110
----, Philip, 78
----, Samuel, 78, 79, 333

Escudé, Abel Léon Philippe, 197, 248, 264, 416, 431
----, Alice Josephine (Prévot), 203, 262
----, Alphonse, 203
----, Arthur Jules, 206, 298
----, Anna Leah, 248, 263
----, Barbara (Lemoine), 263
----, Benjamin, 264
----, Édouard, 203, 264
----, Edward, Jr., 263
----, Edward Leon, 248, 263
----, Émile, 203, 264
----, Gaon, 262
----, Gerard, 263
----, Gloria,(West) 264
----, Henriette Zéline (Willis), 197, 432
----, Ira, 263
----, Jocelyn (Lunn), 263
----, Joseph Leopold, Jr., 262, 300
----, Joseph Leopold, Sr., 205, 262, 298
----, Jules Isaac, 248, 263
----, Landry, 263
----, Louis Philippe, 197, 261-262, 416
----, Marie (Capedeviele), 248, 264
----, Marie Belle (Pearce), 248, 264
----, Philippe, 197

----, Priscilla (Allums), 262
----, Rhoda (Coco), 248, 263

Escudé Funeral Home (Mansura, LA), 262

Essex, USS, 160

Eunice (St. Landry), LA, 97- 99, 107, 109, 394

Evangeline Parish, LA, 76, 97, 98, 100, 101, 104, 115

Evergreen (Avoyelles), LA, 16, 72, 74, 79, 85, 92, 93, 98, 105, 262, 330, 332, 333, 335, 339, 350, 351, 379-388, 393, 409-414, 416, 428, 429, 435, 469, 472- 477, 479, 480, 482, 483, 517

Evergreen Lodge # 139 (Masonic Temple), 413

Ewell, John, 475, 481

Experiment Sugar Plantation, 42

Feibelman, Rabbi, Julian, 227, 513, 514

Feitel, Babette (Heidenheim), 382

Felsenthal, Abraham, 39-46, 52, 473, 517
----, Belvensein (aka Barbara Friedman), 41, 45, 47, 48, 53
----, Benjamin C., 45, 47, 50-52
----, Bernhard, (Rabbi) 39, 48
----, Christopher Columbus, 51
----, David, 39
----, David (bro. Bernhard), 39
----, David Franklin, 43, 45, 46, 48, 49, 53
----, Dennis, 46, 51, 52
----, Dora, 48

----, Emma, 39, 40
----, Estelle, 50
----, Esther (Townsend), 45, 47, 50, 52
----, Eugene Lynn, 51
----, Eva (Bordelon), 50
----, Eva (Scroggs), 50
----, Flora (Seeger), 48
----, Flora, 51
----, Gerard Keith, 52
----, Hannah Louisiana, 41, 45
----, Herman, 41, 45
----, Hobson, 50
----, Jacob, 39, 45
----, Jacobias, 41, 45, 46, 47, 53
----, Lawrence A., 44, 49, 50
----, Lucille (Armitage), 48, 49
----, Marcus, 39
----, Marianna, aka. Hannah (Birkenstein), 45, 47, 48
----, Martha, 41
----, Rothsein, 41
----, Tency Deigo, 46, 51
----, Toby, 51
----, Wallace Russell, 51
----, Wallice Sarah (Meredith), 52

Finklestein, Carl, 393
----, Herbert, 393
----, Israel, 393
----, Solomon, 393

Firment, Alfred, 243, 257
----, Eliza (Gremillion), 256
----, Jules, 243
----, Rose Henriette (Siess), 242, 243, 245, 248, 249, 255-257, 264

Firnberg, Moses Rosenthal, 348, 349, 517

Fisher, Adolph, 443
----, Bella (Anker), 443

Fitzum, Hannah Olevia Walkling (Aaron), 23

Flagon Falls (Rapides), LA, 245

Flauss, Emile Haas Nicholas, 105
----, Nicolas Marie, 105

Florence (Fremont) CO, 218, 219

Foisy, Mary (Aaron), 23

Fontanille, Henri George, 158, 162, 163, 164, 298

Forest Hills (Queens), NY, 340

Forest (Scott), MS, 379, 380, 409

Forest Park Cemetery (Shreveport, LA), 308, 314

Fort de Chartres (Illinois Territory), 146

Fort DeRussy (Avoyelles), LA, 11, 68, 157- 161, 163, 164, 297

Fort-Louis (Alsace), 1,2

Fortlouis, Albert, 15
--------, Augustine (Martin), 15
--------, Ellen, 15
--------, Ernest, 15
--------, Estella, 15
--------, François, 15
--------, Geneviève Stephanie (Carmouche), 7, 15
---------, Georgiana, 15
---------, Henry, 15
---------, Jean Maurice, 3
---------, Leopold, 7, 12, 14
---------, Lionel, 15
---------, Mac Bennett, 15
---------, Madele (Frank), 4
---------, Mathilde, 4, 15
---------, Michel, 4, 12-14
---------, Moïse, 15
---------, Moritz (Maurice), 1-4, 6-8, 12, 15, 16, 23, 115
---------, Maurice (son Leopold), 14
---------, Maurice (son Moritz), 2, 15
---------, Philomène (Isaac), 14
---------, Rosalie (Villère), 4, 14, 15
---------, Théophile, 7, 12, 14

Fort Pillow, TN, Battle of, 12

Fort Worth (Tarrant), TX, 413, 415

Fostoria Glass Co., (Moundsville WV), 441

Français, Fr. Nicolas, 4, 5, 6

Francisco, François, 199-200

François, Céléstin, 203
----, Jean-Baptiste, 203

Franco-Prussian War, 73, 77, 198, 392, 407, 469, 491

Frank, Abraham, 4
----, Adolph (aka Aron), 4,6,7- 10, 16, 18- 23, 37, 196, 337, 473, 517
----, Adolph (son Fremont), 22
----, Albert, 8, 18, 21-22
----, Alicia (Couget,), 9, 17
----, Alicia (dau. Albert), 18
----, Allen, 22
----, Anaïs Albertine (Weeks), 19
----, Aurore (Claverie), 7, 16, 18, 22
----, Bertha (Lareche), 11, 17, 20
----, Bertha (dau. Albert), 18
----, Charles (aka Juda), 4,6-8, 23, 473
----, Charles Wyman, 22

----, Clara (Didier), 9, 18, 19, 20
----, Cléophine (Mayer), 9, 17
----, Edward Joseph, 19
----, Emelie (Huesman)7, 17, 23
----, Émile, 7, 11, 16, 17, 22, 337
----, Emma (Weisenberg, Moncla), 11, 20-21
----, Emma (Marcotte), 18
----, Emma (Long), 18
----, Eugenie, 22
----, Eustis Louis, 17, 22
----, Floyd, 22
----, Fremont Filbert, 17, 22
----, Inez, 18
----, Katheryne, 22
----, Karl Francis, 22
----, Kirtly Mark, 22
----, Lolie Lee, 22
----, Louis (son Charles), 8
----, Louis (son Adolph), 9, 18, 19, 20
----, Marie Siphaée, 18
----, Mathilde (Schwartzenburg, Molenor), 6, 16, 18, 22
----, Matilda (dau. Louis), 18
----, Ovilia, 8
----, Pearl (Posey), 19
----, Rebecca (Schwartzenburg), 9, 17, 18
----, Rebecca (dau. Louis), 18
----, Robert, 17, 22
----, Robert, Jr. 22
----, Roberta, 22
----, Shirley, 22
----, Webster, 19

Frankel, Sidney, 385

Franklin Female College (Holly Springs, MS), 81

Franklin, Rosalie (Erlich), 78

Frank's Hotel, (Marksville, LA), 9-11, 16-18, 19, 20, 22, 162, 337, 517

Free Sons of Israel (Waldheim), Forest Park, IL, 47, 49

Freidheim, Eliza (Levy), 336

French American Claims Commission, 19, 162, 164, 167, 196, 297

Friedman, Bernard, 47
----, Abraham, 47
----, Helena, 47
----, Herman, 47
----, Jacob, 47
----, Jessie Bernette, 47
----, Lena (McIntosh), 47

Friend, David, 410, 411
----, Henry, 225, 226
----, Joseph Emmanuel, 225, 226
----, Joseph Ernest "Joe", 227
----, Julius Weis, 225-227
----, Julius Weis, Jr. "Bill",160, 217,226, 227, 256
----, Lillian (Marcuse), 226, 227
----, Loeb, 225

Frog Canning Co., American, (Metairie, LA) 312

Gainsburgh, Isidore, 510

Gallemand, Louis, 152

Garcellier, Marianne (Gaspard), 6

Garcia, Rosa (Bango), 270

Garrot, Séverin, 336

Gaspard, Caroline (Frank), 6,9, 18, 21

----, Cyriaque, 153, 154
----, Jean-Baptiste, 6

Gates of Prayer (Joseph Street) Cemetery (New Orleans, LA), 217, 229, 230, 391. 449, 450

Gates of Prayer, Congregation (New Orleans, LA), 168, 217, 224, 229, 448

Gatteville-le-Phare (France), 150

Gauthier, Adèle Eunice (Firment), 257
----, Léon, 200

Gebhardt, Amelia (Lopez), 228

Ged Oil Fields (Calcasieu), LA, 272

Geiger, Jacob, 409
----, Valentin, 409, 410

Gemiluth Chassodim Cemetery (Opelousas, LA), 103, 339, 348, 349, 350, 386

Gemiluth Chassodim, Congregation (Alexandria, LA), 52, 96, 109, 202, 205, 270, 296, 300, 337, 341, 347, 386, 435, 504

George Muse Clothing Co (Atlanta, GA), 499

Gérard, Col. Aristide, 157, 163

Gerolsheim (Germany), 100

Gilroy (Santa Clara), CA, 483

Gingrass, J.G., 255

Ginsburg, Florence Nanette (Goldring), 499

Glasscock, Benning Jerrol, 265
----, Benning Jerrol, Jr., 265
----, Giles Ambrose, 265
----, Irene Elmire (Blanchard), 204
----, Louis Downing, 265
----, Louis Downing, Jr., 265
----, Ura Mae (Aymond), 265

Gismonda Mining & Milling Co., (Florence, CO) 218, 219

Glucksman, Alexander, 271
----, Sarah (Bango), 270, 271

Godchaux's Dept. Store (New Orleans LA), 499

Goldberg, Beryl (Pincus), 96
----, Elaine (Meyer), 96
----, Joseph M., 96

Golden Plantation, 102

Goldenberg, Charles, 240, 243, 246
----, Henrietta Julia (Katten), 388
----, Ida (Schilling), 248

Goldring, Abram, 492
----, Anna, 492
----, David, 346, 347, 491, 492, 498-501
----, David Leslie, 499
----, Ferdinand, 346, 499, 500
----, Frederick, 499
----, Herman, (aka Henry) 492, 493
----, Kalman, 491, 492
----, Libbie (Elster), 491-494, 498
----, Louis, 492
----, Martin S., 346, 499, 500
----, Molly, 492

----, Rona, 499
----, Stephen, 499
----, Tilly, 492

Goldring's Department Stores, 345, 347, 499, 500

Goldsmith, Freida, 493
----, Jennie, 493
----, Julius, 493
----, Samuel, 493
----, Simon, 493, 495, 504

Goldstein, Benjamin, 430, 431, 434, 442, 444
----, David, 423, 430, 431, 434, 437, 438, 440- 442, 444, 446, 448, 450,
----, Fanny, 430
----, Isidore Mark, 423, 431, 432, 436, 442, 446,450
----, Mark, 430, 431
----, Sadye Rae (Winsberg), 423, 437, 444, 446, 448, 449, 450

Golub (Poland), 518

Gommersheim (Germany), 328

Gonzales (Ascension), LA, 514, 515

Goodman, Joan (Rich), 450, 451

Gottheil, Edward, 11

Gouazé, Marcelle Reine (Mendelson), 303, 305, 309,313
----, Michel Frédéric, 303

Goudchaux, Abraham, 328
----, Abraham (son Leopold), 334
----, Adèle (Fies), 329
----, Adèle (Davis), 95, 332, 349
----, Babette (Dreyfus), 328
----, Bernard, 333, 351
----, Blanche Mathilde, "Bonnie" (Levy), 331, 382, 386, 388, 390,, 393
----, Callie, 338, 339
----, Caroline "Callie," 331
----, Charles Abraham, 331, 348, 350
----, Elsie (Goldsmith), 334
----, Esther, aka. Estelle, (Kahn), 328, 330, 334, 335, 366, 474, 483
----, Eugene Weill, 338, 339
----, Fleurette (Kahn), 328, 333
----, Henry, 328, 329
----, Henry (son Leopold), 332
----, Herbert, 333, 351
----, Hortense Miriam (Weil), 334, 348
----, Jacob Lehman (aka Jacques), 330, 338, 339
----, Jacob Oppenheim, 332, 333, 351
----, Jacques, 328
----, Julius Joseph, 334
----, Lazard, 329, 330, 332, 333, 350, 383, 384, 411, 433
----, Leon Eilert, 333, 334
----, Leona (Firnberg), 348, 349, 517
----, Leopold, 78, 89, 95, 327, 329-331, 333, 334, 338, 348-350, 382, 518
----, Leslie, 332, 351
----, Lottie (Kahn), 338, 339
----, Lottie Eilert (Morrison), 348, 349
----, Louise (Heyman), 336
----, Madel (Kahn), 338
----, Maline (Lehmann), 328, 330
----, May Louisa (Rosenfeld), 333, 351
----, Rosa (Barnett), 331
----, Rosa, 332
----, Sara (Lazard), 329
----, Sarah (Mayer), 334, 348
----, Sylvan, 334

Goudchaux's Department Store (Baton Rouge LA), 351

Gould, George Jay, 239, 248, 255-256
----, Jay, 239, 248

Gradenigo, Aimée Agathe (Voorhies), 183

Grandpierre, Antoine, 336

Grant, Mary Gerdes (Wolf), 371, 372
----, Richard Henry, 372
----, St. Agnes Loulette (Wolf), 372, 373

Grant, U.S. General Ulysses S., 159

Gray, Scott, 153, 154

Grayson, Inez (Escudé), 262

Green, James Everett, 447
----, General Tom (CSA), 71

Greensburg (St. Helena), LA, 367

Greenwood Cemetery (Shreveport, LA), 389, 414, 415

Greenwood, Coleman, 240

Greenwood Memorial Park (Pineville LA), 114, 371

Gremillion, Alfred, 256
----, Bella, 505
----, Marie Irene (Frank), 22
----, Onil, 191

Grégoire, Firmin, 152

Grey Gables, 85, 139

Grisamore, Capt. Silas T., 156

Gross, Aaron, 432, 438, 444- 446, 448, 449, 466, 467
----, Fannie, 432, 438, 446, 448, 449
----, Herman, 385, 431-433, 438, 446, 448, 449, 504
----, Jacob, 432,
----, Jacob Samuel, 432, 438, 445-446, 448
----, Kalman, 432
----, Regina (Brandt), 448
----, Solomon, 385, 432, 433

Gruenebaum, Johanetta (Felsenthal), 39

Guatemala City (Guatemala), 434, 442, 443

Guillot, Elodie (Mayeux, Felsenthal), 44, 45, 47. 50, 52
----, Marie, 18
----, Valéry, 8

Gus Mayer Department Stores, 342

Gutheim, Rabbi James, 168

Haas, Alexander M., (aka. Alex Haas, or Alexander Murdock Haas)65-67, 69-87, 89- 93, 96, 104-106, 115, 138, 141 348, 385, 394, 473, 475, 476
----, Alexander Marshall (aka. A. Marshall Haas), 73, 80, 88, 89, 92, 95- 97, 104, 112
----, Alexander Murdock, Jr. 74, 80, 81, 84, 100, 115,
----, Alice Bostick, 104

----, Alice Rosalind (Dannenbaum), 80, 86, 88-91, 94, 141
----, Charles, 74, 79, 80, 84, 92, 94, 98, 100, 113, 385
----, Charles Harold, 104, 105
----, Dorothy, 104
----, Douglas Marshall, 104
----, Fanny (Moch), 66,67, 77, 95-96, 112
----, Hattie (Haas), 72, 80, 81, 83, 87, 94, 96, 106, 110, 111, 114
----, Helen, 106
----, Helen Neomi (Ducôté), 104, 105
----, John (son Leon), 103, 104
----, John A., 72, 80, 84, 87, 88, 96, 97, 99-103, 114, 115
----, Jerome, 103, 104
----, Katherine Moore, 104, 105
----, Leon Samuel, 74, 80, 81, 84, 97, 103, 104, 115
----, Leon Samuel, Jr., 103,104
----, Maccie Martha (Harrison), 106, 108
----, Martha Elaine, 100
----, Mary Maccie "Bunkie" (Strouse), 73, 80, 81, 83, 84, 88, 89, 110, 140
----, Mary Maccie (dau. A Marshall), 104, 105
----, Montez Henning (Constant), 110, 115
----, Nanie (Mikell), 106, 110, 111
----, Nanie (Pokorny), 72, 80, 81, 86-89, 93
----, Nathan, 103, 104
----, Salomon (aka Solomon, Sol), 66,67, 73, 77, 95-96, 105
----, Samuel (son Alexander M.), 74
----, Samuel, Jr. (son W.D.), 106, 109, 110, 111, 114

----, Samuel Cerf, 65-69, 71, 73, 74, 77- 80, 82- 84, 87, 93-100, 107, 112, 114, 115, 349, 385
----, Samuel Douglas, 114
----, Samuel, Sr. (aka Samuel Aron), 65-67, 77
----, Sara, 66, 67
----, Sophie, 66
----, Stella, 98
----, William David (aka W.D.), 70, 72, 79- 81, 83, 87, 92-97, 106-114, 385, 386
----, William David, Jr. 106, 109, 110
----, William David, III, 110, 114, 115

Haas Investment Co., 113, 114, 394

Haasville (Avoyelles, LA), See also Tiger Bend, 70, 73, 80, 81, 85, 87, 90- 92, 94, 95, 104, 115

Hamburg (Avoyelles), LA, 367, 368

Hardtner Bros. (Ernest & Henry), 244

Hardy, Carl, Jr., 267

Harper, Rollo Elmer, 260
----, Charmian Fae (Dunckelman), 260

Harrison, Roy Bertrand, 108

Harrisonburg (St. Helena), LA, 68,69

Hatten (Alsace), 204

Haupt, Lulu Susan (Haas), 110, 114, 115

Heard, Maj. T.P., 11

Hebrew Benevolent Assn., 78, 205, 412

Hebrew Rest Cemetery #2 (New Orleans LA), 231, 388, 391, 413, 440, 450, 512, 515

Hebrew Rest Cemetery #2 (Shreveport, LA), 415

Hebrew Rest Cemetery #3 (Shreveport, LA), 389

Heidenheim, Caroline (Cerf), 382, 388
----, Celestine (Katten), 388
----, Josephine (Heymann), 382, 387
----, Moses, 382

Heilperin, Louis, 344
----, Natalie (Weiss), 344

Heiman, Philip, 262, 416

Heller, Rabbi Max, 103, 437, 440, 442, 509

Henderson, Mary Burem, 273

Henning, Montez Sarah, 110, 115

Hep Hep riots, 1

Heptasophs (Order of the Seven Wise Men), 294

Hernandez, Adilie (Levy), 410
----, Charles, 206

Hernsheim, Isidore, 474

Hesse, Sophie (Karpe), 407, 408

Hesse-Cassel (Germany), 388

Hesse-Darmstadt (Germany), 382, 388

Heyman, Abraham (aka Bear), 336, 339
----Heyman, Emmanuel, 336

Heymann, Cora (Levy), 383, 386, 387, 388, 390
----, Fannie (Levy), 382, 383, 386, 390
----, Jacob, 382, 386, 387

Hildenbrand, Emily (Schreiber), 507

Hiller, Abraham, 335
----, Arthur Aby, 337
----, Daniel, 336, 337
----, Edwin Jacob, 337
----, Elie, 197,198, 199, 203, 217, 335, 336, 337, 338, 473
----, Hannah, 199
----, Herz (Hatch), 335
----, Ida Hannah (Gretzner), 336
----, Jonas, 244, 335-337
----, Lawrence Estelle, 337
----, Mabel, 337
----, Matz (Matthew), 335, 336
----, Melvin Errol, 337

Hillsboro (Scott), MS, 408, 409

Hinchin, Rabbi Martin, 270

Hoggatt, Joyce Sophie (Marshall), 81

Hollander, Frederick, 408

Holmesville (Avoyelles), LA, 162, 163, 381

Home Guard, 160, 161, 162

Homer (Claiborne), LA, 381

Hopewell Plantation, 85

Hotel Bentley (Alexandria, Rapides), La, 267, 390, 412

Hot Springs (Garland), AR, 273, 274, 275, 391

Houma (Terrebonne), LA, 370, 494, 495

Hub Dry Goods Co. (Alexandria, LA), 347

Hudson, Daniel Bester, 475
----, Lavinia (Cole), 71

Huesman (Ducôté), Bertha, 17
------, Charles Frederick, 17
------, Harriet (Aaron), 17, 23
------, Herman, 17

Hurtz, Myer, 385

Hyams, Joseph Brooks Joseph, 431

Hydropolis (Avoyelles), LA, 1, 3, 4, 7, 8, 39

Ingwiller (Alsace), 65- 67, 77, 83, 95, 105, 112, 198, 429

Isaac, Alexandre, 14

Isles of Scilly, 225

Israel, Meyer, 329

Jackson (Hinds), MS, 12, 229, 230, 408

Jackson, Israel, 341
----, Selma (Weiss), 341, 342

Jacksonville (Duval), FL, 275

Jacobs, Manheim Harry, 437-438, 442

Janeau, Fr. Jules, 17, 147, 151, 156

Janowski, Diane, 13,14

Jayhawkers, 68, 69, 163, 164, 166, 167

Jean-Baptiste, Martin, 296

Jefferson Medical College (Philadelphia PA), 80, 101

Jennings (Jefferson Davis), LA, 203, 337, 338, 393, 446

Jessica Lumber Co. Ltd., 255

Jewish Congregation of Bunkie (Avoyelles), LA, 433

Jewish Cemetery, Lafayette, LA, 511, 516

Jewish Cemetery, Pineville (Rapides), LA, 8, 46, 53, 196, 205, 240, 259, 261, 270, 300, 304, 340, 342, 347, 348, 350, 380, 381, 386, 391, 394, 411, 423, 435, 446, 449, 497

Jewish Widows and Orphans Home (New Orleans LA), 78, 83, 88, 95, 271

Joffrion, Capt. Eloi, 153, 475

----, Louis A. 476

Johnson, Isaac C., 479, 482
----, Marie (Rooler, Rich), 446

Joseph, Cerf, 248
----, Julius, 248

Judenedikt, 2

Jules Clement # 1, 338

Juneau, Cléophas, 300

Kaffie, Harris, 298
----, Malcolm, 304, 307
----, Retta G. (Siess), 298, 304, 307, 308, 415

Kahn, Aaron, 79, 334, 335, 410, 472, 474, 480, 481, 483, 489
----, Abraham, 78, 333, 334
----. Abraham Aryeh, 328
----, Albert, 339
----, Brunette, 339
----, Cerf, 338
----, Emelie (Weill), 338
----, Estelle, 335
----, Fannie (Fies), 329
----, Helvena (Hiller), 197, 199, 335- 337
----, Henry, 79, 334, 335, 410, 472, 474, 480, 481, 482, 483
----, Jacob (Jake), 78, 333
----, Lazare, 229
----, Leon Simeon, 229, 230
----, Leona (Patterson), 230
----, Lippman , 328, 333
----, Max, 334, 335
----, Medar, 339
----, Rosette (Goudchaux), 328
----, Samuel, 328, 330, 334, 335, 474, 483
----, Sigmund, 335

Karlsruhe (Germany), 1, 4, 15,

Karpe, Anchel, 407, 408
-----,Aaron Charles, 411, 422
----, Arnold Blum, 411, 413, 414, 415
----, David, 407
----, David Burns, 414
----, David Leopold, 411, 413, 414
----, Françoise, 408
----, Harvard Edward, 415, 416
----, Irvin Meredith, 411, 413, 414
----, Jacquetta, 416
----, Lazard, 408
----, Leon, 408
----, Leon (son Anchel), 409
----, Lester Isidore, 411, 413, 415
----, Lion, 407
----, Moïse, 407, 408, 411
----, Pauline 408
----, Salomon, 408
----, Samuel, 407
----, Simon, 335, 350, 384, 386, 407, 408-414, 416, 435
----, Stella, 411, 413-415
----, Wolff, 407

Kaskaskia (Illinois Territory), 146

Kassel, Pauline (Schlessinger), 495, 497

Katten, Arthur Alexander, 388, 389, 391
----, Camille (Baer), 389
----, Edwin, 388
----, Herman, 388
----, Herman (son Arthur), 389
----, Helen (Sperling), 389
----, Simon, 388

Kaufman, Herman, 507
----, Jacob Marcus, 507
----, Maureen (Raiff, Schreiber), 507

Keim, George W., 105

Keirsey, Alexander, 274

Kelone, Patrick, 50
----, Sarah (Felsenthal), 50, 51

Kern, Florence (Liebreich), 259

Kepner, Thomas Henry, 274

Keyes, Frances Parkinson, 228

Khorassan, Dramatic Order Knights of, 295, 301, 303

Kieffer, Emmanuel, 144
----, Julia (Newman), 144
----, Louis, 144

Kirsch, Fanny (Levy), 223, 224, 227, 230

Klein, Leopold, 429, 430, 431
----, Leopold, Jr., 431
----, Rabbi Marx, 204, 383

Klotz, Solomon, 469, 472

Knoll, Wilhelmine, aka Minnie (Felsenthal), 48, 49

Koch & Meyer, 472, 477, 483

Kojis, Regina (Mayer), 518

Kolsky, Rachel (Rich), 427

Kranson, Helen (Siess), 260

Krewes, Carnival
----, Caronis, 310
----, Carthage, 310
----, Eurydice, 309
----, Mendelsonians, 309

Krotz Springs (St. Landry), LA, 101, 114

Kuhne, Frederick, 73

Ku-Klux Klan Act, 469

Kurtz, Annie E. (Elster), 494, 495, 501, 502, 510- 512, 515
----, David, 494

Kutzenhausen (Alsace), 198

Laborde, Sephora (Escudé), 264
----, Sévère, 297- 299

Lacour, Charlotte Marie (Glasscock), 265

Lafargue, A. D., 196
----, Lafargue, A. J. - 195
----, Clara (Edwards), 22

Lafayette (Lafayette), LA, 100, 156, 269, 509, 510- 513, 516, 518

Laff, Joseph, 493

Lake Charles (Calcasieu), LA, 272-274, 338, 339, 345, 350, 391, 393, 447, 518

Lake Providence (East Carroll), LA, 470, 471

Lamsheim (Germany), 336

Landau (Germany), 427

Langlois, Rosalie, 3,

Laresche, John Baptist Félix Léonce, 19, 20
-------, Jean Léonce Guilbert, 20

Laurent, Jr., Joseph, 162, 184, 196

Lauterbourg (Alsace), 409

Lavallais, Jean-Baptiste., 184, 196, 203

Lavies, Elva Mae (Kimball, Weiss), 344

Lawler, U.S. General M.K., 13

Lazard, Calmé (Charles), 329
----, Rosa (Israel), 329

Lazarus, Ziphele (Haas), 65

LeBlond, Fr., 149

Leckie, Albert Gallatin, 264

Lecompte (Rapides), LA, 92, 337

LeConniat, Mother Marie Hyacinthe, 6, 165,166

LeHavre (France), 1, 66, 143-145, 148, 149, 340, 411, 491

Lehman, Paul Marius, 163, 299

Lehmann, Abraham, 328-330
----, Abraham, 143
----, Gustav, 474
----, Isaac, 143-145, 147, 157, 162, 163
----, Louis, 386
----, Michel, 143
----, Salomon, 143, 144, 148-150

Lehman, Abraham & Co., 186, 189, 192, 194. 203

Lembach (Alsace), 143, 144, 145, 148, 150, 198

Lemoine, Clovis, 189, 193
----, Elma Cecilia (Escudé), 263
----, Emma Rita (Abramson), 515, 516

----, Fulgence Z., 162, 297, 298
----, John V. 263
----, Jules, 493

Leone, Bernice (Karpe), 416

Leucht, Rabbi Isaac, 83, 427

Levi, Barbe (Goudchaux), 328, 336
----, Samuel, 379
----, Vogel (David), 407

Levin, now Tioga (Grant), LA, 240-244, 246, 247, 250

Levin, Fannie (Siess), 202, 205, 206, 239-241. 247, 248, 258- 261, 264, 300
----, Flora, 248
----, Jacob, 243, 246
----, Johanna (Sokolosky), 248
----, Julius, 202, 204-206, 239-241, 243, 244, 246, 248, 250, 258

Levy, Armand, 518
----, Benel, 427
----, Benjamin Franklin, 380, 383, 385, 392, 435
----, Bertha (Bodenheimer), 389
----, Celina (Geiger), 409, 410
----, Donald Eilert, 386, 390
----, Édouard, 409
----, Elie, 379
----, Ella (Rich), 427, 429-431, 437, 441, 442
----, Ernest Aaron, 380, 383, 387, 388, 390, 391
----, Ernestine (Klein, Hyams), 429, 430, 431
----, Estelle, 379, 383, 390, 391
----, Estelle (Kaufman), 507
----, Félicie (Levy) , 427, 429,430
----, Florian, 518
----, Gustave, 379, 382-386, 388, 391

----, Helen (Levy), 382, 389, 391, 392
----, Jacob, 379, 382, 383, 386, 388, 390, 391
----, Lieut. Jacques, 68
----, James Roy, 518-520
----, JoEllyn, 391, 392
----, Joseph, Jr., 391, 392
----, Julia (Hiller), 336
----, Julius Meyer, 380, 383, 386, 387, 388, 390, 392
----, Lazarus, 518
----, Leon, 427, 428-430
----, Lillian (Wolbrette), 382, 383, 389, 391, 392
----, Lottie Rhoda (Riff), 386, 390, 391, 393
----, Louis J., 347
----, Lucille Weil (Bodenheimer), 382, 383, 389
----, Malzy (Runkel), 229
----, Marilyn (Silver), 347
----, Marion G. , 382, 386
----, Marion Heymann, 390, 392
----, Mary, 380, 383
----, Marx M., 379, 382, 386, 388, 390, 393
----, Matilda"Maude" (Bloch), 107, 380. 383, 385-388, 390, 393, 394
----, Mayer Arthur, 393
----, Mayer Arthur, Jr., 393
----, Michel, 336
----, Moïse, 379-381, 383, 388, 406, 410
----, Moise (son Elie), 379
----, Moïse (husb. Fanny Kirsch), 230
----, Rhea, 387, 390, 392
----, Rosalie (Hiller), 335, 336
----, Rosalie Weil (Katten), 382, 383, 388, 389, 391
----, Ruth, 383, 386, 390
----, Samuel, 379
----, Selma Jeanne, 386, 390

----, Solomon, aka. Sol, 97, 379, 381- 386, 388, 389, 391
----, Toba Laura (Lopez), 228
----, Victor, 386, 390, 393

Lexington Stables, 74

Liberty Homestead Association, 302

Lichten, Leo Felix, 260, 261
----, Helen Elaine (Solomonson), 260
----, Leo Joseph, 260

Lichtenstein, Isaac, 97

Lieb, Gertrude (Goldring), 499

Liebreich, Adèle (Siess), 259, 260, 300
----, Pincus, 259

Lincecum (Grant), LA, 246, 248, 252

Livingston (Guatemala), 426, 427, 429, 430, 431, 434, 437

Lixheim (Meurthe), France, 427

Lloyd's Bridge (Rapides)LA, 87

Löb, Mundel, aka Mindele, Minette Süss, (Süss, Lehmann)143, 144, 148-150, 226

Loeb, Adelyn Dorothy (Weiss), 345
----, Edward Lee, 100
----, Elias, 148
----, Felix, 473, 474
----, Henriette, 148
----, Joseph, 148
----, Lienhard, 148
----, Mattye (Haas), 84, 100
----, Solomon, 84, 100

Lone Pine (St. Landry)LA, 90, 97

Lone Pine Oil & Mineral Co., 113

Lone Pine Sawmill & Lumber Co., 90, 97

Long, Huey Pierce, 343

Long Bridge (Avoyelles) LA, 92, 206

Loolo Temple D.O.K.K. Band, 302

Lopez, Aristide, 228
----, Arthur 228
----, Blanche, 228
----, Daniel, 228
----, Ernest Daniel, 227- 229
----. Ernest Weil, 229
----, Victoria Rebecca (Runkel), 229

Loring, Maj. General William, 12

Louisiana Dental Society, 293, 300

Louisiana Life Assurance Society, 483

Louisiana Medical College, 389

Louisiana Pythian, 295

Louisiana State Asylum (Jackson, LA), 271

Louisiana State Normal School (Natchitoches, LA), 261, 267

Louisiana State University, aka. L.S.U., 259, 260, 270, 307, 451, 516, 518

Louisville (Jefferson), KY, 39, 95, 342, 493, 495, 496, 497

Loupe, Samuel, 483
----, Seraphina (Kahn), 483

Loupershouse (Moselle), France, 407

Lowenstein, Bella (Abramson), 509

Loyola University School of Dentistry, 301, 307

L. Siess Oil Syndicate, 272

Lubraniec (Poland), 423, 444

Ludington (Beauregard), LA, 439

Luna, Schooner, 148-150, 163

Luneau, Jean-Baptiste, 49
----, Julie Azéma (Robertson), 49

Lusk, Squire, 470

Lynbrook (Nassau), NY, 340

Mackenheim (Alsace), 198

Magnolia (Pike), MS, 336

Maillard, Angèle Marie (Flauss, Keim), 105

Maison Blanche Department Store, 332, 343, 351

Major, Philomène Victoria (Fortlouis), 14

Mamou (Evangeline) LA, 97, 115

Manchester (Great Britain), 423, 430

Mandeville (St. Tammany), LA, 386, 390

Manhattan, NY, 329, 342, 347, 444, 493, 494, 499, 500, 507

Mansfield (DeSoto), LA, 159, 162, 163, 166,

Mansfield, Battle of, 71, 159, 163

Mansura (Avoyelles), LA, 8, 16, 19, 71, 82, 92, 146, 147, 151, 152, 155-158, 160, 162-167, 169, 182- 187, 189, 190, 192-194, 196, 197, 200, 203- 206, 216, 217, 242, 247, 259, 262- 265, 291, 293- 300, 303-305, 307, 309, 314, 324, 339, 367, 393, 473, 475, 480, 501

Mansura, Battle of, 165, 166-167,

Many (Sabine), LA, 346, 498

Marcotte, Josephine (Frank), 18

Mardi Gras, 105, 309, 312, 313

Marix, Cecilia Aline (Dardenne), 512, 513

Marix, Morris, 512

Marks, Fanny (Weil). 198

Markstein, Clara (Pokorny), 93
----, Pauline (Tobias), 441

Marksville (Avoyelles), LA, 7, 9-11, 16-23, 39, 46, 50, 82, 90, 92, 97, 99, 112, 151, 152, 157, 159, 162, 186, 189, 190, 192, 195, 197, 198, 199, 201, 202-204, 206, 217, 218, 229, 231, 242, 243, 245, 249, 256, 257, 263, 264, 267, 271, 275, 292, 293, 314, 330, 331, 335- 337, 339, 346, 372, 381, 384, 393, 435, 473, 475, 480, 482, 492-497, 501- 506, 508- 511, 513-517, 519, 536, 537

Marksville Hospital, 510, 511, 513

Marksville Light & Ice Co., 503

Marmoutier (Alsace), 336

Marshall, Lucy (Rhodes), 84
----, Mary Maccie (Haas), 72, 74, 76, 79-81, 84, 87, 93
----, Robert J., 92, 97, 110
----, Roger Banks, 74
----, Roger T., 87

Martha Manor (Bayou Chicot), 83

Martial law in Avoyelles Parish, 155, 158

Martin, Bishop Auguste Marie, 166
Martin, Augustine, 15
----, Elizabeth, 15
----, Georgina, 15
Martin, Fr. Jean Émile, 3, 5
----, Mary, 15
----, Philibert, 15
-----,William, 15

Martinez, Noella (Weiss), 345

Marx, Flora (Goudchaux), 334, 338, 339, 350, 351
----, Nanette (Hockwald), 334

Masters' Affair, 152-154, 158, 160

Masters, Jr, , Frederick William, 160, 161
----, Frederick William, Sr. , 153

Mastio, Deborah (Kuhner), 266

----, Edmond, 266
----, Glen, 266
----, James, 266
----, Jean, 266

Matamoros, Mexico, 11, 329

Mathis, Charles P. 250-251, 255
----, Minnie Ann (Siess), 251, 255, 273, 274

Mathis & Siess General Store (Winnfield, LA), 251

Maxey, Addie (Rich), 439, 446

Mayer, Alfred, 203, 336
----, George L., 17, 18, 20, 198, 204, 336
----, Guy Andrew, 518
----, John (aka. Jacob Myer Levi), 427
----, Sol, B., 518
----, Solly B., 518

Mayeux, Céleste (Masters), 153, 160
----, V.L., 193
----, Marie Elizordie, 45

McDonald, John, 52
----, Lawrence, 52

McEnery, Samuel D., 474, 476, 478

McLaughlin, James, 204

McNairy, Silas, 331

Melville (St. Landry), LA, 92, 102, 348, 385, 496

Memory Lawn Cemetery (Natchitoches, LA), 394

Memphis (Shelby), TN, 39, 239, 414, 425, 440, 451

Mendelson, Albert Broel, 312, 313
----, Benjamin, 292, 294-296, 300, 301-303
----, Harry, Jr., 305, 306, 309, 310, 312, 313
----, Harry, Sr., 292, 294, 300-303, 305-307, 309, 310, 313, 314
---, Harry, III, 312, 313
----, Musette Mathilde (Gonzales), 303, 309, 313

Mendelson's School of Music, Singing, Dancing & Dramatic Arts, 306

Merchants & Manufacturers' Association, 474

Merchants' & Planters' Bank (Bunkie, LA), 92, 93, 97, 109, 385

Mermelstein, Joseph, 346, 347

Mertzwiller (Alsace), 95

Metairie Cemetery (New Orleans, LA), 94

Metzger, Marie (Goudchaux), 328

Mexia (Limestone), TX, 388

Meyer, Rabbi Abraham, 202
----, General Adolph, CSA, 473
----, Mary Gertrude, 379, 380, 410
----, Rosalie (Levy) 379-381, 410
----, Samuel, 373

Meyerowitz, Rabbi Myron, 270, 300, 304

Meyer, Weis & Co., 82

Miami (Dade), FL, 310, 500

Michel, Edmond, 243, 257, 258

Michel-Firment, Paul, 152, 243

Michelson, Mina (Glucksman), 271

Mikell, Franklin Haas, 111
----, Franklin Trazevant, 111, 112

Miller, Orduna, "Donna" (Clement), 268

Milligan, Albert, 447
----, Rosa Mae (Rich), 447

Milmar Shops, 507

Milwaukee (Milwaukee) WI, 225, 226

Minneapolis (Hennepin) MN, 219, 220, 221

Minoret, Frank, 336

Mississippi Military Institute, 80

Mitau, Russia, 493, 498

Moch, Bertha (Silverberg), 95, 96
----, Elias, 77, 95, 96
----, Laura (Goldberg), 95, 96

Molenor, Alice, 16
-----, Beulah, 16
-----, Leon, 16, 18

Mommenheim (Alsace), 229

Moncla (Avoyelles) LA, 40

Moncla, Ernest, 21

Mondavia Plantation, 115

Monroe (Ouachita), LA, 259, 261, 274, 444

Moore, Sabrina (Wolf), 367-369

Morant, Alberta (Siess), 274, 275

Moreauville (Avoyelles), LA, 92, 152, 263, 371, 472, 477

Morganza (Pointe Coupée), LA, 13, 168

Morrison, Jerome P., 349

Morrow (St. Landry), LA, 92, 386, 393

Moses, Bernard & Gustave, 74-75
----, Esther (Levy), 379
----, Fannie (Gross), 432

Mother of the Redeemer Monastery (Plaisance, St. Landry), LA 263

Moyse, Anna (Wolbrette), 391, 392

Mühlheim an der Eis,(Germany), 143, 205

Münchweiler (Germany), 39

Nancy (Meurthe-et-Moselle), France, 392

Napoleonville (Assumption), LA, 340, 469

Nashville (Davidson), TN, 70, 341, 342

Natchitoches (Natchitoches), LA, 14, 69, 155, 166, 261, 267, 298, 340, 372, 382, 394

Nathan, Jeannette, 410

National Rice Milling Co., 483

Navarro, Héloïse Marie (Siess), 265

Newgass, Benjamin, 78

New Orleans (Orleans), LA, 3, 4, 5, 10, 12, 13, 17, 20, 22, 39, 40, 53, 66, 70-76, 78, 79, 82, 83, 85-92, 94, 95, 97, 98, 102-106, 108, 109, 111, 114, 143-145, 148, 150, 152-155, 158, 163, 164, 168, 169, 184, 186, 191, 197, 198, 201, 203, 204, 206, 217, 221, 222-226, 228-231, 246, 258, 259, 262, 265- 268, 270, 271, 291- 295, 297, 298, 300-310, 312, 313, 327- 330, 332, 334- 337, 341- 348, 350, 351, 370, 372, 379, 381-384, 386- 392, 395, 407- 409, 411- 414, 423, 425, 426, 427, 429- 437, 439- 451, 469, 473, 474, 476, 477, 481, 483, 492, 495, 497- 500, 502, 505, 508- 515

New Orleans Catholic Monthly, 295

New Orleans City Park Concert Band, 301

New Orleans College of Pharmacy, 258

New Orleans Music Festival, 310

New Orleans Dental College, 293

Nickerson, Bella (Chappuis, Abramson), 516

Niederbronn (Alsace), 198, 379

Niederhochstadt (Germany), 389

Niederroedern (Alsace), 198, 335, 379

Nordstetten, (Germany), 4

Normand, L.P., 192

----, Orfila, 153

North Louisiana Sanitarium (Shreveport, LA), 509

Nuclear Regulatory Commission, 260

Nuestra Senora del Carmen (aka Avoyelles Church), 4, 5

Nugent, F.O. & Son, 240

Nugent, J.M. & Co, 240

Nugent, James Monroe, 245, 247, 249

Oakdale (Allen), LA, 50

Oak Hall Plantation (Avoyelles) LA, 76, 96, 106, 108, 110, 112, 114

Oberlauterbach (Alsace), 69, 341

Oceanside (Nassau), NY, 340

Odenbach (Germany), 39

Old Rapides Cemetery (Pineville), LA, 46, 52

Olivier, Edward, 299

----, Ernestine (Fontenot), 299
----, Estelle (Hébert), 299
----, Eunice (Jean-Baptiste), 295, 299
----, Josephine, 295, 299
----, Léonce, 299
----, Louis, 163, 295

Opelousas (St. Landry), LA, 71, 77, 84, 89, 94, 99, 100, 103, 104, 106, 109, 183, 338, 339, 348-351, 382, 386, 433, 496,

Oppenheim, Bernard Benjamin, 332
----, Charles, 332, 351
----, Harriet (Goudchaux), 332, 350, 411
----, Lily (Isaacs), 332

Oppenheimer, Caroline (Hiller), 336

O'Quinn, Rev. John, 475

Orrecchio, Immaculata Maria (Siess), 275

Pacific Fire Co., (Alexandria) LA, 204

Pailet, Andrée Margot, 512
----, Aron Louis, 512
----, Luise Adrienne (Tovar), 512, 515
----, Maurice, 512

Paincourtville (Assumption), LA, 469

Panama Canal, 98, 436, 440

Pan American Exporters, 437, 441, 442, 443, 444, 450

Pearce, Stephen Samuel, 475

Pearson, Carl, 372

Peekskill Military Academy (Westchester Co., NY), 443

People's State Bank (Opelousas, St. Landry, LA), 104

Philippe, Agnès (Roy), 146
----, Michel, 146

Phillipon, Capt. L. 152

Picard, Anona (Weiss), 345

Pierrot, Clément, 184
----, Jean-Baptiste, 19

Pinschowers, Jonas, 424, 426

Pine Prairie (Evangeline) LA, 97, 98, 115

Pine Prairie Oil & Mineral Co., 97, 98, 114

Plaquemine (Iberville), LA, 92, 328, 330, 334, 392, 473, 512, 513

Plaucheville (Avoyelles), LA, 410, 496

Pleasant Hill, Battle of, 71, 159, 163

Pleasant, Col. Ruffin, 498

Plonsky, Edward, 518
----, Frimmit (Levy), 518
----, Hannah (Wolff), 518
----, Jacob, 518
----, Joseph, 518
----, Leon, 518
----, Mary (Bendel), 518

Pointe Coupée Parish, LA, 2, 3, 7, 8, 11-15, 165, 168, 262, 263, 265, 393, 509

Pointe Maigre (Avoyelles), LA, 40-47, 49- 51

Pokorny, Bertha (Kamien), 76
----, David, 76, 87, 88, 93
----, Hannah (Haas), 75, 76, 80, 85, 86, 91, 93, 94
----, John, 75, 93
----, Michael, 75. 76, 87
----, Rosa (Adler), 85, 87, 93

Pollock (Grant), LA, 245, 248, 249, 251, 255, 256

Pollock, Capt. James W. , 248

Porché, Helen (Fortlouis), 2, 15
------, Marie Aurore (Fortlouis), 3,8, 11, 14
------, Michel, 3

Poret, Isidore, 167, 196
----, J.B., 337

Portable Mills Lumber Co., 246

Port Gibson (Claiborne), MS, 144

Port Gibson College, 80

Preus, Caroline (Plonsky), 83

Prévot, Celestin, 304
----, Helen (Seiss), 304, 309, 325
----, Victor, 262

Prostdame, Victor, 8, 151, 162

Provençal (Natchitoches), LA, 382, 386, 393

Puerto Barrios (Guatemala), 427, 434

Puerto Cortes (Honduras), 427

Puerto Limon (Costa Rica), 427

Puklice (Czech Republic), 75

Punta Alegre Sugar Co., (Cuba), 445

Punta Gorda (Honduras), 426, 430, 434

Punta San Juan (Cuba), 445

Puttelange-lès-Farchviller (Moselle), 198, 407, 408, 411

Püttlingen (Elsass-Lothringen), See Puttelange-lès-Farchviller,

Pythian Cemetery (Bunkie, LA), 105, 439, 447

Pythias, Knights of, 295, 296, 300, 301, 303

Quezaltenango (Guatemala), 443

Quilleboeuf, 149

Rabalais, Martin vs. David Siess, 158, 168

Rabalais, Oliver, 163, 299

Raphael, Frommet (Abraham), 143

Rapides Hotel (Pineville, LA), 16

Railroads (Louisiana)
----, Avoyelles, Palmetto & Gulf, 496

----, Avoyelles Railroad Co., 384
----, Chicago, Milwaukee & St. Paul Railway, 48
----, Fischer Logging RR, 349-350
----, Louisiana & Arkansas, 254
----, Louisiana & Texas Railroad & Steamship Co., 239
----, Louisiana East and West 107-108, 109
----, Louisiana Railway & Navigation Co., 254
----, Morgan, 81, 82, 85
----, New Orleans & Mobile, 75
----, St. Louis, Avoyelles & Southwestern Railroad, 384
----, St. Louis, Avoyelles & Southwestern Railway Co., 384
----St. Louis, Iron Mountain & Southern, 239, 248, 250, 255
----, Rock Island, 254
----, Texas & Pacific, 82, 84, 108, 109, 206, 239, 240, 264, 305, 314, 339, 371, 372, 373, 385, 428, 431, 439, 446, 496
----, Virginia & Truckee Railway, 426
----, Winnfield Oil Well Railway, 254

Ray, James Edward, 373
----, Ophelia (Blakewood), 373

Raylass Department Stores, 507

Rayne (Acadia), LA, 339, 518

Rea, Capt. George W., 202

Reconstruction, 43, 45, 51, 168, 184, 369, 469

Red River Campaign, 13, 159

Reed, John, 40, 41

Regard, Férreol, 196

Regard, Férreol vs. USA, 162, 164

Reuben, Natalye (Weiss), 342

Reynaud, Joseph, 184
----, Victor, 187

Rhodes, John T., 84, 97
----, John T., Jr., 93,
-----, Maccie (Haas), 79, 84, 98-100

Rice-Stix Dry Goods Co., 444

Rich, Aaron, 431, 435, 438, 440, 446, 447, 448
----, Abraham, 247, 343, 385, 423, 424-429, 431-436, 446, 447, 451, 466, 473
----, Benjamin, 427,
----, Benjamin (son Abraham), 429, 435, 438, 439, 446, 447
----, Benjamin (son Isidore), 429
----, Carol, 451
----, Esther (Anker), 443
----, Isidore, 423, 424, 426, 427, 429-438, 440, 441, 448, 451
----, Jack, 423, 442, 451
----, Jack Jr., 451
----, Jacob, 424, 426
----, Lena (Warshauer), 432, 444
----, Leon, 430, 437, 438, 441, 442, 446, 450
----, Leon, Jr., 442, 446, 450, 451
----, Leon III, 451
----, Leopold (Lee), 429, 435, 438, 439
----, Minette (Goldstein), 423, 429, 430, 437, 441, 442, 444, 446, 448, 450
----, Miriam (aka Mary Cone), 267, 429, 435, 438, 439, 440, 446, 447
----, Miriam (Green), 439, 446, 447
----, Nancy Rose (Hohlfeldt), 451

----, Raye (Coberly), 423, 431, 435, 438, 439, 446, 447, 468
----, Sadie (Woodson), 423, 431, 435, 438, 439, 446, 448
----, Sadye Zona (Jacobs), 430, 437, 441, 442
----, Sarah (Goldstein), 430, 431

Rich & Warshauer, 424

Richards, Adèle (Adrion), 23

Riché, J.A., 201, 337

Richey, Andrew, 46

Ricord, Fabius, 7,8

Riddle, Sr., Charles, 519

Riedseltz (Alsace), 198, 328

Ries, Minette (Levy), 427
Ries, Moses, 427
----, Jeannette (Mayer), 427

Riff, Henry D., 390
----, Lloyd, 391
----, Maury, 391
----, Sol D., 390, 391, 393

Robeline (Natchitoches), LA, 340, 382

Robertson, Julia Clarice (Felsenthal), 49, 50

Rogozno (Poland), 259

Romanswiller (Alsace), 198, 473

Roos, Adolph David, 84
----, Jeannette (Haas), 84, 101
----, Mary (Haas), 84, 103

Roosevelt Hotel (New Orleans), 230, 343, 344, 442, 447

Root, Joseph Cullen, 219

Roz, Celestine, 146

Rosenbaum, Babette (Carb), 408, 409, 414, 415
----, Hannah (Hollander), 408

Rosenberg, Joseph B., 502
----, Louis, 502
----, Ruth, 502
----, Saul, 502

Rosenfeld, Jesse Sigmund, 351

Rosenthal (Jackson), Hannah, 341
----, Sgt. Jonas, 68, 69

Roser, Marie (Kieffer), 144
----, Rosalie, 144
----, Samuel, 144
----, Simon 144

Roth, Annie (Weiss), 341

Rothbach (Alsace), 65, 66, 115, 198

Rothstein, Rabbi Leonard, 96, 109, 260, 261

Rouensa, Chief, 146
----, Marie (Philippe), 146

Roy, Félonise (Frank), 18
----, Léandre T., 184
----, Marie (Chatelain), 146
----, René, 146
----, Teska, 247

Royal Perfume Company, 265, 266

Rubel, Rose (Rich), 451

Runkel Bros. Chocolate Manufactory, 228

Runkel, Herman, 229
----, Sigismond, 229

Russell, James M., 394

Rymanów (Poland), 493

Saal, John, 371
----, Johnnie Moses, 371

Sacred Heart Catholic Church (Moreauville, Avoyelles), LA, 371

Salomon, Eleanor (Ries), 427

Saltz, Maurice, 393

Samuel, Sarah (Weiss), 340, 348

Samuels, Frances (Friend), 225, 226

Sand Spur (see Siess, LA)

San Francisco (San Francisco), LA, 89, 91, 92, 98, 217, 219, 220, 335, 350, 393, 424, 425, 426, 431, 439, 443, 483
----, Earthquake, 91-92
----, Pacific Heights, 91, 92

Sarstoon River Fruit Co. Ltd., 437

Saucier, Ludoviska (Frank), 17, 22

Saer, Fannie (Finklestein), 393

Savanilla (Columbia), 427

Schiller, SS, 225

Schilling, Louis, 248

----, Ruby, 248

Schirrhoffen (Alsace), 338, 339

Schlessinger, Annie, 495
----, Benjamin, 496, 501, 504, 506
----, Daniel, 495
----, Esther, 496, 497, 498, 501
----, Jacob, 493
----, Major Jacob, 496, 498, 501, 504
----, Mary (Bach), 496-497, 501, 504, 506
----, Moses (Morris), 493, 495, 497
----, Nathan, 495
----, Rosa (Goldsmith), 493, 495, 497
----, Sarah, 495
----, Simon, 493, 495, 496, 497, 501, 503, 504

Schmulen, Fleurine (Kahn), 339

Schneider, Margaretha (Schwartzenburg), 16

Schreiber, Emmanuel Martie, 493, 495, 496, 501, 505, 507
----, Harry, 493, 495, 496, 497
----, Helen Naomi (Spring), 496, 501, 507, 508
----, J.H., 507
----, Julius, 493, 495, 501, 505-507
----, Lynn Carol, 507
----, Rosie, 493
----, Sylvia Dora (Bensinger), 496, 501, 505, 507

Schultz, Pauline (Goudchaux), 329

Schwabacher, Julius, 335, 410
----, Max, 474

Schwartzenburg, Caroline, 16
----, Charles, 16
----, Edward, 16
----, George Washington Xavier, 18
-----, Mary (aka Mollie Gremillion), 16
-----, John, 16
----, John, Sr., 16

Seattle (King) WA, 89, 220

Seeger, Max Albert, 48

Seiss, Barbara Elaine (Langer), 309
----, Beryl (Sykes), 314
----, Carl Anthony, 309
----, Charles Andrew, 309
----, Eugene Daniel, 309
----, Felicia , 314
----, Lorraine, 314
----, Louis André, 296, 299, 304, 309, 314, 325
----Juanita Veronica (Barbin), 309
----, Marjorie Ann, 296, 309
----, Mary Yolanda (Barbin), 309
----,Vincent Nathaniel, 309

Selber Bros. Clothing Store (Shreveport, LA), 348

Selber, Mandel Charles, 348

Selman's H.P., Department Store, 342

Sembach (Germany), 408

Semple John Heiner, 471

Sender, Aron (aka Aron Alexander), 65

Shangarai Chassed (Gates of Mercy) Synagogue (New Orleans, LA), 168, 408

Shannon, Capt. John, 148, 150

Share, Rabbi Nathaniel, 448

Shaw, Helen (Bango, Thompson), 269, 270-272
----, John Morrill, 269
----, John Siess, 269
----, Morrill Edward, 269

Shell Canal, 101

Shirley Plantation, 85

Shopfloch (Germany), 427

Shreveport (Caddo), LA, 22, 114, 159, 160, 203, 217, 221, 223, 260, 266, 267, 304, 305, 307, 308, 314, 344-348, 389, 408, 414- 416, 439, 499, 500, 509, 510

Siegel, Libby (Schlessinger), 496, 501, 504, 506

Siess(Grant), LA, 245-247, 249, 250

Siess, Alice, 196, 197, 215
----, Auger, 147, 184, 185, 189-190, 192, 193, 195, 198, 199, 201, 202, 204- 206, 214, 215, 239- 244, 246-248, 250, 255, 258- 261, 264, 300, 428, 429
----, Camille Nugent, 249, 257, 266-267
----, Caroline (aka Carrie), 196, 203, 206, 293. 294, 299, 305, 308
----, Carolyn Louise, 273
----, Charles Preston, 251, 255, 273, 274

----, Charles Preston, Jr. 247, 273
----, Chester Paul, 259-260
----, Clotile Margery (Shaw), 246, 254, 269, 288
----, David, 143-147, 155, 157, 158, 162- 164, 167-169, 182-197, 199, 200, 203, 204, 206, 207, 291-300, 303, 304, 309, 314, 315, 324, 473, 475, 480, 501
----, Douglas G. , 266
----, Edna Louise (Glasscock), 245, 264, 265
----, Edyne Joan (Gupfert), 249, 267, 440
----, Ella Beth (Treadway), 245, 249, 255, 257, 264, 268, 269
----, Elmo Paul, 243, 257, 266
----, Emmanuel, 169, 184, 192, 193, 199, 215, 242- 250, 255-256, 258, 264, 267-269, 440,
----, Estelle Johanna, 248, 254, 270, 288
----, Eugénie, 185, 203, 206, 293, 294, 299, 302, 305, 306, 308, 326
----, Eunice Vida (Lichten), 242, 260, 261
----, Florestine (Escudé), 151, 184, 197, 203, 216, 247, 248, 261, 264, 275, 298, 416, 431
----Gladys Josephine (Wysong, Simpson), 247, 258, 261
----, Gretchen (Tadlock), 273, 274
----, Guy Edward, 246, 254, 269, 288
----, Harry James, Jr., 299, 305, 307, 308, 314, 325,
----, Harry James, Sr., 203, 293, 294-300, 303,-305, 307, 308, 323, 324, 415, 501
----, Helen Louise (Keirsey), 251, 255, 273, 274
----, Héloïse Marie (Mastio), 266
----, Hermina (Rich), 156, 184, 199, 247, 423, 428, 431, 432, 435, 438, 439 , 447, 468, 473, 501

----, Isaac Édouard, 185, 199, 242-248, 252, 254, 255, 258- 261, 264, 269, 270, 288
----, Jack, 251, 273, 275
----, Jacquelin (Terry), 275
----, John D., 251, 273, 275
----, Judith Ann (Bremseth), 260
----, Leo Chester, 239, 242, 258-260, 300
----, Leon, 185, 217--221, 224, 225, 227, 229, 230, 231, 256, 303
----, Lenox Leopold, 243, 257, 265, 266
----, Lenox Leopold, Jr., 266
----, Leopold, 143-148, 151, 152, 155, 156-157, 160-164, 168, 169, 181, 184, 185, 190, 192, 193, 197, 199, 203, 205, 216, 217, 248, 259, 274, 275, 416, 429, 473, 480, 501
----, Louis Preston, 185, 199, 214, 242, 247, 248, 250-255, 272-274, 290
----, Lucille Beatrice (Crager), 242, 258, 261
----, Mae Rose (Clement), xix, 249, 267, 268, 275, 440
----, Marian, "Marney" (Kepner), 273, 274
----, Marie Isabelle (Leckie), 242, 243, 264, 268
----, Mathilde (Weil), 168, 183, 184, 203, 204, 217- 220, 223- 227, 229, 230, 238
----, Mathilde (Mendelson), 183, 184, 203, 206, 292, 294, 300-303, 305, 308
----, Nellie Adèle (Hardy, Hymes), 245, 257, 267
----, Philip L. 266
----, Rae Ethel (Harper), 240, 260, 261
----, Robert Edward, 251, 255, 273, 274
----, Simon, 90, 143, 144, 146, 147, 151, 155-158, 163, 164, 167-

169, 182-195, 197- 204, 206, 217-220, 223-225, 229- 231, 256, 300, 303, 335, 336, 429, 473, 475, 480
----, Terri Lynn, 275

Siess & Campbell Drugstore (Alexandria, LA), 259

Siess Boarding House, 292

Siess vs. Siess, 187-195

Silber, Rabbi Mendel, 229

Silberman, Sarah (Winsberg), 448

Silver, Harry, 347, 499
----, Ted, 347

Silverberg, Isaac, 96

Silverstone, Elizabeth (Siess), 220, 224, 227, 230, 231
----, Emmanuel, 220
----, Solomon, 220

Simmesport (Avoyelles), LA, 71, 92, 157, 165, 263, 265, 334, 384, 385, 496

Simon, Agathe (Karpe), 407

Singer, Fanny (Pokorny), 75, 87

Slaves.......
----, Ben, 151
----, Bill, 41
----, Elizabeth, 151
----, Emeline, 44
----, Geneviève, 147
----, Hannah, 44
----, Mary, 44

Smith, U.S. General A.J., 159, 164
----, Charles, 203

----, Edward A., 415
----, Lieutenant-General Kirby, CSA, 12
----, Merle (Frank), 22
----, Murrell Smith (Siess), 298, 305, 307, 308, 314
----, Robert Hill, 112,113

Snelling, John P., 84, 86, 97

Sofnas, Rosine (Pailet), 512

Sokolosky, Isaac, 248

Solomon, Bertha (Abramson), 508

Somers, Annette (Weiss), 340

Sommer, Lazarus, 144
----, Rosalie, 144
----, Thérèse, 144

Soniat Oil Co., 91

Sophie B. Wright High School, 224

Soulé Business School (New Orleans, LA), 312, 511, 512

Southard, Dorothy (Karpe), 414, 415

Southern Development Co. of Alexandria, 250

Spindeltop (Texas) Oil Production, 250, 338

Spring, Julius J., 507, 508

St. Anthony of Padua RC. Church (Bunkie, LA), 83, 89, 104, 105

St. Francis Xavier Cathedral (Alexandria, LA), 371

St. Joseph's Catholic Cemetery (Marksville), LA, 16, 21, 264

St. Joseph's RC Church (Marksville), LA, 242

St. Landry State Bank, 97, 102

St. Louis Cemetery # 3, (New Orleans, LA), 303, 307, 313, 314

St. Paul's Cemetery (Mansura, LA), 8, 259, 264

St. Paul the Apostle RC Church, (Mansura, LA), 9, 16, 147, 165, 185, 197, 263, 264, 296, 304

St. Roch Catholic Cemetery (New Orleans, LA), 105

Standard Oil Company, 269, 373, 439

Starn, Johanna (Davis, Berger) ,246

Stern, Frances (Elster), 495
----, Isabelle (Kahn), 483
----, Rosa (Cohn), 513

Stolar, Claire (Weiss), 342

Strassburg (Russia), 491

Strouse, Clarence B., 88

Sugar, Solomon (see Solomon Zucker)

Sulphur Timber & Lumber Co., 252-253

Summit (Pike), MS, 97, 335, 338

Surbourg (Alsace), 334

Süss, Michael (aka Ayel Süssel), 143

Suss Mill School, 242

Sutton, William D., 372

Sweet Home Lumber Co., 240

Tadlock, Ardis Lyndon, 274
----, Ardis Lyndon, Jr., 274

Tangipahoa (Tangipahoa), LA, 369, 370, 371

Tarnów (Austria) , 491, 494

Tassin, Blanche Marie (Escudé), 262
----, Symphorien, 204

Taylor, General Dick, CSA, 159, 165
----, Zachary, 159,

Temple Gemiluth Chassodim (Alexandria, Rapides, LA), 96, 109, 270, 296, 300, 341, 347, 386, 504

Temple Sinai (New Orleans, LA), 448, 510, 513, 514

Tepper, Olga (Broel), 310-312

Thalsheimer, Henry, 204

Thalsheimer, Minette, See Mundel Löb

Théard, Major P.E., 158, 163

Thomas, Casimir, 188

Thomas Douglas Marshall Cemetery (Evergreen, LA), 79, 93, 105

Thompson, Harriet (Lehman), 163

Tiger Bend (Avoyelles),LA, 72, 73, 76, 77, 81, 82

Tillery, Virgil H., 471

Tioga (see also Levin, LA), 250, 261

Tioga High School, 261

Timmons, Theora (Friedman), 48

Tobias, Sylvia (Rich), 441, 442, 446

Touro Infirmary (New Orleans, LA), 88, 224, 391, 392, 413, 449, 450, 508, 510, 514

Touro Synagogue (New Orleans, LA), 83, 106, 304

Townsend, George, 52
----, Mary, 52

Trans-Mississippi Department, 12, 70, 71, 159

Treadway, Betty Jo (Smith, Chilton, Benoit), 268
----, Carmen Elaine (Boleyn, Lirette), 268
----, Gloria Henriette (Blaylock, Porter, Smith, Persky), 268
----, Henry Jerome, 268, 269
----, Mary Nell (Trahan, Davenport, Myrick), 268

Tri-State Sanitarium (Clinic) (Shreveport, LA), 262, 307

Tropical Clothing Manufacturing Co., 445, 449, 450

Tujague's Restaurant (New Orleans, LA), 223

Tulane Medical School (New Orleans, LA), 80, 244, 509, 510, 514

Tulane University (New Orleans, LA), 80

Turci's Italian Garden Restaurant (New Orleans, LA), 303, 305

Turner, Notie Fay (Weiss), 344

Uhry, Henriette (Haas), 65, 66, 77

Ungvar (Hungary), 340, 341, 343, 345, 346, 432

Union Bank (Marksville, LA), 263, 504, 513

Union Field Jewish Cemetery (Ridgewood, NY), 506, 507, 508

United Daughters of the Confederacy, 88, 105

United Confederate Veterans, 71, 93

United Musicians' Local Industrial Union, C.I.O., 309

Uzhorod (Ukraine), See Ungvar

Vandenburg Cemetery (St. Landry) LA, 83, 96, 99

Van Couvenhoven, Marretje Gerretse (Van Voorhies), 183

Van De Ven, Bishop Cornelius, 89

VanVoorhies, Coert Stevense, 183

----, Cornelius, 183

Veit, Gladys, 415

Ventress (Pointe Coupée), LA, 14, 15

Vermillionville (See also Lafayette, LA), 156, 157

Veteran Confederate States Cavalry Assn. 71

Ville Platte (St. Landry)LA, 87, 92, 97, 98, 101, 107, 113,

Villère, Charles W., 14, 15

Vilna (Russia), 512

Vinton (Calcasieu), LA, 255, 272

Virginia, University of, 81, 103

Virginia City (Storey), NV, 424-428

Volk's Department Store, 345

Voorhies (Avoyelles), LA, 263

Voorhies, Chrissa Eliza (Cochrane), 183
----, Cornelius, 183
----, Peter Gordon, 183

Wachenheim (Germany), 507

Waddil & Barbin vs. Simon Siess, 185

Wagner, John Thornton, 447

Waller, Nolan T., 200

Walsh, Gladys Leona (Siess), 273, 274

Ware, Dr. James, 201, 202

Warsaw (Poland), 425, 508, 513

Warshauer, Aaron, 432, 444
----, Bella (Gross), 431, 432, 438, 444, 446, 449
----, Erna, 446, 449
----, Herman (aka. Herman Bratman), 444, 445, 446, 449
----, Irving B. , 446, 449
----, Louis, 444
----, Morris James, 444, 445, 446, 449, 450
----, Sigmund, 445, 449

Warshawski, Lewin, 444

Washington (St. Landry) LA, 73, 75, 78, 101, 348, 518

Warner, T. R., 332

Waters & Bringhorst, 239-240

Watsky, Mathile (Abramson), 514

Weekly Pelican, The, 477-478

Weil, Alexander, 381
----, Bertrand, 482
----, Blanche, 381
----, Camille, 381
----, Carrie Justine (Levy), 381, 382, 383, 388, 389, 391
----, Conrad, 482
----, Elise (Friend), 90, 219, 223-227, 230, 231
----, Eliza, 389
----, Ernest M., 198, 203, 217, 218-225, 238, 407, 473
----, Flora (Kahn), 218, 223, 229, 230

----, Jeanne (Lopez), 218, 223, 227, 229
----, Jonas, 380, 410
----, Omega (Levy), 381, 382, 383, 389, 391, 392
----, Rosa (Bauer), 482
----, Samuel, 482

Weil Bros. & Bauer, 482

Weill, Charles, 338
----, Emelie (Weiss), 347, 348
----, Fanny (Weiss), 340, 500
----, Jacob, 347
----, Jonas, 347
----, Josephine (Goudchaux), 338, 339. 340
----, Jules, 340, 347
----, Rachel (Loupe), 483

Weinburg, Leon, 204

Weis, Henrietta (Godchaux), 227
----, Ida Sophie (Friend), 225-227
----, Julius, 82, 226
----, Marion, 89, 90
----, Samuel, 226

Weiss, Annette (Selber), 346, 348
----, Barbara Ann, 344
----, Bernard E., 344, 345
----, Charles, 340, 500
----, Claire (Weisman), 342
----, David Bernard, 340, 341, 342, 347
----, Edda (Steinfeld), 341
----, Gustave Waldorph, 341, 342
----, Gustave Waldorph, Jr., 342
----, Herman, 340, 347, 348, 385, 433, 500
----, Johnny, 345
----, Joseph M., 340, 341, 385, 435, 498, 504
----, Joseph M., II, aka Jack- 341
----, Julius, 344, 499
----, Lillian R., 341, 342, 343
----, Louise, 344
----, Martin, 340, 348, 385, 431, 432
----, Mervin, 340
----, Mervine, 340
----, Meyer Roth, 341, 342
----, Milton Eli, 344, 345
----, Miriam (Levy), 346, 347
----, Morris Joseph, 340, 343, 345, 346, 347, 498, 499, 500
----, Richard, 340
----, Rosa (Goldring), 340, 346, 348, 498, 500
----, Samuel, 340, 343, 385
----, Samuel C., 346, 347
----, Samuel Joseph, 345
----, Seymour, 343, 344, 347
----, Seymour II, 345
----, Selma H., 341, 342
----, William Morris, 345

Weiss Bros. Department Stores, 340, 342, 345

Weiss & Goldring Department Store (Alexandria, LA), 340, 343, 346, 347, 499, 500, 504

Weissbach, Lee Shai, 23

Weisenberg, Charles Maximilien, 20, 21

Weldon, Alice (Siess), 269

Whitfield, Carrie Labertha (Wolf), 372

Whitstine, Emma (Wolf), 371

Wickliffe (Pointe Coupée), LA 15

Wickliffe, Col. John, 475-477, 479, 480, 481

Wilhelmi, Dana Margaret (Abramson), 516

William David Haas Memorial Methodist Church (Bunkie, LA), 83, 115

Williams, Barney (born Sheftelowitz), 518
----, Minnie Pearl (Levy), 518

Winnfield (Winn), LA, 251, 252-255, 272, 274, 275, 288-290, 373

Winnfield, Bank of, 254

Winnfield Oil Co. Ltd., 251, 254

Winnfield Oil Well # 1, 251, 290

Winnfield Parish Bank, 254

Winn Parish Medical Society, 252

Winsberg, David Jacob, 440, 450
----, Jacob, 448
----, Jerome Meyer, 423, 450
----, Winfred Julius, 448

Wissembourg (Alsace), 84

Witkowski, Eugenia Florence (Semple), 470
----, Julius, 470
----, Simon, 470-472, 477, 478, 479, 483

Wloclawek (Poland), 432, 434, 444, 445

Wolbrette, Bertha (Feitel), 392
----, Betty, 391, 392
----, David,, 391, 392
----, Henri, 391, 392
----, Henri, Jr., 391, 392
----, Hermance (Oppenheimer), 392

----, Jules, 392
----, Moyse, 392
----, Samuel, 392
----, Sidney, 392
----, Thérèse (Sommer), 392

Wolf, Andrew Jackson, 369, 370, 371, 372
----, Andrew Jackson, Jr., 372
----, Anna, 372
----, Anna (Ray), 370, 373
----, Benjamin, 370
----, Bessie, 372
----, Caroline Godchaux (Mayerson), 227
----, Clara (Pearson), 372
----, Cornelius N., 367, 369, 370
----, Eva, 370
----, George Lawrence, 373
----, Henrietta (Weil), 381
----, Henry Overton, 372, 373
----, James Adolph, 367, 369, 370, 371
----, Joseph, 367
----, Joseph Adolph, 373
----, Joseph Bernard, 369, 370, 371, 372
----, Kingston Grant, 373
----, Mary Myrtle, 372
----, Mattie R. (Saal). , 367, 368, 369, 370, 371
----, Moses, 367-369, 370, 373, 374, 378
----, Moses Hamilton, 370, 372, 373
----, Moses Hamilton, Jr., 372
----, Nettie M. (Sutton), 370, 372
----, Robert L., 367, 369, 370
----, Rosalia, 369

Wolff, Florence (Goudchaux), 348, 349
Wolff, Leon, 73, 77, 78, 83, 101, 112, 348

----, Mae (Weill), 348
----, Zerlina (aka Caroline Haas), 66, 67, 73

Woodcraft, Cadets of, 222

Woodmen Circle, 222

Woodmen Mutual Health & Casualty Co., 222, 223

Woodmen of the World, 104, 219-221, 223, 224

Woodmere (Nassau), NY, 502

Woodson, James Raymond, 439, 446
----, Raymond Rich, 439, 446

Woodville (Wilkinson), MS, 146, 245, 252

World Panama Exposition, 98

Yellow Bayou, Battle of, 71, 165

Yoist, Judge John, 194

Zemurray, Sam (the banana man), 437, 438

Zucker, Solomon, 336

Zurawie (Poland), 508

Zwolle (Sabine) LA, 346

www.ingramcontent.com/pod-product-compliance
Lightning Source LLC
Chambersburg PA
CBHW021348290426
44108CB00010B/157